EXPERIENTIAL DESIGN SCHEMAS

Experiential Design Schemas

Authors | Conception
Mark DeKay   Gail Brager

Graphic Design | Art Direction
Hansjörg Göritz

Layout | Graphic Coordination
Zachary Dulin

Production Assistance
Brittaney Bluel, Emily Miller

Editorial Assistance
Susanne Bennett

Illustrations
Zachary Dulin, Ethan Guthrie,
Megan McConnell, Matea Montanaro

Research
Tya Abe, Ethan Guthrie, Phoebe Johanassen,
Amy Loy, Emily Miller, Stephanie Robertson,
Kevin Saslawski, Cullen Sayegh, Aaron Waldrupe,
Jing Yuan

Foreword
Joshua Aidlin, William Browning

ORO EDITIONS
Novato, CA

Cover

Meditation Hall, SAN Museum
Wonju, Gangwon Province
South Korea, 2019
Tadao Ando, architect

Photo Junho Jang (Image Joom)

ORO Editions
Publishers of Architecture, Art, and Design
Gordon Goff: Publisher

www.oroeditions.com
info@oroeditions.com

Published by ORO Editions.

Authors: Mark DeKay + Gail Brager
Book Design: Hansjörg Göritz
Project Manager: Jake Anderson

10 9 8 7 6 5 4 3 2 1 First Edition

ISBN: 978-1-957183-73-2

Color Separations and Printing: ORO Group Inc.
Printed in China

ORO Editions makes a continuous effort to minimize the overall carbon footprint of its publications. As part of this goal, ORO, in association with Global ReLeaf, arranges to plant trees to replace those used in the manufacturing of the paper produced for its books. Global ReLeaf is an international campaign run by American Forests, one of the world's oldest nonprofit conservation organizations. Global ReLeaf is American Forests' education and action program that helps individuals, organizations, agencies, and corporations improve the local and global environment by planting and caring for trees.

dedication

To the student in all of us

Contents

Foreword

Joshua Aidlin

In the Spring of 1998, 25 years ago, my college classmate David Darling and I were discussing the direction of our newly-founded architecture studio, Aidlin Darling Design, and the direction of the profession itself. Half of the studio space was devoted to a woodshop that I had inherited from my father, a sculptor, who had passed away years before. We shared a wariness of the inundation of computer-driven architecture upon the profession. At that time the temptation to quickly adopt, apply and reproduce architecture—driven by seductive visuals—was consuming the industry. The firms creating these buildings worked in hermetic white offices, with designers lined up in rows with three linear feet of desk space each. These studios could have been mistaken for accounting firms, law offices, or call centers, given their isolation from the physical materials and three-dimensional forms for which they were responsible. The results sadly are what you see in every metropolis and suburb today: completely synthetic buildings with equally soulless environments. David and I wanted to build a language of practice that is more emotionally and psychologically attuned.

Our shared focus was to help, one building at a time and with great care, swing the pendulum in the opposite direction. We created a studio that embraces materials in all their reality and architecture in all its sensuousness. We surround ourselves with endless shelves and tabletops filled with physical models, wood, stone, and steel; our environment feeding a mode of design for all the senses, not merely the visual. This is an environment where one can pick up materials and understand how they feel, weigh, smell and sound when one knocks against them; where you can pick up a model and spin it around, understanding instantly how the proportions of both the interior spaces and exterior forms "feel" when sunlight strikes them.

Mark DeKay and Gail Brager share our interest in soulful Architecture. Mark is a registered Architect and Professor of Architecture at the University of Tennessee, specializing in sustainable design theory and tools. He holds M.Arch degrees from Tulane University and University of Oregon. Mark has written extensively and lectured internationally on climatic design and integral sustainability. Gail's experience in the field of Architecture is deep, with a Ph.D. in Mechanical Engineering and a Professorship of Building Science and Sustainability in the Department of Architecture at the University of California, Berkeley. She has been teaching, writing and conducting research for over 35 years, addressing issues directly connected to sensory experience in buildings.

Together these two minds have created a rare tome focused on the process of designing for all the senses. To me, this research is fascinating, as it takes a very intuitive process that unfolds every day in our studio and structures it as a highly rational matrix or catalog of design schemas. It reads as if a master chef has taken the recipe for a subtle dish and made its workings intelligible to a novice by categorizing the ingredients and cooking processes. Not only this, but for each ingredient they offer a real-world example and detail the qualitative metrics that guide its success. This innovative strategy of cataloging the intangible is both ingenious and revelatory in its potential to help create soulful works of Architecture.

Joshua Aidlin is a founding partner in Aidlin Darling Design, an award-winning San Francisco architecture firm.

We think of design as a sensory art, one where the way a space feels is as important as how it looks.

— Aidlin Darling Design

The timing of this investigation is critical. As Aidlin Darling Design has begun to create a library of structures whose programs are focused on meditation and contemplation for the youth of our society, the evident need to create and provide environments that heal the soul is undeniable. The damage that is being done to our society with its addiction to the digital screen—large and small—is, at this point, indisputable. The need for our buildings, both private and public, to assist in reconnecting the mind and the body is crucial.

I feel the research that Gail and Mark have done, and the highly approachable manner in which the data has been dissected and formatted, will make this document required reading for all environmental design students and professionals. This is the first important step in a long process to realize nurturing and soulful environments for all.

William Browning

We will know that we have succeeded when we walk into the building and feel it through our skin.

— Deborah Butterfield, sculptor

Until very recently the vast majority of human existence has been outdoors, with the sun, moon, wind, rain, dirt, water, plants and animals engaging all of our senses. Today most Americans spend more that 90% of our time indoors. While four walls and a ceiling can provide shelter from the elements, we need light, air and more to support our health and wellbeing. We need sensory and spatial variability; without it we get bored or worse.

Unfortunately, somehow we all got trapped in the fantasy of the International Style office design, sealed, air-conditioned spaces with blinding uniform light levels. The thermal conditions were optimized for middle-aged white men in suits, and the high illuminance was based on reading black ink on white sheets of paper on a desk top. While lighting and thermal standards have evolved somewhat to address a greater diversity of tasks and demographics, we are still stuck in a mindset that uniform conditions are optimal. The natural world is anything but uniform. There is evidence that children have better academic performance in classrooms with areas of variable light levels and temperatures. Daylight access also makes a difference in academic performance.

Daylight is not the same over the course of the day. It is yellow in the morning, bluer at midday and shifts to red in the afternoon. Our bodies change temperature and heart rate. The balance of serotonin and melatonin shift with those color changes; this is our circadian rhythm. All too many buildings separate us from the marvelous variability of daylight. Even the patterns of light and shadow can make a difference.

Throughout nature there are statistical fractals—self-repeating patterns that have levels of variation. Fern leaves, snowflakes, waves rolling onto a beach, flames dancing in a fireplace, and the dappled light under a tree are all statistical fractals. They occur so frequently in nature, that when we see them in a human-designed object or space, our brain is predisposed to easily process the image and lower our stress level. This condition, referred to as fractal fluency, can be created with light shining through perforated metal screens, a lath structure, fritting on glass or a pattern silk screened onto fabric window shades.

There is strong evidence that introducing the richness of natural experiences into our buildings has psychological, physiological and emotional benefits. This connection to nature, biophilia, is getting increasing attention. The default strategy is to introduce views to nature, even if just a photograph or potted plant. Such perfunctory interventions are beneficial, but there are many more ways to engage our senses.

As designers, we all too frequently respond to a design as a function of how it looks. That's not a huge surprise, given that the majority of our sensory processing is visual, but if we just design for looks, then we miss out on a much richer experience of the world. We have so many senses: touch, taste, balance, sound, smell, pressure, temperature, distancing; the catalogue continues to increase. Memories are richer when the underlying experiences are multisensory, therefore designers need to be more intentional about crafting the experiences we engender in our built environment.

These can be haptic experiences. The Bank of America Tower at One Bryant Park in New York, by COOKFOX Architects, is a beautiful crystalline skyscraper, designed to maximize views to the adjoining Bryant Park. But the first direct experience of the building is your hand grasping a heavily-grained white oak handle on the door. The core wall in the lobby is covered in Jerusalem stone that is filled with ammonites and other fossils. People love tracing the fossils with their fingers, while the elevator banks are wrapped in red leather that continues to patina as people touch it.

These can be olfactory experiences. A pop-up forest in Valextra's flagship store in Milan used tall live-edge slabs of wood to display a seasonal collection of handbags. Designed by Kengo Kuma and Associates, the space was visually gorgeous and had many biophilic qualities, but the scent of the wood was what people remembered. Scent triggers deep memories and can have psychological and physiological benefits. Linalool, the predominate compound in the scent of lavender, triggers the same neural pathways as Valium. Limonene is also found in citrus Similarly, Stone Pine can improve cardiorespiratory response

Or these can be acoustic experiences. Paley Park, designed by Zion and Breen is a 30 foot by 90 foot south-facing park on busy 53rd Street in Midtown Manhattan, New York. The design is simple: two side walls of ivy, decomposed granite gravel on the ground, a canopy of honey locust trees and a water fall as the back wall. Research in psychoacoustics indicates that the sound of falling water is by far the most effective masking sound and that it lowers our stress. When you are walking down the street, the sound of this water feature pulls you down the street to the entrance of the park. Once you are inside Paley Park. the water feature masks out the other sounds of the city.

Bill Browning is a founding partner of Terrapin Bright Green, consultants for biophilic, ecological and high-performance design. He is co-author of *Nature Inside: a biophilic design guide* and *14 Patterns of Biophilic Design*.

Good design means better performance in terms of both human and natural environments. Good design also means that we must make our buildings beautiful.

—Bill Browning

The form of the space itself can also influence our psychological and physiological responses. A clear prospect view through a space lowers our stress and increases a sense of safety. Spaces that protect your back and provide some canopy overhead create the sense of refuge, which reduces stress. The front porch of a craftsman bungalow combines these spatial schemas where you can sit under the shelter of the overhanging roof and have a view up and down the street—creating prospect and refuge together. The form of a space can also induce a sense of mystery, offer a bit of pleasurable risk or inspire awe.

These sensory experiences of nature are, unfortunately, overlooked in architectural education and practice, which seems too focused on the celebration of form as a theoretical exercise. It is time to shift to asking about the space's actual impact on health and wellbeing. Fortunately, there are a few important books about experiences in architectural space. Jun'ichirō Tanizaki's masterpiece, *In Praise of Shadows*, along with Lisa Heschong's *Thermal Delight in Architecture* and Juhani Pallasmaa's *Eyes of the Skin*—all make compelling arguments for us to think differently about architectural space.

What has been needed is a toolkit of design schemas that help us to celebrate all the senses. Now with *Experiential Design Schemas*, Mark DeKay and Gail Brager give us the tools to create spaces that are far from static, spaces that engage wonder and make us more alive.

Authors

Mark DeKay, AIA, is a Full Professor of Architecture specializing in sustainable design theory, research and design tools. His current work is in various applications of Integral Theory and in the experience of sustainable design. He is a registered architect and has taught at the university level since 1992. He is author of *Integral Sustainable Design: transformative perspectives* and primary co-author of, *Sun, Wind, and Light: architectural design strategies, 3rd ed.* Professor DeKay received two national AIA teaching awards, was a Fulbright Fellow to CEPT University in Ahmedabad, India, and recently served as a Fulbright Specialist at Iuav University, Venice, Italy. At the University of Tennessee he has been twice awarded University Scholar of the Week, along with the Chancellor's Awards for both Teaching Excellence and for Research and Creative Practice. Along with his wife Susanne, he lectures internationally on *Solving the Climate Crisis by Design.* He collaborates on research with scholars in Australia, Canada, China, Greece, Italy, Lebanon and Scotland.

Gail Brager earned a Ph.D. in Mechanical Engineering and is a Distinguished Professor of Architecture in the Building Science, Technology + Sustainability program at the University of California, Berkeley. Since joining the faculty in 1984, Professor Brager remains passionate about teaching and conducting research addressing the design, operation and assessment of buildings to minimize energy consumption while enhancing indoor environmental quality and occupant experience. She serves as Director of the Center for Environmental Design Research and Associate Director of the Center for the Built Environment, a collaboration with 50+ partners who are diverse leaders in the building industry. She currently is Associate Dean of UC Berkeley's Graduate Division. Author of 100+ publications, leader in the Women in Green movement and recipient of numerous local, national and international awards, Professor Brager's greatest pride comes from mentoring students and watching them grow and excel in their own journeys to have an impact on the world.

Preface

Mark DeKay

"I believe that a work of art reaches perfection when it conveys silent joy and serenity," Luis Barragán said in presenting the sum of the ideology behind his work (1). The best architects seem eternally on a quest for building feeling into their forms.

(1) Barragán, Luis. 1980. Laureate Acceptance Speech for the Pritzker Architecture Prize

In 1986 I traveled from New Orleans to New Haven, Connecticut in a pilgrimage to Paul Rudolph's Yale Art and Architecture Building, a dramatic expression of bush-hammered concrete and industrial steel-framed glass. It was monumental and spatially complex, composed in 37 levels overlooking a central atrium. I had admired it as a student in Rudolph's precise pen and ink drawings and especially in published black and white photographs. After two days of driving, the visit lasted less than ten minutes. As much as I admired Rudolph's other works, particularly the Florida buildings, the spatial drama and raw expressionism could not override its difficulty, the disorienting tensions it evoked and the atmosphere of angst combined with a cold melancholy.

Walking out of the Art and Architecture Building, I could see the two museums by Louis Isadore Kahn, and because I was there anyway, I decided to visit the Yale Center for British Art. The 1973 building had always struck me in photos as a bit of a dull box, austere matte steel panels set in a concrete frame against a rarely clear New England sky. Walking along the street, that mental construct changed rapidly, passing the active shops on its lower level, finding the cave-like entrance, seeing and touching the steel skin up close as it wrapped to the interior, walking onto the grounded travertine floor, subtly pulled by its lines and by the light beyond. From the compression of the single-storey corner entry to the expanded feel of the sunlit four-storey entrance court, ascending within the enclosed, cylindrical toplighted concrete stairwell, isolated from views, hand gliding over the cool, smooth perfectly-detailed railing, returning to overlook the warm oak-paneled court and finally circling back to the serene library court with its generous filtered soft ambient daylight—such was the delightful symphonic multi-sensory sequence of light and space, temperature, touch and view. Sitting in the carefully placed leather sofas, gazing upon the grand-scale British masterworks in a building become inhabited luminaire, awe resounded. It was a present moment active first-person feeling of the intentions embedded by a conscious architect in form.

I realized this as my first experience in a building of silent joy and serenity.

In 2016, returning to our hotel from a conference dinner, Gail and I struck up the kind of conversations that seems only possible while walking. We were lamenting about, both being teachers of environmental systems, how difficult it seemed to be to enroll our students in the high-performance sustainable design ideas that we were both so passionate about. Much of the energy consumed in buildings is devoted to providing occupants with comfort, which gets very technical in its standardization. Gail suggested that what we needed was a language of environmental design that was more experiential, more about pleasure and performance, a language connecting sustainability to human feeling beyond comfort. Someone mentioned Lisa Heschong's *Thermal Delight* as raising the bar (1979). But, what, we wondered was beyond delight? "Thermal nirvana!", she exclaimed. This began our six-year conversation to understand, explore, define and communicate concepts and methods to help students and practitioners achieve positive experiences beyond comfort.

Returning to Barragán's speech, he continued: "It is alarming that publications devoted to architecture have banished from their pages the words Beauty, Inspiration, Magic, Spellbound, Enchantment, as well as the concepts of Serenity, Silence, Intimacy and Amazement. All these have nestled in my soul, and though I am fully aware that I have not done them complete justice in my work, they have never ceased to be my guiding lights."

In exploring the terrain of experiencing architecture, our work in this book is to both expand the realm of delight-beyond-comfort and to venture into the peaks and potentials of human experience that guided Barragán, to which we might only add the felt sense of connecting to Nature. In providing some conceptual scaffolding and, we hope, some practical tools, our overall intention is to catalyze design that joyfully connects people to nature.

Gail Brager

I have a collection of scrawled notes, hastily written in spontaneous moments of multi-sensory delight. They include scribbles on a paper plate while sitting with my feet in the gentle current of Squaw Creek in Tahoe, on a napkin while cooling off under the punkah of a shaded bhang lassi café in the Indian holy city of Varanasi, and on the back of a receipt while under the bed covers listening to the symphony of rain pounding on the metal and thatch roof portions of a cottage in Caye Caulker, Belize. When I would read each of these the next day, I smiled at the personal memory, but wished I had more poetic proficiency.

Over nearly 40 years of teaching, I have also built a collection of exercises that invite students to observe their environment and connect design decisions with building performance and human experience. Academic readers will be familiar with my early inspirations from the Vital Signs curriculum materials project, developed in collaboration with my UC Berkeley colleague, the unparalleled Professor Cris Benton. My series of thermal awakenings and experiential programming exercises sought to awaken students' senses to the ability of thermal qualities to add to the richness of one's overall experience, expand their sensory-based language, and serve as fodder for their subsequent design project. Students were unequivocally enthused and inspired by these exercises, as was I by their presentations. Yet there was often a disconnect between their excitement and their subsequent ability to translate experiential goals to architectural strategies. I frequently ended the semester wishing I had more explicit experientially-based design guidelines to offer them.

My research has always explored the connections between building, environment and experience. Mentors played a strong role in my development, and hence have had an indirect hand in this book. One of my earliest projects with UC Berkeley Professor Ed Arens asked how to link wind tunnel studies of natural ventilation to physiological/psychological modeling, and give designers a tool for understanding the impacts of their design on occupant comfort. My work on adaptive thermal comfort with Professor Richard de Dear (then a Professor at the University of Macquarie in Sydney) transformed building standards by asking how thermal experiences differ in laboratory experiments compared to real buildings, focusing on the context of climate and conditioning strategies. Some of my biggest inspirations, and avenues for impact, are the Industry Partners of my research group, the Center for the Built Environment (CBE). These architects, engineers, building owners, manufacturers and more, deeply understand the value of bridging research and design decisions. CBE Partners' clear enthusiasm for evidence-based design guidelines made me wish for evermore ways to better articulate and visually represent the design impacts of our research. This project represents an amalgamation of those things I wished for.

The story of how Mark and I came to embark on this book writing journey together is one of serendipity and synergy, forged first on a walk through the streets of Edinburgh. We had known each other for years, and were both attendees of a 2017 conference where I presented a pedagogy paper about experiential aesthetics as a basis for design. The conference kicked off with a workshop led by the Society of Building Science Educators (SBSE), a beloved and loosely organized network of like-minded faculty. During a welcome gathering, Mark was one of the first people to share as we went around describing current activities. He talked about his ideas for a book focusing on experiential design schemas. My ears perked up immediately, this was eerily familiar. I flipped through my small journal and there it was—a page of notes that began "Book Idea: Experiential aesthetics of sustainable design". At the time, I was mostly focused on science, research evidence, and architectural case studies. Mark leaned more towards his strengths in phenomenology and design guidelines. Our intellectual passions and core principles were strikingly similar, even while we brought different perspectives and skill sets to the table. And I confess here—I was mesmerized by how eloquently and poetically Mark expressed his ideas. I knew I had to steal a moment with him before we left Scotland, and caught him on the walk between the conference dinner and hotel, which he describes. Our animated conversation made it clear that this synergistic partnership was worth exploring!

My journey towards this project was built on my profound love of nature, sensitivity to the environment, fondness for architecture, passion for teaching, and gratification from decades of collaborative building science research focused on human response to indoor environmental qualities. Every reader will have their own journey. Our hope is that this book speaks to many different audiences—design professionals, students, and perhaps even building owners and occupants who want to enrich the sensory experiences in spaces they live and work in. Experiential delight can be within reach of everyone, through both small and large design moves, and even simple ways one operates and inhabits an existing space. After reading this book, we are heartened by the prospect that our enthusiasm for this territory will be contagious. We hope we can change your professional directions, but also the ways you personally think about and experience buildings.

Experiential Design Schemas Outline

Contrast · Gradient · Rhythm · Flux · Sequence · Narrative

Levels of scale + complexity

1 Materials
2 Elements
3 Systems
4 Rooms
5 Room Organizations
6 Whole Buildings

Contrast	Gradient	Rhythm	Flux	Sequence	Narrative
C1 Thermic Hues	G1	R1	F1 Melodic Materials	S1 Veridical Patina	N1 Perceptible Provenance
C2 Haptic Connection	G2 Adaptive Altitude	R2 Aperture Engagement	F2 Current Prehension	S2 Aromatic Transit	N2 Authentic Matters
C3 Scintillating Sun	G3 Existential Datum	R3 Biorhythmic Radiance	F2 Water as a Mirror	S3	N3 Roof Terrain
C3 Water You Can Touch	G4 Incalescent Center	R4 Dawn + Dusk Places	F3 Fans First	S4	N3 Distinguishable Durability
C4 Engage the Rain	G4 Euphonic Water	R4 Circadian Space	F3 Revealed Conveyance	S5 Territorial Tuning	N4
C4 Inhabited Periphery	G4 Zephyr Spectrum	R4 Radiant Sailing	F3 Water-Animated Surfaces	S5 Ingress Transitions	N5 Three Realms
C4 Lightrooms	G4 Shades of Brilliance	R4 Habitat Fringe	F4 Compluvium Shower	S5 Light + Dark Procession	N6 Situated Scenes
C4 Tempered Pathway	G5 Pockets of Shadow	R5 Heliotropic Rooms	F5	S5 Phototropic Catenation	
C5 Thermal Enclave	G6 Engagement + Retreat	R6 Cooling Conversions	F6	S6 Topophilic Perambulation	
C6					

Alphabetic Schema Contents

Distributions of conditions

C Contrast
G Gradient
R Rhythm
S Sequence
F Flux
N Narrative

Detailed Schema Contents

Levels of scale + complexity

1 Materials
2 Elements
3 Systems
4 Rooms
5 Room Organizations
6 Whole Buildings

Contrast

Gradient

Detailed Schema Contents

Rhythm

Flux

Sequence

Narrative

Levels of scale + complexity

1 Materials
2 Elements
3 Systems
4 Rooms
5 Room Organizations
6 Whole Buildings

Schemas by Elements + Distribution Type

	Air	Earth	Life	Light
Contrast	C3 Water You Can Touch C4 Engage the Rain C4 Inhabited Periphery C4 Tempered Pathway C5 Thermal Enclave	C1 Thermic Hues C2 Haptic Connection C4 Tempered Pathway	C1 Thermic Hues C4 Tempered Pathway	C1 Thermic Hues C3 Scintillating Sun C4 Inhabited Periphery C4 Lightrooms C4 Tempered Pathway
Gradient	G1 Adaptive Altitude G4 Zephyr Spectrum G6 Engagement and Retreat	G3 Existential Datum	G3 Existential Datum G6 Engagement and Retreat	G4 Shades of Brilliance G6 Engagement and Retreat
Rhythm	R2 Aperture Engagement R4 Radiant Sailing R6 Cooling Conversions	R4 Dawn + Dusk Places R4 Radiant Sailing R4 Habitat Fringe R6 Cooling Conversions	R2 Aperture Engagement R4 Habitat Fringe	R2 Aperture Engagement R3 Biorhythmic Radiance R4 Dawn + Dusk Places R4 Circadian Space R5 Heliotropic Rooms
Flux	F1 Melodic Materials F2 Current Prehension F2 Water as Mirror F3 Fans First F3 Water-Animated Surfaces F4 Compluvium Shower		F2 Current Prehension F2 Water as Mirror F3 Revealed Conveyance	F2 Current Prehension F2 Water as Mirror F3 Water-Animated Surfaces F4 Compluvium Shower
Sequence	S1 Veridical Patina S2 Aromatic Transit S5 Territorial Tuning S5 Ingress Transitions	S1 Veridical Patina S6 Topophilic Perambulation	S1 Veridical Patina S2 Aromatic Transit	S1 Veridical Patina S5 Territorial Tuning S5 Ingress Transitions S5 Light + Dark Procession S5 Phototropic Catenation S6 Topophilic Perambulation
Narrative	N5 Three Realms	N1 Perceptible Provenance N2 Authentic Matters N3 Distinguishable Durability N5 Three Realms N6 Situated Scenes	N1 Perceptible Provenance N2 Authentic Matters N3 Distinguishable Durability N5 Three Realms N6 Situated Scenes	N5 Three Realms N6 Situated Scenes

Sun

C3 Scintillating Sun
C4 Inhabited Periphery
C4 Tempered Pathway
C5 Thermal Enclave

G4 Shades of Brilliance
G5 Pockets of Shadow
G6 Engagement and Retreat

R2 Aperture Engagement
R4 Dawn + Dusk Places
R4 Radiant Sailing
R4 Habitat Fringe
R5 Heliotropic Rooms

F3 Water-Animated Surfaces

S1 Veridical Patina
S5 Ingress Transitions
S6 Topophilic Perambulation

N5 Three Realms

Water

C3 Water You Can Touch
C4 Engage the Rain
C4 Inhabited Periphery
C4 Tempered Pathway

G4 Euphonic Water
G6 Engagement and Retreat

F2 Water as Mirror
F3 Revealed Conveyance
F3 Water-Animated Surfaces
F4 Compluvium Shower

S1 Veridical Patina
S5 Ingress Transitions

N3 Roof Terrain
N5 Three Realms

Levels of scale + complexity

1 Materials
2 Elements
3 Systems
4 Rooms
5 Room Organizations
6 Whole Buildings

Distributions of conditions

C Contrast
G Gradient
R Rhythm
S Sequence
F Flux
N Narrative

Schemas by Condition Dynamics + Scale

Environmental Conditions

Experiential Scale	uniform in space: steady state	uniform in space: dynamic in time	non-uniform in space: steady state	non-uniform in space: dynamic in time
local	N1 Perceptible Provenance N2 Authentic Matters N3 Roof Terrain N3 Distinguishable Durability	F1 Melodic Materials R3 Biorhythmic Radiance	C1 Thermic Hues C2 Haptic Connection C3 Water You Can Touch G1 Adaptive Altitude G3 Existential Datum	C3 Scintillating Sun S1 Veridical Patina S2 Aromatic Transit R2 Aperture Engagement F2 Current Prehension F2 Water as a Mirror F3 Fans First F3 Revealed Conveyance F3 Water Animated Surfaces
whole spaces		R4 Radiant Sailing	C4 Lightrooms G4 Euphonic Water	C4 Engage the Rain C4 Inhabited Periphery C4 Tempered Pathway G4 Incalescent Center G4 Zephyr Spectrum G4 Shades of Brilliance R4 Dawn + Dusk Places R4 Circadian Space R4 Habitat Fringe F4 Compluvium Shower
multiple spaces	N5 Three Realms N6 Situated Scenes		C5 Thermal Enclave G5 Pockets of Shadow S5 Territorial Tuning S5 Ingress Transitions S5 Light + Dark Procession S5 Phototropic Catenation S6 Topophilic Perambulation	G6 Engagement + Retreat R5 Heliotropic Rooms R6 Cooling Conversions

Schemata Language Map

The nested hierarchy of the schema language

The Schemata Language Map is one way to look at the structure of the knowledge base for experiential design. It shows the relationships potential in the many design schemas and organizes them into a nested, lattice-like hierarchical network. Every architectural experience takes place *in a place.* As chapter 2 will outline, architectural space and form combine with natural forces to establish a distribution of conditions that forms the basis for human experiences. We call these the fields of experiential possibilities. Because architectural experience is a phenomena of inhabitation in space, each schema has a dominant spatial scale.

The map's organization is based on the idea that each schema is both *a whole and a part.* Each is made up in some way of schemas at a lower order of complexity and a smaller scale. Each schema also has a *context*, which is another larger, more complex schema. The structure of the map is based on observations about the relationships of parts and wholes first formally identified in general systems theory and later in ecological hierarchy theory. An informal version was employed by Alexander and co-authors (1977) in *A Pattern Language.* Philosopher Ken Wilber (2000) clearly articulated the logics of such systems structures that apply to many knowledge domains in what he called "the twenty tenets."

Levels of scale + complexity shows the hierarchical logic in the Schemata Language Map, the idea that the nesting of schemas within schemas follows levels of scale, where each larger scale also increases in complexity. The complexity spectrum is organized in a system of six levels, from materials to whole buildings, as shown in the sidebar. These six are a subset of the larger set of nine levels first used in *Sun, Wind + Light, 3rd edition* (DeKay + Brown, 2014). Using this logic of parts and wholes, an architectural or landscape *Element* (level 2), for instance a window or garden wall, is made up of and cannot exist without its constituent *Materials* (level 1), such as (for the window) glass and wood. Elements help to build larger, more complex schemas at level 3 *Building Systems,* which might be walls, roofs or floors. In turn, building or landscape Systems are configurations of Elements. Similarly, level 4 *Rooms,* indoors or outdoors, configure schemas at the level of Systems; while level 5 *Room Organizations* are arrangements of level 4 Rooms in plan, section and/or three-dimensions. Level 6 *Whole Buildings* schemas are combinations of two or more Room Organizations. Additionally, level 6 considers the building's plot or immediate site. Each increase in complexity proceeds in this way, a nested hierarchy of both experience and spatial order.

This is but one way to look at the order of parts and wholes; there could be more fine gradations or a logic with fewer levels. This particular system fits designers' common logics and the building professions' language about architectural components and scales. It is a simple system that accounts for all design's physical elements and the empirical observations of parts combining to form larger patterns. Consider the possibility that these scalar relationships may be required for a whole and complete experiential environment. Schemas at several scales are needed to support an *architecture beyond comfort,* that is, places of richness and pleasure, fecundity and felicity.

Levels of scale + complexity

1 Materials
2 Elements
3 Systems
4 Rooms
5 Room Organizations
6 Whole Buildings

Distributions of conditions

C Contrast
G Gradient
R Rhythm
S Sequence
F Flux
N Narrative

These six types of stimuli patterns are outlined at the beginning of chapter 4.

Schemata Language Map

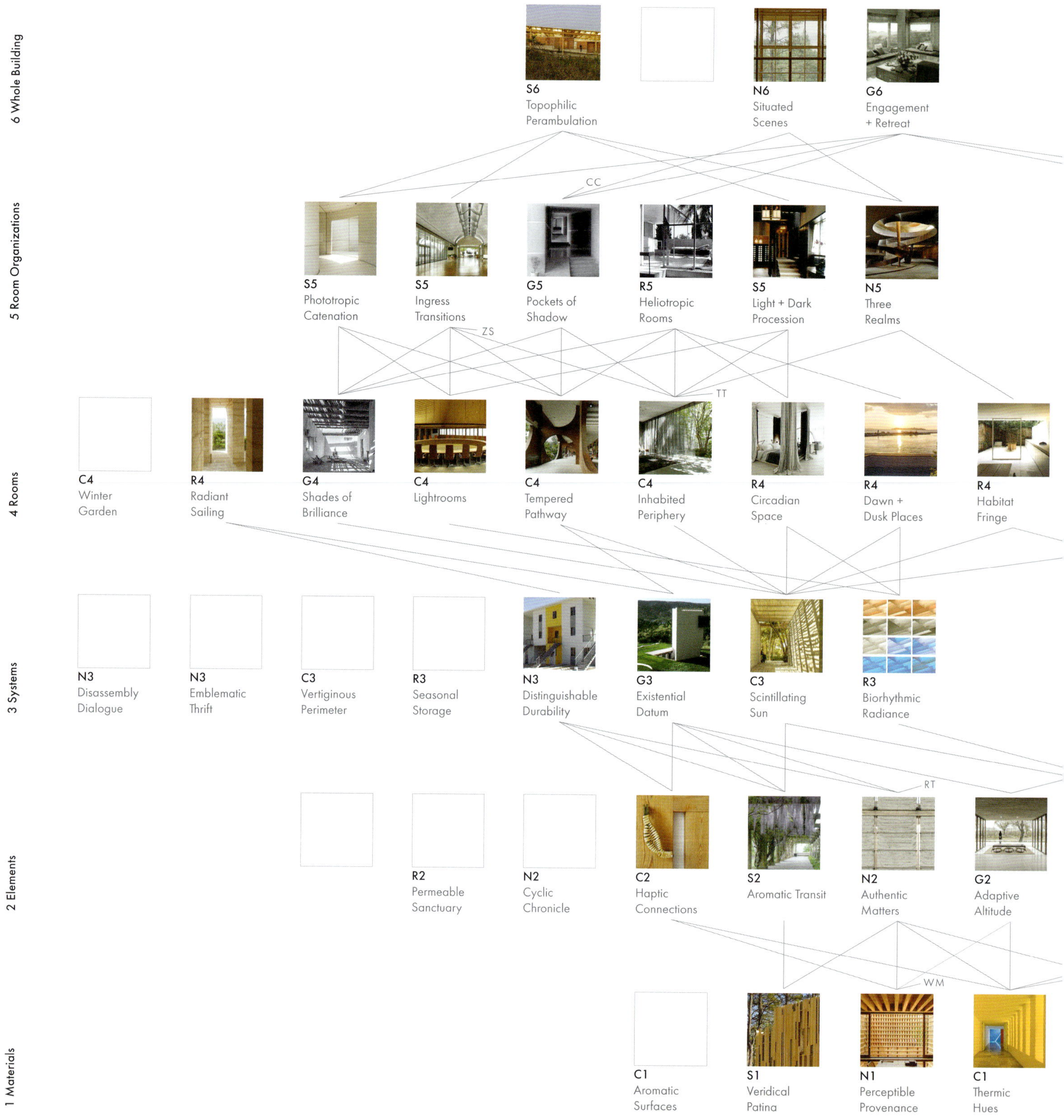

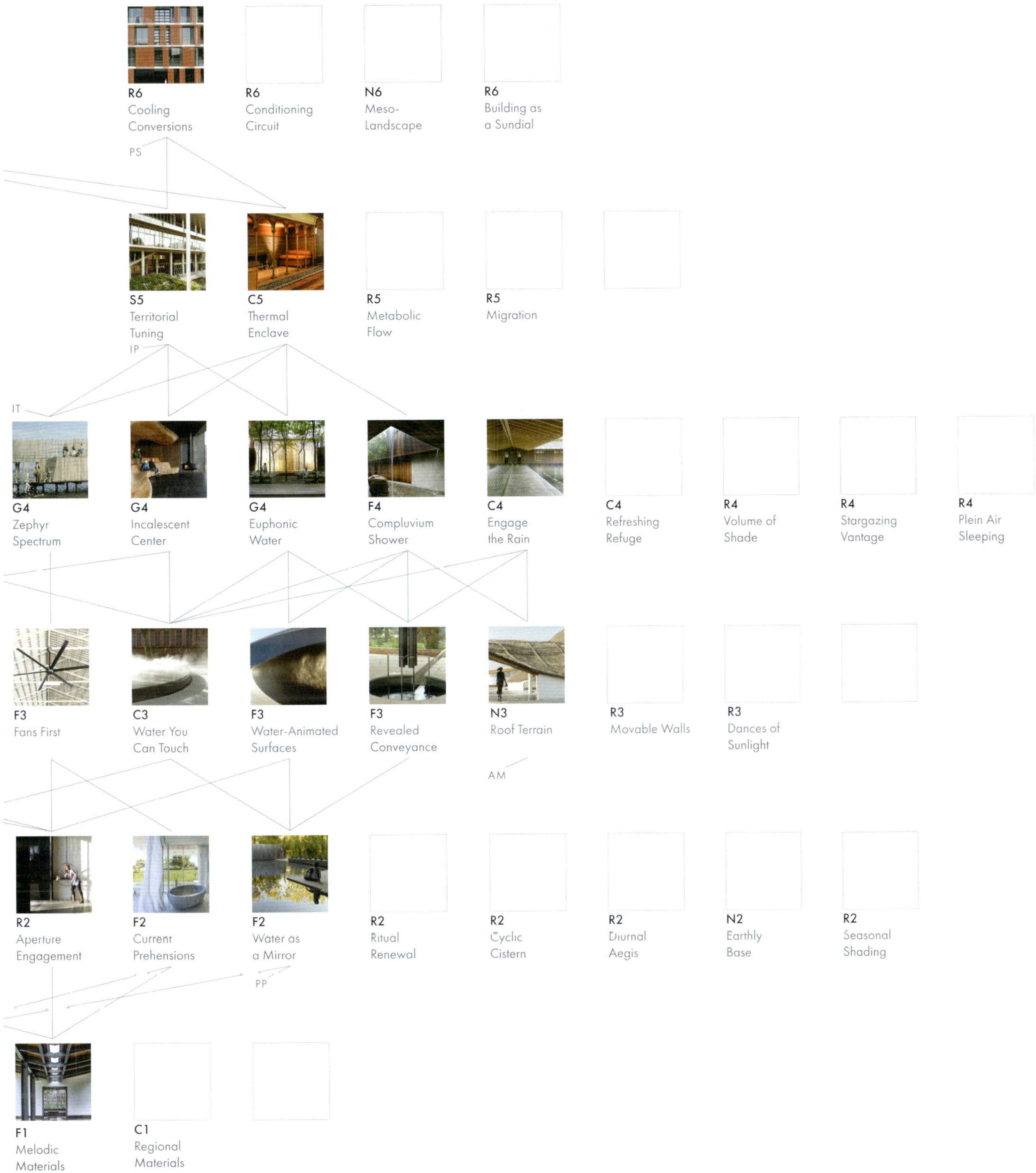

C Contrast
G Gradient
R Rhythm
S Sequence
F Flux
N Narrative

1

Beyond Comfort

opposite
Acropolis Museum

Athens, Greece, 2009
Bernard Tschumi Architects

photo Pygmalion Karatzas

Every good book needs a great hook, something to enroll the reader in getting past page one and investing the mind energy to go on the journey with the authors. If we were to have a hook, an intellectual seduction for the peculiar audience interested in buildings, we might begin with the fundamental human feeling of up and down, sky and earth, that gives the sense of axis though the body to the heavens. We would mention how the sun moves from east to west everywhere, giving the four directions. From there we could link to how the sun's heat drives the wind and fuels plants and then arrive at climate's rhythms, varieties of life and the many beings that share the planet with all of us. There—the stage is set and all the stimuli in place to enroll the reader in the importance of sense perception and its potential polymorphic pleasures. The reader, being clever, would of course know this hook was meant to enroll them, even if we had not already told of it. Nevertheless, we would persevere in emphasizing the root of architecture in the timeless typologies of hearth, oasis, courtyard and several more that become the spatial context for social and Nature connections. We would talk of time at various scales, measured in buildings' life-spans, season-to-season, day-to-night and in moments. The aim would be the reader's pondering what is durable, even true for all time, or to awaken to buildings' changing nature, despite how they seem static—to glimpse of the idea that what humans know of themselves and of Nature might be found in how they inhabit buildings built for rhythm.

Perhaps elder readers might note some homage to a writing motif of von Meiss (1986) and think, as he wrote of the cosmic, territorial and temporal in archetypal terms, that he would likely enjoy the motif's return. While here, why not a quote from that classic author in the margin? There, we have our quote, yet we should, as von Meiss, desire to quote Bachelard for some mystery and poetics, but having consumed our quotation quota, that would be saved for a design schema to come.

Perhaps I shall suggest a very simple planning law: 'from each house and from each place of work one must be able to perceive the rhythm of the seasons and the weather'.

—Pierre von Meiss

We would be remiss if our overture did not mention that the work comes from our own struggles with the slippery subject of human feeling; whatever wisdom occurs here is built on the shoulders of giants. For us the effort has seemed at times like a Sisyphean task, so there would be some humility in the writing. We would certainly emphasize that we are laser-focused on bringing the person back to the center of design intentions in the context of conventional practice that has tended to treat all people and space the same. We shall mention the value of variability, not only because we enjoy the sound of the term's alliteration, but also because we are going to tell you about some new ways to think about interior conditions as dynamic in time and nonuniform in space.

Sooner or later, we would remember that we were introducing both the first chapter and the book as a whole—which reminds us, if we were to enlist your attention with such a précis, to say that there are some critiques to come that will seem radical to some, but please be patient, gentle reader, as these will be followed with new possibilities and solutions. We will suggest the need for a dynamic experiential aesthetic that includes (beyond the simply visual) a full-body phenomenological aesthetic and the intellectual beauty of processes in time. Readers, we expect, will be intrigued by allusions to the many ways to think about positive experiential states in buildings as something aspirational for which one can plan.

We would write the introduction over and over and critique it and look for what we left out and add in a couple of teasers, such as the idea that one may be surprised at the breadth of what can be considered as evidence for design, or that there is not one idea of Nature but many, and you will hear about five. We would express our fervent hope that you care about architecture's impact on climate change and mention that solving the climate crisis by design requires that other people care, too. Evidence shows that people care about Nature more when they have experiences of it, therefore we would end with sharing the idea that almost everything in the rest of this book will help you, if that's what you want, figure how to counteract the rising trend for Nature deficit disorder and instead design to connect people to Nature.

We would not try to convince you of anything. We shall invite you.

Transformations

For architecture, climate change is the most significant issue of our time. Attentive design of the built environment—a large contributor to the problem—can go a long way towards solving the climate crisis. We believe that requires designing for human experience, a paradigm shift for most architects and engineers. Climate-responsive, bio-inspired buildings use less energy and generate less greenhouse gases, but more importantly, they have the potential to engender greater Nature affiliation and understanding. From this human-Nature connection, individuals develop care and sustaining, protective action for buildings and the planet. Along the way, there is delight, joy, serenity, place-empathy and belonging. Our advocacy for this transformation is born first of noticing problems found in contemporary practice, ultimately expressing these more neutrally as *realities*, then reframing them into affirmative *possibilities*.

Realities and Possibilities

We say *realities* because the word is latent with greater opportunity than interpreting situations as problems. This section expands on a few of the many realities in contemporary buildings that occur to us: the neutrality fallacy that brings sensory monotony, buildings that isolate occupants from Nature, the authoritarianism of centralized heating, cooling, ventilation and lighting controls that reduce individual choice, the societal addiction to air-conditioning that results in reduced Nature awareness, and the homogenizing effect of minimum universal standards. Each of these we can say, without negative judgment, is a real effect originating in good intentions. Yet, each comes with a cost, often in the form of complaints from occupants about the impoverished life settings associated with conditions these realities foster. In the next section, we create a new context of interpretation by unpacking five realities of normative architecture and their well-founded *aims*. These are followed by suggesting new *commitments* that can lead to richer human experiential possibilities.

Gando Primary School Library
Gando, Burkina Faso, 2018
Kéré Architecture

Daylighting, non-uniformly varied across space, is also dynamic in time, waxing and waning in intensity over the day and moving with the changing sun path. Strong contrasts such as this are well fit to short duration uses, non-critical activity and moments of drama.

photo left GandoIT
photo right Kéré Architecture

Neutrality fallacy

Imagine for a moment—what life would be like if you and everyone around you ate the same foods at every meal, never experienced weather or the sky's changing light, heard only a constant monotone with no music or bird song, and life was devoid of art to delight the eye. That is essentially what is happening in most buildings when designed for static, uniform, neutral conditions. The cost is inhabitants' dissociation from Nature and its inherent cycles, along with a state of deprivation and monotony. Sensory neutrality has somehow become the building community's ideal. Neutrality in this sense means that environmental conditions are held relatively constant within narrow criteria so that as few people as possible will complain that the room is too noisy, the air too humid, the temperature too cold or the light too dim. These are scenarios built on healthy intentions. Underneath the practice of neutrality is the aim to improve health and minimize discomfort. Its ambitions are many: less mold and mildew, guaranteed rates of fresh air, light wherever it is needed at any time and greater occupant satisfaction with thermal conditions, no matter what the weather. Unfortunately, many buildings fall short of these aspirations. What is missing are patterns of environmental conditions that people actually sense, such as air freshness, changing temperature and moisture, air movement, patterns of dark and light and Nature sounds. As indoor environments become more experientially bland, one's hunger for more stimulation and delight escalates.

Our proposed transformation of neutrality calls for a new commitment to enhanced *vitality*. Vitality can be presenced when the building community abandons homogeneous targets and creates possibilities for more environmental variation and sensory stimulation. This call is not new. Arguments for variability's importance in buildings began with lessons learned from the behavioral sciences. Woodburn Heron, a research psychologist at Ontario's McMaster University, was one scholar who studied the effects of sensory deprivation. Some of his experimental conditions were a bit severe, yet sensory deprivation can be understood as an extreme form of the environmental monotony found in many buildings today. Heron's results are thought-provoking and still relevant. In his most well-known paper, *The Pathology of Boredom* (1957), he wrote, "Prolonged exposure to a monotonous environment has definitely deleterious effects......A changing sensory environment seems essential for human beings. Without it, the brain ceases to function in an adequate way .....Variety is not the spice of life: it is the very stuff of it."

Jack Wohlwill, a central figure in environmental psychology, made significant contributions to understanding human perception and experience of the built environment in *The Physical Environment: A Problem for a Psychology of Stimulation* (1972). He pointed out the psychological benefits of sensory stimulation in terms of the dimensions of intensity, novelty and complexity. He notes that reduced sensory monotony has positive impacts on people's motivation, perception and cognitive functions. Similar findings come from building researchers. Kenny Gerlach (1974), environmental engineer with Arup Associates, discovered that cognitive processes are more attuned to perceiving relationships and variation than to absolute conditions: "Exposure to unchanging stimuli has been shown to induce satiation and boredom." Looking more specifically at thermal response, Donald McIntyre (1980), a leading figure in the field of thermal comfort research from the UK's Electricity Council Research Centre, argued that humans have an inherent need for sensory stimulation and made a plea for using fluctuating interior temperatures to counteract thermal boredom. Evidence for the positive impacts of environmental variance have been around longer than most of the buildings that North Americans inhabit today.

We advocate for dynamic non-uniform indoor conditions as a counter to an ideal constancy and support the longstanding research arguments against neutrality. Giving people choices to seek their preferred settings is particularly important for happiness. Difference deserves its due. Along the way, such heterogeneous conditions yield some surprising possibilities for delight. Forsaking neutrality will mean crafting spaces that give the opportunity for stimulating contrasts or rhythms in formerly dull situations. In the midst of chaotic contexts, it means creating places of repose and stillness. Developing architectural thought to transcend constancy requires recognizing the validity of neutrality's underlying aims, occasionally appropriate, yet most times not.

Nature disconnection

Parallel to conventional practice's lack of embracing the vitality possible in conditional variability stands the congruent reality of how buildings have progressively dissociated from Nature. People today are spending less time outdoors, and this impacts health, well-being and Nature stewardship. Richard Louve (2005) coined the term *nature-deficit disorder* in his ground-breaking book, *Last Child in the Woods*. With a particular focus on child development, he presents a range of scientific evidence for how Nature disconnection contributes to people's diminished use of their senses, attention difficulties and longer-term illness, both physical and emotional.

From Nature disconnection to affinity with Nature

Center for Health + Social Welfare
Laongo, Burkina Faso, 2014
Kéré Architecture

Open to sky, changing light, fresh air, framed landscape views. Water channels irrigate a young tree for future shade, surrounded by wood, stone, earth materials.

We are in a beautiful area. I wanted people to have a connection to this fantastic landscape. I wanted patients to have a view of the nature around them, whatever position they are lying in.—*Frances Kéré*

photos Kéré Architecture

This reality can be viewed at various scales, from societal to the individual. Christopher Ives, a sustainability scientist in the School of Geography at the University of Nottingham, examined the spectrum of how people connect with or disconnect from Nature (Ives et al. 2018). These relationships range from external physical and sensory interactions, to internal cognitive and emotional responses and, ultimately, to how Nature relationships affect a person's worldview. These interactions are interrelated. For example, direct experiential connections with Nature can shape emotional engagement, environmental knowledge and attitudes, and foster a worldview that embraces planetary care. Conversely, Nature disconnection can lead to people caring less about the environmental consequences of their actions, such as the way their energy use contributes to climate change. The Nature disconnection reality is seen in buildings with impoverished views of outdoor Nature, where workers are distant from basic cues to weather outside. Common examples include small tinted windows, deep floor plans that ignore daylight and fixed windows that optimize for the machine but shut out all possibility of feeling a breeze or hearing outdoor sounds. Still, even underneath these practices we find the well-intentioned aim of efficient energy use and predictable indoor conditions in service to better life quality.

We encourage architects, engineers and code officials to fuse these admirable aims with a recognition of humanity's four-billion-year evolutionary connection of organism to environment. The new commitment is for *affinity with Nature*. In inhabitants' affiliative Nature relationships emerge the possibilities for increased Nature awareness, understanding natural rhythms, biophilia and varieties of meaningful connection, from membership to merging. Buildings, as the prime mediator between contemporary humans and Nature, can simultaneously bring elements of the outdoors inside and encourage people to go out. Indoor plants are lovely, but offer a poor substitute for an outdoor lunch place where one can revel in changing colors and smells of seasonal foliage, watch the passing clouds, tune in to the movement and sounds of birds and ground one's feet on the earth. Ultimately, these individual lived encounters with Nature matter most.

Conditioning monarchies

The architecture-Nature disconnect coincides with an inward-oriented, isolated building occupation and a paradigm of centralized building environmental control systems. While lighting and HVAC systems become increasingly sophisticated, their capabilities are rarely marshaled to apply a nuanced qualitative palette. It is as if occupants live under a monarchy of environmental conditioning in which an unseen autocrat works to satisfy a mythic median preference while building citizens have no right of petition. Under the monarchy, conditioning and lighting systems are based on predictable machines and electronics producing uniformity across large zones or an entire residence.

Today's commercial buildings typically have large, electrically-lighted, constantly cooled interior zones and flush-skin facades without shading depth. They depend completely on centrally-controlled HVAC, where occupants have little role in self-determining their interior environments. We call this tyrannical situation a *space-based approach*; it is relatively oblivious to individual voices. Remember, beneath this approach lie laudable aims: to achieve the highest comfort for the most people, eliminate human error and reduce feedback delay.

We propose an evolved commitment for a *democracy of personal control*. Democratic inhabitation depends on what we term a *person-based approach*, which starts with the intention that heating, cooling, ventilation, lighting and shading solutions transcend comfort and provide people pleasure. It considers difference and gives individuals or small groups the means for tuning local domains. Its experiential possibilities manifest as a sense of personal freedom and agency, greater physical and affective pleasure, and a more active user participation in building operation. The latter is explored more in the R2 Aperture Engagement schema, which encourages occupants to consciously control climatic relationships by adjusting openings and layers, thereby also building place connection and empathy.

In transcending the limits of traditional buildings' vernacular and decentralized conditioning, Modern approaches threw out the baby with the bathwater, and systems with centralized controls won out in the 20th century. Premodern commercial buildings typically had shallow floor plates where open windows cooled occupants with breezes. High ceilings allowed heat to rise away from occupied zones, fans provided cooling in localized areas, and natural lighting for desks near the perimeter minimized electrical lighting needs. In such buildings, people controlled their situation by regulating clothing, moving from space to space, engaging with the architecture by opening windows, employing shades and operating heating sources, which were themselves most often distributed around the building. These traditional strategies still work. There is also value in the capacity for well-designed intelligent

From conditioning monarchy to democracy of control

Burkina Institute of Technology (BIT)
Koudougou, Burkina Faso, 2020
Kéré Architecture

Local, independent control for light and air. A screened veranda buffer zone brings variety to conditions and sequence with adaptive opportunity.

photos Jaime Herraiz

centralized mechanical conditioning and electrical lighting systems to provide for human needs, especially at night, in public spaces with many people or when climatic conditions become extreme. Buildings need the workable aspects of both traditional and modern approaches. A newly reimagined person-based approach builds on these and integrates centralized and dispersed order, manual with automated regulation, large and small spatial domains, individual with collective agency.

Balancing the benefits of space-based and person-based approaches integrates three strategies:

1 Architectural patterns fundamentally responsive to perennial climatic rhythms
2 Smart, efficient active systems used only when and where needed
3 Opportunities for inhabitants to engage the architecture and systems to modify conditions.

Air-conditioning addiction

Harmonizing these approaches is essential for reversing a trend dangerous for both people and planet. In developed countries, occupants are increasingly addicted to air-conditioning—whether at home, in the office or the automobile—an illness spreading globally. While the term *addiction* may seem excessive, many previous authors refer to this predicament.

University of Delaware Professor Willett Kempton (1992), in a presentation on The Anthropology of Comfort, determined from field data that attitudes about and use patterns of air-conditioning (AC) appeared to satisfy the same definition of addiction used by clinicians with respect to drugs. Examples include using AC for longer than

Startup Lions Campus
Turkana County, Kenya, 2021
Kéré Architecture

Landmark stack ventilation towers take inspiration from termite mounds. Low wall inlets filter dust, for an IT building with no AC in a hot-arid climate. Pergola-covered roof terraces shaded by creeping vegetation offer spaces for informal meeting and landscape connection. The layout creates a climate-protected oasis that doubles as gathering courtyard.

photos Kinan Deeb

required, wanting to reduce use but not managing to do so and continuing to use AC even when one knows it is causing problems (such as climate change). In a provocative essay, London School of Economics Professor Gwyn Prins (1992) examined the anthropological dimensions of air-conditioning in the US. He presented a scathing argument that "the physical addiction to air-conditioned air is the most pervasive and least noticed epidemic in modern America."

Similar to many of the realities already identified, at this one's base are aims for improved life quality and reduced suffering. Willis Carrier, the inventor of modern air-conditioning, was motivated by wanting reduced humidity for printing presses and later, delight for (and tickets sales from) cinema patrons, not addiction and global warming. Yet, that which relieves suffering or delights the senses, when indulged over the long term, becomes the suffering of craving and attachment. The Buddha would have predicted it.

Design-for-experience has implications for energy use and climate change, perhaps most strongly in the area of space cooling. The global demand for air-conditioning is surging; residential use is predicted to more than triple by 2050 (IEA 2018). AC is the fastest growing energy user in buildings and contributes significantly to greenhouse gas emissions from electricity production and refrigerant leakage. This growth is changing the way buildings are designed, operated and experienced. Indoor coolness has become an unfortunate prestige symbol. Yet the problems of overcooling (both more hours and cooler temperature) are pervasive and well-documented. This is a particular problem in US workplaces where buildings are being operated to run colder in summer and warmer in winter than in the past—in contrast to many people's preferences and the opposite of what both common sense and the comfort standards suggest. UC Berkeley researcher Tom Parkinson (2021) used an innovative method combining large field study datasets with Twitter crowdsourced data to demonstrate a significant gender inequity caused by this overcooling, with the associated impacts on well-being borne predominantly by women. Understanding and changing cooling expectations can have significant implications for both improving thermal satisfaction and mitigating the climate crisis.

We are not arguing against all air-conditioning; rather, we encourage limiting its use to just when and where it is actually needed. We advocate reversing the trends of excessive space cooling and thermal monotony—shifting to the possibility for "gourmet thermal experiences", as Lisa Heschong (1979) framed it in *Thermal Delight in Architecture*. The associated commitment becomes *healthy delight*. Reducing air-conditioning reliance aligns with creating experientially-rich environments. The possibilities that surface are thermal places that provide epicurean occasions, variable conditions and congruence with climatic rhythms of the day and season.

An approach to cooling committed to healthy delight is that of an architecture of thermal moderation that avoids saturating pleasure centers, which fuels addiction. Occupants, building envelopes and conditioning systems would dynamically respond to the ever-changing climatic patterns. While bodily sensations are stimulated from the immediate environment, one's perception and relative enjoyment of sense experience depends in part on broader contextual factors and cultural interpretations. While context is key to creating situated experiences, designers are bound by codes and standards, which typically do not embrace or facilitate this approach.

Universal standards

People notice their environment mostly because it occurs that something is wrong: bad odors, dripping faucets, and noisy neighbors. Common perception is dominated by negative impressions, such as stuffy air, poor lighting, annoying background noises or arid indoor air that dries the nostrils. In parallel, conventional building standards and the practices they drive are based on aims to reduce negative perceptions and complaints by setting minimum acceptability thresholds. They are built on the premise that if no one actually notices the indoor environmental qualities, then success has been achieved.

Building standards are perhaps the most influential mechanism for transferring information from research to practice. However, they constitute the floor that defines minimum acceptable performance for buildings, rather than an aspirational ceiling. By focusing on avoiding complaints, rather than enrichment or *joie de vivre*, such standards further promote everyday life's homogeneity. Because codes and standards target universal application, the architecture generated from them disregards social, cultural, regional and other contextual influences on individual's approbation. These include the ways men and women dress differently, demographic and health-based variations in metabolism, cultural or employment dress codes and expectations arising from how cultures have adapted to climates other than North American temperate zones. Standards disregard how the building

From universal standards to differential flexibility

Lycee Schorge Secondary School
Koudougou, Burkina Faso, 2016
Kéré Architecture

Interior spaces are wrapped with shading on sides and top to create a layered microclimate facilitating flexible location. Flexible operation supports flexible, adaptive comfort standards using local, not universal, criteria. Adaptive comfort supports natural ventilation via wind catcher towers to each classroom.

photos
left Andrea Maretto
right Francis Kéré

itself influences inhabitant inclinations, such as the way, over time, sealed envelopes and full-time mechanical conditioning can narrow inhabitants' temperature tolerances. Over time, occupants come to expect warmer temperatures in winter and cooler temperatures in summer, thus thwarting their natural bioclimatic adaptation.

We recognize that the purpose of standards is to set minimum thresholds rather than to be aspirational, which is more in the purview of green building, living building and wellness certifications. Nevertheless, there is room for improvement. To supplement existing standards, we propose a new commitment to *differential flexibility*. Greater flexibility can account for the diversity of individual, regional, climatic and cultural differences. This forwards the possibility that occupants can be more engaged and connected to their environment, helping to shape their own positive and pleasurable affections.

Optimistically, we see some movement in this direction. The 2020 edition of ASHRAE Standard 55 (2020) incorporates several addenda that begin deconstructing conditional monarchies. Based on research done at UC Berkeley's Center for the Built Environment, the standard now has thermal environmental control classification levels based on the degree of occupant personal control (see graphic in R2 Aperture Engagement). The applicability of the climate-based Adaptive Comfort Model (described further in Chapter 3), which shifts comfort limits upward as the season warms, has also been expanded. Previously limited only to purely naturally-conditioned spaces, it is now applicable to mixed-mode buildings that combine mechanical cooling and natural ventilation. The WELL Building Standard (2020) focuses on assessing how buildings impact health and well-being. It equitably considers experiences from diverse populations, encouraging opportunities for personal control and engagement.

Conventional Realities	Underlying Aims	Transformed Commitments	Experiential Possibilities
Neutrality Fallacy	improved health + minimized discomfort	Vitality	mental acuity, happiness, satisfaction, alertness
Nature Disconnection	efficient energy use + predictable indoor conditons	Affinity with Nature	nature awareness, understanding rhythms, biophilia, memberhsip, merging
Contitioning Monarchies	highest comfort for the most people, reduced human error + feedback delay	Democracy of control	freedom + agency, pleasure, active participation
Air-Conditioning Addiction	improved life quality + reduced suffering	Healthy delight	gourmet thermal experiences + dynamic climatic congruence
Universal Standards	reduced negative perceptions + avoiding complaints	Differential flexibility	environmental engagement, well-being, cultural + regional diversity

From conventional realities to experiential possibilities

Each current practice reality has well-intended aims, yet comes with associated disasters. Each can be transformed to a new aspirational design commitment with greater possibilities for pleasure, satisfaction and Nature appreciation.

Summary

These five pairings (see table) of conventional realities and their transformation to new experiential possibilities conceptually frame ways for practice to shift its internal, mostly tacit, aims to more conscious commitments that serve human flourishing. To reiterate: while conventional practice realities are founded in well-meaning intentions, results often fall short. The design community can aim higher. In each of these five realities, the Modern, 20th century approach could be replaced with a more complex and diversified, greener, pluralist approach, yet collages and amalgamations alone provide no coherent living world. A building is not a complicated assemblage or montage. Our propositions are not easy; rather, they call for increasingly adaptable sophistication and a complex order. A more integral, evolutionary approach transcends what has historically been unworkable, unsustainable and life-degrading, and instead forwards what is workable, sustainable and life-affirming.

Delightful Aspirations

Designing for experience requires considering in concert spatial composition and order, aesthetic perception and interpretive cultural meaning. Towards this aspiration, we explore two underlying themes:

1 Designing for the expanded experiential possibilities described above embraces a broader-than-normative view of building aesthetics, expanding from visual perception alone to encompass multi-sensory and time-based phenomenal beauty.

2 Emotional connections can be borne from social rituals that connect people and buildings to climate and other natural processes.

Most human beings have essentially the same biological sense systems for perception. One person takes in the same colors, light patterns and temperatures as the next. Aesthetic perception, however, is an inside job. It is an interior, subjective phenomenon of individuals. To know if someone finds a scene beautiful, they must be asked. We depend on one another for reporting subjective responses. At the same time, the very language used for that reporting is given by one's social and cultural contexts that provide the means for communication, and interpretation. Thus, any expanded exploration of aesthetic feeling situated in architectural form and space requires making sense of that feeling by employing an expanded experiential aesthetic conception.

Experiential Aesthetics

Aesthetics is the philosophical attempt to explain first-person aesthetic experience in response to beauty. It is commonly cast in visual terms, as vision dominates human perception, and other senses are often united through visual impressions. Architectural thinker Juhani Pallasmaa (2012), a proponent of multisensorial space, writes, "The perception of sight as our most important sense is well grounded in physiological, perceptual and psychological facts." Pallasmaa argues that fully multisensorial space is an existential necessity that creates life-enhancing architecture. Each sense has its own way of stirring pleasure and emotion, and of course, the senses overlap and reinforce each other. In addition to the familiar visual and spatial composition elements, experiential designers fashion ever-fluctuating warmth and coolness, sun and shade, breeze and stillness, light and dark, stillness and sound. We explore the science of these different sensory systems further in Chapter 3.

To unpack this, consider a framework developed in *Integral Sustainable Design: transformative perspectives* (DeKay 2011, 2012) that identifies five nested levels of sustainable design aesthetic complexity: visual, phenomenological, process, ecological and evolutionary. In the current work, what we refer to as *experiential aesthetics* is a combination of the first three (see table).

Experiential aesthetics. Experience is inclusive. Each level of aesthetic complexity requires a different perceptual perspective, a distinguishable prospect. Each also apprehends different phenomena not disclosed by the others. These are summarized in the table. While the primacy of vision may be the fundamental basis for an aesthetic architectural experience, it is just that: fundamental. *Visual aesthetics* refers to one's visual experience and perception of order; this is often termed *formal aesthetics* because the objects considered occur as objective form. More complex and inclusive, a *phenomenological aesthetic* includes the visual, along with the full range of multi-sensory information, as stimulus for aesthetic response. Design transcends architecture-as-image to evoke a sense of awe, moments of surprise and feelings of joy, peace, pleasure or rejuvenation. *Process aesthetics* appreciates the elegant interplay of events in time with patterns of form and space. Process is always dynamic and allows one to find beauty in natural rhythms.

More complex apprehensions include the less complex level. Appreciating experience engages all three degrees of human faculties. An individual can develop capacity at each level on this aesthetic line.

Complexity	Aesthetic Perspective	Perceptual Objects
Visual fundamental perception	– Vision-dominated – Beauty as the seen – Leads to appreciation [1]	– Static form, color, unity, balance, variety, repetition, texture, proportion – Appears as composition
Phenomenological transcends + includes visual	– Multiple senses – Beauty as whole-body experience of form + forces in concert – Leads to above [1] + awareness [2]	– Natural forces interact with static or changing form, changing conditions – Appears as direct experience of contrasts, gradients, fluxes
Process transcends + includes phenomenological	– Multi-sensory + memory + thought – Beauty as order of space revealing process – Leads to above [2] + understanding	– Dynamic process as the order of change (growth, seasons, processes) – Appears as experiential rhythms, sequences, narratives

In Chapter 4, we advance dozens of applied concepts, grounded in this expanded view of experiential design aesthetics, engaging the visual beauty beheld by the eye, phenomenological beauty perceived by the whole body and process beauty apprehended by the mind. Great chefs can turn simple ingredients into delectable feasts of taste, smell and visual composition, delivered in ritual sequence. In the same way, architects imaginatively organize sensory elements to create epicurean phenomenal events engaged in ritualistic or commonplace sequences. Over time, such elevated life events become established as the constituents for generating significant meanings of place and Nature.

Ritual Connection

English primatologist and anthropologist Jane Goodall once remarked, "Only if we understand can we care. Only if we care will we help. Only if we help shall we be saved." In the built environment, we find a parallel with her idea of stewardship for other creatures. When buildings are designed to create harmony with the natural world, then people develop greater environmental sensitivity and feel more motivated to protect Nature. Similarly, when inhabitants feel emotionally connected to their buildings, they are more motivated to take care of them (Kellert 2012). Over time, building owners will more likely restore and renovate as needed, rather than neglecting, demolishing and replacing.

What creates emotional connections among people and their homes, schools, markets and workplaces? Connection often arises from finding social meaning in situations. When individuals share experiences, they

Villa Sarabhai

Ahmedabad, India, 1954
Le Corbusier, architect

Opportunities for engagement with or retreat from the complex Ahmedabad climate are afforded by spatial migration, earth-sheltered thermal mass and operable elements, bringing residents into participatory relationship with architecture-in-place.

photo left Manuel Bougot
photo right Arnout Fonck

develop empathy for each other. In the same way, when people share uniquely enjoyable life places, they potentially build an individual sense of relatedness and belonging set in a field of shared resonance. While emotional response to buildings and places has a personal aspect, collective experience generates the potential for shared understanding and meaning.

The prospect for emotional connections to buildings and Nature is enhanced when perceptions are associated with social rituals. These, in turn, may be connected to diurnal and seasonal rhythms that are particularly revealed in a climate-responsive building attuned to those cadences. Ralph Knowles explored these themes over a long career in teaching design students and in his books, *Sun, Rhythm, Form* (1981) and *Ritual House* (2006). Lance LaVine (2001) eloquently elaborates on this idea in his book, *Mechanics and Meaning in Architecture,* where he argues that the role of architectural elements and technologies is to "place people into significant relationships with nature" by providing both literal and figurative connections to events that happen each day and every season.

Buildings can host phenomenal and atmospheric episodes that bring awareness to Nature's pulsations. Rather than beholding buildings as static objects, one can recognize them as settings for dynamic temporal interplay. In her paper, The Dance of a Summer Day, an exposition of family life in Le Corbusier's Villa Sarabhai, Susan Ubbelohde (2003) details occupants' cyclic rituals as tightly tied to daily climatic variations. Simple moments, such as waking up after sleeping in the roof garden, walking barefoot across cool stone tiles or operating the pivoting windows that connect indoors to the garden are revealed as layered events. They occur as palpable thermal experiences steeped in psychological and emotional connections to daily life. The temporal patterns of dawn-to-dusk and summer-to-monsoon-to-winter are reflected in both the rhythms of the home's climatic response and its associated social use, creating physical and spiritual refuge. The house displays an ability to "reveal the world" to residents, bringing a love and understanding of place.

Heschong (1979) provides wonderful examples where ritual connections are revealed in places with strong variable thermal qualities from diverse cultures and times. With poetic and critical insights, she describes *necessity, delight, affection* and *sacredness* as design constructs. Favorite examples include the archetypes oasis and hearth, the Islamic walled garden, the Japanese art of associating thermal experiences with other senses and room-to-room migration rituals in Baghdad courtyard houses.

Masaya Saito and his colleagues (2000), in research conducted at Japan's Musashi Institute of Technology, reveals the evolved sensory perceptions of Japanese culture, where *suzusisa* means "a pleasant thermal sensation to be sensed under rather dynamic conditions; for example, a hot and humid environment with some breeze". Japanese architecture reveals a sensitivity towards crafting subtle moments. Similarly, Jun'ichirō Tanizaki (1977) describes in a perennial architects' favorite, *In Praise of Shadows*, the Japanese sense of beauty and environmental relationship that stems from an appreciation of soft gradients, subtle contrasts and the association of luminous patterns with non-visual senses. Inhabitants often develop a deep sense of affection for their homes or celebration for event moments.

We take the stand in this work—based on experience, on built precedent and on hope—that environmentally, experience begets relationship begets meaning, which leads to action. The deep work of the thinkers, scholars and designers mentioned above, and many others, give us confidence that buildings can be designed to elevate occupants' experience of Nature and its forces, linking these to social events and rituals both mundane and extraordinary. We imagine a more profound inhabitation in which occupants become place-empathetic residents of buildings that reveal the world and place people into significant relationships with Nature—that is, a human ecosystem where, as architect and author William McDonough (2016) puts it, "we could become, once again, native to place".

What Experience Means

In this work, we address only a subset of the many experiences possible in buildings, while acknowledging that they can mean many things to individuals. Here we outline the positive nature of this agenda: the intention for buildings to engender mental flow, delight, joy and peace, centeredness—not boredom, drowsiness, angst, tension, stress, transgression, confrontation or disorientation. Broadly considered, experience can be understood in individuals as both transitory body-mind *states* and as more permanent consciousness *stages*. Stages are studied

Nested experiential state complexity

More inclusive states seem to depend on less inclusive ones.

adapted and expanded from Watchman et al. 2021

Sensation Environmental stimuli affect sensory organs		Affect Feelings + thoughts about a sensation		Understanding Knowledge of abiotic, biotic + ecologic		Affiliation Significant relationships	
hot	cold	safe	playful	aware	comprehension	empathy	merging
bright	dark	private	curious	knowing	appreciation	bonding	kinship
quiet	loud	exposed	imaginative	orderly	wholeness	companionship	affinity
smooth	rough	protected	inspired	meaningful	integrity	membership	unity
wet	dry	excited	fascinated	enrichment	coherance	genus loci	compassion
humid	arid	suprised	attracted	discernment	significance	community	rapport
calm	busy	satisfied	confident	literacy	utility	belonging	solidarity
still	breezy	comfortable	healthy	recognition	tolerance	connection	identity
odourless	fragrant	pleased	bored	familiarity		oneness	acquaintance
enclosed	open	delighted	sleeply			alliance	intimacy
hard	soft	joyful	alive				
		wonderful	awestruck				

by developmental psychology and more recently in environmental psychology (Piaget 1972; Kegan 1982, 1998; Kellert 2005). The distinction is important because the same event can be interpreted differently, and thus design may engender various experiences, depending on a person's developmental stage.

As examples (adapted from Watchman et al. 2021): In a covered outdoor room, a kindergartner may sense and enjoy the diverse colors and fragrances of outdoor vegetation during this *magical* stage (Gebser 1985) in which children are fully immersed in Nature. A third grader may appreciate the same space during rainy-day recess or the delight of choosing options to read in sun-filled or shaded areas, illustrating this stage's focus on individual interests and desires. Kegan (1982) identified this as the *second order of consciousness,* when children can translate their own perceptions into concrete categories and consequences. By sixth grade, as *rational stage* cognitive capacities develop, a student may have a greater understanding of solar rhythms and times during which direct sunlight penetrates the space. Experience gets registered in time and begins to form larger patterns. Experiences at this stage help develop *pluralistic stage* environmental values, particularly as children explore and create bonds with their place (Kellert 2005; Sobel 1999). Finally, adult teachers might embrace a host of multi-sensory experiences in seasonal planting rituals, understanding with complex *integral stage* thought their contribution to the larger ecosystem of the schoolyard and nested larger scales beyond. These later, more complex value and cognition stages are found in Beck and Cowan (1996) as *flex-flow* and in Kegan's fifth-order consciousness as "the *self-transcending mind*".

Nested experiential state complexity, shown in the diagram, provides an orienting framework illustrating four hypothetical aspects developed from ideas presented by scholars of biophilic design (Beatley 2016, Browning et al. 2014; Heerwagen + Gregory 2008; Kellert 2018; Watchman et al. 2021). Moving from left to right, more complex states are built on less complex ones.

At the simplest level, bodily *sensation* can sometimes be sufficient unto itself, such as *witness consciousness*, or the practice of detached observation and mindfulness; that is, noticing without judging, interpreting, evaluating or adding valence, as when sensing "the air right now feels hot and dry." Sensation then manifests as a mental perception or *affect,* which is essentially how one feels about that sensation. At the next more inclusive level, *understanding* occurs as direct knowledge through affective experience over time, but can also be influenced by socialization and education. Knowing what patterns to look for eases the effort to spot them. Finally, *affiliation* is about connection. In one sense, affiliation depends on understanding; it is hard to feel connected to or care for something unknown. In this way, it is the most complex and inclusive of the four and is often associated with higher developmental stages, yet, like all temporary states, affiliation can be experienced at any stage.

Our work attempts to address all of these nested levels. The framework can be used to explain how the body-mind experiences architecture in multifarious ways. In terms of sensation, this book focuses on the visual, thermal, acoustic and olfactory qualities of the built environment, with some additional attention paid to the way materials, textures and the ground plane affect the haptic sense of touch and the kinesthetic and proprioceptive senses of movement. These empirical qualities of physical and living elements occur within and are shaped by organizations of architectural space and one's movements within that order. People quickly translate sensation to register physiological, affective (psychological/emotional) and cognitive responses. We describe or present evidence for these responses where available, while acknowledging that they can vary significantly among individuals, even for the same set of environmental conditions. Having encountered them, individuals make sense of the occurrence as different understandings about the natural forces and process at work, such as a radiant field in a room with a fireplace, or the cyclic patterns of daylight that follow short and long days in a year. In recognizing significant patterns, humans are meaning-making beings, with the potential for deep affiliation with Nature as their home territory.

Experiential Hierarchy

Psychology offers various theories to explain human experience. Among them, environmental psychologist Jacqueline Vischer (2008) describes an environmental comfort sequence that begins with basic *habitability,* and then moves upward to levels that she termed *physical comfort, functional comfort* and *psychological comfort.*

Spectrum of occupant experiences

Building standards begin with habitability. Conventional practice targets sufficiency. Good designers aim beyond comfort.

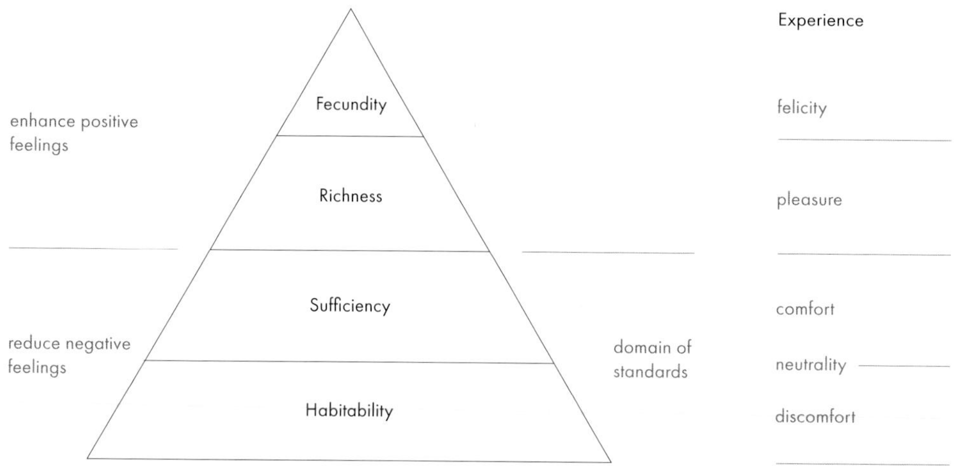

Spectrum of Occupant Experiences (diagram next page) started with Vischer's basic model. Then we created a modified diagram to elaborate on the meaning of these levels for architecture. The words within the triangle represent the overall goals of each level, while the words on the right suggest experiential states. The most fundamental level of shelter begins at the lowest level to establish a *habitability* zone, offering enough protection from the elements to ensure health and safety, such as avoiding extreme heat and cold stress. While occupants might feel a range of discomfort, this zone rises above otherwise uninhabitable deprivation conditions. This most basic level is expressed as habitability guidelines for passive survivability in resilient buildings during natural disasters, heat waves and power outages. While this may seem a low bar, most contemporary buildings would in fact operate below this threshold—unsafe, unhealthy and uninhabitable—without their utility feeds and constant throughput of water and waste and energy for heating, cooling, lighting, refrigeration, even fresh air.

Buildings are generally operated to meet the second level, *sufficiency*, where many codes and standards aim. This territory spans from imperceptible neutrality to satisfying basic comfort, but not beyond. Conventional building engineering practice is targeted to reduce negative feelings, but not necessarily to enhance positive feelings. For lighting, this might include a range of illuminance levels specified for different kinds of activities or contrast ratio limits to reduce glare. For the thermal environment, standards equate comfort with neutrality. As we argue later, we see neutrality as sitting near the threshold between habitability and sufficiency, while a state of comfort is higher. Thermal standards define sufficiency in terms of a "comfort zone", prescribing conditions that 80% of occupants will find acceptable, and providing various ways in which "acceptability" can be directly or indirectly determined. While it is sometimes necessary for building standards to address responses of the average person or large groups, that is not aspirational. If a manufacturer set a goal that no more than 20% of customers would be unhappy, or

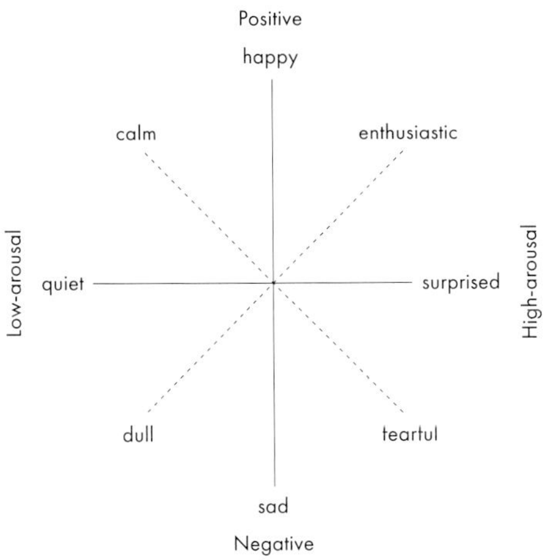

James Russell's circumplex model

All affective states mapped on a two-dimensional system of positive-negative valence and high-low arousal (emotive energy).

for a restaurant owner, a maximum 20% negative patron reviews, they would never stay in business! We argue that experiential goals be routinely set higher than neutrality—or an absence of feeling and complaint—since environments without stimulus approach sensory deprivation.

This book is mostly focused on the third level in the diagram, an environment of sensory *richness* which produces emotive form and felt pleasure states. From there, our highest aspiration is for spaces of *fecundity*, designed experiences that elicit a deep, long-term, multi-faceted sense of well-being. Well-being is an overall experience of physical and mental health, emotional and social wellness, strong cognitive capacity and a sense of life satisfaction (Altomonte et al. 2020). More specific to our task, fecundity implies opportunities for creativity, inventiveness, fruitfulness and the quality of assisting healthy growth. Imagine designing to intentionally elicit great happiness, bliss, well-being, joy—an architecture of felicity. While this sounds ambitious and is almost certainly unmeasurable, we believe that designs that invoke positive responses, built on dynamic and variable qualities and conditions, deeper Nature connections and personal choice, move occupants toward felicity and eudaemonia.

Mapping Experiential States

James Russell's circumplex model (1980) describes affect as the product of cognitive processes generating emotional interpretations as positive or negative. He showed that nearly all affect constructs could be mapped onto a two-dimensional bi-polar map with a displeasure-pleasure axis (negative to positive valence) and an arousal axis (sleepy to alert). Versions of this mapping have been employed by many psychological researchers.

Framework for affective states in buildings

Using dimensions similar to Russell's, we map the universe of potential states for building occupants. Conventional practices target the neutral zone; more profound buildings, farther right.

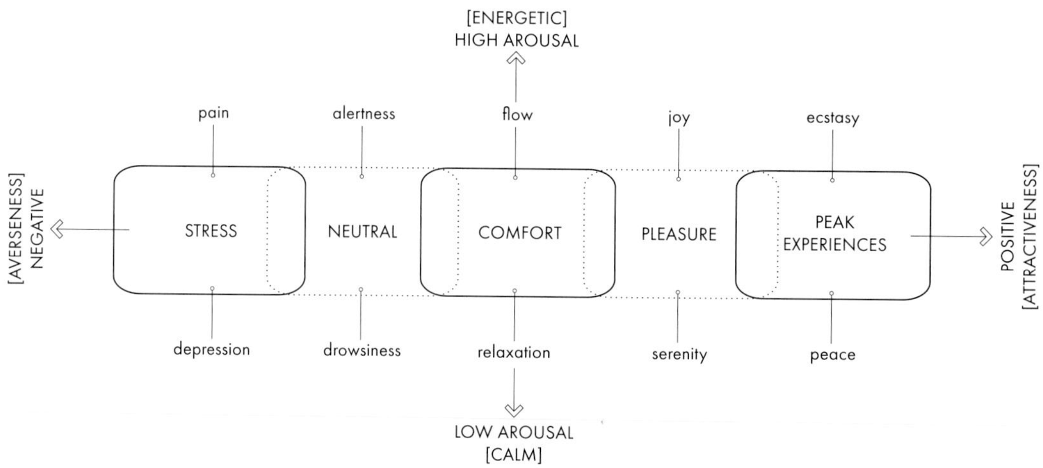

Framework for affective states in buildings (diagram) offers a reinterpretation of Russell's framework, mapping experiential states for building environments. Whereas Russell's original work is based on experimental research, our interpretations are representative generalizations for buildings. In the figure, valence is mapped on the horizontal axis. It is closely related to the right side of the Spectrum of Occupant Experiences illustration shown previously. Human nature finds positive states attractive and seeks them out; conversely, people are averse to negative states and effort to avoid them. The vertical axis maps low to high emotional arousal, that is, how calm or energetic the feeling is or how much emotional power it entails. For example, in the *neutral* zone, one can feel drowsy or alert, or a state somewhere on a spectrum in-between. At the *comfort* region, feeling relaxed is on the calm end, while a creative flow state might engage the body and mind in a more energetic experience. Even at the higher valence of *pleasure* and beyond that, *peak experiences*, one can feel a relatively calm serenity or inner peace, or a more energetic sense of joy or ecstasy. Again, these states represent degrees of arousal on spectra within each zone; many other feeling states could be used and mapped.

Using the thermal environment as an example, ASHRAE's Standard 55, Thermal Environmental Conditions for Human Occupancy (a default standard), describes a comfort zone and associates that with thermal sensations where neutral is a center point, assumed to be ideal. In this representation, we argue that these are not necessarily the same—that comfort constitutes a higher and more positive state between those of neutral and pleasure.

We advocate for more ambitious affective goals that move even further to the right. Indeed, conditions in buildings frequently engender pleasure states, such as delight, as captured in Heschong's original work (1979) and more recently in her *Visual Delight in Architecture* (2021). Although rarer, one can have peak experiences, not just in Nature, but in profound examples of places, such as Chartres Cathedral, the cave temples at Ellora, India, or in the works of Kahn, such as the Kimbell Art Museum. The intention embodied in this book is to have professional practice move from neutral as the most common state (and conventional goal) towards increasingly positive feelings, bringing the opportunity for more frequent aspirational feelings within everyday environments.

Referencing the diagram, designing for conditions that move to the right of neutral is better for learning or working spaces, while designing to move towards low arousal is better for relaxation at home and especially in the evening. We could, of course, get more complex, adding duration and other variables. Nevertheless, the illustration serves to show that, mostly, the building community is ill-focused on engendering positive states. We hope that this model could provide a basis for shifting the industry's agenda and expectations toward constructing buildings as the habitat for lives well-lived.

Spaces of Experience

In the end, designers' work results in configurations of form and space that are accomplished by locating a building on a site, orienting windows, proportioning rooms, linking spaces in movement sequences, determining dimensions, orchestrating views and detailing materials. These configurations shape and negotiate the forces of weather, climate, sound, smells and light. Nature acts on buildings, and buildings shape Nature. Ordered form orders flows. "Form follows flow follows form," as architect Sim Van der Ryn (2005) asserted. What inhabitants experience is a totality of the influencing conditions as distributed in space, re-shaped by the architectural *form-space* itself. Change the architectural organization and the experience also alters. The light needs the room. Heat's rhythms need the structure's mass. Airflow needs the window and its arrangement in the room and in relationship to other windows. Environmental forces, built elements and human experience, these in concert become transformational.

Sensibility

Sensibility is the capacity for feeling, an individual's ability to perceive and respond to stimuli. We apply to architecture, encouraging students and professionals by challenging them to generate experiential goals as the basis for strategies, patterns, schemas and narratives used to craft designs that manifest their intentions for occupants. For example, a designer—architect or engineer—might intend for inhabitants a sense of wonder in which they notice and appreciate their environment and are induced to contemplation or impelled to express joy. To do this, designers have to develop their own sensibility aptitude. This practice of being intentional in the early stages of design is what we call *experiential programming*.

In our collective decades of research and teaching, we observe that the language available to designers to describe architectural experience, Nature connection and affective states is underdeveloped. Even the word *beauty* is rarely uttered in the design reviews of our contemporary schools. As we considered, or more accurately struggled with, how the built environment can bring significance, poignancy, emotional power and spiritual openings to architectural denizens, we started with the recognition that all human experience happens somewhere, in some place. Patterns of experience are anchored in patterns of space. A special evening with friends happens around the kitchen table. The rituals of greeting and parting happen from the front steps to the porch to the entry hall to the living room and back again. Just as this is so of social events, it is also true of Nature's events.

In this way, an imagined experience to be created for others cannot be separated from the forms that they inhabit or the natural processes at play with those forms. The process of experience is grounded by *form-in-place*. Enjoying the memorable sweet smell of jasmine occurs on a walkway; the refreshing cool breeze is felt through an open window; the warmth of sunlight, engaged in the thermal pocket formed by a window seat. Winter coziness lives within the fireplace inglenook; the musical sound of rain fills the space below a metal roof. To intend sensibility is at once to intend design formation and to do so within a Nature context. The design propositions in Chapter 4 are based in these insights.

In her content-rich book, *Creating Sensory Spaces,* Barbara Erwine (2017) addresses many of these topics with eloquence and skilled storytelling. She is a kindred spirit advocating for ideas similar to those explicated here. We encourage readers to explore her work. Erwine employs evocative metaphors: cathedrals of smell, caves of sound, alcoves of warmth, thresholds of texture and cones of light. These suggest metaphoric ways for the building community to speak more articulately about architectural experience in spatial terms.

Describing Delight

We intend for this book to give people an expanded language and set of strategies to engage in a shared conversation about design for experience, beginning here with highlighting a few foundational ideas.

That conversation begins with clear objectives for experiential qualities established during programming, providing architectural composition opportunities to shape distributions of conditions. Early decisions often have profound, even irreversible, effects on the phenomena that define an atmosphere. The upcoming section on a novel Variability Framework details conditions in terms of spatial distribution (uniform or varied conditions in space) and dynamic patterns (constant or changing conditions in time). Early design objectives offer the chance to be explicit about *adaptive opportunity,* which is occupants' prospects for exerting personal control over how environmental conditions vary. This regulates the relationships among indoor and outdoor environmental forces. More surprising is that one's very experience of those conditions can be modified by whether or not adaptive opportunity is provided.

Engineering + Technology University

Barranco, Peru, 2015
UTEC /Grafton Architects +
Shell Arquitectos

Generative metaphoric thought: building as a human-made cliff, a "carved mountain" forming stepped gardens, a "matrix-scaffolding within which life happens", architecture as a "new geography." In the equatorial temperate desert of Lima, a porous vertical university of "structure holding space" as social infrastructure of stairs, terraces, balconies, walkways, and gardens, open to cooling ocean breezes and views, sun-shaded.

photos Iwan Baan

For example, people are more satisfied with indoor conditions if they have operable windows—whether they actually use them or not. The presence of adaptive opportunity upgrades experience.

Certainly, designers may employ normal, everyday language to describe feelings and emotions generated in buildings: affection, awe, surprise, mystery, delight, peace, centeredness, focus, alertness. The more technical language, concepts and mappings from psychology also help, as introduced previously. Yet, none of these linguistic approaches anchor experiences in their contexts of habitable built space or in Nature's patterns. To intend positive outcomes alone, even comfort and joy, is insufficient, lacking fecundity. A richer, more fertile language is required, one more suggestive of possibilities, a speaking capable of encompassing without overly specifying the triad of experience, conditions and space.

Metaphoric thought is a common means designers use to both express ideas for which finding literal words can be difficult and to connect disparate ideas. *Hearth* is metaphor for home and all its associated safety and comforts, at once an experience of space, warmth, sustenance and emotion, combined with layered histories of meaning, whether actual or symbolic. Simon Unwin (2019) explores in his book, *Metaphor, an exploration of the metaphorical dimensions and potential of architecture*, the idea that metaphors, in addition to their traditional linguistic, poetic role "can also be non-verbal–visual, spatial, experiential." As he argues, "metaphors live at the conceptual core of architecture." Walls are climate-separating *skins* or heat-retaining, enclosing *envelopes*. Windows become *eyes* looking outwards or inwards, reconnecting occupants to Nature. Structural *skeletons* hold the sky aloft and visually map Nature's gravity. Stone buildings are *caves* and *wombs*, while wood and steel structures become hierarchically branching *trees*. A hundred others have names.

> It is important to recover the use of living water, of water which runs in culverts and channels... Architecture is an occurrence which forms different spaces, places that become diverse because of the incidence of light, the sound of water or the passing of a cloud.
>
> —*Rogelio Salmona*

Metaphoric thought is employed even in building science and engineering. In objective terms, *healthy buildings* is an organismic metaphor, requiring monitoring of multiple *vital signs* to diagnose sick buildings or healthy ones. Architect and educator Donald Watson (1984) in his essay, Model, Metaphor and Paradigm, framed five metaphors for energy-efficient design: building as a natural light diffuser, as a heat-exchanger, as creator of microclimates, as an integrated biological system and building as a functional part of its environment. Each offers a means to free the design imagination in ways that science and engineering conventions and quantitative reasoning do not. Although framed in objective and inter-objective terms focused on energy, even these metaphors quickly suggest subjective human experiences and inter-subjective relationships.

LaVine (2001) develops an argument for architecture's inhabited technologies as metaphors that place people into relationship with Nature. He identifies four, "different ways of metaphorically portraying Nature through the buildings that people create":

1 *Nature as tangible transactions* reveals that Nature can be understood by contemplating how it appears to work as it interfaces with buildings.

2 *Nature as sensually revealed belief* proposes that architecture presents Nature as the embodiment of mythic interpretations via its support of ritual.

3 *Nature as embedded origins* describes Nature as indirectly contained in what humans learn of it by their making things.

4 *Nature as dialectic distinctions* suggests, Nature is what technological form argues about it convincingly.

The point of such metaphors is the expression by means of built design to convey the significance of being in the world, about human inhabitation, about belonging in Nature. LaVine suggests that design's role is to "define Nature in a manner that allows people to belong within it physically, emotionally and spiritually".

One of our favorite design metaphors, the *oasis*, was articulated as a holistic sensory experience generative for design at the first retreat of the Society of Building Science Educators (SBSE) in 1986 on the Oregon coast. Literally, an oasis is a fertile or green area in an arid region, and is often thought of first in terms of thermal qualities and its life-sustaining water supply. Metaphorically, an oasis implies a place of refuge, relief or pleasant contrast from a larger, contrasting field of less pleasant or more challenging conditions. Oasis and context taken together constitute the antithesis of the uniform, monotonous conditions typically maintained in contemporary buildings. The oasis provides places where people find sensory-rich moments within larger and less stimulating fields, or from a tumultuous milieu find a still place. These might be edges where harsh light becomes dappled or locations where stillness gives way to breeze, and ambient temperature is punctuated with delightful transitions. Classic examples in the thermal realm include a hammock on a shaded porch, a sunny window seat on a cold day or seats around a wood stove. Additional metaphoric ideas can be found throughout the Chapter 4 schemas, either as perspicuous metaphoric associations or as underpinning, even if not explicit. Examples to

Oasis: Casa del Fuerte de San Juan de Manzanillo
President's Guest House

Cartagena de Indias, Colombia
1981, Rogelio Salmona, architect

Seven courtyards are entered from their corners. The Patio of the Purple Oak is bounded by galleried paths serving guest rooms and is shaded by a large oak and other vegetation, together providing a sense of enclosure and protection from the climate and outside views. Water spouts from a wall fountain and "flows through the geometry of the *atarjeas*, small channels made of brick and embedded in a floor of stone tiles" (Castro 1998).

photos Ricardo L Castro

look forward to include the hearth as pattern in G4 Incalescent Center, buildings as evoking heaven, earth and underworld in N5 Three Realms; and pools of light in C4 Lightrooms, to name a few.

Variability Framework

When leaving the paradigm of steady-state spatially-uniform settings behind, how to conceptualize variable conditions becomes challenging. If architects and engineers are to collaborate in creating more dynamic and pleasurable places, they need a language both graphic and verbal inside of which they can think, ideate and communicate. We could not find one comprehensive or rigorous enough for the task. Developing this section helped us to make sense of the subject, and we hope it empowers the reader as well.

Framework of environmental conditions in and around buildings (see matrix on next spread) proposes a novel conceptual framework to organize the multiple kinds of static and variable conditions that inhabitants might experience and designers can configure. *Environmental conditions*—light, temperature, humidity, air flow, sound and more—can be either *uniform* or *non-uniform* across a space. They can also occur as either *steady-state* or *dynamic in time*. Physical distributions for a singular environmental condition (temperature or light, for example) present as one of four combinations shown in the matrix columns. The rows represent three *experiential scales* of a person's bodily engagement with conditions. The scale is partly influenced by whether occupants are stationary or moving between spaces. This framework can be used as a means to generate intentions for experiential diversity. While it was developed to graphically represent thermal conditions, versions could be developed for other stimuli.

Framework of environmental conditions in and around buildings

Most conventional buildings target conditions that are steady-state + uniform in space across all scales. Most of the design schemas in this book facilitate conditions that are more dynamic in time, non-uniform in pace, or both.

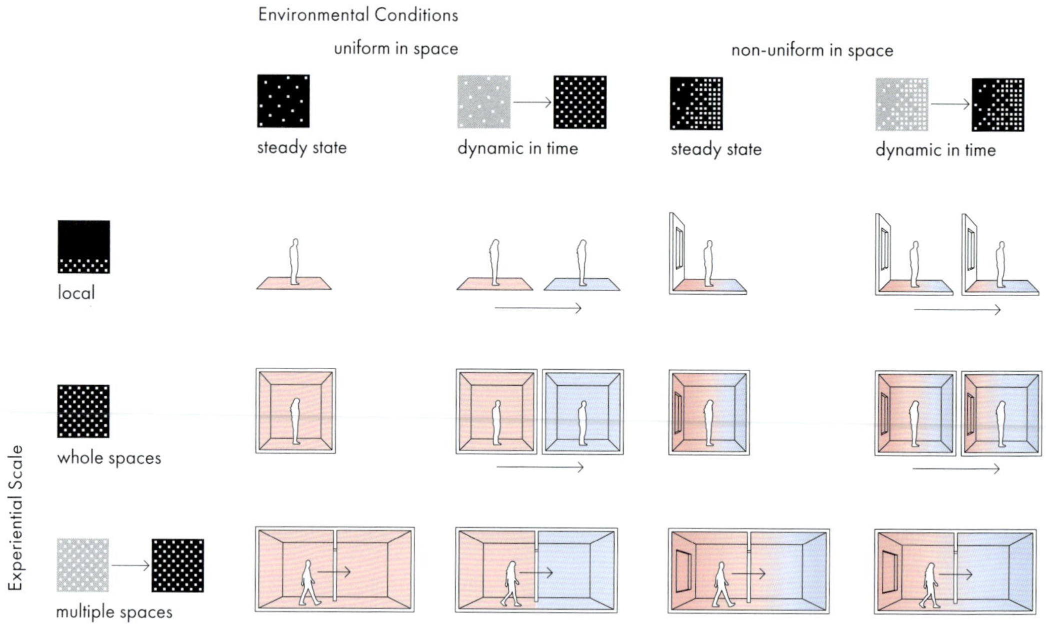

Spatial variability

Environmental conditions can occur as uniform or non-uniform in space. In contemporary design, engineers often attempt to create uniform indoor conditions of light and thermal factors throughout a whole space. Building standards often bias toward uniform lighting conditions and limit thermal differences in both vertical and horizontal dimensions. Because standards have driven the dominant environmental conditioning culture to consider neutrality as the norm, HVAC or lighting engineers refer to standards as *best practices,* often considering variability as an inherent sign of failure. In contrast, we argue that non-uniformity often offers many benefits, one being occupants' adaptive opportunity.

An instance of spatial non-uniformity is the differences in sound transmission and reverberation among rooms in the same building, for example, private offices, classrooms, public lobbies and music performance rooms. Others include lighting and thermal conditions that vary between building interior and perimeter zones and pools of light that attract social gathering or draw occupants to points of wayfinding orientation. Asymmetric temperature distribution can be intentionally created by radiant conditioning systems with warm floors or cool ceilings. Room air can be stratified vertically, such as in a displacement ventilation system or by an open sectional organization that

North King Street Housing

Dublin, Ireland, 2000
Grafton Architects

The project shows both spatial and temporal variety between layers of control for the lively orientation and occupiable layers of balconies walkways and glazed rooms facing a quiet outdoors (McCarter 2108).

The street wall is 530 mm (21 in) thick and is constructed of brick and timber with large sliding shutters which offer security, privacy, and environmental and acoustic protection from the busy streets. The courtyard walls by contrast are constructed of brick, steel and glass.

photos Ros Kavanagh

makes for warmer upper and cooler lower-level zones. Similarly, lighting conditions commonly vary from a work surface, to lower ambient workspace levels to lower again in adjacent corridors.

Temporal variability

Environmental conditions can be steady-state or dynamic in time. When light, temperature and airflow change over time, this is referred to as *non-steady state*, *dynamic* or *transient* conditions. A daylit building celebrates changing light levels and colors across the day. In contrast, the goal for a mechanically-conditioned space is often to hold the room temperature constant within a very small tolerance controlled by the thermostat. However, in a passively-cooled or solar-heated building, the room temperature is expected to fluctuate more broadly on a daily cycle. In thermal comfort research, laboratory studies of comfort during transient conditions create air temperature dynamics in patterns of cycles, drifts or ramps, stochastics (random) or step changes, designed to represent conditions that can occur in buildings or in Nature. These are described further in Chapter 3. Temporal examples include varying light levels or radiant conditions from the facade, such as when the sun is hitting a window but then is covered by a cloud, or when there is variable breeze and bird sounds through an open window.

Experiential scale

The human body experiences combinations of spatial and temporal variability differently depending on the scale of the event. We think of these experiences at three scales: *local*, *whole space* and as sequences of *multiple spaces*.

Local scale conditions are experienced simultaneously as one condition in one place on the body and a different condition in another, for example, when a person is sitting near a sunlit window, warmer on one side than the other. Other instances include sitting on a cool stone bench with heat conducted away from the body only through the parts in direct contact with the bench, or dark clothing facing the sun that heats faster than the same clothing in the opposite orientation. A breeze cools the windward side of the face but not the leeward. These situations can bring delight if in contrast to otherwise uncomfortable conditions. In the top matrix row, local scale asymmetric conditions are represented as a warm or cool floor. Instead of heat, the force could be light, air, moisture or sound. In buildings, such conditions are usually specific to particular places or surfaces within a room.

Whole space conditions are experienced primarily by the entire body when one is relatively stationary in a room. The main distinction is that wherever one is located, conditions are approximately the same over the whole body. While immersed in a set of conditions, they can change over time. At the whole-space scale, these changes affect the whole body, as when an entire daylighted space brightens from early morning to mid-day.

Multiple space conditions are whole-body experiences that occur when moving between spaces, a common progression that designers account for in every building, as when designing circulation and entries as functional and experiential sequences (see S5 Ingress Transitions). Sequences from inside to in-between spaces to outdoor rooms (or in reverse) usually have the greatest conditional range.

In summary, patterns of environmental conditions can vary in several ways with relation to space and scale:
- At a single point in a room
- Across a single room
- From space to subspace or alcove
- From room to room
- From indoor space to in-between space (porch, arcade) to outside space.

Nature connections

Finding joy, beauty and love being immersed in Nature seems universal. In addition to ideas for designing more pleasure within buildings, this work addresses the ways architects can place people into meaningful relationships with Nature.

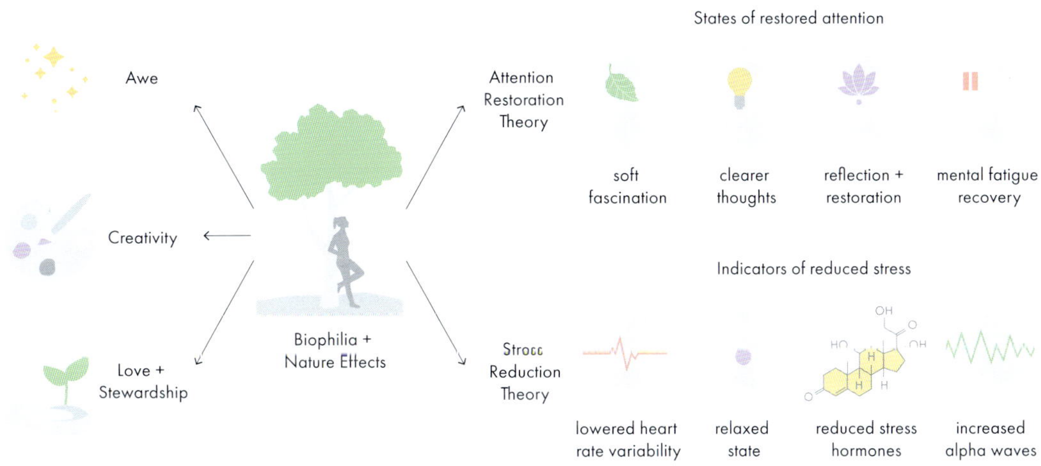

Scientific biophilia theories

Nature contact generates love, awe, creativity and stewardship. Attention restoration theory and stress reduction theory attempt to explain the mechanism for some effects with measurements using experimental subjects.

Biophilia

Many of the design schemas that follow overlap and complement biophilic design. *Biophilia*, from the Greek "love of life", describes humans' tendency to be drawn toward Nature. Biophilic design uses the built environment to satisfy this innate desire for affiliation. The concept of *forest bathing*, developed in Japan in the 1980s, is the contemplative practice of fully engaging the sights, sounds, smells and microclimates of the forest. Biophilic design embraces those same inclinations by connecting to Nature with buildings.

Scientific biophilia theories (diagram) addresses three current scientific explanations: an evolutionary argument for why biophilia matters and how it stimulates positive and inspired human responses, plus two explanations for how it affects people physiologically, emotionally and cognitively.

The biophilia hypothesis, developed by biologist, naturalist and writer Edward O. Wilson, based on principles of evolutionary biology, argues that humans evolved in a biocentric world and maintain emotional relationships with features of Nature that had early consequences for survival. People are attracted to what is beneficial, avoiding what might be harmful. Environmental psychologist Judith Heerwagen offers a perspective about biophilic design and sensory aesthetics in her co-authored book on *Biophilic Design* (Kellert et al. 2011). She describes how the desire for humans to develop a harmonious relationship with the biosphere is genetic and therefore a basic need and stable trait, not a culturally determined preference. Another aspect of this evolutionary theory is that love of Nature comes from "our capacity to experience empathy with other creatures and respond to their concerns as our own" (Goodenough 1998). Such empathy leads to a greater sense of environmental stewardship, elaborated on

Windhover Contemplative Center

Stanford University, Stanford, California, 2014
Aidlin Darling Design, architects
Andrea Cochran Landscape Architecture

The center is designed "to promote personal renewal and well-being", where art, landscape and architecture integrate "to replenish and invigorate the spirit", combining spiritual sanctuary, art gallery and contemplative garden in a "unique typology for contemplation and reflection" (ArchDaily 2015; Windhover 2021).

photos Matthew Millman

previously in the section on ritual connection. Enhanced creativity is evident by the countless Nature-inspired works of visual art and literature. The Greater Good Science Center, a UC Berkeley research center for the study of the psychology, sociology and neuroscience of well-being, recently published a white paper on The Science of Awe, demonstrating the transcendent experiences that comes from qualities associated with Nature (Allen 2018).

Stress Reduction Theory (SRT), pioneered by Roger Ulrich, professor of architecture at the Center for Healthcare Building Research at Chalmers University of Technology, focuses on the physiological and emotional benefits of how Nature contact lowers anxiety and promotes relaxation (Ulrich 1983). It begins with the physiological understanding of stress response. When faced with a stressful situation, the body enters an instinctual fight-or-flight mode, which evolved as a survival mechanism but still occurs in non-life-threatening situations. By SRT, stress effects are reversed when people view scenery containing greenery or water. This has short-term effects by easing anxiety states, creating a sense of calm and mitigating long-term health implications of chronic stress. Ulrich's studies found that natural settings having forest vegetation and water elements created a relaxation response similar to an awake, eyes-open, meditation-like state (Ulrich 1981; Ulrich et al. 1991).

Attention Restoration Theory (ART) is the product of research by Rachel Kaplan and Steven Kaplan, professors of psychology at the University of Michigan specializing in environmental psychology. ART proposes that fatigue and reduced cognitive capacity is a result of the kind of sustained mental effort that requires focused or direct attention (S Kaplan 1995; R Kaplan 1993). It focuses on the cognitive benefits of how Nature contact quiets the brain's prefrontal cortex activity, thus enabling a person to restore attention and perform thinking tasks better (Kaplan +

	Natural Forces abiotic	Living Organisms biotic	Living Systems abiotic + biotic
Steady State	air light water earth	micro-organisms plants animals	current landscapes + ecosystems
Variable	wind sunrise + sunset falling snow earthquake climate change	organic growth deciduous vegetation wind-blown foliage animal migration	changing landscapes + ecosystems natural succession plant migration

Degrees of Nature complexity

Complexity increases from abiotic to living systemic Nature. Each of these increases in complexity when temporally varied.

adapted from
Watchman et al. 2021

Kaplan 1989; S Kaplan 1995).To recover from fatigue and regain critical thinking abilities, one needs to rest the directed attention mechanisms. The idea of ART is that Nature views or contact allows all these states of cognitive restoration to happen. The growing body of research supporting these biophilic theories is heartening.

What is Nature?

In contemplating the possibilities for designing Nature connections, the question quickly arises, What is Nature? Answers and definitions abound, each with different implications for design. If Nature occurs differently to designers, how they design-with-Nature also varies. The next section considers some complexities found in the empirical view of Nature.

Degrees of Nature complexity (table) develops a map that illustrates how Nature connotes many things. In this work, we take an inclusive view. The figure, adapted from Melanie Watchman and co-authors (2021), builds on descriptions of Nature from various scholars (Kellert 2018, Beatley 2016, Browning et al. 2014, Chawla 2002, Kaplan + Kaplan 1989). Nature can be understood as a broad field of increasing complexity for experience: from abiotic natural forces (such as light, wind and water) to biotic living organisms (animals and plants) to more complex living systems (landscapes and ecosystems). This illustration relates to our previous framework because each of these Nature types occurs with both spatial and temporal variations—daily, seasonal and annual. All of these variations are potentially enriching when experienced, understood and appreciated. In the contemporary world, buildings create, as either expansion or limitation, Nature's relationships to humans. Configuration crafts connection.

Connecting to varieties of Nature

Multiple worldviews operate simultaneously in society. How design forges Nature connections is contingent on Nature's occurrence from a worldview. Designers can navigate these to address a diverse public.

Worldview	Metaphor Nature as the...	Intention Connect people to Nature as...
Transpersonal	The universal Self manifesting	Access to the unity of Spirit
Integral	Matrix of perspectives	Complex living systems
Postmodern	Web of life	Community
Modern	Biosphere	Resources and services
Traditional	Primeval garden	Primal force and structure

Architecture can shape the experience of air or focus a resident ritualistically on the setting sun or rising moon. Buildings can give occupants a window on plant and animal life or participate directly in the living ecosystems on site. When Nature is defined in this range of complexity, there are a thousand ways buildings give people access to interacting with Nature's complex forces and beings. How those facts of human-Nature interplay get perceived and interpreted is not singular, but depends in large part on the worldview lens one looks through.

Metaphoric ideas of Nature

Connecting to varieties of Nature (table) presents from among the manifold coexisting contemporary perspectives, five broad categories of contemporaneous worldviews, along with their primary metaphoric nature ideas: those from traditional, modern, postmodern, integral and transpersonal prospects (DeKay 2011). These distinctions help to frame how to think about designing Nature connections for inhabitants. Each worldview can be associated with a different definition and understanding of Nature.

The design schemas in Chapter 4 help with shaping form to engender sensing and feeling weather and Nature's abiotic phenomena. They name concepts and offer guidance to establish relationships with its biotic members and with more complex living systems. Some schemas, such as C2 Haptic Connection and G4 Incalescent Center, draw from fundamental *Traditional* ideas of Nature as primal felt force sensed in materials and fire, or from timeless events, such as in R4 Dawn and Dusk Places. Others, such as N2 Authentic Matters and F3 Fans First rely on *Modern* logical understandings of structural and thermal forces and how to order them. *Postmodern* thought understands nature as the web-of-life, as suggested in R4 Habitat Fringe, and as energy, material and water cycles, as given visible expression in N3 Roof Terrain and R4 Radiant Sailing. Contextual thought is a hallmark of a postmodern worldview and can be seen in multiple schemas, such as N6 Situated Scenes, which designs for view to and from a building set in site context. An *Integral* view engages complex living systems at multiple scales, as represented by the design schema maps that link concepts across six interrelated scales. Integral-oriented schemas include R6 Cooling Conversions, where multiple kinds of cooling strategies can be employed in spatially complex ways, attendant to daily or seasonal rhythms or more stochastically as the weather shifts. The integral prospect on Nature engages a matrix of perspectives that finds what is valuable in each worldview, sometimes reveling in the contemporary employment of both archaic and modern, such as seen in N5 Three Realms.

A transpersonal state is a potential available to anyone at any stage of human development and has been authentically reported so often that such noetic and unification experiences must be accounted for by any comprehensive approach. In addition to transpersonal and adult developmental psychology, all the great wisdom traditions identify not only peak experiences, which often occur in Nature, but also an idea of a transpersonal stage where the state becomes more permanently established as a *Transpersonal* worldview, as an ever-present awareness. A characteristic of the transpersonal is a sense of self that disidentifies with the individual personality and ego and experiences a more universal Self. As the sense of a separate self as distinguished from Nature diminishes, experiences—from small and local, such as C3 Water You can Touch, to room-scale spatial domains, as in C4 Lightrooms, to larger organizational and movement patterns, like S6 Topophilic Perambulation—become opportunities for first-person, present-moment encounters with Nature as the access to the unity of spirit.

Finally, the schemas navigate freely for inspiration among these varied and ever-present multiple natures. A built example of a schema becomes an artifact of the consciousness that built it and may transmit some of that awareness, at least as potentiality; yet each building will be engaged by a public with a range of different worldviews, each interpreting through their own lens, which may or may not match that of the designer. The meanings available through these worldviews are indeterminate and multifarious. For this reason, a designer is well-served to become aware of and take responsibility for their own idea of Nature while also becoming literate in the multiple ways to define Nature from inside different worldviews inhabited by clients and building occupants. This opens more possibilities for connecting with Nature via design.

Evidence for designing experience

In this work, evidence informs the development of schema design guidance by helping answer several questions: What general valid principles can be asserted for a design situation? What background of authenticity makes the design guidelines trustworthy? How can suggestions or precepts be sourced in knowledge relevant to the essential core characteristics of the schema? What is the likely effect of a spatial configuration on human mood, feeling, health and well-being?

We use evidence in a wide-ranging way because at least four great knowledge traditions offer support for our work: building science, social sciences, humanities and art—in addition to the architectural design discipline itself. Architecture is an ongoing discourse that generates new insights and knowledge by research strands within practice and academia. Murray Fraser (2015) describes architectural design research from within the profession as: "processes and outcomes of inquiries and investigations in which architects use the creation of projects, built or unbuilt, or...design thinking," in a process involving "research activities of thinking, writing, testing, verifying, debating, disseminating performing, validating, etc." In considering the topic of variable human environments, we find incredible value in this and the entire diversity of modes of research and the evidence they produce.

Buildings are created as a collaborative effort between architects, engineers and other design professionals. They uniquely bring to each project both shared and distinctive understandings of space and inhabitation and of how to manage the complexity of natural forces and human behavior. They may even employ entirely different languages or resonate with dissimilar types of evidence. LaVine (2001) offered some insightful, if quite polemic, distinctions between the approach to knowledge about buildings taken by architects and engineers. While individuals may develop capacities to bridge these disciplines or even to master both, articulating the polarities of the disciplines is instructive as the intent and challenge of this book's work is integration and reweaving. To summarize his in-depth distinctions, engineers understand space primarily as physical conditions, what we describe later as from the "outside"; architects may think of space from the person's experience, "inside", as a terrain of inhabitation. "The spaces organized by architects are populated by human beings rather than forces." This inside view is fraught with the complexity of human life and is therefore clearly less dependable, while the outside view is inevitably a reduction "to a manageable set of understandable interchanges."

Both views are valid, yet partial; each contains something useful not disclosed by the methods of the other. We argue that professionals from either discipline who might think about experience still lack the language and tools to adequately design for it. This is the aim of our work. Engineers use mostly numerical symbols (formulas and algorithms) while architects employ mostly formal symbols (drawings, diagrams and models) in an entirely different language. Each describes different aspects of human habitat. Engineers apply physical principles to particular situations while architects generate abstractions about validity from inside the messy design process using a sequence of judgements. Both processes can be employed by either discipline—for example, a figure like Santiago Calatrava—but the crossover is relatively rare even if growing. Engineers quest for elegance in economy, efficiency and knowable truth, while architects search for forms that "reveal the ideas that make our place on the earth knowable." Good buildings need both.

These two noble streams each have something to offer, and we find value in the viewpoints and evidence from both. Because buildings require knowledge from several disciplinary domains, good design is informed by knowledge from disparate thought modes. Where possible in this work, we employ an evidence-based approach, engaging multiple perspectives in an effort to reintegrate and compliment the differentiated traditions. Our shift toward multi-sensory experience, conditional variability and higher-level states is an effort to move engineering thought in the architectural direction of inhabitation. Our effort to validate human subjective experience in empirical and experimental evidence is intended to ground architectural design thought about form in its scientific and engineering correlates. This book as a whole can be understood as an effort to attune these multiple domains of knowledge and method in practical terms that become feeling and form-generative. Chapter 2 unfolds these distinctions and relationships further.

Scientific evidence is empirical or experimental and depends on scientific methods using rigorous research standards set by scientific culture. Anyone who has attempted an evidence-based approach to design knows that such rigorous objective standards for evidence are often hard (often impossible) to find for building applications. Abundant evidence about building physics may be found but much less about human feeling in buildings. The methods themselves limit the questions that can be asked and simplify the complexity of practice. Nevertheless, where possible, we use scientific evidence to develop design recommendations, sometimes directly, often by inference and extrapolation.

Roadmap

This work is about how designers can choreograph experiences of dynamic environmental conditions and connect people to Nature's rhythms. The chapters that follow bridge perspectives from phenomenology, architectural theory, building science, engineering and the health disciplines, translating them into a practical design language, all in the service of helping people thrive.

Chapter 2, Integral Experience, kicks off the rest of the journey. We address the deep contemporary need for a cogent explanation for how designers might make sense of elusive subjective experience and then how to access that understanding in terms concrete enough to make form that engenders gratifying dwelling. From thinkers and researchers representing several major human knowledge domains, we summarize how others have understood and explored architectural experience. These include: 1. As individually lived phenomena; 2. As neurobiologic function; 3. As meaning situated in particular places; and 4. As the pleasure of evolutionarily-purposed archetypes. We then describe an underlying theoretical framework that helps us understand architecture and its relationship to Nature, natural forces and environmental variability. This framing is built around four fundamental knowledge perspectives: Experiences—self and consciousness; Behaviors—science, mechanics and performance; Cultures—meaning, worldviews and symbolism, and Systems—social and natural ecologies and contexts.

Chapter 3, Excited by Evidence, provides a glimpse into the science of sensory perception. We filter the vast literature intending to understand how people respond physiologically to environmental stimuli, and how sensation influences perception and feeling. Each of these can be personally mutable and challenging to generalize

from research. Nevertheless, we take them as groundwork for the book. The chapter introduces how the body's sensory systems work, highlighting characteristics of how each sense responds to environmental heterogeneity. For each—eyes, skin, ears and nose—we select one or two topics for deeper exploration, including circadian stimulus, views from buildings, alliesthesia (the physiological basis for thermal delight), the adaptive comfort model, positive soundscapes, water sounds and scent walks. The chapter concludes with a brief discussion of multi-sensory research evidence as it relates in particular to Nature connections, providing a segue for the next chapter.
Chapter 4, Experiential Design Schemas, constitutes the heart of the work. To organize sensory stimuli, we identify six patterns of conditions, based in how they are distributed in space and time, : Contrast, Gradient, Rhythm, Flux (random or stochastic), Sequence and Narrative. These become the structure for organizing the dozens of experiential design schemas. Schemas are further typed at six levels of scale and complexity: material, element, building system, room, room organization and whole building. Each schema follows a template as a four-page spread with elegant precedents, supporting evidence and design guidelines. They are intended as a preliminary design resource for students and professionals in this nascent field. We define a schema as the organization of form and space marshaling environmental conditions to create a field for rich human experiences. They integrate our understanding of human perception, spatial patterns and broadly defined evidence. Schemas provide design guidance aimed at occupants' experiential delight, health and well-being, awareness of natural process and Nature connection.

Sources

Allen, Summer. 2018. *The Science of Awe*. Greater Good Science Center, Univ of California, Berkeley

Altomonte, Sergio, Joseph Allen, Philomena M Bluyssen, Gail Brager, Lisa Heschong, Angela Loder, Stefano Schiavon, Jennifer A Veitch, Lily Wang + Pawel Wargocki. 2020. Ten Questions Concerning Well-Being in the Built Environment. *Building and Environment* 180

ArchDaily. 2015. Windhover Contemplative Center/ Aidlin Darling Design. *ArchDaily*, 18 Mar, archdaily.com/608268

ASHRAE 2020. *Standard 55: Thermal Environmental Conditions for Human Occupancy*. Atlanta, GA: American Society of Heating, Refrigerating and Air-Conditioning Engineers

Beatley, Timothy. 2016. *Handbook of Biophilic City Planning + Design*. Washington, DC: Island Press

Beck, Don + Christopher C Cowan. 1996. *Spiral Dynamics: Mastering Values, Leadership, and Change: Exploring the New Science of Memetics*. Cambridge, MA: Blackwell Business

Browning, William D, Catherine O Ryan + Joseph O Clancy. 2014. *14 Patterns of Biophilic Design: Improving Health + Well-being in the Built Environment*. New York: Terrapin Bright Green

Castro, Ricardo L, Rogelio Salmona + Benjamín Villegas Jiménez. 1998. *Salmona*. Bogota: Villegas Editores

Chawla, Louise. 2002. Spots of Time: Manifold Ways of Being in Nature in Childhood. in *Children and nature: Psychological, sociocultural, and evolutionary investigations*. Cambridge, Massachusetts, USA: MIT Press

DeKay, Mark. 2011. *Integral Sustainable Design: Transformative Perspectives*. ed. Susanne Bennett. London: Earthscan

Erwine, Barbara. 2017. *Creating Sensory Spaces: The Architecture of the Invisible*. New York: Routledge

Fraser, Murray. 2015. Design Research in a Globalized Age. in *Perspectives On Architectural Design Research: What matters-Who Cares-How*, eds. J Moloney, J Smitheram + S Twose. Baunach, Germany: Spurbuchverlag

Gebser, Hans, Jean Gebser + Algis Mickunas. 1985. *The Ever-Present Origin*. Athens, Ohio: Ohio University Press

Gerlach, Kenny A. 1974. Environmental Design to Counter Occupational Boredom. *Journal of Architectural Research* 3(3):15–19

Goodenough, Ursula. 1998. *The Sacred Depths of Nature*. Oxford, UK: Oxford University Press

Grafton Architects. 2000. North King St. Housing, Dublin. graftonarchitects.ie/North-King-St-Housing-Dublin

Heerwagen, Judith + Bert Gregory. 2008. Biophilia and Sensory Aesthetics. in *Biophilic Design: The Theory, Science and Practice of Bringing Buildings to Life*, eds. S Kellert, J Heerwagen + M Mador. Hoboken, New Jersey: Wiley

Heron, Woodburn. 1957. The Pathology of Boredom. *Scientific American* 196: 52–56

Heschong, Lisa. 1979. *Thermal Delight in Architecture*. Cambridge, Massachusetts, USA: MIT Press

Heschong, Lisa. 2021. *Visual Delight in Architecture: Daylight, Vision and View*. New York: Routledge

IEA. 2018. *The Future of Cooling: Opportunities for Energy-Efficient Air Conditioning*. *Technology Report*. Paris: International Energy Agency

Ives, Christopher D, David J Abson, Henrik von Wehrden, Christian Dorninger, Kathleen Klaniecki + Joern Fischer. 2018. Reconnecting with Nature for Sustainability. *Sustainability Science* 13(5):1389–97

IWBI. 2020. *WELL Building Standard v2*. New York: International Well Building Institute. wellcertified.com

Sources

Kaplan, Rachel. 1993. The Role of Nature in the Context of Workplace. *Landscape and Urban Planning* 26(1):193–201

Kaplan, Stephen + Rachel Kaplan. 1989. The Visual Environment: Public Participation in Design and Planning. *Journal of Social Issues* 45(1): 59–86

Kaplan, Stephen. 1995. The Restorative Benefits of Nature: Toward an Integrative Framework. *Journal of Environmental Psychology* 15(3):169–82

Kegan, Robert. 1982. *The Evolving Self: Problem and Process in Human Development*. Cambridge, Massachusetts: Harvard University Press

Kegan, Robert. 1998. *In Over Our Heads: The Mental Demands of Modern Life*. 3rd ed. Cambridge, Massachusetts: Harvard University Press

Kellert, Stephen R, Judith Heerwagen + Martin Mador. 2008. *Biophilic Design: The Theory, Science and Practice of Bringing Buildings to Life*. Hoboken, New Jersey: Wiley

Kellert, Stephen R. 2012. *Building for Life: Designing and Understanding the Human-Nature Connection*. 2nd ed. Washington, DC: Island Press

Kellert, Stephen R. 2018. *Nature by Design: The Practice of Biophilic Design*. New Haven, Connecticut: Yale University Press

Kempton, Willett, Daniel Feuermann + Arthur E McGarity. 1992. "I Always Turn It on Super": User Decisions about When and How to Operate Room Air Conditioners. *Energy and Buildings* 18(3):177–91

Knowles, Ralph. 1981. *Sun Rhythm Form*. Cambridge, Massachusetts, USA: MIT Press

LaVine, Lance. 2001. *Mechanics and Meaning in Architecture*. Minneapolis, Minnesota: University of Minnesota Press

Louv, Richard. 2008. *Last Child in the Woods: Saving Our Children From Nature-Deficit Disorder*. Updated and Expanded. Chapel Hill, NC: Algonquin Books

McCarter, Robert. 2018. *Grafton Architects*. London: Phaidon

McDonough, William. 2016. Cradle-to-Cradle Design, Education and a Future of Abundance. Lecture, Global Institute of Sustainability and Innovation, Arizona State University

McIntyre, Donald A. 1980. *Indoor Climate*. London: Applied Science Publishers

Meiss, Pierre von. 1986. *Elements of Architecture: From Form to Place*. Lausanne, Switzerland: EPFL Press

Pallasmaa, Juhani. 2012. *The Eyes of the Skin: Architecture and the Senses*. 3rd ed. London: John Wiley & Sons

Parkinson, Thomas, Stefano Schiavon, Richard de Dear + Gail Brager. 2021. Overcooling of Offices Reveals Gender Inequity in Thermal Comfort. *Scientific Reports* 11(1)

Piaget, Jean. 1972. Intellectual Evolution from Adolescence to Adulthood. *Human Development* 15(1):1–12

Prins, Gwyn. 1992. On Condis and Coolth. *Energy and Buildings* 18: 251–58

Russell, James A. 1980. A Circumplex Model of Affect. *Journal of Personality and Social Psychology* 39(6):1161–78

Ryn, Sim Van Der. 2005. *Design For Life: The Architecture of Sim Van Der Ryn*. Salt Lake City, Utah: Gibbs Smith

Saito, Masaya, Atsuko Hojo, Tomomi Kozuka + Masanori Shukuya. 2000. Investigation of the Characteristics of Outdoor Air Movement Providing with "Suzusisa" Sensation. in *Proceedings of the Seventeenth International PLEA Conference, Cambridge*. London: James + James Science Publishers

Sobel, David. 1999. *Beyond Ecophobia: Reclaiming the Heart in Nature Education.* 2nd ed. Great Barrington, Massachusetts: Orion Society

Tanizaki, Jun'ichirō. 1977. *In Praise of Shadows.* New Haven, Connecticut: Leete's Island Books

Ubbelohde, Susan. 2003. The Dance of a Summer Day: Le Corbusier's Sarabhai House in Ahmedabad, India. *Traditional Dwellings and Settlements Review* 14(2): 65–80

Ulrich, Roger S, Robert F Simons, Barbara D Losito, Evelyn Fiorito, Mark A Miles + Michael Zelson. 1991. Stress Recovery during Exposure to Natural and Urban Environments. *Journal of Environmental Psychology* 11(3): 201–30

Ulrich, Roger S. 1981. Natural Versus Urban Scenes: Some Psychophysiological Effects. *Environment and Behavior* 13(5): 523–56

Ulrich, Roger S. 1983. Aesthetic and Affective Response to Natural Environment. in *Behavior and the Natural Environment, Human Behavior and Environment,* eds. I Altman + J F Wohlwill. Boston, Massachusetts: Springer US

Unwin, Simon. 2019. *Metaphor: An Exploration of the Metaphorical Dimensions and Potential of Architecture.* New York: Routledge

Vischer, Jacqueline C. 2008. Towards an Environmental Psychology of Workspace: How People Are Affected by Environments for Work. *Architectural Science Review* 51(2): 97–108

Watchman, Mélanie, Mark DeKay, Claude M H Demers + André Potvin. 2022. Design Vocabulary and Schemas for Biophilic Experiences in Cold Climate Schools. *Architectural Science Review* 65(2):101–19

Watson, Donald. 1984. Model, Metaphor and Paradigm. *Journal of Architectural Education* 5–9

Windhover. 2021. Windhover Contemplative Center. orsl.stanford.edu

Wohlwill, Joachim F. 1972. The Physical Environment: A Problem for a Psychology of Stimulation. *Journal of Social Issues* 22(4): 29–38

opposite
Novartis Campus Forum 3

Basel, Switzerland, 2005
Diener + Diener Architekten

photo Pygmalion Karatzas

2

Integral Experience

How do architects design to engender for building inhabitants rich human phenomenal body-mind states, such a pleasure and peak experiences? Architects find the nature of human feeling in buildings an enigma. On one hand, the pressing objective requirements for economy, function and safety capture their attention as fundamental needs for shelter and earthquake-resistant structure, minimizing energy use and greenhouse gas emissions, and staying within budget. Complex interobjective overlays of production systems, building codes, planning regulations and construction finance bind multiple decisions. In the architectural mind, these objective and interobjective concerns create constant tension with the equally important concerns to provide for subjective, qualitative human livings.

Architectural practice in the current century becomes increasingly complex—and sustainable design, more sophisticated. Performative design methods achieve higher standards and computational approaches optimize for more variables, yet something fundamental feels simultaneously lost. Such increases in formal, performative and process complexity offer many benefits and transcend some limits of earlier approaches. Simultaneously, the same practice regularly rebuffs the rooted, real, lived human experience that was supported by preindustrial and the best Modern architecture. Ironically, the sensory, emotional and cognitive building blocks that underpin complex thought, upon which more complex production methods and interpretation depend, are being eroded. At the same time, many designers, especially those of the digital generation, generate proposals and construct buildings that can often be distant from the preferences, desires and felt aesthetics of the people who occupy them.

As Nikos Salingaros and Kenneth Madsen (2008) point out in describing the Modern shift from building as the guild-based product of innate neurological processes to architecture as an intellectual profession, "Architectural design and the study of design methodologies were all but severed from those processes that had served for millennia to render the built environment as something intrinsically human." It is as if by expanding on one line of architectural development—perhaps technological performance or formal composition or response to urban context—that other lines, subtler and less subject to being modeled with an algorithm or reduced to a formal diagram, have been forgotten. On the optimistic side, the importance of first-person human encounters with buildings and Nature, along with how to explain them, come from more than a single quarter.

Four Explanations for How People Experience Buildings

As a starting point, let us examine how thinkers and researchers representing each of the major human knowledge domains addresses architectural experience. Four approaches are presented briefly. Each considers the similar topic by applying different lenses, methods and thought disciplines.

Experience as individually lived phenomena

In his classic work, *The Eyes of the Skin*, Juhani Pallasmaa (2012), a Finnish architect, educator and prolific writer, proclaims a *sensory architecture* with the "body in the center". He is interested in a multisensory inhabitation in

Thermal Vals Spa

Graubünden Canton
Switzerland, 1996
Peter Zumthor, architect
with Loeliger, Durisch + Rainer

photos Fernando Guerra, FG+SG

Architecture is experienced by laymen without thinking...I want an emotional reaction.

—Peter Zumthor 2013

which the human being returns from the Modern era's visual-eye dominance to a *natural perception* that integrates all the senses "in the very constitution of the body and the human mode of being". His is an existential engaging with buildings in which a person's inner life and the world itself, including the built environment, interpenetrate and co-influence each other. The foundation of this architectural phenomenology is the idea that reality is revealed through the lived human experience, which becomes an opportunity to construct meaning.

Scott Poole (2019) writes that Pallasmaa's inquisitiveness over a long writing career orbits around the question, "How does the experience of architecture help us to more fully grasp the meaning in our existence?" It may seem obvious to those outside the discipline that architecture is a multi-sensory event, yet much of contemporary design is driven by abstractions rather than concreteness—by ideas of buildings as economic commodities, functional utility or aesthetic and compositional novelty. It has become a radical stance for architects to put trust in and value human perceptions as based in a grounded reality, biologically rooted, and revealing "essential things about human life".

Architecture, in Pallasmaa's words (Pallasmaa 2019), is "an extension of nature into the man-made realm". One's experience in buildings—and of the natural forces interacting with them—"concretizes the cycle of the year, the course of the sun, and the passing of the hours of the day". In such a first-person, participatory perspective, the act of sensing and knowing the world is also to sense and know one's self. This gives rise to precepts, such as the need for dim spaces to facilitate imagination, the understanding of architectural space as articulated through sound and echo, the essentialness of silence that generates states of tranquility, the fireplace as an intimate zone merged with its utility, the door handle as the *handshake of the building*, and how gravity and the ground's density and texture are sensed and measured by the foot's sole.

Pallasmaa understands architecture as an interior (human subjective) phenomenon in which experience is an action of everyday life, such as the act of movement when entering a building or the act of looking through a window. These experiences *as verbs* are the interaction of the engaged occupant with a dynamic world, which in turn provides the basis for a psychological response and mental construction by which one can know both Nature and the nature of being human. Previous mental concepts are considered unnecessary, as are preexisting interpretive systems. Pallasmaa's explication of architectural experience reports how building-in-environment occurs from the view within the body-mind and through the senses of a keen life-long designer and multi-sensory monitor of built environments. He presents, not what a third-person scientific observer sees of an inhabitant's first-person perception, but rather what architecture looks like from the inside first-person view of the first-person human interior.

Thermal Vals Spa is designed from the phenomenological approach that considers the first-person engagement of bathers, the baths exemplify an architecture of multiple senses (Frearson 2016). As the architect explains, "Architecture is experienced by laymen without thinking....I want an emotional reaction (Zumthor 2013).

Experience as neurobiologic response

Neuroscientists and architects have become interested in each other's fields, as evidenced by The Academy of Neuroscience for Architecture, established in 2003. The goal of this interest is to understand how the brain perceives architecture and conversely, how architecture can be designed to generate particular positive responses. John Eberhard (2009), founding president of the Academy, believes that "the key to understanding how our brains enable our minds to experience architectural settings is *consciousness*". Although neuroscience does not understand exactly what consciousness is, it quests to scientifically uncover how consciousness emerges from the interactions of sensory systems, the brain, the human body and the world humans inhabit, especially the world of architectural space and its qualities.

For neuroscientists, emotion is fundamental to understanding how humans experience architecture. They distinguish *emotion* as a biological response to a stimulus, something that is precognitive and immediate, while *feeling* comes later and invokes cognition. Harry Mallgrave (2013), professor of architecture at Illinois Institute of Technology, frames this as a sequential process in which building experience is initially not conscious or cognitive; rather, it originates with the physical body and its "physiological (emotional) responses to the environment."

Pavilion of the Nordic Nations at the Venice Biennale 1962 is one of architect Sverre Fehn's well-known early works. His approach is considered a prime example of an experience-driven approach (Lindman 2016). Neuroscience seeks to explain the acknowledged effects of buildings like the Nordic Pavilion on their occupants' body-minds. Neuroscientist Antonio Damasio (2010), often referenced by other architectural writers, describes *feelings* as "composite perceptions of what happens when the body is emoting". In the brain stem and subcortical brain areas, sensory data is processed to generate *felt body states*. The idea is that, in response to the environment,

Pavilion of the Nordic Nations
Venice Biennale

Venice, Italy, 1962
Sverre Fehn, architect

The pavilion creates careful views outward and toward itself. Using a double layer of concrete beams, Fehn creates a column-free space, weaving around the existing trees. The roof, pigmented to glow, a metaphor for sunlight falling on a quilt of snow (Taylor-Foster 2016) is felt as "concrete manifestations of the living presence of nature" (Norberg-Shulz + Postiglione 1997).

photos Mark DeKay

these felt emotional states serve an evolutionary purpose of keeping the body in balance, regulating life functions such as thermal balance, food access and physical safety. What Demasio (2018) and others call feelings are built "on top of" emotions:

Feelings are mental experiences, and by definition they are conscious; we would not have direct knowledge if they were not. But feelings differ from other mental experiences on several counts. First, their content always refers to the body of the organism in which they emerge. Feelings portray the organism's interior—the state of internal organs and of internal operations...

Demasio's second characteristic of feelings is that they have *valence* as their defining element; that is, humans fundamentally experience them as a spectrum of good to bad, or positive and negative valence—as a moment-to-moment mental translation of exterior life conditions.

How this gets translated to architecture is that *architectural emotion* can be thought of as the body's physiological response to the built environment. How one feels about being in a building arises first from these emotions and *then* become conscious. Repeated over time, feelings can become concepts, the material for intellectual abstractions. Like the phenomenologists, the body is considered as foundational for any architectural perception, yet neuroscience is more interested in the biological explanation for how the body responds to and interacts with the world, a third-person objective view, rather than the first-person view of the experiencer.

As Professor Robert Condia (2018) puts it, "We perceive architecture by moving and acting with and through the body," considered as "always an embodied multisensory experience". Architectural experience is, therefore, kinesthetic. Condia's reading of neuroscience is that "aesthetic experience is always a combination of thinking and emotion", being "bodily, not merely cognitive," which is a radical shift from common aesthetic explanations that emphasize the intellect's role. The implication is that all sensory perception of architecture is emotional to one degree or another, to a valence. This is true not only for great works, monuments, landmarks or churches, but also for everyday rooms, gardens, windows and construction. To have people respond to a building with positive valence emotion, the design has to operate on a non-verbal level. What forms and organizations would generate these responses? This is a mostly unexplored research area.

Experience as progenitor of place-situated meaning

Lance LaVine (2010), professor emeritus of architecture at the University of Minnesota, distinguishes between two streams of architectural thought:

1 *Construct-challenging design*, which constantly searches for new expressions in a series of revolutionary overthrows and rejections of ideas that came before—an ongoing avant–garde.

2 *Place-empathetic design*, which targets developing long-lived core disciplinary constructs rooted in the ongoing evolution of material expressions, form language and community identity with particular places.

LaVine explains, "Place-empathetic architecture is inherently an architecture of intimacy," employing knowledge that emerges only when situated in a local or regional culture. In this view, architecture evolves slowly, in part as knowledgeable climatic and landscape response. It is constructed from local materials and thus mastered by local craftspeople, rather than built from industrially manufactured materials meant for universal distribution and factory-like assembly. This type of form language interacting with sun, light, rain and temperature regimes encourages occupants' bodily responses and emotions within architectural expressions that become built metaphors of place.

Desirable Nature connections and joy from encounters with natural forces shape building design, especially in places where industrialized construction and mechanical heating or cooling subordinate. Nature-responsive design can order building massing, orientation, room organization, window size and location, shading design and materials choices. However, these are not simply objective or utilitarian responses. Architectural form responding to a particular locale's climate and landscape also engenders occupants' place experience—deep shade or animated sun moments, connections to or isolation from the smells, sounds and temperatures outside, panoramic or controlled views, and whether the core or perimeter of buildings are occupied at a moment.

Stamp Museum

Oaxaca, Mexico, 2002
Daniel López Salgado +
Associates, architects

The courtyard endures as a spatial pattern with rich sensation, feeling and associative cultural meaning.

photos Mark Aronica

Stamp Museum in Oaxaca exemplifies this kind of design work in its use of courtyards as enduring structural patterns with both rich human experience and associative cultural meaning (Salgado 2000; Arrieta 2001; Braun 2009). Overcast areas like northern England cannot get enough natural light, and the size of windows in their buildings reflect this paucity. Hot, sunny climates like southern Mexico feel just the opposite. Shade befriends the court as it moves three-dimensionally with the sun's path. Sky enters the building's center. Surrounding arcades provide tempered circulation and an in-between sheltered zone that extends the territory of each room connected to it. Local climate's rhythm becomes the seasonal rhythm of lives lived.

LaVine (2001) argues cogently that such fundamental inhabitation within an architectural technology links people to places, locating them in relationship with Nature. Over time, when shared with others in a community, these mutual place connections promote cultural continuity. What occupants live within is an architecture influenced by its local customs and fashioned by the building community's response to its locale. Thus, a conservative form language (rather than construct-challenging designs) emerges from this intimate fitness of architecture to its cultural and natural place. Architecture and Nature combine to set the patterns of conditions-in-space, a product of the environmental conditions interacting with architectural patterns. This diad contains and directs the options for human feeling. In doing so, it presents Nature as modified by human construction in response to that local variety of Nature. People have access to both inhabited form that reveals Nature by how architecture interacts with it—a *metaphorical* communique—and a *direct lived* experience, as Pallasmaa describes it, of the momentary changes and seasonal rhythms. The result of being in and experiencing place-empathetic architecture is the possibility of architecture, "to reflect on and reinforce a people's cultural identity" (LaVine 2010, 180).

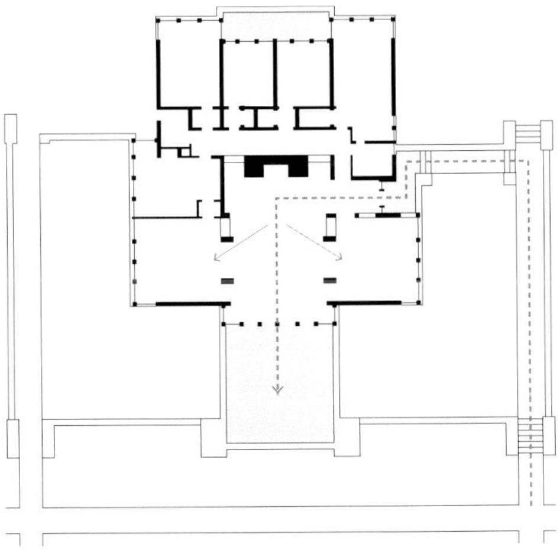

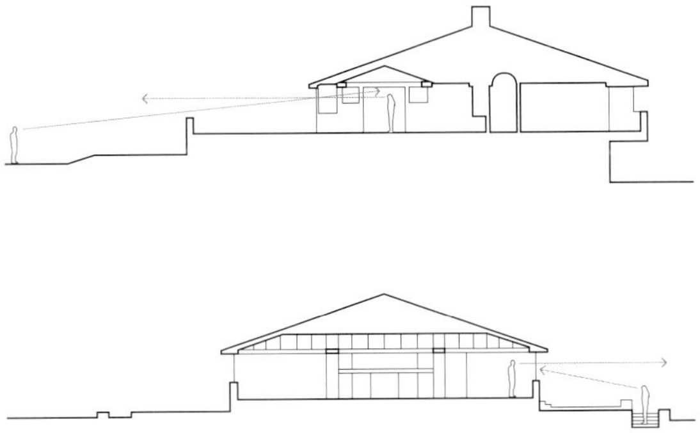

Edwin Cheney House

Oak Park, Illinois, 1904
Frank Lloyd Wright, architect

left
Plan with dashed entry sequence path shown from street to common areas and terrace

right top
View from living room and restricted public view from street

right bottom
Residents' view from library of approaching visitors

based on Hildebrand 1991

Experience as evolutionarily archetypal pleasure

A fourth approach to explaining architectural experience focuses on buildings' spatial patterns, along with their animating natural forces. Together, these complex physical situations afford occupants sensual and perceptual opportunities. *Prospect-refuge theory*, proposed in 1975 by British geographer Jay Appleton (1975), forwards the idea that innately, perhaps genetically hard-wired by evolution, humans prefer and seek places that offer both the territorial survey ability (prospect) and safety without being seen (refuge).

Edwin Cheney House is one of several buildings by Frank Lloyd Wright that Brandt Hildebrand (1991) analyzed in *The Wright Space: Pattern and Meaning in Frank Lloyd Wright's Houses*. He identified several architectural features of Wright's spatial compositions that he associated with prospect-refuge, helping to explain their enduring attraction. These include a circuitous entry path that could be observed by residents, combined with a cave-like hearth where one's back can be protected. The hearth space is characterized by significant enclosure and lower ceiling height. A sense of prospect was accentuated by opening into a less enclosed, taller living area, which in turn links through filtered (psychologically-protected) views and a lowered-ceiling transition zone. The linking periphery opens broadly onto an outdoor terrace, also with a view of surrounding landscape, provided with a low solid perimeter wall (more refuge) and an elevated plinth for additional prospect. Later, Hildebrand (1999) proposed the idea of *internal prospect-refuge*, that is, not only protected views to landscape, but also views from one interior space to another, patterns seen in many Wright buildings. His thesis for both versions of prospect refuge and by extension, other phenomena, was that survival-driven instinctual preferences can drive some aspects of contemporary architectural pleasure.

Vocabulary of archetypes in architecture (excerpts)

Thiis-Evensen 1987, 443, 301
Scandinavian University Press

left
Essence of the skeletal frame archetypes

right
What the roof does

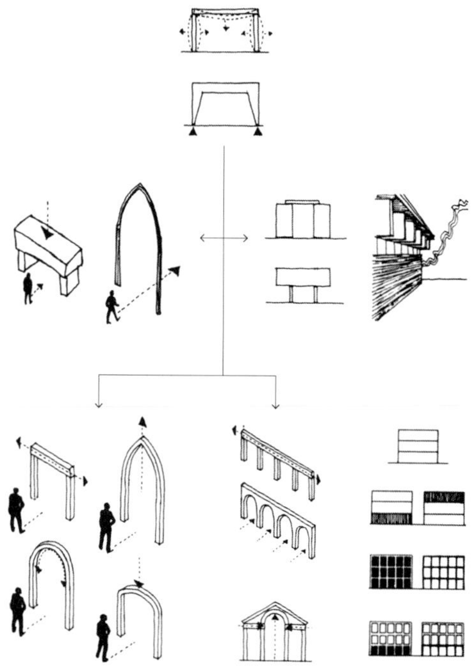

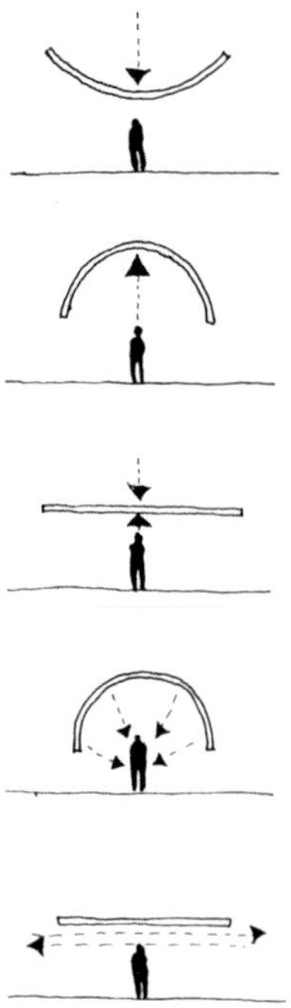

The phenomena of people's preference for conditions of prospect and refuge may indeed have an evolutionary origin, as Appleton hypothesized, and if so, may have developed as emotional responses based in the reptilian and mammalian brain and its interaction with environments that contributed to life-enhancing conditions, as investigated by neuroscience. However, neither a third-person objective neurological explanation, nor a first-person subjective felt perspective can identify recurrent spatial patterns that engender the positive emotional valence of comfort, safety or being in control. The first measures physiological correlates to feeling and the second reports the feelings themselves. Spatial order, however, is not found in behaviors of people or things, not in genetics or the brain and sensory systems. It is of another different, interobjective order found in architecture's own discipline.

Vocabulary of archetypes in architecture shows excerpts from a detailed language developed by Thomas Thiis-Evensen (1987) in his landmark, *Archetypes in Architecture*. He took up the question of how particular primary form and space patterns are correlated with human psychology. The work expanded on the more generalized project of his pioneering mentor, Christian Norberg-Shulz (1965) who outlined in *Intentions in Architecture* the view of architecture as a psychological phenomenon. Thiis-Evensen developed a detailed multi-leveled theory of archetypes and their classifications, proceeding from the proposition that one core purpose of architecture is generating occupant feeling or *mood*. Various architectural *atmospheres* that lead to human responses can be associated with particular forms. Thiis-Evensen (1987, 15) asks, "How can one plan specific architectural effects?" He answers his own question:

The first condition for such planning is that the architect must be acquainted with the expressive characteristics of form before he starts designing. Another condition is that one is able to choose those forms which are appropriate to the intended expression.

For both Hildebrand and Thiis-Evensen, experience in buildings is a product of form and its careful organization into universal spatial order patterns. Human experience's constancy is foundational to all individual difference. Up is up, and down is down; gravity is the same across the planet, and since no person is over 10 ft (3 m) tall, human scale always applies. As investigators of space and sequence, they are more interested in the ways that recurring patterns of forms in both buildings and their settings engender experiences across individuals and cultures. In the polarity of deep versus surface structures, they look for the deep. Thiis-Evensen writes that his aim is, "to show that there is a common language of form which we can immediately understand, regardless of individual or culture."

The Integral Context for Experience

How is one to make sense of the four explanations for architectural experience we just presented? How might they relate to each other, and to the arguments and solutions we present in this book?

A theoretical model that can help address this complexity is expressed by four fundamental perspectives introduced by integral philosopher Ken Wilber (2000a, 2000b). At its most essential level, Integral Theory organizes variables for any problem into a matrix of quadrants that intersect individual and collective phenomena with objective and subjective knowledge. These combined variables reveal the following considerations (DeKay 2014):

1 *Experiences:* self and consciousness
2 *Behaviors:* science, mechanics and performance
3 *Cultures:* meaning, worldviews, and symbolism
4 *Systems:* social and natural ecologies and contexts

The theory begins with the proposition that everyone is right—at least *partially*. These four approaches represent what Wilber calls a *quadrivia*. Quadrivia means "Literally 'four ways,' the use of all four quadrants as perspectives with which one can view any occasion" (DeVos 2017). "A quadrivial analysis is achieved by looking through

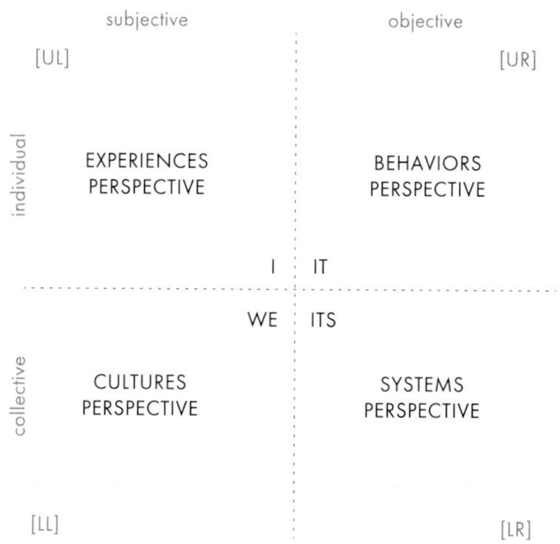

Integral theory's four quadrants

Two essential universal distinctions frame four fundamental perspectives on any occurrence. Each employs different methods that reveal and obscure. They differ significantly in what counts for value, yet represents the basic knowledge approaches humans have developed.

based on illustration from DeKay's 2011 framing of Wilber's model for sustainable design

The quadrant perspectives correspond generally to the four ways in which universities divide research methodologies (that is , truth-claim generating practices or paradigms): fine arts [UL], humanities [LL], natural sciences [UR], and social and systemic natural sciences [LR].

—*Michael Zimmerman, philosopher, 2004*

the four perspectives at one phenomenon, person, occasion, or issue" (Mcgregor 2015). Each perspective, using its own methods, reveals the object of attention differently, focusing on some aspects and occluding others. The combination reveals a more complex reality. One can read in the four approaches presented that, while operating from a clear dominant paradigm, each has some knowledge and appreciation of at least one other quadrivium [singular perspective] and makes attempts to relate their work to it.

Integral theory's four quadrants (diagram) frames this most fundamental aspect of Wilber's (2005) integral theory model (one of five major frames) that he terms *quadrants* due to its representation in this simple two-by-two matrix. For shorthand, we will refer to the individual perspectives as found in the diagram, such as LR for the lower-right quadrant's Systems Perspective, UL for the upper-left quadrant's Experiences Perspective, and so on.

Integrating architectural experience

We can now see how a multiperspectival approach reveals our topic in ways that individual prospects can not. The proposition is that more sophisticated understandings and solutions will emerge from this endeavor.

Four perspectives on architectural experience maps onto the four-quadrant integral model the previously outlined distinct approaches to architectural experience:

[UL] *Pallasmaa and the phenomenologists* take a first-person, subjective perspective, appreciating the experience as it occurs to the individual in consciousness. This exemplifies the I-realm of the Experiences Perspective in which to be known an inhabitant has to report on their own feeling.

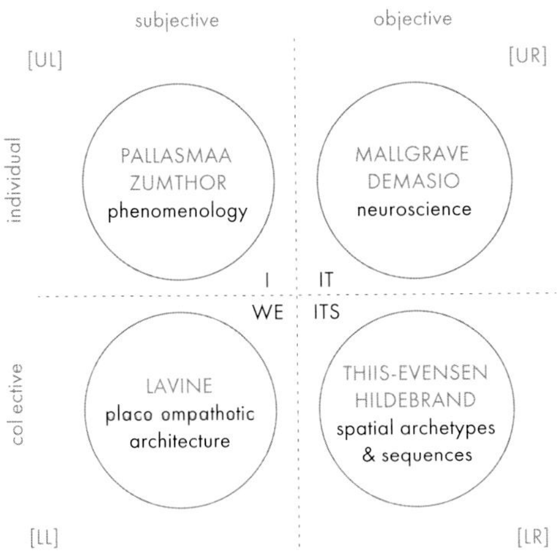

Four perspectives on architectural experience

Each researcher, looking through a distinct yet valid lens, employing different methods, taking a distinguishable prospect, arrives at unique results. Each contributes a valuable aspect to understanding the topic. None frame the whole picture.

[UR] *Mallgrave, Demasio and the architectural neuroscientists* take a third-person, objective perspective that seeks explanations for experience in their biological, evolutionarily-developed origins. This can be considered an IT-realm where the fundamentals of biology and physics rule the Behaviors Perspective, named so because behaviors of people and things in the empirical world can be observed, measured and weighed.
[LL] *LaVine,* a rare constructive example of theorists taking a second-person plural, intersubjective Cultural Perspective, finds experience as intertwined with meanings associated with place-empathetic architecture that arises from the particulars of a culture situated in a material and climatic place. This approach occupies the WE-terrain in which meaning and belonging arise inside the conversations of cultural communities of which individuals are members (not parts).
[LR] *Hildebrand, Thiis-Evensen and the typologists* take a more formalist approach approximating a third-person, interobjective perspective where the physical patterning and organization of universal architectural archetypes are the drivers of human experience. This kind of systemic, multi-scalar thinking defines a complex ITS-terrain of the Systems Perspective in which phenomena are mapped, diagrammed and drawn, rather than measured.

While each researcher uses the tools of a primary domain, they are also interested in the correlations with others. The phenomenologists, such as Pallasmaa, are quite interested in how the biological brain and sensory mechanism correlates to lived experiences. As architects, they want to understand how design choices affect atmosphere and feeling. The neuroscientists know that they are trying to explain expressions of feeling generated by contextual environments and conditions outside the body that architects understand much better than they do and that the lived experiences reported by people are the complex results of the core processes they seek to know. LaVine's place-empathetic architecture, while centered on collective identity and meaning, is situated in the empirical reality of particular places with their vegetation, materials, climate and so on, along with how people in such cultures experience being related to place and Nature. Similarly, Thiis-Evensen and the typologists, while developing a relatively universal formal grammar of architecture, use objective empirical approaches to classifications in ways analogous to 19th century biologic taxonomy, while appealing directly to their own first-person phenomenological experiences as real and reliable evidence. To generalize about architectural expressions, they take a third-person view on the first-person experiences of others who experience the same forms. Intersecting these four perspectives (quadrivia) reveals more than any of them taken individually.

In the sections that follow, we unpack the integral model further to apply it as a meta-framework for understanding architectural experience and creating a foundation to support designing. Each of these fundamental perspectives can be used to help understand architecture and its relationship to Nature. In this case, we use this framework in subsequent discussion to set architectural experience, an upper-left, individual, subjective perspective, into a larger context and to articulate how this perspective is different from, yet correlated with, the other three.

The core of this book is the experiential design schemas in Chapter 4, design guidance that begins with experiential intentions, which we then relate to actionable means to accomplish them via built form, based in supportive evidence from design and related disciplines. In attempting to give rather objective design guidance about how to design to engender subjective experiences, we had to develop a more holistic and comprehensive way of thinking about and explaining experience that was, as we have seen from the four examples, clearly missing from the professional practice and research literature. What was required was an approach that could empower building designers and engineers making sense of the environmental conditions that give rise to experience, the way those conditions occur, how they impinge on and are morphed by architecture, the effect of the space and form itself on experience, and the role cultural context and worldview play in framing feelings, interpretation and meaning.

The integral context of architectural experience (diagram) outlines the complex terrain where conditions, space, experience and meaning are *co-defining*. Let us start with the complexity of the situation in which design-for-experience is situated and then, one piece at a time, go a little deeper, using this diagram as the framework. What architects generate in the world when they design for occupants from the Experiences Perspective is actually Fields of Experiential Possibilities [UL], which are the situations in and around buildings in which occupants have the opportunity (not the requirement) to have particular experiences. Individuals can be more or less developed to different stages of consciousness and at any moment can inhabit various bodily and mental-psychological states. Both stages and states may constrain or open the Field of Possibilities.

Such fields of experiential possibilities are based mainly (not wholly) on a Behaviors Perspective about how objective Distributions of Environmental Conditions [UR] occur in both space and time (as covered in Chapter 1) and manifest in ways we describe later as contrasts, gradients, rhythms, sequences and fluxes (see Chapter 4 for

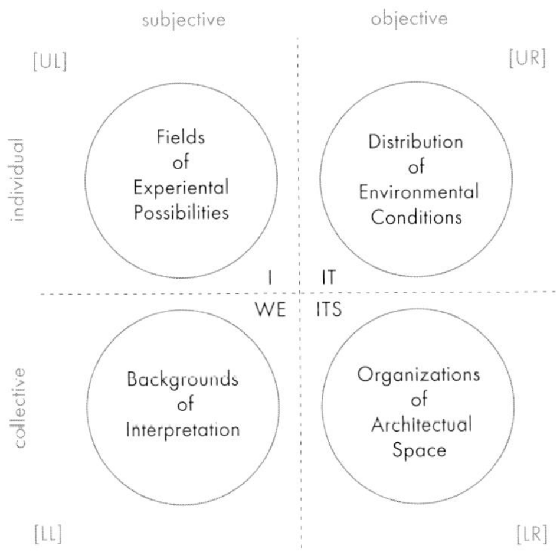

The integral context of architectural experience

Architecture generates potentials for individuals. Each of these four fundamental perspectives is necessary to understand architectural experience. None can be reduced to any of the others. The data reveled from each perspective's methods is valid in its own domain. Each influences the other as they co-arise.

UR *Behaviors Perspective*
LR *Systems Perspective*
UL *Experiences Perspective*
LL *Cultures Perspective*

details). These distributions of conditions, whether light, temperature, moisture, air movement, sound, rain, sun or shade, among others, are disposed within Organizations of Architectural Space [LR]. Such formal organizations of space and the elements that define them are reveled from the multi-scalar Systems Perspective familiar to designers: site plans that organize buildings, open spaces and streets; floor plans that organize rooms, courtyards and circulation; rooms shaped and oriented in particular ways; and windows of certain shapes, sizes and arrangements. Structural and mechanical systems can, if treated so, also define space and shape environmental conditions. These scales are defined as six *levels of complexity* (or more simply, *levels*) in the design schemas. Further, each design of a room or building is set in particular design situations (contexts), including climate dynamics, which are in turn constituted of complex configurations of natural forces.

Viewed from the Cultures Perspective, one can see that inside those fields of experiential possibilities individuals can have a range of responses and experiences that are narrowed by often tacit narratives as Backgrounds of Interpretation [LL] that constrain what and how they see the world. Such backgrounds are informed by several contemporaneous *worldviews*, as introduced in Chapter 1. Once an individual has an experience, they give it meaning or interpret it in relationship to their operative interpretive background(s). Whether a mythic, rational or pluralistic interpretation, each frames how the phenomena occur. Over time, individuals in localized groups having similar experiences develop a sense of local identity and shared meaning about their home place and their place in Nature. As Levine articulated, this is especially so for those grounded in the climatic, material and cultural conditions of particular places and is also common for people living every day in locally-adapted and expressive buildings. That shared meaning supports society at taking collective Nature-supportive actions.

In summary, spatial organizations [LR] shape the environmental dynamics [UR], such as natural forces, generating new distributions of conditions [UR], creating settings for experiential fields [UL], in which individuals have first-person experiences [UL] and give them meaning through their interpretive backgrounds [LL] that operate from one or more larger collectively-determined worldviews [LL]. There are modifiers of and iterative feedbacks between each of these steps. For example an inhabitant, through their sense receptors [UR] receives information about environmental conditions [UR], giving rise to felt-experience and the cascade of interrelated emotions, thoughts, belief-associations, and judgments [UL]. This, in turn, generates additional neurobiologic responses, leading to adaptive behavioral actions [UR] that may change physical conditions [UR], such as when adjusting building controls. That is about the simplest model that covers all the bases. In what follows, we unpack these related parts.

Setting the field for experience

Several interconnections and feedbacks work in a system to generate the situations people inhabit. These situations set what is possible as empirical stimuli, architectural mood and inhabited atmosphere.

Spatial organizations and natural force dynamics as interlinked (left graphic). As climatic forces on the sites around buildings vary with the day and season, the way they interact with buildings also changes in time. Nature's dynamics vary; buildings vary them further. Architectural space organizes natural force flows; in turn, such forces act on architecture. Change the spatial organization as defined by architectural components, such as walls, windows, roof and floors, and the natural forces' dynamics respond. Both the forces' intensity and their spatial distribution are reshaped. Buildings locate within a site microclimate, then create new microclimates. How deep the sun penetrates through a window, how the air moves across a room or leaves a stagnant corner, how light is reflected off a wall when a window is near the room's corner—these and many more environmental force behaviors constitute an often unseen and mutable life context. Nature arrives at the door anything but static and uniform. In whatever way humans build, they impact Nature and change its pattern. Buildings can modify Nature with or without designers' awareness of the consequences. However, this basic interaction between building form and natural force sets up the new disposition of conditions that forms the contextual stimuli for human experience.

Passive architecture that is heated with the sun, cooled by the wind and earth, and lighted by the sky, is an especially variable phenomenon. As Heraclitus wrote, "All entities move and nothing remains still." All built and natural entities flow and none abide, even if they appear so at times. It takes some practice to shift the architect's consciousness from building as static form to building as a set of dynamic processes. Physically, passive, climate-responsive architecture is characterized by formal and spatial organizations that guide patterns of natural flows and forces in space. As natural forces change over time, they can vary in their spatial distribution, such as changes in wind direction, which then changes the path of air flow through a building, even resulting in switching an opening from a ventilation inlet to an outlet. Natural forces can also keep their spatial distribution essentially the same while altering their magnitude, such as a south wind that blows softly at one moment and more intensely in the next; or, as when solar radiation increases over the day, wind speeds also increase, yet the direction may stay constant.

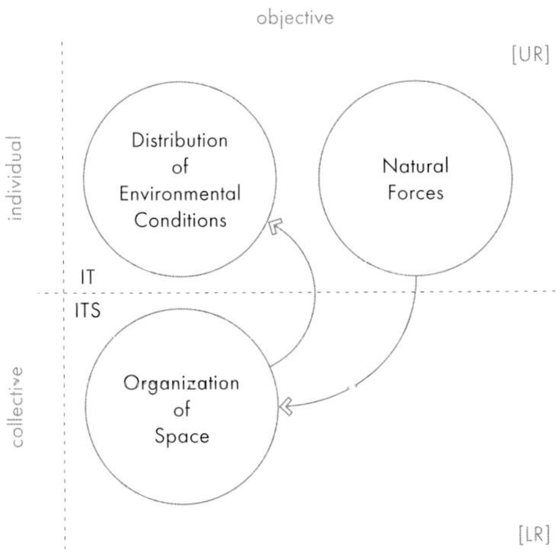

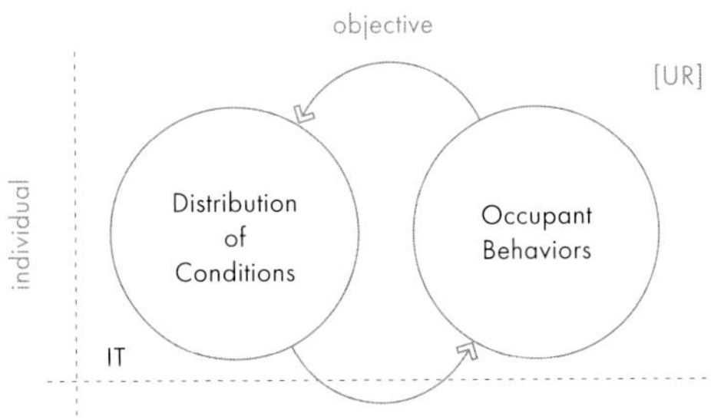

left
Spatial organizations and natural force dynamics as interlinked

The dynamics of Nature vary; buildings vary them further. The perceptual shift in the designer's mind is from architecture as structure to process to dynamic unfolding.

right
Occupant behaviors modify dynamic natural conditions

People affect in multiple ways the conditions they sense. They are inter-actors in setting their own field of possibilities.

Occupant behaviors modify dynamic natural conditions that have been already modified by buildings (right graphic). As they interact with the building, inhabitants engage doors, windows, blinds, fans, awnings and thermostats, further adapting the building's configurations and operation, its anatomy and physiology, to switch, redirect or transform the natural forces distribution. As the patterns of Nature change, for example in the Northern Hemisphere summer, when the sun moves from east toward south in the morning, attuned occupants adjust adaptive elements, such as deploying a shade that reduces the sun's intensity; then, as the east windows no longer receive direct sun, people open the shades to take in an expanded view, receive better cross-ventilation and accept more diffuse daylight. The insight here is that people are not merely passive recipients of conditions they inhabit; rather, they are actors that change the conditions by their own presence, interventions and daily activity.

Settings and experience fields as interlinked. Beginning in 1960 and into the 1980s, one of the first books on architecture that students often read in US design schools was Danish architect Steen Rasmussen's (1962) *Experiencing Architecture*. It forwarded the idea that spatial design influences human experience. During a Modernist period when architectural space could be thought of in purely formal, mental and abstract terms, he promoted high-quality, everyday human experience by regular people as a worthy and fundamental purpose for buildings. For Rasmussen, experiencing architecture was fundamental to understanding it. The place's character and features create the opportunity for felt inhabitation in two ways: both experiencing space as a three-dimensional environment, occupied and navigated, and experiencing the environmental conditions in and around buildings. The situational conditions [UR], together with the spatial organization [LR], provide the context in which personal experience [UL] may be engendered.

86 **Distribution of conditions-in-space generate fields of possibilities**

The product of Nature and architecture, patterns of conditions-in-buildings provide the basis for a first-person life-world.

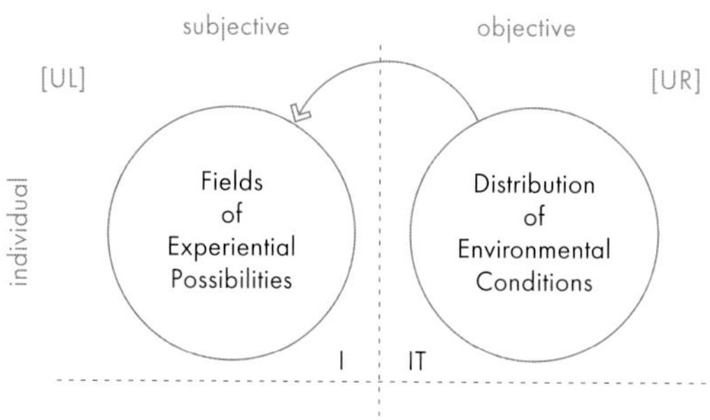

Another way to think of setting the field for occupation is the idea that a building cannot be understood fully without its context. The basic unit of consideration is *architecture-in-environment*, similar in logic to Gregory Bateson's (1972) fundamental unit of analysis as *organism-in-environment.* In the same way, sun, wind, rain, light and other natural forces do not merely form the context outside of buildings. Natural forces are also on the *inside* of rooms. Nature is in everyday architecture's interiors, always, moment-to-moment living within human habitat. Therefore, consider as another unity: environmental *conditions-in-buildings.* Neither make any sense without the other. These dyads of architecture-in-environment, of environmental conditions-in-buildings are the physical situations in which architectural-natural experience can happen. In the built environment, Nature is ever-present. John T. Lyle (1985, 1994) used the term *human ecosystems* to describe this synthesis of human and natural in an integrated whole. In this sense, one cannot separate a view of Nature from the window nor light from the room surfaces that reveal it. The human experience is not separate architectural and Nature experiences. Rather, in most buildings, occupant experience can more accurately be thought of as an integrated *architecture-Nature* experience.

Distribution of conditions-in-space generate fields of possibilities (diagram). In the field generated by the multiple agents interacting to organize conditions-in-buildings, perception and experiences arise. At times these are universal. Sitting in light clothing, all humans perceive freezing temperatures combined with windy conditions as cold. A wooden floor always feels different than a concrete one. In other cases, the distribution of conditions gives the opportunity for a particular feeling or for a range of emotional responses. Alternately, in a featureless and uniform steady-state landscape, no distinctive sensation at all may arise, even a numbing or soporific effect from deprivation. Occupant behavior and perception of opportunity modify subjective perception of the same conditions. This is the concept of adaptive opportunity. As occupants lose control over their environment, as in buildings where a centralized system automatically regulates interior conditions, they are less tolerant of changes and less satisfied if conditions move away from their preferred optimum. If, however, one can control the environment, whether or not actually doing so, one becomes happier with change and with a wider range of variable conditions indoors.

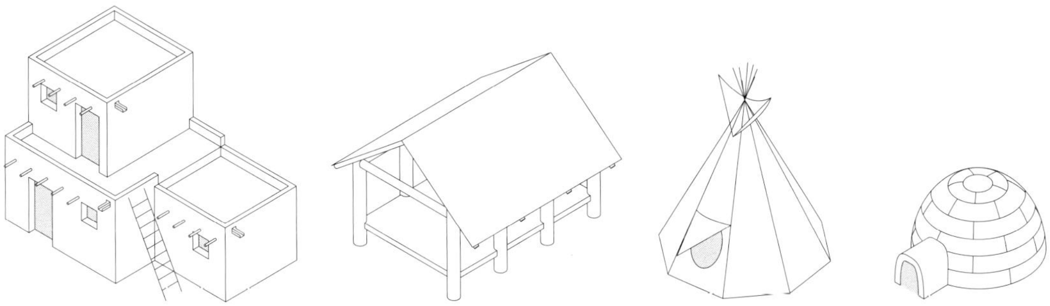

Pueblo Seminole Crow Inuit

Native North American architecture

Examples show regional form language responding to climate as modified for inhabitation and constructed from local material resources. The forms become culturally significant.

adapted from
Grondzik + Kwok 2019

Phenomena and experience are related in several ways, sometimes based simply on sensation. Others situations require basic perception, or noticing, the recognition of patterns or phenomena. Some events entail directed or focused attention to the phenomena or require greater focus one the body. To complicate it all, individuals have knowledge and personal history. Some phenomena occur in consciousness only if the perceiver has prior knowledge and the readily available mental concepts to organize sensory data into recognizable patterns. For example, the momentary sky conditions and color at sunrise and sunset can easily be appreciated by anyone, but prior repeated experience is need to recognize the evening sequence of the golden hour beginning before sunset, followed by the blue hour after sunset, with twilight fading to night. Perhaps more rare is one's lived familiarity to apprehend the inverse sequence in the morning hours around sunrise (see the R4 Dawn + Dusk Places schema).

Cultural meaning as ever-present context

Individual perspectives are embedded in collective ones. The collective worldviews humans inhabit are often unseen or unconscious. They frame and limit what is possible to perceive and think, providing the lenses through which these are interpreted and made meaningful or meaningless.

Form languages as linking experience fields and meaning backgrounds. When people live in a particular place, with its regional patterns of climate—if the building's machines do not ameliorate it—they adapt their architecture to smooth out the climate's extremes, to reduce the energy flows to the point where the relatively weak and distributed forces of sun, wind, daylight and rainfall can provide for most of their needs. Such climatically-adapted types or styles of architecture come to signify and express the region and its inhabitants. European settlers of North America developed new versions of vernacular indigenous regional prototypes or adapted European models, as seen in adobe construction, the Pueblo Style and Territorial Revival in New Mexico, Creole cottages and galleried plantation houses along the Gulf of Mexico coast, Cape Cod types and saltbox houses in New England. The architectural forms, born of their places, evolved into styles and types reproducing architectural responses that serve well in their particular locations.

left
Underpinning backgrounds of interpretation

Objective perspectives provide the elements for shared interpretations. Shared meaning occurs in the presence of communal situations.

right
Nature encounters and meanings as co-arising

Experiences of Nature engender shared meanings. Meaning frames care.

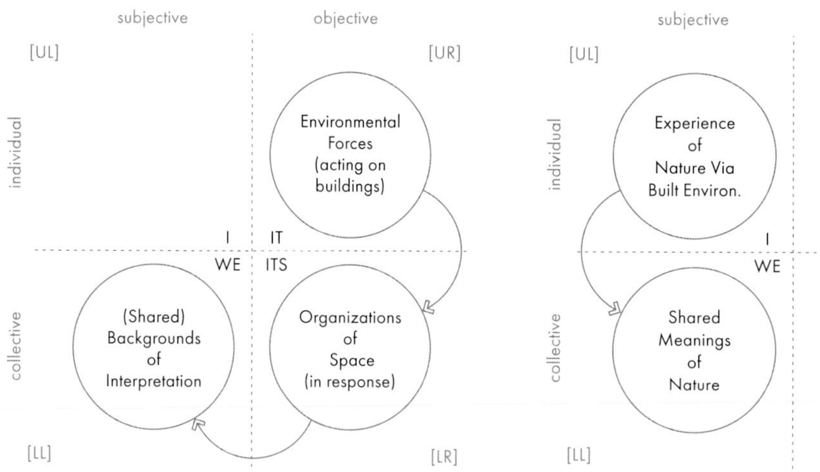

Native North American architecture (diagrams) studies find Acoma pueblos and Navajo hogans in the arid Southwest, raised Seminole chickees in the swampy Florida lowlands, Cheyenne and Crow tepees on the Great Plains and Inuit igloos in the Arctic (Grondzik + Kwok 2014, 195)—along with Algonquin wigwams and Iroquois longhouses in the Northeastern forests, Chinookan plank houses in the Pacific Northwest and Cherokee asi [wattle and daub houses] in the Appalachian valleys.

Such local architectural languages, when repeated and varied over time come to hold meaning for their inhabitants and build a sense of local identity. Climate can shape architectural form and space, even when interacting with strong cultural norms that ask architecture to be shaped differently.

Underpinning backgrounds of interpretation (left diagram above). Referencing again the four-quadrant model, architectural form languages develop as organizations of space [LR] in response to patterns of environmental forces [UR], thus providing the objective correlates and sources for interpretations that are geographically, culturally associated, which manifest as regional identity [LL].

Backgrounds of meaning can be thought of as arising in another compelling way. When individuals share experiences, they develop empathy for each other. When people live in the same place, they experience in similar ways the climate and biota that flourishes in their home-place. When they live in and move about in cities constructed of similar architectural patterns, their lives are bounded correspondingly. Meaning arises out of the collective cultural resonance with each other that is present in common experiences and their expression in

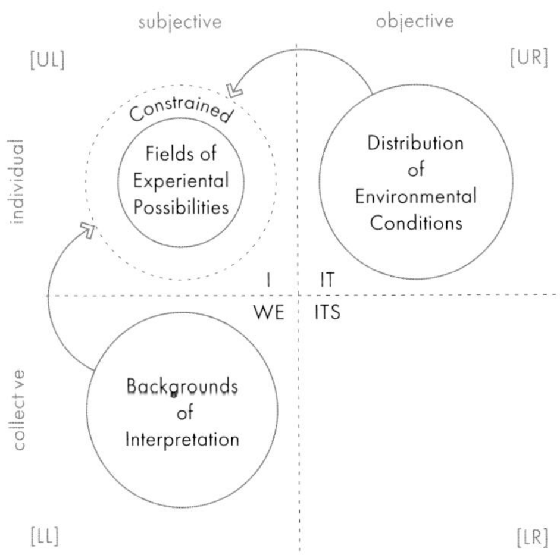

Interpretive backgrounds constrain possible experiences

Objective inputs provide stimuli for sensation, perception and emotion, but what is perceived and how the perceptions are interpreted are both limited by worldview.

everyday dialogue. Individual experience is set within the background of one's life situation, which is necessarily collective. The urban context is communal with the others in one's neighborhood or polis. While people may live in individual dwellings, the dwellings within a regional culture share many similar features and orders, from the design of kitchens and bathrooms to the zoning of public entry, entertainment space, living room, private zones and bedrooms. Buildings therefore shape the potential for much experience of the world and how meaning is given.

Nature encounters and meanings as co-arising (right diagram above). This book is about humans' experience of their habitat, whether driven by Nature and natural forces in buildings or, secondarily, by increasingly sophisticated conditioning systems. If designed well, both history and evidence suggest that building inhabitants can live a more fulfilling, aesthetic, stimulating and healthful life. In the best situations, their building inhabitation brings individuals into contact with Nature in each moment [UL]. Such experiences develop relationship. If occupants know Nature—even if contemporary lifestyles have Nature mediated almost entirely through buildings where life is predominantly lived—then it is likely they will care more deeply about Nature. When people care about something or someone with which they are in relationship, they act in the favor of the loved one. To the extent that numerous people in a particular place have similar Nature experiences via buildings, then common cultural meanings potentially develop [LL]. Buildings can shape individuals' Nature encounters and, since buildings are mostly an inhabited collective social phenomenon, architectural design offers a route to an environmental activism based in transformations of a culture's collective ideas about the meaning of Nature. Shared Nature encounters engender shared Nature meanings. It is probably more accurate and rigorous to say that these phenomena co-arise.

Interpretive backgrounds constrain possible experiences available to individuals (diagram). While common life events shared can give rise to collective meaning, cultural meaning also frames, limits and places injunctions on the field of experiential possibilities, further constraining the resulting meaning. The worldview inhabited by an individual embedded in a culture shapes the very idea of what Nature is understood to be, providing a powerful lens for shaping one's interpretation of experiences and their ultimate meaning (DeKay 2018).

The cultural stories, myths and values that form background collective conversations, inside of which individuals live, are powerful drivers of interpretations about individuals' experiences. Once shared cultural meaning emerges, the sensations that individuals have of Nature, such as weather in buildings or the structure of plant and animal life outside, are interpreted and made sense of, often unconsciously, though the mostly tacit background interpretations. As examples: Is 27 °C (81 °F) hot or comfortable, or even cool? Is that urban yard messy and unkempt, or is it a healthy urban ecology? Are high levels of daylight associated with comfort or discomfort in this location? Is perspiration acceptable or to be averted? Is 80% relative humidity muggy or normal? Is being seen from the street or sitting on your front porch safe and socially acceptable? Does Nature exist for humans to make use of, or is humanity's task to protect it? Many more examples could be given. Answers to all of these questions are not found entirely in the phenomena of Nature, space, conditions, or even experience. The balance resides in the backgrounds of meaning through which humans interpret all their observations, concepts and feelings.

Conclusions

This chapter has articulated four explanations for architectural experience and mapped these using the four fundamental perspectives of the Integral Theory quadrants. While Pallasmaa, Demsaio, LaVine and Thiis-Evensen, as examples of each perspective, offer distinct methods and reveal architectural experience in contrasting ways, each also engages at least one other perspective's view. The figures and ideas given as examples of each perspective are not comprehensive, but illustrate common kinds of conversations and approaches in the field. Perhaps more examples would reveal a subtler but more complex reading of the territory. The proposition here in this chapter is to outline an integrating theory, a decent map, to help fit together these contrasting views.

The chapter engaged the fundamental problem of situating human experience in the context of knowledge and phenomena arising from multiple perspectives. A basic model explaining a holistic co-arising of architectural experience as an all-quadrant occurrence has been outlined. In perhaps a simplified form—for reality is more complex than the map offered—the analysis reveals the intricate co-defining of experiential phenomena in its quadrivia.

Wilber's (2005) full integral model inlcudes quadrants, levels of complexity and lines of development in each quadrant, along with states and types at many levels. It is often referred to as all-quadrant/all-level, or AQAL for short. This chapter has only addressed *quadrants*, the fundamental perspectives. The discussion has only briefly mentioned human developmental levels and how various human capacity lines influence individual experience. The framing for further research into the impact of levels of both self and culture has been laid in the chapter, Unfolding Prospects of the Interior Perspectives, in *Integral Sustainable Design: Transformative Perspectives (ISD)* (DeKay 2011). Readers are referred there for more detail. Similarly, transitory states of human experience and feeling have only loosely been addressed, although a new approach to characterizing these in buildings was proposed in Chapter 1, moving across a valence spectrum from neutrality through comfort and pleasure to peak experiences and, in another dimension, across an intensity/arousal spectrum. Much investigation awaits concerning relationships among specific state experiences and the conditions-in-space that engender them. Nevertheless, buildings are designed and built every day, therefore the design schemas that follow propose ways to connect these with disciplined thought, beginning from what we do know.

The influence of worldview stages, from Traditional to Modern to Postmodern to Integral, that constrain fields of experiential possibilities, occlude or amplify certain phenomena. These culturally-embedded interpretive systems that transform the same architectural experience into different meanings have not been developed in detail here. The *nature of Nature* from different worldviews, along with injunctions and strategies from five worldviews is developed in some detail as, "Designing relationships to Nature: Metaphors and Injunctions for Deep Connections," also in *ISD* (319–429). That approach articulates general ways to connect people to Nature, beginning with how they experience Nature via buildings. The practical application of worldviews in designing for experience, also fertile territory for further research, is addressed more in the design schemas of chapter four.

As in most applications of an integral approach, the added complexity is both enlightening and simultaneously identifies many unanswered questions. Despite the vastness of what is unknown about such everyday occurrences as how people feel in buildings, this chapter offers thought progress significant enough, and from our perspective, trustworthy enough, to build upon its ideational ecology a rapid advancement in experiential design guidance. The work's goal is to support and empower practitioners at creating sumptuous spaces that bring occupants to a more immediate experience of themselves and a deeper connection with Nature. In the next chapter, we take the reader on a journey through some of the most important scientific research evidence that supports this approach to experiential design guidance.

Sources

Appleton, Jay. 1975. *The Experience of Landscape*. New York: Wiley

Arrieta, José. 2001. Moderna Intromisión. *Arquine: Revista Internacional de Arquitectura*, January, 9–10

Bateson, Gregory. 1972. *Steps to an Ecology of Mind.* Chicago: University of Chicago Press

Braun, Verlagshaus Braun. 2009. *1000x Landscape Architecture.* Salenstein, Switzerland: Braun Publishing

Condia, Robert. 2018. Applied Neuroscience for Architects: How Architecture Means Something. Lecture, New School of Architecture, San Diego, CA

DeKay, Mark. 2011. *Integral Sustainable Design: Transformative Perspectives.* ed. Susanne Bennett. London: Earthscan

DeKay, Mark. 2014. The Four Perspectives of Integral Sustainable Design. in *Proceedings, 30th International PLEA Conference Passive and Low Energy Architecture.* Ahmedabad, India

DeKay, Mark. 2018. Designing Relationships to Nature: Five Kinds of Stories and Five Kinds of Connection. *Integral European Conference.* Siofok, Hungary

Demasio, Antonio. 2010. *Self Comes to Mind, Constricting the Conscious Brain.* New York: Pantheon

Demasio, Antonio. 2018. *The Strange Order of Things: Life, Feeling and the Making of Cultures.* New York: Pantheon

DeVos, Corey. 2017. Integral Life Glossary. integrallife.com/glossary/quadrivia/

Eberhard, John P. 2009. Applying Neuroscience to Architecture. *Neuron 62: 753–56*

Grondzik, Walter T + Alison G Kwok. 2019. *Mechanical and Electrical Equipment for Buildings.* 13th ed. Hoboken, New Jersey: Wiley

Hildebrand, Grant. 1991. *The Wright Space: Pattern and Meaning in Frank Lloyd Wright's Houses.* Seattle, Washington: University of Washington Press

LaVine, Lance. 2001. *Mechanics and Meaning in Architecture.* Minneapolis, Minnesota: University of Minnesota Press

LaVine, Lance. 2010. *Architecture, Place, Empathy: the work of Enrique Lastra + Daniel Lopez.* Mexico City: Editorial Piso + Daniel Escotto Editores

Lindman, Åke e:son. 2016. Sverre Fehn: *Nordic Pavillion at the Venice Biennale.* Feb 18. *Divisare.* divisare.com/projects/310739

Lyle, John T. 1985. *Design for Human Ecosystems: Landscape, Land Use and Natural Resources.* New York: Van Nostrand Reinhold

Lyle, John T. 1994. *Regenerative Design for Sustainable Development.* New York: John Wiley

Mallgrave, Harry Francis. 2013. *Architecture and Embodiment: The Implications of the New Sciences and Humanities for Design.* Abingdon, Oxon, UK: Routledge

Mcgregor, Sue L T. 2015. Integral Dispositions and Transdisciplinary Knowledge Creation. *Integral Leadership Review*, Jan-Feb, integralleadershipreview.com/12548-115

Norberg-Schulz, Christian. 1965. *Intentions in Architecture.* Oslo: MIT Press

Norberg-Schutz, Christian + Gennaro Postiglione. 1997. *Sverre Fehn: Works, Projects, Writings, 1949-1996.* New York: Monacelli Press

Pallasmaa, Juhani. 2019. in Wall, Scott, ed. *Rooted in Experience: An Encounter with Juhani Pallasmaa.* Knoxville, Tennessee: University of Tennessee, 11

Pallasmaa, Juhani. 2012. *The Eyes of the Skin: Architecture and the Senses.* 3rd ed. London: John Wiley + Sons

Poole, Scott. 2019. in Wall, Scott, ed. *Rooted in Experience: An Encounter with Juhani Pallasmaa.* Knoxville, Tennessee: University of Tennessee, 3

Rasmussen, Steen Eiler. 1962. *Experiencing Architecture.* 2nd ed. Cambridge, Massachusetts, USA: MIT Press

Salgado, Daniel López. 2000. Museo de Filatelia de Oaxaca (MUFI) IDEAS. daniellopezsalgado.mx/mufi/

Salingaros, Nikos A + Kenneth G Madsen II. 2008. Neuroscience, the Natural Environment, and Building Design. in *Biophilic Design: The Theory, Science, and Practice of Bringing Buildings to Life*, eds. S R Kellert, J H Heerwagen + M L Madore. Hoboken, New Jersey: Wiley

Taylor-Foster, James. 2016. AD Classics: Nordic Pavillion in Venice/ Sverre Fehn. *ArchDaily*, Mar 30. archdaily.com/784536

Thiis-Evensen, Thomas. 1987. *Archetypes in Architecture.* Oslo: Scandinavian University Press

Wilber, Ken. 2000a. *A Theory of Everything: An Integral Vision for Business, Politics, Science, and Spirituality.* Boston, Massachusetts: Shambhala

Wilber, Ken. 2000b. *Sex, Ecology, Spirituality: The Spirit of Evolution.* Boston, Massachusetts: Shambhala

Wilber, Ken. 2005. Introduction to Integral Theory & Practice: IOS Basic and the AQAL Map. *Journal of Integral Theory and Practice* 1: 1–38. integralinstitute.org

Zimmerman, Michael E. 2004. Integral Ecology: A Perspectival, Developmental and Coordinating Approach to Environmental Problems. *World Futures* 61(2): 50–62

Zumthor, Peter + Tony Chapan. 2013. Talking Architecture, Pether Zumthor in conversation with the RIBA's Tony Chapman, video, Royal Institute of British Architects (RIBA). YouTube, Feb 7

3

Excited by Evidence

Every day, nearly every moment, the human body-mind is experiencing the surrounding *sensescape*. We are fascinated by uncovering how this happens and delight in exploring the qualities of architecture people enjoy and love. An intriguing disciplinary range investigates this topic, yet the architectural and engineering vocabularies used to describe sensations and the feelings they invoke require expansion. This chapter summarizes the science of sensation and perception as one foundation for this remarkable journey. When possible, we translate evidence to inform design practice guidelines. The word *sensescape* was coined by David Howes (2005) and refined by many others. We define *sensescape* as the distributions in space and time of environmental conditions that can be sensed, perceived, felt and interpreted by people. In perceiving the sensescape, all of the senses interconnect to create a holistic experience. This chapter covers: 1. Visual elements sensed by the eyes in the *lightscape*; 2. Thermal factors perceived by the skin in the *thermscape*; 3. Acoustic stimuli heard by the ears in a *soundscape*; and 4. Olfactory elements smelled by the nose in a *scentscape*. While we emphasize these, other bodily sensory systems, like proprioception and touch are also addressed in the Chapter 4 schemas.

Sensations affect people physiologically, psychologically, emotionally and cognitively. Sometimes the effects are momentary; some are a lingering consequence of an ephemeral encounter. In other circumstances, effects happen after prolonged immersion. Architectural experiences can impact one's health, well-being and sense of place. Sometimes the interpretation of a sensescape is borne from a deeply conscious way of observing the minutiae of environmental conditions, understanding their source and putting names to sensations and the feelings evoked. Other times, the cause can be entirely subconscious: one notices the effect without understanding how it occurred, remembering the influence of past experience or being aware of a broader influencing cultural context. Human response to the environment is incredibly complex and fascinating, offering endless opportunities for discovery.

We hope that the more deeply designers understand the complexity of human response, the more likely they are to consider such knowledge when designing. Extensive empirical research from the physical and social sciences has documented a range of likely responses to sensescapes, as well as how architecture shapes the distribution of conditions. Lessons from the neuroscience of sensory adaptation and psychological perception help explain both fleeting and sustained delight. Such research results can inspire building professionals and offer evidence-based guidance, helping create evocative first impressions and more enduring influences.

While peer-reviewed research is rigorous and well documented, it is often written in a way foreign to practice. Our aim is to bridge analytic scientific language and poetic sensorial architectural perspectives to provide a basis for creating positive, holistic aesthetic experience. Chapter 2 built a framework for multi-disciplinary thinking about human experience, sensorial conditions, spatial order and meaning, including a phenomenological perspective and the cultural context for interpretation. This chapter offers a scientific perspective about the body's sensory systems, selectively highlighting research on the merits of variable stimuli and connecting people to Nature, in order to help practitioners make sense of sensescapes.

opposite
National Library of Greece
Stavros Niarchos Cultural Center

Athens, Greece, 2016
Renzo Piano Building Workshop

photo Mark DeKay

The broader one's understanding of the human experience, the better design we will have.

—*Steve Jobs*

Science of Architectural Experience

Architectural perception begins with the senses, whether or not one notices, understands or emotionally processes the sensations. Scholars from many disciplines explore this territory: cultural studies, engineering, history, neuroscience, phenomenology, physiology, psychology and others. There are many trajectories through this sphere. For example, one can begin with how building design and operation shape the environmental elements of a sensescape—or start from the environment, exploring how it impacts the body's sensors or how the body's physioneurologic systems transit those sensations to the brain. That could lead to deeper examination of the static and dynamic character of environmental conditions and how the associated neuroreceptor firing influences affective response. Some investigators prefer to skip all that and focus on how minds and hearts interpret affect and assign significance. The sequence of events in the human-environment system are viewed by some scientists as a given, and for others, debatable. Regardless of order, the process of learning about any of these fundamental underpinnings of experience can feel enlightening and can empower the experiential designer.

While much can be learned from historic or phenomenological research, and from computational simulations, the emphasis here is on direct empirical research about the physical attributes of the environment, especially indoors, and people's physiological and subjective response to these attributes. Some of this work has been done in laboratory experiments, which offer the benefits of carefully controlled and more easily replicable conditions. Other research is based on field studies, which offer realism and all its complexities, yet often with multiple confounding factors. Before learning about examples from each, we begin with the body.

Environment, senses and perception (diagram), along with their relationships, provide a starting point to design for delight. Whether enjoying the crashing ocean waves' salty mist or the desert chaparral's earthy fragrance, the outdoors is teeming with stimuli. This is eloquently described by Michael Cabanac (2010), a Professor of Psychiatry and Neuroscience at Laval University in Quebec, in his book *The Fifth Influence* or, the *Dialectics of Pleasure*. From a purely physiological perspective, environmental conditions first *stimulate* sensory organs. These include, but are not limited to sensors in the eyes, ears, nose and skin. *Sensitivity* describes the sensors' ability to notice environmental changes and send information to the nervous system, which then sends signals via nerve impulses to particular brain regions. The frequency profile of transmitted impulses manifests for people first as a *sensation*, essentially the physiological detection of a stimulus. For thermal response, Parkinson (2021) hypothesizes that the frequency, or firing rate, of impulses indicates how sensors respond to changes in, rather than absolute values of, a stimulus. How quickly receptors adapt is central to how bodies respond to constant or variable conditions. For example, temperature sensors are relatively slow compared to instantaneous olfactory registration.

Disciplines that study the stimulus-sensation relationship offer many theories about the complexities and attributes of sensation. Architectural designers will benefit by knowing how people *feel* about their sensations. They might

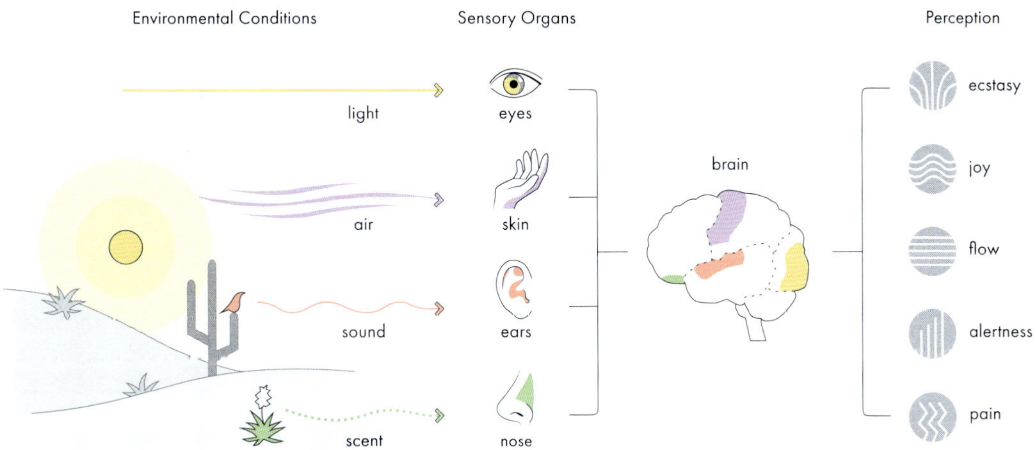

Environment, senses + perception

Environmental data is processed by sensory organs that send impulses to the brain, which then interprets the information. Sensation is a physical process and perception is psychological.

be annoying or pleasurable; if pleasurable, then the nuance could be calming or relaxed, alert or energized. This affective state of mind is *perception*, essentially one's most fundamental interpretation of the information processed by the senses. Simply put, "We sense the presence of a stimulus, but we perceive what it is" (Levine + Shefner 2004). Perception depends on one's activities, behavior and purpose for presence in an architectural space. For example, a person's perception of a room's conditions can vary widely, depending on whether the person is relaxing at home, concentrating at work, healing in a hospital or socializing at a pub. Perception is influenced by sensation, activity and sociocultural factors, such as memory, preferences and expectations. As described in Chapter 1, interpretations and emotions lead to higher-level understanding and affiliation, giving rise to meaning; however, these more subjective and intersubjective phenomena are more complex than what the physical sciences aim to discover.

Research methods

Designers shape buildings, which shape environments. When envisaging occupants' experience, evidence from diverse and perhaps unfamiliar literature can help, especially when designers have a general understanding of the approaches used by researchers. The scientific method broadly includes problem formulation, testing and analysis, yet there is rarely consensus on measurement protocols. This can present difficulties in comparing and generalizing findings from different sources. The relatively easy part is how to measure or simulate the physical environmental conditions. The more challenging task is assessing human response—physiological, psychological or cognitive. Within buildings, occupant psychological studies are intended to evaluate people's behavior and subjective responses to the environment—how they use, sense and perceive it. Post-occupancy evaluation (POE) studies can be part of robust research, often accompanied by physical measurement. They constitute the most accessible approach for practitioners who want to learn about the occupants' lived perspective in their buildings. Common methods include focus groups, interviews and surveys. Questions can help collect quantitative or qualitative responses. *Likert scales* measure attitudes, perceptions, and behavior, typically using a five or seven-point range from which participants answer questions. The most commonly used Likert questions address specific sensations—for example, bright-to-dim or loud-to-quiet. A classic thermal sensation scale, used in research and standards, ranges from cold (−3) to neutral (0) to hot (+3). These are then accompanied by questions about perceptual constructs, among them comfort, satisfaction, preference and acceptability. Studies of more complex human experience and emotion may have additional nuanced questions that address a multitude of qualitative perceptions. Among these we find pleasure, happiness, alertness, ability to concentrate, fatigue, boredom, stress or anxiety, adaptability and air freshness. Most surveys also include open-ended questions for more narrative responses, which can be especially revealing. Content analysis tools can be used to identify themes and relationships that emerge from even the qualitative text. UC Berkeley's Center for the Built Environment (CBE) created one of the first digital post-occupancy surveys and has collected a large database of over 100,000 responses from over 1000 buildings, producing vast and meaningful insights about how building occupants perceive their spaces (Graham et al. 2021). Originally developed as a research tool, the survey has become widely used as a way for companies and design teams to receive feedback about inhabitants' experiences.

While it's relatively easy for practitioners to directly engage in survey research, they are more likely constrained to learn from others about physiological and cognitive effects. These studies are more complicated and require specialized equipment or techniques. Creating healthy buildings starts with eliminating negative impacts, which we consider necessary but insufficient. The primary focus of physiological research in the built environment is to reduce problems, such as stress reduction or sick building syndrome symptoms, rather than engender positive affect. While stress is typically measured in the moment, it can indicate long-term health implications. Researchers directly measure heart rate, heart rate variability, blood oxygen saturation and respiration rate, diastolic blood pressure, stress hormone (cortisol) levels, visual acuity and illness symptoms. Such physiological measurements have been the most common basis for biophilia studies that demonstrate Nature's restorative effects. Physiological research can also use surveys to assess subjective symptoms or specific physical health conditions, for example, headaches or dryness of skin, eyes, nose or mouth. Cognitive performance studies often examine how conditions affect workplace task performance or students' academic success. Researchers might give subjects tasks to test their mental agility—typing, math problems or puzzles—while measuring speed, error rate, time for completion or ratio of correct answers. Experimental researchers evaluating the elusive constructs of creativity, logical thinking, memory, collaboration and motivation confront a more difficult challenge than physiological, cognitive or psychological factors.

Valuing variability

Nature offers soothing, invigorating and restorative effects. It is replete with sensory variability. Chapter 1 introduced how the biophilic pleasure that people derive from Nature connection arises from the fact that homo

Nature's variability embraced by architecture, indoors and out

Thorncrown Chapel
Eureka Springs, Arkansas, 1980
E Fay Jones, architect

Situated in a dense forest, the chapel has no cultivated landscape. Structure and trees express oneness of subject and object, inside and outside, person and place, Nature and spirit. Soaring walls, transparency, light and dark, breeze and motion, the forest canopy, awe. Slender struts, branches, columns, trunks. Peace. Lightness that lives.

photo Dustin Holmes

sapiens evolved in a landscape where sensitivity for and responsiveness to dynamic environmental stimuli insured survival. Biophilic theory proposes that this survival-based sensitivity has evolved into pleasure discrimination, reflected in people seeking outdoor climate variability in their recreational lives. Given the preponderance of time people spend indoors, they hunger in parallel for alternatives to the relatively bland technology-dominated environmental constancy of contemporary buildings. Sensory monotony is not necessarily problematic unless it predominates, while excess variability can lead to complaints. Balance is key. Some alternative scenarios for sensescape composition include:

1 *Matching the degree of variability to activity* and intended sensory qualities, such as hushed private versus lively collaborative spaces in an office

2 *Contrasting variability within a steady-state context*, such as a breezy entrance to a hospital in a hot climate

3 *Contrasting stillness against chaotic context*, such as a quiet pocket park in the bustling city or a contemplative chapel in a crowded airport

4 *Creating rhythms*, randomness or other patterns between relatively dynamic and static conditions within the same space, such perimeter study carrels surrounding larger core zones in a library

5 *Determining the range of comfortable variability* associated with predictable responses, such as progressions from light to dark spaces in a museum to allow for visual adaptation
6 *Varying one or more environmental parameters* while holding others constant, such as hearing the sounds of rain and wind while within the warm refuge of home

Chapter 1 introduced how variability occurs in different timeframes—momentary, hourly, daily, seasonally, annual or quasi-random. It introduced spatial scales—human, rooms, spatial sequences and buildings. In the sections that follow, time and space get unpacked for four sensory systems, as variable conditions hold a different significance for each.

Smell is the most fleeting sense, scent fading quickly after the first whiff, while simultaneously the most lasting by invoking long-term memory. Building designers tend to pay the least attention to the, beyond eliminating noxious odors. In contrast, landscape architects find scent an essential element. Several design schemas in Chapter 4 offer examples to link indoor and outdoor scentscapes, including S2 Aromatic Transit, C4 Engage the Rain and C4 Inhabited Periphery.

Sound wave variance is fundamental for interpreting what one hears. Enjoyment requires contrast to distinguish notes in a simple song or an elaborate symphony, identifying forest bird sounds or relishing quietude after immersion in the cacophonous city. In other circumstances, the temporal patterns become irritating, as with the jackhammer's repetition or the office's white noise. Embracing soundscape variation underpins schemas like G4 Euphonic Water, F1Melodic Materials and F4 Compluvium Shower.

It is easy to take for granted the visual system's functional latitude, yet when considered, its breadth astounds. Daily life is marked by light and dark cycles. Pupil dilation and constriction allow sight over a vast range of light levels. Of all the sensory systems, designers are most adept at using lighting spatially and temporally to shape experience. Familiar associations may be found in the design schemas, such as the diurnal pattern of light's regulatory function in R4 Circadian Space, the role of adaptation in S5 Light and Dark Procession or the outdoor gradations in G4 Shades of Brilliance.

The skin is the only sensory organ covering the entire body, uniquely enabling temperature or texture differences to be felt locally by the hands, feet or face. Thermal sensations are affected not only by air temperature, but also by humidity, air movement and heat radiation. Architectural organizations and mechanical systems influence each of these, resulting in distributional permutations, as addressed by the design schemas R2 Aperture Engagement, S5 Territorial Tuning and C4 Tempered Pathway.

The scientific understanding of how sensory variability induces pleasure remains limited, as conducting such research remains challenging for many reasons. First, it is easier to measure coarse discomfort thresholds than comfort, satisfaction or pleasure nuances. Hedonic feelings tend to be more transitory than the less explicitly pleasurable neutrality or comfort states. Context becomes increasingly important for higher affect levels, increasing difficulty of generalizing beyond the circumstances of a particular experiment. For example, feeling air on the face or dipping feet into cool water is pleasurable when feeling warm but unwelcome if already cold. The effect also depends on activity level at the time. Fortunately, the nature of research is expanding, with growing evidence for delight and greater support for the arguments forwarded in this book—evidence to be excited about!

Adaptive opportunity

Inhabitants' choice and control factor heavily in ensuring that variability indeed leads to pleasure. Imagine for a moment a regularly-occupied space shared with others. Perhaps one prefers a warm house and another prefers coolness. Maybe one likes working in quiet, while an officemate enjoys interactive hubbub. Such discord is common. Individuals differ substantially in the sensescape qualities they find pleasurable. Many factors contribute to these differences, among them activity level, emotional state, recent or distant experiential history memory associations and social or cultural norms that affect expectations.

Given these multifarious influences, designing buildings to offer inhabitants *adaptive opportunity* is an approach towards ensuring individualized delight, offering the possibility for people to interact with and modify their location, personal factors, or environmental conditions of a space. This term was first coined by University of Cambridge Professors Nick Baker and Mark Standeven (1995), referring primarily to building inhabitants' ability to achieve thermal comfort through personal factors and building controls. We believe it has broader implications for experiential design. When occupants are provided flexibility to behaviorally adapt (either spatially, temporally or operationally) to any environmental condition, their agency for pleasure increases. Designing for such adaptive opportunity means providing a range of places with different conditions, freedom to relocate and physical control of their local conditions through architectural, mechanical or electrical means. These opportunities for behavioral adaptation can be thought about in four main ways:

Spatial flexibility encourages and facilitates occupants to migrate to areas that they find most comfortable at different times of the day and year, for example, relocating to sunny east-facing spaces on cold winter mornings, or avoiding the sun by moving from a shaded western terrace on a summer morning to a shady east-facing porch in the afternoon. An agile workplace provides alternative zones to match physical space to activity and sensory needs, such as small rooms for quiet concentration and privacy, open collaborative space where clamorous conversation is more acceptable, breakout relaxation areas or technology enhanced suites for group brainstorming.

Temporal flexibility means that occupants can shift their schedules, either as a group or individually. Shifts might be based on seasonal conditions. In Greece, shops close during the hot afternoon hours and reopen in the evening. Office and school schedules in Ahmedabad, India, shift to begin and end earlier to avoid a similar afternoon peak during the hottest April and May months before the June monsoon. In schools, classrooms are often scheduled for only a portion of the day, so some schools allow a vacant period in-between classes to let the room cool before the next class's people, occupants and equipment loading; this allows for natural ventilation in place of AC. While many of these strategies are cultural or depend on company policy, there can be implications for design or operational accommodations. Design for temporal flexibility may also reflect daily cycles, such as having different favorite places in one's home to enjoy morning coffee or afternoon cocktails, or be circumstantial, such as the ability to move from the perimeter to interior work spaces when there is temporary outdoor construction.

Personal flexibility describes the physical and psychological adjustments occupants can make to adapt to their surroundings, including changing the amount and type of clothing from lighter in summer to heavier in winter, drinking warm or cold beverages in response to an opposite condition, changing posture with a sit-stand desk or otherwise moving about. Occupants' personal flexibility can be partly determined by the building's type and use, it's interior design or a company's dress code.

Environmental flexibility can be thought of as operational, or providing technical controls. It includes the ability to open a window, operate blinds or other shading, use a fan, turn on sound masking, or access individualized bright task lighting within a context of lower level ambient lighting. This approach could create interior sensory zones or microclimates, employing a person-based conditioning approach such as using low-energy, personally-controlled fans, foot warmers or heated/cooled chairs.

Adaptive opportunity toolbox (table) provides examples of these four behavioral flexibility categories, each intersecting architectural design, technological solutions, and building operation. This concept serves as an underlying principle of many design schemas, and figures heavily in large or shared spaces where satisfying everyone with the same conditions becomes difficult.

The notion of personal control is so central to adaptive opportunity that it is worth exploring more. Monica Paciuk at the National Building Research Institute at the Technion in Haifa, Israel, did pioneering work on this area as part of her dissertation on the role of personal control (1990). In it, she distinguishes three aspects of control:

1 *Available control* is purely *physical*, for instance, access to operable windows, blinds, task lighting, fans and thermostat. It is perhaps the easiest and most commonly researched metric of personal control.

2 *Perceived control* is the psychological recognition that one can control local conditions. Her research tied it to the confidence that one's actions will have, if enacted, on the desired effect.

3 *Exercised control* is the frequency of actual behavioral adjustment of the available control elements.

Adaptive opportunity toolbox

Examples of how culture, company policy, and building design, operation, and technology can support the four types of behavioral adaptation

Spatial	Temporal	Personal	Environmental
Migration internally or indoor-outdoor	Seasonal patterns of operation or space use	Clothing: more or less, flexible dress codes	Task lighting, blinds + louvers for light redirection/glare control
Range of microclimates + activity zones	Siesta, daily open + closed periods based on climate	Metabolic: activity or stillness, activity-based zones or breakouts	Personal comfort systems, zone controls, ceiling + desktop fans
Variation of ambient vs local conditions	Intermittent occupancy, staggered start times, peak load shifts	Posture: sit or stand, adaptive furniture	Operable windows + other ventilation apertures
Spatial transformations: expansion + contraction	Daily rhythms, morning vs evening inhabitation of favorite spaces	Consumption: hot or cold, accessible beverage stations	Personal sound masking, acoustic screens

Examining the relationship among these control types and thermal comfort, Paciuk conducted a field study of over 500 workstations in ten office buildings featuring a variety of components that occupants could control. These included windows, exterior shading devices, interior blinds and ventilation louvers. She found that 25% of the variance in individuals' thermal comfort responses could be accounted for collectively by these three aspects of control. Her further analysis showed that thermal satisfaction was *positively* correlated (improved) with increases in *available* and *perceived* control. In other words, if people *have* or *think they have* control over the thermal environment, they will be more satisfied than others exposed to the same conditions but without control. In contrast, satisfaction was *negatively* correlated (reduced) with *exercised* control. This suggests that if occupants frequently adjust controls, it often indicates an unsatisfactory environment.

Many other researchers found that perceived control had the highest correlation with thermal satisfaction (Haghighat + Donnini 1999; Langevin et al. 2012; Boerstra et al. 2013). Similarly, investigating lighting, researchers found a strong relationship between occupants' available and perceived lighting control and their visual comfort, personal wellbeing and acceptance of broader ranges of visual conditions, such as dimmer lighting (Robertson et al. 1989; Sadeghi et al. 2016). These discoveries suggest that *available controls* are necessary but not sufficient. Occupants educated to understand their adaptive opportunities and how to use them gain *perceived control* and greater satisfaction.

The following sections explore four sensory systems: eyes, skin, ears and nose, while remaining cognizant that other senses also perceive the environment and the body's movement in it. Entire books and multitudinous scientific publications have been written on each sensory system and the physical characteristics that affect them. Our intention is not to explain each sense's physiological, neurological and psychological network in detail. Instead, we highlight characteristics that help designers understand how people respond to variable conditions, turning from basic comfort toward the direction of delight. A deeper dive into selected topics for each sense follows.

Eyes: luminous environment

Vision is the dominant sense, the primary way humans process information from their world. Of all the sensory systems, it is the most influential for sighted people in how the first impression of a space forms. Vision is primary for architects pondering how people will see the form, structure, texture and color of the rooms and buildings they design. It is the basis for designing apertures to bring in daylight's nuanced qualities and for framing views connecting people to outdoors. Indoors, the lightscape distributes the pleasurable and performative attributes of daylight and electric light. It provides pragmatic requirements for specific visual tasks. All of this can have a profound effect on the full range of nested experiential states described in Chapter 1, that is, sensation, affect, understanding and affiliation. These states include, among many others, sensing dark and light patterns or smoothness and roughness, emotional delight and aesthetic response, awareness and comprehension, belonging and identity.

The eyes also contribute to the non-image-forming effects of light. To be precise, the term *visible light* is defined as the subset of the electromagnetic spectrum wavelengths that elicits a visual response. We will be employing the more colloquial usage found throughout the literature, where *light* refers to stimulus that causes both visual and non-visual responses. While a rapidly evolving field, there is growing evidence that demonstrates how the daily light and dark cycle supports people's circadian rhythms—the body's natural cycle of physical, mental and behavioral changes, sometimes called the body clock. Before describing these effects, let us briefly consider the eye's physiology.

Eye physiology (diagram) has recently evolved in scientific understanding. The retina has multiple photoreceptor cell types. The two most familiar are the rods and cones, which are part of the visual system, and the *intrinsically photosensitive retinal ganglion cells* (ipRGCs) regulate hormones and circadian health. Daytime vision and spatial acuity depend primarily on the cones, which are active at higher light levels and feed color perception. The rods facilitate sight at low light levels; while they do not substantially contribute to color vision, new research indicates they play a minor role. These two photoreceptors send impulses along optic nerve fibers to the brain's primary visual cortex, which then processes vision's fundamental building blocks (color, edges, direction and movement) to produce an image. This allows one to determine higher order perceptions, for instance, shape, size and distance.

Humans perceive light across a vast range of illuminance levels. The eye adjusts from a starlit sky to a bright sunny beach, a change in illuminance levels well over a million-fold! The iris adapts to dilate and contract, controlling how much light enters; by itself, this accounts for a maximum visible illuminance range of about 16:1. The visual system has three additional adaptation mechanisms that make the retina more sensitive in low light and less sensitive in bright light. This allows humans to perceive light across a mind-boggling range, such as about 100,000 lux on a sunny day to 0.001 lux under a moonless, starlit sky. These adaptations occur in the photoreceptors themselves as:

1 *Switchover* from rods to cones
2 *Bleaching or regeneration* of the photopigments, with less photopigment available at high light levels
3 *Neural feedback* to control photoreceptor responsiveness.

Designers will be interested in the considerable research about the benefits of daylight and view, persuasively described in Heschong's *Visual Delight in Architecture* (2021). Views of Nature from buildings are particularly relevant to an architecture of variability and delight. Intriguing daytime views encourage building occupants to focus their gaze outdoors, which, in turn, enhances the circadian stimulus they receive, a topic expanded below.

In the brain, visual association areas surround the primary visual cortex. There, information is compared to past experiences so that a person can recognize something familiar, which in turn can be connected to emotional response. The relationship between one's visual system and emotions is complex. Lang and colleagues (1998) used functional magnetic resonance imaging (fMRI), which is similar to MRI but is particularly sensitive to brain activity, to demonstrate that emotional processing typically begins with vision. Schupp and team (2003) measured event-related potentials (ERPs) to study how visual cues were responsible for emotional categorization. ERPs are very small voltages generated in the brain as a response to specific sensory or cognitive stimuli, or to bodily movements. Both researchers found strong responses associated with emotion in the visual cortex.

In addition to rods and cones, the third type of photoreceptors, the ipRGCs, were discovered at the turn of the 21st century. This breakthrough has had a revolutionary effect on understanding light, its non-image-forming functions and, ultimately, its more subtle and complex effects on human experience. The ipRCGs play a very minor, indirect role in modifying visual perception through increasing contrast sensitivity at night and enhancing pupil dilation. More importantly, they play an essential role in light's biological impacts. They have been found to connect to multiple locations in the brain, helping to regulate the basic physiological rhythms of sleep, body temperature, digestion, immune response and hormone release. These circadian rhythms, primarily attuned to 24-hour patterns of light and dark exposure, are integral to overall health. This new knowledge has elevated the importance of designing to connect people to daily lighting rhythms.

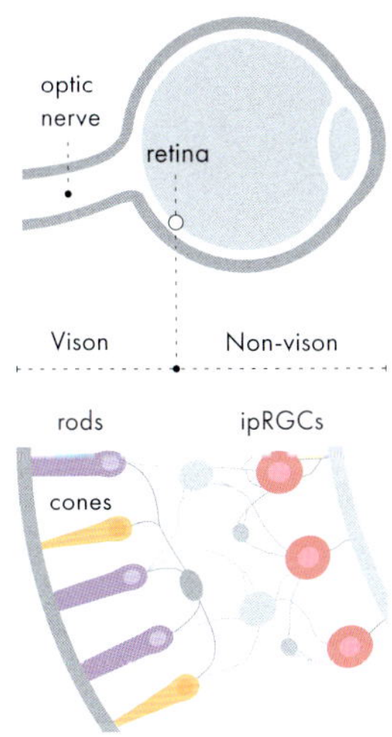

Photoreceptor Cells

Ancestral versus modern daily light exposure

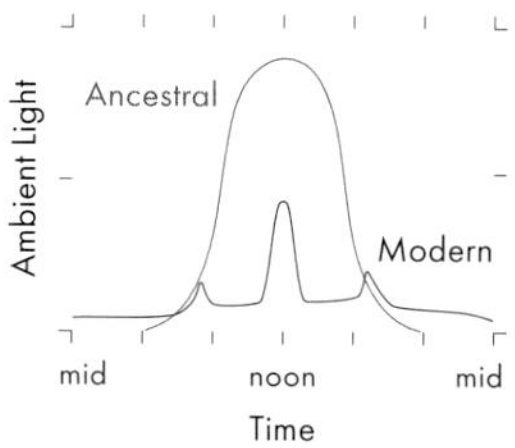

Adapted from Heschong 2021

Temporal and spatial patterns of light distribution and intensity matter. Pupil contraction and glare perception when transitioning from dim to bright conditions can be almost immediate. Adaptation when moving from brightness to dimness takes much longer; how long depends on the degree of brightness change. These patterns are an important element of S5 Light and Dark Procession. Light's effects on alertness and mood can occur over hours or the course of a whole day. Longer term health effects or seasonal depression might not be evident for months or years. Like all human sensory systems, not everyone responds to the same conditions in the same way. In particular, response to illuminance contrast is highly age-related. Older adults generally perceive a smaller illumination range and adapt slower than younger people by a factor of 10 to 100, highlighting the importance for designers to understand the building inhabitants' demographic profile.

Circadian stimulus

The word *circadian*, coined in 1959, comes from Latin *circa*, meaning about and *diem*, meaning day; the term refers to an approximately 24-hour cycle that controls various biological processes. Humans' evolution as outdoor, daytime beings means that the visual system has adapted to be sensitive to light across the visible spectrum at wavelengths of 400–700 nm and is particularly sensitive to blue sky colors, short-wavelengths in the range of 450-480 nm (Lockley et al. 2006). It also means that people's biological systems are tuned to ancestral temporal patterns of experiencing bright light during the day and near-darkness at night.

Ancestral versus modern daily light exposure (diagram) offers a compelling illustration of contemporary lifestyles. As an indoor species, with perhaps occasional outdoor excursions during the workweek, the daily pattern of our illumination exposure has become much flatter, with potentially significant health implications. In Chapter 4, the design schema R3 Biorhythmic Radiance provides guidance on electric lighting, while R4 Circadian Space addresses architectural daylight to support circadian health. For both, the most important elements of a healthy, integrative lighting strategy are, in order of priority, temporal patterns of light and dark (timing and duration of exposure), light level (luminous intensity), light spectrum (color temperature), and spatial patterns (gaze direction and luminous distribution in field of view).

Diurnal cycle and hormone production (figure) illustrates the human biological clock's calibration of metabolism and hormone cycles that naturally support physical and mental activity during the day, nightly rest, supporting memory formation and boosting the immune system health. In general, people thrive when following these natural rhythms and suffer if deprived of a regular light-dark cycle. Evidence indicates health problems for people who work irregular night shifts and for airline staff who routinely travel across multiple time zones (Write et al. 2013). The science of light's effects on non-visual systems is complex. A highly simplified explanation starts with light from the eyes that causes the photoreceptor ipRGCs to send signals to the brain's hypothalamus area, which triggers, among others, the amount of melatonin or serotonin released. These two hormones work in harmony—serotonin stabilizes mood and helps one feel energized, while melatonin helps wind the body down. Together, they explain

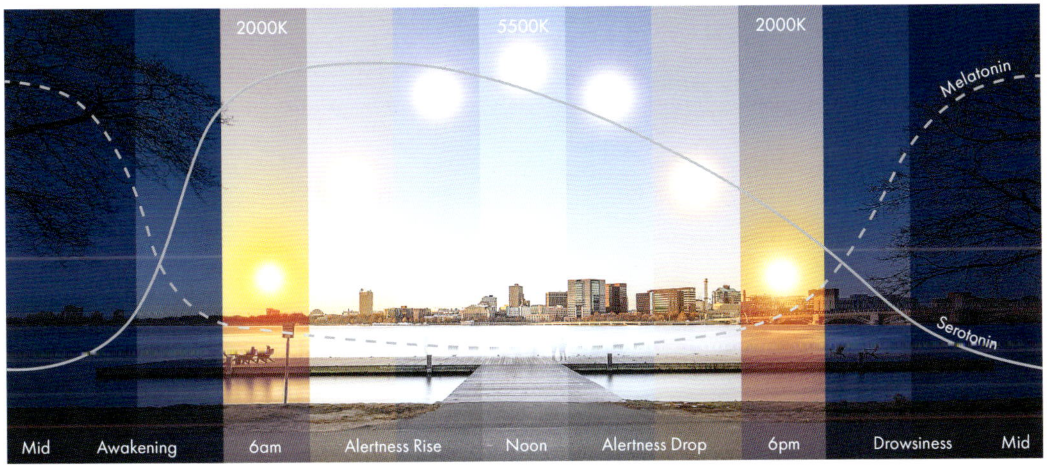

Diurnal solar cycle and hormone production

Daily changes in daylight intensity, color temperature and spectral distribution affect hormone production. This affects alertness and other biological functions. Sun path varies by latitude and season; times illustrate mid-latitude spring/fall; color temperatures are generalized.

why patterns of light can affect one's immediate alertness state, sleep-wake cycles, cognitive function and longer term health (Badia et al. 1991; Vandewalle et al. 2009). When outdoors, the eyes see two dynamic rhythms of full-spectrum daylight:

1 *Intensity gradually shifts* from low in the early morning, higher as the day progresses, and lower again in the evenings.

2 *Color temperatures* are warmer/redder (< 2000 K –3500 K) when the sun is rising and setting; cooler/bluer at noon—from about 5000K for clear sky conditions to 7000–10,000K for a slightly-to-heavily overcast sky.

The rise in intensity and cool blue-rich light during the day suppresses melatonin release and increases serotonin, allowing one to feel more alert. The evening's lower intensities and warm amber light triggers the production of melatonin and brings on drowsiness.

Research is offering greater understanding of how designing for daylight and dynamic electrical lighting can have profound effects on circadian health (Lucas et al. 2014) and how views from buildings can bring benefits beyond the daylight provided, partly becuase a view encourages an outward gaze, which then increases light exposure (MBC Aries et al. 2015; Heschong 2021). There is also a growing but less understood body of research investigating ways that ipRGCs are responsible for mood and behavioral state beyond mediating hormone release (Milosavljevic 2019). As this research grows, it will be increasingly important for understanding not only how to treat seasonal affective disorder (SAD) and other psychiatric disorders (Wirz-Justice et al. 2013), but also how to design lighting systems to enhance daily health and well-being.

Laboratory research demonstrated that light enhances alertness (as measured by EEG beta activity) and psychomotor performance (Badia et al. 1991; Phipps-Nelson et al. 2003). Exposure to light at 6500 K led to cognitive improvement for activities requiring sustained attention but not for those that required higher order executive function, in this case measured as attention, calculation ability, and information processing speed (Chellappa et al. 2011). Field research has primarily been in workplace and school settings. Studies of office electric lighting revealed that blue-enriched polychromatic light improves daytime alertness, concentration ability, sleep quality, overall mood and mental health (Boubekri et al. 2014; Mills et al. 2007; Viola et al. 2008). Studies of school dynamic lighting that follows natural cycles revealed improved student performance in standardized tests of concentration, reading speed and comprehension (Barkmann et al. 2012; Figueiro et al. 2017; Mott et al. 2012).

Metrics for describing circadian impact are in flux, currently being debated by researchers. While the conventional unit of *lux* tracks with the way vision cones register light intensity, new metrics are required for circadian lighting's biological effects, and there is not yet consensus about which of those proposed is best.

– *Melanopic Equivalent Daylight Illuminance* (EDI or m-EDI) is the circadian metric adopted by the International Commission on Illumination (CIE 2019). Research seems to be pointing to this being the best path forward, although there are still many other metrics being used. EDI has units of lux, and is weighted to the ipRGS's sensitivity using calculations that are somewhat complicated, but viewed as the most accurate to date.

– *Equivalent Melanopic Lux* (EML), introduced by Lucas et al. (2014), is used in the WELL Building Standard (IWBI 2022). It predates EDI and has a simpler calculation method, multiplying the traditional lux measurement by a *melanopic ratio* as the weighting factor, which is dependent on the spectral power distributions of the light source.

– *Circadian Lux* (CLA) is one of two metrics developed by The Lighting Research Center (LRC) at Rensselaer Polytechnic Institute. CLA is based on a mathematical model that calculates the irradiance at the cornea weighted by the spectral sensitivity of the body's circadian system, as measured by melatonin suppression after a 1-hour exposure. It is based on a scientific model of human circadian phototransduction, the process by which light is converted into electrical signals in the eyes receptors (Rea et al. 2010).

– *Circadian Stimulus* (CS), transforms CLA into simpler relative units, ranging from zero (the threshold for activation) to 0.7 (response saturation). Another way to interpret those same numbers is as the percentage of melatonin suppression that the light causes (from 0% at night to a maximum of 70% suppression during the day).

To support human health and vitality indoors, we suggest an overall design goal for circadian health as any combination of daylight, as addressed in R4 Circadian Space (preferred) and electric light that generally mimics the brightness and color spectrum of the outdoor lighting rhythm. This also implies very low lighting levels in the evening and darkness for sleeping. For rooms more dependent on electric light, there is growing attention toward circadian lighting systems that offer intensity and color tuning based on the time of day, as covered in the R3 Biorhythmic Radiance schema.

Time to B Cafe

Yongin-si, South Korea
NONE SPACE, architects

This no-plug, no-Wi-fi cafe encourages analog time for resting and relaxing in Nature.

The space becomes a single place by becoming a touch point between the time of 'nature' and 'individual.' By spatially interpreting the time of 'real' nature, we have created various sequences and gaze flow.

—*None Space architects*

Photos Kiwoong Hong

ArchDaily 2022

Nature views

When one cannot be outdoors, having a view of Nature while indoors, either from perimeter windows or viewed into interior courtyards, is the next best thing. A visual connection to the outdoors has been shown to have numerous positive effects on people's physiology, psychological and emotional state, cognitive performance and overall sense of well-being. A group of over 50 experts recently drafted a position statement related to the complexities of window view quality, adopting a framework developed at UC Berkeley for its primary components—content, access, and clarity—and describing areas were research is needed (Ko et al. 2022). The most important constituents of window views include nature (greenery, water, weather), three horizontal layers (ground, horizon and sky), and movement (human-related activities, or natural movement such as falling leaves or passing clouds). Access refers to the relationship between the occupants and the windows, affecting the amount of view that can be seen. This is an important purview of designers, from early decisions about building orientation to later choices about furniture layout. Clarity is affected by glazing properties, including dynamic and spectrally selective glass, and the material and operation of blinds or shading systems. These decisions are often made during later phases of the design process, and can present tradeoffs with managing glare control.

Research covers a wide range of circumstances, from being immersed in nature, having views through windows and substituting imagery. In her recent book, Heschong (2021) offers a comprehensive summary of the increasing evidence that Nature views from buildings, particularly of water, reap for viewers similar benefits to being outdoors. As one example, she describes the causal reasons behind cognitive improvements in the case where student academic performance is improved in daylighted classrooms and even more with an outdoor view. The phenomenon of mind wandering, where a person's thoughts divert from an attention-demanding task, could be at cause (Shepherd 2019). In certain situations this is not a good thing, such as when driving. However, mind-wandering is beneficial in many settings, such as schools and workplaces; evidence supports that it can facilitate memory, creativity and problem-solving (Baird et al. 2012).

The diversion of an outdoor view can have parallel physiological effects. At the office, a view inspires workers to turn away from their desks or computer screens and focus on something at a distance. This can reduce dry eyes and eye strain, while improving overall eye health by maintaining muscle tone and lubrication. Many optometrists recommend that workers refocus their eyes at least every 20 minutes by viewing something at least 20 ft (6 m) away (Altomonte et al. 2020). Shin (2007) found that office workers with a forest view reported lower stress levels, as well as higher job satisfaction, than those without that view

Ko and team (2020) studied the impact of window view on emotions, cognitive performance, and thermal comfort. They found that people with views had higher rates of positive emotions (happy, satisfied content), lower rates of negative emotion (sad, lonely, unhappy), performed better on cognitive tests (ability to concentrate and working memory),and were less drowsy. Compared to people without views but in the same thermal conditions, subjects with views felt slightly cooler and were more comfortable. Other research focusing specifically on views of movement demonstrated the delight of connection to weather's variations, and the effects of helping one's sense of time passage (Aries et al. 2010 ; Farley + Veitch 2001).

Some studies have confirmed that an outdoor view's broader benefits depend not on illumination levels but on other aspects, including size of sunlight areas and the proportion of natural elements in the view (Ulrich 1984; Stone + Irvine 1993; Boubekri 1991). Related evidence about preferences for outdoor connection versus illumination levels and lighting distribution patterns comes from a study done in a university library. Shunning study carrels with carefully controlled, glare-free diffuse lighting, patrons preferred carrels near a window, where conditions varied strongly with outdoor weather. Some users experienced direct sunlight and glare, traditionally considered as negative, but chose the location for its view of a river and surrounding landscape (Steemers + Stean 2004).

Nature views are an integral part of many design schemas in Chapter 4, including C4 Tempered Pathway, R4 Habitat Fringe, N5 Three Realms and N6 Situated Scenes.

Skin: thermal environment

Habitability and comfort are the primary purpose for mechanical heating and cooling systems, which significantly contribute to contemporary buildings' carbon footprints, a fact that underscores the importance of thermal conditions. The thermscape is complicated because ambient temperature and many additional factors, particularly air movement, affect thermal response and can, with intelligent design, collude to create thermal delight.

Like other sensescapes, thermal conditions and experiences vary over different time scales. When a person moves between outdoors and in, or between perimeter and interior zones, it is their own movement that participates in creating the dynamic experience. Climate-responsive, envelope-dominated buildings (having low internal heat gains from lights, people and equipment) do not have deep interior core zones that require constant cooling, as do thick-plan buildings. Their indoor environment is more connected to weather fluctuations. In such buildings, even a sedentary occupant can experience the outdoor climate's daily and seasonal rhythms.

Skin physiology (diagram) illustrates cold and warm thermoreceptors. When environmental conditions are constant, the frequency of the receptors' impulses sent to the brain is steady, referred to as *static response*. When the thermal environment and the body's associated skin temperature changes, the *dynamic response* of generated impulses can vary quickly. This distinction has several implications for both human experience and design; it is particularly relevant when experiencing outdoor environments, with their fluctuating air motion, light and sound. Compared to the warm receptors, cold receptors tend to be denser, located at shallower skin depth and have a stronger dynamic response. This means that people typically react to rapid decreases in temperature more quickly than to increases. Similarly, a person reacts rapidly to being cooled by air motion. Such phenomena form the physiological basis for the thermal delights engendered in design schemas that use air motion, from natural ventilation or fans. Thermoreceptors are distributed unevenly; consequently, different body parts vary in their sensitivity to temperature changes, suggesting alternative design opportunities in response, as developed in C2 Haptic Connection.

The relationship between physical thermscape elements (temperature, humidity, air movement, radiation) and people's thermal sensation and comfort has been researched extensively. A smaller but growing body of research about thermal pleasure, or *alliesthesia*, is described below. Recently, a predictable neurophysiological link was discovered between thermal delight and the skin's dynamic thermoreceptor activity (Parkinson et al. 2021). Before exploring these details, let us consider the nature of thermal variability, its description and related research.

Skin physiology

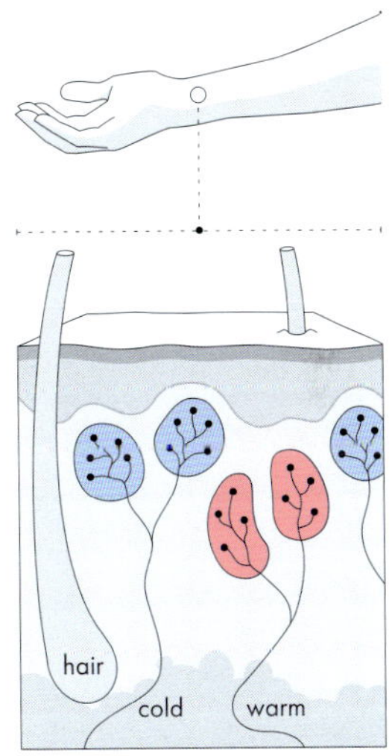

Thermoreceptors

Describing thermal patterns

Mishra and cohorts (2016) offer a synopsis of thermal variety research, presenting myriad situational and environmental conditions affecting thermal sensation and its relationship to comfort and pleasure. Variation, such as differences in temperature between rooms or over time, are often termed *heterogeneous, transient* or *dynamic* thermal conditions. Historically, thermal comfort research and its associated standards for buildings have been aimed at investigating thresholds for imperceptible change rates, or targeted at finding the limits of variations that might cause discomfort. In contrast, this present work highlights research surpassing conventional approaches to identify milder desirable variability. Chapter 4 defines several categories to organize patterns of variability, or what we call *distributions of conditions*, that can vary in time and across space.

Dynamic thermal patterns

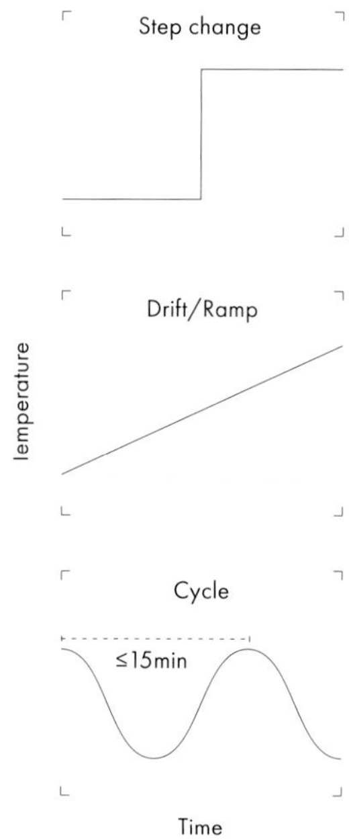

Dynamic thermal patterns (diagrams) for temporal variation of conditions are described in the research literature and standards as being of three types, with standards prescribing acceptable limits for each:

1 *Step changes* are considered instantaneous from one condition to the next.
2 *Drifts and ramps*, are smooth, gradual, noncyclic transitions.
3 *Cycles* are repeated rising and falling temperature patterns, described by amplitude, and frequency.

Step changes can be seen as a subset of the Contrasts and Sequence distributions of conditions, such as entering an air-conditioned lobby from the hot outdoors. Research on the pleasurable potential of step changes, which we espouse, is described below under *alliesthesia*. Building comfort standards say very little about how to address these relatively instantaneous changes, other than to use the same conventional methods one would use for steady-state thermal environments. In standards ASHRAE 55 (2020) and ISO 7730 (2005), this steady-state analysis is done with the Predicted Mean Vote (PMV) method (Fanger 1970), a laboratory-based empirical model that predicts thermal sensation and comfort in response to inputs about the thermal environment and people's clothing and activity. ISO 7730 suggests that the steady-state analysis can be applied immediately after an up-step, while waiting approximately 30 min following a down-step, while noting this depends greatly on circumstances.

Drifts and *ramps* both describe temperatures that rise or fall at a fairly steady rate. They are defined differently by whether they are passively created (drift)—such as in a thermal mass building where temperatures slowly rise over the course of a warm day, or actively created (ramp)—which might occur as a load shedding strategy during peak energy demand times. For both, ASHRAE Std 55 presents a singular table specifying the acceptable rate of temperature change over different time periods ranging from fifteen minutes to four hours. ISO 7730 more simply states that steady-state analysis applies if the rate of change is lower than 2.0 K (3.6 °F) per hour. We advocate for the variable delight of passive strategies, and associated drifts can be found in many of the Gradient and Sequence schemas. The concept is also relevant for fragments of some Rhythms schemas' cyclical patterns, where conditions change in an almost linear fashion for segments of the day.

Cycles of temperature, within the context of comfort standards, are defined as having a peak-to-peak period of 15 minutes or less. ASHRAE Std 55 prescribes a maximum peak-to-peak amplitude of 2.0 °F (1.1 °C), and ISO 7730 is similar. Longer periods are considered by mechanical engineers as a drift or ramp in terms of ASHRAE's prescriptive requirements. One common example of short-period cycles is when indoor conditions fluctuate within an overly narrow *deadband* —the range around the thermostat setting when neither mechanical heating nor cooling activates. For example, if a thermostat is set to 70 °F (21 °C) and the HVAC system has a 2 °F (1.1 °C) wide deadband, this means that the temperature will fluctuate between 69 and 71 °F (20.6–21.7 °C), with the heater turning on at the lower threshold and the air-conditioning turning on at the higher end. This would be undesirable due to excessive energy use and hardship on the system, and evidence shows that such tight temperature ranges are also not necessary for maintaining comfort. We recommend wider deadbands for single-setting thermostats,

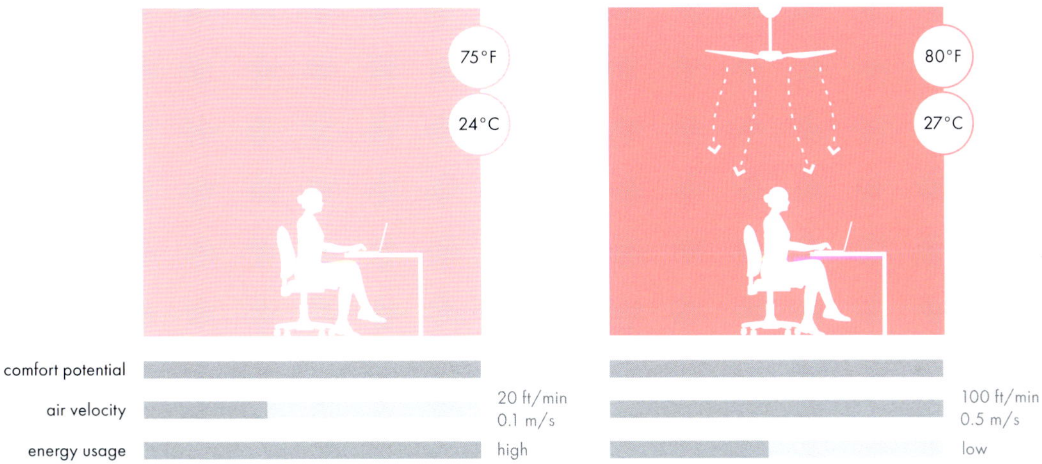

Air movement's cooling effect

People experience equivalent comfort at warmer temperatures with increased air movement. Values are calculated with CBE Thermal Comfort Tool (Tartarini et al. 2020), at typical values of 1.3 met (metabolic rate), summer 0.65 clo (clothing insulation). Still air means ≤20 ft/min (0.1 m/s).

or wider differentials between heating and cooling setpoints when possible, allowing conditions to float over a broader ranges. People easily adapt to wider daily cycles in passively heated and cooled buildings and can do so in mechanically conditioned buildings as well (Parkinson et al. 2020).

Air movement's magic

Moving air is a particularly effective, low-energy way for people to control and enrich their own thermal experience. Conventional air-conditioning design pays no attention to the positive potentials of moving air. When air-conditioning was adopted, control over temperature and humidity alone were all that was considered to be required for creating the ideal environment. Multiple generations of designers abandoned fans and operable windows as no longer important comfort control elements, but these have been recently reemerging. Moving air across people at rates they can feel is a prime example of people-based conditioning that can easily offer both gradients in a room and velocity changes over time to suit individual preference.

Air movement's cooling effect (diagram) illustrates how a fan (or breeze through a window) feels at a warmer temperature equivalent in comfort to a cooler condition with still air. For example, a relatively gentle air speed of 100 ft/min (0.5 m/s)—similar to what one would feel at a very slow walking pace—provides a cooling effect of approximately 5°F (2.8°C), as compared to still air conditions. Slightly higher speeds for a ceiling fan of 250 ft/min (1.3 m/s) would provide the equivalent cooling effect of 7°F (3.9°C).

Moving air's value is included in several schemas. G4 Zephyr Spectrum focuses on providing spatial variety and choice to match individual preferences in both indoor and outdoor settings. R2 Aperture Engagement offers occupants personal control over air flow, among other conditions. R6 Cooling Conversions integrates passive (natural) ventilation and active (mechanical) cooling strategies in mixed-mode conditioning cycles. F3 Fans First integrates the cooling effect of air movement with air-conditioning controls by operating fans prior to and simultaneous with the AC to reduce energy use and foster occupant comfort. Lastly, air movement provides fast-acting cooling after physical activity or when entering a building from the hot outdoors, as described in the S5 Ingress Transitions schema.

People perceive air movement as desirable. Using a *right now* research method, including both physical measurements and survey questions, a greater number of people in extensive office building field studies preferred *more* air movement than they currently had, compared to wanting *less*, across a broad temperature range and even when already feeling slightly cool (Arens et al. 2009; Zhang et al. 2007; Toftum 2004).

Alliesthesia

While most research and standards focus on the limits of discomfort, alliesthesia research takes the opposite approach. Alliesthesia can be thought of as the physiological basis for thermal delight—experienced walking past a fountain's mist on a hot day, or warming one's hands in front of a roaring campfire. Alliesthesia research aims beyond comfort, driven by the proposition that spatial and temporal variety in the built environment can be pleasurable. Investigators seek to find out how the phenomenon works and why it engenders delight. This is one of the most exciting new areas of thermal comfort research, connecting understanding in neurophysiology with psychology and suggesting new design possibilities.

One explanation for alliesthesia suggests that hedonic feelings come, in part, from the skin thermoreceptors' dynamic behavior. Therefore, the best potential for this mechanism of thermal pleasure arises from one of two modes, either temporally dynamic conditions or contrasting conditions felt in different body parts (Zhang 2003, Parkinson + de Dear 2015). The first—*temporal alliesthesia*—is the pleasure arising from thermal conditions that help the body's heat balance return to normal, such as the rapid cooling of a breeze from the wind or a fan when sweating. The hypothesis is that dynamic thermal experiences are pleasant when they elicit a fast response from thermoreceptors, suggesting that step changes are the most likely type of thermal dynamic to be pleasurable. This has implications for schemas such as S5 Ingress Transitions, which choreographs sensory progressions for people entering buildings, and for S5 Territorial Tuning, which diversifies thermal zones for inhabitants' elective agency and transitional enjoyment. Not all dynamic environments elicit delight. For example, while the slow and subtle changes of drifts and ramps might indeed be comfortable, they are less likely to produce pleasure, acute body awareness, relief or appreciation.

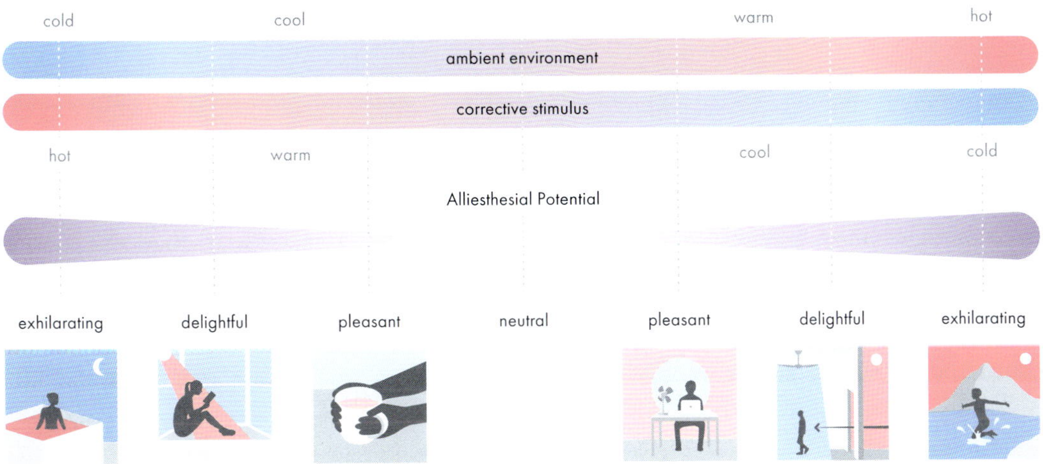

Alliesthesia framework

Thermal pleasure comes from rapid thermal contrast or differentiation across different skin areas. Greater pleasantness comes from increased corrective stimulus.

The second type is referred to as *spatial alliesthesia*, or *asymmetric alliesthesia*. In this case, *spatial* does not describe architectural space; rather, it refers to the body and describes pleasure that arises from differences in temperature or heat flow in different areas of the body. This is called an asymmetric condition. The feeling tends to occur when differences in conditions (temperature, radiation, air movement or moisture) are localized on the body, such as dipping one's feet into a cool pool on a hot day. Example schemas include:
— *C2 Haptic Connection*, which creates thermal differentiation on surfaces that occupants touch or on which they sit, for example, a sunny bench that is warmer than the posterior sitting on it.
— *G4 Zephyr Spectrum*, a schema utilizing air movement for cooling joy that is typically felt more in one part of the body than another. This can happen when a breeze cools the windward side of the body but not the leeward side.

Alliesthesia framework (diagram) illustrates how contrast in environmental conditions can influence people's thermoregulatory system and pleasurable psychological response. The top bar represents the ambient environment's thermal conditions, which can also be taken as the mean skin temperature that thermoreceptors sense. The middle bar shows the contrasting thermal stimulus, always opposite the ambient condition, that moves a person toward pleasure; this can be temporal or asymmetric contrast, as described above. Both bars become thermally more extreme at their endpoints. The lower bar indicates the resulting alliesthesial pleasure, arising from a body experiencing heating in a cool environment, or cooling in a warm situation; this also becomes greater with distance from the neutral center. Example experiences and settings are shown at the bottom. In the center of the diagram, people feel neutral or comfortable—a good thing but not rising to pleasure.
Examining further, look first at moving from the center towards the left side, where the body is feeling an increasing

Saw-tooth thermal transition

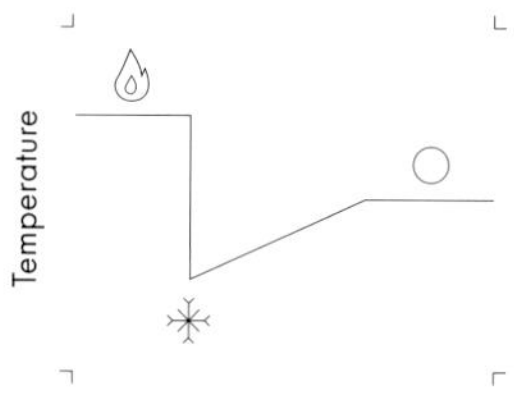

degree of coolness. A familiar example of mild asymmetric alliesthesia comes from holding a warm cup of coffee in a cool morning room. This would not be nearly as pleasant on a warm day with the coffee just as hot. Sitting in a window seat in winter, basking in the sun brings delight. More extreme, a dip in the hot tub on a cold night combines temporal alliesthesia on entry and asymmetric alliesthesia arising from a cooler head and upper body while the lower body soaks in the heat.

Moving from the center towards the right represents warm settings. Localized cooling from a breeze on the face can generate distinct pleasure. Transition spaces can be more delightful. For example, after rushing to work on a hot day, a cool building lobby or one with a strong ceiling fan will help purge body heat. This initially feels delightful, but might then feel neutral or cool after an extended time in the same conditions. At the far right, jumping into a cool mountain river on a hot day stimulates an exhilarating temporal alliesthesia. That instantaneous and intense feeling is memorable, if fleeting. Temporal alliesthesia most commonly occurs when the body begins in a slightly less-than-comfortable, but not extreme state. Transition spaces, where a person moves from a hot to cool space, serve as a perennial challenge.

A saw-tooth thermal transition (diagram), a rapid step change stimulation onset followed by a gradual drifting return to steady-state conditions, could be an ideal resolution. More subtle sequences of moving between thermally differentiated spaces, such as a home's warm south-facing sun room and cooler north-facing studio, can still offer delight without a person necessarily feeling uncomfortable first. Similarly, asymmetric alliesthesia does not require preceding discomfort and offers greater potential for creating pleasurable sensations for longer periods of time. Examples include people-based conditioning strategies, such as personal fans or using materials with higher conductivity, like marble or stone, to elicit sensory experiences localized on the body.

Adaptive Thermal Comfort

Variability, adaptive opportunity and climatic design intersect in naturally ventilated buildings. Chapter 1 introduced how the universal approach of *laboratory-based* thermal comfort standards has started to erode, with the adaptive (thermal) comfort model as one example. Gail described in her Preface how her development of this work was personally transformative, leading her to search for ever more opportunities to bridge building science research and architectural design applications. What is exciting for buildings about this new evidence is that inhabitants can feel comfortable at temperatures much warmer than previously thought. This seemingly simple discovery has enormous implications for the viability of passive cooling, a shift of resources from machines to buildings, helping to solve the climate crisis and much more.

The *adaptive comfort model* describes a relationship between people's acceptable indoor temperature (on a thermal preference scale) and seasonal fluctuations. It is a *field-based* empirical model, originally developed for naturally-ventilated buildings. The hypothesis is that contextual factors, such as dynamic thermal experiences and occupant-controlled windows, shift inhabitant preferences to indoor temperature that more closely follow outdoor climate rhythms. We find this underlying concept compelling, separate from the generated statistical model.

Beginning with the premise that people relish outdoor climate diversity, how much climatic variety do they want *indoors*? It turns out to depend on what kind of conditioning approach a building employs. Buildings with conventional centralized heating, ventilation and air-conditioning (HVAC) systems have the capacity to maintain nearly constant indoor thermal conditions year-round. People get physically and mentally accustomed to the convenience and predictability of unchanging conditions, but this comes with a high energy cost, a perilous contribution to climate change and—as we have been arguing—unhealthy thermal monotony. In contrast, passively heated, cooled and ventilated buildings inherently generate an indoor thermscape that more closely follows seasonal and diurnal climatic cycles. They are moderately warmer in summer, cooler during winter and operate with a wider daily temperature range. People typically accept and enjoy such rhythms in their homes and other buildings where this process of thermal adaptation has three components—physiological acclimatization, psychological habituation or expectation, and behavioral adjustment.

Initially, adaptive comfort research studied the extent to which this adaptive temperature tolerance shift happens in the workplace. Gail and her colleague Richard de Dear, a world-renown thermal comfort researcher and professor from the University of Sydney, built on some of the original pioneering adaptive comfort work by Michael Humphreys (1978). From the start, their intentions were ambitious: to bring the adaptive approach into mainstream thinking and practice, to change Std 55's tight limits on recommended indoor thermal conditions and to support more widespread adoption of natural ventilation strategies in lieu of buildings fully dependent on AC.

The research assembled a meta-database of 21,000 sets of raw data compiled from previous thermal comfort field experiments in buildings on four continents, covering a broad spectrum of climate zones, and conditioning strategies (de Dear 1998). The data included physical measurements and subjective survey responses. Analysis examined the data of *observed* thermal comfort responses in the buildings and calculated *predicted* sensations using the conventionally accepted method, the Predicted Mean Vote (PMV) model that is the basis for the Std 55 comfort zone.

Calculated versus field-observed comfort preference in office buildings (graphs) illustrates a persuasive argument for why the PMV-based comfort standard needed to be updated. The graphs each compare two different methods for assessing indoor comfort in office buildings, applying them to two different sets of buildings: one for buildings with centrally controlled HVAC systems (left) and the other for buildings cooled by natural-ventilation alone (right). Each plots indoor comfort temperature against mean outdoor air temperature recorded during the time of each field study. Each graph shows two lines: one based on observations from the field-based data, the other from predictions made using the PMV model. For simplicity, the graphs omit original data points to which

Calculated versus field-observed comfort preference in office buildings

PMV model predicted well for HVAC buildings but poorly for naturally ventilated ones. People in HVAC buildings tolerate change poorly, while occupants in naturally-ventilated buildings increase their preferred temperature as outdoor climate warms (de Dear + Brager 2001).

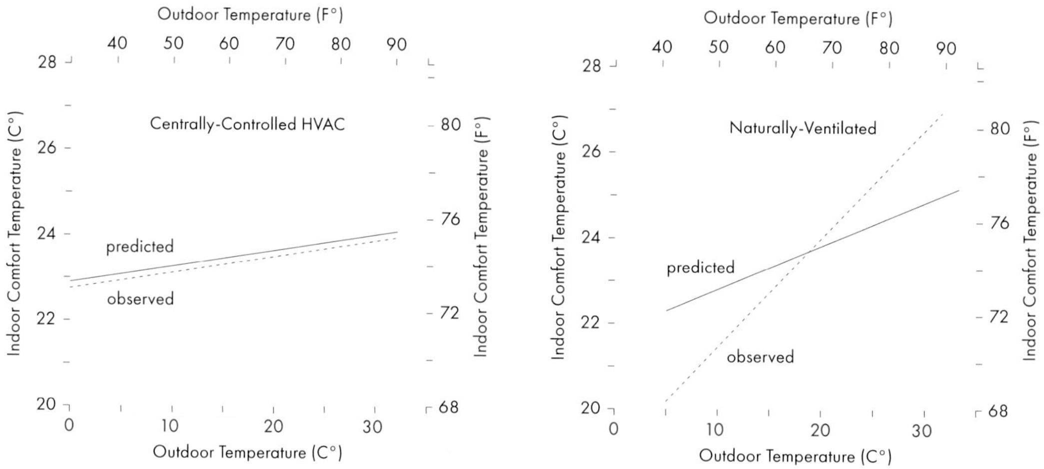

the weighted regression lines were fit. Indoor comfort temperature (y-axis) is derived from comparing survey responses to experienced thermal conditions. *Temperature* refers to *operative temperature,* the metric commonly used in building heat transfer and comfort analysis, essentially defined as the average of air and mean radiant temperatures in a room. More details about the calculation methods can be found in deDear and Brager (2001).

Two strong patterns emerge from these graphs. First, look at the dotted lines of observed responses in the two graphs. The flatter slope in HVAC buildings suggests that occupants became more finely adapted (or *addicted*) to the narrow, constant conditions typically provided by mechanical conditioning. Comparatively, the steeper slope in the right graph illustrates that inhabitants of the naturally ventilated buildings prefer a wider range of conditions that are more closely linked to changes in outdoor climate.

Secondly, within each graph, compare the dotted line (observed response) to the solid line (predicted response). In the HVAC buildings, PMV was remarkably successful at predicting occupants' preferred comfort temperatures. This suggests that climate-based factors that *are* accounted for in the PMV model fully explained the relationship between indoor comfort temperature and outdoor climatic variation. These include seasonal changes in clothing and indoor air speed, although these adjustments are both slight in HVAC buildings. In the naturally ventilated buildings, PMV-based predictions did a very poor job of matching observations, clearly displaying that inhabitants' experiences were strongly influenced by factors not accounted for in the laboratory-derived predictive model. The conclusion of this research is that, in naturally ventilated buildings, people do not merely tolerate but actually *prefer* a significantly wider range of temperatures that track with outdoor patterns. Further, these preferences are

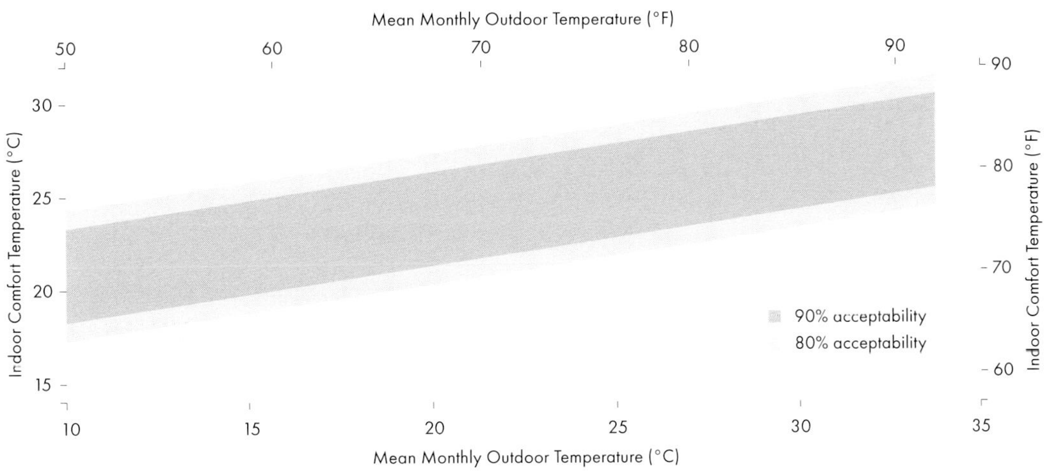

Adaptive Comfort Model in ASHRAE Standard 55

As the mean outdoor temperature rises seasonally, occupants adapt and the comfort zone shifts correspondingly upward, a radical departure from 20th century assumptions.

strongly influenced by shifting thermal expectations resulting from a combination of higher levels of actual and perceived control and greater thermal experience diversity (Brager + de Dear 1998).

Adaptive Comfort Model in ASHRAE Standard 55 (graph) shows how the results from research were the basis for creating 80% and 90% acceptability comfort zones for naturally ventilated buildings. (We note that the European Standard EN 16798-1 (2019), replacing the more familiar EN 15251, has a similar adaptive comfort standard but based on multiple categories ranging from 75-94% acceptability). There have been some important new developments since the ACM was first incorporated into Std 55 in 2013. Originally, the ACM was only allowed to be applied to buildings that were purely naturally ventilated with occupant-controllable windows. In 2020, new research into adaptive comfort revealed that more indoor seasonal variability was equally acceptable to occupants in mixed-mode buildings that combined natural ventilation and mechanical cooling and even to occupants of purely air conditioned buildings (Parkinson et al. 2020). This work was the basis for a change to the eligibility criteria of the ACM in Std 55 In 2020, which now allows the ACM to be applied to mixed-mode buildings. The actual modification of the wording of the eligibility criteria is astonishingly slight. The requirement that there is no mechanical system "installed" was changed to "in operation". The impact on the design and operation of buildings is potentially profound, not only in terms of the potential for energy and cost savings, but also for the experiential qualities of comfort, delight and greater Nature connection.

Adaptive Comfort Model: annual comfort range

The laboratory-generated PMV-based comfort zone depends on clothing (which may or may not vary seasonally or by location, particularly if people become accustomed to constant indoor temperatures). The field-based ACM climate zone relates indoor comfort temperatures to a running mean outdoor temperature. For Phoenix, the graph shows a substantial difference in the summer, and potential related energy savings.

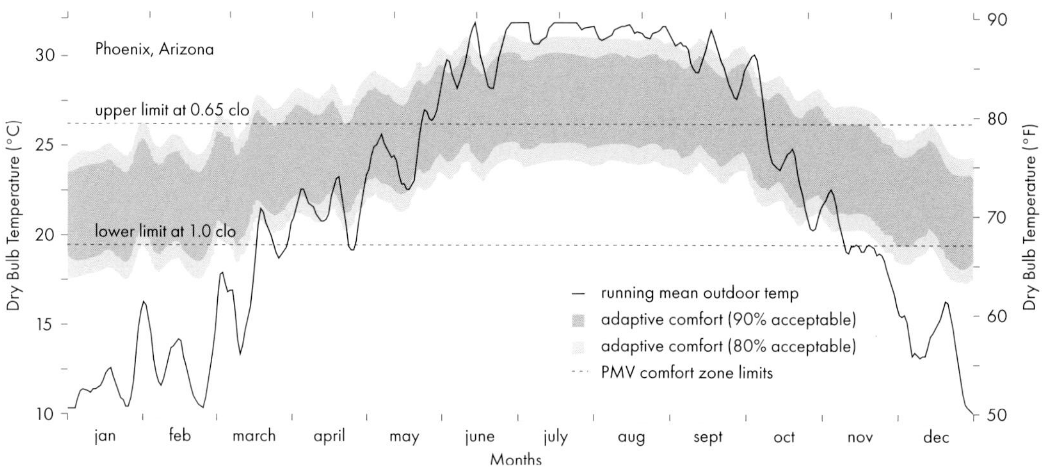

Adaptive Comfort Model: annual comfort range (graph) illustrates the potential differences in the ACM and PMV-based comfort zones over the course of a year, using Phoenix, Arizona as an example. The PMV zone limits vary based only on clothing, which can vary seasonally and quite differently by location. For comparison, upper and lower limits are shown for representative summer clothing insulation (clo) of 0.65 and indoor winter clothing at 1.0 clo, respectively. In Phoenix, clearly the ACM allows for warmer indoor temperatures from April to October. While the ACM is based on occupants being able to operate windows, comfort in warmer temperatures would also be enhanced if occupants are free to wear lighter clothing and also have access to enhanced air movement from fans.

Adaptive Comfort Model: regional differences (map) illustrates how the climate-based impacts on comfort preferences vary on a regional basis. Using the continental US in July as an example, we compared ACM and PMV-based recommended indoor comfort maximum temperatures. The difference between the two is an indication of the potential impact of using the ACM, allowing for more hours when natural ventilation can maintain comfortable indoor conditions before needing air-conditioning. This comparison is based solely on climate. Determining exactly what the interior temperatures would be (and their comfort degree) for any particular building, such as one using natural ventilation and thermal mass, requires a thermal simulation.

This evidence provides support for redirecting conventional practice from its sole reliance on mechanical heating and cooling within tight temperature ranges toward more creative thought about both cooling strategies and indoor conditions. The potentials are enormous to reduce energy use and magnify delight by prioritizing climate-responsive strategies for environmental conditioning. Letting conditions float over wider ranges while providing a

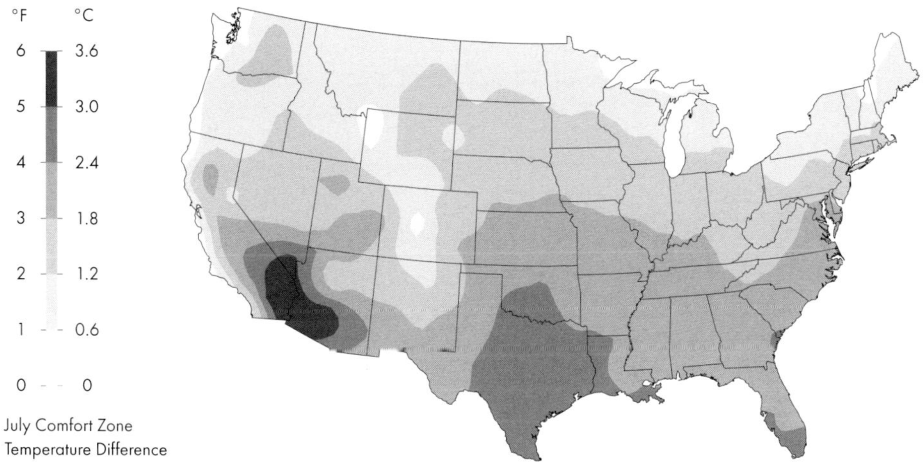

Adaptive Comfort Model: regional differences

Map indicates how much ACM raises top of comfort zone above 27°C (80.6°F) allowed by ASHRAE Std 55 [1]. Darker areas indicate larger differences, therefore larger energy savings using ACM.

analysis Tom Parkinson

1 Upper limits based on 50% RH, summer 0.65 clo and office work activity at 1.3 met (ASHRAE Std 55 Fig 5.2)

variety of adaptive opportunities allows mechanical system use only as needed. As the season warms from spring to summer, if indoor temperatures are nudged upwards slowly enough to allow for adaptation, then over weeks or a season, the typical persistent over-cooling in buildings could be avoided while reducing energy use. This can be done without sacrificing occupant comfort and could instead enhance it. The evidence for adaptive comfort criteria supports several schemas, among them: R6 Cooling Conversions, S5 Territorial Tuning and F3 Fans First.

Ears: acoustic environment

People do not merely inhabit the soundscape; they are part of it. Occupants generate sound and absorb it. They speak to each other, make noise in conducting their activities, wear sound-absorptive clothing and walk about leaving footfall, thereby influencing the resonance, reverberation and patterns of sound waves. Architecture is instrumental in creating sonic experiences by collecting, amplifying, mitigating and distributing sounds for ears to receive, brains to process and human beings to emote. Designers can configure a room's shape, volume and surface materials, which amalgamate to absorb, reflect, color and transmit sounds. Aurally great buildings compose multiple spatial acoustic signatures into a rich, positive, life-enhancing soundscape that can create a sense of intimacy or a shared orchestral experience.

As one example, the reverberation time of sound in space is a particularly important part of acoustic experience. This signature architectural acoustic quality, wrought by form and materials, can suggest a place's significance.

Ear physiology

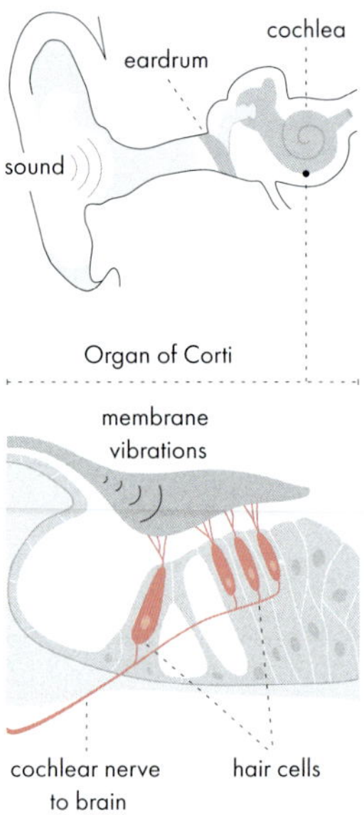

Consider the great Gothic cathedrals , built with high ceilings and massive, sound-reflective stone construction, causing very long reverberation times where sound seems to hang in the air for many seconds before dissipating; music had to be composed specifically for the cadence of the echoes there. In contrast, smaller rooms padded with rugs, soft upholstery and wall hangings absorb sound to create minimal reflections and very short reverberation time for quietness and a sense of tranquility.

Ear physiology (diagram) works through a cascade of sensory processing that begins in the outer ear, where changes in air pressure from sound waves are funneled into the ear canal to the ear drum. The ear detects multiple characteristics of sound waves: the wavelength (frequency), which determines perception of pitch, and the amplitude, which is perceived as loudness (measured in decibels). The inner ear is composed of the vestibular system for balance and the cochlea for hearing. Sound waves vibrate through the eardrum to the cochlea, where membranes amplify the sound across hair cells that then convert the kinetic feedback to electrical impulses—the language of the brain. The brain's auditory cortex instantly compares them to stored knowledge, aiding in interpreting the sound's meaning.

Sound stimuli evoke many neurophysiological and emotional responses: positive or negative, tranquil or stimulating, supportive or stressful. Auditory experience richness is particularly impacted by the ability of the ear and brain to differentiate between foreground and background sounds and between discrete acoustic events and perception of *sound textures.* Example textures include crowd noise, insect swarms or rain sounds. Design for the latter is described in F1 Melodic Materials, C4 Engage the Rain and F4 Compluvium Shower. Perhaps more than any other sense, acoustic experiences in buildings are defined more by variable, often highly unpredictable *sonic events* set against relatively steady-state background conditions. While the human ear is able to detect a wide range of sounds, it is particularly sensitive to the frequency of the human voice. Hearing others' laughter can bring a smile. The ability to easily recognize a singular voice from a host of others is a wonder, yet can also be distracting when surrounded by conversation while concentration is required.

Several models provide a framework for the science of how people hear and perceive soundscapes (Davies et al. 2013). While they vary in scope and details, they each have ways of distinguishing three types of components:

1 *Objective physical aspects* of the sonic environment (soundscape)
2 *Psychological or behavioral perception* of and response to the soundscape, the acoustic experience
3 *Context that situates and influences* the relationship between soundscape and experience.

Acoustic science studies the production, control, transmission, reception and effects of sound on humans. It employs physics principles, addressing how a room's three-dimensional shape and materials impact the sound's physical characteristics. The variables are complex and include transmission, reflection, absorption, frequency, echo, resonance, reverberation and pressure levels (loudness). The design of acoustic experiences in buildings is aligned with the branch of psychophysics called *psychoacoustics,* meaning the science of sound perception and audiology concerned with how humans perceive sounds. In this work, we are curious about how inhabitants perceive and recognize sounds, then respond to them as subliminal moods or deeper emotions.

When crafting an acoustic experience, recognize that people's sonic preferences differ— both among people (inter-individual) and for the same individual at alternate instances (intra-individual). This highlights the importance of providing a diversity of quiet and lively settings and opportunities for inhabitants' migration among them, such as in G6 Engagement and Retreat. How people characterize aural qualities as *pleasant sounds* or *unwanted noise* is often subjective, varying by individual and circumstance. One might embrace the city's frenetic excitement, while another seeks retreat from traffic to a pocket of stillness. One worker thrives in the collaborative atmosphere of a boisterous open-plan office, while another seeks quiet privacy for head-down concentration. A recent study of workplace acoustics and personality found that more extroverted and more emotionally stable employees are less sensitive to sounds, while tending to be more distracted, particularly by others' conversations (Graham et al. 2021).

Sound emotions

The auditory sense's strong connection to emotion is apparent when listening to music or hearing voices. Researchers have seen that emotion is associated with increased activation in the brain's right anterior auditory cortex, indicating that auditory systems process emotions before speech content (Gradjean et al. 2005, Ethofer et al. 2006). Another project focused on the connection between psychological and physiological measures, revealing that sounds perceived as pleasant are associated with lower skin conductance, an indirect measure of the body's autonomic activity associated with emotion and attention (Medvedev et al. 2015). These findings are important for several reasons. First, they suggest that subjective interpretations of sound are more important for stress recovery than loudness. They also validate self-reported surveys as a tool for researching soundscapes. Further studies of design features that contribute to positive soundscapes are elucidated below.

Sound colors (graphs) refer specifically to the power spectrum, the amount of vibration at each individual frequency, as shown in the illustration. Each type of power spectrum is perceived differently.

White noise has equal energy intensity across all audible frequencies, low to high. Calling it *white* is an analogy to white light which, at the time the term was coined, was mistakenly thought to have a flat power spectrum. The physical characteristics do not translate to a similar perceptual pattern. To the human ear, white noise sounds slightly high-pitched, like radio static; listening to it can be uncomfortable because the ear-brain connection picks up higher frequency sounds better, amplifying their perception. Examples of white noise in the built environment include whirring fans and humming air-conditioners.

Pink noise is adjusted for the human hearing deficit to low-frequency. Instead of being a flat spectrum, the lower frequencies have more power and the higher frequencies less, therefore sounding relatively balanced in loudness

Sound colors

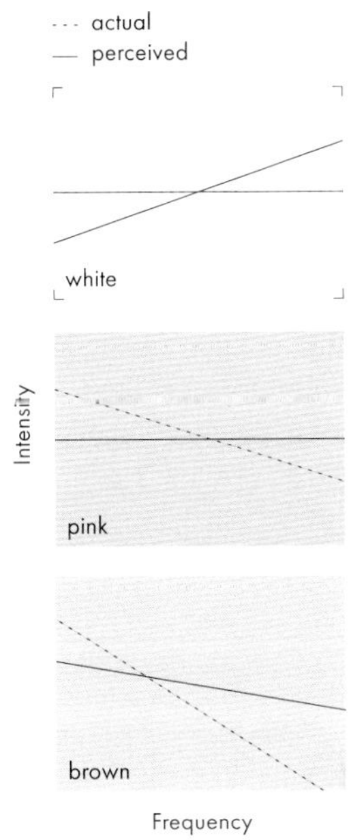

to the human ear. People perceive it as less abrasive than white noise. The name originated as a parallel to the pink appearance of visible light, which has a similar power spectrum. Pink noise is one of the most common patterns found in biologic systems and Nature, such as heartbeats, the sound of leaves rustling in the wind or ocean waves.

Brown noise lowers the power of high frequencies even more, with more randomness, sounding rougher and deeper, like rumbling traffic, thunder or a strong waterfall. Brown noise is named, not after a color, but for botanist Robert Brown, whose name is also associated with the discovery of Brownian motion (of random particles).

All of these *sound colors* can be used to mask other distracting noises by providing the brain with an even stimulus. White noise is the most well-known, but evidence suggests that listening to pink noises is more relaxing, and brown noise is often associated with aiding in concentration. Outdoor sounds entering through open windows are likely to pink or brown noise. Pink noise is commonly used as a sleep aid in sound machines or digital applications. Papalambros and colleagues (2017) along with Jesper and team (2010) found that people who fell asleep listening to the pink noise of rushing water or falling rain slept more deeply, boosted their memory and recovered better from stress. In the workplace, sound masking systems historically generated white noise, but increasingly provide pink and brown background sounds, including Nature soundtracks, particularly water sounds.

Workplace soundscapes

People spend a great portion of their day at work, often with minimal control over their acoustic environment. In this context, designers need to address but move beyond the conventional acoustic focus—enabling speech privacy and speech clarity while minimizing distracting noise. Acoustic engineers emphasize reducing reflected sound energy and mitigating undesirable, unpleasant or intrusive noise levels. Managing these factors mostly requires control of absorption and sound levels, which constitute only two factors in an aurally aesthetic workplace.

Nigel Oseland extensively studied sound perception in open-plan offices, finding that only 25% of differences in workers' annoyance could be attributed to the sound level itself, with the remainder attributed to psychoacoustic factors, including perceivers' ascribed meanings (Oseland + Hodsman 2015). People tend to pay more attention to sounds that are important to them—the human voice for one. This has utility when paying attention to another and explains the *cocktail party effect*, where, in a noisy environment, one can easily focus on a specific conversation. The same faculty distracts and annoys when one is trying to concentrate on work inside a context of nearby conversations that become difficult to ignore.

Designing pleasant workplace acoustics is challenging. Three broad types of approaches can be identified:

1 *Behavioral adaptations* have workers employ their own masking or dampening, such as wear earplugs or headphones with their own music. Another example is migrating to alternative workspaces, separate from a personal desk in the open office, for private concentrated work, phone calls or meetings. Both designers and office managers play roles in enabling these approaches

2 *Passive interventions* employ sound-absorbing surfaces, partitions and furnishings, along with sound isolating and blocking construction between rooms and for exterior walls and windows.
3 *Active interventions* include broadband sound masking strategies, which can be either generated purposefully or endemically as background noise generated by the mechanical system. Active strategies are intended to reduce the intelligibility of surrounding sounds but not themselves be noticeable.

As described above, sound masking comes in different *colors*, or frequency power profiles. Some people find broad-band white noise irritating, and studies show it can have negative impacts, ranging from dissatisfaction to more prolonged health impacts due to increasing stress hormones (corticosteroids, catecholamines). This can lead to more serious health impacts, including impaired higher brain functions, learning and short-term memory, higher blood pressure and increased incidence of coronary disease. Where active pink and brown noise systems are employed, some of these problems are reduced.

Workplace acoustic interventions are intended to mitigate acoustic challenges, yet they potentially replace one negative experience with another; in most cases neutrality, the absence of badness, is the best that can be hoped for. Such approaches fall far short of this book's aims for pleasure and states beyond. The potential is untapped for evidence-informed design to create positive soundscapes in both everyday buildings and civic architecture.

Positive soundscape project

Amidst the vast research on noise, we are particularly interested in what has been learned about the *benefits* of soundscapes. The physics of sound waves is quite robust, as compared to the less-developed body of evidence about enjoyable building acoustics. The Positive Soundscape project stands as a noteworthy exception; it included multiple interdisciplinary investigations utilizing soundwalks, interviews, focus groups and other research methods. While this project generated multiple publications, the scope of work is best summarized by Davies and co-authors (2009) in the paper The *Positive Soundscape Project: a Synthesis of Results from Many Disciplines.*

The studies describe diverse constructs for subjective soundscape assessment, including "the individual's knowledge and prior experience of the soundscape, the meaning they derive from it, their attitude towards the sound source, their behaviour, their noise sensitivity, demographic and cultural dimensions, and their sense of control over the noise" (Payne et al. 2009). Researchers concluded that personal meaning was much more strongly connected to the positive emotional response evoked by a soundscape than to any physical acoustic metrics.

The Positive Soundscape project documented Nature and people as contributions to a pleasant sonic environment. In one of their studies, using 150 soundscape stimuli, semantic differential rating scales assessed attributes such as calmness, relaxation, comfort, assurance, vibrancy, arousal, informativeness, intrusiveness and pleasantness. Natural sounds were associated with relaxation and tranquility and were viewed as more positive than mechanical sounds. Human voices were generally perceived as positive, associated with feelings of vibrancy and conveying a sense of social connection. More details can be found in Cain et al. (2009).

Consistent with other research, the project also found that acoustic perceptions and preferences varied widely among individuals. As with smell, affective response to a particular soundscape can be strongly influenced by associations with memory, particularly ones that have strong emotional attachments (Snyder + Gregg 2011). Architecturally, this can further enhance the pleasure of soundscapes. For example, crafting an acoustic connection to the outdoors allows one to listen to the sound of rain, which might conjure memories of family gathering for shelter on stormy nights.

Sound perception can be complex and somewhat capricious. The research found that positive soundscape impressions are most related to whether an individual:

1 *Believes* they have some control over the sonic environment
2 *Interprets* that sounds meet their expectations a particular place
3 *Resonates* compatibly with the sounds in their mood or sense of purpose in the space

Control over the sonic space can be behavioral or cognitive. *Behavioral control* can be direct sound modification, disconnecting from the sound, such as putting on headphones, or moving to another space with different sounds. Auditory cognition describes how the brain makes sense of the sound world, and *cognitive control* affects how and what one hears, mentally selecting the sounds we pay attention to or tuning out unwanted sounds.

Researchers Tjeerd Andringa and Jolie Lanser, from the Netherlands' University of Groningen, studied how behavior and cognitive functions affect perception and health effects of soundscapes (2013). They present a cognitive model of pleasurable sounds, a framework, where acoustic experience is affected by the extent of required attention and the sounds' information content. People find soundscapes positive when less attention or effort is required, such as if foreground and background sounds blend together. This condition is commonly found in Nature and in more intimate residential settings. Positive perceptions are more likely when the sounds provide some information that would be expected from its source, such as hearing a waterfall that can also be seen. This is why office sound masking systems that distribute ambient water sounds are most effective if accompanied by a visible water feature, offering at least a visual association with the sound even if it is not its actual source. F2 Current Prehension is an example in which wind sound might be accompanied by seeing swaying branches or light curtains blown. Soundscapes with a strong distinction between foreground and background sounds require more directed attention, such as focusing on vocal music in a noisy club. These can be viewed negatively, especially if the background sounds are loud, persistent or erratic.

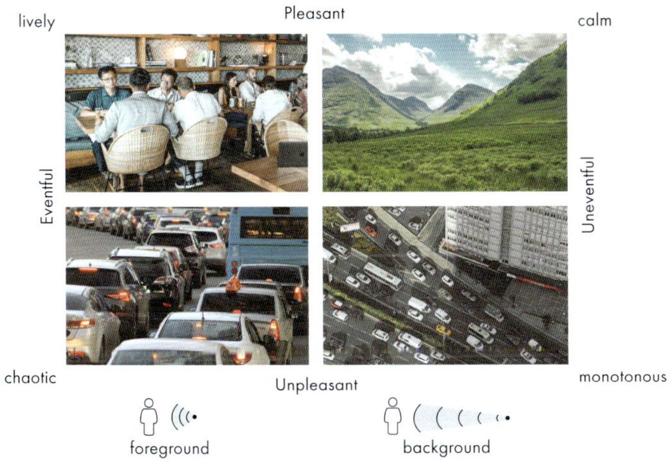

Sound pleasure model

Pleasurable sounds are characterized by lively environments with discernible foreground sounds or calm atmospheres with eneventful background sounds.

based on Andringa + Lanser 2013

Sound pleasure model (illustration) offers a cognitive framework for environmental sound with two characteristic dimensions: pleasant and eventful. Pleasant *calm* responses are associated with uneventful background sounds; *lively* experience, with eventful foreground sounds. *Monotonous* sounds are unpleasant and linked to uneventful background noise; *chaotic* atmospheres, with eventful but unpleasant foreground noise. The team explains why certain soundscapes promote health, arguing that more subtle environmental sounds promote proximal awareness and provide an abundance of safety indications. These, in turn, generate more mind-state freedom, requiring less vigilance and reducing stress-related health effects. These results are consistent with the World Health Organization report on environmental noise, which found that "there is overwhelming evidence that exposure to environmental noise has adverse effects on the health of the population" (WHO 2011).

Water sounds

Designers can orchestrate aquatic soundscapes by creating resonating shapes and materials for water to move through and land on, varying volumetric flow and form, as suggested in G4 Euphonic Water, or by considering acoustic behaviors of materials exposed to rain, as described in F1 Melodic Materials. From an evolutionary perspective, water is key to survival, so it is not surprising that people are attracted to the sights and sounds of moving water in Nature. Research on the role of water in biophilic design initially focused on views of water, then expanded to sound. Nasar and Lin (2003) focused specifically on urban water features, studying various nuanced emotional responses that theorists had speculated on but had never been empirically tested. Participants viewed five kinds of water features (still, flowing, falling, jet and combination), and responded to nine semantic differential scales organized under Preference, Calming, and Exciting categories—the three components of environmental appraisals proposed by Russell + Snodgrass (1987). While participants viewed all water features favorably, they preferred jets and combinations, rated still water as more calming, while flowing water's visual and auditory qualities evoked excitement. G4 Euphonic Water presents additional evidence about the cognitive and emotional effects of water sounds.

Water is an excellent example of a soundscape being accompanied by multisensory stimuli, which research shows enhances perception and improved psychological and physiological responsiveness. Complex, naturally fluctuating multisensory stimuli induce cognitive effects of improved concentration and memory restoration, emotional states of relaxation and tranquility, and physiological responses such as reduced stress hormone (cortisol) production, lower heart rate and diastolic blood pressure (Alvarsson et al. 2010; Biederman + Vessel 2006; Hunter et al. 2010; Windhager et al. 2011; Barton + Pretty 2010; White et al. 2010; Karmanov + Hamel 2008; Ruso + Atzwanger 2003; Orians + Heerwagen 1993; Ulrich 1983; Part et al. 2009).

To evoke tranquility, gentle, natural flows, such as a small stream or waterfall, are the most effective (Watts et al. 2009). Natural water sounds are increasingly introduced to workplaces for their biophilic effect. They provide effective sound masking and positive impacts on emotional states and cognitive performance (DeLoach et al. 2015; Haapakangas et al. 2011) . Active sound masking systems are intended to be noticeable but not distracting. Moving water sounds are particularly good at obscuring noise, especially the sound of human voices. This is useful in open-plan offices where content-rich conversations are a major source of distraction (Ragonesis 2009; Cai et al. 2019). The growth of open-plan offices is motivated partially by economics and the impracticality of manifold small, cellular private offices and partially by an intent to facilitate more spontaneous interaction and collaboration. The resulting soundscape of these open-plan environments presents an enormous challenge, supported by ample anecdotal evidence, as well as post-occupancy evaluations. In shared open-office plans, high workstation density, sound reflective materials and the constant buzz of conversation, equipment and ringing telephones contribute to a cacophony often noted for concentration disruption and privacy erasure. Because water sounds are mostly pink noise, they are pleasant sound maskers.

Nose: olfactory environment

A human being breathes in and out over 20,000 times a day, each inhalation accompanied by aromas, whether noticed or not. The idiom *stop and smell the roses* could be a call to literally relish the pleasurable *smells* in the environment as much as its admonition to simply slow down. Olfactory language is relatively limited, compared to that of the other senses; it often utilizes analogy, comparing a scent to *smelling like* a set of familiar objects or foods. People have visceral reactions to smells, quickly distinguishing whether or not they characterize an odor as pleasant, but with less capability to name or explain *why* they like it. The challenges in noticing, identifying and describing smells all contribute to architectural design's tendency to ignore this unsung sense. Landscape architecture and garden design are exceptions. Building design and management's focus on the indoor olfactory environment has primarily been based on *smell editing*, the notion that anything smelled must be objectionable, a problem to be eradicated, rather than an opportunity for delight. The goal becomes eradicating unwanted odors with an arsenal of source reduction, ventilation and cleaners to eliminate odor or mask with synthetic scents.

We advocate an alternative approach, one that reclaims the positive olfactory experience, informed by an understanding of scent science. Note that this discussion is different from indoor air quality (IAQ) and pollution issues, which mostly involve contaminants that cannot be detected by smell. Some harmful pollutants are odorless, and unpleasant odors are not always considered pollutants. IAQ is beyond our scope. The challenge to designing positive scentscapes is that, despite extensive personal observations, researchers still know very little about how olfactory perception impacts emotional response. In parallel, designers have limited insights from evidence about how to shape the scentscape.

Nose physiology (diagram) illustrates that smell happens when scent particles, volatile (vaporized, airborne) *odorants* first land on the nasal cavity's mucus, which can detect several hundred thousand different scents. A second form of detection is a chemical sense by receptors on all the mucous membranes in the nose (and eyes); they are particularly sensitive to *irritants*. In combination, these receptor cells send signals along nerve fibers to the brain's olfactory bulb and, along with learned references, help to distinguish pleasant from irritating scent. Like other senses, scent awareness is triggered by changes and becomes dormant under monotony. The mind quickly filters and adapts to familiar smells, generally noticing only when there is variety. One explanation is this as an evolved mechanism to avoid frequent distraction. The power of smell in invoking memory is directly linked to the human anatomy, particularly the close proximity of the olfactory bulb to the limbic system, which supports a variety of functions including emotion, behavior and long-term memory. This adjacency allows a more direct route, compared to other senses, that sends messages from the olfactory bulb to be processed through the thalamus, before being sent to the cerebral cortex. Because the nose's nerve cells are more directly connected to the limbic part of the brain, smells are processed simultaneously with cognitive and precognitive responses, causing smell memory to be deeply embedded.

Some aspects of smell perception are innate, confirmed with studies of newborns, but the predominant valence of a scent—what one likes or not—is primarily shaped by memory, experience and learning. It is often directly tied to the earliest experiences of that aroma, particularly if there is an emotional association, often solidifying into lifelong olfactory preferences. This is not surprising, given that smell is the only sense fully developed in a fetus and remains the most refined sense in a child until about age ten, when vision becomes relatively more developed. In *A Natural History of the Senses*, Diane Ackerman (1990) refers to this primacy, describing how "smell was the first of our senses, and it was so successful that in time, the small lump of olfactory tissue atop the nerve cord grew into our brain.....we think because we smelled."

Nose physiology

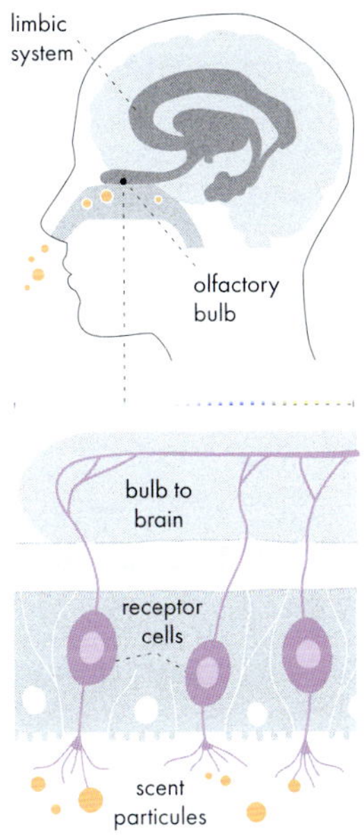

While researchers know that early experience is important, there is relatively little evidence about the mechanisms behind why individuals might like or dislike a particular smell. A unique study done in collaboration between UC Berkeley's Helen Wills Neuroscience Institute and The Weizmann Institute of Science in Israel mapped *olfactory perceptual* space to the *olfactory stimulus space* (Khan et al. 2007). In this context, *perceptual space* refers to how one describes the scentscape experience, while *stimulus space* refers to the physiochemical descriptors of odors; in both cases, the term space is used metaphorically. Researchers found that for all the many available descriptors of scent type and character (for example, floral, sweet, sharp, rancid), it is the degree of *pleasantness*, a metric also referred to as valence or *hedonic tone*, that constitutes the primary dimension of scents' perceptual space. Pleasantness is most correlated with physiochemical odorant properties and occurs as relatively consistent across cultures. The Berkeley-Weizmann research team also showed that, generally, heavier, more spread-out molecules are associated with bad smells, while lighter, more compact molecules are perceived as more pleasant. Hopefully, these discoveries can lead to more collaborations among scientists and designers to build knowledge that can inform scentscape composition. This potential comes with a caveat. The researchers acknowledge significant differences among individuals and note olfactory perception plasticity for individual occupants; these can be influenced by factors not easily predicted, such as context, expectation and multisensory convergence.

One approach to designing indoor scentscapes is to leverage the aromatic qualities of building materials. Historically, smells were often employed as a design element. The sweet scent of an old villa often arises from cedarwood's abundance, also serving as a natural insect repellent. Homes each have a unique scent signature; for example, historic homes rich with oak tannin, leather and terracotta contribute to a notable profile. Natural fibers used in rugs, like jute and grasses, exude fragrance, especially in humid weather. In contrast, many contemporary materials, for instance, glass, aluminum and steel, effuse no odor because they do not evaporate microscopic particles at typical room temperatures. Redwood or eucalyptus saunas and cedar closets are examples of spatially contained aromatics that contrast with relatively unscented ambient conditions, bringing surprise and pleasure.

Outdoor rooms and in-between spaces offer opportunities, either fleeting or lingering, for people to inhabit aromatic places without the constraints of indoor conditioning that often requires the envelope's thermal closure. Inhabitants may thus experience sublime events if fragrant plantings are carefully selected and located. Purposeful placement of aromatic plants can link indoor, in-between and outdoor realms, as described in S2 Aromatic Transit. This might include creating an ambrosial promenade at a building approach and entry or planting sweet-smelling herbs just outside an open window on the windward facade, a future schema we might call Upwind Flowers.

Scent walks

Designing to elevate appreciation for this relatively neglected sense requires designers to refine their own first-person aromatic perception. One discipline for this development is the urban *scent walk*. The idea is to survey the city's unique olfactory signature, seeking spatial and temporal variation while noticing sources and how they reveal

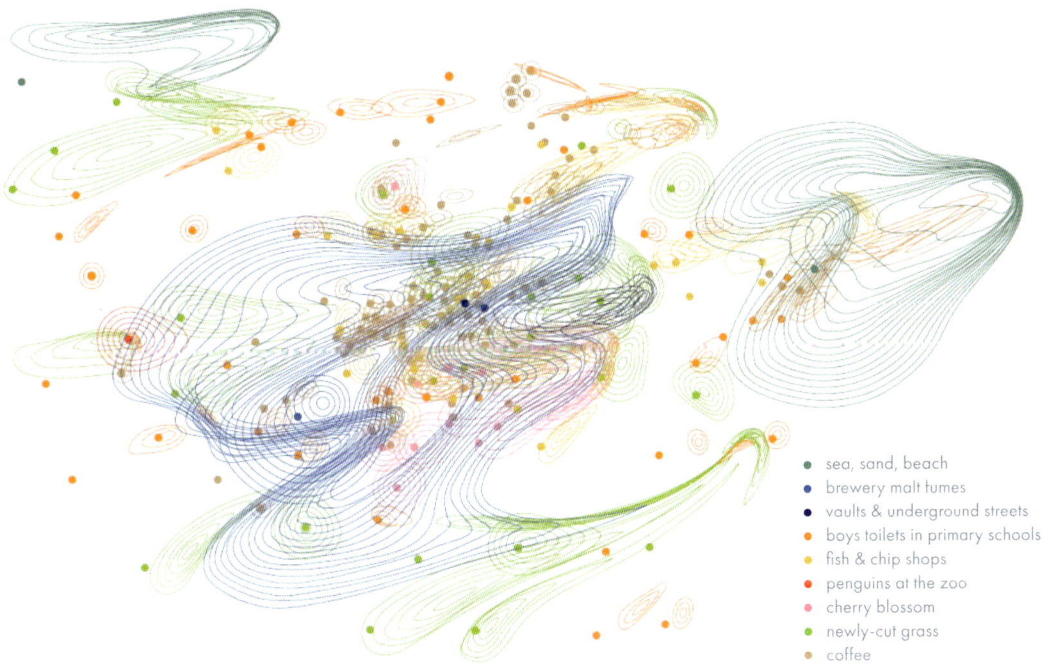

Smells of Auld Reekie on a very breezy day in 2011

Auld Reekie emits a plethora of scents and smells; some particular to Edinburgh, some ubiquitous city aromas. It is the smell combination and how they are distributed by the prevailing southwesterly winds that make them city-specific. Coloured dots indicate the point of origin of the scents, the contour lines shows where they blow to in the wind.

—*Kate McLean*, sensorymaps.com

Scent walks employ groups of people and various visualization techniques to reveal the sources, spatial pattern and movements of urban smells.

the place's activities and rhythms, along with ways they shape behaviors and elicit emotional response. This nose-first sensory exploration is exemplified by the pioneering work of urban planner Victoria Henshaw (2013), known for conducting scent walks and surveying the olfactory identity of cities around the world.

Smells of Auld Reekie, a compelling visualization of the city's scentscape by designer Kate McLean, builds on Henshaw's work by integrating sensed data and cartographic techniques. It depicts relative areas of olfactory vibrancy and lightness. McLean leads teams of participants through a city where they log odors and characterize attributes that include intensity, pleasantness and familiarity. Participants are asked to differentiate pervasive, omnipresent background scents from episodic foreground aromas. Physical mapping layers assessments of affective response, revealing how smells influence the atmosphere toward calm and intimate feelings or energetic and social expressions. Discussions distinguish common and contested aromas, comparing expected smell locations and surprising discoveries, while developing an olfactory language using both descriptive and metaphorical naming. This map of Auld Reekie (a historical term for Edinburgh), was created on a breezy day in late spring of 2011, showing the local prevailing south-westerly winds. McLean's maps create a visual synthesis of the smellwalkers' unique experiences, negotiating different perceptions as part of the discussions, to preserve the olfactory memory of a place and its relation to momentary conditions of weather. The more delectable scentscape qualities of Edinburgh include smells of sea, sand and beach; brewery malt, cherry blossoms, and coffee.

These scent walks are an excellent urban scale example of raising sensory awareness. Most of this book focuses on buildings and the territory just beyond them, since that is where we have spent the bulk of our professional lives. We anticipate that readers will be able to expand the ideas herein to other scales. Working in reverse, one could easily imagine extending the urban scent walk to architecture by asking designers (or students) to comparatively smellmap the interiors of multiple buildings. At either scale, the goals are to enhance designers' olfactory sensibilities and to discover aromatic design patterns they can proactively incorporate into their work. Perhaps Japan may serve as model, with its celebration of scent as vital to local character. Japan has declared "One hundred sites of good fragrance" that now have protected status. Most sites have been selected for their natural scentscapes, such as Furano's lavender fields, the Kushiro sea fog, or Kairakuen's plum grove. Some reveal local industry, including Southern Morioka's roasted beer, Kashiya Yokocho's sweets, Nada Gogo's sake brewers, and Yoshino River's indigo dyeing plants. And other sites honor local establishments and rituals, such as the smell of ancient documents on Kanda's old bookstore street, the aroma of incense from Buddhist altar shop neighborhoods and temples, and the fragrant scent of roasting tea from many street corners and tea gardens.

Conclusions

This chapter is based on the premise that the more deeply designers understand the complexity of human response and its relationship to the sensory environment, the more likely they are to be inspired by and consider such knowledge when designing. Towards this end, this chapter began broadly with the science of architectural experience, describing the relationship between the environment, the body's physiological sensors and perception. We described the significance of spatial and temporal variability for the different sensory systems and introduced the idea of adaptive opportunity—designing for inhabitant's choice and control by providing a range of places with different conditions, freedom to relocate and physical control of local conditions through architectural, mechanical or electrical means. We then explored four of the body's sensory systems—eyes, skin, ears and nose—summarizing the science of how each works, and highlighting characteristics that relate to environmental variety.

While we organized this chapter by sensory system, and the significant majority of research is domain-specific, in reality people experience their surroundings with all of their senses simultaneously. Unfortunately there is a glaring paucity of work that looks at human response to multisensory stimuli, even though that is inherently the way humans perceive the environment. One cannot simply add the effects of unisensory stimuli. What evidence does exist is often in the fundamental sciences of neurophysiology or cognitive neuroscience; relatively little research focuses on perception of indoor environmental parameters or explores human responses in the domains of comfort, emotion, health and overall well-being.

Professor Marcel Schweiker and a large interdisciplinary team (2020) provide a comprehensive summary of multi-domain approaches to indoor environmental perception. To provide a segue to Chapter 4, we offer just a few examples. The most common type of multisensory studies look at two sensory modalities acting together. Since vision is the primary sense by which humans interact with the world, most multisensory researchers study the interaction between visual response and another sense, often thermal perception. As one example, the hue-heat hypothesis suggests that environments with dominant light frequencies toward the red end of the visible spectrum will feel relatively warm compared to environments with more blue light at the same temperature. While research findings are mixed, this serves as an inspiration for C1 Thermic Hues. te Kulve et al. (2016) found that both warm and cool discomfort could be partially relieved by lighting conditions rated with higher visual comfort. This suggests that if building temperatures float over a range wider than conventional, as explored in S5 Territorial Tuning, then more occupants would be satisfied at the comfort zone edges by employing multisensory solutions. For example, strategies like high visual quality lighting could greatly expand the thermal design opportunities. Ko et al. (2020) found that people who sit next to a window with a nature view had cooler thermal sensations than those without the view, even under the same thermal conditions. This could have implications for many view-related schemas, such as C4 Inhabited Periphery.

An example of thermal-acoustic interactions comes from Yang and Moon (2019), who studied water sounds relevant to G4 Euphonic Water. They found that in cool conditions, water sounds were perceived negatively (with increased perceptions of noisiness, loudness and annoyance), while in warm conditions the water sounds were perceived positively (with improvements in perceptions of pleasantness, calmness, naturalness and overall acoustic comfort). Other thermal-acoustic studies found that if sounds originate outdoors, the inhabitants' valence responses are tied to the desirability of open windows at any particular moment. It can be complicated enough figuring out when opening a window will have a positive effect on comfort based on relative indoor and outdoor thermal conditions. That same open window can bring in either undesired sounds in an urban setting (traffic, construction) or a delightful chorus of birds and connection to the outdoors in a less dense setting. These findings relate to schemas such as R2 Aperture Engagement and G6 Engagement and Retreat.

In the next chapter, we take the reader to the heart of this book—the experiential design schemas, where evidence informs each generative design idea.

Sources

Ackerman, Diane. 1990. *A Natural History of the Senses.* New York: Vintage Books

Altomonte, Sergio, Joseph Allen, Philomena M Bluyssen, Gail Brager, Lisa Heschong, Angela Loder, Stefano Schiavon, Jennifer A Veitch, Lily Wang + Pawel Wargocki. 2020. Ten Questions Concerning Well-Being in the Built Environment. *Building and Environment* 180:106949

Alvarsson, Jesper J, Stefan Wiens + Mats E Nilsson. 2010. Stress Recovery during Exposure to Nature Sound and Environmental Noise. *International Journal of Environmental Research and Public Health* 7(3):1036–46

Andringa, Tjeerd + J Lanser. 2013. How Pleasant Sounds Promote and Annoying Sounds Impede Health: A Cognitive Approach. *International Journal of Environmental Research and Public Health* 10(4):1439–61

Arens, Edward, Stephen Turner, Hui Zhang + Gwelen Paliaga. 2009. Moving Air for Comfort. *ASHRAE Journal* 51(5):18–28

Aries, Myriam B C, Jennifer A Veitch + Guy R Newsham. 2010. Windows, View, and Office Characteristics Predict Physical and Psychological discomfort. *Journal of Environmental Psychology* 30: 533–41

Aries, Myriam B C, Mariëlle P J Aarts + Joost van Hoof. 2015. Daylight and Health: A Review of the Evidence and Consequences for the Built Environment. *Lighting Research + Technology* 47(1): 6–27

ASHRAE 2020. *Standard 55: Thermal Environmental Conditions for Human Occupancy.* Atlanta, Georgia: American Society of Heating, Refrigerating and Air-Conditioning Engineers

Badia, Pietro, Brent Myers, Maren Boecker, Janice Culpepper, + J R Harsh. 1991. Bright Light Effects on Body Temperature, Alertness, EEG and Behavior. *Physiology + Behavior* 50: 583–88

Baird, Benjamin, Jonathan Smallwood, Michael D Mrazek, Julia W Y Kam, Michael S Franklin + Jonathan W Schooler. 2012. Inspired by Distraction: Mind Wandering Facilitates Creative Incubation. *Psychological Science* 23(10):1117–22

Baker, Nick + Mark Standeven. 1994. Comfort Criteria for Passively Cooled Buildings, a Pascool Task. *Renewable Energy* 5(5): 977–84

Barkmann, Claus, Nino Wessolowski + Michael Schulte-Markwort. 2012. Applicability and Efficacy of Variable Light in Schools. *Physiology + Behavior* 105(3): 621–27

Barton, Jo + Jules Pretty. 2010. What Is the Best Dose of Nature and Green Exercise for Improving Mental Health? A Multi-Study Analysis. *Environmental Science + Technology* 44(10): 3947–55

Biederman, Irving + Edward Vessel. 2006. Perceptual Pleasure and the Brain. *American Scientist–AMER SCI* 94

Boerstra, Atze, Tim Beuker, Marcel Loomans + Jan Hensen. 2013. Impact of Available and Perceived Control on Comfort and Health in European Offices. *Architectural Science Review* 56(1): 30–41

Boubekri, Mohamed, Ivy N Cheung, Kathryn J Reid, Chiao Hui Wang + Phyllis C Zee. 2014. Impact of Windows and Daylight Exposure on Overall Health and Sleep Quality of Office Workers-A Case-Control Pilot Study. *Journal of Clinical Sleep Medicine.* 10(6): 603–11, Jun 15

Brager, Gail S + Richard J de Dear. 1998. Thermal Adaptation in the Built Environment: A Literature Review. *Energy and Buildings* 27(1): 83–96

Cabanac, Michel. 2010. *Fifth Influence or the Dialectics of Pleasure.* Union City, New Jersey: BookWhirl

Cain, Rebecca, Paul Jennings, John Poxon + Alec Scott. 2009. Emotional Dimensions of a Soundscape. *INTER-NOISE and NOISE-CON Congress and Conference Proceedings.* Institute of Noise Control Engineering

Chellappa, Sarah Laxhmi, Roland Steiner, Peter Blattner, Peter Oelhafen, Thomas Götz + Christian Cajochen. 2011. Non-Visual Effects of Light on Melatonin, Alertness and Cognitive Performance: Can Blue-Enriched Light Keep Us Alert? *PLoS ONE* 6(1): e16429

Cheung, Toby, Lindsay T Graham + Stefano Schiavon. 2022. Impacts of Life Satisfaction, Job Satisfaction and the Big Five Personality Traits on Satisfaction with the Indoor Environment. *Building and Environment* 212:108783

CIE 2019. *Position Statement on Non-Visual Effects of Light: Recommending Proper Light at the Proper Time*. Vienna, Austria: International Commission on Illumination.

Davies, William J, Mags D Adams, Neil S Bruce, Rebecca Cain, Angus Carlyle, Peter Cusack, Deborah A Hall, Ken I Hume, Amy Irwin, Paul Jennings, Melissa Marselle, Christopher J Plack + John Poxon. 2013. Perception of Soundscapes: An Interdisciplinary Approach. *Applied Acoustics* 74(2): 224–31

Davies, William, Mags Adams, Neil Bruce, Rebecca Cain, A Carlyle, Peter Cusack, KI Hume, Paul Jennings + Christopher Plack. 2009. The Positive Soundscape Project: A Synthesis of Results from Many Disciplines. *INTER-NOISE and NOISE-CON Congress and Conference Proceedings*. Institute of Noise Control Engineering

de Dear, Richard + Gail S Brager. 2001. The Adaptive Model of Thermal Comfort and Energy Conservation in the Built Environment. *International Journal of Biometeorology* 45(2):100–108

de Dear, Richard. 1998. A Global Database of Thermal Comfort Field Experiments. *ASHRAE Transactions* 104:1141–1152

DeLoach, Alana G, Jeff P Carter + Jonas Braasch. 2015. Tuning the Cognitive Environment: Sound Masking with "Natural" Sounds in Open-Plan Offices. *The Journal of the Acoustical Society of America* 137(4): 2291–2291

Ethofer, Thomas, Silke Anders, Sarah Wiethoff, Michael Erb, Cornelia Herbert, Ralf Saur, Wolfgang Grodd + Dirk Wildgruber. 2006. Effects of Prosodic Emotional Intensity on Activation of Associative Auditory Cortex. *Neuroreport* 17(3): 249–53

Fanger, Povl Ole. 1970. *Thermal Comfort: Analysis and Applications in Environmental Engineering*. Danish Technical Press

Farley, K M J + Jennifer Veitch. 2001. *A Room with a View: A Review of the Effects of Windows on Work and Well-Being*. Research Report. Institute for Research in Construction, National Research Council Canada

Figueiro, Mariana + Mark Rea. 2017. Quantifying Circadian Light and Its Impact. *Architect Magazine,* Feb 13. www.architectmagazine.com

Graham, Lindsay T, Thomas Parkinson + Stefano Schiavon. 2021. Lessons Learned from 20 Years of CBE's Occupant Surveys. *Buildings and Cities* 2(1):166–84

Grandjean, Didier, David Sander, Gilles Pourtois, Sophie Schwartz, Mohamed L Seghier, Klaus R Scherer + Patrik Vuilleumier. 2005. The Voices of Wrath: Brain Responses to Angry Prosody in Meaningless Speech. *Nature Neuroscience* 8(2):145–46

Haapakangas, Annu, E Kankkunen, Valtteri Hongisto, Petra Virjonen, David Oliva, + Esko Keskinen. 2011. Effects of Five Speech Masking Sounds on Performance and Acoustic Satisfaction: Implications for Open-Plan Offices. *Acta Acustica United with Acustica* 97: 641–55

Haghighat, Fariborz + Giovanna Donnini. 1999. Impact of Psycho-Social Factors on Perception of the Indoor Air Environment Studies in 12 Office Buildings. *Building and Environment* (34): 479–503

Henshaw, Victoria. 2013. *Urban Smellscapes: Understanding and Designing City Smell Environments*. New York: Routledge

Heschong, Lisa. 2021. *Visual Delight in Architecture: Daylight, Vision and View*. New York: Routledge

Humphreys, Michael. 1978. Outdoor Temperatures and Comfort Indoors. *Batiment International, Building Research and Practice* 6(2)

Hunter, Michael D, Simon B Eickhoff, Robert J Pheasant, Molly J Douglas, Greg R Watts, Tom F D Farrow, Declan Hyland, Jian Kang, Iain D Wilkinson + Krill V Horoshenkov. 2010. The State of Tranquility: Subjective Perception Is Shaped by Contextual Modulation of Auditory Connectivity. *NeuroImage* 53(2): 611–18

ISO. 2005. *International Standard 7730: Ergonomics of the Thermal Environment—Analytical Determination and Interpretation of Thermal Comfort Using Calculation of the PMV and PPD Indices and Local Thermal Comfort Criteria*. Geneva, Switzerland: International Standard Organization

IWBI. 2020. *WELL Building Standard v2*. New York: International Well Building Institute. wellcertified.com

Karmanov, Dmitri + Ronald Hamel. 2008. Assessing the Restorative Potential of Contemporary Urban Environment(s): Beyond the Nature versus Urban Dichotomy. *Landscape and Urban Planning* 86(2):115–25

Khan, Rehan M, Chung-Hay Luk, Adeen Flinker, Amit Aggarwal, Hadas Lapid, Rafi Haddad + Noam Sobel. 2007. Predicting Odor Pleasantness from Odorant Structure: Pleasantness as a Reflection of the Physical World. *Journal of Neuroscience* 27(37):10015–23

Ko, Won Hee, Stefano Schiavon, Hui Zhang, Lindsay T Graham, Gail Brager, Iris Mauss + Yu-Wen Lin. 2020. The Impact of a View from a Window on Thermal Comfort, Emotion, and Cognitive Performance. *Building and Environment* 175:106779

Ko, Won Hee, Stefano Schiavon, Sergio Altomonte, Marilyne Andersen, Ayesha Batool, William Browning, Galen Burrell et al. 2022, Window View Quality: Why It Matters and What We Should Do. *LEUKOS* 18:3, 259–267

Lang, Peter J, Margaret M Bradley, Jeffrey R Fitzsimmons, Bruce N Cuthbert, James D Scott, Bruce Moulder + Vijay Nangia. 1998. Emotional Arousal and Activation of the Visual Cortex: An FMRI Analysis. *Psychophysiology* 35(2):199–210

Langevin, Jared, Jin Wen + Patrick L Gurian. 2012. Relating Occupant Perceived Control and Thermal Comfort: Statistical Analysis on the ASHRAE RP-884 Database. *HVAC+R Research* 18:179–94

Levine, Michael W + Jeremy M Shefner. 2004. *Fundamentals of Sensation and Perception*. 3rd ed. Oxford, UK: Oxford University Press

Lockley, Steven, Erin E Evans, Frank A Scheer, George C Brainard, Charlies A Czeisler + Daniel Aeschbach. 2006. Short-Wavelength Sensitivity for the Direct Effects of Light on Alertness, Vigilance, and the Waking Electroencephalogram in Humans. *Sleep* 29:161-168

Lucas, Robert J, Stuart N Peirson, David M Berson, Timothy M Brown, Howard M Cooper, Charles A Czeisler, Mariana G Figueiro, Paul D Gamlin, Steven W Lockley, John B O'Hagan, Luke L A Price, Ignacio Provencio, Debra J Skene + George C Brainard. 2014. Measuring and Using Light in the Melanopsin Age. *Trends in Neurosciences* 37(1):1–9

Medvedev, Oleg, Daniel Shepherd + Michael J Hautus. 2015. The Restorative Potential of Soundscapes: A Physiological Investigation. *Applied Acoustics* 96: 20–26

Mills, Peter R, Susannah C Tomkins + Luc J M Schlangen. 2007. The Effect of High Correlated Colour Temperature Office Lighting on Employee Wellbeing and Work Performance. *Journal of Circadian Rhythms* 5: 2

Milosavljevic, Nina. 2019. How Does Light Regulate Mood and Behavioral State? *Clocks + Sleep* 1: 319–31

Mishra, Asit K, Marchel G L C Loomans + Jan L Hensen. 2016. Thermal Comfort of Heterogeneous and Dynamic Indoor Conditions—An Overview. *Building and Environment* 109: 82–100

Mott, Michael S, Daniel H Robinson, Ashley Walden, Jodie Burnette + Angela S Rutherford. 2012. Illuminating the Effects of Dynamic Lighting on Student Learning. *SAGE Open* 2(2): 2158244012445585

Orians, Gordon H + Judith H Heerwagen. 1992. Evolved Responses to Landscapes. *The Adapted Mind: Evolutionary Psychology and the Generation of Culture.* Oxford, UK: Oxford University Press

Oseland, Nigel + Paige Hodsman. 2015. *Planning for Psychoacoustics: A Psychological Approach to Resolving Office Noise Distraction.* Research Report for Saint-Gobain Ecophon

Paciuk, Monica. 1990. The Role of Personal Control of the Environment in Thermal Comfort and Satisfaction at the Workplace. *Environmental Design Research Association* 21: 303–12

Papalambros, Nelly A, Giovanni Santostasi, Roneil G Malkani, Rosemary Braun, Sandra Weintraub, Ken A Paller + Phyllis C Zee. 2017. Acoustic Enhancement of Sleep Slow Oscillations and Concomitant Memory Improvement in Older Adults. *Frontiers in Human Neuroscience* 11:109

Parkinson, Thomas + Richard de Dear. 2015. Thermal Pleasure in Built Environments: Physiology of Alliesthesia. *Building Research + Information* 43(3): 288–301

Parkinson, Thomas, Hui Zhang, Ed Arens, Yingdong He, Richard de Dear, John Elson, Alex Parkinson, Clay Maranville + Andrew Wang. 2021. Predicting Thermal Pleasure Experienced in Dynamic Environments from Simulated Cutaneous Thermoreceptor Activity. *Indoor Air* 31(6): 2266–80

Parkinson, Tom, Richard de Dear + Gail Brager. 2020. Nudging the Adaptive Thermal Comfort Model. *Energy and Buildings* 206(Jan):109559

Payne, Sarah R, William Davies + Mags Adams. 2009. *Research into the Practical and Policy Applications of Soundscape Concepts and Techniques in Urban Areas.* Report. London: HMSO Publisher

Phipps-Nelson, Jo, Jennifer R Redman, Derk-Jan Dijk + Shantha M W Rajaratnam. 2003. Daytime Exposure to Bright Light, as Compared to Dim Light, Decreases Sleepiness and Improves Psychomotor Vigilance Performance. *Sleep* 26(6): 695–700

Rea, Mark S, Mariana Figueiro, Andrew Bierman + John Bullough. 2010. Circadian Light. *Journal of Circadian Rhythms* 8(0): Art. 2

Ruso, Bernhart + Klaus Atzwanger. 2003. Measuring Immediate Behavioral Responses to the Environment. *The Michigan Psychologist* 4:12

Sadeghi, Seyed Amir, Panagiota Karava, Iason Konstantzos + Athanasios Tzempelikos. 2016. Occupant Interactions with Shading and Lighting Systems Using Different Control Interfaces: A Pilot Field Study. *Building and Environment* 97:177–95

Schupp, Harald T, Junghöfer Markus, Almut I Weike + Alfons O Hamm. 2003. Emotional Facilitation of Sensory Processing in the Visual Cortex. *Psychological Science* 14(1): 7–13

Schweiker, Marcel, Eleni Ampatzi, Maedot S Andargie, Rune Korsholm Andersen, Elie Azar, Verena M Barthelmes, Christiane Berger, et al. 2020. Review of Multi-domain Approaches to Indoor Environmental Perception and Behaviour. *Building and Environment* 176:106804

Shepherd, Joshua. 2019. Why Does the Mind Wander? *Neuroscience of Consciousness.* Vol 2019(1): niz014

Shin, Won. 2007. The Influence of Forest View through a Window on Job Satisfaction and Job Stress. *Scandinavian Journal of Forest Research* 22: 248–53

Snyder, Joel S + Melissa K Gregg. 2011. Memory for Sound, with an Ear toward Hearing in Complex Auditory Scenes. *Attention, Perception + Psychophysics* 73(7):1993

Steane, Mary Ann + Koen Steemers. 2004. *Environmental Diversity in Architecture.* New York: Routledge

Tartarini, Federico, Stefano Schiavon, Toby Cheung, + Tyler Hoyt. 2020. *CBE Thermal Comfort Tool: Online Tool for Thermal Comfort Calculations and Visualizations.* SoftwareX 12:100563

te Kulve, Marije, Lisje Schellen, Luc J M Schlangen + Wouter van Marken Lichtenbelt. 2016. The Influence of Light on Thermal Responses. *Acta Physiologica* 216(2):163–85

Toftum, Jørn. 2004. Air Movement—Good or Bad? *Indoor Air* 14: 40–45

Ulrich, Roger S. 1983. Aesthetic and Affective Response to Natural Environment. in *Behavior and the Natural Environment, Human Behavior and Environment,* eds. I Altman + J F Wohlwill. Boston, Massachusetts: Springer US

Ulrich, Roger S. 1984. View through a Window May Influence Recovery from Surgery. *Science* 224(4647): 420–21

Vandewalle, Gilles, Pierre Maquet + Derk-Jan Dijk. 2009. Light as a Modulator of Cognitive Brain Function. *Trends in Cognitive Sciences* 13(10): 429–38

Viola, Antoine U, Lynette M James, Luc J M Schlangen + Derk-Jan Dijk. 2008. Blue-Enriched White Light in the Workplace Improves Self-Reported Alertness, Performance and Sleep Quality. *Scandinavian Journal of Work, Environment + Health* 34(4): 297–306

Watts, Greg R, Rob J Pheasant, Krill V Horoshenkov + Laura Ragonesi. 2009. Measurement and Subjective Assessment of Water Generated Sounds. *Acta Acustica United with Acustica* 95:1032–39

White, Mathew, Amanda Smith, Kelly Humphryes, Sabine Pahl, Deborah Snelling + Michael Depledge. 2010. Blue Space: The Importance of Water for Preference, Affect, and Restorativeness Ratings of Natural and Built Scenes. *Journal of Environmental Psychology* 30(4): 482–93

WHO (World Health Organization). 2011. *Burden of Disease from Environmental Noise: Quantification of Healthy Life Years Lost in Europe.* World Health Organization. Regional Office for Europe

Windhager, Sonja, Klaus Atzwanger, Fred L Bookstein + Katrin Schaefer. 2011. Fish in a Mall Aquarium—An Ethological Investigation of Biophilia. *Landscape and Urban Planning* 99(1): 23–30

Wirz-Justice, Anna, Francesco Benedetti + Michael Terman. 2013. *Chronotherapeutics for Affective Disorders: A Clinician's Manual for Light and Wake Therapy,* 2nd ed. Basel, Switzerland: Karger Medical + Scientific Publishers

Wright, Kenneth P, Andrew W McHill, Brian R Birks, Brandon R Griffin, Thomas Rusterholz + Evan D Chinoy. 2013. Entrainment of the Human Circadian Clock to the Natural Light-Dark Cycle. *Current Biology* 23(16):1554–58

Yang, Wonyoung + Hyeun Jun Moon. 2019. Combined Effects of Acoustic, Thermal, and Illumination Conditions on the Comfort of Discrete Senses and Overall Indoor Environment. *Building and Environment* 148: 623–33

Zhang, Hui, Edward Arens, Sahar Abbaszadeh Fard, Charlie Huizenga, Gwelen Paliaga, Gail Brager, + Leah Zagreus. 2007. Air Movement Preferences Observed in Office Buildings. *International Journal of Biometeorology* 51(5): 349–60

Zhang, Hui. 2003. *Human Thermal Sensation and Comfort in Transient and Non-Uniform Thermal Environments.* PhD Dissertation, University of California, Berkeley

4

Experiential Design Schemas

Contrast | Gradient | Rhythm | Flux | Sequence | Narrative

opposite
Texas A+M Engineering College in Education City

Doha, Qatar, 2007
Legorreta + Legorreta, architects

photo Pygmalion Karatzas

C1 Thermic Hues	**G1**	**R1**	**F1** Melodic Materials	**S1** Veridical Patina	**N1** Perceptible Provenance
C2 Haptic Connection	**G2** Adaptive Altitude	**R2** Aperture Engagement	**F2** Current Prehension	**S2** Aromatic Transit	**N2** Authentic Matters
C3 Scintillating Sun	**G3** Existential Datum	**R3** Biorhythmic Radiance	**F2** Water as a Mirror	**S3**	**N3** Roof Terrain
C3 Water You Can Touch	**G4** Incalescent Center	**R4** Dawn + Dusk Places	**F3** Fans First	**S4**	**N3** Distinguishable Durability
C4 Engage the Rain	**G4** Euphonic Water	**R4** Circadian Space	**F3** Revealed Conveyance	**S5** Territorial Tuning	**N4**
C4 Inhabited Periphery	**G4** Zephyr Spectrum	**R4** Radiant Sailing	**F3** Water-Animated Surfaces	**S5** Ingress Transitions	**N5** Three Realms
C4 Lightrooms	**G4** Shades of Brilliance	**R4** Habitat Fringe	**F4** Compluvium Shower	**S5** Light + Dark Procession	**N6** Situated Scenes
C4 Tempered Pathway	**G5** Pockets of Shadow	**R5** Heliotropic Rooms	**F5**	**S5** Phototropic Catenation	
C5 Thermal Enclave	**G6** Engagement + Retreat	**R6** Cooling Conversions	**F6**	**S6** Topophilic Perambulation	
C6					

C Contrast
G Gradient
R Rhythm
F Flux
S Sequence
N Narrative

Building a place in the world for elevated feeling is a difficult thing—to link the measurable and the unmeasurable. To have something to say about form and space that ennobles subjective inhabitation and offers utility for designers turns out to be even more challenging than we imagined. We count among our colleagues and friends those experts in the quantitative domain, a few masters of the artistic qualitative approach to design and the occasional practitioner of the "dark art "of architectural hermeneutics. Our work, a quest for which there can be no ultimate answers, somehow lies at the intersection of these multiple perspectives. Nevertheless, it occurs to us as a worthwhile, if humbling enterprise.

It is the inquiry itself that seems to be where the power is. We have tried to be rigorous in the way one can be rigorous with a thorny and multivariate problem. Information is present but the result is not, in the end, answers or solutions. Rather, we hope what becomes present as a result of this effort is an opening, a field of possibilities for both inhabitant and designer. In this realm, the realm of inhabited built environments, every way to look at it is partial—true but partial. We ask you simply to consider these schemas as possibilities. Stand in the perspective they present and look at architecture and life that way, and see what becomes possible for you and your life, your work, and those whom your work serves.

In the sections that follow we offer the results of our inquiry, not as definitions, but as suppositions. We draw inspiration from our mentor and colleague G Z Brown, who would say "Suppose this were the case......then what could be present?", calling this approach a design *supposal,* in contrast to a proposal. Each opens a world of potentials that might occur, not as a formula for designing feeling, nor as forms or things, but as thought domains inside of which many particular forms and expressions of the schema may emerge. We encourage you, when reading these, to form your own interpretations.

Five Distributions of Conditions

There are many frameworks for organizing thought about architectural experience and no singular right way to organize design knowledge or to access it. In developing our approach, we look at the conditions that drive experience and how people experience those different kinds of conditions. Often beginning from direct empiricism, we asked, What *am I* feeling? and, What is going on here *that* I am feeling? It can't be proven that the categories that follow are absolute or complete. What can be said is that they seem useful and, most of the time, in line with a first-person encounter with the phenomena. We first identify five types of *distributions of conditions*. Later, we add a sixth type, related to the phenomena but significantly different from the relatively more direct sensory concreteness addressed in the first set. The types of conditions constitute distinctions of conceptual domains that open and expand potential perceptions. Once a conditional type is distinguished (such as *rhythms*), one finds many occurrences of the type emerging for different forces at various scales.

Dai-ichi Yochien Preschool

Kumamoto City, Japan
Youji No Shiro + Hibino Sekkei architects

photos Studio BAUHAUS

ArchDaily, 2015

Contrasts

Contrasts are found when opposing conditions, such as warm and cool, humid and dry, or dark and light are experienced simultaneously or in rapid succession. Contrasts place sharp or distinct steps from one condition to another adjacent condition without significant gradients between them. The body feels contrast when walking barefoot on a warm radiant floor in a room with cooler air. Contrasting conditions typically exist within a single space, such as when direct sun enters a room through windows and provides a strong pattern of sun and shade on the walls or floor. During a rainstorm, the contrast between rain in a courtyard and dryness under the porch is extreme and abrupt. Contrasts can be architecturally mediated by transitional or linking spaces that have access to both types of more extreme conditions. For example, a porch or arcade can link and provide a transition between indoor and outdoor conditions of temperature, air movement, sun, moisture and light. If contrasting conditions occur when a person moves from one space to another, we distinguish this condition as a sequence, explained below.

The room scale schema, C4 Engage the Rain, *contraposes wet exposure with dry protection at occupied building edges to engender pluvial pleasures.* The Dai-ichi Yochien Preschool atrium has an operable roof. When open its court collects water; after a downpour, a grand puddle awaits eager children to play in it. On dry days, the courtyard becomes a sports court, or in winter, an ice skating rink. Students can appreciate the falling rain from under the protected adjacent open plan *piloti* zone; sliding walls allow the entire interior to become semi-outdoors.

 Pérez Art Museum

Miami, Florida, 2013
Herzog + De Meuron Architects

photos Pygmalion Karatzas

Gradients

Gradients are relatively smooth transitions between one condition and another within the field of one's perception. For example, a sidelighted room with windows on one wall will be bright by the windows and gradually becomes darker away from the window wall. This lighting gradient is typically within the field of one's vision. Similarly, the warmth of a fire decreases with distance from the hearth. In rooms without significant air circulation, warm air will rise toward the ceiling and cool air will move toward the floor, creating a vertical thermal gradient. Acoustic gradients are most familiar day-to-day as people move away from the sound source. Typically, gradients occur within a single space, however the organization of spaces and subspaces can also create gradients, such as when an atrium building is open to vertical air movement, so higher floor levels become warmer than lower floors.

Gradient conditions can be seen in the design schema, G4 Shades of Brilliance. The Perez Art Museum creates public verandas, covered with an expansive pergola roof, connecting a park on one side with bay views on the other, "offering gradual transitions from the outside to the inside, from the warm to the cool, from the humid to the dry and from the street to the art" (Herzog + de Meuron, 2013). Louvered sunshades promote views, support *hanging gardens* and protect large windows. The result is a variety of fully protected, partly shaded and full sun options. The left image depicts an afternoon view, of the northeast terrace. In the morning, more of the terrace is sunny and chairs can move back. Fixed benches at the edge are sunny in the morning, while broad steps beyond, remaining mostly sunny all day, lead down to the bay promenade. (ArchDaily, 2014; A+U, 2014).

Villa Elxis

Paros Island, Greece, 2016
Studio 265 + Vazaios Petropoulos architects

left
Sunrise view over the Aegean

right
Moonset view from covered dining terrace allowing the appreciation of the *blue hour*. Also aligns with sunset.

photos Pygmalion Karatzas

Rhythms

Experiential rhythms allow occupants to experience Nature's periodicity. Much of Nature works in daily and annual cycles, particularly those processes that are driven by the sun's energy, which includes climate, seasons and daily patterns. Conditions in buildings and how people occupy them have historically been closely tied to the rhythms of Nature: when to cut firewood, when to plant crops, when to sit by the fire and when to cook and eat outdoors. Mechanized conditioning and the sealing of the building envelope in the 20th century, along with the corresponding increase in time spent indoors—coupled with ubiquitous electric lights, cheap energy to run them and the resulting out-of-phase condition with light-regulated sleep cycles—have conspired to disconnect people from knowing, experiencing, and relating to Nature.

An experiential rhythm can be seen in the design schema, R4 Dawn and Dusk Places, which focuses occupants' attention on the light and color transitions around sunrise and sunset and their lunar equivalents. The master bedroom of Villa Elxis is oriented toward the rising sun and opens onto a large veranda overlooking the Aegean Sea. The bathroom, located opposite the sea view, has a large interior window in the wall behind the bed, connecting occupants back to the sky and water view. The spectacle can be appreciated while indoors or from the terrace. From the west-facing side of the breezeway lounge, both moonset and sunset are framed from under cover or, again, on the terrace (Karatzas, 2007; Divasare, 2007).

146 **Water/Cherry House**

Eastern Japan coast, 2012
Kengo Kuma, architect

photo left Botond Bognar
photo right Balázs Bognár

Fluxes

Fluxes are continuously changing stochastic conditions perceived as random or chaotic, such as leaves blowing in the wind, or the intensifying and lightening of rain and its concomitant sounds. The formation, movement and dissipation of clouds is relatively stochastic. On partly cloudy days, daylight variation caused by clouds passing over the sun or the darkness of an approaching rainstorm manifest unpredictability that we term *flux*, meaning "constantly changing" (Merriam-Webster, nd). Nature can be rhythmic, yet it can also be arhythmic. Such frequent changes, suddenness and randomness are characteristic of weather at times. Similarly, sun sparkling on rippling water, birds moving, insects and other wildlife, flowing water in a stream or fountain and even the intermittent scents wafting on the breeze fit what Browning et al (2014), call *non-rhythmic sensory stimuli*. These are "stochastic and ephemeral connections with nature that may be analyzed statistically, but may not be predicted precisely." The space "feels as if one is momentarily privy to something special, something fresh, stimulating and energizing."

In the schema F3 Water-Animated Surfaces, walls or ceilings receive dancing sunlight reflections from water, when it is disturbed by wind. In the Water/Cherry House (JA+U, 2012, video; Yin et al, 2017 video), flat pools reflect the sun onto walls and ceilings of nearby rooms. When breezes disturb the water surface, the reflection becomes animated and light refracts more through the water. The surface of the moving water has concave and convex conditions, and as light is shown through those ripples of water, it is refracted or reflected (Upstill, 1979). This playful, moving light quality connects occupants to wind movement and sky qualities.

NY Carlsberg Glyptotek Addition

Copenhagen, Denmark, 1996
Henning Larsen, architect

Visitors journey "through a rich sequence of daylight infusions and blacked out rooms" (Larsens 2010).

left
underground Egyptian Sarcophagi exhibit
photo Jens Lindhe

right
toplighted circulation
photo Thomas Flensted

diagram
See S5 Light + Dark Procession schema

Sequences

Sequences take two forms. The most common is people moving from one space to another; in the process, they experience heterogeneous conditions. Another mode is when conditions change over time but occupants don't relocate. Experientially, both are dynamic in time. Entering a building by a well-designed sequence, path direction and elevation often change, offering different views; an extended or carved-away volume encloses the body with a *spatial compression* and reduced light, helping the eyes adjust from bright exterior to dimmer interior. The building entry is usually shaded, offering sun and rain protection and a cool summer zone or greater wind protection. Airlocks, foyers and lobbies continue transitions of light reduction, shade and wind, plus greater thermal control. The whole sequence can be orchestrated as a delightful series of multi-sensory moments. Another common sequence employs people's attraction to light. Designers often select light levels or locate windows so that people naturally move toward the light, especially at points of orientation where circulation decisions are made.

In the schema S5 Light and Dark Procession, light intensity varies between spaces, defining significant features and enlivening the luminous experience. In the Ny Carlsberg Glypotek addition, Larsens created a series of darker galleries alternating with skylighted circulation (Plummer, 2012; Larsens, 2010). The darkest, subterranean level is the Egyptian exhibit. Toplighted circulation illuminance crescendos from lower darker floors to a bright open-to-sky roof terrace. Thick walls link bright and dim. As in many museums, the intended visitors' route is planned, therefore the exhibit path and a designed lighting sequence can be orchestrated together.

148 **University of Tennessee Art + Architecture Building**

Knoxville, Tennessee, USA, 1980
McCarty Holsaple McCarty architects

photos Jeff Goldberg/ESTO

Narratives

The landscape architect and author, John Lyle (1994), enjoined designers to "shape form to manifest process", by which he meant that built environment design can communicate its relationship to Nature, particularly the ways it engages with ecological processes, such as the hydrologic cycle. This was distinct from his injunction to "shape form to guide flow", which describes instead the ecological function of buildings and designed landscapes. To *manifest process* is to present it visibly, even pedagogically, to occupants via design. In contrast, to *guide flow* is to organize the built environment in functional ways to work with climate, habitat, water, and other environmental dynamic exchanges of energy, information and matter. To organize space and form in ways that convey how a building and site are *designed-with-nature*, to use landscape planner Ian McHarg's (1971) terms, or to express what is meaningful about a building's relationship to how humans understand Nature, is a new category of how we consider experiential design. It is based on the human sensation of conditions, and yet also transcends sensation to require an understanding of the metaphoric and symbolic communication employed in the work. To manifest process is one example of how design narrates to connect people to Nature. It requires a designer-author to embed the narrative in the work and an aware occupant to read and interpret the narrative. In between the designer and the experiencing occupant are the combinations of spatial order, conditions and human experiences that we have already been discussing.

Magney House

Bingie Point, New South Wales
Australia, 1984
Glenn Murcutt, architect

photos Anthony Browell

Embedded narratives in two buildings

In the building where Mark teaches, the impoverished awareness of the hydrologic cycle is constituted only by the 6 in (15 cm) between restroom faucet and basin drain. In a football field sized flat-roofed building, rooftop rain cannot be heard, nor a single drop seen once captured. Its path from the roof is concealed in interior pipes painted to match the ubiquitous concrete structure, runoff disappears beneath the floor, hurtled underground, presumably arriving via storm drains to the nearby Tennessee River. In a water landscape, it seems that rainfall does not exist. In *The Architecture of the Well-Tempered Environment,* Reyner Banham (1969) articulated two approaches to environmental controls, such as mechanical, electrical and plumbing systems: *concealed power* and *expressed power.* The University of Tennessee's Art & Architecture Building (Architectural Record, 1982) expresses power with color-coded exposed ductwork, electrical conduits and sprinkler systems, yet it conceals every aspect of water. It has clear and visible narratives about active building systems and opaque suppressed narratives about its passive systems and its relationship to natural site processes. Without the expressed architectural narrative there would be little experience of the building's mechanical system order; with it, occupants gain interpretive opportunity.

Contrast this with a house by Glenn Murcutt. Situated on a wind-swept Australian site overlooking the ocean, Magney House (OZ.E.Tecture, nd) is sited for access to sunlight and ventilation (Mosconi, 2016). The asymmetrical butterfly roof, oversized scupper, conical leader head and cylindrical downspout express a relationship to the hydrologic cycle. The rain sounds on the metal roof and in the water swirling in the down-pipe animate the home's occupancy. Its deep sun-shading overhang, operable sun and light control louvers, high equator-facing wall and sloping light-reflecting roof all express a careful fitting to the climatic processes of the site. A high level of intelligence is embedded into simple forms expressed for all to see, feel and interpret.

Turtle Creek House

Dallas, Texas, 1993
Antoine Predock, architect

Entrance through a metaphorical stone cave. The view opens to the lawn at ground level and into the forest understory. The "theater of the trees" house, built for a birdwatcher, offers multiple varied vantage points on nature. A sky bridge enters the canopy. A roof terrace frames sky and star watching.

photos Tim Hursley

Buildings as metaphors for ideas of Nature

As humans spend most of their time indoors, architecture has become a powerful mediator of the relationship between humans and Nature. What occupants know of Nature, how they understand it and how it is defined and experienced in everyday life, has accordingly become a contemporary challenge and responsibility for designers. The Tennessee Art & Architecture Building and the Magney House express different relationships to Nature and natural hydrology. Indeed, they express radically different ideas of what Nature is. They manifest distinctly different narratives about Nature and about how buildings should be designed in the mental and moral space of those differing ideas of Nature. These originate from different worldviews originating in different regions, and from different cultural and intellectual generations.

Narrative, as the sixth category for conditional distribution, stretches the idea of environmental stimuli in the metaphoric direction and into longer time spans. Narratives, as stories humans tell each other in words or in symbols, frame human life. They help people interpret their being in the world while shifting time in ways that allow them to make sense of dynamic phenomena from the past and future: "When it has rained or will rain, the building interacts like this...." Narratives can compress time, allowing occupants in moments or minutes to understand processes that take days, seasons, years, or decades, such as how materials age with natural forces over many years. It is not merely the specific colors or textures in the aging of wood or the patina of copper that people enjoy. Embedded history read in them enriches momentary sensory input. In such ways, some rich human experiences cannot be extracted from the cultural narratives that members of that culture associate with them.

Schema N5 The Three Realms, forwards connecting occupants to the diverse worlds of the subterranean, surface and sky. Turtle Creek House is entered through a cave-like passage into massive limestone tiers and emerges to a ground level forest view (Predock, 1998; Pearson, 1994). Stairs ascend to a second-level bridge, while a *sky ramp* extends into the avian home canopy. Each level reveals different aspects of Nature that can be enjoyed and amplified in the human perception. Forests have vertical structure with different micro-communities at each level: roots, burrowers and the living soil below, ground dwellers and understory species in-between and canopy life, from insects to raptors to air mosses above.

Some critics argue that merely having a good story is the mark of good architecture and that the best buildings are the ones with the best stories, even if most people don't follow along with the plot. We don't agree. Often occupants do not get the point because the designer's narrative is too esoteric or the symbolic language poorly employed. It seems essential that people *do* follow along, that they *get it,* at least a little bit. Narrative is a fundamentally mental form of experience, or of giving meaning to it, so we can't argue that it makes or breaks a building's success. Yet to overlook these conditional narratives would be a substantial omission. The power of buildings as embodied values, as culturally situated storytellers, reinforces other kinds of experience and adds a deeper level of potential understanding.

Schema alpha-numeric coding

Distributions of Conditions

C Contrast
G Gradient
R Rhythm
F Flux
S Sequence
N Narrative

Levels of Scale + Complexity

1 Materials
2 Elements
3 Building Systems
4 Rooms
5 Room Organizations
6 Whole Buildings

What Is a Design Schema?

The schemas are the heart of the book, providing a set of knowledge modules as a design process resource. An *experiential design schema* is a narrative/graphic generative design aid that helps designers find and employ experiential concepts. As defined in this work, a *schema* is the organization of form and space that disposes environmental conditions to create a field of potential positive human experiences. They are conceived in harmony with the four approaches described in Chapter 2. The schemas integrate human perception, related evidence (from scientific research where available) and spatial patterns, providing design guidance aimed at increasing occupants' experiential delight and awareness of natural process, their psychological and physical health and their cognitive functions. Each schema connects a configuration of architectural space with the distribution of conditions (usually environmental forces), such as temperature, moisture, sound, air and light, but also terrain, plants, animals and living systems. The schema links these to fields of potential human experiences—for example delight, comfort, security, peace, connectedness and joy.

Anatomy of a design schema illustrates the organization of each schema's four-page spread. The idea is to convey the essentials of each experiential design possibility in a very concise way. The top of each layout begins with an alpha-numeric *schema level* designation, such as G4 or R5. The letter refers to a distribution type (see sidebar), for example G = Gradient and R = Rhythm. The numbers refer to a level of scale and complexity in a system from Level 1 (materials) to Level 6 (whole buildings), as elaborated in the *Schemata Language Map* section in the front matter (See the sidebar list). A *header* gives the schema's name and frames its essence in one sentence. Two *precedent* images illustrate how designers have used the schema in an elegant way. *Captions* for each image are located in the margins. An original *haiku* sets the tone and invites the reader to slow down. These haikus are further explained subsequently. The text begins with an *introduction* paragraph that completes the first page, explaining the phenomena, and including the potential positive human experiences.

Two paragraphs on the schema spread's second page offer *precedent analysis* to briefly explain how the selected projects exemplify the schema. These are often chosen to illustrate some significant variable, such as a cold versus hot climate example, or two different building types or different strategic solutions that both fulfill the schema's experiential intent. At page two's outer edge, there are two sets of original icons. The top set helps with *schema navigation* by identifying the conditions distribution type, such as Narrative, Sequence or Contrast (see sidebar for all six). The active type will be black, while the other five are grayed out. The lower set of icons identifies the most applicable *natural elements* that are engaged by the schema. There are six possible, and more than one element may be addressed by a single schema. The elements that are active will be black and the others, gray.

Page three opens with a *header* that reminds the reader of the schema being read. A typical schema has an *evidence diagram* that translates the often cryptic world of scientific research into a visual language that, we hope,

Anatomy of a design schema

Each schema is presented in a consistent four-page spread that inlcudes precedents, supporting evidence, design guidelines and a navigational system.

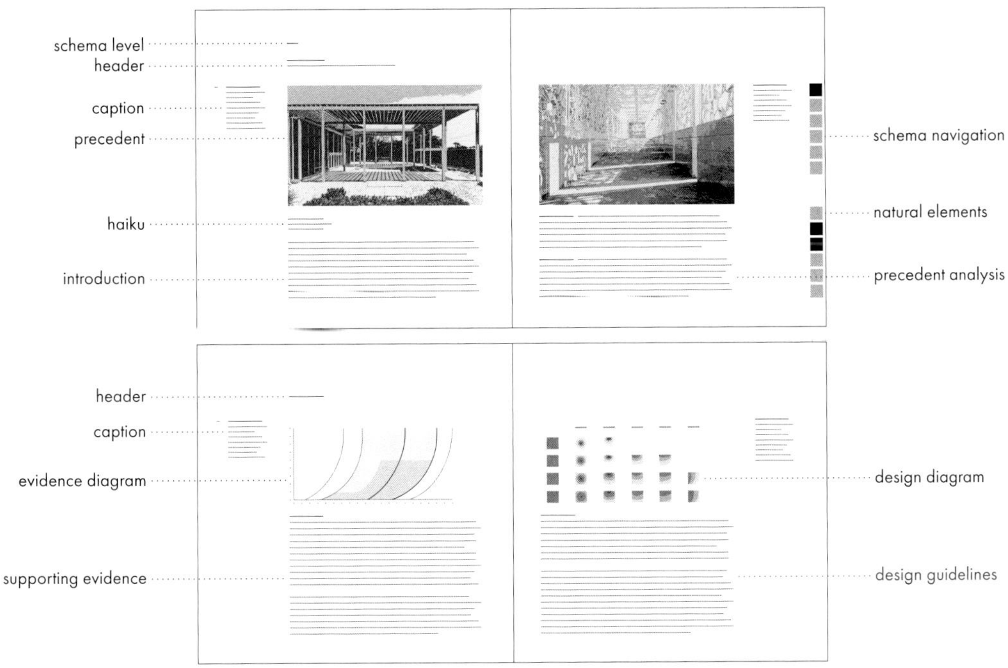

becomes more accessible for the visually-oriented designer. A few schemas do not include this graphic. Each schema inlcudes a concise text section of *supporting evidence* that culls the literature for a few gems of relevant positive evidence that can provide some information to the informed art of architecture. The evidence subhead is followed by a concise one or two sentence summary of the overall takeaways. A broad range of evidence types and epistemologies are included as evidence. For further explanation of our diverse and inclusive approach to evidence, see the end of Chapter 1.

Page four addresses *design guidelines*, which are based both in the authors' many decades of experience and in our reading of the evidence. The guidelines subhead is followed by a concise one or two sentence summary of the overall guidance for designers. To the degree we feel certainty, the guidance is framed in active terms. When we are less certain, the language is qualified. Because we can not know all the specifics of the reader-designer's situation, we ask the readers to rely on their own judgment or seek the advice of licensed professionals. As the schema format is concise, the evidence employed in the recommendations is not always fully covered in the supporting evidence summary. Often, but not always, we provide a diagram or illustration related to the design guidelines. Sometimes they outline a typology of alternatives or frame the choices designers have. Each set of guidelines concludes with a section that identifies refiner schemas at the same scale or at smaller scales that the schema helps to organize. It also calls out larger scale schemas that the outlined schema helps to build.

Haikus

Each schema opens with an original English language haiku. Initially inspired by a component of Gail's experiential teaching assignments, these were either written by Mark, or initially drafted by student assistants and then edited and revised by Mark. We are not professional poets, and we ask the literary critics among our readers some forbearance for any shortcomings. That said, the poems are purposeful: the idea is that each helps to concretize some aspect of what is presented in the design schema that follows, to set a tone as both pedagogical and performative metaphor. Just as the book concerns designing form to engender feeling, so the aim of the haiku is to put the reader in a particular state—the kind of attentive, reflective mental space that allows for fully opening to the rich, multiperspectival material that follows in the rest of the schema.

Like all haikus in English, they differ significantly from the Japanese form, such as the English convention of being written on 3 lines instead of one, using a syllable structure in contrast to the Japanese *on* (phonetic units similar to the English syllable), and so on. The haiku, derived from the earlier *hokku*, usually has a *kigo*, a seasonal reference. In our case, the reference is broadened to nature in general, including its forces and weather that can be sensed. Ideally, they coax or perhaps startle the reader into presence within a life of flux.

Situated experience

The architecture-Nature experience is always situated. In this sense, schemas are a variation of other related design knowledge systems. In *A Pattern Language (APL)*, Alexander and colleges (1979) articulate their design patterns as repeated events anchored in space. The events are primarily social phenomena. In the authors' definition, the pattern resolves a context of conflicting forces, or a situational tension. In *Sun, Wind + Light (SWL)*, DeKay + Brown (2014) define design strategies that relate spatial and formal configurations to patterns of energy use and bio-psychological human comfort responses. These spatial strategies shape the force of climate in particular sites and regions. Thus, the languages of both design guidance systems are situated, one mostly in social context, the other mostly in climatic context. The design schemas in this book identify human experiences set in a context of both natural forces and spatial order.

In all three approaches, the outcomes cannot be specified precisely. The contextual variety ensures that an *APL* pattern, an *SWL* strategy or a *Forming Feeling* experiential design schema will also have variety of expression. Each specifies something concrete, characteristics at the core of the social, energetic or felt pattern, but each also leaves open many other influencing variables, including the designer's voice. In this way, each schema has a thousand possible manifestations.

Fundamental yet complex

Schemas specify and articulate in open-ended, non-deterministic ways. They name simple, sometimes everyday occurrences in collective shared experience. In one sense, they are very basic, yet in another they are not purely fundamental or platonic or like some elementary particle of buildings. In fact, schemas depend on several other language distinctions, each developed throughout a long disciplinary history, including:

– *Distinctions of form and space,* of their types and organizations of scale: material, element, room, court, plan, section, and the languages of their composition.
– *Distinctions of conditions in time and space,* of the distributions and measurement of sun, wind, light sound, moisture, other species: steady state dynamic, uniform and non-uniform, linear, cyclic, and seasonal.
– *Distinctions of the human interior,* of sensation, emotion and feeling: joy as distinguished from happiness, calm from serenity, comfort from neutrality, and hundreds more.
– *Distinctions of culture and worldview,* of meaning and interpretation: the ideas of Nature and of culture and of their relationships, of stewardship and value, of tradition and progress.

All these and more constitute the many systems of distinctions that make schemas possible, the intellectual antecedents on top of which they are built. One can now see schemas as confluences, intersections, in-betweens and complexes that build new, more complex patterns out of existing distinctions. This makes them more significant and less fundamental than their constituents.

Satisfying indeterminacy

A single schema accesses distinctions from each quadrant and integrates them. The whole schema can be thought of as a field of bounded possibilities. Conditions that inhabitants sense are possibilities, rhythmic, dynamic, often indeterminate, even random. Occupant behaviors and adaptations are possibilities, unknown in their specifics, subject to individuality. Even aspects of the building's space and form can be possibilities dependent on design and operation, on opening windows and transforming enclosure, and on changes to the building through its life.

These establish partially determinant fields with boundaries and rules of the games that can be played within their fields. Given this complexity and indeterminacy, together with the multiplier of cultural interpretative varieties, one might easily argue that the whole endeavor to type experience and give design guidance for engendering feeling is tilting at windmills. Yet, therein also lies the fascination of architecture—that from a few simple components and variables arises an infinitely permutational art, each building unique, like each individual tree of a species or leaf on the tree. We hope you enjoy creating with the palette.

Sources

A + U. 2014. Herzog + de Meuron: Pérez Art Museum, Miami, FL 2013, *A + U: architecture and urbanism* 10(529) Oct: 94–107

Alexander, Christopher, Sara Ishikawa + Murray Silverstein. 1977. *A Pattern Language: Towns, Buildings, Construction.* New York: Oxford University Press

ArchDaily. 2014. Perez Art Museum/Herzog + de Meuron, *ArchDaily*, 7 Apr, archdaily.com/493736

ArchDaily. 2015. D1 Kindergarten and Nursery/ HIBINOSEKKEI + Youji no Shiro, *ArchDaily*, 23 Jun, archdaily.com/645730

Architectural Record. 1982. Art and Architecture Building, University of Tennessee, Knoxville, Tennessee; architects: McCarty Bullock Holsaple, Inc. *Architectural Record* 170(8) Jun:108–113

Banham, Reyner. 1969. *The Architecture of the Well-Tempered Environment.* Chicago: University of Chicago Press

DeKay, Mark + G Z Brown. 2014. *Sun, Wind + Light: Architectural Design Strategies*, 3rd ed. Hoboken, New Jersey: Wiley

Divsare. 2007. Studio 265, Villa Elxis in Paros Island, *Divasare*, divisare.com/projects/369686

GA. 2012. Kengo Kuma + Associates: Water/Cherry, East Japan, 2007–12, *GA (Global Architecture) Japan: environmental design.* 117 (Jul-Aug): 22–45

Herzog + de Meuron. 2013. 306 Perez Art Museum Miami, herzogdemeuron.com/index/projects

JA+U. 2012. *Water/Cherry* [video]. *Shinkenchiku (New Architecture), Japan Architecture + Urbanism*, Dec. vimeo.com/user11358352. Also at archdaily.com/339130

Karatzas, Pygmalion. 2007. Villa Elxis, Paros Island, Greece. pygmalionkaratzas.com/villaelxisparos

Kuma, Kengo. kkaa.co.jp/works/architecture/watercherry/

Larsens, Henning. 2010. Ny Carlsberg Glyptotek. henninglarsen.com

Lyle, John T. 1994. *Regenerative Design for Sustainable Development.* New York: John Wiley

McHarg, Ian L. 1971. *Design with Nature.* Garden City, New York: Doubleday/Natural History Press

Merriam-Webster. n d. Flux. In Merriam-Webster.com dictionary. Retrieved 9 Jan, 2022

Mosconi, Léa. 2016. En prise avec les éléments (Welcoming the climate): Magney house, Cap de Bingle, Australie, 1984– Glenn Murcutt. *Architecture d'aujourd'hui* 411(Mar): 54–59

OZ.E.Tecture [nd] Magney House Bingie Point. ozetecture.org/

Pearson, Clifford A. 1994. For the Birds: House on Turtle Creek, Dallas, Texas, Antoine Predock, Architect. *Architectural Record* 182(4): 76–83

Plummer, Henry. 2012. *Nordic Light: Modern Scandinavian Architecture*, London: Thames + Hudson, 92–95

Predock, Antoine. 1998. *Turtle Creek House: Antoine Predock.* New York: Monacelli Press

Upstill, Colin. 1979. Light Caustics from Rippling Water. *Proceedings of the Royal Society A: Mathematical, Physical and Engineering Sciences* 365(720): 95–104

Ying, Kok Xuan, Liew Cherng Qing, Lim Woo Leon, Lu Chiao Er, Michelle Wong Sook Yin, Phares Phung Chi Meng + Teoh Jun Xiang. 2017. *Water Cherry House* [video], Taylors University Lakeside Campus, School of Architecture, Building & Design, youtube.com/watch?v=QKyp1soemVA

158 **Hospital of San Sebastián**

Badajoz, Spain, 1694
Nicolás de Morales Morgado
architect

renovation 2017
José María Sánchez García,
renovation architect

Patches of sun from the bright court roof contrast with the shadows of the arcade, animating the space.

photo Roland Halbe

Contrast Schemas

C1 Thermic Hues

C2 Haptic Condition

C3 Scintillating Sun

C3 Water You Can Touch

C4 Engage the Rain

C4 Inhabited Periphery

C4 Lightrooms

C4 Tempered Pathway

C5 Thermal Enclave

C6

The human nervous system responds more strongly to changes in the environment than to steady–state conditions. Erwine (2017) frames the sensory situation as, "We experience everything in relation to a larger context. If the whole world is blue, then color becomes meaningless. Everywhere we look, smell, hear or feel, we perceive these experiences against a contrasting field." When contrasting climatic polarities exist together, in events such as watching a summer thunderstorm under a deep porch or warming by a fire in an outdoor room, contrast *is* the context.

People regularly experience one polarity in the context of an awareness of its opposite. In *The Good House: contrast as a design tool* (1990), Max Jacobsen and his colleagues, all architects, argue that six interrelated contrast dimensions are characteristic of the ideal good house. In addition, they propose that each contrasting elements pair is linked by a transitional space or *joint*, which is itself an architectural element, in the case of a door, portico, gate, hall or balcony. The linking can be momentary, perhaps a special doorway, or a place to linger, such as a porch that links inside and outside. Finally, they suggest that these contrasts and transitions should occur at all scales, from the site to the detail—in this book's system, from Level 1 Materials to Level 6 Whole Buildings.

The design schemas in this section identify how buildings can be shaped to forward perennial patterns of contrasting environmental conditions that engender rich human experiences, such as delight, beauty, affection, calm and a sense of refuge. C1 Thermic Hues addresses thermal associations of warm and cool colors. Two schemas, C2 Haptic Connection and C3 Water You Can Touch, forward the momentary direct body contact with materials and their thermal qualities. C3 Scintillating Sun and C4 Lightrooms focus on the aesthetics and social dimensions of luminous distribution. C4 Engage the Rain suggests ways to be present with drizzles and downpours without actually getting wet, while three schemas, C4 Inhabited Periphery, C4 Tempered Pathway, and C5 Thermal Enclave purvey patterns of immersive thermal environmental contrasts at the larger scales.

The designer's challenge with contrast schemas is to combine multiple reinforcing contrasts for greater effect and to intervene in their intensity by creating transitional linking and filtering elements. Another complex design challenge is to orchestrate at the right moments the contrasts that are pleasant. A strong contrast of light and shadow can be pleasant when it animates the room during a time of relaxed activity, as in a lunchroom during the noon hour. Yet, the same pattern can be distracting or stressful if it falls on a critical visual task, for instance reading fine print or working on a computer screen.

Six contrast dimensions

adapted Jacobsen et al. 1990

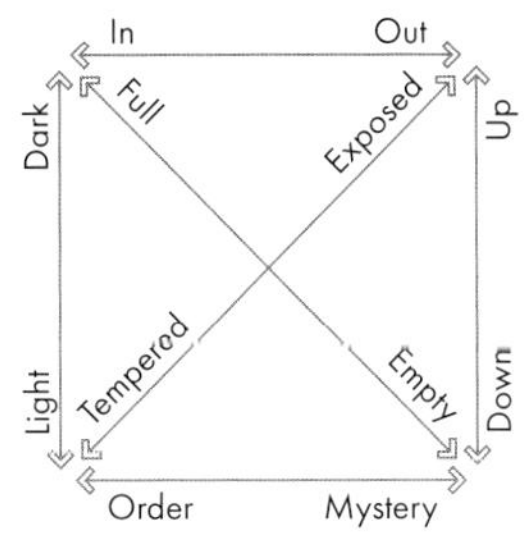

C1

Thermic Hues

employs warm or cool colors to reinforce multi-sensory appreciation and emotional response.

160 **New York Times Building Lobby Garden**

New York City, New York, 2003
HMWhite, landscape architects
Cornelia Oberlander Architects
Renzo Piano Building Workshop + FXFowle Architects

The warm-hued interior contrasts with the cool indirect daylight from winter snows in the courtyard.

photo Scott Norsworthy

deep amid hoarfrost
distant fires illumine snow
i remember warmth

Red hot, ice blue, golden sun, sea-foam green, fiery orange, forest green—even the names that we use for many colors evoke an inner thermal association. Some colors remind us of the sun or fire and connote warmth. Others suggest coolness, reminding us of water, or shade or the evening sky after sunset. Color attributes, emotions and arousal states are all connected, yet hue is more psychologically than physiologically associative with temperature. Even so, inhabitants feel the totality of a multi-sensory atmosphere, thus *thermic hues* comprise an emotional palette. Surface colors can align with the ambiance of human activities, while color variances, along with their thermal intimations, can reinforce the spatial order of zones, define rooms or mark transitions between adjacent spaces. A building's complexion helps visually distinguish and signify contrasting thermal differentiation. Warmer reds, oranges and yellows suggest a place of relative warmth, especially contrasted with a cooler ambient context. Cool blue, green and purple can indicate relative coolness and relief on a hot summer day.

Casa Gilardi

Mexico City, 1976
Luis Barragán, architect

Bright warm daytime colors in the hall contrast with cool blue of the dining room pool to amplify both the apparent spatial depth of the journey and the sense of coolness on arrival.

photo Flavio Coddou

New York Times Building offers a lobby with bold shades of red and marigold yellow, warmly lighted with oak flooring that promises relief from the cold exterior blanketed in snow. Warm shelter is reinforced by the color palette providing a perceptual contrast with the coldness outdoors remembered, yet not felt directly. Summer reveals a lush, verdant green fern and sedge garden with paper birches of the Hudson River Valley woodlands, a visual association to coolness against the muggy New York heat (ArchDaily 2011; Architect 2013; AV 2017). Color contrast is associated with a shift in atmosphere, the serene courtyard an evocative counterpoint to the bustling energy of Times Square. The view through the transparent ground floor to the garden remains open from the street.

Casa Gilardi, Barragán's final design, uses deep, sumptuous color, beautifully associated with thermal experience. "The corridor (with its yellow light) prepares the voyage through the house to arrive at an important space, a dining room with a pool. Suddenly, from the pool a magenta wall cuts the water and almost touches the ceiling. The wall gives a sense to the space, makes it magic, creates tension over the space. From the ceiling a light well bathes that wall, emphasizing its role." (Underwood 1991). The painted glass and hall window surrounds illuminate the space with the bright yellow of sunshine even on cloudy days, while the blue increases depth (Pauly 2002).

Thermic Hues

162 left
Heatmap of hue-emotion association

Darker cells symbolize higher percentage of participants endorsing the color-emotion association.

Jonauskaite et al. 2020

right
Emotional arousal from color

Brighter and more saturated colors are associated with higher levels of emotional arousal.

adapted from
Wilms + Oberfeld 2018

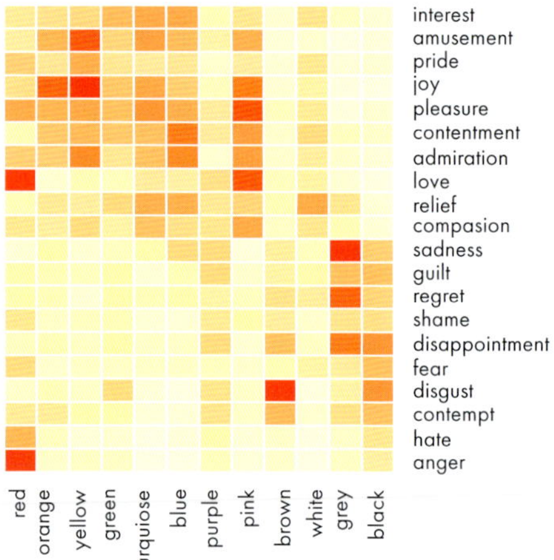

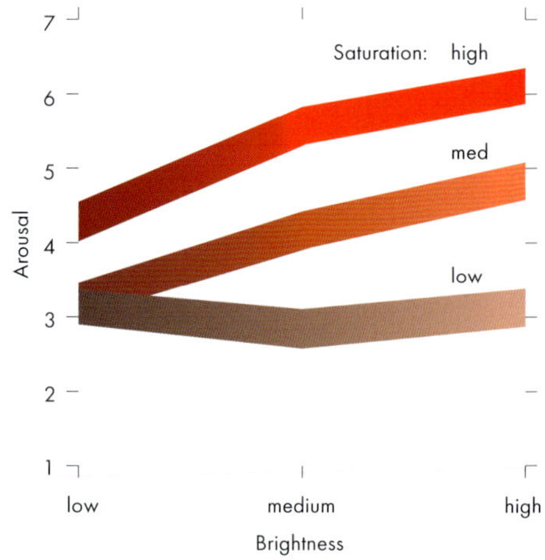

Supporting Evidence

Decades of research have tried to link color attributes to physiological and emotional response, behavior, and cognitive performance. The literature is replete with a mix of substantiated theories and questionable claims, making it sometimes difficult to differentiate. We present a few that seem most valid and useful for the profession.

Three color attributes include *hue,* as the term commonly used for the basic color name (red, green, blue etc) as determined by its wavelengths in the visible spectrum; *saturation,* for how pure a color is (from gray tones to vivid, based on how much white is added), also known as *chroma;* and *brightness,* which describes relative darkness or lightness. All three elements have been studied for their potential thermal response.
Heatmap of hue-emotion association, from Jonauskaite and team's (2020) studies of color and affective response, shows examples of positive associated emotions, such as red-love, yellow-joy, blue-contentment, pink-pleasure.
Emotional arousal from color illustrates a stronger and more universal trend: saturated and brighter colors tend to be energizing (higher emotional *arousal*), while less saturated and lower brightness colors are more relaxing to view (Wilms + Oberfel d 2018; Valdez + Mehrabian 1994; Suk + Irtel 2010). Similar patterns were found for *valence* (degree of pleasantness), although with a smaller difference between medium and high saturation.
Physiological response studies centered on effects of hue have been mixed, showing heightened cortisol in red (vs blue) rooms on one occasion, and lowered heart rate in red rooms on another (Mikellides 2017).
Hue-heat hypothesis states that people will subjectively feel warmer in environments with colors toward the red end of the spectrum, and cooler with colors toward the blue end. While hues are often characterized as warm or cool, there is no clear consensus about the relationship between color and biophysical thermal response. Related

research is distinguished by how color is created in the environment, such as painted surfaces, colored daylight from tinted or spectrally selective glass or colored electric lighting. Literature reviews suggest that colored daylight is more likely to have a measurable effect on *psychological perception* than the color of objects or architectural surfaces, but neither affect *physiological* response (Chinazzo et al. 2018). Thermal perception was warmer in a red-colored cubicle than a blue-colored one (Hettiarachchi + de Silva 2015). Behaviorally, people held a cold and hot beverage longer in warm-colored and cool-colored rooms, respectively (Ziat et al. 2016), which relates to C2 Haptic Connection. When given personal control, occupants adjusted their desired temperature about 0.4°C (1.3°F) lower in red-colored rooms as in blue rooms (Fanger et al. 1977).

Performance effects of color are mixed. In one example, performance for complicated tasks was higher in a blue room compared to a red room of the same saturation level. Conversely, performance for easy tasks was higher in the red room. These results suggested that blue is a more calming or less stimulating color and may have allowed people to focus more (Stone 2003). Performance completing problem-solving and proofreading tasks was better in a soft orange-colored office compared to a gray office (Öztürk Gül et al. 2012).

Design Guidelines

Color can be a powerful design element when selected intentionally to achieve particular effects for an audience. Vary brightness and saturation among spaces for neurodiversity and options. Use color to psychologically offset climatic extremes. Leverage cultural associations.

Fit brightness and saturation to effect. Employ lighter, less-saturated colors in spaces for relaxation, respite, or focus. Use bright, highly-saturated colors to create excitement, spark creativity or encourage social interactions. To provide for neurodiversity and accessibility, vary saturation and give occupants options, as some find brightly-colored spaces overstimulating and unpleasant, even if highly preferred by others. Conversely, neutral-colored spaces feel monotonous to some, but provide valuable stimulation refuge for others (Sargent 2019).

Associate color with seasonal or climatic context and a desired thermal experience. Prioritize warm colors for predominantly cool climates and cool colors for predominantly warm climates. For mixed climates, create warm and cool zones for variety, and use colors to support each atmosphere.

Tailor associations to culture, as hues have different cultural or regional connotations (Aslam 2006) and cannot necessarily be universally relied on to affect behavior or mood in the same way. However, local trends can be significant. Leverage cultural color associations to engender feeling safe, interesting, happy or relaxing (Ou et al. 2004). In general, people prefer colors linked to things they like, such as blue skies and water bodies, and avoid color references to what they shun, such as the browns of dirt and decay (Palmer + Schloss 2010).

Help build C2 Haptic Connection, where the tactile sense can supplement the visual, by using hard, conductive materials for coolness and soft, insulative materials for warmth, and N2 Authentic Matters.

C2

Haptic Connection

highlights pleasure moments from occupants touching materials that thermally contrast with the body.

164 **Säynätsalo Town Hall**

Säynätsalo, Finland, 1952
Alvar Aalto, architect

Brick benches are warmed by hydronic heaters beneath, creating a direct heating of the body in contrast with the cooler windowpane: a warm seat and cooler upper body.

photo Tero Takalo-Eskola
Terotemedia

a warm brumal hearth
a cool rail in canicule
delighted the hand

Wrapping cold hands around a hot cup of coffee or tea is a familiar ritual, a fleeting moment of thermal pleasure that both precedes and accompanies the internal warmth of the beverage. Designers can create similar experiences in buildings. The secret is in the skin, the body's largest sensory organ, mediating between person and world. "Skin reads the texture, weight, density and temperature of matter," Pallasmaa (2012) writes in *The Eyes of the Skin*. While haptic connections include a variety of tactile sensations, this schema focuses on how well-planned furniture and the right materials for contact components create perceived thermal contrast and bring pleasure when touched. This delight arises from the experience of heat flow by body contact, an example of *alliesthesia* when body parts are warmed or cooled in contrast to ambient conditions. More insulative materials that resist heat flow, like wood or fabric, feel warmer than more conductive materials that are cooler than skin temperature, such as stone or metals. The opposite is true for heated materials.

left
Villa Mairea door handle

Noormarkku, Finland, 1952
Alvar Aalto, architect

Textured leather-wrapped door handle feels warm to the touch, as it conducts little heat in a cold climate.

photo Emmi Pullinen
Alvar Aalto Foundation

right
Museu Brasileiro da Escultura (MuBE) handrail

São Paulo, Brazil, 1995
Paulo Mendes da Rocha, architect

Cool conductive smoothness of a metal handrail offers momentary relief in a warm climate, encouraging lingering contact along the path.

photo Paul Clemence

Säynätsalo Town Hall has long, highly glazed hallways that by themselves might feel chilly in a climate with cool summers and cold winters (Weston 1993; Fiederer 2002; Erwine 2017). To counteract the cold radiant heat sink effect of the large glazing, buoyant warm air rises up from hydronic radiators below the window seats and through slits in the brick bench at the base of the windows. The brick then becomes a warmed thermal mass seat providing direct conductive body contact and thermal delight in a radiantly asymmetric space. Archival drawings show the architect's intent noted as "aukko ilman kiertoa varten" (opening for air circulation).

Villa Mairea's library door handle in cold climate Finland is made of brass wrapped in leather to make the touch warmer (Pallasmaa 1998; Gullichsen + Kinnunen 2009). It is typical of Aalto's exquisite attention to detail and sensuous tactile experiences. Pallasmaa (1996) notes, "The door handle is the handshake of the building", a recognition of the important but often unappreciated role of what is often one's first haptic experience in buildings. In addition to the pleasing sense of texture, the material of the door handle can offer a thermal experience as well. Museu Brasileiro de Escultura's handrail offers a contrast to the Finnish response. On a hot day, touching highly conductive metal handrails provides a delightful burst of cooling alliesthesia (Pisani et al. 2015; Landon 2013).

166 **Body thermal sensitivity mapping**

This study's 310 sensor points on a person is the densest microscale thermal sensitivity testing to date.

adapted from Luo et al. 2019

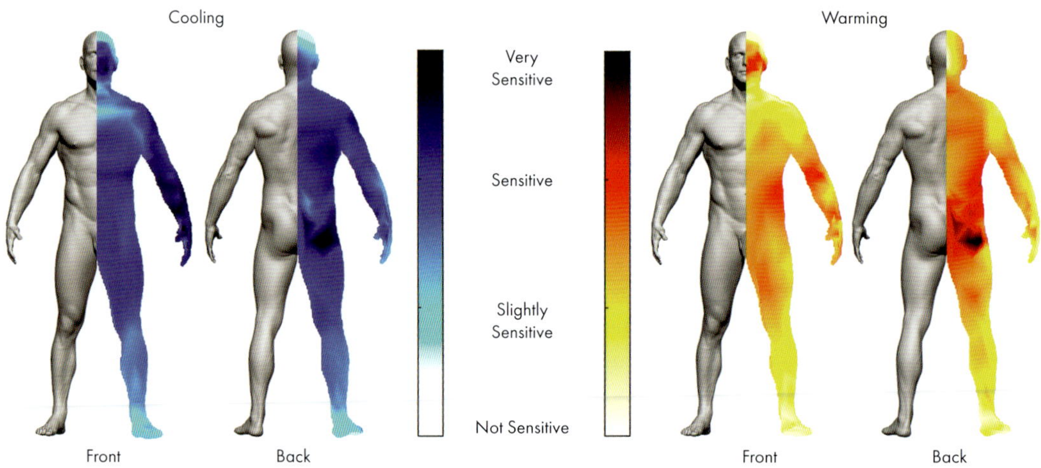

Supporting Evidence

The non-uniform and varied sensitivity of warm and cold thermoreceptors, and the influence of their neural firing rates, reveals opportunities for momentary but meaningful hedonic feelings of thermal delight.

Nuanced haptic pleasure. Thermoreceptors are part of the somatosensory system of sensory neurons and neural pathways that respond to four primary sensation types: heat and cold, texture, pain and movement. They sense heat flow, rather than temperature; as long as a surface is cooler than the skin temperature, it feels cool when touched. The human hand is quite sensitive to the relatively high heat loss rate from warm skin to a highly conductive metal door handle or stair rail. This is pleasurable if the body is already feeling warm, but less so in a cold situation.
Body thermal sensitivity mapping of receptors shows how they vary significantly; thus, haptic experience greatly depends on which body parts touch cool or warm surfaces (Luo et al. 2019). Hands, feet and buttocks are most sensitive to cold, predominantly contributing to whole body cold discomfort. This means that localized heating of these areas in a cold environment will be particularly delightful. In comparison, the face is more sensitive to warm environments. Therefore, when feeling overheated, cooling around the head is most welcome (Arens et al. 2006).
Dynamic experience. While the thermoregulatory system is primarily geared towards keeping one's core temperature constant, emerging studies focus on how the dynamic behaviors of thermoreceptors are responsible for pleasure. While receptors are rapidly adapting, responding quickly to even small changes in temperature, they quickly stop firing as temperature reaches steady-state. Thermal pleasure (alliesthesia) is related to these neural firing rates, which in turn is related to dynamic environmental characteristics (Parkinson et al. 2021).
Bodies are more sensitive to cold than heat because there are about 3.5 times more cold receptors, the receptors are located closer to the skin's surface and they generate more frequent impulses for a similar magnitude of

temperature difference (Hensel 1982). Minimizing haptic cold is facilitated by the relative ease of heating surfaces by mechanical or electrical means, as compared to cooling them. A warm radiant floor is a delightful source of barefoot haptic delight. Even though the physics shows that longwave radiant heat flow from the floor to the whole body has a stronger effect than direct heat conduction through the feet, the cozy feeling is undeniable.

Spatial alliesthesia refers to the thermal pleasure that comes from differences in temperature or heat flow across the skin's surface, especially when these differences are localized on the body, such as sitting on a heated bench or feeling a breeze on the face. Asymmetric differences in conditions between different body parts can offer more sustained pleasurable experiences than when the whole body is warmed or cooled by changes in room air temperature (Zhang et al. 2010; Parkinson et al. 2016, 2017).

Personal comfort systems. Studies of heated and cooled chairs have demonstrated the effectiveness of personally-controlled comfort systems. Controlled lab conditions produced more than 90% thermal satisfaction when room temperatures varied across a wide range of 64–84°F (18–29°C) (Pasut et al. 2015), and field studies with even longer exposure times revealed 96% satisfaction across 71.4–77.5°F (21.9–25.3°C)(Kim et al. 2019).

Design Guidelines

Provide for haptic connections in warm weather with materials that have high conductivity or are cooled actively. In cooler conditions, warm the body contact surfaces actively or with sun, or use low conductivity materials. In either case, intentionally create experiences of thermal contrast for hands, feet and seat.

Design a touchable building by specifying materials with effective conductive, textural and hardness properties to bring moments of attention to both building and experience. Pay attention to door handles (particularly at the entry), push plates, stair railings, drawer pulls, furniture (especially in lobbies) and other places hands touch.

Arrange conductive building elements and furniture for passive conditioning, so users can feel thermal contrast by bodily contact. In winter, locate mass materials where the surfaces are in the sun and become warmer than other elements in the room. Sunny brick, tiled or stone seating that stores solar heat amplifies and prolongs the effect. In summer, keep the same surfaces cool by shading and ventilation, especially at night when they can cool most.

Actively condition seating, such as benches or chairs, with mechanical heating or cooling. Use personal conductive (body contact) heaters, which are twenty times more efficient at comfort than convective (air) heaters (Cohn 2017).

Conceive floor feelings in cool climates and winter spaces by providing either radiant floors, passive solar mass floors or insulating materials like wood and carpets. In hot climates and summer use rooms, where inhabitants sit on or closer to the floor, use thick, massive stone, tile, earthen and concrete materials (especially if softened with earth additives). Provide night ventilation so the mass gets cooled close to the low overnight temperature.

Plan for adaptation when utilizing active conditioning, providing user flexibility and choice with controllable heating or cooling elements to ensure that asymmetric conditions from local heating or cooling create pleasure.

Refine with C1 Thermic Hues, N1 Perceptible Provenance, G2 Adaptive Altitude and N2 Authentic Matters. Help build G3 Existential Datum and N3 Distinguishable Durability.

C3

Scintillating Sun

filters direct light to achieve dynamic, visually complex patterns, evoking a calming and primal Nature moment.

168 **House on the Sand**

Trancoso, Brazil, 2019
studio MK27, architects
Marcio Kogan + Marcio Tanaka

The rustic eucalyptus pergola casts shadows onto open circulation and shaded terraces, generating a "fundamental emotional gradient that harmonizes architecture with nature," says architect Filippo Bricolo (2019).

photo Fernando Guerra | FG+SG

see also R4 Habitat Fringe

magnifying light
in tuning restless shadows
walk in the forest

Behaviors of natural light in and their images remembered can be generative models for daylighting design. The intent may be metaphoric of Nature elsewhere, as in a forest, or a more direct engagement of the similar dynamics interacting with *in-situ* building and natural elements—that is, Nature referenced or Nature here and now. Two factors seem critical: a degree of randomness and complexity in light and shadow patterning, together with foregrounding the dynamic changing light. For example, *dappling* in nature occurs when sunlight filters through a layered tree canopy, a nature encounter appreciated wherever it occurs. Beyond literal dappling, sunlight that is filtered, atomized, fragmented or refracted creates irregular light patches on building surfaces that change with sun position and sky conditions when clouds move, or in the case of vegetation or flexible elements, with wind currents. Such poetic dynamic daylight evokes positive biophilic associations, also bringing to inhabitants' awareness their existence in a unique moment, being witness to dancing Nature arising in pantomime and shadowgram.

Ceremonial Court

Education City, Doha, Qatar, 2010
Arata Isozaki + Assoc, architects

Light-atomizing screens based on the traditional *mashrabiya* cast dynamic sun patches that slowly animate the ambulatory and temper the Qatar heat.

photo Pygmalion Karatzas

House on the Sand on Brazil's Atlantic coast, "expresses the dissolution of architecture into its natural surroundings" (Bricolo 2019). Corridors and entrance halls are open air; five separate single-function volumes sit upon a raised deck under the eucalyptus wood parasol pergola that expands to cover a wrapper of outdoor terraces (housedeco 2021). The architect explains that, "Atmospheric agents, such as sunlight and rain, are filtered by the covering to create suggestive shadows that converse with the shades caused by the foliage of the numerous trees that surround the house" leaving one feeling "immersed in a suspended atmosphere in which shadows and leaves split the sun rays creating a constant and poetic rain of shadows throughout the day" (Bricolo 2019).

Ceremonial Court in Education City shows how perforated architectural skins can create a delightful variegated light effect. The facility hosts graduations, lectures and concerts, with formal and informal amphitheaters. The site's two courtyards are "bounded by a shaded, glass reinforced, concrete panel pergola system on three sides" (Karatzas 2018). The abstracted, open-air screen on walls and ceiling, referencing the traditional *mashrabiya*, combined with the opaque base and structural frames, creates a partially shaded dynamic pattern, the experience of which is animated even by walking along the ramps. Such transitory uses are excellent locations for this schema.

Scintillating Sun

Facade types: interior views and subjective response

left
Interior views of three facades with equal transparency and opaque proportions under two sky conditions. Labels refer to non-uniform distribution of rectangular openings (Irregular), uniform distribution of the same openings (Regular) and venetian blinds (Blinds). Chamilothori et al. 2016

right
Subjective responses for social vs working contexts under clear sky (graphs refer to top row images)

adapted from
Chamilothori et al. 2019

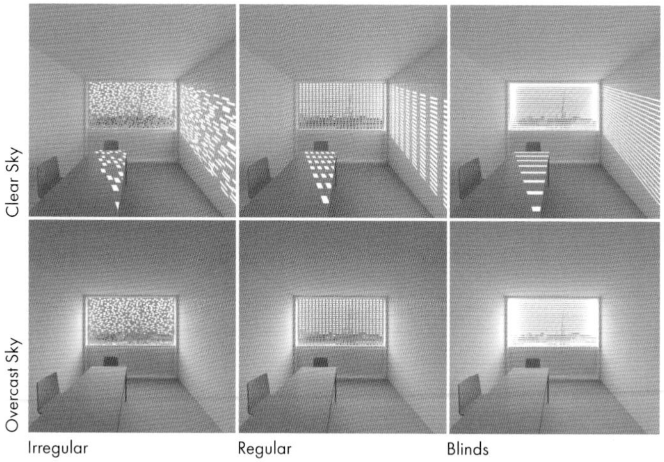

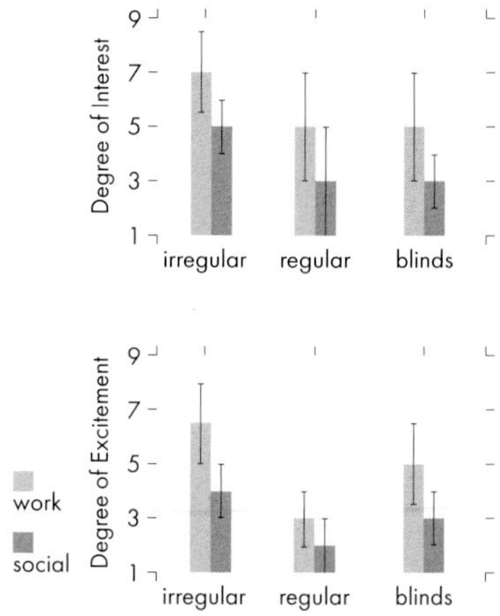

Supporting Evidence

Responses to irregular and fractal light patterns depend on complexity as perceived by the observer. The experience of nature patterns is significantly influenced by the built and social context and by sky condition.

Visual complexity of medium to high fractal dimensions and their projections onto room surfaces were found significantly more visually interesting and visually preferred than a rectangular window or horizontal stripes, such as from shading louvers (Abboushi et al. 2019). Self-similar at multiple scales, fractal patterns are found in clouds and trees. People found more complex light projections and horizontal stripes more exciting. Lower complexity patterns and a simple rectangular opening were judged more relaxing.
Facade types were studied by Chamilothori and team (2016, 2018). In the images, irregular, regular and striped pattens admit the same light, yet people identified the irregular pattern as more interesting and more exciting in social and work contexts. In these virtual reality studies, sky condition was not a significant factor. Expanded studies are shown on the next page. The same researchers (2018) surveyed 80 architects in Switzerland, showing them a different set of complex facades to assess which patterns would make a space feel relatively calm or exciting.
True dappled effect occurs when sunlight filters through layers of tree leaves and complex light and shadow patterns appear on the ground. Small spaces between leaves create pinhole cameras that cast solar disc images onto surfaces (Tufte nd). Light patches are round if intercepted normal to the rays and elliptical if projected onto a surface at an angle, such as horizontal ground or a vertical wall (Minnaert 1995).
Nature associations. Lighting designer Christina Augustesen (2015) describes how humans experience fluctuating dappled or patterned light: "most often it reminds one of being close to nature and origins." This interpretation is common in both research and professional literature.

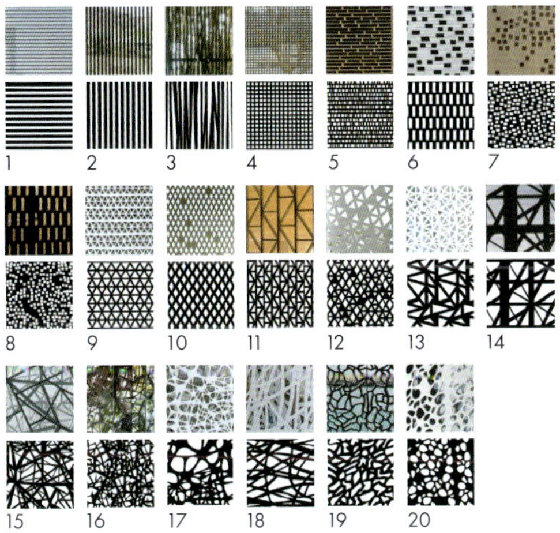

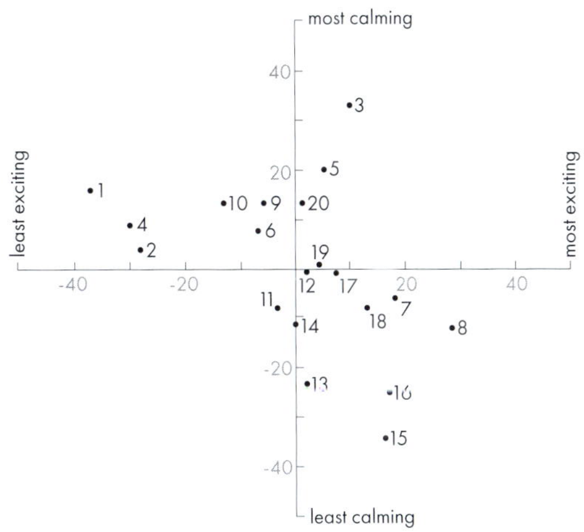

Facade types: architect assessments

left
20 built facades and their abstracted patterns adjusted to 40% perforation for simulation

right
20 patterns assessed for degree of excitement and calmness in a survey of architects

adapted from
Chamilothori et al. 2018

Design Guidelines

Be careful with this schema; it is easy to get wrong. Engage complex and dynamic light and shadow patterns in outdoor spaces and circulation and on building surfaces. Avoid contrasting light on work surfaces. Keep views open and permeable enough for daylighting. Complex or screen-like facades can impede views to the outside.

Moderate complexity. Greater uniformity and temporal regularity for work settings helps avoid contrast on work surfaces or in the field of immediate view when concentration or safety is important. Circulation, lobbies, lunch rooms, terraces and other outdoor rooms may be the best locations for greater complexity.
Preserve views from inside to outside. This suggests careful placement of unobstructed openings dedicated to views, or using the overhead horizontal plane for perforated designs, rather than an entire wall of patterned facade. In contrast, detailed screening has been used for centuries to allow a close-up view out, but deny views inward.
Design for clear sky, which creates a more dappled and dynamic effect, but brings more solar heat gains and high-contrast glare potential. Exterior shading elements during hot periods and parasol roofs seem excellent opportunities for this schema. Perforated building elements will still be experienced under overcast sky, but light cast will be very soft with mostly indistinct patterns.
Ally with plants. Trees overhead add a filtering, dynamic layer to light-piercing roof or wall elements. Overhead pergola vines and vegetated wall screens can stand on their own or become a layer in a constructed composition.
Build mock-ups. Again, this schema is easy to get wrong. Model and test with a physical, full-scale mock up that can be experienced in the real sun. Do not rely on only the designer's perception of a computer simulation.
Refine with R2 Aperture Engagement and R3 Biorhythmic Radiance. Help build G4 Shades of Brilliance, C4 Tempered Pathway and R4 Circadian Space.

C3

Water You Can Touch

encourages hydrotropic behavior and provides instant alliesthesia.

172 ***Silence***

Carlos Place, Connaught Hotel
London, 2011
Tadao Ando + Blair Associates architects

A raised oval pool gives child-height touch access, as water spills over granite edges all around. The still pool alternates with hidden-sourced misting.

photo Peter Berthoud

shaking ocean's hand
from restless seas to dewdrops
water's joying floods

Contact with water creates a readily available physiological and psychological cooling portal, carrying with it some deep cultural and archetypal associations—from Baptism and ablutions to the unknown and unconscious. When air is warm, water brings immediate cooling pleasure from direct touch, reinforced by attendant sights and sounds. Just witnessing water being touched by another seems to evoke vicarious empathetic cooling. Due to its mass, water temperature lags behind that of the ambient air, often by many hours, and with increasing volume, temperature extremes are reduced both day and night in all seasons. Water is highly conductive, so one feels the flow of heat from skin to water rapidly and intensely. An *alliesthesia* example, that is, delight from thermal contrast, water can be touched with the hand in a fountain or with feet dangling in a pool. It is felt on the face from fountain spray or with the whole body immersed in misting or plunging into a pool.

Triton Hotel

Ahungalla, Sri Lanka, 1982
Geoffrey Bawa, architect

In a warm tropical clime, a shallow pool penetrates under cover into the open-air lobby, inviting all manner of aqueous contact while visually dematerializing the ground plane for a designed horizon that is even more aligned to eye level when swimming.

photo Geoffrey Bawa + Lunuganga Trusts

video Sobeautifulsrilanka 2013

Silence water feature surrounds two trees in busy Carlos Place with an elliptical pond only 2-3 cm (1 in) deep. Atomizing fog rings sit beneath metal grates at the base of the preserved London Plane trees and generate hazy mist in fifteen-second intervals for fifteen minutes at the top of the hour (Roe 2019). Inbetween, the water seems placid. With a granite base raised to child access height, the water is easy touched by passers-by of all ages, and spills slowly and elegantly over the edges to disappear before recirculation. At night, underwater glass discs illuminate with LED lights as the atmospheric glow further attracts and mesmerizes. Ando explains his intention as "expressing the dualities that embrace the project" in dual pairs, such as, "silence and dynamism, light and shadow, nature and technology," to "form a square where people can gather and interact" (Ando, 2011).

Triton Hotel public areas are mostly without walls, organized as an axial sequence with views from reflecting pond and porte cochère entry, through the lobby to the partly-covered interpenetrating swimming pool and onward to the ocean. The polished stone floor and water are set at the same elevation, giving the appearance of continuity. Guests can cool their feet at the edge, immerse in the shaded shallows, venture beyond the coconut palms to the open pool or further on to meet the sea (Taylor 1986; Rupert 1983; Jayewardene 1986; Robson 2002).

Water You Can Touch

Water touching alliesthesia

Pleasure from water contact depends on contrast between the initial body state and water's temperature. A *cold body* feels more pleasant touching very warm water, while a *warm body* maximizes thermal pleasantness in contact with cooler water.

adapted from Mower 1976

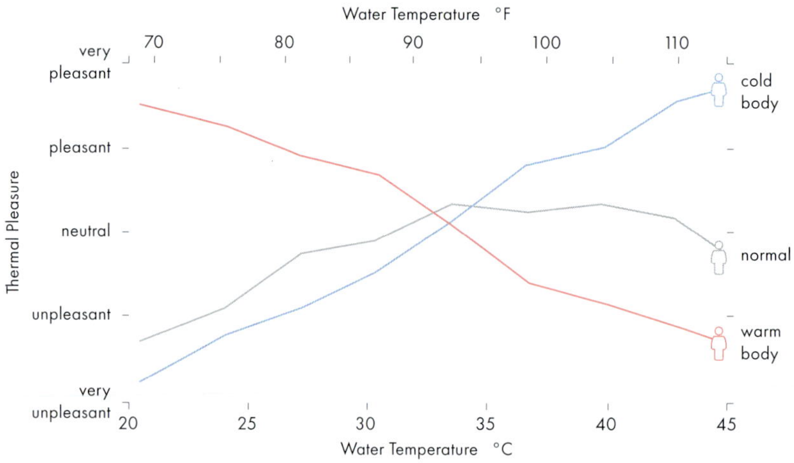

Supporting Evidence

Most studies of water have focused on people's preference for water views and sounds, finding that they are perceived as having restorative and calming effects, and speed up recovery from stress. Limited studies of physical contact with water focus on its effect on thermal pleasure, emotional response and stress reduction.

Water touching alliesthesia research demonstrated that contrast was essential for thermal pleasure. Researchers found that a person starting out feeling neutral can never reach higher levels of thermal pleasure, compared to a warm or cool body touching water of a contrasting temperature (Mower 1976). More recent studies reported that a temporary over-cooling of a small portion of the body when hot, or over-heating when cold, is perceived as highly comfortable even without impacting the body's overall core temperature (Arens et al. 2006).
Environmental Education. Water provides a memory-forming learning context for education about water cycles and sustainable water management practices. Greater water knowledge is associated with water-saving behaviors and alternative methods harvesting rainwater (Dean et al. 2016), especially when accompanied by emotional response (Carmi et al. 2015).
Emotion. Touching water has benefits beyond the immediate thermal experience, amplifying broad positive emotional responses such as pleasure and arousal, particularly when linked to other senses (such as seeing or hearing the water)(Schreuder et al. 2016). A greater sense of calm may be achieved by features that have still, glassy moments while part of an underlying slow circulation or gentle fountaining (Biederman + Vessel 2006).
Stress Reduction. Entering water can lead to significant reductions in physiological and psychological stress indicators (White et al. 2010). Floating relieves stress on muscles and joints. Without immersion, hearing, seeing and especially touching water may induce positive recollections and swimming or floating associations.

Microclimates. A water feature can cool air immediately around it, even if outdoors, creating a cool pool effect. One simulation study of lakes with fountains showed a reduction of up to 6°C (10.8°F) and 2°C (3.6°F) in the surrounding areas (Martins et al. 2016). Thus, touch extends to the wash of cool air that accompanies fountains.

I have overcome impatience, nervousness, haste. I enjoy every single second of these simple moments I spend. Happiness, I think is a simple everyday miracle, like water, and we are not aware of it.

—Nikos Kazantzakis, 1935 Greek novelist and poet, written after his first Japanese bath

Design Guidelines

Design for accessible water in indoor, inbetween and outdoor locations. Provide options for the lesser commitment of hands and feet, for fountain sprays and mists in warm weather, and for full immersion in cool or warm pools, appropriate to the situation. Consider cool plunge pools and hot spas or enlarged bathing for two or more.

Program for pleasure. Set an intention for soothing, quiet respite or for vibrancy and excitement (Hunter et al. 2010). Develop a vision in the brief for both warm and cool seasons.

Choose degree of enclosure among inside, inbetween (like Bawa's Triton pool) and outside (like Ando's *Silence*) options, as addressed in greater depth in C4 Inhabited Periphery. Exposed water indoors undeniably changes a room's atmosphere. For an example with all three enclosure conditions for water, see the Alhambra plan in G6 Engagement and Retreat.

Fit water temperature to climatic context. Induce greater pleasure by supplying the opposite of ambient conditions. An immersed hot-tub bather can delight in a starry frigid night outdoors. A summer desert dweller exhilarates in plunge pool water cooled by the night sky, which can be lower than the air temperature by 20˚F (11˚C).

Provide access options, perhaps with multiple contact points. Water can be a full-body experience, such as immersion in a cool mist, or a more subtle fountain's spray from a few steps away. Design pools and fountains for play and dipping the feet, with shallow feathered edges or a seating edge and descending steps. Tempt with an option for simple finger-brushing under streams, along paths or embedded in handrails. Signal invitations to touch and participate. Insure access for all ages and abilities.

Expand bathing room possibilities for residences beyond the conventional five-foot (1.5 m) tub. Alexander and team (1977) in the Bathing Room pattern recommend a larger bath for two or more with access to an outdoor balcony or walled garden. Bathing becomes centered on regenerative pleasure and supplemented with efficiency utility shower and basin in a separate room.

Public baths are a special case, with their range from *caldarium* to *frigidarium* and inbetween, with precedents from Budapest's thermal baths to Japan's public *sento* bathhouses. See Zumthor's Thermal Vals in Chapter 2.

Add more senses, to increase pleasantness and restoration, including auditory, visual and touch (Pheasant et al. 2010; Alvarsson et al. 2010). Water's visual presence, its movement intensity and sound and scent add to its effect. Fluctuate moving water in more naturalistic ways to create relaxing effects. Nonrhythmic flows achieve pink noise.

Clean and clear water affects attraction to water and, therefore, its possibility for psychological restoration.

Refine with F2 Water as Mirror, F3 Revealed Conveyance and F3 Water-Animated Surfaces. Help build G4 Euphonic Water, F4 Compluvium Shower and C4 Engage the Rain.

C4

Engage the Rain

contraposes wet exposure with dry protection at occupied building edges
to engender pluvial pleasures.

176 **Casa Butantã**

São Paulo, Brazil, 1967
Paulo Mendes da Rocha, architect

The house is completely elevated, deeply protected and thoroughly ventilated, providing living sheltered from rain, engaging moisture, breeze, sounds and nature context.

photo Leonardo Finotti

see also Dai-ichi Yochien Preschool example in Chapter 2

tears descend glass panes
their rooftop march echoes clear
within dry chambers

Water is necessary for life. People dig wells for it, drink it, bathe in it. They collect rain water and even sometimes dance in it when the monsoon relieves drought. Rain connects earth and sky, its path diverted and often obscured by the structures people create to keep it out. This schema aims to supplement the instinct to seek shelter by creating experiences that contrast dry security with rainy exposure, providing excitement and some feeling of risk or a bit of peril, as viewers of lightning and audience for thunder, while simultaneously enabling inhabitants' safety and ability to feel in control. Carefully designed schemes having both protected refuge and options for exposure and rainfall prospect can counter negative connotations of a rainy day and provide access to rain's refreshing pleasure, elemental nature and the often surprising patterns of humid cooler air that accompany showers. Rainstorms encourage everyone to slow down, relax and reflect. The effect seems so calming to many people that relaxation and meditation recordings commonly feature pluvial sounds.

Zuishoji Temple Priests' Quarters

Tokyo, Japan , 2018
Kengo Kuma + Assoc, architects

As rainfall curtains to the central pool, deep eaves shelter courtyard paths, recalling the traditional protected-edge Japanese *engawa* [1] found outside the *shoji* but under the roof.

photo Balázs Bognár

1 *engawa* (or *yen-gawa*): see JAANUS 2001; Morse 1883

Casa Butantã, built for the architect's family without mechanical conditioning, occupies a warm-humid rainy summer climate at the tropics' edge. The challenge was to protect from rain while allowing light and ventilation. The house is lifted from the damp ground on *pilotis*, providing parking and sheltered play space below. Two continuous glazed peripheral living zones, protected by extremely wide overhanging eaves, wrap five inner skylighted bedrooms. Structural beams extend to form the pergola edge. Large ingenious tilting windows rotate awning-like to shield from blowing rain. Air flow is provided throughout with partitions that do not reach the ceiling and louvered shutter doors that can be opened broadly for through-flow (da Rocha et al. 2016; Pisani et al. 2015; Leal 2015).

Zuishoji Temple Priest's Quarters were rebuilt as a U-shaped cloister around a courtyard with a water pool and stage in the center. As the temple is for one of the earliest Zen schools brought to Japan, its deep eaves are derived from features of traditional Chinese temple architecture. Joists of the pitched roof extend beyond the walls of the halls, forming a continuous sheltering overhang along the whole perimeter path. A multi-purpose hall opens by large sliding glass doors to connect rear garden hall and court, providing the opportunity to be present with the frequent rain events in Tokyo's long hot-humid monsoon-influenced summer season (Futagawa 2017; AV 2019).

Engage the Rain

178 **Engage rain with protection**

left
Rain porch with outboard columns and extended roof (below) and deeply protected, screened *sleeping porch* (above)

center
Arcade (below) and roofed *gallery* (above), both with direct access from adjacent rooms

right
Window seat with awning window and horizontal exterior shade (below) and *bay window* with horizontal ventilation inlet to admit air without rain (above)

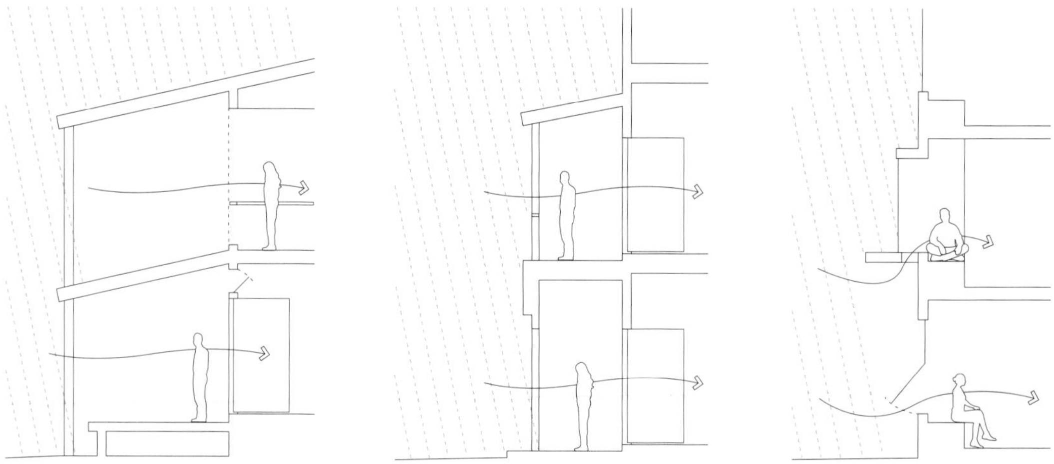

Supporting Evidence

The significance for humans of rain sounds and smells has evolutionary origins. Experiencing the rain provides numerous health and relaxation benefits. Rain brings multiple associations and encourages contemplation.

Scent. The sweet, earthy smell of rain comes from a blend of oils that accumulate in dry rocks and soil and are released into the air during rain; these combine with *geosmin*—a chemical produced by soil-dwelling bacteria. Humans can smell geosmin at concentrations as low as 5 parts per trillion (Polak + Provasi 1992). One argument for instinctual affection for rain scent is that early humans relied on rainy weather for survival. Social anthropologist Diana Young (2005) hypothesizes that rain smell pleasure is anchored in collective memory and associated with expectations for plant growth and its links to grazing game.
Meanings. Rain scent exemplifies *cultural synesthesia*, where populations share cross-sensory associations among perceptions and larger meanings. Rain can be celebrated as "a cleansing element, a climate control or ecological balance element, a visually refreshing element, a spiritual element" or even "a nourishing element of refreshment" (Krenz 2008). Psychotherapist and Columbia University Professor Laurel Steinberg notes that "Stormy weather reminds people that the world is made up of forces bigger than they are, which makes their woes pale in comparison." (Keppler 2017)
Well-being benefits. Rain protection offers refuge, which reduces stress, irritability and perceived vulnerability, while improving concentration, attention and safety perception (Browning et al. 2014). Rain features in relaxation recordings because its sounds result in the brain processing it as calming and non-threatening (Mendez 2019). Rain's *pink noise* mixes high and low frequencies that sound more natural than *white noise*. It can reduce brain wave complexity and improve sleep quality (Zhou et al. 2012).

Design Guidelines

The essence of this schema is to create an intentional contrast between enclosure and exposure, providing just enough sense of *peril*—to hear and see the rain and feel its effects on the air, while offering inhabitants an affective range from edgy to cozy and snug.

Engage rain with protection, in-between space options, are shown in the left and center diagrams. A *rain porch* (left-below), or a protected courtyard edge under an *arcade* (center-below), provides a place of contrasts where one is exposed to the multi-sensory stimuli of rain while remaining under the safe, dry shelter of a deep roof, as in the Zuishoji Temple. Similarly, a covered *gallery* (center-above) provides continuous engagement opportunity on upper floors. Design these spaces deep enough to sit closer or further from the edge of contrast to be able to feel a splash or mist or to retreat and sit against a protected back wall in full dryness. Deep protection and a sense of safety is even more critical for a *sleeping porch* (left-above), usually insect-screened, common in many warm summer climates before air-conditioning.

Engage rain with protection, indoor space options, are shown in the right diagram. The key to engaging the rain from indoors is the ability to ventilate and admit sound without admitting rain. Like the Casa Butantã, deep overhangs can sometimes be enough. In climates where it rains during warm weather, ventilation needs to be maintained. Often large awning windows next to a *window seat* (right-below), louvered shutters, high transoms under the eaves (left-below), and other variations are employed to keep rain out while allowing people indoors to experience delightful cooling breezes. A *bay window* (right-above) affords the opportunity to bring air through a non-glazed ventilation aperture from below. Sounds travel easily on the air, so almost any ventilation opening also provides access to rain sound, as well as scent, temperature, freshness and humidity.

Provide migration options. The sound of rain seems to be universally pleasing, yet its sounds do vary; the auditory qualities (and the potential to get wet) correlate with the desire to engage or to retreat. Such occupant choices may depend on whether the falling rain is a drizzle, light rain, downpour, thunderstorm or monsoon.

Set rain porch depth at 6–9 ft (2–3 m) or more. Elevate the porch floor above ground level with a sloped roof and deep overhangs that allow variations in how close to or far from the rain a person can locate, provide shelter for driving or blowing rain from an angle, and offer protection for furniture or a porch swing. Provide ample rear wall protection and, possibly full or partial side protection to enhance a refuge feeling.

Linkages. Connect indoor spaces to the rain porches or other in-between spaces though the use of moveable walls or multiple doors and windows to allow user control of exposure to adjacent rooms. Small transparent portions of a sloped roof provide occupants, in addition to daylight, a visual and acoustic animation of the rainfall and runoff.

Variations. Create rain-engaged spaces of different sizes to accommodate a range of social settings, such as solitary contemplation or to serve social seating or dining. Consider a rain-protected sleeping porch.

Refine with N3 Roof Terrain, F3 Revealed Conveyance and C3 Water You Can Touch. Help build C4 Inhabited Periphery and F4 Compluvium Shower.

C4

Inhabited Periphery

links distinct indoor and outdoor conditions by treating the building envelope as a thick occupied zone.

180 **Home for Elderly People**
Santa Casa de la Misericordia health center

Alcácer do Sal, Portugal, 2010
Aires Mateus e Associados architects

In this sculpted monolith with porous periphery, filter-space loggias, engaged and accessed through recessed glass faces that are obscured to avoid sun, create shade, access to breeze and a link to the outside world for limited mobility elders.

photo Fernando Guerra, FG+SG

within and without
the territory between
ambit granted life

Spaces between indoors and outdoors offer dynamic opportunities where occupants can encounter environmental contrasts and transitions of many types. These encounters with Nature's elements are deeply satisfying when occupants experience one polarity in the presence of its opposite—and when they have options for which condition to occupy. Such *in-between rooms* express as many different types (such as balcony, gallery, portico, colonnade, veranda, porch, lanai, conservatory) that are often specific to climate and culture. Peripheral spaces allow users the opportunity to participate in or withdraw from breezes, sun, sounds, smells, and daylight from a relatively protected position. They link in and out, warm and cool, breezy and calm, light and dark, sun and shade, wet and dry, noisy and quiet, private and public. An inhabited periphery is a type of *threshold space* with often ambiguous and complex spatial structure, multiple functions and challenges for the senses. From the inhabited perspective indoors, such peripheral zones serve as *filter space,* typically moderating the incident natural and social forces.

Optical Glass House

Hiroshima, Japan, 2012
Hiroshi Nakamura, architect +
NAP, architects

A sound and thermal buffer glass block wall and opaque side walls offer a filtered range of natural force experiences, along with solitude, although the dwelling enfronts a main traffic artery.

photo Nacasa & Partners Inc.

see also R4 Habitat Fringe

Home for Elderly People offers assisted living in sunny Portugal. The inhabited peripheral zone is intended to express and provide for social life and solitude by forming a thick boundary layer, seeming massive with deep voids, each with a large glazed wall, shaded in wedge-shaped recesses. Residents, often with reduced mobility, prefer time outdoors; each of the 38 rooms on the upper two floors has an individual semi-enclosed balcony with access to the outdoors and a glass balustrade for unobstructed views into shared gardens linked to ambulatory paths and the town. White walls reflect sunlight into the single or double occupancy rooms; in places, the deeper gaps also let light through full-height corridor windows (El Croquis 2011; A+U 2014, 2018; Barac 2011).

Optical Glass House fronts a busy street with cars and trams. Blocking urban sound for tranquility and view for privacy, a two-storey, clear glass block facade bounds a layered garden viewed from all rooms. The living room wall fully opens to extend its space, occupants can engage the outdoors or withdraw. "Filtered light through the garden trees flickers on the living room floor, and a super-lightweight curtain (to further filter light to the indoors) of sputter-coated metal dances in the wind" enabling inhabitants to "enjoy the changing light and city moods, as the day passes, and live in awareness of the changing seasons" (Nakamura 2012; Frearson 2013; Oshima 2012).

Inhabited Periphery

In-between space lexicon

anteroom
atrium
arcade
arbor
balcony
bay window
bower
breezeway
buffer space
canopy
carport
conservatory
courtyard
covered walk
cloister
colonnade
cuisine d'été
dog-trot
engawa
Florida room
foyer
French balcony
gallery
galleria
gazebo
glasshouse
greenhouse
hot house
lanai
loggia
patio
pavilion
pergola
peristyle
piazza
porch
portál
porte-cochère
portico
ramada
sas d'entrée
screened porch
shadow pocket
sleeping porch
solarium
stoa
stoop
sunroom
sun porch
sunspace
summerhouse
veranda
vestibule
window seat
windfang
wintergarden
zone tampon

Supporting Evidence

Humans characteristically occupy architectural and natural edges where contrast maximizes. Sumptuous Nature engagements situate in spatial adjacencies and sequences found at building perimeters.

Center and edge. Lance LaVine (2004) described Kahn's Exeter Library as a dialogue between center and edge, the center representing a "mental abstraction of the changelessness of an idea," while at the perimeter, "order is produced....from an interpretation of nature." Light on the identical walls is a function of orientation and sun position. Study carrels, which are "micro-places" are located next to windows, encouraging patrons to "see the world beyond their individual windows as seasonal vegetation changes color."

Thigmotaxis. Sussman and Hollander (2015) point out that biologists classify humans as *thigmotactic,* that is, as a wall-hugging species, along with other animals from spermatazoa to zebrafish. As an evolutionary inheritance of protection and observing safely, people seek edges, whether in restaurant booths, arriving at a party, navigating an urban arcade or crossing a square. More strictly, *thigmotaxis* refers to human movement and assists with orientation and cognitive spatial mapping, but also applies to interiors, and as we suggest here, to in-between spaces, providing places for Appleton's (1975) hypothesis of *prospect and refuge*.

Social relationships. *A Pattern Language* (Alexander et al. 1977) address the inhabited periphery in several patterns, including Six-Foot Balcony, Gallery Surround and Building Edge. Each intends to connect building occupants and the community, as a zone of social relationships in which "the building and the larger world are intertwined." Periphery spaces connected to interior rooms bring activities to an enlivened perimeter interface with social and natural contexts.

Insideness and outsideness. In *The Good House* (Jacobsen et al. 1990), the architect-authors develop a theory of design based on contrasts and propose that each polarity, such as inside and outside, should be linked with spaces in-between. They point out that more transparent enclosing surfaces create a greater feeling of *outsideness,* while more opaque surfaces generate more feeling of *insideness.*

Design Guidelines

Rather than a thin wall, think of the building's edge as a thick, inhabitable zone that links indoor and outdoor conditions and provides options for occupants to experience the range of environmental and social contrasts.

Type variants for designing in-between spaces. Inhabited periphery spaces can create a *sense of enclosure* (greater feeling of interiority) or a *sense of exposure* (more experience of connection with the outside environment). A recently developed biophilic design vocabulary (Watchman et al. 2022) organized horizontal and vertical adjacencies of three space types: *indoor, semi-enclosed* and *outdoor.* These are intersected to generate type variants that engender different fields of experiential possibility based on spatial context and sequence. Configurations are grouped into seven formal categories: alignment, interposition, boundary, elongation, encasement, closeness or containment.

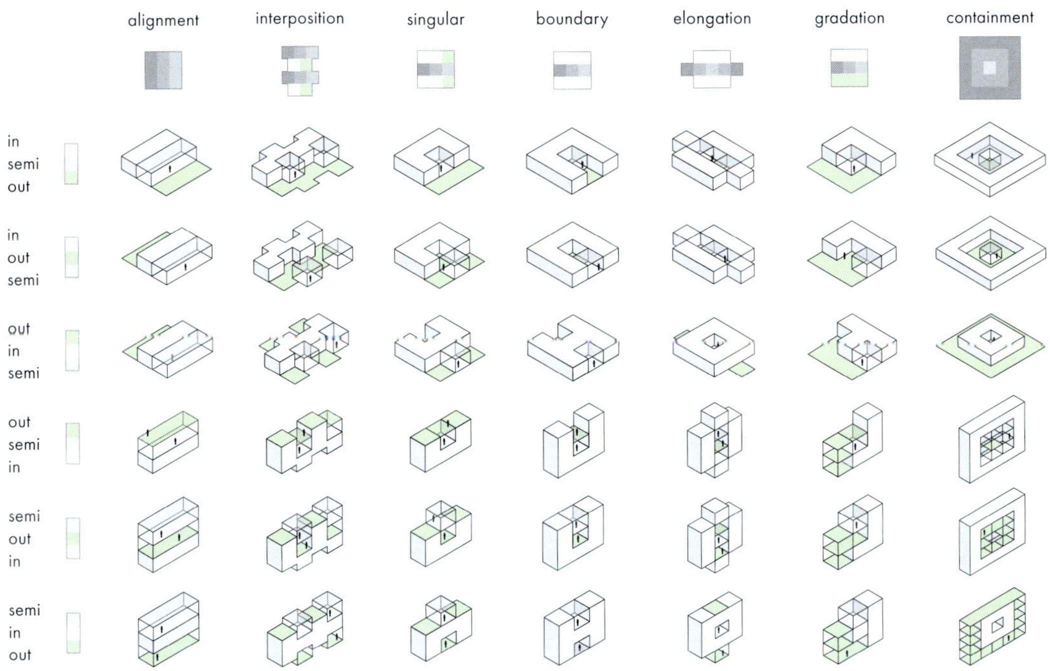

Type variants for designing in-between space

Horizontal and vertical adjacency arrangements among inside (in), semi-enclosed (semi) and outdoor (out) spaces.

based on Watchman et al. 2022

see also Sea Ranch Condo One *saddlebag* space example in G6 Engagement + Retreat

Choose an enclosure variation and scale. The periphery zone may be *outside the envelope*, such as a built-in bench or plinth (common in Indian urban buildings), or *inside the wall*, such as a window seat or bay window alcove (common in overcast sky cities like San Francisco). The inhabited edge may also be expanded from the scale of furniture to the scale of a room between in and out.

Dispose liberally. This schema might be part of an S5 Ingress Transitions—as a portico, ante-room, waiting or reception area—or part of circulation, such as a courtyard arcade. It can also be placed at the edge of classrooms, offices, hotel rooms, living areas and other spaces not part of the building's primary circulation sequence.

Connect periphery space to its indoor companion with multiple windows and doors, so that it is easily accessible and can become an extension of the indoor space. This suggests a strong bias for horizontal connections between indoor and semi-enclosed spaces, rather than vertical adjacencies that require access stairs.

Vary transparency to views and to various natural forces with filtering elements, in addition to providing fully blocking or admitting elements. Filters can be translucent skins, lattice, louvers and vines that supplement the formal degree of enclosure by calibrating preferred degrees of feeling insideness or outsideness.

Refine with C3 Scintillating Sun, C4 Engage the Rain, C4 Tempered Pathway, G4 Shades of Brilliance and R4 Habitat Fringe. Help build R5 Heliotropic Rooms and G5 Pockets of Shadow and N5 Three Realms.

C4

Lightrooms

are delineated by nonuniform brightness and darkness zones that encourage social interaction or private focus.

184 **Liechtenstein State Assembly**

Vaduz, Liechtenstein, 2008
Hansjörg Göritz Studio

A ridge-line skylight caps a steep roof of the assembly house washing light over the warm brick ceiling to center and highlight *res publica.*

photo Jürg Zürcher

drawn by Surya's call
brilliance beckons life to come
convivial room

Light attracts people and invokes affection for places. People rarely congregate in the dark places within buildings. Instead, they are *phototropic*, attracted to light and its instinctively associated feeling of clarity, unhiddenness and safety. Variable light levels non-uniformly distributed in space create allure and hierarchies of importance. To the extent designers give spatial significance an order with built form language, its meaning is amplified by how light reveals and reinforces that order. Pools of light over a kitchen or restaurant table define the space of luminous experience congruent with social space. Paradoxically, similar conditions on a smaller scale impart a sense of individual territory and control. When people gather and share with others, social relationships develop positive affiliations with these social locales. In the same way, when outdoors, people may congregate beneath shade structures or within sunny patches, depending on conditions. Within a context of relative darkness, at night or in the shorter, dimmer days of winter, people tend to congregate where pools of light are provided.

Van Wassenhove House

Sint-Martens-Latem, Belgium, 1974
Juliaan Lampens, architect

A pool of skylight sets a focus on a private study loft above and communal dining place below, reinforcing their domains.

photo Rik Vannevel
Museum Dhondt-Dhaenens

Campens, 2010a
Lampens, et al. 2014, 2020

Liechtenstein State Assembly meets around a circular table under a steeply sloped gable roof of the *High House* (Neitzke 2008; Weckesser 2008). The space, 18 m (59 ft) high, is topped by a linear, deeply-baffled skylight along its ridge. Sand-toned brick materializing the roof form spreads toplight in a soft gradient over textured surfaces, creating a highly centered space. Above the table, a large circular chandelier of 9 m (30 ft) in diameter further defines the democratic light-room for discourse and provides warm downlight, fitted for both directional and diffuse lighting components, combined for good facial recognition (Vaduz nd). Depth of adjacent edges and visitors' gallery are subtly darker. Here, daylight and electric light combine with archetypal form in "pure and meticulous materialization" to help create "an architecture of space and timelessness" (Göritz 2011).

Van Wassenhove House insures adequate light-room contrasts between the bright circular skylight and the gray unfinished concrete ceiling and walls. A light cone casting onto the study loft helps define perceptual boundaries of a room without walls within a room. Warm wooden surfaces seem more so in natural light, adjacent to cooler concrete. Lampens' housing idea was an open column-free interior privileging community while focusing on life together and a shift from contemporary complexity to more basic living (Campens 2010b; Van Den Berghe 2014).

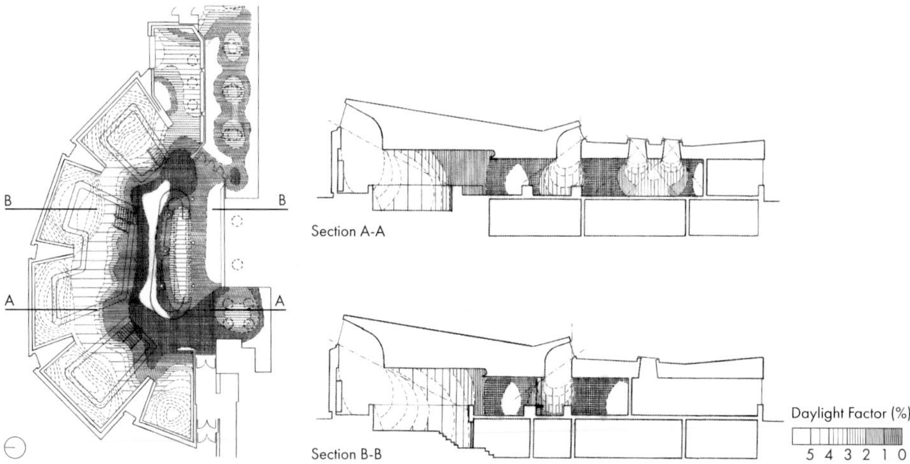

186 **Light zones in Rovaniemi Municipal Library**

Rovaniemi, Finland, 1965
Alvar Aalto, architect

Skylights define distinct light-zones in activity areas while shadow-zones limit and define their edges. Five reading niches are illuminated by skylight scoops. No electric lighting is used in the darker circulation zone inbetween the brightly toplighted circulation desk and the fan-shaped reading room.

analysis + illustrations
Merete Madsen 2004

Supporting Evidence

Whether termed light pools, cones, islands or hotspots, nonuniform light distribution can define activity and space. Based in daylight or electric light, such perceptual light-spaces are always ephemeral. Depending on scale and organization, they can define individual or collective spaces. Light color and relative contrast have a key influence.

Experienced illuminated space can be characterized, among other ways, as: 1. *Coincidence* of light-defined space and physical space borders or 2. *Incongruence* of light-defined space and physical space, typically as discrete zones defined by light qualities set within a larger physical space (Lindh 2012). Both types extend three-dimensionally, and hybrid overlapping is common.

Hotspot as an archetype for electric lighting is defined by Kwan (2010) as "an isolated pool of bright downlight that operates in contrast to its surroundings. Hotspots encourage a pause in movement and collection around or within it." The same phenomena can be attributed to a similar daylight-generated pattern.

Light-zones and shadow-zones were explored by Madsen (2006) as linked design concepts in which light-zones "create areas, places or zones to be in," whereas darkness-zones "create thresholds and transition zones." Light reveals form, space and matter, while shadows conceal and suggest. One does not exist without the other.

Inside and outside perceptions define fundamental distinctions of being within the light pool or viewing it from without. Inside, there is often a sense of security and control; from outside, an attraction towards the light (Krautter + Schielke 2009). Warm-tinted lighting can amplify the sense of insideness and separation from surroundings.

Social effects. People tend to gather in or around a pool of light, as the light influences a different interpretation of physical space, encouraging social discourse. Barazawa + Hanyu (2013) showed that nonuniform lighting influences *prospect and refuge* (Appleton 1975) in rooms and can create a more defined sense of refuge, which is important when people have no interaction in a shared space; it can also form a "sense of unity" for people's conversation by "illumination wrapping them together."

Public and private zones both make use of brightness distinctions. Private settings, being well-known to inhabitants, can have darker zones than less familiar public settings that require more environmental information for occupancy by a wider population (Krautter + Schielke 2009).

Design Guidelines

Vary lighting distribution to create zones of light and surrounding or transitional darkness. Align larger, more central lightrooms with collective uses to encourage social conviviality; employ smaller light zones to define individual territories. When safety allows, increase contrast to sharpen experience-space definition. Warm the light.

Distribute light variably within individual rooms and from room to room. Order lightrooms within physical rooms. Zones within larger rooms are perceived as more private as only the people lighted are participants in the group. At night or on winter afternoons when daylight dims, ambient illuminance can be lower than needed for particular tasks, allowing task lighting or more focused electric light to define the space of work and give individuals the sense of being *in their own space*.

Light social space with pools of more intense light in areas where people gather, on tables for groups, or any place where social interaction is to be encouraged. Consider that gathering as a social pattern may be functional and symbolic, as in the Lichtenstein parliament meeting room, or more conversational and ritualistic, as in a dining table. Sociality may take the form of being together while engaged in individual activities, such as silent reading in a library reading room, as in the bright public daylighted reading zones of Aalto's libraries.

Contrast light pools with darker surroundings or transition areas. Moderate the light-zone and its surrounding ambient condition so the contrast is not too extreme and thus discomforting glare is avoided. However, the sharper the contrast at the edges, the more a light pool will be perceived as a space—as a lightroom defined. In non-residential spaces control transitions more carefully and keep enough illuminance for navigation and a sense of security. Darkness zones may have lower illuminance in familiar private settings.

Create daylight pools primarily by the size and location of apertures, such as with Daylight Apertures and Skylight Wells strategies, and by roof and facade designs, such as employing Daylight Roof and Window Placement strategies (DeKay + Brown 2014).

Supplement daylight zones with electric lighting zones as complimentary patterns. Utilize electric lighting sources at low heights and select controls that support occupant adjustments and that vary patterns or intensity in time, such as to support experiencing the full sequence of sunset and twilight. Bille and Sorensen (2007) find a Danish preference: "The movement of the shadows and inability of the candlelight to fully light up the room are considered more *hyggelig* (cosy)". Warm the light with combined color effects of source, luminaire and surfaces.

Refine with R3 Biorhythmic Radiance and R4 Circadian Space. Help build S5 Light + Dark Procession, S5 Phototropic Catenation and S5 Ingress Transitions.

C4

Tempered Pathway

creates climate-moderating passages that promote year-round walking and connect pedestrians to their surroundings.

 Ayub National Hospital

Dhaka, Bangladesh, 1962
Louis Kahn, architect

A portico stretching the entire building length provides two layers of sun-shading depth for open-air circulation. Light floors and ceilings reflect and diffuse the strong South Asian sun.

photo Cemal Emden

close contained inside
open free-changing outside
walk the middle way

In contrast to the range of conditions within a single room, the activity of walking between rooms or buildings contrasts path conditions with those of origin and destination places. Like many in-between spaces, the greater exposure of outdoor or unconditioned circulation provides more contact with the ambient air and broader views of the landscape, sky and horizon. If life and work require a degree of isolation from the outdoors, moving about can be an opportunity to reconnect, to sense the temperature, breezes and more of the sky than when sedentary indoors. Some outdoor environments require modulation of nature's forces to create enjoyable conditions. Exterior passageways exhibit as various archetypes across the globe, yet maintain similar characteristics. They are partially exposed to the elements, allowing or blocking breezes, sheltering from sun or rain, and admitting mediated daylight—acting as intermediary between indoors and out. Pathways may be freestanding linkages, such as covered walks, or be located adjacent to buildings, as are arcades.

Allen Lambert Galleria

Toronto, Ontario, Canada, 1992
Santiago Calatrava, architect
with Bregman + Hamann

A glass roof five stories above shelters facades and pedestrians in this winter city.

photo Thomas Guignard

360 image, see 360 Cities 2009
video, see Machado 2014

Ayub National Hospital, designed as part of the national capital complex, faces the western sun with a double layer of brick arcades. Recognizing the problem of glare, Kahn (1964) explained in sketch notes, "Glare greatly modified as walls against the light receive light themselves. The light is reflected off the wall to light the wall against light, thereby modifying glare." The outer layer is composed of multistorey circular openings inset with more arches in their upper half, serving as multiple entries and porches. Lateral bracing arches connect to a second layer of circular openings, further protecting the primary building ambulatory. As Ashraf (1994) describes it, "Nature—sun, wind and air—invades a man-made artifact, erodes its envelope, makes it porous, and finally repossesses it" producing "a sense of eternal timeless place unparalleled in modern architecture (McCarter 2005).

Allen Lambert Galleria covers Front Street five stories above, sheltering pedestrians from the cold Toronto weather. Its five-storey freestanding steel vaults connect buildings and streets and support a glazed roof and in some places walls, bringing daylight to adjacent offices and shops, while buffering temperatures and blocking urban winds (Slessor 1994; Kapusta 2000). The arcade was "conceived as a free-standing element between existing buildings. It appears as a new typology for weather-protected precincts" (Calatrava nd).

Tempered Pathway

190 **Tempered pathways**

Warm weather types
A Cool walk
B Trellised path
C Shady arcade

Cool weather types
D Warm walk
E Warm loggia
F Glazed way

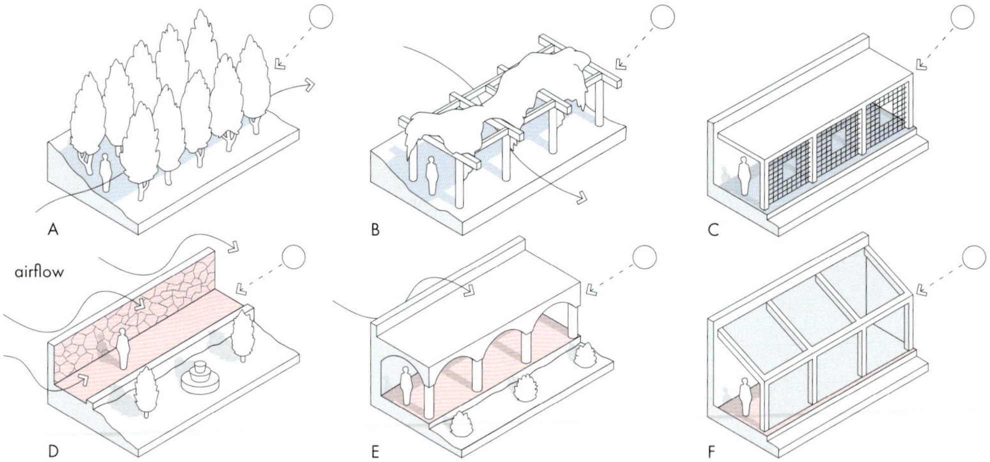

Supporting Evidence

The period of daily and seasonal outdoor comfort and use can be greatly extended and extreme conditions moderated by tempering sun and wind. This promotes the pleasure of walking and greater connections to Nature.

Landscape pathways. In *Garden and Climate*, Chip Sullivan (2002) offers several historical patterns with numerous examples for pathways in gardens and sites. Among them: A *cool walk* (A) creates *an avenue of shade* with closely spaced trees shadowing narrow paths, oriented in the direction of prevailing breezes. When managed it can be a *shady tunnel* with trained plants, which can be trees or hedges, such that no sun reaches the pedestrian. A *trellised path* (B) grows vines on light structures or wires to provide primarily overhead shade and opening to breezes below. It can be attached to or detached from buildings. A *warm walk* (D) of heat-absorbing masonry materials is built into sun-facing terraces. Its tall equator-facing wall enables a solar-heated radiant warmth. A *warm loggia* (E) covers the path with a roof and arcade, closed on the polar side and open to the sunny side. They often include seating facing a garden or courtyard. Extending Sullivan's types, a *shady arcade* (C) shelters from mid-day sun and may be supplemented with vertical screening, while a *glazed way* (F) shields from wind and collects sun.
Hot climate urban passages. Mücahit Zildirim studied ten traditional shady passageways in hot and dry Sanliurfa, Turkey. The streets were typically about 3 m (10 ft) wide with buildings taller than the street width, some covered, and oriented to the breeze. Open-ended passages were cooler than dead-end conditions, covered paths cooler than those open-to-sky, and larger height-to-width ratio configurations (taller buildings) cooler than lower. In summer, temperatures were 1–4°C (2–7°F) cooler than unshaded areas, depending on design.
Spatial diversity. Vasilikou and Nikolopoulou (2020) found that sequences of interconnected urban spaces of high diversity result in a "differentiation of thermal pleasantness" and more "thermally interesting transitions."

Design Guidelines

Provide tempered linkages between buildings; in buildings with thin plans, place circulation at one edge. Where possible, make the links open to the outdoor air, but protected from the extremes of summer sun and winter wind. Design overhead layers primarily to protect while ensuring that vertical layers connect visually.

Balance climatic protection with admitting desired forces, such as light and air to the adjacent indoor space. Awnings, arcades and building step-backs can all reduce winter wind down-wash effects on pedestrians. However, during warm periods such urban air flows can be a comfort asset. In their classic *The American Vitruvius*, Hegemann and Peets (1922) identify the *arcade* and *colonnade* as elegant means to unify a street while allowing individual buildings' their expression on upper stories. Simultaneously, "it consists in the charm and feeling of security enjoyed by the pedestrian" while being "sheltered from the rain and sun without being deprived of fresh air." Daylight reduction to adjacent shops can be addressed by tall arcades or clerestory windows above.

Create outdoor linkages with tempered circulation in sites with building groups, such as educational buildings, university and corporate campuses and downtown areas. Connect the tempered pathways to buildings and to a variety of outdoor rooms, squares and open spaces. Designing one scheme that works in both cool and warm seasons is difficult. Sequences of more sunny/open conditions alternating with more shady/narrow conditions (squares vs streets for example) offer options and a seasonal reversal of where comfort is found. Outdoor circulation provides greater views of sky and landscape; locate paths to enhance this.

Bias in cool climates to block wind; admit sun as a second priority; ideally, do both. In cold places, the paths may be glass-enclosed, with or without conditioning. In cold Anchorage, Alaska, planners recommend sidewalk arcades rather than awnings or canopies because they "avoid obstructing sunlight or views along the existing sidewalk and can provide a more comfortable, sheltered transition space between the indoors and outdoors." They also recommend transparent roofs that allow sunlight to reach the sidewalk (Anchorage Planning Dept 2007). Design awnings to avoid shedding snow and rain drip lines on the sidewalk.

Bias in warm climates to admit breeze and create shade. Keep the vertical dimension open for airflow. Locate circulation along the edges of courts, or along building street edges, especially on the north edges of either (in Northern Hemisphere). Guidelines for designing a layer of Overhead Shades that can protect outdoor spaces and buildings from high sun is addressed in DeKay and Brown (2014). Hot climates suggest opaque overhead shade, roofs with smaller daylight openings or vertical screens for westerly sun. Alternately, locate pathways in narrow north-south oriented spaces or streets between buildings that can provide for shade from low-angle sun.

Cover pedestrian paths with glazing in cool, snowy or rainy climates. Glazed streets, such as in shopping arcade buildings, can be used like atria both for lighting adjacent rooms and for providing light to plants and activities that occur in their climate-buffered space. Potentially, they have the additional advantages of increasing marketability, reducing conductive heat loss and gain in the building (Buffer Zones), providing winter solar heat gain (Sunspaces) and serving as a passive ventilation stack (Stack-Ventilation Rooms)—strategies found in DeKay an Brown (2014).

Refine with C3 Scintillating Sun, G3 Existential Datum, G4 Shades of Brilliance and C4 Inhabited Periphery. Help build G5 Pockets of Shadow, R5 Heliotropic Rooms, S5 Phototropic Catenation and S5 Ingress Transitions.

C5

Thermal Enclave

provides a sub-space with conditions and atmosphere contrasting with the larger ambient space.

192 **William Winslow House**

River Forest, Illinois,1893
Frank Lloyd Wright, architect

Cool climate: An extra-warm alliesthetic reception for the visitor at the end of a cold journey, opposite the formal entry.

photo Jim Tschetter, IC360 Images

there within the field
modest respite, place apart
a niche oasis

Steady-state uniform conditions can create monotony. The opposite is the oasis, or in its building-scale, the *thermal enclave*, a pleasure place distinguished as a room, zone or alcove with conditions purposely warmer or cooler than the adjacent or surrounding areas. The enclave always manifests as a special atmosphere, as a feeling apart. One can retreat on a cool evening to the fireside inglenook with no need to keep the whole building warm. On a snowy day people bask in a sun-warmed window alcove. In both cases, their sense of coziness depends on some enclosure in context of the cooler field. In warm weather, residents of tropical Singapore often air-condition only their sleeping rooms at night while the rest of the home remains naturally ventilated. Similarly, the Southern US dogtrot house provides a breezeway room whose delight is its deep shade enclave and increased air velocity set in a hot-humid ambient climate. Differential spatial configuration shapes the thermal processes at play, constraining volume to contain heat or concentrate breeze toward an occupied spot.

Zachary House

Zachary, Louisiana, 2005
Atkinson Architecture

Hot-humid climate: The shotgun type intersects the dogtrot —a shaded breezeway open on two sides, the coolest place in the environment.

photo Tim Hursley

Winslow House, described by Wright as his first *prairie house*, locates the fireplace inglenook at the edge of the reception hall, opposite the front door, in a slightly narrowed inset alcove. Screened with an arcade for partial enclosure, a lowered ceiling and raised three steps, the fireplace is flanked by cushioned benches. Heat-storing brick wraps on three sides. These elements combine to amplify social, physical and psychological warmth. Imagine the extreme contrast felt by a visitor having just journeyed through the cold Chicago winter and the symbolic welcoming effect of the hearth on immediate theatric display (Hitchcock 1942 ; Secrest 1998; Brooks 2006).

Zachary House in subtropical hot-humid Louisiana locates a covered breezeway between two enclosed rooms, each opening onto it with double doors. As the architect describes, "A removed chimney anchors the house and the *dogtrot* configuration with a central yet exterior breezeway adding emphasis to the cooling of the house." Shade and air movement offering the only relief in such a climate, the Venturi effect increases channeled breeze velocity through the opening, making the void space a cooling enclave. A deck extended on the cross-axis organizes landscape vistas and encourages local migration, while the fireplace paradoxically generates a warm primal attractor within the cooler evening air (Cramer 2000; Richardson 2001; Willoughby 2003; Green 2012).

Thermal Enclave

Organizations for warm and cool enclaves

A Rocky Mtn. Inst. Innovation Ctr.
Basalt, Colorado, 2015, ZGF

B Winslow House
River Forest, Illinois, 1893
Frank Lloyd Wright

C Cloud House
Otis, Oregon, 2012, G Z Brown

D Zachary House
Zachary, Louisiana, 2005
Atkinson Architecture

E Carnegie Inst. for Global Eco.
Stanford, California, 2004, EHDD

F Olnick Spanu House
Garrison, New York, 2008
Alberto Campo Baeza

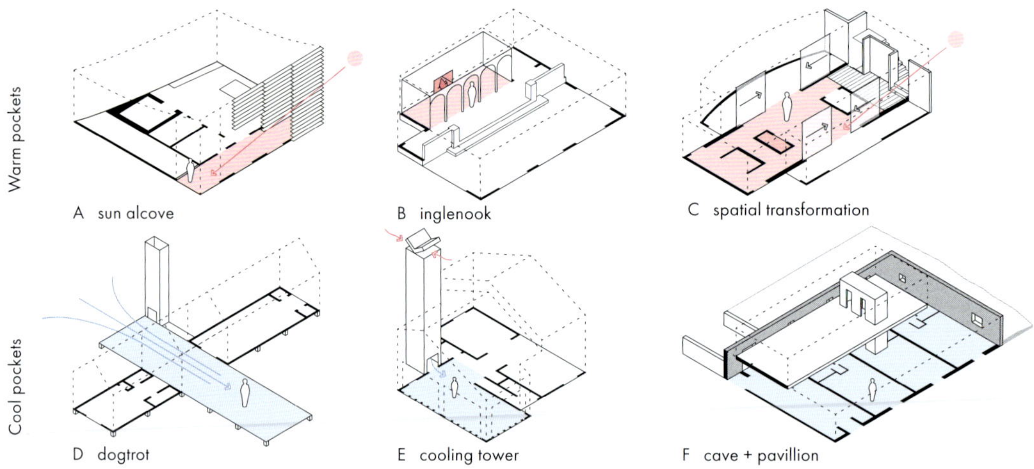

Supporting Evidence

A thermal enclave is an intensified thermal zone with different thermal criteria yielding nonuniform thermal space.

Thermal zoning practice has several approaches. Conventional HVAC zoning organizes areas by activity (internal gains) and orientation, rarely recognizing significantly different experiential criteria for each, estimating loads to provide different supply rates to create uniform conditions. DeKay and Brown (2014) describe in Heating Zones and Cooling Zones strategies how to intentionally vary thermal criteria and conditioning strategies. The conventional approach takes spatial order as given by non-thermal drivers, while the alternative begins with thermal experience, grouping and ordering rooms to use the same strategy at the same time for non-uniform effect. Zonal variations can be significant. A solar sunspace can be 5–30°F (2.8–16.7°C) warmer than adjacent spaces. Sleeping alcove temperatures can be steady while ambient conditions fall by 5–10°F (2.8–5.6°C). The inglenook holds warmed air and adds radiant heat, as described in G4 Incalescent Center. Unconditioned buffer zones will be between indoor and outdoor temperature. Increased air movement raises comfort temperatures by up to 8°F (4.4°C). Air exiting an evaporative cooling tower can be 15–25°F (8.3–13.9°C) cooler than outdoors. Below ground, uninsulated mass walls and floors can be close to cool ground temperature (DeKay and Brown 2014). The *takhtabush* is used in traditional Egyptian architecture to induce breeze by locating an outdoor room between a shaded garden and sunny court, which pulls air from the cool court as warmed air in the sunny court rises (Fathy et al. 1986); the air passes through a screen wall, reducing dust and increasing velocity, as in Hassan Fathy's Akil Sami House (Steele, 1997; ARCHNET, nd). Ahmed (2018) studied two similar Cairo houses on a summer day, finding the takhtabush cooler by 2°C (3.6°F) at night and 6°C (14.4°F) in the afternoon, peaking at 2:30-3:00 pm when air velocity in the takhtabush was 3.6 times that of the other court (1.2 vs 0.34 m/s or 2.7 vs 0.8 mph).

Design Guidelines

Inside an ambient thermal domain, create smaller thermal refuge places with attention to accessing pleasant forces and isolating from unpleasant ones. As people will naturally congregate in the thermal enclaves during more extreme periods, provide comfortable seating in arrangements that reinforce social connections.

Organize for warm enclaves in cool situations. A *sun alcove* (A) warms a smaller space with sun through larger glazing, as at the Rocky Mountain Institute (RMI 2022, Hill 2016, CBE 2018). In the extreme, it can take the form of a passive solar *sunspace* (DeKay + Brown 2014). Farther from the perimeter, the *inglenook* (B), as in the Winslow House, intensifies the zone near a fire or heating stove. The warm pocket requires relative thermal and air movement isolation, as in the Marriage Bed and Bed Alcove from *A Pattern Language* (Alexander et al. 1977), employed to heighten the experience. In cold conditions, the retreat and isolation is from outdoor temperatures, so locations that are more interior and have but one or even no exterior walls make sense. A *spatial transformation* (C), like in the Cloud House, uses large sliding doors to enclose a warmer night inner space. During the day, the doors are open to admit passive solar heating (see Periodic Transformations strategy in DeKay + Brown 2014).
Organize for cool enclaves in warm situations. A *dogtrot,* like in the Zachary House (D), amplifies wind velocity. A passive downdraft evaporative *cooling tower* (E), such as at Carnegie IGE (CBE 2007, 2013; DeKay + Brown 2014, Mixed Mode) provides cool humid air with lower temperature and fastest movement near tower outlets. Full or partial spatial enclosure keeps the cool air from mixing with ambient air (Evaporative Cooling Towers strategy in DeKay + Brown 2014). The cool pocket can be a high-mass cave-like retreat, such as in R4 Radiant Sailing or in the subterrane of N5 Three Realms. The Olnik Spanu House offers a *cave + pavilion* (F), combining a partially below-ground sleeping and lounge level with a glassed daytime living pavilion above (Baeza 2008, Crespi 2009). The cave eschews wind in favor of earth-contact cooling (see Earth Edges in DeKay + Brown 2014) and the *flywheel* capacity of thermal mass. The character of the enclave will then be dimmer, with few windows, and is more enclosed than the ambient order. In either variation it will be a place of migration during the hot periods.
Provide switching elements. Conventionally, interzonal airflow promotes air mixing and even temperature distribution among zones and rooms (O'Brien et al. 2011). However, for this schema, *uneven distribution* is the target, at least sometimes. Therefore any vents, louvers or transoms in internal walls require switching control, whether manually or automatically, allowing the enclave to be isolated when needed. This can be with additional layers of insulation, such as door and curtains, or with Movable Insulation (DeKay + Brown 2014).
Migration. If the enclave is primarily used at night, then it can be thermally open to the larger spaces during the day and more closed at night while surrounding spaces cool more rapidly. Smaller volumes are more easily heated and induce lesser convection currents. This *small space/thick wrapper* strategy can be supplemented by point-source heating, such as an inglenook heating stove, creating a G4 Incalescent Center operated periodically to create a winter evening social space or a warm enclave on a cool morning as a contrast to cooler sleeping spaces.
Engender a quiet, still atmosphere in both warm and cool enclaves as the dispersed activities that occur during less extreme conditions give way to sedentary peace in a place of pleasure and relief.
Refine with G4 Zephyr Spectrum and N5 Three Realms. Help build R6 Cooling Conversions.

Contrast Sources

Introduction

Jacobson, Max, Murray Silverstein + Barbara Winslow. 1990. *The Good House: Contrast as a Design Tool.* Newtown, Connecticut: Taunton Press

C1 Thermic Hues

ArchDaily. 2011. The New York Times Building, Lobby Garden/HM White Site Architects + Cornelia Oberlander Architects. *ArchDaily.* archdaily.com/102398

Architect Magazine. 2013. The New York Times Building, Lobby Garden. *Architect Magazine, 7 Feb.* architectmagazine.com

Arquitectura Viva. 2017. The New York Times Building, Nueva York—Renzo Piano. *Arquitectura Viva.* arquitecturaviva.com/works/edificio-del-new-york-times-2

Aslam, Mubeen M. 2006. Are You Selling the Right Colour? A Cross-cultural Review of Colour as a Marketing Cue. *Journal of Marketing Communications* 12(1): 15–30

Chinazzo, G, Jan Wienold + Marilyne Andersen. 2018. Combined Effects of Daylight Transmitted through Coloured Glazing and Indoor Temperature on Thermal Responses and Overall Comfort. *Building and Environment* 144: 583–97

Fanger, Povl Ole, N O Breum + E Jerkig. 1977. Can Colour and Noise Influence Man's Thermal Comfort? *Ergonomics* 20(1): 11–18

Hettiarachchi, Anishka + Nimal Silva. 2015. Colour Associated Thermal Perception, Manifestation and Contributing Factors with Reference to Red and Blue. 8th FARU Int. Conf., Colombo, Sri Lanka, Dec

Jonauskaite, Domicele, Alejandro Parraga, Michael Quiblier + Christine Mohr. 2020. Feeling Blue or Seeing Red? Similar Patterns of Emotion Associations With Colour Patches and Colour Terms. *i-Perception* 11(1): 2041669520902484

Mikellides, Byron. 2017. Colour Psychology: The Emotional Effects of Colour Perception. *Colour Design (2nd Ed)* 8: 193–214, in J Best, Ed, *Woodhead Publishing Series in Textiles.* Sawston, UK: Woodhead Publishing

Ou, Li-Chen, M Ronnier Luo, Andrée Woodcock + Angela Wright. 2004. A Study of Colour Emotion and Colour Preference. Part I: Colour Emotions for Single Colours. *Color Research + Application* 29(3): 232–40

Öztürk, Elif, Semiha Yilmazer + Sibel Ertez Ural. 2012. The Effects of Achromatic and Chromatic Color Schemes on Participants' Task Performance in and Appraisals of an Office Environment. *Color Research + Application 37*

Palmer, Stephen E + Karen B Schloss. 2010. An Ecological Valence Theory of Human Color Preference. *Proceedings of the National Academy of Sciences* 107(19): 8877–8882

Pauly, Danièle, Luis Barragán + Jérôme Habersetzer. 2008. *Barragán: Space and Shadow, Walls and Colour.* Boston, Massachusetts: Birkhäuser

Sargent, Kay. 2019. Designing for Neurodiversity and Inclusion. *Work Design Magazine,* 6 Dec

Stone, Nancy J. 2003. Environmental View and Color for a Simulated Telemarketing Task. *Journal of Environmental Psychology* 23(1): 63–78

Suk, Hyeon-Jeong + Hans Irtel. 2010. Emotional Response to Color across Media. *Color Research + Application 35(1): 64–77*

Underwood, Max. 1991. Architect of the Intangible. *Americas* 43(4): 6

Valdez, P + A Mehrabian. 1994. Effects of Color on Emotions. *Journal of Experimental Psychology, General* 123(4): 394–409

Wilms, Lisa + Daniel Oberfeld. 2018. Color and Emotion: Effects of Hue, Saturation and Brightness. *Psychological Research* 82(5): 896–914

Ziat, Mounia, Carrie Anne Balcer, Andrew Shirtz + Taylor Rolison. 2016. A Century Later, the Hue-Heat Hypothesis: Does Color Truly Affect Temperature Perception? *Haptics: Perception, Devices, Control, and Applications,* 273–80, in F Bello, et al., Eds, *Lecture Notes in Computer Science.* Cham, Switzerland: Springer Int Pub

C2 Haptic Connection

Arens, Edward A + Hui Zhang. 2006. The Skin's Role in Human Thermoregulation and Comfort, in N Pan + P Gibson, Eds, *Thermal and Moisture Transport in Fibrous Materials*, Woodhead Series in Textiles, 560–602

Arens, Edward, Hui Zhang, Gabe Fierro, Michael Andersen + David Culler. 2019. Occupant Comfort and Behavior: High-Resolution Data from a 6-Month Field Study of Personal Comfort Systems with 37 Real Office Workers. *Building and Environment* 148: 348–60

Cohn, Sebastian A C. 2017. Development of a Personal Heater Efficiency Index, MS Thesis, Dept of Architecture, University of California, Berkeley. escholarship.org/uc/item/4dv241wd

Erwine, Barbara. 2017. *Creating Sensory Spaces: The Architecture of the Invisible.* New York: Routledge

Fiederer, Luke. 2016. AD Classics: Säynätsalo Town Hall/ Alvar Aalto. *ArchDaily*, 9 March. archdaily.com/783392

Gullichsen, Kirsi + Ulla Kinnunen. 2009. *Inside the Villa Mairea: Art, Design, and Interior Architecture.* Jyväskylä: Alvar Aalto Museum + Mairea Foundation

Hensel, Herbert. 1982. *Thermal Sensations and Thermoreceptors in Man.* Springfield, Ill: Thomas

Kim, Joyce, Fred Bauman, Paul Raftery, Edward Arens, Hui Zhang, Gabe Fierro, Michael Andersen, and David Culler. 2019. Occupant Comfort and Behavior: High-Resolution Data from a 6-month Field Study of Personal Comfort Systems with 37 Real Office Workers. *Building and Environment* 148: 348–360

Landon, Robert. 2013. Museu Brasileiro de Escultura (MuBE)/ Paulo Mendes Da Rocha. *ArchDaily.* archdaily.com/444881

Luo, Maohui, Zhe Wang, Hui Zhang, Edward Arens, Davide Filingeri, Ling Jin, Ali Ghahramani, Wenhua Chen, Yingdong He + Binghui Si. 2019. High-Density Thermal Sensitivity Maps of the Human Body. *Building and Environment* 167: 106435

Pallasmaa, Juhani. 2012. *The Eyes of the Skin: Architecture and the Senses.* 3rd ed. London: John Wiley + Sons

Pallasmaa, Juhani. 1999. *Alvar Aalto: Villa Mairea, 1938-39 (2nd ed).* Helsinki, Finland: Alvar Aalto Foundation + Maiera Foundation, Ram Publications + Distributors.

Parkinson, Thomas + Richard de Dear. 2016. Thermal Pleasure in Built Environments: Spatial Alliesthesia From Contact Heating. *Building Research + Information* 44(3): 248–62

Parkinson, Thomas + Richard de Dear. 2017. Thermal Pleasure in Built Environments: Spatial Alliesthesia. *Building Research + Information* 45(3): 320–35

Parkinson, Thomas, Hui Zhang, Ed Arens, Yingdong He, Richard de Dear, John Elson, Alex Parkinson, Clay Maranville + Andrew Wang. 2021. Predicting Thermal Pleasure Experienced in Dynamic Environments from Simulated Cutaneous Thermoreceptor Activity. *Indoor Air* 31(6): 2266–80

Pasut, Wilmer, Hui Zhang, Ed Arens + Yongchao Zhai. 2015. Energy-Efficient Comfort with a Heated/Cooled Chair: Results from Human Subject Tests. *Building and Environment* 84: 10–21

Pisani, Daniele, Leonardo Finotti + Francesco Dal Co. 2015. *Paulo Mendes Da Rocha: Complete Works.* New York: Rizzoli

Weston, Richard. 1993. *Town Hall, Säynätsalo: Alvar Aalto* London: Phaidon

Zhang, Hui, Edward Arens, Charlie Huizenga + Taeyoung Han. 2010. Thermal Sensation and Comfort Models for Non Uniform and Transient Environments, Part III: Whole-Body Sensation and Comfort. *Building and Environment* 45(2): 399–410

Contrast Sources

C3 Scintillating Sun

Abboushi, Belal, Ihab Elzeyadi, Richard Taylor + Margaret Sereno. 2019. Fractals in Architecture: The Visual Interest, Preference, and Mood Response to Projected Fractal Light Patterns in Interior Spaces. *Journal of Environmental Psychology* 61: 57–70

Augustesen, Christina. 2017. *Architecture for the Senses*. The VELUX Group. thedaylightsite.com/architecture-for-the-senses-2/

Bricolo, Filippo. 2019. On the Sand. studiomk27.com.br/sand/

Chamilothori, Kynthia, Jan Wienold + Marilyne Andersen. 2016. Daylight Patterns as a Means to Influence the Spatial Ambience: A Preliminary Study. *3rd International Congress on Ambiances*, Volos, Greece

Chamilothori, Kynthia, Jan Wienold + Marilyne Andersen, eds. 2018. Façade Design and Our Experience of Space: The Joint Impact of Architecture and Daylight on Human Perception and Physiological Responses. *Proceedings of the Light Symposium*

Chamilothori, Kynthia, Giorgia Chinazzo, João Rodrigues, Elise Dan-Glauser, Jan Wienold, + Marilyne Andersen. 2019. Subjective and Physiological Responses to Façade and Sunlight Pattern Geometry in Virtual Reality. *Building and Environment* 150, March: 144–155

HouseDecor. 2021. The House On The Sand By Studio MK27. *HouseDecor*. housetodecor.com

Karatzas, Pygmalion + Arata Isozaki. n.d. Ceremonial Court by Arata Isozaki Architects. *Divisare*. divisare.com/projects/398376

Minnaert, Marcel. 1993. *Light and Color in the Outdoors* (Len Seymour, trans). New York: Springer-Verlag

Tufte, Edward. n.d. Dappled Light. *Edward Tufte Forum*. edwardtufte.com

C3 Water You Can Touch

Alexander, Christopher, Sara Ishikawa + Murray Silverstein. 1977. *A Pattern Language: Towns, Buildings, Construction*. New York: Oxford University Press,#144 Bathing Room, 681–686

Ando, Tadao. 2011. Carlos Place, "*silence*" (Connaught Hotel), *GA Document* 118, Sep: 116–117

Arens, Edward, Hui Zhang + Charlie Huizenga. 2006. Partial and Whole-Body Thermal Sensation and Comfort—Part II: Non-Uniform Environmental Conditions. *Journal of Thermal Biology* 31(1–2):60–66

Biederman, Irving + Edward Vessel. 2006. Perceptual Pleasure and the Brain. *American Scientist* 94(3): 247-253, May–Jun

Carmi, Nurit, Sara Arnon + Nir Orion. 2015. Transforming Environmental Knowledge Into Behavior: The Mediating Role of Environmental Emotions. *Journal of Environmental Education* 46(3):183–201

Dean, Angela J, Kelly S Fielding + Fiona J Newton. 2016. Community Knowledge about Water: Who Has Better Knowledge and Is This Associated with Water-Related Behaviors and Support for Water-Related Policies? *PLoS ONE* 11(7)

GA. 2011. Tadao Ando: Carlos Place "Silence" (Connaught Hotel). *GA Document* 118:116–17. Global Architecture

Hunter, M, S Eickhoff, R Pheasant, M Douglas, G Watts, T Farrow, D Hyland, J Kang, I Wilkinson + K Horoshenkov. 2010. The State of Tranquility: Subjective Perception Is Shaped by Contextual Modulation of Auditory Connectivity. *NeuroImage* 53(2): 611–18

Jayewardene, Shanti. 1986. Bawa: A Contribution to Cultural Regeneration. *Mimar* 19: 47–67, Jan–Mar

Kazantzakis, Nikos. 1964. *Travels in China + Japan* (George C Pappageotes, trans). Oxford, UK: Cassirer

Martins, Tathiane A L, Luc Adolphe, Marion Bonhomme, Frédéric Bonneaud, Serge Faraut, Stéphane Ginestet, Charlotte Michel + William Guyard. 2016. Impact of Urban Cool Island Measures on Outdoor Climate and Pedestrian Comfort: Simulations for a New District of Toulouse, France. *Sustainable Cities and Society* 26: 9–26

Mower, George D. 1976. Perceived Intensity of Peripheral Thermal Stimuli Is Independent of Internal Body Temperature. *Journal of Comparative and Physiological Psychology* 90(12):1152–55

Robson, David. 2002. *Geoffrey Bawa: The Complete Works.* London: Thames + Hudson

Roe, Michelle. 2019. Fountain Fog Effects at Tadao Ando's Masterpiece in London: Koolfog. *Koolfog.Com*

Schreuder, Eliane, Jan van Erp, Alexander Toet + Victor L Kallen. 2016. Emotional Responses to Multisensory Environmental Stimuli: A Conceptual Framework and Literature Review. *SAGE Open* 6(1): 2158244016630591

Scott, Rupert. 1983. Two Bawa: Parliament Building, Sri Lanka, Hotel, Ahungalla, Sri Lanka. *Architectural Review* 173(1035):17–29

Sobeautifulsrilanka. 2013. *The Heritance Ahungalla beach hotel in Sri Lanka* [Video]. youtube.com/watch?v=NZJ7W3pyTKQ

Taylor, Brian Brice. 1986. *Geoffrey Bawa.* Singapore: Mimar/Concept Media

White, Mathew, Amanda Smith, Kelly Humphryes, Sabine Pahl, Deborah Snelling + Michael Depledge. 2010. Blue Space: The Importance of Water for Preference, Affect, and Restorativeness Ratings of Natural and Built Scenes. *Journal of Environmental Psychology* 30(4): 482–93

C4 Engage the Rain

Arquitectura Viva. 2019. Zuishoji Temple, Tokyo - Kengo Kuma. *Arquitectura Viva.* arquitecturaviva.com/works/templo-zuishoji-tokio-3

Browning, William D, Catherine O Ryan + Joseph O Clancy. 2014. *14 Patterns of Biophilic Design: Improving Health + Well-being in the Built Environment.* New York: Terrapin Bright Green

Futagawa, Yoshio. 2017. *GA houses 151: project 2017 (Global Architecture).* Toyko: ADA Edita

JAANUS. 2001. *engawa.* Japanese Architecture and Art Net Users System. aisf.or.jp/~jaanus/deta/e/engawa.htm

Keppler, Nick. 2017. Stormy Weather Is Great For Anxiety. *Vice.* vice.com

Krenz, Jacek. 2008. Rain in Architecture and Urban Design. In L Nyka, Ed, *Water for Urban Strategies, DAAD,* 12–19

Lago, André Corrêa do + Yukio Futagawa. 2016. *Paulo Mendes Da Rocha House. São Paulo, Brazil 1964–66.* Tokyo: ADA Edita

Leal, Ledy Valporto. 2015. Projetada por Mendes da Rocha, casa dos anos 60 foi laboratório modernista. *Universa UOL.* uol.com.br

Mendez, Emily. 2019. in Ginger Wojcik, How the Sound of Rain Can Calm an Anxious Mind, *Healthline,* 26 Dec. Healthline.com

Morse, Edward S. 1883. Ch V, Entrances and Approaches. *Japanese Homes and Their Surroundings.* Cambridge: John Wilson + Son. kellscraft.com/JapaneseHomes

Pisani, Daniele, Leonardo Finotti + Francesco Dal Co. 2015. *Paulo Mendes Da Rocha: Complete Works.* New York: Rizzoli

Polak, Ernest H + Joëlle Provasi. 1992. Odor Sensitivity to Geosmin Enantiomers. *Chemical Senses* 17:23

Contrast Sources

Young, Diana. 2005. The Smell of Greeness: Cultural Synaesthesia in the Western Desert. *Etnofoor* 18(1): 61–77

Zhou, Junhong, Dongdong Liu, Xin Li, Jing Ma, Jue Zhang + Jing Fang. 2012. Pink Noise: Effect on Complexity Synchronization of Brain Activity and Sleep Consolidation. *Journal of Theoretical Biology* 306: 68–72

C4 Inhabited Periphery

A+U. 2014. Houses for Elderly People in Alcácer Do Sal, Portugal, 2010. *A + U: Architecture and Urbanism*, 156–59

Alexander, Christopher, Sara Ishikawa + Murray Silverstein. 1977. *A Pattern Language: Towns, Buildings, Construction.* New York: Oxford University Press; #160 Building Edge, 752–756; #166 Gallery Surround, 777–780; #167 Six-Foot Balcony, 781–784

Appleton, Jay. 1975. *The Experience of Landscape.* New York: Wiley

Barac, Matthew. 2011. Housing for the Elderly, Alcácer Do Sal, Portugal. *Architectural Review* 229(1369): 62–67

El Croquis. 2011. *Aires Mateus: 2002-2011—construir el molde del espacio = building the mould of space.* Madrid: El Croquis Editorial

Frearson, Amy. 2013. Optical Glass House by Hiroshi Nakamura + NAP. *Dezeen*, 27 Jan. dezeen.com/2013/01/27

Jacobson, Max, Murray Silverstein + Barbara Winslow. 1990. *The Good House: Contrast as a Design Tool.* Newtown, Connecticut: Taunton Press

LaVine, Lance A. 2004. *Constructing Ideas.* Dubuque, Iowa: Kendall Hunt Publishing

Nakamura, Hiroshi. 2012. Optical Glass House. *Hiroshi Nakamura + NAP.* nakam.info/en/works/optical-glass-house

Nakamura, Hiroshi + NAP Co, Ltd. 2013. *Optical Glass House*, video. vimeo.com/58181421

Oshima, Ken Tadashi. 2012. Optical Glass House, Hiroshima, Japan. *The Architectural Review* 232(1390): 40–45

Sussman, Ann + Justin B Hollander. 2015. *Cognitive Architecture: Designing for How We Respond to the Built Environment.* New York: Routledge

Watchman, Mélanie, Mark DeKay, Claude M H Demers + André Potvin. 2022. Design Vocabulary and Schemas for Biophilic Experiences in Cold Climate Schools. *Architectural Science Review* 65(2):101–19

C4 Lightrooms

Appleton, Jay. 1975. *The Experience of Landscape.* New York: Wiley

Barazawa, Natsuki + Kazunori Hanyu. 2013. Effects of Nonuniform Lighting on the Evaluation of Spaces: A Comparison Between the Situations With and Without Conversation. *Japanese Psychological Research* 55(3): 273–83

Bille, Mikkel + Tim Flohr Sørensen. 2007. An Anthropology of Luminosity: The Agency of Light. *Journal of Material Culture* 12(3): 263–84

Campens, Angelique. 2010a. *Juliaan Lampens.* Brussels: ASA

Campens, Angelique. 2010b. Juliaan Lampens: A Fundamentalist Vision of Living a Shift of Perception. domusweb.it/en/architecture/2010/06/15/juliaan-lampens.html

DeKay, Mark + G Z Brown. 2014. *Sun, Wind + Light: Architectural Design Strategies*, 3rd ed. Hoboken, New Jersey: Wiley; #66 Daylight Roof, E.177–179; #68 Window Placement, E.182–184; #83 Skylight Wells, E.223; #85 Daylight Apertures, E.227–228

Göritz, Hansjörg. 2011. National Parliament Principality of Liechtenstein. *ArchDaily*, 3 Oct. archdaily.com/62491

Krautter, Martin + Thomas Schielke. 2009. *Light Perspectives, Between Culture and Technology: Light, Space, Perspectives.* Lüdenscheid, Germany: ERCO GmbH/Tim Henrik Maak + Kay Pawlik

Kwan, Joanne Pui Yuk. 2010. *Theory Studies: Archetypal Artificial Lighting Practices in Contemporary Interior Design.* MA Thesis, Ithaca, New York: Cornell University
Lampens, Juliaan, Nobuyuki Yoshida + Asami Naito. 2014. *Feature: Juliaan Lampens.* Tokyo: A+U Pub

Lampens, Juliaan, Gerard Vandenhaute, Paul Vermeulen + Kunstcentrum deSingel. 2020. *Juliaan Lampens 1950–1991* (Simpson, Helen, trans). Antwerp: Vlaams Architectuurinstituut

Lindh, Ulrika Wänström. 2012. *Light Shapes Spaces: Experiences of Distribution of Light and Visual Spatial Boundaries.* PhD Dissertation, HDK–School of Design and Crafts, University of Gothenburg

Madsen, Merete. 2006. Light-Zone(s): As Concept and Tool. *ARCC Journal* 4(1): 50–59

Neitzke, Peter. 2008. Ausdruck und Gebrauch: Landesforum und Landesparlament des Fürstentums Liechtenstein, Vaduz. *Baumeister* 105(5): 56–67

Vaduz, Hochbauamt. n.d. The New Parliament Building for the Principality of Liechtenstein by Licht Kunst Licht. *Architonic.* architonic.com/5100486

Van den Berghe, Jo. 2014. House Van Wassenhove: Sint Martens-Latem, Belgium, 1974. *A + U: Architecture and Urbanism* (4): 60–73

Weckesser, Annette. 2008. Landesparlament in Vaduz, Fürstentum Liechtenstein—Entwurf (Design), Prof. Hansjörg Göritz. *Architektur, Innenarchitektur, Technischer Ausbau* 12:148–155

C4 Tempered Pathway

360 Cities. 2009. Allan Lambert Galleria, Toronto by Udo D. 360cities.net/image/allen-lambert-galleria-toronto-canada
Anchorage Planning Dept. 2007. *Ch 6 Urban Design. Destination Downtown: Anchorage Downtown Comprehensive Plan.* City of Anchorage, Alaska

Ashraf, Kazi K. 1994. in Kahn, Louis I, Yukio Futagawa + Kazi K Ashraf. *Louis I. Kahn, National Capital of Bangladesh, Dhaka, Bangladesh, 1962–83.* Tokyo: ADA Edita
Calatrava, Santiago. n.d. BCE Place: Galleria + Heritage Square/ Toronto 1992. Santiago Calatrava, Architects and Engineers. calatrava.com/projects/bce-place-galleria-heritage-square-toronto.html

DeKay, Mark + G Z Brown. 2014. Sun, Wind + Light, Architectural Design Strategies. 3rd ed. Hoboken, New Jersey: Wiley; #23 Overhead Shades, E.66–67; #29 Buffer Zones, E.83–85; #49 Sunspaces, E.134–136; #53 Stack-Ventilation Rooms, E.145–146

Hegemann, Werner + Elbert Peets. 1922. *The American Vitruvius: An Architect's Handbook of Civic Art.* reprint, A J Plattus ed. New York: The Architectural Book Publishing Co

Kahn, Louis I. 1964. *The Development by Louis I. Kahn of the Design for the Second Capital of Pakistan at Dacca.* Raleigh, North Carolina: School of Design, North Carolina State University

Kapusta, Beth. 2000. Calatrava in Canada. *The Canadian Architect* 45(5): 30–33

Machado, Robert. 2014. *Allen Lambert Galleria* [video]. youtube.com/watch?v=KKuvliRC7LQ

McCarter, Robert. 2005. *Louis I. Kahn.* London: Phaidon

Slessor, Catherine. 1994. Glorious Galleria. *The Architectural Review* 194(1165): 24–30

Sullivan, Chip. 2002. *Garden and Climate.* New York: McGraw-Hill Professional

Vasilikou, Carolina + Marialena Nikolopoulou. 2020. Outdoor Thermal Comfort for Pedestrians in Movement: Thermal Walks in Complex Urban Morphology. *International Journal of Biometeorology* 64: 277–29

C5 Thermal Enclave

Alexander, Christopher, Sara Ishikawa + Murray Silverstein. 1977. *A Pattern Language: Towns, Buildings, Construction.* New York: Oxford University Press, #187 Marriage Bed, 864–865; #188 Bed Alcove, 868–871

ARCHNET. n.d. Akil Sami House, Dashur. *Archnet.* archnet.org/sites/2588

Baeza, Alberto Campo. 2008. Olnik Spanu House, NY. *Alberto Campo Baeza.* campobaeza.com/olnick-spanu-house

Brooks, Allen H. 2006. *The Prairie School.* New York: W W Norton

CBE. 2007. Livable Buildings Award Winner: Global Ecology Research Center, Stanford, CA. *Center for the Built Environment.* University of California, Berkeley. cbe.berkeley.edu/livable-building/global-ecology-research-center/

CBE. 2013. The Carnegie Institute for Global Ecology. Mixed Mode Case Studies and Project Database. *Center for the Built Environment.* University of California, Berkeley. cbe.berkeley.edu/mixedmode

CBE. 2018. Livable Buildings Award Submission: Rocky Mountain Institute (RMI) Innovation Center. *Center for the Built Environment.* University of California, Berkeley. cbe.berkeley.edu/wp-content/uploads/2018/12/Livable-Building-2018-RMI.pdf

Cramer, Ned. 2000. Studio Atkinson: The Zachary House, Zachary, Louisiana. *Architecture* 89(1): 68–73

Crespi, Giovanna. 2009. Alberto Campo Baeza: Casa Olnick Spanu, Garrison, NY. *Casabella* 73(777): 42–49

DeKay, Mark + G Z Brown. 2014. *Sun, Wind + Light: Architectural Design Strategies.* 3rd ed. Hoboken, New Jersey: Wiley; #25 Periodic Transformations, E.74; #26 Cooling Zones, E.76–78; #27 Mixed Mode Building, E.79–80; #28 Heating Zones, E.81–82; #46 Evaporative Cooling Towers, E.126–128; #49 Sunspace, E.134–136; #76 Earth Edges, E.208–210; #89 Movable Insulation, E.235–236

Fathy, Hassan. 1986. *Natural Energy and Vernacular Architecture: Principles and Examples with Reference to Hot Arid Climates.* eds. W Shearer + A A Sultan. Chicago: University of Chicago Press

Green, Penelope. 2012. One Shed Fits All. *The New York Times* Section D:1, 4 Oct (print), 3 Oct (online), nytimes.com

Hill, David. 2016. Inside the Rocky Mountain Institute's New HQ. *Architect* 105(3): 69

Hitchcock, Henry-Russell. 1942. *In the Nature of Materials: The Buildings of Frank Lloyd Wright, 1887–1941*. New York: Da Capo Press

O'Brien, William, Andreas Athienitis + Ted Kesik. 2011. Thermal Zoning and Interzonal Airflow in the Design and Simulation of Solar Houses: A Sensitivity Analysis. *Journal of Building Performance Simulation* 4(3): 239–56

Richardson, Vicky. 2001. *New Vernacular Architecture.* New York: Watson-Guptill

RMI. 2022. Innovation Center Virtual Tour. *Rocky Mountain Institute.* rmi.org/our-work/buildings/scaling-zero-net-carbon/rmi-innovation-center/

Secrest, Meryle. 1998. *Frank Lloyd Wright: A Biography.* Chicago: University of Chicago Press

Steele, James. 1997. *An Architecture for People: The Complete Works of Hassan Fathy*. London, UK: Thames + Hudson

Willoughby, William T. 2003. Between Land and Sky: Reduction in the Work of Stephen Atkinson. *Oz: Journal of the College of Architecture, Planning, and Design* 25 (1 Jan): 22–29, article 5. Manhattan, Kansas: Kansas State University

204 **Hospital of San Sebastián**

Badajoz, Spain, 1694
Nicolás de Morales Morgado
architect

renovation 2017
José María Sánchez García,
renovation architect

Subtle gradients of light from courtyard to arcade and across the vaults.

photo Roland Halbe

Gradient Schemas

G1

G2 Adaptive Altitude

G3 Existential Datum

G4 Incalescent Center

G4 Euphonic Water

G4 Zephyr Spectrum

G4 Shades of Brilliance

G5 Pockets of Shadow

G6 Engagement + Retreat

Both a cool northerly glass expanse and a large sunny southern window can create a thermal asymmetry in plan and add convective currents to a vertical gradient. In apprehending gradients, one becomes aware of being related to the energetic structure of spaces, the seen and unseen forces that envelop the body—and often of the happy opportunity to change that relationship at any time. Social gradients ofttimes emerge as people distribute or concentrate, depending on preferential conditions. In summer, folks may gather in the shade, while in winter they are attracted to the sun and hearth. At such times, the space, its conditions, human experience and social relationships align in subtle yet significant ways that are ephemeral and partly invisible, yet still linger as quiet impressions. For example, the hushed voices and often-silent experience of social closeness on a cold winter evening around the flickering light and glow of a fireplace or wood stove, with its radiant field, is not simply a thermodynamic occasion. The feeling of a warm front and a cool back body adjusting closeness to the fire, is a timeless joy. This evening cool-climate hearth ritual binds people together in space, sharing the thermal gradient of an incalescent center. Such experiential linkages make buildings significant in everyday life.

The design schemas in this section suggest ways to organize and shape architectural elements to produce gradients that elicit sumptuous and stimulating experiences, such as reflection, awareness, sense of place, peacefulness, the pleasure of choice, and sensory delight. G2 Incalescent Center and G6 Engagement + Retreat both address at different scales the spatial implication of human attraction and aversion to environmental conditions. G3 Existential Datum identifies a range of fundamental floor to ground relationships. G4 Shades of Brilliance and G5 Pockets of Shadow offer organizing patterns in response to primordial sun and light forces. In addition to thermal and lighting gradients sensed by the skin and eyes, conditions associated with most of the senses can occur as gradients, such as sound, as developed in G4 Euphonic Water, air velocity in G4 Zephyr Spectrum, scent and humidity.

The designer's challenge with gradient schemas is to offer variety and choice by configuring space such that occupants always have a range of possibilities within which to locate themselves, a small-scale migration opportunity. Historically, building engineers considered the unevenness of most gradients to be problematic. Their thermal standards limit asymmetry. Overhead electric lighting methods strive to create uniformity. In contrast, designers can fashion felt fields with conditional variety, spatially distributed in smooth transitions. Such fields of conditions provide unique affordances and occasions for agency in personal pleasure.

G2

Adaptive Altitude

gives occupants options to adjust body position to the climatic context or room's vertical thermocline.

206 **Yue Library**

Hangzhou, China, 2019
Yi + Mu Design Office, architects
Yi Chen + Muchen Zhang
Beijing Fenghemuchen Space Design, interiors

Many positional body opportunities are possible across multiple levels in zones of vertical thermal-spatial gradient and stratification.

photo Xiangyu Sun

fluxes in moments
small adjustments high to low
miniature joys

This schema is simple and subtle. In rooms without mechanical churning, less dense warm air rises to the ceiling and cooler, denser air falls toward the floor. A natural vertical temperature gradient develops; the air stratifies into a perceptible *thermocline.* Within this gradient a small-scale adaptive potentiality for occupants lies latent. Seemingly prosaic, an incremental lyricism abides. In many places, traditional architecture developed furniture, floor level profiles and spatial section designs that facilitate occupants' adaptation to a heterogeneous indoor weather. In hot climates, seating is often near or directly on the floor where the air is cooler; if the floor is massive, such as with stone, its haptic coolness delights. Furniture in this case can be low or simply cushions on a short platform. In cooler places, such as northern Europe, chairs and beds are taller. In mixed climates and to accommodate individuals anywhere, varied seating height and terraced or tiered floor levels provide options. The extreme version of this schema's pattern can be felt in a sauna's tiers.

Waterside Buddhist Shrine

Tangshan, China, 2017
ARCHSTUDIO, architects

Japanese *zaisu* floor seating provides a felt ground connection and cooler conditions near the floor for the warm-humid summer.

photo Ning Wang

Yue Library is "designed to be a representation of the warmth of life," explain the designers. It is constructed mostly of oak, "a material filled with vitality, whose temperature and touch are quite similar to those of human beings" (ArchDaily 2019; DesignBoom 2019). The 10 m (33 ft) tall central space is divided into multiple levels with stepped seating and mezzanines throughout. Patrons can sit directly on the wood terraces, on movable cushions, upholstered chairs at reading tables or, in places, at counter-height stools. The lower level coffee shop offers conversation and reading at three heights on two tiers. The topographic stepped floor and the incremental seating options allow inhabitants to position themselves to their liking in thermal and social space (Wujie video 2019).

Waterside Buddhist Shrine's tea room projects between two outdoor trees; its glass wall opens fully to the lotus-filled, slow-moving river pool just beyond the gravel surface. In the monsoon-influenced Tangshan climate, summers are long and warm-humid, similar to Japan. Traditional height, low seating cushions paired with Japanese *zaisu* style legless tatami chair backs accommodate pilgrims for tea and nature viewing at the low wooden table. Interior flooring is woven natural fiber over smooth terrazzo with white pebbles outdoors, intended to create "a difference in sense of touch" for patrons close to the ground (Keskeys 2018 video; Metalocus 2017).

Adaptive Altitude

Satisfaction with vertical gradients

Recent research shows that older standards for thermal gradients were too restrictive and that most seated people find acceptable a gradient between head and feet of about 5°C/m (3°F/ft). For the average seated person, that is a temperature difference of about 7°C (12°F) from head to toe.

adapted from Liu et al. 2020

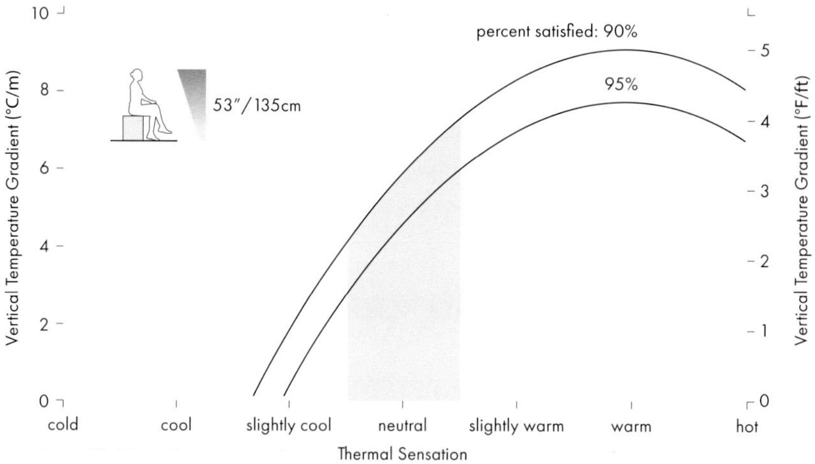

Supporting Evidence

Historic and vernacular examples worldwide demonstrate furniture and design practices using height to respond to climatic conditions. Vertical gradients and stratification occur naturally and can be amplified or reduced. Contrary to early standards, research demonstrates satisfaction with vertical gradients at a relatively wide range (diagram).

Sleeping. Hot-humid Japanese summers call for futons on the floor. In arid Indian regions, rooftop sleeping accesses the cool night sky, water poured over tile floors evaporatively cools, and short portable netted rope *charpoy* beds allow ventilation and cooling from below. In cool climates, antique beds were often tall, even requiring steps to access. The American colonial canopy bed created a raised thermal enclave above the uninsulated wood floor, while cold Norway developed the raised bed alcove combined with insulating curtains.
Sitting. Heschong (1979) notes, "Europeans have the custom of using furniture, chairs and beds, which conveniently raise them above the cold air that accumulates at the floor level. [Indians].....use no such furniture, but sit directly on the floor, where they benefit from the extra coolness held in the ground." Stone floors support the feeling of coolness. Dining can be on low tables or trays set on a carpet. Floor sitting has the feeling of *groundedness*, as Suzuki (1959) writes, "To raise oneself from the ground even by one foot means a detachment, a separation, an abstraction, a going away to the realm of analysis and discrimination. The Oriental way of sitting is to strike roots down to the center of earth and to be conscious of the great source ...." An exception to low warm-weather seating is the social Indian platform swing, and the Southern US porch swing, which generate their own breeze.
Floor warming. Radiant floors generate warmth at the feet. In cooler parts of China people sat and slept directly on heated raised *k'ang* platforms; in Korea, on sophisticated hypocaust *ondol* floors; and Alaska's Aleutian Island residents employed a hypocaust system as early as 1000 BCE (Bean et al. 2010).

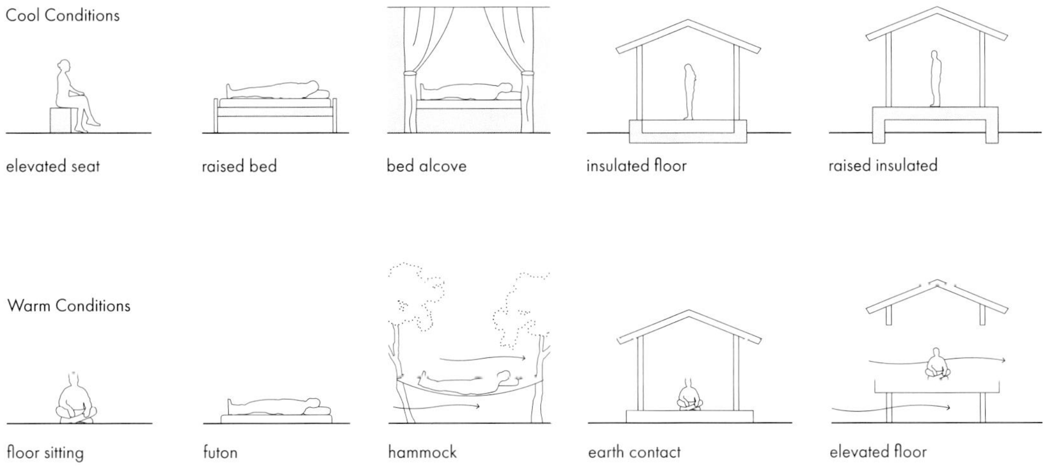

Altitude adjustments in cool vs warm conditions

Cool
Elevated sitting and sleeping; floors insulated from cold earth and cold outside air

Warm
Floor level or low sitting and sleeping, or elevated for breezes; floors in contact with cooler earth or elevated for breeze and isolation from ground moisture

Design Guidelines

In spaces with several occupants, provide a range of thermal conditions that approaches the comfort zone limits. In this vertical temperature gradient context, provide various furniture heights, seating options or floor levels within a room. This accommodates both individual preferences and seasonal changes in whether people are drawn toward warmth or to coolth. In predominantly hot or cold climates, respond accordingly with low or high seating.

Supply fresh air for ventilation and use radiant delivery for the primary heating or cooling loads to reduce air mixing rates and promote a wider interior weather range. Commercially, this is known as a dedicated outdoor air system (DOAS). As an alternative to all-air HVAC systems that maximize air mixing, use displacement ventilation and underfloor air distribution systems to create varying degrees of thermal stratification.

Shape floors to form *cool pools* with sunken areas and *warm perches* by elevated tiers. Terracing the floor as a stepped interior landscape allows for locating the whole body in thermal space.

Plan three seating tiers to diversity occupant adaptive choices. Provide options for low seating on or near the floor, conventional seating at about 16–18 in (46 cm), and stool height seating about 24–30 in (60–76 cm) high.

Accommodate seasonal sleeping in mixed climates by adjustable height bed furniture or by migration between summer and winter sleeping spaces with different heights.

Fit furniture materials to cool or warm circumstance: insulating materials for cool settings and conductive, ventilated materials for warm conditions. Practicing in cold Finland, Aalto (1935) argued, "A piece that comes into the most intimate contact with man, as a chair does, shouldn't be constructed of materials that are excessively good conductors of heat."

Refine with C2 Haptic Connection. Help build G3 Existential Datum and C3 Water You can Touch.

G3

Existential Datum

fits buildings to the ground, connecting inhabitants visually, phenomenally and symbolically to the land.

Fallingwater (Kaufmann House)

Mill Run, Pennsylvania, 1935
Frank Lloyd Wright, architect

The house, integrated with the site, expresses an extension of geomorphology and terrain that carries powerful feeling, full of opportunity for meaning conveyed.

photo Christopher Little, Western Pennsylvania Conservancy

she meets us on plane
Gaia and the builders clasp
a deep-felt union

Building structures are the visible expression of gravity, a context of a force that terminates in the earth. How a building meets the ground is an important moment of expression about the human relationship to terra firma—the most fundamental datum of human existence. Depending on the solution, one can feel angst or security. Buildings can perch lightly on slender piers, hovering above the ground or sit firmly upon it. They can in contrast, settle partly or wholly within the soil. Columns and bearing walls can pierce the ground or foundations can rise up to meet them. Each of these relationships carries a rich metaphorical meaning and induces a unique embodied feeling, from a sense of groundedness to an affect of detachment or freedom. This schema asks designers to give people the psychological satisfaction of structure with a solid and visible grounding and to carefully relate floors to the Earth with a conscious recognition of the implications; for example, consider the solidity of a massive raised plinth in contrast to the lightness of a suspended wooden floor.

Casa de Retiro Espiritual / House of Spiritual Retreat (Casa Cordoba)

Seville, Spain, 1975
Emilio Ambasz, architect

A dramatic descent from land surface into occupation of the subterrane

photo Michele Alassio

Fallingwater anchors to its steep landscape with stone walls, fireplace and floors. Structure is anchored to natural boulders, and more boulders protrude around the hearth. Massive stone walls form the cliff-side edges of rooms open on other sides to valley light and views (Stoller 1999; Waggoner 2010). "The visible bedrock is important psychologically in an otherwise bold and 'perilous' architecture" of cantilevered balconies (Thiis-Evensen 1987). Similarly, concrete beams tied to rock outcroppings signal permanence with rational transparency, forces resolved.

Casa de Rietro Espiritual is entered through a portal in the corner of tall, massive angled walls. One then descends broad stairs to a fountained, sunken court wrapped by banked rooms of the mostly subterranean home. The descent is marked by increasing enclosure and a transition from open distant landscape views to an upward sky view and a near horizon of the enclosed court. Along the way, the wayfarer's eye passes level with the horizontal green roof, only to have it disappear. Inside, the rooms are curved and cavernous, evoking a living experience rooted in the earth. A sinuous perimeter of private courts brings light from above and places the retaining wall surface into visual relief. The physical building interior calms and quiets the human interior, establishing an atmosphere for reflection, grounding and turning within (Ambasz et al 2005).

Existential Datum

Platforms + plateaus

Sketches by Jørn Utzon, 1962
Utzon Archives/ Utzon Center

left
Monte Alban
pre-Columbian Zapotec + Mixtec
Oaxaca state, Mexico

right
Chinese + Janese houses
grounded vs detached floors

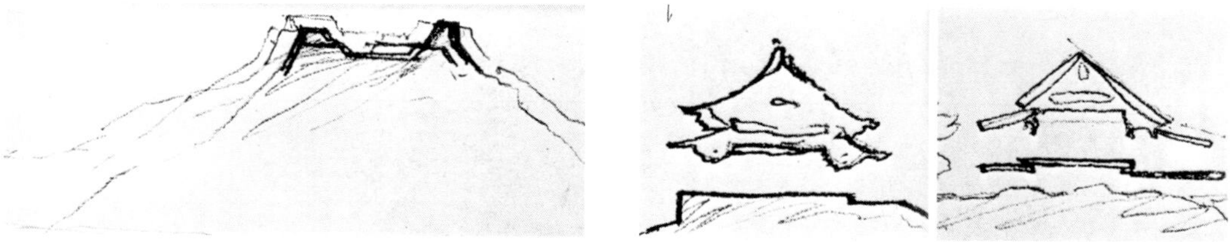

Supporting Evidence

Flattening of the ground is the first act of human settlement. The felt experience is based on the density of the floor material, the floor's structural rigidity and the degree of enclosure by the earth.

Platforms and plateaus is a seminal essay by Jørn Utzon (1962) in which he identifies the raised plane of the architectural plateau as conveying detachment from the earth and orientation towards the sky. When the plateau is sunken but open-to-sky, it can further emphasize views and connection to the heavens, as in Monte Alban. Phenomenology of the floor is detailed by Thiis-Evensen in *Archetypes in Architecture* (1987) in several variations. The shaping of ground and floor together, if *sunken*, gives a feeling of interiority, enclosure, and centering. An *attached* floor at grade relates occupants more to the horizontal landscape, linking inside and outside. A *detached* floor raises the view, creating distance between subject and object while also disconnecting from the ground. Floor structure can be, as in Chinese houses, an extension of the earth, giving a solid "feeling of firmness and security" (Utzon 1962). When *stone or concrete* is set directly on the ground, the effect is emphasized and sensed through the feet. If the floor itself is *earthen* or partly of earthen material, such as Wright's cement-stabilized earth floors, then the feeling is softer, more timeless and earth-connected, especially when soft tile and brick are employed (Alexander et al 1977). By contrast, in the detached raised floors of the Japanese house, the vibrations and deflections of wooden structure communicate directly that one is suspended. Utzon expresses it as feeling like "one is standing on a small wooden bridge, dimensioned to take just your weight and nothing more." Structural psychology of bearing. Structural forces can be conveyed visually. People tend to prefer columns with a base and walls that anchor on a foundation. A foundation that rises up visibly from the earth to meet the downward thrust of walls and columns—in turn holding aloft the weightiness of upper stories and the roof—is especially satisfying. Christopher Day explains in *Places of the Soul* (1990) that, "A wall is more solid, rooted in the earth, more timeless, quiet, reassuring and restful if its base is wider than its top......How buildings meet the ground makes all the difference to whether they belong in this particular place or have merely been parked there."

Design Guidelines

Choose with clear intention the feeling qualities and desired relationship between inhabitant and Earth. Match the shaping of ground and floor—of structure and surface—to achieve that intention.

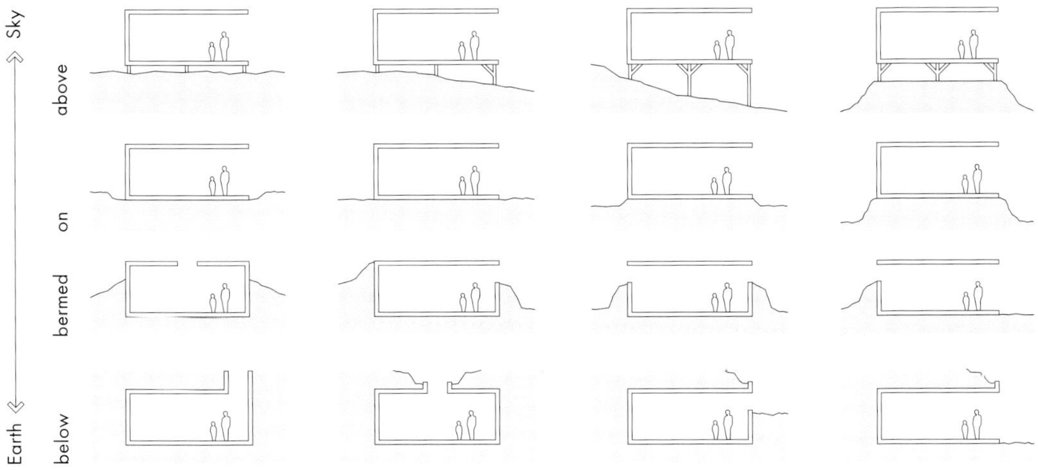

Floor + Ground Relationships

Vertically
From detached above ground to submerged, each condition engenders a different feeling, sensed directly.

Horizontally
From more (left) to less (right) enclosure by earth

adapted and expanded from Watchman et al. (2021)

Connect feeling with floor + ground relationships. The adjacency of a space to the ground can generate different experiences of the sky, horizon and earth (Watchman et al 2021). To connect people more to the earth, submerge portions of the ground floor or use earth berming. Floors above ground give an orientation to the sky that increases with elevation above ground. All of these conditions are mediated by apertures for view and light. Decrease spatial enclosure to give an affect of openness; increase enclosure with more solid boundaries to engender more grounded psychological interiority.

Solidify flooring structure. Build floor slabs or paving directly on the ground to maximize solidity experience. For raised structure, use short spans and stiffen floor structure with solid, more massive secondary structure.

Ground with flooring material. The earth does not shake under footsteps. Employ relatively dense, massive floor materials to support groundedness and earth connections. In some cases, designing a floor system with stiff structure and low deflection, combined with a floor surface with some softness (wood, earth, cork) may be preferable for long periods of standing or walking, as these materials are more sympathetic to the human foot.

Express foundations. Give visible manifestation to the vertical forces where buildings meet the ground. Allow column bases and bearing walls to thicken, as this visibly conveys in built metaphor the inevitable spreading of loads to the wider foundations below. If greater softening and blending of building and living land is desired, employ plantings at the building-ground junction and climbing vines on walls.

Insure daylighting and ventilation. More submerged buildings have improved insulating qualities, a dampening of the diurnal temperature cycle and potential in some climates for earth-contact cooling. However, they require special attention to daylighting and fresh air ventilation. For design guidance, see the Earth Edges design strategy in DeKay + Brown (2014).

Refine with the schemas G2 Adaptive Altitude and N2 Authentic Matters. Help build R4 Radiant Sailing.

G4

Incalescent Center

radiates heat that decreases with distance from the source,
encouraging choice of thermal location and social clustering.

214 **Trennemoor House**

Kirchhorst, Germany, 1992
Hansjörg Göritz Studio

right
Radiant stone wall

below
Thermal patterns, plan diagram

A stone core inside a renovated timber barn, heated hydronically from the center of the wall, radiant from the center of the house, creates a warm center with cooler perimeter.

photo Hansjörg Göritz

in chilled fields
fire's glow a circle domain
this gloom burned through

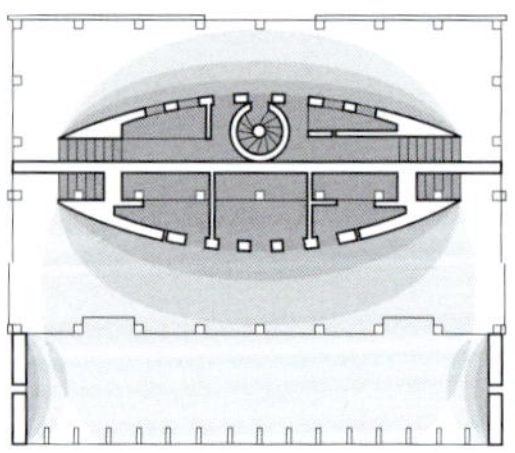

A family gathers around the hearth. In a Vermont country store, a pot-bellied wood stove organizes the circle of working men and their morning coffee ritual. Campfire light defines a room as its thermal rings draw some closer to its center, others sent farther afield towards cooler edges. Heat is a spatial phenomenon in plan and section. Anyone who has lived with a centralized radiant heat source knows these two patterns: 1. Social gathering near warmth within a relatively cool field, attended by relationships that develop by repeatedly shared ritual; and 2. Locating one's body along the thermal gradient from warm center to cooler periphery, often changing orientation and proximity for the pure pleasure and variety of it. Steady-state conditions, especially when spatially uniform, offer none of this personal delight and no gradient to draw people together. Most buildings in most climates can heat with passive solar much of the time. When back-up heat is needed, bring to the coldest days the communal fire and its relatives, the feeling for which there is no substitute.

Norwegian Wild Reindeer Pavilion

Hjerkinn, Dovre, Norway, 2011
Snøhetta, architects

A fireplace opposite a glass wall fosters a temperature range throughout the space and in the tiered seating arc.

photo Ketil Jacobsen, Snøhetta

Trennemoor House sets a metaphorical stone house inside an existing timber barn retrofitted with an insulating wrapper (Göritz 2009). The brick masonry monolith acts as a central thermal mass, its curved walls embedded with hydronic heating coils. The stereotomic core radiates toward the cooler tectonic wood-framed perimeter, creating gradated arcs of warmth that vary depending on the inhabitant's position. Sleeping is in a loft above the warm nucleus, which also houses the heat-producing kitchen and bath; inbetween them, a mezzanine with bath and library. The architect writes, "To make and inhabit such an internalized world demands and creates strength, and makes us return to the essentials of things—which is a challenge and a gift" (Göritz 2021). The plan diagram (left margin) shows the radiant core with an accessory apartment on one side and the main residence on the other.

Norwegian Wild Reindeer Pavilion creates varying thermal fields with a suspended metal fireplace that yields a radiant heat point source, expressed and amplified on its open side oriented towards wooden seating shaped in a loose arc around the fireplace. Tiers allow visitors to take an adaptive altitude by sitting on a warmer upper tier that is deeper in the alcove of a subtle thermal enclave. Opposite the seating, a large glass wall amplifies the gradient toward the cold outdoors with lower thermal resistance and thus cooler surface temperatures.

Source surface area and temperatures

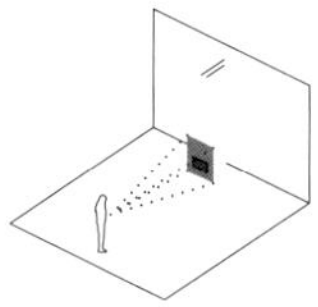

A Wood stove
small delivery area
400 °F/200 °C

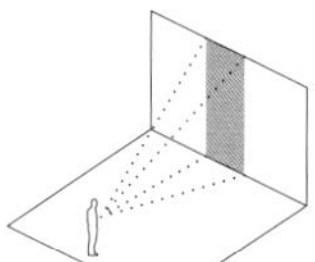

B Concentrated radiant wall
medium delivery area
150 °F/65 °C

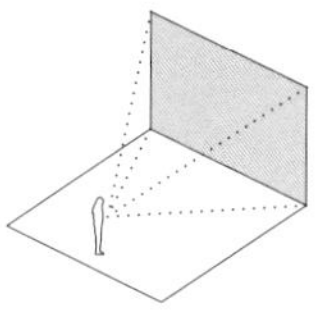

C Dispersed radiant wall
large delivery area
80 °F/27 °C

C Trombe wall (passive)
large delivery area
average 100 °F/38 °C
peak 20–130 °F/49–54 °C

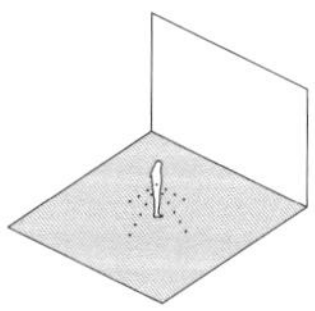

D Active radiant floor
largest delivery area required
75–85 °F/24–29 °C

Supporting Evidence

Radiant heat defines a sensory field where its character heavily influences social patterns and relaxation responses. The open flame is a unique, mysterious case known for inducing contemplation. Radiant heat transfer intensity depends on heated surface area, source temperature and the geometric relationship with an occupant.

Social domain, shaped in a circle, was first defined by the fire pit. Humans likely tamed fire some 1.8 million years ago, built the first hearth in Kenya 1.4 million BCE, and began constructing chimneys in China about 2,000 years ago (Tabb 2019). "The beginning of association among human beings, their meeting and living together, thus came into being because of the discovery of fire," wrote Vitruvius, circa 30–20 BCE (Gwilt 1874).
Reverie by fire, is "the invitation to repose" wrote Bachelard (1938) in *The Psychoanalysis of Fire*. "In these circumstances, reverie becomes truly fascinating and dramatic; it magnifies human destiny; the small to the great, the hearth to the volcano, the life of a log to the life of a world."
Ritual healing hypothesis proposed by McClenon (2006) speculates that hypnotic campfire-watching influenced *Homo erectus* to be relaxed and prosocial. Fire-induced *relaxation response*, studied by Lynn (2010) with visual and sound recording, showed that fire, with its associated sounds, is "visually and aurally naturalistic, allowing for multi-sensory absorption into the experience, and thereby provided the greatest relaxation effect."
Source surface area and temperatures. Source *delivery temperature* impacts radiant heat transfer by the 4th power of the temperature difference between source and person (or other surface), a dramatic impact of this variable. See sidebar for examples. In contrast, heat source *delivery area* and the total heat flow are directly proportional. The hotter the surface, the smaller area required to deliver the same thermal experience. A wood stove (A) has a small surface area that gets very hot, while a relatively cooler hydronic wall surface (C) must be much larger to create the same radiant effect on people or surrounding surfaces.

Design Guidelines

Whereas the G2 Adaptive Altitude schema engages a vertical thermal gradient, the incalescent field allows people to locate themselves primarily in the horizontal dimension relative to a heat source. Create heating distribution as concentrated delivery or asymmetric radiant and non-radiant walls. Locate active walls to the interior of rooms or buildings; the exception is a Trombe wall. Employ fireplaces or wood stoves with visible flames of renewable fuels to maximize reverie. In common areas, hotter, more concentrated sources amplify the thermal gradient and readily engender an atmosphere for social gathering.

Radiant thermal space geometry can be complex. Receiving surfaces and occupants will feel warmer when closer to the source, mostly because they intercept a larger sector of the source's radiation. Sources can either be a spatially centralized *point* source, located on a room edge like a typical wood *stove* or fireplace, or embedded in walls. Heated from within, radiant wall heating can have a smaller, more *concentrated* surface if hotter or a larger *dispersed* surface area with a lower supply temperature. Like a fireplace, a radiant-heated wall will be more

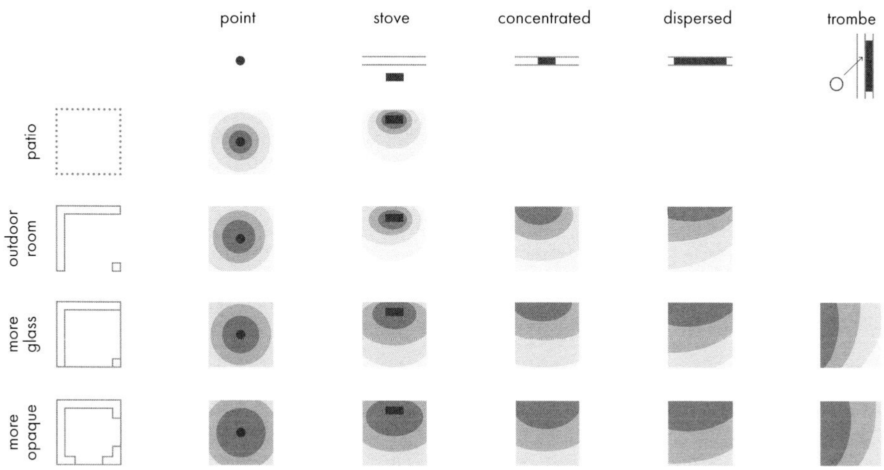

Radiant thermal space

A radiant field's spatial pattern is a product of both heat source and room design.

Principles

_ Less enclosure = more temperature range. Edge is closer to outdoor temperature.

_ More glass = more temperature range.

_ Centralized sources generate circular fields. Wall sources generate more linear fields.

More thermal contours in same distance = steeper gradient = greater social gathering effect.

efficient if located on the interior where it will not lose heat to the outdoors. In contrast, a passive solar Trombe wall heats a room's sunny equator-facing edge. Radiant thermal space is shaped by source type and temperature, along with room design, collectively affecting gradient steepness and user experience. The diagram contours show gradient steepness increasing among from *dispersed* to *concentrated walls* to a hot *stove*. High temperatures do not require fossil fuels. Renewable biomass and active solar can supply high temperatures for greater concentration. Photovoltaics (PV) can supply energy for efficient systems, such as a ground source heat pump.

Envelope permeability and thermal insulation also help define the radiant field. A super-insulated envelope has a low skin heat loss rate and small heating need, thus a less discernible thermal gradient. In contrast, an outdoor fire creates a steep gradient in less distance. It is accompanied by a strong asymmetric warm front and cool back.

Choose appropriate space types for strong thermal gradients, such as in buffer spaces, a glazed atrium, lobbies and other spaces where a wide comfort range, spatially non-uniform, works well. When one radiant source heats several linked rooms, the gradient can extend long distances and support S5 Territorial Tuning.

Plan incalescent events that bring dynamic temporal pleasure by cycling heating relative to climate rhythms, such as a heat pulse at night when residents are present, or in the early morning when workers begin their day.

Locate for visibility, as recommend in The Fire pattern from *A Pattern Language* (Alexander et al. 1977). An incalescent center viewed from circulation or adjacent rooms activates the schema by drawing inhabitants toward the warmth. Provided an alternate visual focus for when the fire is out, such as with an outdoor view.

Provision moveable seating or plan for a range of exposures that allow inhabitants to organize for social interaction and to regulate their heat balance and feeling intensity, such as in the Reindeer Pavilion.

Refine with G2 Adaptive Altitude, C4 Inhabited Periphery, R4 Radiant Sailing for a Trombe wall and R4 Circadian Space at night to provide the darkness needed. Help build C5 Thermal Enclave and S5 Territorial Tuning.

G4

Euphonic Water

employs refreshing aquatic timbre with calm and cool associations that intensify nearer the source.

218 **Paley Park**

New York, NY, 1967
Zion Breen Richardson Associates
landscape architects

Forming a small oasis in the middle of New York City, the soothing cascade sound of Paley Park's waterfall offers masking respite from frenetic street life.

photo Saitowitz, Flickr

cacophony day
sounding cascade mystifies
calmness resounding

Everyone enjoys the soothing, mesmerizing sounds of flowing water. Rhythmic surf crashing against rocks, spray in the air, a lake's lapping perimeter or mountain stream cascades—people seek these aquatic nature moments to become immersed in their atmosphere. In evolutionary terms, water is key to survival, therefore humans are attracted to moving water's acoustics. Architecture can bring this aural pleasure to daily life. Designers can orchestrate flows, resonating shapes and materials for the fluid to move through and strike. In urban settings, water features help build a restorative oasis within the noisy, assaulting soundscape. Moving and falling water sounds foster a sense of serenity and rejuvenation. Flowing water in most forms generates *aural space* situated within the volume bounded by physical elements—its own acoustically defined territory with soft edges and sound that builds in density, gathering attention, drawing people into its center. Meanwhile, contextual sounds fade while the sense of being within a *water-space* grows, bringing one to daydreams, reverie and introspection.

Contemporary Art Museum of Monterrey (MARCO)

Monterrey, Nuevo León, Mexico
Legorreta Arquitectos, 1991
Ricardo Legorreta, architect

A dramatic cascade periodically fills the patio floor with water and the arcades with sound.

photo Lourdes Legorreta

videos see Galvan 2011, Valdes 2011, Aguirre 2022

Paley Park, an original *vest pocket park,* masks midtown Manhattan's street bustle. Creating a peaceful acoustic oasis in the midst of urbanity, the park is elevated above the street level; dense sound-absorptive ivy shrouds the adjacent attenuating masonry walls and a 20 ft (6 m) water-wall flanks the rear. The honey locust canopy defines an urban room's ceiling. From the street to the waterfall, the three-sided space dampens city noise as the sonic gradient of falling water ramps up with each pace. Lightweight movable metal mesh chairs allow patrons to situate for sun, shade or within the hydric crescendo (Tate 2015; de Wit 2018; Bernstein 2017).

MARCO is organized around a central skylit courtyard, surrounded by arcades that access adjacent art galleries (Arellano 2022). "Daily, just about every 15 minutes, the central courtyard is covered by a 2-inch flow of water which energizes and refreshes the environment" (Legorretta nd). "Water comes out of a huge outlet and floods the courtyard. The sound of water is part of the experience of the museum" (Legoretta 2000). From a dramatic single jet it floods a shallow pool that feathers from 60 mm to 2 (2.4–0.1 in) at the edges, filling in rhythmic arcing waves, forming a water mirror as it calms over the polished marble floor. When the court is needed for public events, it can be easily drained. "Given the acoustics of the Patio, the jet rumbles throughout the museum" (MARCO 2012).

Euphonic Water

Cognitive impacts of water sounds

left
Creative effect of sounds

Water sounds support creative thought.

adapted Haapakangas et al. 2011

right
Urban soundscape semantic profiles

A variety of water sounds are preferred across a range of qualities.

adapted Jeon et al. 2012

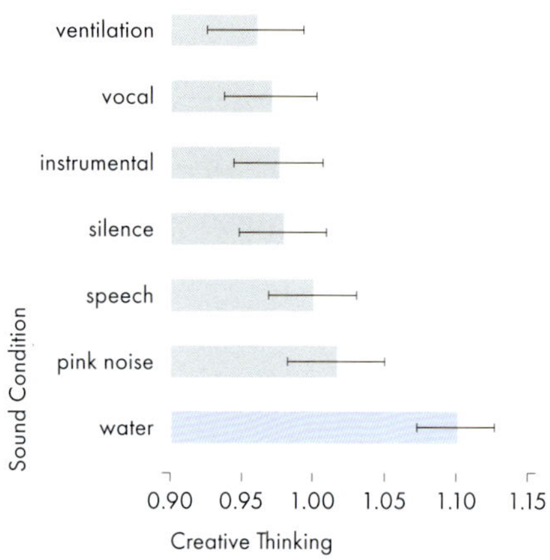

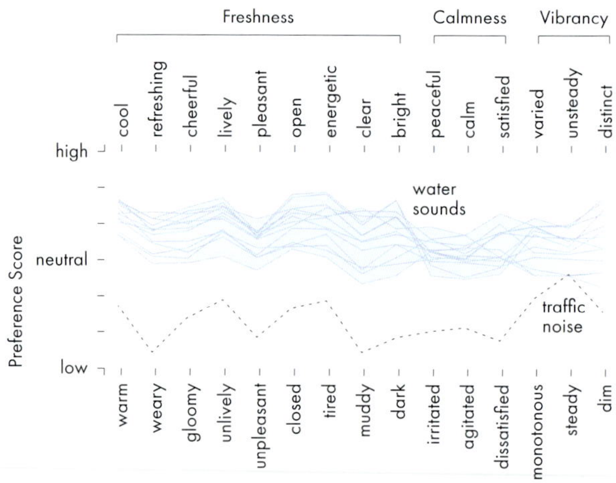

Supporting Evidence

Water sounds promote creative thinking. Effects can be calming, exciting or annoying, depending on the kind of water feature, and the various deployment of light and color vividness, landscape harmony and naturalness.

Cognitive impacts of water sounds. The left graph shows the *creative effect of sounds*. The x-axis shows the *c-score*, a metric used to measure ideational originality based on creative thinking tasks (Haapakangas et al. 2011). Among seven different sound conditions, water clearly engendered more original creative thinking. In studies of *urban soundscape semantic profiles* on the right, Jeon and partners (2010, 2012) used semantic differential tests (matched adjective pairs on top and bottom) to evaluate how people characterized urban sounds. Factor analysis is a method to find dataset patterns, reducing a large number of variables into smaller sets of common themes, seen in the groups of related adjectives. The dashed line shows traffic noise of 75 dBA. Compared to 55 dBA (not shown), results demonstrated that people were more sensitive to water sounds in noisier background situations. Besides demonstrating the expected—that a variety of water sounds all had more positive effects than traffic noises— researchers also studied the water's psychoacoustic characteristics of loudness, sharpness, roughness and fluctuation strength. Sharpness, the high frequency content of a sound, was the most dominant factor affecting water soundscape perception. Among the water sounds, fountains had the greater sharpness while streams had smaller. Behavior. In contrast to more common perceptual studies, Ruso and Atzwanger (2003) investigated how people's *behavior* might change in an environment with and without water elements. Their observational methods involved video-taping activity over three months near a shopping mall water fountain during periods with and without water. They concluded that the water increased the time people spent near the fountain by 21%, increased interactions

with others by 109%, and increased the likelihood people explored their environment by 69%.
Type. Nasar and Lin (2003) studied people's responses to five kinds of water features. Compared to *flowing* or *combinations*, *still* water was most calming. *Jets* or *falling* water evoked the strongest feelings of excitement.
Character. A study by Bulut et al (2010) used 25 photos grouped into five waterscape types, and participants evaluated them for visual preference and difference characteristics. The most preferred types had characteristics of *vividness* (intensity of light and color), *harmony* (rhythm between natural and cultural landscape elements) and *naturalness*. Ekman and Rådsten (2015) determined that, for urban water features, positive reactions were most related to the *temporal variability*—that is, when flows and sounds change over time, while negative reactions were related to the overall loudness of the water sound.

Design Guidelines

Map the place's existing acoustic character. Define desired sonic qualities and noise abatement. For a new soundscape, ensure a volume gradient that promotes choice for locating closer or further away from moving water.

Analyze the site to understand its acoustic qualities. Identify surrounding sound sources and propagation paths, distinguishing between preferred and unwanted sounds.
Enclose euphonic space to some degree, if ambient sounds are significant. Sound blocking with massive walls, as in Paley Park, is more effective than distance. A semi-enclosed space also enhances the evaporative cooling effect because the moist air is better contained. An indoor location, as in the MARCO precedent, will amplify loudness, reflections and reverberation time. A greater degree of built enclosure increases the distance at which the water sounds can be heard, while sound from a similar source in an open field would quickly dissipate.
Locate listening points with water sound as both foreground and background. Integrate a variety of seating arrangements, preferably movable. Organize seating for varied solitude or social interaction.
Complement sound with microclimate to include a variety of thermal experiences fit to context, such as sunny, wind-protected places in cool weather or shady, breezy locations with fountain mist during warm periods.
Ripple and vary the water patterns. Incorporate movement that creates ripples and cascades. Naturalistic randomness in flow and timing is more pleasing than regularity or constancy. For masking effects, water flow sound level should be similar to level of the urban noises but not more than 3 dB below them (Jeon et al 2010).
Supplement with multi-sensory delights, such as water's coolness, surrounding with fragrant plants (see S2 Aromatic Transit) and accessible places where the water can be touched. Where feasible, incorporate fish, which carry positive psychological associations and can reduce stress. Clean water is critical to its attractiveness. Use materials and color to create the appearance of darker blue and green shades, which seem deeper and more dense. See color guidance in F3 Water-Animated Surfaces and for calm pools, F2 Water as a Mirror.
Refine with C3 Water You Can Touch, F3 Revealed Conveyance and F3 Water Animated Surfaces. Help build C5 Thermal Enclave and S5 Territorial Tuning.

G4

Zephyr Spectrum

creates a range of pleasurable breezy and calm conditions that promote adaptive choices fit to transitory conditions.

222 **Kastrup Sea Bath**

Copenhagen, Denmark, 2004
White Arkitekter

The structure provides a range of wind, water and sun exposure or protection options with open slats, solid walls and a variety of levels and orientations.

photo Åke E:son Lindman
Lindman Photography

at autumn's edges
a cat's paw or pleasing gust
adapted content

Zephyr (or *Zephyrus*) was the Greek god of the west wind, considered the gentlest of the winds in mythology. Think of the thermal delight brought by soft breezes on a warm day. These are often quite variable and accompanied by other stimuli, such as fragrances of surrounding flora, moist salty ocean air or Nature sounds arriving through open windows. Air movement is one of the fastest ways to cool off, whether indoors or out, particularly in humid conditions where the body's capacity for cooling by perspiration is stifled. Zephyrs can invoke refreshment and invigoration and improve people's perception of air quality. Inhabitants' preferences for air movement differ widely and are highly dependent on activity level and other contextual factors. Natural ventilation can be thought of as heat-removing *space cooling* or as *people cooling,* where individuals locate themselves within calm or more breezy conditions in a room. Orienting and arranging apertures to organize intentional irregular air distribution engenders the pleasure of adaptive opportunity.

Khoo Teck Puat Hospital

Singapore, 2010
CPG Consultants Pte Ltd +
RMJM Architects

left
Courtyards, external walkways, and balconies provide a range of access to outdoor breezes.

right
Wing wall facade fins, louvered lower wall and operable jalousie windows maximize natural ventilation to patient rooms in a warm-humid city.

photos CPG Consultants Pte Ltd

We just took those original technologies and reintroduced them in a 21st century way.

—Chris Johnston, chief architect RMJM 2015

Kastrup Sea Bath uses slats in a curved wall to create a patchwork of conditions where breeze is admitted and blocked to differing degrees. As the sun moves during the day, portions of the deck are in sun or shade, accommodating every microclimatic preference. The surrounding wall gradually elevates to 5 m (16 ft) above the sea. The circular shape is open to the south, concentrating the sun and biased toward wind protection. For maximum contrasting wind exposure, the path to the high diving platform is on the breezy outer shady side of the wall. The structure itself has a dynamic quality as its silhouette changes when viewed from different perspectives and as users animate it by moving through and around it (Ohtake 2009; White Arkitekter AB 2008).

Khoo Teck Puat Hospital provides a range of calm and breezy zones, indoors and out. Courtyards and walkways are open-air; balconies extend inhabitation. A narrow space between two towers creates a Venturi effect that increases cross-ventilation through the adjacent tower. Facade fins provide shade and capture breezes, enhancing flow by 20–30%, based on wind tunnel tests (Yen 2012). Rooms in the naturally-ventilated ward have a louvered lower wall, a large mid-section of modular jalousie windows and an upper clerestory with light shelves. Air movement is supplemented with individual ceiling fans for each patient bed (Schröpfer et al. 2016; ILFI 2017).

Zephyr Spectrum

left
Air movement preferences

Building occupants generally prefer more air movement than that with which they are provided.

Zhang et al. 2007

right
Wind type preference

Compared to other patterns, people prefer air flow patterns that follow the fluctuations of natural wind.

Zhao + Li 2004

Air Movement Preferences vs. Thermal Sensation

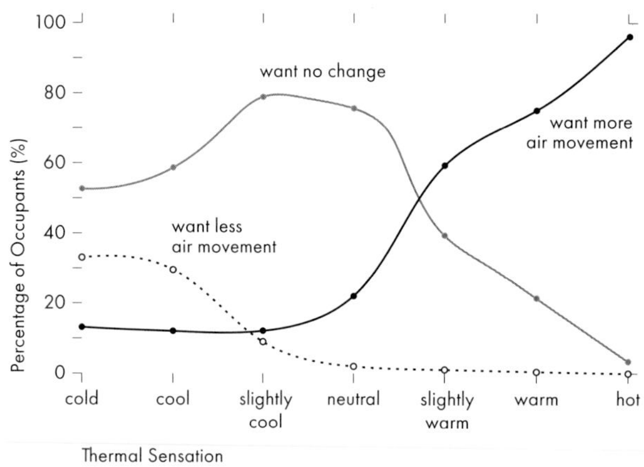

Wind Type Preference

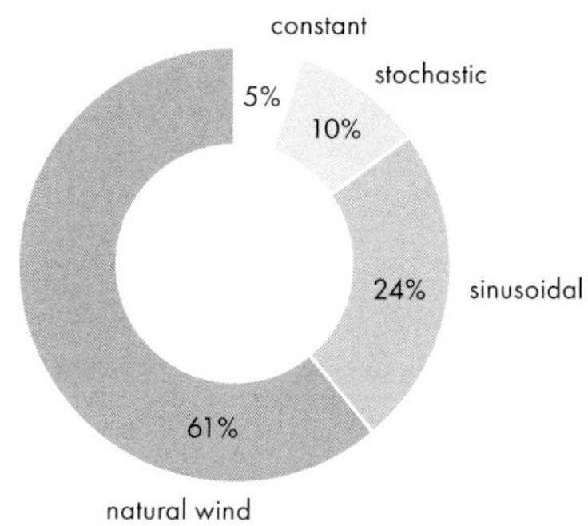

Supporting Evidence

Air movement research and building standards have shifted in the 21st century from emphasizing reducing negative draft discomfort to focusing on air's positive hedonic qualities. Air movement provides fast-acting, user-controlled, energy-efficient comfort, delight, refreshment and Nature connections. Providing personal control is essential.

Language used to describe air movement has changed to acknowledge positive perceptions. Past research methods typically referred to air movement as either non-existent or used negative terms, such as *draft* and *nuisance*. Happily, researchers are increasing their use of more affirmative terms, such as *breeze, pleasure, thermal delight* and descriptions of air's aesthetics (de Dear et al. 2013).
Air movement preferences among building occupants show desires for greater sensations of breeze than previously predicted. Extensive surveys, particularly in office buildings, indicate that 40% prefer more air movement under neutral conditions, and 59% prefer more when conditions are at least *slightly warm*. Even for people who are slightly cool, current standards overestimate the probability of draft discomfort by over twice the rate of dissatisfaction found in these field studies (Arens et al 2009; Zhang et al 2007).
Wind type preference. The pleasurable thermal experience of a breeze comes from more than air speed. Natural winds differ significantly from artificially created air movement in velocity distribution, turbulence intensity and power spectra (energy distribution across different wind frequencies). In contrast to constant, stochastic or sinusoidal patterns, people greatly prefer flows that follow natural wind fluctuations (Zhao + Li 2004). When airflow characteristics resemble natural wind and its mean speed is like a gentle breeze (0.8 m/s or 157 ft/min), comfort can be achieved up to 30°C (86°F). Draft complaints were significantly reduced in conditions imitating natural wind, as compared with the other types of airflow at the same mean speeds (Hu et al. 2009).

Wind direction. A unique study done in both laboratory and field settings found that air blowing on the front of the body (compared to the back) led to higher energy levels and enhanced creative engagement (Izadi et al. 2019). This has implications for orienting people and desks towards operable windows or front-facing fans.
Comfort and perceived air quality. In addition to cooling effects, the perception of air as stuffy often has more to do with the thermal characteristics than the air quality itself. A study of personally-controlled air movement from both floor-fans and ceiling fans demonstrated that air movement improves these perceptions. Thermal comfort was maintained to 30°C (86°F) and 60% relative humidity (RH), while perceived air quality was acceptable to 30°C (86°F) and 80% RH, all without discomfort from humidity, air movement or eye-dryness (Zhai et al 2013, 2015).

Design Guidelines

Locate and size windows to create air movement gradients within a room such that velocity distributions are non-uniform in space; they may also be dynamic in time. Use window types and facade elements to direct air flows. Provide local occupant controls, movable seating or other options for occupant relocation and adaptation.

Zone spaces to create higher and lower velocity areas within more discreet rooms and in open plan areas. At the room organizations scale (level 5), rooms can be arranged to align higher cooling requirement uses with orientations and areas in the building that have the greatest access to breezes. For additional guidance, see Cooling Zones strategy in DeKay + Brown (2014).
Locate and size windows so their relative size and the position of inlets and outlets, along with interior partitions alignments, create the intended air flow patterns. For example, windows on opposite or adjacent walls create more opportunities for variable indoor air flow patterns and higher ventilation rates than do windows on a single wall. Equal size inlets and outlets create the highest air flow rates; smaller inlets create highest velocities just inside the opening, and larger inlets create more uniform interior velocities. The relative location of inlets on a wall has a greater effect on directing the internal air flow than the location of outlets. For additional guidance, see Ventilation Openings Arrangement strategy in DeKay + Brown (2014).
Direct airflow with elements such as exterior wing walls, operable fins, casement or jalousie windows, operable shutters or movable horizontal louvers. Each modifies the relative pressure differentials across openings in different ways, catching more available wind and directing the flow, for instance upwards or downwards, towards or away from occupants. For additional wing wall guidance, see Cross-ventilation Rooms strategy in DeKay + Brown (2014). Provide adaptive opportunity to adjust air flow velocity and direction.
Supplement windows with fans, which can be ceiling or personal fans or mechanical ventilation systems with variable velocity delivery options (such as a *breeze* setting). Give occupants control over setting the speed. For additional guidance, see the *CBE Ceiling Fan Design Guide* (2020).
Outdoor rooms. In occupied exterior or in-between spaces, create windward facades with varying permeability.
Refine with R2 Aperture Engagement and F3 Fans First. Help build C5 Thermal Enclave and S5 Territorial Tuning. Air movement is also addressed in R6 Cooling Conversions.

G4

Shades of Brilliance

generates subtle microclimates for inhabitants' hedonic and thermoregulatory choices.

Georgia O'Keefe House

Abiquiu, New Mexico, 1948
Maria Chabot, designer

The "roofless room" of this renovated traditional adobe house creates a complex gradient of sun, partial shade and full shade.

photo Balthazar Koráb

morn break, mid-day's sun
countless pleasure hues abide
mine alone to choose

Particularly when conditions are somewhat warm or cool, rather than extreme, people feel delightfully alive when poised at the edge of comfort. They find an appreciation of the relief offered from the simple alignment of the body with elemental forces. To position oneself in either sun or shade is one of the most primal mammalian moves toward pleasure. Even greater is the gratification present in the opportunity to move from one location to another as conditions change. Outdoor rooms offer the pleasant, dynamic opportunity for local migration between the extremes of sun and shade. At extremely cold or hot times, Homo sapiens will seek the opposite condition, while in moderate conditions, individuals will often choose from within a range of microclimate conditions to suit their pleasure. People have different and finely tuned individual thermal preferences and often wear a range of clothing levels in the same conditions. Thermal thrill-seekers revel in willfully driving their own alliesthesia by first either overcooling or overheating themselves and then moving to the opposite condition.

Hiss Residence [Umbrella House]

Sarasota, Florida, 1954
Paul Rudolph, architect

A latticed, sun-filtering parasol roof covers the house and pool area. A low suspended panel offers full shade. Full sun penetrates the edges and pool opening.

photo Nicholas Ferris Photography

Georgia O'Keefe's House. The *ceiling* of the *roofless room*, as its court is known, offers a combination of partial shade and full shade by different densities of pergola structure and full sun where the rustic trellis is omitted. The full-height walls offer zones of full shade and (sometimes) sun through the unglazed window (Lynes + Lopez 2012). The graded zones of sun, shade and in-between conditions change shape and location as the sun and clouds move. The result is a visual interest from both rhythmic and arhythmic changes, along with locational adaptive opportunity in an extreme climate, accomplished with elegantly simple materials and composition.

Hiss Residence, built without air-conditioning, is covered with fine wooden louvered shades over wood joists (the umbrella) extending front and back over the entire house and the outdoor space, filtering the Florida sun. Above the pool itself, the umbrella roof is open to give an area of full sun. The pool is located to the south of the house, shown in the image near mid-day; the projected shaded area moves with daily and seasonal sun position. An opaque plane is suspended over part of the terrace to give a localized area of full shade with a lowered ceiling that makes the shade patch more predictable. Deeper shade is provided indoors, ventilated by full-height jalousie windows (Olgyay + Olgyay 1957; Moholy-Nagy + Schwab 1970; Paul Rudolph Heritage Foundation 2021).

Outdoor shade + thermal stress

Conditions on a typical June day in Knoxville, Tennessee (zone 4-A mixed-humid climate). UTCI calculations were based on average hourly data for temperature, solar radiation, humidity and wind speed for each daylight hour, based on TMY-2 weather files. Summer outdoor conditions in full shade cause no bodily thermal stress all day.

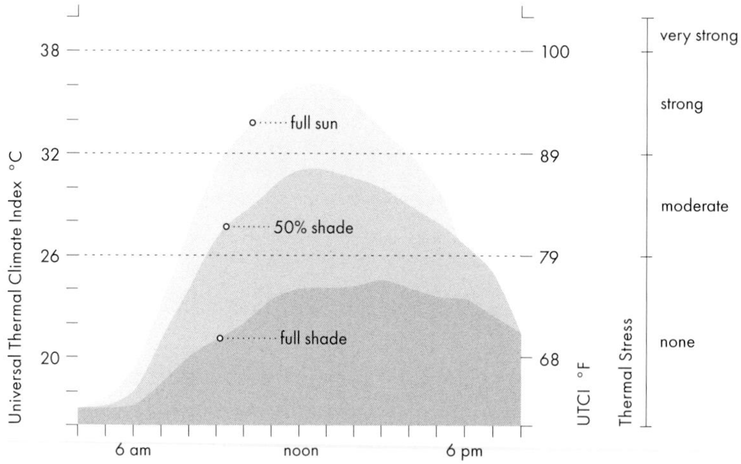

Supporting Evidence

Adding solar radiation warms a body and shifts the comfort zone to a cooler temperature range. Constructed shade reduces temperatures, illuminance and UV exposure.

Outdoor shade and thermal stress. Most bioclimatic chart comfort zones assume a person in shade with no air movement. However, in outdoor rooms, this is often not the case. The graph shows calculated Universal Thermal Climate Index (UTCI), an equivalent temperature that accounts for ambient temperature, humidity, wind and solar radiation, and is then divided into stress categories (Fiala et al. 2012). In full shade, conditions remain in the UTCI's *no thermal stress* zone (none); in full sun, under the same other climatic conditions, a person would most likely experience *moderate* or *strong thermal stress*. Partially shaded conditions would fall in-between.

Shaded courtyards and furniture. Galán-Marín et al. (2018) studied shaded and unshaded courtyards in Cordoba, observing a mean temperature difference of 12 °C (22 °F) during the hottest hour. Holman et al. (2018) found that outdoor shade promoted furniture use: "People will use shade structures if they are available."

Light levels. Architecturally-provided shade, in addition to blocking or filtering solar radiation, reduces daylight to the shaded space and adjacent rooms. Diffuse skylight on an overcast day ranges from 3,000 to 18,000 lux (280–1680 fc). Greater permeability of roofs blocks less sun and admits more light.

UV Exposure. Shade provides an effective means for UV protection, serving as a skin-cancer prevention tool. The degree of protection for opaque elements is proportional to the occupant's sky view. For partial shade, more shade density is also more UV protection, but reflected light can also add UV, which can be reflected (UV albedo) at different rates than visible light, depending on materials (Holman et al 2018).

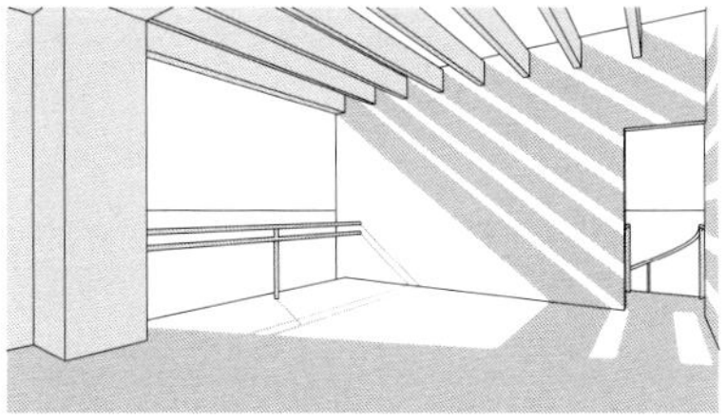
A
Gropius House

B
My Montessori Garden

C
Hiss Residence

D
Villa Buggenhout

Outdoor room configurations

A Lincoln, Massachusetts, 1938
Walter Gropius + Marcel Breuer
Unglazed south facade, parallel overhead louvers + opaque west wall (Process Architecture 1980)

B Ha Long City, Viet Nam, 2020
HGAA, architects
Overhead metal panels, vines mesh grid, tree openings, wire mesh walls (Astbury 2021)

C Fine overhead slats, opaque plane + pool opening. See precedent.

D Buggenhout, Belgium, 2013
Geers + van Severn, architects
Opaque overhead and bounding vines on metal grid (Divsare 2016)

Design Guidelines

In outdoor rooms, create three conditions: 1. *Sunny, open-to-sky space* without shade where users can warm themselves; 2. *Partial shade with filtered sunlight* where occupants can get just enough sun to stay comfortable; and 3. *Full shade with opaque surfaces* to block the sun, so people can escape the sun's heat but enjoy being outdoors.

Celebrate the sky. The sun marks time and places all earthly things in relation to its passage; configure outdoor surfaces to make the phenomena visible by moving the edge between sun and shade through the occupied domain. As the roof covers and protects occupants from the sky and its weather, so its openings reconnect occupants symbolically and functionally with *Nature's roof*. Construct the roof with degrees of transparency.
Locate outdoor rooms mostly used in summer for access to prevailing breeze directions; if primarily for cool weather, locate them to the lee side of the building, or construct wind barriers. If the room is used year-round in a mixed climate, locate for access to summer breeze and add a switch to block winter wind.
Ensure adaptation opportunity with seating options in each of the three conditions—or select furniture that can be easily moved from one place to another.
Distinguish shading periods between times and dates needed for fixed shading and those for operable shades. Operable shades can extend the season from that of fixed shades alone. Indoors needs shade longer than outdoor rooms. Vines provide seasonally-responsive shading (Shading Calendar technique, DeKay + Brown 2014).
Solve for shading geometry. Shade for east and west-facing space requires significant horizontal depth or vertical shading. Find guidelines in DeKay + Brown (2014), Overhead Shades and Layer of Shades strategies.
Refine with C3 Scintillating Sun, C4 Tempered Pathway and G4 Zephyr Spectrum. Help build G5 Pockets of Shadow and R5 Heliotropic Rooms.

G5

Pockets of Shadow

treats building edges as thick, sun-protecting, layered zones, giving a sense of shelter and peace.

Lalbhai Dalpatbhai Institute of Indology

Ahmedabad, India, 1962
Vastu Shilpa Consultants/
Balkrishna Doshi, architects

A full-length covered veranda with outboard sun-breakers creates a continuous layer of shade.

photo Mark DeKay

marginal thickness
life in layered shadow
sanctuary here

In a cold climate, people feel that more sunlight is better, but in hot places, retreating into the shadows is innate. Viewed from within cooler shaded space, inhabitants better appreciate both the coolness itself and the dynamic sun patterns outside. This schema's name is borrowed from Indian architect, Anant Raje, who wrote, "The focus is to develop *pockets of shadow*... keep the sun out and have peace within" (Raje + Raje 2012). Even in temperate climates, people near windows can feel visual discomfort from glare or excessive brightness, and thermal discomfort from too-warm radiant surfaces. This schema transforms these typical problems of unshaded sunny windows found in thin walls into a spatial pattern of thick occupiable edges, reducing the experience of excess glare and unwanted heat and establishing the building as a place of sanctuary. Another Indian architect, Charles Correa, distinguished between the typical North American building enclosure as a thin line of separation between inside and outside and the Indian facade that becomes a deep, transitional, inhabitable territory of gradation.

Indian Institute of Forest Management

Bhopal, India, 1988
Anant Raje, architect

Layers of shade over outdoor rooms, rhythmic dark and lightness in exterior circulation, and thickened zones at the building edges protecting windows.

photos Mark DeKay

Lalbhai Institute of Indology was designed to house ancient manuscripts and a research center. "All the elements one finds in Indian buildings are present," Doshi says, referring to the raised plinth, natural ventilation and generous veranda employed for regulating climate and light to preserve the ancient artifacts. The peripheral shade zone with sun-breakers becomes an occupiable *brise-soleil* at the level of public access (Curtis 1997; Steele 1998).

Indian Institute of Forest Management has shaded circulation that protects offices and alternates with covered outdoor meeting terraces (Bhatt + Scriver 1990). Outdoor public rooms are shaded with large sun-breakers. "The openings that receive operable windows are recessed into shadow pockets and these pockets become the dominant architectural features..." (Raje + Raje 2012). Raje's career is a study in variations on this theme of layered edges of shadow and light, as shown in the plans on the next page.

Pockets of shadow variations (next page) illustrate three Raje plans. *Mudra Institute of Communications Classroom Building's* southwest wall is opaque; apertures face a court through a sheltered layer. Classrooms and offices on other sides are wrapped in a shaded terrace layer about one-quarter the room depth. *ATIRA Staff Housing* uses

Pockets of shadow variations
Anant Raje, architect

Shaded areas show partly-enclosed shadow pockets open to outdoor air; boundaries to interior have operable windows and doors.

left
Mudra Institute of Communications Classroom Building
Ahmedabad, India, 1990

top right
ATIRA Staff Housing
(Ahmedabad Textile Industry Research Association)
Ahmedabad, India, 1984

bottom right
Bhopal Development Authority Headquarters
Bhopal, India, 1990

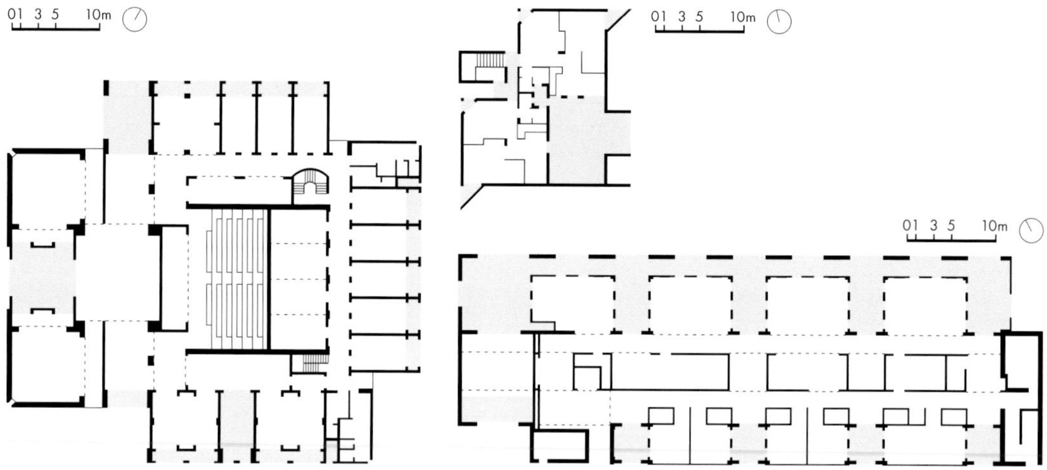

large exterior vertical fin wall shading, oriented towards prevailing breezes. Covered open-air circulation between apartments shields entries. Bathroom cores open to ventilation shafts with indirect light. Kitchen/dining areas face semi-protected courts. *Bhopal Development Authority Headquarters* windows are never set to wall faces (A+D 1991). Openings are recessed in thick walls, sometimes with additional separated walls having large exterior openings. Raje gave large volumes of vertical space over to light and often spoke of *light space* and *light volumes*. All Raje projects also covered in the same monograph as the quotes (Raje + Raje 2012).

Supporting Evidence

The psychological benefits of this schema can be connected to a respite from solar heat, leading to improved comfort conditions, elimination of glare and its liabilities, controlled views from less toward more extremes and a more fluid relation between in and out with options to inhabit the in-between.

Shading. When fully shaded, no direct sun hits windows, and reflected heat gain is about 75-80% less than full sun. A building's shade needs can be determined using the Shading Calendar technique. When shading periods are understood, the geometry can be studied using the External Shading strategy. Find both in DeKay + Brown (2014).
Glare. Windows provide access to daylight and view, which generally improve cognitive performance, circadian health, and visual delight. However, unshaded they can also lead to glare and eyestrain, particularly in bright sky climates. Glare is a function of brightness contrast within occupants' field of view. The use of reflection surfaces and the prevention of direct sun entering a room reduces the glare experience. Further glare reduction occurs when the sources of light, both direct sun and diffuse sky, are obscured from any direct line of view.

Glare and view. Investigating window technologies that both reduced glare and insured a view, a study by the Well Living Lab (Jamrozik et al. 2019) found that, when shading was employed, occupants experienced improved satisfaction with lighting and the indoor environment, improved well-being and performance, reduced eyestrain and better working memory.

View and porosity. Stamps' (2013b) experiments found that increased porosity of spatial boundaries, allowing *views through*, increased participants' sense of spaciousness via less feeling of enclosure. His other studies (Stamps 2013a) show that both permeability and, to a lesser extent, depth of boundary condition decrease sense of enclosure. In his *theory of permeability*, he argues that enclosure without view increases fear feelings from danger (such as enemies) that may be close but not seen. Similarly, seeing out while not being seen from outside gives feelings of safety, which is a known prerequisite to calmness. O'Brien (2020) concludes, "These findings suggest that an ability to perceive the layering of space through multiple surfaces can increase our sense of spaciousness."

Design Guidelines

In hot climates, protect inset windows by means of thickened edges and gallery layers, or face them to shielded terraces or sun-breaking courts. Make these volumes inhabitable, connected to interior rooms and integral to the form, rather than as attached shading *devices.*

Inhabit the linkages. The essence of this schema is creating with a lighting gradient linkage of indoor, in-between and outdoor space, such that outdoors is viewed though shadow space, bringing a feeling of mental and bodily sanctuary. Make the shading pocket layer inhabitable whenever possible and link indoor rooms to it with doors.

Subtract from volumes as the essential tactic for this schema. Raje's examples illustrate the importance of conceiving pockets of shadow as three-dimensional volumetric, potentially inhabitable spatial elements that occupy area in the plan and section, providing sun protection and privacy. Use the schema to establish fundamental building massing and solid/void compositions during preliminary design.

Explore variations. Many forms are possible: 1. Corner volumes with two rooms facing into the pocket; 2. Gallery or arcade layers with several rooms that parallel repeating pocket subdivisions; 3. Vertical opaque walls alternating with multistory inset pockets and windows from three sides facing into them; or even 4. A thickened wall in which the larger frames shade wall elements set back inside the structural grid.

Organize servant pockets to support served rooms. Outdoor zones can form layers around indoor rooms. The uncovered North American deck or patio is the antithesis of this. Bound indoor rooms with partially-enclosed frameworks of columns, beams, piers, arches or brise-soleil. Roofs may combine covered, trellised or open details. Begin with addressing west and southwest orientations, with their low sun angles and high afternoon temperatures.

Avoid add-on shading devices, such as louvered screens and attached protrusions, which are easy to delete when inevitable cost-cutting evaluations are taken. Integral spatial compositions are more difficult to change

Refine with G4 Shades of Brilliance, C4 Tempered Pathway and C4 Inhabited Periphery. Help build G6 Engagement and Retreat and R6 Cooling Conversions.

G6

Engagement and Retreat

creates an outdoor connection spectrum by providing locational options across varying degrees of enclosure.

234 **Sea Ranch Condominium One**

Sea Ranch, California, 1965
Moore, Lyndon, Turnbull +
Whitaker [MLTW] , architects

Unit nine: from engaging daylight and sun, close to weather, to inside retreat close to others and a warm fire.

image: Morley Baer Photography Trust

periodic place
sequestered or allied
hosts my inner state

Locomotion is a fundamental human freedom that brings at will options for seeking privacy and community, light and dark, or exposure versus protection. In buildings, workers who must sit at the same desk all day feel confined, while at home they find liberty in relocating from room to room as inclined. Architecturally, variations of privacy, exposure, light and liberty can all be correlated with enclosure. A range of spatial enclosures—from street and site to arcade and court to perimeter and interior rooms—constitutes a spectrum for climate control and an array of choices for intense or mediated sensations. Such options, among many further degrees of refinement, also facilitate a fundamental phenomenological distinction. One can connect to the outdoor environment in more open or transparent spaces and, by association, psychologically affiliate with the context, climate and surrounding life. In contrast, by retreating to greater enclosure, into more interior realms, one is protected, sheltered from weather and noise, isolated from over-stimulation and thus impelled to reflect internally and connect with the essential self there.

Sea Ranch Condominium One

left
Unit nine: further retreat, sleeping safely enclosed in the tower

photo Morley Baer Photography Trust

right
Protected common court

photo Dan Klyn

next page, axonometric
Degrees of enclosure

Sea Ranch Condominium One, a 10-unit structure and the first building in this Northern California coastal development, offers residents four degrees of daytime enclosure and a fifth private sleeping loft. 1. A sunny wind-protected court provides a communal open-to-sky terrace with a framed view of the sea; 2. Protected inward, court-facing entries and arcades create in-between spaces. Units are organized as multistorey timber-framed 24 ft (7.3 m) cubic volumes. 3. Inside, four freestanding columns, independent of the heavy timber frame, define a fire-warmed interior social *aedicula* space (Futagawa + Turnbull 1970). Windowless itself, "to enhance the sense of enclosure," the lowered ceiling creates a sheltered feeling of interiority (Turnbull et al. 2000). 4. At the ocean-side edges, a glass-bounded *saddlebag* window seat pushes outside the corner of the primary structure and weather envelope, vulnerable and exposed on multiple sides, suspended between protected interior and wild outside coastal conditions. The rest of the loosely defined living and dining space situates between these poles of protected and exposed. 5. In a tower atop the living space lies the bed loft under a large skylight from which to watch the stars or rain. Apart from life below, the sleeping space is surrounded by fabric enclosure and drop-down curtains to further increase the sense of security and shelter. The project "records a dynamic balance in the interaction between disparate life forces—in this case between shelter and exposure..." (Lyndon + Alinder 2014).

Degrees of enclosure

left
Sea Ranch Condos, Unit 9

Exposed window seat and entry court; enclosed four-poster living space and isolated bed loft.

right
Palace of the Lions (Palacio de los Leones), The Alhambra
Grenada, Spain, 14c

1 Open-to-sky Court of the Lions
2 Three-sided open pavilions
3 Arcaded surrounding gallery
4 Interior *salas* (halls)
5 Protected alcoves
6 More remote/enclosed alcoves

analyses
Zachary Dulin + Mark DeKay

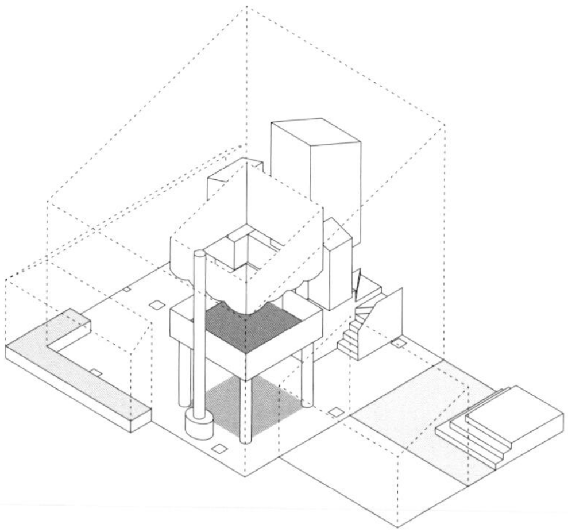

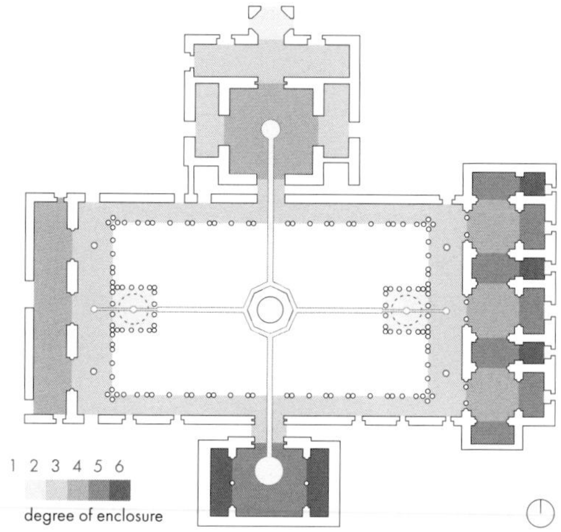

Supporting Evidence

Inhabited space's degree of enclosure is a fundamental ground of place-making and orientation to the world, influencing occupancy activity and impacting connection to or isolation from weather and Nature.

Palace of the Lions exemplifies degrees of enclosure. It is known for its spatial variety and complexity in the Granada climate that cycles from cool winter to very hot summer. The Nasrid culture used moveable furniture, rugs and tapestries, allowing rooms to be used for more than one activity and for activities to relocate on a daily and seasonal basis. Spatial enclosures gave options for residents—ranging from full outdoor weather exposure (1) to deep retreats in small spaces bounded by masonry walls with few windows (6). A north-facing, shady, wind-exposed *mirador* provides maximum summer engagement (2), while the south-side domed hall offers the most stable and sun-protected space for extreme heat (5 +6). Fountains and moving water brought indoors provide cooling both evaporatively and psychologically. The Hall of the Kings at the east end provides the option for all six levels of enclosure in one sequence from sheltered alcove (6) to the central sunny Court of the Lions (1) (Willmert 2010; Alcalá 1999).

Insideness is the phenomenological quality of living that geographer Edward Relph (1976) identifies as key to transforming space into place. He distinguished seven types of place identities, the most profound being *existential insideness*, in which "a place is experienced without deliberate and self-conscious reflection yet is full of significance." Place identity at any scale, he articulates, is a product of three interrelated yet irreducible components: physical features, human activity and meanings.

Inside and outside, according to Norberg-Shulz (1988), is a distinction that allows humans to take "possession of space" and only then "we may say he dwells." How inside is defined relates directly to what is outside and therefore to the cardinal directions and horizon, and expresses in how openings are placed in walls to establish a relationship between inside and the particulars of outside. Architecture becomes a "complex field of occurrences." Shell-space and core-space distinguish inside and outside as *architectonic space* (shell) defined by exterior walls, defining a void within the fullness of nature, in contrast to *experience-space* (core) as defined by inhabitation and activity, "the idea of fullness surrounded by emptiness." A courtyard, therefore, has characteristics of both architectonic space and experience-space (van der Laan 1983). Within the spectrum of room to arcade to court, one can choose to locate according to desires for a degree of fullness or emptiness, engagement or retreat. Architectural space density, an index of spatial enclosure was studied by Csanady (2018), who found a relationship between space density and activity: people tend to choose enclosed (spatially high-density) locations for low-level activities, such as sitting or studying, while selecting more open (spatially low-density) locations for higher level activities of standing and walking.

Design Guidelines

To provide inhabitants climatic and psychological adaptive opportunity, organize buildings with room options that have a range of more open and contained enclosures. Compose the spectrum from fully indoor retreat to fully outdoor engagement by combinations of spatial position, orientation and envelope permeability.

Program for locational flexibility. Mobility, the freedom to relocate, becomes essential to this schema. A few uses, such as cooking or bathing are tied to particular rooms, yet many activities can be moved among places. Establish an enclosure gradient by locating a range of three or more degrees of enclosure adjacent to one another, such that inhabitants can move easily among them in increments of exposure. More protected and enclosed spaces can naturally be wrapped in layers of decreasing spatial enclosure. The Palace of Lions shows multiple arrangements for this horizontal adjacency; it also provides a vertical gradient of enclosure (not illustrated) from basement level earth-sheltered space opening to a north garden, to a south-facing upper floor exposed lookout. Organize an intimacy gradient. In some measure, people associate enclosure with privacy and intimacy with the self or others. In concept design, search for congruences between the physical outdoor engagement gradient and the social intimacy gradient. Activities of bathing, sleeping, dressing, reflecting, meditation and creativity may require a high degree of privacy and separation. Sea Ranch shows that degrees of intimacy can be zoned vertically. Though more challenging, careful design can provide simultaneous outdoor connection and privacy. Orient toward or away from sun and wind to support enclosure facilitating either engagement or retreat on a seasonal or daily basis. Glass can face toward winter or away from afternoon sun; terraces can be in the summer wind or winter lee. East versus west exposure facilitates alternating morning and afternoon occupancy. Vary exterior envelope permeability to drive a sense of enclosure. Small windows, thick walls and deep shade provide retreat, which can be from either cold or hot conditions. Multiple large apertures, arcades and thin layers encourage exposure. Shading that helps retreat from sun can combine with perimeter openness engaging breeze. Refine with C5 Thermal Enclave, R5 Heliotropic Rooms and G5 Pockets of Shadow.

Gradient Sources

G2 Adaptive Altitude

Aalto, Alvar. 1935. Rationalism and Man, in Alvar Aalto + Goran Schildt, eds. *Alvar Aalto: Sketches* (Stuart Wrede, trans). Cambridge, Massachusetts: MIT Press, 48

ArchDaily. 2019. Yue Library/Beijing Fenghemuchen Space Design, *ArchDaily*, 15 Oct, archdaily.com/926534

Bean, Robert, Bjarne W Olesen + Kwang Woo Kim. 2010. History of Radiant Heating and Cooling Systems. *ASHRAE Journal* 52(1): 40–47

DesignBoom. 2019. Beijing Fenghemuchen Space Design Builds Yue Library as Wooden Forest of Books in Hangzhou. *DesignBoom*, 17 Oct, designboom.com

Heschong, Lisa. 1979. *Thermal Delight in Architecture*. Cambridge, Massachusetts: MIT Press

Keskeys, Paul, 2018. 2018 A+ Awards Project of the Year: Waterside Buddhist Shrine by ARCHSTUDIO [with Video]. *Archisizer*. architizer.com

Liu, Shichao, Zhe Wang, Stefano Schiavon, Yingdong Hea, Maohui Luoa, Hui Zhanga + Edward Arens. 2020. Predicted Percentage Dissatisfied with Vertical Temperature Gradient. *Energy and Buildings* 220:110085

Metalocus. 2017. ARCHSTUDIO Designs Buddhist Shrine into a Small Mound in Hebei. *Melatlocus*, 15 Jun. metalocus.es

Suzuki, Daisetz Teitaro. 1959. *Zen and Japanese Culture*, 2nd ed. New York: Pantheon Books, 105

Wujie, Li. 2019. *Yue Library* [video]. *YouTube*, 2 Oct, youtube.com/watch?v=CdFXl5EaTWM&t=2s

G3 Existential Datum

Alexander, Christopher, Sara Ishikawa + Murray Silverstein. 1977. *A Pattern Language: Towns, Buildings, Construction*. New York: Oxford University Press, #248 Soft Tile and Brick, 1141–1144

Day, Christopher. 1990. *Places of the Soul: Architecture and Environmental Design as a Healing Art*. London: Aquarian Press/HarperCollins, 62-63

DeKay, Mark + G Z Brown. 2014. Sun, *Wind + Light: Architectural Design Strategies*. 3rd ed. Hoboken, New Jersey: Wiley, #76 Earth Edges, E.208–210

Emilio, Ambasz, Michele Alassio + Peter Buchanan. 2005. *Emilio Ambasz: Casa de Retiro Espiritual*. Milan: Skira

Stoller, Ezra. 1999. *Frank Lloyd Wright's Fallingwater*. New York: Princeton Architectural Press

Thiis-Evensen, Thomas. 1987. *Archetypes in Architecture*. Oslo: Scandinavian University Press, 55

Utzon, Jørn. 1962. Platforms and Plateaus: Ideas of a Danish Architect. *Zodiac, International Magazine of Contemporary Architecture* 10:112–142

Waggoner, Lynda S, ed. 2011. Western Pennsylvania Conservancy. *Fallingwater*. New York: Rizzoli

Watchman, Mélanie, Mark DeKay, Claude M H Demers + André Potvin. 2022. Design Vocabulary and Schemas for Biophilic Experiences in Cold Climate Schools. *Architectural Science Review* 65(2):101–19

G4 Incalescent Center

Alexander, Christopher, Sara ishikawa + Murray Silverstein. 1977. *A Pattern Language: Towns, Buildings, Construction*. New York: Oxford University Press, #181 The Fire, 838–843

Bachelard, Gaston. 1938. *La Psychanalyse du Feu, Librarie Gallimard*, reprint, *The Psychoanalysis of Fire*. Boston, Massachusetts: Beacon Press

Göritz, Hansjörg. 2009. Vast Vicinity: Learning from Essential Settling and Dwelling. *Transactions on Ecology and the Environment* 120: 339–351

Göritz, Hansjörg. 2021. Stone in a Tent: Trennemoor House Narrative, unpublished, personal correspondence, trans. from original 1993 German

Lynn, Christopher. 2014. Hearth and Campfire Influences on Arterial Blood Pressure: Defraying the Costs of the Social Brain through Fireside Relaxation. *Evolutionary Psychology* 12(5): 983–1003

McClenon, James. 2006. The Ritual Healing Theory: Therapeutic Suggestion and the Origin of Religion. in Patrick McNamara + J Harold Ellens, eds. *Where God and Science Meet: How Brain and Evolutionary Studies Alter our Understanding of Religion*. Westport, Connecticut: Praeger, 35–158

Tabb, Phillip. 2019. *Elemental Architecture: Temperaments of Sustainability*. London: Routledge, 35

G4 Euphonic Water

Aguirre, Jamie Guana. 2022. *Monterrey, N L Museo Marco, Fuente Y Efecto De Agua Cruzado* [Monterrey N L Marco Museum, Fountain and Crosswater Effect]. video. *YouTube*, 27 Jan. youtube.com/watch?v=shAJIF5aJ0U

Ekman, Maria Rådsten, Peter Lundén + Mats E Nilsson. 2015. Similarity and Pleasantness Assessments of Water-Fountain Sounds Recorded in Urban Public Spaces. *The Journal of the Acoustical Society of America* 138(5): 3043–3052

Galvan, Manu. 2011. *Fuente Museo MARCO* [MARCO Museum Fountain], low res video with jet sound. *YouTube*, 26 Jul. youtube.com/watch?v=wVRuSbTOI_Q

Haapakangas, Annu, E Kankkunen, Valtteri Hongisto, Petra Virjonen, David Oliva, + Esko Keskinen. 2011. Effects of Five Speech Masking Sounds on Performance and Acoustic Satisfaction: Implications for Open Plan Offices. *Acta Acustica United with Acustica* 97: 641–55

Jeon, Jin Yong, Pyoung Jik Lee, Jin You + Jian Kang. 2010. Perceptual Assessment of Quality of Urban Soundscapes with Combined Noise Sources and Water Sounds. *The Journal of the Acoustical Society of America* 127(3):1357–366

Jeon, Jin Yong, Pyoung Jik Lee, Jin You + Jian Kang. 2012. Acoustical Characteristics of Water Sounds for Soundscape Enhancement in Urban Open Spaces. *The Journal of the Acoustical Society of America* 131(3): 2101–2109

Nasar, Jack + Yi-Hsuan Lin. 2003. Evaluative Responses to Five Kinds of Water Features. *Landscape Research* 28(4): 441–450

Ruso, Bernhart + Klaus Atzwanger. 2003. Measuring Immediate Behavioral Responses to the Environment. *The Michigan Psychologist* 4:12

Ulrich, Roger S, Robert F Simons, Barbara D Losito, Evelyn Fiorito, Mark A Miles + Michael Zelson. 1991. Stress Recovery During Exposure to Natural and Urban Environments. *Journal of Environmental Psychology* 11(3): 201–30

Valdes, Jorge Elias Guiterrez. 2011. *Museo Marco* [Marco Museum]. video. *YouTube*. 16 Jun. youtube.com/watch?v=68yFR5iD-I8

G4 Zephyr Spectrum

Arens, Edward, Stephen Turner, Hui Zhang + Gwelen Paliaga. 2009. Moving Air for Comfort. *ASHRAE Journal* 51(5):18–28

de Dear, Richard J, Takashi Akimoto, Edward A Arens, Gail Brager, Christhina Candido, David K W Cheong, Baizhan Li, N Nishihara, Chandra Sekhar, Shin-ichi Tanabe, Jorn Toftum, Hui Zhang + Yingxin Zhu. 2013. Progress in Thermal Comfort Research over the Last Twenty Years. *Indoor Air* 23(6): 442–461

Gradient Sources

DeKay, Mark + G Z Brown. 2014. *Sun, Wind + Light: Architectural Design Strategies*. 3rd ed. Hoboken, New Jersey: Wiley; #26 Cooling Zones, E76–78; #44 Cross-ventilation Rooms, E120–122; #69 Ventilation Openings Arrangement, E185–186

Hu, S, Y Xin, G Liu, G Wang, J Zhou, K Liu, M Chen + A G Zhou. 2009. Preliminary study on influences of plateau low-pressure environment on human thermal comfort. *Heating, Ventilation and Air-Conditioning* 39(7):18–21

ILFI. 2017. Khoo Teck Puat Hospital (Stephen R. Kellert Biophilic Design Award). *International Living Futures Institute*. living-future.org

Izadi, Anoosha, Melanie Rudd + Vanessa M Patrick. 2019. The Way the Wind Blows: Direction of Airflow Energizes Consumers and Fuels Creative Engagement. *Journal of Retailing* 95(4): 43–157

Ohtake, Miyoko. 2009. Dunkin' Danish. *Dwell*. 17 Jun, dwell.com

Raftery, Paul + David Douglass-Jaimes. 2020. *Ceiling Fan Design Guide*. March. Center for the Built Environment. University of California, Berkeley. cbe.berkeley.edu/wp-content/uploads/2020/04/CBE-Ceiling-Fan-Design-Guide-V0.pdf

RMJM. 2015. The Architect's Perspective: Khoo Teck Puat Hospital. *RMJM Company*. 28 Sep. rmjm.com/the-architects-perspective-khoo-teck-puat-hospital/

Schröpfer, Thomas, Heng Chee Chan + Kees Christiaanse. 2016. Khoo Teck Puat Hospital, in Thomas Schröpfer, Heng Chee Chan + Kees Christiaanse, *Dense + Green: Innovative Building Types for Sustainable Urban Architecture*. Basel: Birkhäuser, 114–119

White Arkitekter AB. 2008. Kastrup Sea Bath/ White Arkitekter. *ArchDaily*. archdaily.com/2899

Yen, Tan Shao. 2012. The Practice of Integrated Design: The Case Study of Khoo Teck Puat Hospital, Singapore. Masters Dissertation, 31 Jan. Nottingham, UK: University of Nottingham

Zhai, Yongchao, Hui Zhang, Yufeng Zhang, Wilmer Pasut, Edward Arens + Qinglin Meng. 2015. Thermal Comfort and Perceived Air Quality with Ceiling Fans in Warm-Humid Conditions. *Building and Environment* 90: 178–185

Zhai, Yongchao, Hui Zhang, Yufeng Zhang, Wilmer Pasut, Edward Arens, + Qinglin Meng. 2013. Comfort under Personally Controlled Air Movement in Warm and Humid Environments. *Building and Environment* 65:109–117

Zhang, Hui, Edward Arens, Sahar Abbaszadeh Fard, Charlie Huizenga, Gwelen Paliaga, Gail Brager, + Leah Zagreus. 2007. Air Movement Preferences Observed in Office Buildings. *International Journal of Biometeorology* 51(5): 349–60

Zhao, Rongyi + J Li. 2004. The effective use of simulated natural air movement in warm environments. *Indoor Air* 14(7): 46–50

G4 Shades of Brilliance

Astbury, Jon. 2021. Plant-Covered Mesh Panels Surround Preschool in Vietnam by HGAA. *dezeen*, 10 Oct. dezeen.com/2021/10/10

DeKay, Mark + G Z Brown. 2014. *Sun, Wind + Light: Architectural Design Strategies*. 3rd ed. Hoboken, New Jersey: Wiley; #A26 Shading Calendar, E.344–349; #23 Overhead Shades, E.66–67; #63 Layer of Shades, E.170–172

Divasare. 2016. Office Kersten Geers David van Aevern Office 39—Villa Buggenhout. *Divasare,* 27 Jan. divisare.com/projects/308813

Fiala, Dusan, George Havenith, Peter Bröde, Bernhard Kampmann + Gerd Jendritzky. 2012. UTCI-Fiala Multi-Node Model of Human Heat Transfer and Temperature Regulation. *International Journal of Biometeorology* 56(3): 429–441

Galán-Marín, Carmen, Victoria López-Cabeza, Carlos Rivera-Gómez + Juan Rojas-Fernández. 2018, 30 Oct. On the Influence of Shade in Improving Thermal Comfort in Courtyards. *Proceedings* 2(22):1390, Economy, Sustainable Development and Energy International Conference (ESDEIC), Edinburgh, Scotland, UK, 25–27 June. mdpi.com

Holman, Dawn M, George T Kapelos, Meredith Shoemaker + Meg Watson. 2018. Shade as an Environmental Design Tool for Skin Cancer Prevention. *American Journal of Public Health* 108(12) Dec:1607–1612

Lynes, Barbara Buhler + Judy Lopez. 2012. *Georgia O'Keeffe and Her Houses: Ghost Ranch and Abiquiu*. New York: Abrams/ Georgia O'Keeffe Museum

Moholy-Nagy, Sibyl + Gerhard Schwab. 1970. *The Architecture of Paul Rudolph*. New York: Praeger

Olgyay, Adalar + Victor Olgyay. 1957. *Solar Control and Shading Devices*. Princeton, New Jersey: Princeton University Press, 196–197

Paul Rudolph Heritage Foundation. 2021.Hiss Residence—Umbrella House. paulrudolph.institute/ 195308-hiss-residence

Process Architecture. 1980. Katsuhiko Ichinowatari, Ed. *TAC, The Heritage of Walter Gropius* (Process Architecture 19). Tokyo: Process Architecture Pub.

Curtis, William. 1997. L D Institute of Indology, Ahmedabad, India 1957–1962. *A + U: Architecture and Urbanism* 7(322): 32–39

DeKay, Mark + G Z Brown. 2014. *Sun, Wind + Light: Architectural Design Strategies,* 3rd ed. Hoboken, New Jersey: Wiley, #A26 Shading Calendar, E344–349; #91 External Shading, E239–246

Jamrozik, Anja, Nicholas Clements, Syed Hasan, Jie Zhao, Rongpeng Zhang, Carolina Campanella, Vivian Loftness, Paige Porter, Shaun Ly, Selena Wang + Brent Bauer. 2019. Access to Daylight and View in an Office Improves Cognitive Performance and Satisfaction and Reduces Eyestrain: A Controlled Crossover Study. *Building and Environment* 65:103–379

O'Brien, Darragh. 2020. Layered Boundary Spaces: How does the Layering of Boundaries Effect our Sense of Spaciousness? *EBD: Evidence Based Design*. ebdjournal.com

Raje, Shubhra + Amita Raje. 2012. *Anant Raje Architect: Selected Works 1971-2009*. New Delhi: Tulika Books, 64, 190

Stamps, Arthur E, III. 2013a. Permeability Theory and Palace Athena. *Perceptual and Motor Skills* 116(3) Jun: 806–815

Stamps, Arthur E, III. 2013b. Effects of Multiple Boundaries on Perceived Spaciousness and Enclosure. *Environment and Behavior* 45(7) Oct: 851–875

Steele, James. 1998. *Rethinking Modernism for the Developing World: The Complete Architecture of Balkrishna Doshi*. New York: Whitney Library of Design

G5 Pockets of Shadow

A+D. 1991. Headquarters, Bhopal Development Authority, Bhopal, 1990. *Architecture + Design* 8(3) May–Jun:17

Bhatt, Vikram + Peter Scriver. 1990. *Contemporary Indian Architecture After the Masters*. Ahmedabad, India: Mapin Publishing, 204–207

G6 Engagement + Retreat

Alcalá, Benito Jiménez. 1999. Natural Cooling in Hispano-Moslem Residential Architecture: The Case-Study of The Court of The Lions and The Court of Comares In The Alhambra (Granada), PLEA 99 Conference. *Passive and Low Energy Architecture*, 399–406

Gradient Sources

Csanady, Pal. 2018. Architectural Space Density: Effect of Enclosure. *Symmetry: Culture and Science* 29 (X), 499–504

Futagawa, Yukio + William Turnbull. 1970. *MLTW : Moore, Lyndon, Turnbull and Whitaker: The Sea Ranch, California. 1966.* Tokyo: ADA Edita

Lyndon, Donlyn + James Alinder. 2014. *The Sea Ranch: Fifty Years of Architecture, Landscape, Place, and Community on the Northern California Coast, rev ed.* New York: Princeton Architectural Press

Norberg-Schulz, Christian. 1988. The Concept of Place, in *Architecture: Meaning and Place, Selected Essays.* New York: Rizzoli, 27–32

Relph, Edward C. 1976. *Place and Placelessness.* London: Pion, 55

Turnbull, William, William Stout + Dung Ng. 2000. *William Turnbull, Jr: Buildings in the Landscape.* San Francisco: William Stout

van der Laan, Hans. 1983. *Architectonic Space: Fifteen Lessons on the Disposition of the Human Habitat.* Leiden, Netherlands: Brill

Willmert, Todd. 2010. Alhambra Palace Architecture: An Environmental Consideration of its Inhabitation. *Muqarnas* 27: 57–188

244 **Hospital of San Sebastián**

Badajoz, Spain, 1694
Nicolás de Morales Morgado
architect

renovation 2017
José María Sánchez García,
renovation architect

Nature inside: direct sun, modulated by the court roof, follows rhythms of the day and season, visibly mapping the progression on floor and walls.

photo Roland Halbe

Rhythm Schemas

Because architecture is actually the prime mediator between contemporary humans and Nature, it has the possibility to connect people to Nature. The human biological clock requires a daily reset with a high dose of sunlight. As the sun crosses the sky on a summer day, different rooms are heated; occupants respond by employing and retracting shades. The sunrise and sunset are universally attractive. The star-filled night sky encourages contemplation of one's place in the universe. Buildings can help people experience these profound events. They can facilitate inhabitants' engaging and understanding these and other of Nature's rhythms. Warm and cold seasons, long and short daylight hours, humid and arid cycles, rainy and dry periods, harvesting and storage of food—these are fundamental to the pulsation of life on Earth.

While Nature's rhythms drive conditions for buildings, humankind's habitat is characterized by its interior conditions, which are experiential progenitors and can be steady-state or dynamic. When dynamic, they often follow rhythms. People prefer cooler sleeping temperatures and expect warmer daytime conditions. Winter clothes are associated with expectations for cooler indoor temperatures, as are the lighter clothes of summer linked with acceptably warmer conditions. Bright daylight required for work gives way to dimmer illumination for evening story-telling.

The design schemas in this section provide generative starting points for designing buildings that can respond to, amplify and celebrate rhythms of the day and season, bringing the potential for occupants to feel alertness, happiness, a sense of belonging in and connection with Nature, environmental awareness, deep sleep, and the satisfaction of everyday ritual and memory. R2 Aperture Engagement has inhabitants participating directly with Nature and knowing it by how they operate the building's response to Nature's rhythms. R3 Biorhythmic Radiance and R4 Circadian Space address the human diurnal need for light. R4 Dawn + Dusk Places and R5 Heliotropic Rooms suggest ritualistic and appreciative acknowledgment of solar and lunar arcs. R4 Radiant Sailing and R6 Cooling Conversions forward the cyclic awareness that manifests when the building's structure embodies space heating and cooling intelligence, depending less on machines. R4 Habitat Fringe recognizes the fascination and curiosity humans have with seasonally rich garden ecology, bringing life to the edges of rooms.

The designer's challenge with rhythmic schemas is to find the fit between the rituals of occupants' social lives, the configuration of architectural space and the periodicity of Nature. This leads people to know Nature more intimately and to feel more situated in place; thus, the repeated events of life gain more significance.

R2

Aperture Engagement

encourages conscious control of climatic relationships by adjusting openings and layers, building place connection.

246 **242 State Street Building**

Los Altos, CA, 2014
Olson Kundig Architects
Tom Kundig, design principal

The large, operable window wall is allowed to be opened freely as a means of adjusting the interior climate and linking to the outdoors

photo Bruce Damonte

video see OlsunKundig 2014
more images see ArchDaily 2014

joy in agency
open windows draw the blinds
feel one with weather

Operating a well-designed building is a bit like sailing. In buildings designed to link with daily and seasonal climatic rhythms, engaging apertures is how users regulate their experience of light, sun, wind, view, glare, outdoor sound and privacy. As Glenn Murcutt (1996) thinks of it, "You modify and manipulate its form and skin according to seasonal conditions and natural elements, and work with these to maximize the performance of the building. This involvement with the building also assists in the care for it." It brings occupants into a participatory ritualistic relationship, which in time becomes significant to how they make meaning about living in a place. Habitual patterns of controlling windows, shutters, daylight louvers, ventilation openings and shades create relationships among the person, building and Nature. Preferences for thermal, lighting and acoustic qualities vary dramatically among individuals and for a single individual. People want to be in control over their lives and environment. Even the mere presence of control opportunity makes a difference to their satisfaction, but participation is transformational.

58 House

Nai Hiên Đông, Vietnam, 2020
85 Design [To Huu Dung] architect

Movable layers of curtains, glazing and louvered panels allow multiple modes of engagement for occupants to modulate the connection to outdoors.

photo 85 Design

video see HPC 2021

Contrast
Gradient
Rhythm
Flux
Sequence
Narrative
Air
Earth
Life
Light
Sun
Water

242 State Street Building is an adaptive re-use of a 1950's building where user needs drove the space's transformation. The entire double-height, floor-to-ceiling front facade becomes an engageable aperture. Occupants operate a large floor-to-ceiling window by a foot pedal to unlock the safety mechanism, and then turn a hand wheel that activates a counterweight and series of gears and pulleys. This façade replacement converted a previously enclosed structure into an inviting inward public view of its exhibit in a relatively moderate climate that can accommodate an open-air environment during a significant portion of the year (Domus 2014).

58 House employs full storey louvers on the east and west facades to mitigate the impacts of sun and admit wind in this warm-humid climate. The movable louver panels can be collapsed to easily adjust the amount of shading desired in the balconies and rooms beyond them – for example, fully closed on the east side in the morning yet open for full view in the afternoon. With a full height sliding glass facade behind the balcony, occupants can vary ventilation aperture to admit or reject breeze, creating degrees of visual and thermal conditions. A layer of curtains behind the glass adds another option for privacy and light filtering. When it is colder, the louvered shutters can be collapsed and the windows closed to allow for solar heat to enter (85 Design 2020; ArchDaily 2020).

Aperture Engagement

248 **Cooling effect of air movement**

Faster air flow, lighter clothing and local user controls all increase the temperature occupants find acceptable.

ASHRAE Std. 55 defines comfort zones where 80% of people find conditions thermally acceptable. The graph shows zones calculated for 0.5 and 1.0 clo (clothing factor), defined by PMV (Predicted Mean Vote) within limits of +/– 0.5. Separate (dark and light gray) zones are defined for occupant *local control* over air movement vs *no local control*. Additional colored curves (outer edges) show comfort at more relaxed *slightly warm* (+1) and *slightly cool* (–1) PMV limits.

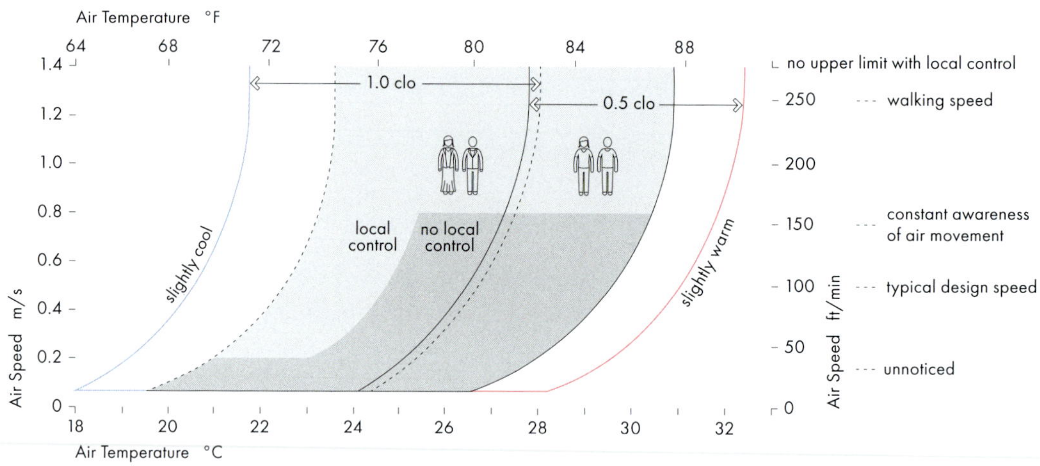

Supporting Evidence

Occupants want to connect with the outdoors, and when they have greater adaptive opportunity to regulate their environment, they tend to be more accepting of fluctuations that might not conform with norms of constancy.

Cooling effect of air movement. ASHRAE Standard 55 (2020), Thermal Environmental Conditions for Human Occupancy, allows for warmer temperatures when air is moving, permitting both temperature and velocity to be higher when occupants have local control. It is widely accepted that even these expanded limits are conservative and that people can be comfortable over even wider ranges. Using the CBE Thermal Comfort Tool (Tartarini et al. 2020), we recalculated lines of equivalent comfort (curves in the graph) for slightly warm and slightly cool perceptions and added them to the figure to better show the comfort-enhancing potentials of air movement.
Adaptive comfort, a model developed by de Dear and Brager (1998) incorporated in ASHRAE Std. 55, demonstrates that when people have control over operable windows in a naturally ventilated building, combining both behavioral and psychological adaptation, they prefer a wider range of indoor temperatures that follow the seasonal rhythms of the outdoor climate. This applies to both naturally ventilated and mixed mode buildings (Parkinson et al. 2020), and is covered more in R6 Cooling Conversions.
Rating systems. Some energy codes and green building rating systems acknowledge the importance of operable windows. The Living Building Challenge (ILFI 2019) requires full control of windows. To meet the WELL Building Standard (IWBI), at least 75% of regularly occupied spaces must have operable windows that provide access to outdoor air, and the openable window area should be equivalent to at least 4% of the net occupied floor area of that space. Many building codes set minimum operable area at 5–10% of the floor area.

Design Guidelines

Design apertures for combinations of light, sun, view, privacy and ventilation, while explicitly putting control in the hands of the occupant.

Avail inhabitants of operable openings as their essential connection to the outdoor environment, providing views of Nature and urban life, an awareness of passing weather and sensation of sounds and smells of the world outside. Apertures and their associated interior and exterior layers precipitate the building skin's filtering, blocking, connecting with, transforming, directing and switching climatic forces. Ensure that all regularly occupied spaces have occupant-controlled, operable apertures.

Separate aperture types to individually control different natural elements. It is difficult or impossible for one aperture to provide all the functions. For example, Kahn's Esherick House separates fixed view glazing from operable opaque screened ventilation panes in a thickened facade that provides fixed exterior and movable interior shade layers. For more guidance see the Separated or Combined Openings strategy in DeKay + Brown (2014).

Layer multiple aperture controls in the facade that allow inhabitants to separately admit, filter or exclude environmental conditions as desired. Examples include operable windows or sliding glass walls, fixed or seasonal exterior shading, movable exterior louvered shutters or interior blinds, and opaque or translucent elements such as curtains or privacy screening.

Insure rational transparency of user controls by their visibility and accessibility, including by people with mobility challenges. Place them at the point of need and ensure they are not blocked by furniture. Make controls straightforward, understandable and intuitively obvious, easy to operate by occupants and management. When users employ controls, provide for a rapid and unambiguous outcome with quick feedback.

Limit automated controls, placing self-regulating windows only where they are most needed, such as in high or out-of-reach places, or in public spaces not perceived as any individual's territory. In buildings occupied only during the day, automated ventilation apertures might be needed for a night-cooled mass strategy. In some cases, automation helps maintain minimum ventilation requirements, controlled airflow during high winds and rain or the operation of unglazed apertures not visibly evident to occupants. Automated controls can be triggered by relative indoor and outdoor temperatures or humidity, CO_2 concentrations for demand-controlled ventilation or by wind speed and direction.

Integrate automation with user control. Ensure that algorithms for opening and closing apertures, shades and other layers are understood by the occupants. Integrate non-residential building HVAC systems with window switches that turn off conditioning supply to the zone when an aperture is opened by occupants. Provide personal control of window operability and local overrides to operable shading while preventing energy waste. Also see the Manual or Automated Controls strategy in DeKay + Brown (2014).

Refine with F1 Melodic Materials and F2 Current Prehension. Help build inhabited experiences in R3 Biorhythmic Radiance, C3 Scintillating Sun, F3 Fans First and F3 Water-Animated Surfaces.

R3

Biorhythmic Radiance

supplements daylight with electric lighting intensity, timing and color that harmonize with bodily cycles.

250 **Novo Nordisk NN2 Headquarters atrium canopy lighting variations**

Bagsværd, Denmark, 2013
Henning Larsen, architects
Christina Augustesen, lighting design, with Sweco Architects

Dynamic electric lighting responds to changing daylight, twilight and darkness with ten programmed sequences. Winner of 2014 Danish Lighting Award (arc 2015)

photos Søren Aagaard

video lecture *see* Augustesen 2017

daylight keeps a beat
light manufactured marches
i awake with ease

People need the right amount of light of the right color at the right times to sleep well and be healthy, energetic and happy (CIE 2019). The body's circadian cycle is triggered by intense morning light that syncs the body's wake/sleep cycle with the 24-hour day. While controlled daylight is the most beneficial light, sometimes climate, location or existing design renders indoor daylight insufficient to support the body's rhythmic circadian needs. When it's not possible to employ daylight for circadian stimulus, electric light can mimic "the morning, daytime and evening periods in spectrum, intensity and dynamics"(Velux 2013). This is especially valuable in basements or the rare windowless room, during early morning hours, in winter months and at high latitudes. In these cases, strategic electric lighting design can supplement good daylighting design, helping provide some of the missing circadian stimulus and its accompanying experiential benefits. The designer's challenge is to key the lighting to the region's natural daylight patterns and together provide the daily lighting variability humans require.

Children's Hospital of Philadelphia Medical Behavioral Unit typical patient room

Philadelphia, Pennsylvania, 2017
ZGF with Architecture+, architects
AKF, lighting

Lighting color and intensity varies through the day to support circadian health.

left
6:30 am, dim orange ambiance, gradually increases like sunrise.

middle
11 am, brighter blue light mimics mid-day daylight

right
3 pm, warming afternoon light gradually decreases toward sunset, similar to sunrise, becoming very dim in the evening and dark at night.

photos Halkin/Mason Photography

Novo Nordisk NN2 Headquarters employs fifty baffled skylights in the atrium roof to deliver daylight to the building interior (ArcDog 2017). The dynamics of the daylight is supplemented by LED electric lighting that varies in "intensity, direction and color temperature" (Augustesen 2017). The lighting system supplements available daylight when needed—and during the evening and dark winter hours. A sophisticated control matrix was designed to vary the electric light based on the sky color and occupancy schedules. Ten programs operate at different times and seasons. The conditions are designed to "control the light in a rhythm and variation that makes us sense a dynamic without distracting us or stressing the mind and body" (Mondo Arc 2015).

Children's Hospital of Philadelphia utilizes a specialized lighting program to supplement daylight in all patient and staff areas to mimic outdoor lighting patterns and support healthy circadian rhythms, syncing sleep and wake cycles. The day starts with a dim orange ambient light in the early mornings, gradually working it's way up to a bright white light around noon, and mellows out toward the end of the day, dimming to the lowest levels possible for a hospital setting at night. Patients are given control over their lighting to modify brightness to their preferences. Just for fun, children can choose between a rainbow of accent light colors (Burling 2018, ZGF 2017).

Circadian Lighting Standards

Underwriters Labs (2019)
CS ≥ 0.3 7 am–4 pm
CS ≤ 0.2 5–7 pm
CS ≤ 0.1 after 8 pm

WELL Buildings (2020)
CS > 0.3 2 hr min in morning

WELL Vertical illuminance
≥ 200 EML 2 hrs, 9 am–1 pm
≤ 50 EML evening hours

Supporting Evidence

Circadian sleep cycle disruption has been linked to a variety of maladies, including poor cognitive function, increased stress and depression, and long-term health challenges. Sleep improvement has been an increasing focus of research about tunable light, targeted to effectively regulate circadian function. Chapter 3 defines various circadian lighting metrics, including Melanopic Equivalent Daylight Illuminance (EDI), Equivalent Melanopic Lux (EML), Circadian Light (CLA) and Circadian Stimulus (CS).

Integrative human-centric lighting refers to electric lighting designed specifically to manipulate temporal patterns, magnitude, spectrum and spatial patterns for users' visual, biological and behavioral responses. Of these characteristics, the greatest impacts on people come from temporal patterns of bright days gradating to dim evenings and dark nights (Vetter et al. 2021).

Improved sleep. Reduced evening blue light supports healthy sleep, since it suppresses melatonin production (Zeitzer et al. 2000; Chellappa et al. 2011). A study of healthy men found that low level evening lighting eased falling asleep by suppressing melatonin production less than lighting at conventionally higher illuminance (Stefani et al. 2021). Limiting evening video screen exposure or dimming displays offer notable benefits (Figueiro + Overington 2016; Escofet + Bará 2017).

Thermoregulation and heart rate are similarly affected by different light wavelengths and intensity. Both core body temperature and heart rate lower with dimmer and longer-wavelength evening light (Cajochen et al 2005).

Improved health. Exposure to controlled bright light (CS 0.5) during the day and low night levels decreased depression and increased sleep quality and duration in both dementia patients and healthy caregivers (Figueiro et al. 2014, 2015). Studies in Alzheimer's patients showed that continuous, bright, indirect white light (>1000 lux at the eye) during daytime consolidated activity and rest rhythms, slowed cognitive and functional deterioration, and eased depression (Riemersma-van der Lek et al. 2008). Seasonal depression linked to reduced winter light exposure can be improved with morning artificial bright light therapy (Figueiro et al. 2016; Schwartz + Olds 2015).

Preference for dynamic lighting that changes regularly is expressed by office workers, as compared to static lighting, even if lighting variability was momentarily distracting (De Kort + Smolders 2010; Begemann et al. 1997).

Design Guidelines

Design for a combination of daylight (preferred) and electric lighting to provide a daily cycle beginning with bright cool daytime light, shifting to moderate white mid-day light, dimming and warming in the evening, ensuring dark night-time conditions. Circadian-supportive electric lighting best practices are rapidly evolving; readers are advised to consult recent recommendations from the lighting industry's professional and standards organizations.

Target vertical illuminance, as suggested by recent consensus experts (Brown et al. 2019), who recommend daytime EDI > 250 lux and night EDI < 10 lux, starting at least three hours before bedtime. These levels are specified at approximately 1.2 m (4 ft) above the floor (about seated eye level).

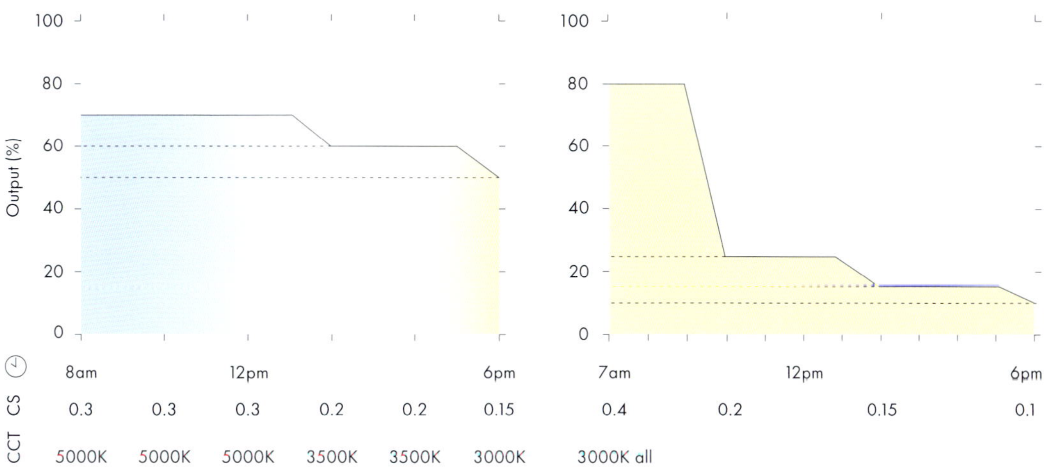

Programming to Support Circadian Stimulus (CS)

Specific schedules support occupant CS (0 for no light to 0.7 max). Y-axes show relative system output (intensity) as %. Both axes are examples, not prescriptions.

left
Color temperature variability. Tunable LED lights programed to change correlated color temperature (CCT) across day; light intensity changes slightly.

right
Light intensity vaiability. CCT constant at 3000K; primary control for regulating CS is light intensity.

both from Figuero et al. 2016

Target activity-based vertical illuminance. Referring to the same vertical planes and height, the WELL Building Std (sidebar) sets daytime targets of at least 125 EML in learning areas, 200 EML in work areas and living environments and 250 EML in break rooms. Luminaires that create little vertical illuminance (V) and mostly horizontal illuminance (H) require greater intensity (Lux) than for those with a higher V:H ratio.

Program for combined spectral power distribution (SPD) and intensity. While cool-white light is typically more CS-stimulating that warm-white light, lights with the same correlated color temperature (CCT), for example, 3000K, can have vastly different melanopic intensities (diagram). A source low in the blue spectrum requires higher illuminance to achieve the same morning CS effect. Support circadian health with programing to dim lighting intensity in late afternoon and evening hours, along with dimming computer monitor blue light after a set hour.

Balance general and local illuminance, such as with local workstation lighting, so that light intensity can be focused, for instance as illuminating privacy panels or by individualized lighting. For related guidance, see the Electric Lighting Zones and Task Lighting strategies in DeKay + Brown (2014).

Combine light and materials. Light vertical wall surfaces in the field of view, not just horizontal work plane. Most combinations of white light sources and white or off-white surfaces perform similarly (UL 2019). Higher reflectance surfaces are important to overall visual comfort and system efficiency.

Control glare. The CS objective is to get the right light to occupants' eyes, which can be difficult in a large office space. Be careful to avoid uncomfortable screen glare, which can result from poorly directed high CS lighting.

Design *light oases* for morning activity spaces, by emphasizing brighter, blue-enriched light that offers high-CS and kick-starts daytime alertness (Chellappa et al. 2011).

Refine with C3 Scintillating Sun and C1 Thermic Hues. Use this schema to help build R4 Circadian Space.

R4

Dawn and Dusk Places

focus occupant attention on the light and color transitions around sunrise, sunset and their lunar equivalents.

254 **Adobe Canyon House**

Patagonia, Arizona, 2005
Studio Rick Joy, architects

right
Sunset terrace. The house has protected sunrise and sunset terraces with covered and open-to-sky options.

photo Bill Timmerman

below
Plan. Occupants can migrate to opposite terraces, close doors to control low-angle sun, choose an exposed edge or a shaded retreat. In heat, western doors can be closed and sunset light appreciated indirectly on the landscape from the eastern terrace.

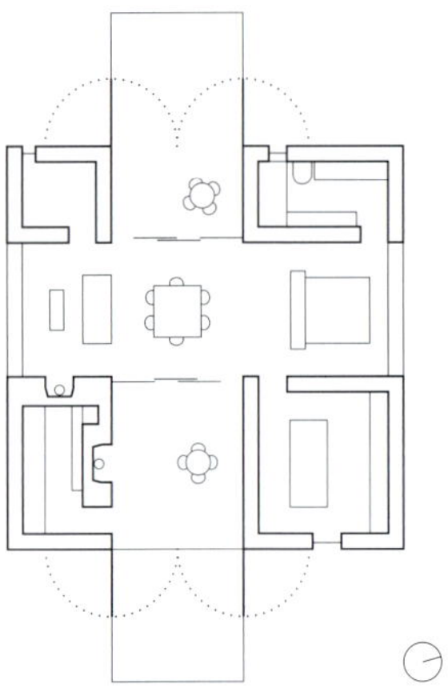

first light's golden break
twilight's fading splendor blue
awe in today's life

Heliophiles are sun-lovers while *selenophiles* (for the Greek moon goddess) find the moon captivating. At the beginning and end of each day, as the sun rises and sets, inhabitants observe dramatic shifts in color and light intensity—the so-called *golden hour,* followed in the evening by the *blue hour*—and the rapid movement of the solar orb as measured against the datum of the Earth's edge. Around sunrise the color sequence reverses, blue then gold. Humans never tire of participating in this ancient ritual. A second drama, a lunar one, repeats monthly in similar orientations, rising easterly and setting westerly. Its most dramatic period is the eastern full moonrise against blue hour sky, just after observing a westerly sunset. Rooms occupied during sun and moon periods of rise and set can be oriented toward those directions. Since the time of megalithic observatories, alignments to these phenomena have built local place empathy. Their movements position humans in a phenomenal cosmos, heavenly events registering on the horizon's radial scale, as seen from an inhabited site—thus situating the inhabitant as well.

Shapes Suites

Ermoupoli, Syros Island, Greece
Loukas Fotopoulos, architect

The view from twin rooftop pool terraces aligned with sunset and moonset also allows appreciation of the *golden hour* and later, the *blue hour*.

photo Pygmalion Karatzas

Adobe Canyon House (Joy 2018) has deep terraces facing east and west, backed by full glass walls of sliding doors that allow the central dining area to be fully open to the breezeway or closed off (see plan). Their alignment, slightly rotated from cardinal, gives a bias toward summer sunsets and winter sunrises. Each terrace can be fully or partially closed off with large hinged metal doors that can be pinned in various positions as vertical shading or security. The wonder of east and west views come with possibly uncomfortable glare and heat. In this scheme, the experiential conflict is addressed simply: combined with the shading fin doors, furniture can be moved from full environmental exposure on the terrace to deep retreat, allowing landscape views even when the sun is very low.

Shapes Suites in the ancient city of Ermoupoli on the island of Syros, Greece, offers small twin suites that open toward the harbor. The roof-top units were added during renovation of a three-story stone building in the historical center into a small hotel, capitalizing on a southwest orientation (Human Point 2019). On the terrace, guests can enjoy their private spa, separated by a planter wall while enjoying the view and ambiance of the golden hour, sunset (and moonset), blue hour and twilight views over the harbor and Aegean Sea. Additional online documentation by Pygmalion Karatzas (2019) shows blue hour views from terraces and from indoor rooms.

Dawn and Dusk Places

left
Moonrise + moonset *azimuth*

Plan view. Darker tones indicate the azimuth range (compass orientation) between major and minor lunar standstills. Inner ring is moon; outer ring, sun. Rising of both is in east and setting of both in west.

right
Golden hour + blue hour *altitude*

Elevation view. Gray shaded sectors show twilight ranges with astronomical definitions. Dawn + dusk definitions are marked as points. Blue and golden hours are approximate culturally-defined ranges. Labels apply am and pm.

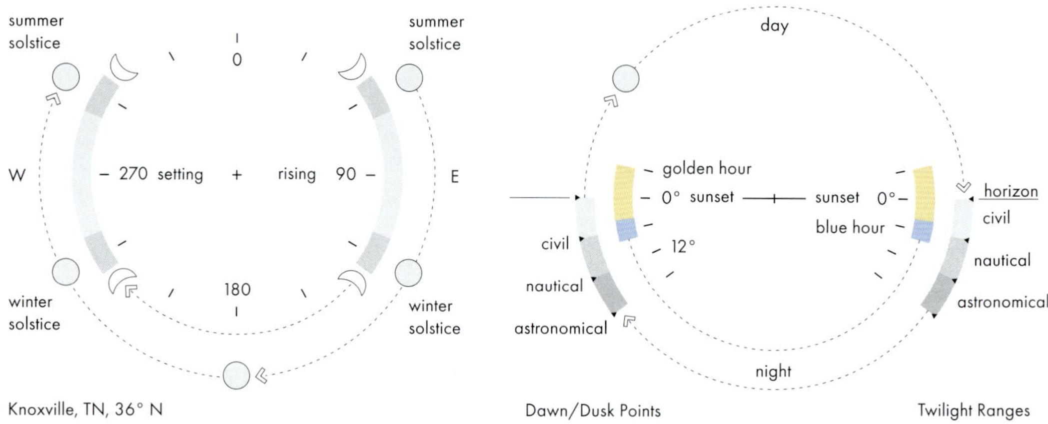

Supporting Evidence

The hour before and after sunrises and sunsets offers particularly dramatic and fascinating colors with rapid momentary transitions, varying with latitude and season. The direction of sunset and sunrise also varies seasonally and with latitude, while moon path is generally similar and varies monthly.

Moonrise and moonset azimuth change daily on a lunar monthly cycle. Because the lunar ecliptic is about 5° from Earth's solar ecliptic, the azimuth range changes on an 18.6-year cycle, the extremes known as major and minor *lunar standstills* (Vincent 2105). New moons rise near sunrise time, while full moons rise opposite the setting sun.
Dawn, twilight and dusk periods just before sunrise and just after sunset are designated by the sun's altitude below the horizon as *civil twilight* (0 to –6°), *nautical twilight* (–6 to –12°) and *astronomical twilight* (–12° to –18°). At *astronomical dawn* (–18°), light in the sky can be detected; at *nautical dawn* (–12°), the horizon and some objects can be distinguished, while at *civil dawn* (–6°) skylight provides enough illumination for most activities (USNO 2011). After sunset, similar twilight periods and dusk definitions are also observed.
Golden hour periods just before, during and after sunset can produce dramatic, beautiful color and intensity shifts in sky and illuminated objects. Photographers refer to the *golden hour,* sky conditions just before and after sunset and sunrise, about +6° to –4° (Marqués 2017). Actual golden hour length varies with latitude and season. The period exhibits changing warm colors of red, orange and yellow soft light of low contrast.
Blue hour periods occur when the sun is below the horizon where blue wavelengths dominate (Marqués 2017), a result of sunlight's atmospheric refraction, scattering and selective absorption. Observers view saturated deep blue colors and a strong gradient from cool zenith to warmer horizon. Blue hour occurs morning and evening during twilight and has a colloquial, perceptual definition. Actual blue hour timing is longer at high latitudes and in winter.

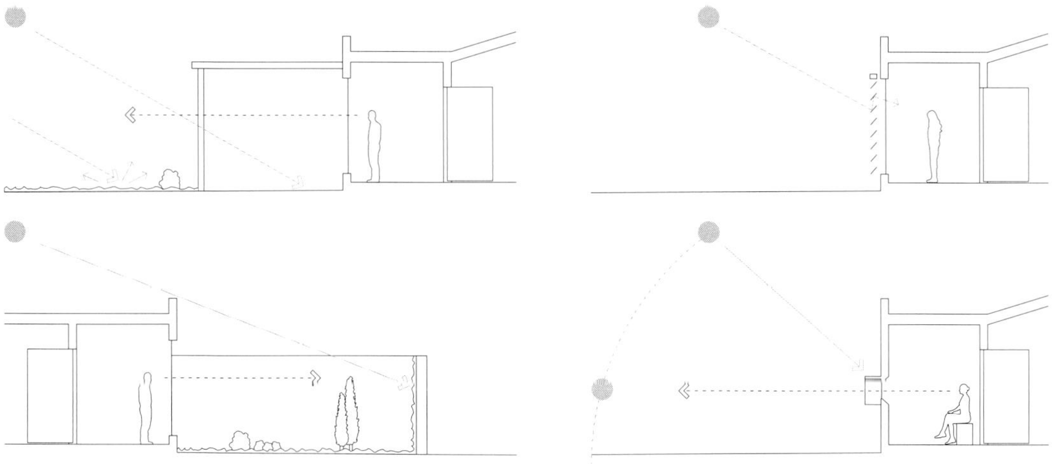

Low-glare views

upper left
Deep covered terrace, low reflectance, diffusing ground

lower left
Walls receive early or late light and golden hour color (*alpenglow*) lights buildings and landscapes (Lynch + Livingston 1995)

upper right
Adjustable louvers allow reflected light and color. Movable screens support daily open/close cycles.

lower right
Small shielded apertures and splayed edges

Design Guidelines

While humans enjoy sunrises and sunsets, low angle sun can cause glare; on late afternoons in summer, the hours preceding sunset bring unwanted solar gain. The design challenge is orchestrating view and aesthetic experience without glare and overheating. Easterly and westerly orientations address sun and moon rise and set directions.

Orient for sun and moon. An open-to-sky outdoor room adjacent to indoor spaces allows full sky experience. Direct views toward the sky phenomena based on occupancy seasons: a mid-summer terrace at 40°N views sunset about 30 degrees north of west, while all latitudes see the sun set due west at the equinox. Sun path diagrams can be found in Dekay + Brown (2014). In general, orient spaces for sunrise and sunset views; the moon's rise and set azimuth range is somewhat wider. Higher viewing position and a horizon view amplify the experience because both sun and moon appear larger and more dramatic near the horizon.
Link occupancy schedules to sun's path, not moon's. Locate spaces used in the early morning easterly for sunrise and late afternoon and early evening-use spaces westerly for sunset. The moon can rise or set at any hour, so daily occupancy schedule can not be linked to moon observation.
Shape low-glare views and reduce heat from summer afternoon sun with alternatives shown above. Low angle sunrise and sunset times, and the hours near, can coincide with heat and glare. Provide deep covered terraces, reflected light from walls, operable shades or shutters, or smaller shaded splayed edge windows sized just for view.
Visualize with sun + sky tools. Several calculators for twilight, blue hour and golden hour times and dates are available. Mobile device apps are available. Tools to aid design include detailed moon positions and moon-path map visualization, along major and minor lunar standstill prediction. See sidebar for sources.
Refine with R3 Biorhythmic Radiance and C3 Scintillating Sun. Help build R5 Heliotropic Rooms.

Sun + moon tools

twilight, blue + golden hours
BlueHourSite (2018)
Twilight Calc (Kossmagk 2019)

moon path visualization
MoonCalc (Hoffman 2021)

moon positions
Spreadsheet (Giesen 2020)
Online (Daily Moon Position 2021)

lunar standstills (azimuth extremes)
Online tools (Reijs 2020)

sun path visualization
SunCalc (Hoffman 2021)
Sun path diagrams (DeKay + Brown 2014)

Circadian Space

keeps people healthy and energized with bright blue morning light and warmer-hued, subdued evening illuminance.

258 **New York Loft**

New York, NY, 2012
Studio Rick Joy, architects

Blackout sleeping curtains create the darkness needed for the body to produce sleep-inducing hormones. Light surfaces maximizes daytime daylight exposure.

photo Joe Fletcher

order's own mirror
brightness then deep dark
within as without

The right daylight in buildings helps occupants feel focused and alert during the day, stay in a good mood and sleep better at night. The human body has a natural 24-hour circadian rhythm affecting its cycles of wakefulness and sleepiness, as well as other bodily functions, such as hormone release, digestive and immune systems function and body temperature. Inhabitants' circadian rhythm is regulated by exposure to daily patterns of daylight—especially early morning light and dark nights; this impacts the suppression and release of melatonin, the master regulator of all body rhythms. This luminous rhythm presents a generative architectural design opportunity to create buildings for a life in-sync with light: bright daylit rooms where people can experience a *lumen-shower* of full-spectrum daylight at high levels, lower illumination settings for quiet focus, low-level amber-colored lighting after sunset, and serene blackness for sleep. Together, these temporal indoor illumination patterns, along with window views outdoors, provide robust diurnal circadian stimulus and a fluid interior atmosphere in cadence with climate.

Federal Center South Building 1202, US Army Corps of Engineers Regional Headquarters

Seattle, Washington, 2012
ZGF Architects

Work spaces facing the atrium and north-facing offices get higher levels of daylight and circadian stimulus, which is especially important in winter. Conference rooms and shared amenities at the building core compel employees to regularly come together near the atrium (ZGF 2012).

photo Benjamin Benschneider

New York Loft's light-colored surfaces and sheer privacy curtains on the windows are needed to bring daylight into the narrow side-lighted apartment. At night however, the body's melatonin production can be suppressed by too much light, making sleep difficult. Instead of using heavier darkening window coverings, the bed is located at the back of the room, where light levels are lower, and is enveloped in curtains of two layers: an opaque black inner side to block night light and eliminate internal reflections, plus a white reflective layer that helps lighten the living and dining zones (Joy 2018; Leoncio 2013).

Federal Center South provides workstations facing daylight-reflecting surfaces in a bright atrium and perimeter sidelight in a narrow 60 ft (18 m) plan with 90% of the area daylit. Informal social spaces project into the light providing a high dose for breaks or collaboration. Studies showed circadian stimulus (CS) higher in summer than winter, and higher for those sitting near windows or the atrium. Perhaps counter-intuitively, higher CS was found in perimeter north-facing offices, because there fewer shading blinds get employed than in perimeter offices facing other directions. During winter, employees got most of their CS at work. In summer they spend more time outdoors on longer days, so more of their CS exposure is away from the office (LRC 2016a, 2016b; ZGF et al. 2012).

Circadian Space

260 **Circadian Stimulus vs Circadian Light**

People need CS ≥ 0.3 in the morning, deceasing in the afternoon, and low CS ≤ 0.1 in the evening (Figueiro + Rhea 2017).

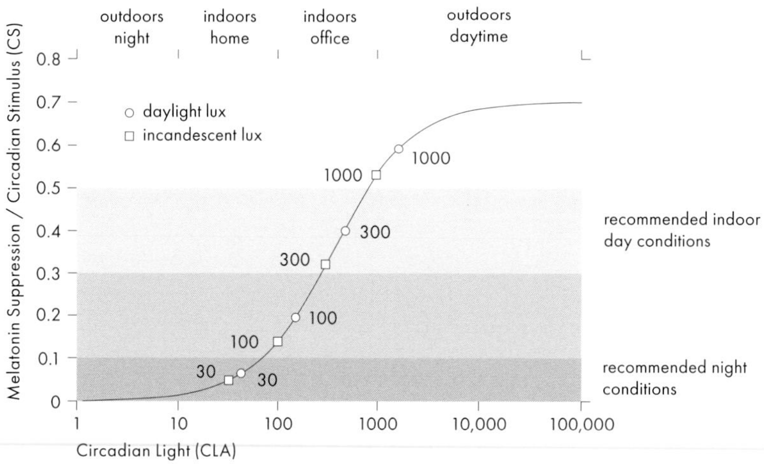

Supporting Evidence

The evidence for health and mood benefits of light-regulated circadian rhythms is extensive, although the details of common metrics, illuminance thresholds and the full range of physical and psychological impacts are still being studied. There is much agreement on the benefits of exposure to daylight, while evidence for the effects of electric circadian lighting technologies is still in its infancy.

Circadian Stimulus vs Circadian Light is based on the Lighting Research Center (LRC) recommendations using a *Circadian Stimulus* (CS) metric that indicates the hormonal effect of spectrally-weighted light received by the eye, and defined earlier in Chapter 3. The LRC recommends that electric lighting provide a "CS greater than 0.3 during the day, particularly in the morning, and less than 0.1 in the evening." This equates to 300 lux (28 fc) of circadian light (CLA) in the day and 30 lux (3 fc) at night, although the graph clearly shows that even higher levels are better during the day. "30 lux for 30 minutes from 'white' light" can be used as a "working threshold for light-induced nocturnal melatonin suppression" conclude Figueiro + Rhea (2017). The graph also shows the greater effectiveness of cooler daylight (tested with CIE 6500K 'daylight' light source) as compared to a warmer incandescent source.
Circadian regulation and health. While the term *circadian* refers to a 24-hour cycle, the biological effects of these light rhythms extend to more than daily sleep/wake patterns and affect many aspects of psychological and physiological health. A broad consensus of circadian researchers (Knoop et al. 2020) wrote: "Daylight has many particular benefits including excellent visual performance, permitting good eyesight, effective entrainment of the circadian system as well as a number of acute non-image forming effects and the important role of vitamin D production." We refer the reader to Knoop's paper for a comprehensive summary of the characteristics and benefits of daylight versus electric light and its strong argument for daylight's relative advantages.

Seasonal Affective Disorder (SAD). Daylight is an anti-depressant that can treat a variety of disorders, including SAD, which is particularly problematic in fall and winter and at higher latitudes. Bright light has a stronger antidepressant effect than dim light at all times, but morning light is superior to evening light (Wirz-Justice et al. 2013). While that research used electric light, the findings are even more relevant to daylight's rhythms.

Design Guidelines

Program occupant schedules and activities to rhythmically align with bright morning and mid-day daylit spaces, and dimmer, warmly-lit evening spaces. Focus lighting design on brightening daytime *vertical surfaces.*

Provide open-to-sky space. Outdoor light is much brighter than indoor light, therefore create walking trails, balconies, sunny terraces, courtyards and other places people can go for time under the open sky. Organize the built form and open space on site to shape a sunny, equator-facing, outdoor room that is wind-protected in winter.

Include lumen shower places, such as a greenhouse, conservatory, atrium or other highly-glazed room. Use clear glass to admit full-spectrum sunlight, and operable shading systems to control for excessive solar heat gain or glare. Where heat gain is not an issue, admit direct sunlight, particularly in winter. Highly glazed room types combine well with passive solar designs, like Direct Gain Rooms and Sunspaces strategies, as found in DeKay and Brown (2014). Especially in overcast climates and high latitude locations, create well-daylit break rooms, lounges and lunch rooms as *lumen showers* or *light cafes* where occupants can get doses of bright light to combat SAD.

Zone for daylight by locating rooms where people spend the most time in the building areas with the most daylight, typically upper floors and building perimeters. See the Daylight Zones strategy in DeKay and Brown (2014). Locate morning activities near windows and bright light; late afternoon or early evening activities, in dimmer places.

Plan agile workplaces that facilitate occupants taking their work or other activity to the brighter parts of the room or building, or to outdoor workspace, as desired.

Ensure vertical illuminance. More CS is experienced when occupants look at light coming from vertical than from horizontal surfaces. Therefore, face primary work-space seating towards brightly-lighted wall surfaces. Arrange interior partitions to not block views or daylight penetration. Partitions and workstation privacy panels that are perpendicular to a window wall work better than arrangements parallel to windows.

Avoid glare. Provide a high level of diffuse daylight that does not create glare, reflections on computer screens or direct sun on people; this minimizes the coping deployment of shades or blinds, which reduces daylight. Typically, arrange video screens perpendicular or at a 45° angle to windows to avoid window reflections (when facing away from windows) or direct glare (when facing toward windows) and allow workers to glance out the window as desired. Provide occupants with control of local shades or blinds.

Refine with C3 Scintillating Sun. When electric light is needed to supplement daylight, supplement with R3 Biorhythmic Radiance. Use this schema to help build R5 Heliotropic Rooms.

R4

Radiant Sailing

creates with mass, pleasant thermal asymmetries and
slow perceptual calid transitions related to climatic waves.

262 **Can Lis, Utzon Residence**

Majorca, Spain, 1971
Jørn Utzon, architect

The house is constructed of high mass materials for all surfaces, including built-in furniture, allowing it to ride daily temperature fluctuations in summer.

photo Torben Eskerod

unseen tides roll in
following the sun instead
washing me in warmth

Silent, high-mass radiant heating or cooling (passive or active) is delightful and almost magically invisible, compared to air-based mechanical conditioning systems. Experientially, the inhabited nature of *passive* buildings designed to dynamically work with local, site-based natural energy is fundamentally different from steady-state machine-age buildings. Because the rhythms of human life and those of renewable energy supply can sometimes be out of sync, passive energy buildings often use high levels of thermal mass for heat (or cool) storage. A passive high-mass building's operation drives an inhabitants' periodic connection with and isolation from the outdoor environment. When structural mass in room surfaces is used in a passive heating or cooling mode, occupants can experience both an indoor cycle of cooler night to warmer day and a complex radiant field that depends on a person's location in the room, the room's geometry and its furniture. The metaphor of *environmental surfing* (Loftness 2013) connotes practices of working with the ebbs and flows of climate to temper the indoor environment.

Stoneflower
[Shaheen-Goodfellow Residence]

Eden Isle, Arkansas, 1965
E Fay Jones, architect

A light frame upper level over an earth-connected, high mass, cool retreat below.

photo Balthazar Korab
courtesy Library of Congress

below
Ground floor plan

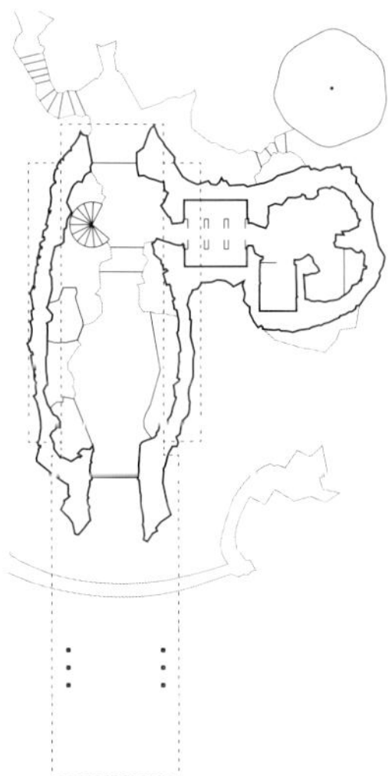

Can Lis, Jørn Utzon's first house on Mallorca, is organized as five volumes linked by courts (Arkitektur DK 1996; Andersen nd; Wilcox 2016). The living room walls are built of local sandstone blocks, the double-height ceiling of vaulted ceramic tiles between concrete beams (Spanish *bovedilla*) and the floor, a denser sandstone. Even the furniture is concrete, carved stone and Spanish tile. Built as a summer house, there is no mechanical heating or cooling. Glazing in the deep angled reveals is set to the outside of the wall, blocking strong sea winds, while less exposed openings provide day and night ventilation. The room thermally sails over a daily cycle, cooling the mass at night and absorbing heat during the day. Sunlight creates a gradient from warm sunny edges to cool shade.

Stoneflower is metaphorically a tree-house on top of a cave (Ivy 1992; DAH 1999). A rock foundation, stone floor and rock walls incorporating existing outcroppings ensure extensive earth contact and large thermal mass. In summer, the partially underground level is always cooler than the lighter wood-framed upstairs. With skylights and a walk-out end, natural light reconnects occupants with the day's dynamics. Water stores about four times more heat than masonry in the same volume. Stoneflower's pool, fountain and waterfall shower in the bathing grotto add to the huge thermal flywheel. A fireplace relieves the coolness in winter and generates a dramatic thermal gradient.

Radiant Sailing

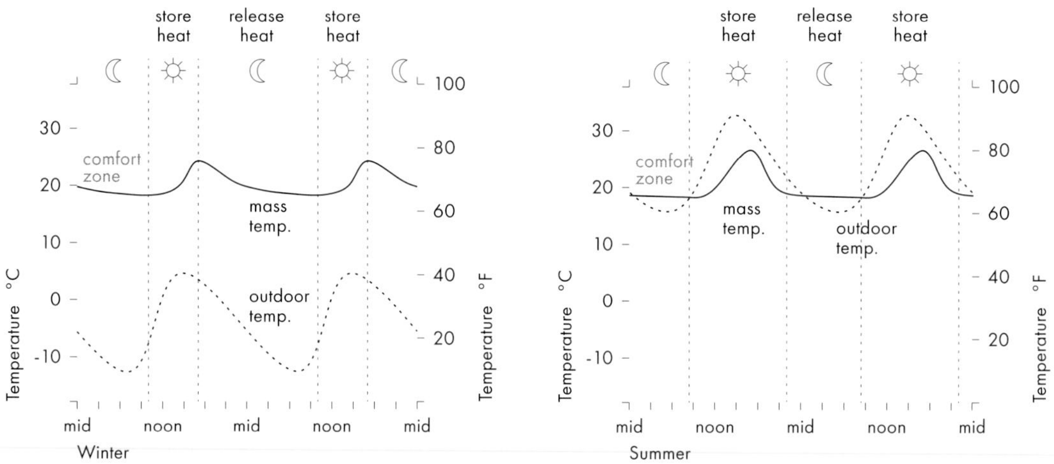

Passive building daily cycles

left
Passive solar building: mass warms rapidly with daytime sun, cools slowly as it heats the room at night.

right
Passively cooled building: mass warms slowly with daily heat gains, cools rapidly with night air.

Supporting Evidence

Independently, indoor air temperature is less important for comfort than *operative temperature*, which includes the effect of radiant temperatures. Passive buildings typically offer variable conditions that change over time and space, which as presented throughout this book, people prefer.

Passive building daily cycles. Conventional commercial building HVAC systems typically operate over a narrow range of setpoints year-round, approximately 22–24°C (71.5–75°F), varying only a little seasonally (Mendell + Mirer 2009; Gunay et al. 2018). Passive buildings will have a wider temperature range, and greater connection to the natural variations of climate; people often find this variability pleasurable (Heschong 1979).
Passive solar buildings have radiant surfaces that absorb heat and sunlight during the day. At night, the mass releases stored heat, warming the space. During a sunny winter day, mass surfaces (particularly those in direct sun) can be warmer for a time than other surfaces in the room. Engineering logic for air-based systems tries to minimize any thermal asymmetries, yet warm radiant floors in winter are widely accepted as pleasurable. According to Prof. Alexandra Rempel (2020), "after collection ends, I've also found that mass remains tens of degrees warmer than the overlying air for hours, if it's properly sized." In passive sunspaces, where temperature swings are wider than in the adjacent rooms they serve, the warm mass effect is amplified as a room-to-room spatial sequence.
Passively cooled buildings fluctuate on a daily cycle rather than maintaining constant temperature. Following nighttime ventilation, mass is cool on a summer morning. Over the day, mass stays cooler than room air, which warms faster. There is both a delay in and dampening of mass temperature compared to outdoors, with maximums typically reached in the evening (Samuel et al. 2013). Similarly, heavy uninsulated walls, floors or roofs that are in contact with the ground can stay cooler than the indoor air, beneficial in warm conditions (but less so in cold).

Delight. Bainbridge and Haggard (2011) argue that "in dwellings, thermal radiation will be about equal in importance to the combined effects of air temperature, humidity and air motion" explaining in part why passive systems "are so delightful." Both warm mass and cool mass can create a pleasurable radiant field within the room. Experience depends on proximity to the radiant surface, how much of it the body sees, referred to as *view factor*.
Floors. Mazria (1979) noted that floors in passive solar buildings are warmer than in buildings with a convective (air) heating system, regardless of passive solar system type, thus alleviating the discomfort of otherwise cooler floors, especially in systems that supply warm air near the ceiling.
Temperature swings. Radiant sailing requires a cycle of indoor conditions but too much fluctuation is undesirable. Techniques for estimating and limiting interior temperature swings in passive solar buildings are covered in Mazria (1979), and in Grondzik and Kwok (2015), based on Balcomb (1984).

Design Guidelines

Use large exposed interior surface areas of high-density materials that store heat, such as stone, brick, concrete, rammed earth or adobe. Interior temperature swing is decreased by larger exposed mass areas and by using mass materials with higher thermal conductance (absorbs heat faster).

Integrate mass with a responsive envelope that collects sun in the cool season, shades glass in the warm season, and opens to admit cooling air at night.
Size mass large enough. For heating use a mass surface area to floor area ratio of about 1:1 or greater in a moderately passive solar heated building. Use 2:1 for a night-cooled mass building in a hot climate. In summer, shade mass from sun. To assess the climate's potential for Night-Cooled Mass, see DeKay + Brown (2014).
Choose good mass locations. Use the floor as a first choice for warm massive radiant surface. The experience is a combination of radiant heat and a C2 Haptic Connection. Use the ceiling for cool radiant surfaces, as passive cooling requires more surface area than solar heating, cool air next to the ceiling naturally falls and better mixes with room air, and occupants have a greater radiant geometric view factor relationship with the ceiling (no obstructing furniture or rugs). Mass walls can be warm or cool as needed, with the added benefit of access to human touch. People can come close and increase their radiant experience.
Get the details right. For design and technical details, see strategies for Mass Arrangement, solar Thermal Mass, Night-Cooled Mass and Mass Surface Absorptance in DeKay + Brown (2014).
Delete the ducts, which becomes possible in passive high mass buildings. They have the potential for reducing air ducts to, at most, a dedicated outdoor air system (DOAS) for fresh air and humidity control, especially if backup heating or cooling is radiant. In some combinations of climate and use, active systems can be eliminated entirely, resulting in a ductless building. Mass used for heating and cooling can also be coupled with air-to-air heat exchangers or with air-flow windows that provide heat exchange for ventilation air with a minimum of ductwork.
Refine this schema with R6 Cooling Conversions and G4 Incalescent Center.

R4

Habitat Fringe

brings plant and animal life to the boundary of indoor rooms.

266 **Palmyra House**

Alibag, India 2007
Studio Mumbai
Bijoy Jain, architect

The house serves as an archetype for maximized edges, its double-height living room opening on three sides to the palm forest.

photo Enrico Cano

an ancient wonder
garden, my house a garden
can you find its edges?

Buildings connect inhabitants to Nature when design becomes habitat. In turn, incorporating other plant and animal species on and adjacent to buildings generates a richer human habitat. The city is an ecosystem with many species, including *Homo sapiens*, and bird diversity can actually be substantially higher in residential suburbs than in forests. Gardens afford urban dwellers many opportunities to observe and cultivate relationships with plants and animals while making a contribution to urban wildlife habitat. A garden can be an outdoor room to occupy, yet residents indoors also need regular access to and views of Nature. The locus for the relationship between shelter and Nature, humans and their larger life context, is the room and its boundaries. In this cause, walls transcend their separation role to become connectors to nearby natural neighbors. Particularly along the sunny edges of occupied rooms, gardens at the building edges—and openings from rooms to gardens—create community relationships between people and Nature, offering solace, companionship or connection.

Sam Walton Residence

Bentonville, Arkansas
1960, rebuilt 1972
E Fay Jones, architect

A linear pergola with translucent roof and open wall provides a sheltered garden edge along the entry path, continuing beyond the door as a glazed solarium adjacent to living spaces.

photo Tim Hursley

Palmyra House is formed of two almost parallel linear boxes set among coconut palms with a 25 ft (7.6 m) wide court and pool between (Barba, 2013). Its open cage-like structure is wrapped in wooden louvers from the local Palmyra tree. The louvers are mostly fixed permanently sloped and open, in other places hinged to disappear entire walls. The linear, single-room depth plan and constant openness infuses the space with tropical sea breezes and the sounds of ocean and rustling palm leaves, engaging occupants in intimate sensory contact with the place. The result is a structure almost entirely of site-related edges, each room opening to its dense living surroundings planted with a variety of cycads, ferns, smaller palms and shrubs to gradually fill the understory (Low, 2010).

Walton Residence incorporates a glass-roofed entry arbor that continues through to an east-facing glass conservatory along one edge of the living space and on to landscaped terraces beyond (DAH 1999). The sense is one of continuous outdoor space, amplified by plantings on both sides of the column line. Enclosure blends with openness by means of, as architect Fay Jones expressed, "transitional areas that flow to outdoor spaces and the garden." Nature is brought close. As one of the residents said, "You are constantly aware of what's going on [in the changing seasons]. In the winter there is snow; in the Spring the birds" (Ivy 1992).

Habitat Fringe

View + habitat layering

Good views are often layered. Include *horizontal view layers:* foreground, middle ground and background (Gorlin 2018). Also arrange *angular view layers:* sky, in-between and ground sectors (Matusiak + Klöckner 2015).

Biodiversity increases with the number of layers. Include *vertical landscape layers:* tree canopy, understory trees, shrubs, herbaceous and ground. Also arrange *lateral landscape layers:* water, wetlands, meadows, grassland (Darke + Tallamy 2014).

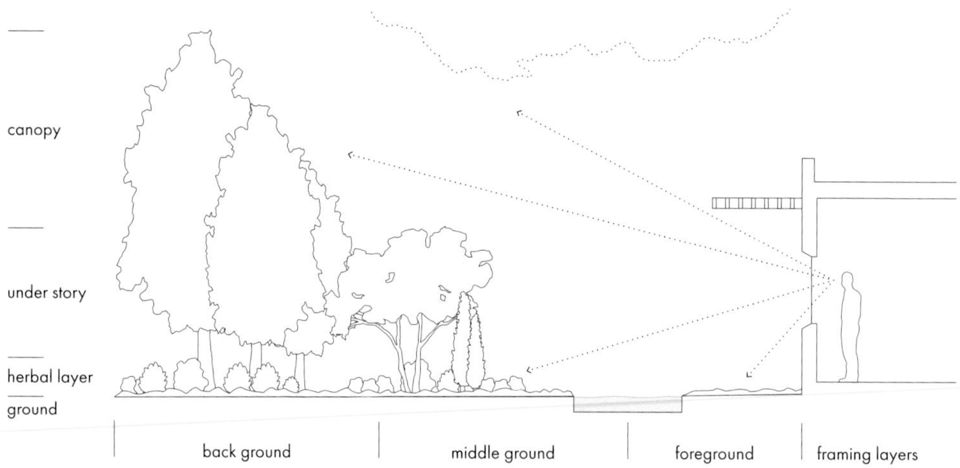

Supporting Evidence

The evidence for the psychological and health benefits of plants and nature contact is well documented. Beyond the standard stress reduction effects, some surprising research results show that either simple planting or complex nature can help inhabitants feel happier, more caring and compassionate, calmer and can induce introspection.

Just a few plants, found Chalmin-Pui et al. (2021), added to a bare lawn had residents reporting significant decreases in perceived stress and physical indicators, and feeling more relaxed, along with improved mood, happiness and sense of pride in their living environment.

"Flowers Generate Happiness," writes Hall + Dickson (2011), in reviewing the multiple benefits of plants from many studies. "Flowers around the home and office greatly improve people's moods and reduces the likelihood of stress-related depression. Flowers and ornamental plants increase levels of positive energy" (Hall 2011).

Nature makes people more caring, as research by Weinstein et al (2009) suggests "that full contact with nature can have humanizing effects, fostering greater authenticity and connectedness and.....enhance valuing of and generosity toward others." The authors explain that "nature helps to connect people to their authentic selves" which "are inherently communal." Rich complex natural environments encourage introspection" (Ryan 2009).

Watching and Feeding Birds, relaxes people, motivates them for greater nature interactions and encourages feelings of pleasure and nature connection, "halting the extinction of [Nature] experience" (Cox + Gaston 2016). Psychological well-being is enhanced by number of birds, especially by species richness (Cox + Gaston 2015).

More mindfulness is linked to greater extents of green space and, in the absence of nearby public access to Nature, to having a private garden (Trapasso 2021). Mindfulness is easier to learn and practice in natural settings, with longer-lasting positive effects (Lymeus 2019).

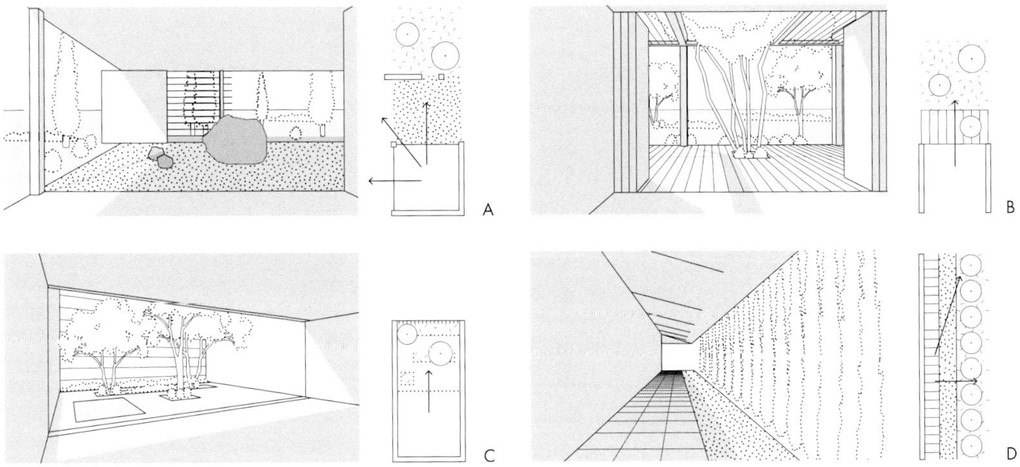

Habitat fringe design variations

A **Creek House**
Truckee, California, US, 2018
Faulkner Architects (Brillon 2018)

B **House on the Sand**
Trancoso, Brazil, 2019
Studio MK27, architects
(The Plan 2019)
See also C3 Scintilating Sun

C **Optical Glass House**
Hiroshima, Japan, 2012
Hiroshi Nakamura + NAP architects
(Frearson 2013)
See also C4 Inhabited Periphery

D **Nezu Museum**
Minato City, Tokyo, Japan, 2009
Kengo Kuma, architect
(Frampton + Kuma 2012)

Design Guidelines

Organize the garden along the edges of the building so that many rooms have a direct view of and, ideally, physical access to the garden plants and the wildlife attracted there. Plant flowers, fruit, and scented herbs that attract hummingbirds and butterflies. Increased biodiversity enhances pleasure and biophilia.

Habitat fringe design variations are shown in the diagrams. Gardens on two sides of a room, as in the Creek House, A, improve access and immersion. Gardens on one side can be extended into the landscape, as in House on the Sand, B, or an enclosed outdoor room, like the Optical Glass House, C. The habitat fringe might define a room-place or bound circulation for experience while moving, as in the Nezu Museum, D. Each example shows a version of occupiable adjacent in-between space that can be covered (A, D), partially covered (B) or open-to-sky (C). Planting can be naturalistic (A, B), combined with occupiable space (A, B, C), or formal (D).

Plan physical access options that allow inhabitants to move between degrees of indoor shelter or outdoor exposure where Nature contact can be maximized. Place usable outdoor space immediately adjacent to indoor rooms and at the same level. Connect with windows, doors and operable walls.

Create visual continuity of materials, compositional lines and planes from indoors to outside (Walton Residence). This suggests an integrated human and natural world and that outdoors is a place to inhabit.

Combine visual and activity layering to add complexity and interest. Each of the diagrammatic examples illustrates a form of layering with fore, middle and background. Sand House and Optical Glass House show a gradient from occupation toward predominantly visual experience of the garden. In all cases, there is a degree of immersion.

Refine with C3 Water You Can Touch, C3 Scintillating Sun and C4 Tempered Pathway schemas. Help build the N5 Three Realms schema.

R5

Heliotropic Rooms

orients activities toward or away from heat and light, fitting to climate, linking daily life and location.

270 **Fredensborg Houses**

Fredensborg, Denmark, 1963
Jørn Utzon, architect

A housing complex of 63 units, walled sun-facing courts combine with single banked rooms facing southeast and southwest.

photo
Ramblersen/Wikimedia Commons

below
Typical unit plan

framing the sunlight
framing the present this room
our future charted

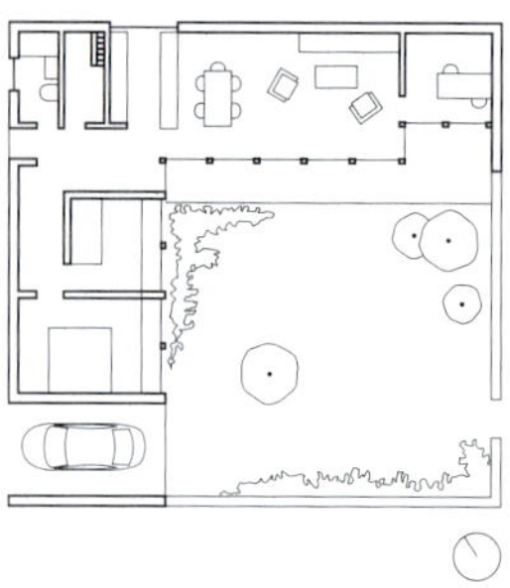

Rising with the easterly first light, living one's day with the sun—or in opposition to it—and experiencing the shifts from sunset to twilight to night, connects one to the primordial rhythms of a place. To be *heliotropic*—tuning life to follow the sun by season or by day—is to know the four directions, to distinguish the animator of life in location. On a clear day, as the sun arcs from east towards zenith to setting west, rooms receive sunlight and heat in sequence, while those not facing the sun receive diffuse daylight. Sun can be an asset or liability. Some rooms are occupied all day, but many are used during only a portion. Especially when occupancy schedules have people in particular rooms at known times, the sun and its more intense light and heat can be intentionally embraced or rejected. In hot climates or seasons, activities and their associated rooms can follow the timing and orientation of the shade. Such occupants are *shade-seekers*. In cold climates or seasons, the pattern reverses: rooms and activities follow the sun. Occupants become *sun worshipers*. Both may find, enjoyment, delight and a situated delectation.

Tempe à Pailla (Tempe a Païa)

Castellar, Alpes-Maritimes
France, 1933
Eileen Gray, architect

Partially shaded south-facing terrace is easily accessed from adjacent day-use rooms.

photo CNAC/MNAM

next page
Solar site plan

Fredensborg Houses in high-latitude Denmark are organized in L-shaped plans around walled, landscaped gardens (Fernandez-Galioano 2018). Living rooms are consistently aligned 12° west of south. The plan either has bedrooms oriented slightly south of east or north of west. Courtyard walls are low enough to allow the 56°N Danish winter solstice sun to penetrate to the back of the living area. South or southwest living space orientation is common in Utzon's houses. Ecabriano's thesis (2014) is that, "the sun can be an organizing element for how you live in the houses designed by Jørn Utzon." Utzon's expresses his attitude: " The houses are arranged like flowers on the branch of a cherry tree, turning towards the sun from each flower's particular position," reflecting his intention to establish functional, "meaningful and intangible" connections with nature (Utzon 1948).

Tempe à Pailla is organized on a *solar site plan* (next page) that arranges rooms and activities to synchronize occupancy periods with sun movement. Gray's bedroom is situated facing northeast for morning sun and spring lemon orchard blossoms. The living room, emphasizing daytime occupancy, has southeast and southwest orientations with a covered terrace, exterior passage and sliding louvered shutters to alternately admit, reflect or block sun, while accessing summer breezes and opening to a sea view. Dining faces southwest to the sun

Heliotropic Rooms

left
Solar site plan

Tempe à Pailla (Tempe a païa)
Eileen Gray's studied rooms, views and circulation in relation to sun.

right
Activity locations + sun path

diagram, 36°N lat., mixed climate

Inner ring suggests cool season daily events in buildings that follow the sun path.
Middle ring recommends warm season events in orientations opposite the sun's position.
Outer ring marks seasonal solar path and sunrise/sunset extremes.

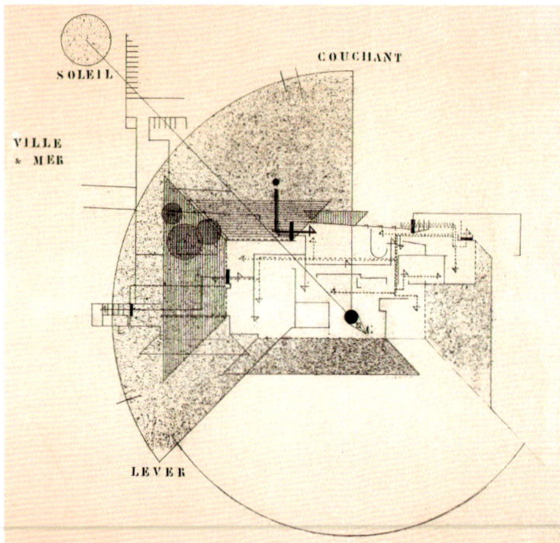

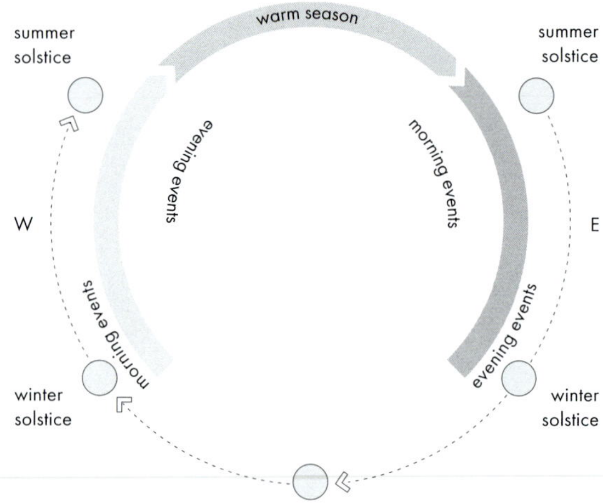

during sunset and evening meals, with a smaller window, allowing views and light for meal times, while heat-producing service areas are located in northwest areas with the least exposure. The bath is tucked mostly inside. Leatherbarrow (2021) suggests that this "scheduling of a sequence of facings"... "represented but never insured synchronization." There is simultaneously the response of aligning habitual domestic rituals with the patterns of nature in the site and the provision of flexible controls that allow spontaneous activity in different locations as a way of tuning to the ambient forces. A flagpole surmounts the symbolic prow of the southeast terrace, a signal of "her ritualistic attention to the sun's diurnal path", serving as a shadow-caster like a sun-dial's *gnomon* (Constant 2000).

Supporting Evidence

Admitting higher levels of winter sun and lower levels in summer fits bodily circadian cycles and thermal comfort needs to annual climate patterns. Room orientation fit to activity schedules is practical from an energy and illuminance perspective while connecting inhabitants to place on a daily basis.

Bodily circadian rhythms depend on light intensity, color and timing (Chapter 3, R3 Biorhythmic Radiance and R4 Circadian Space). In winter, daily activity maximizing sun exposure on the short days ensures circadian stimulus. In summer, daylight intensity is greater and days longer, so shade-seeking does not disrupt the body's internal clock. **Heliotropism** in biology refers to the orienting response of organisms to the sun, such as seen in sunflowers. The moniker, *heliotropic housing* was employed by Catherine Bauer (1934) in reference to the German *Zeilenbau* system of solar orientation. The systematized approach was used to maximize direct sun exposure to as many rooms as possible for its health-giving properties (rather than winter heat gain): "a row-direction of north-north-west to south-south-east. The living-rooms and kitchens are then put on the west side and the bedrooms and bathrooms, in so far as possible, on the east." Of course, this had many problems, including expensive winter heating and excessive summer overheating, as we now know that a south orientation collects more winter sun and less summer sun than a west or east facade. The *Zeilenbau* architects were therefore more interested in *heliotherapeutic* buildings (Denzer 2014).

Orientation and time of use. Mazria's (1979) heating-biased design pattern, Location of Indoor Spaces, exemplifies a contrasting attitude, recommending (for Northern Hemisphere) an east-west elongated plan with occupied spaces distributed from southeast to southwest, according to their daily use schedule: sleeping to the east; kitchen and dining, southeast; living and continuously occupied spaces facing south; and rooms with little need for heat or light on the north as thermal buffers. This reduces energy use and promotes nature-responsive experience.

Rooms following light. Max Jacobsen and co-authors (2002) articulate a Capturing Light pattern, giving guidance for houses "shaped in response to the sun, with its rooms located and organized so that all important spaces receive abundant and balanced light." One of the pattern's tenets: "Plan the placement of rooms so that each space receives light at a suitable time of day for activities that occur there." The authors believe that shaping buildings for sun and light likely has the most significant impact on occupant perception and comfort of any design choice.

An understanding of walking, standing, sitting and lying comfortably, of enjoying the sun, the shade, the water on our bodies, the earth and all the less easily defined sense impressions. A desire for wellbeing must be fundamental to all architecture if we are to achieve harmony between spaces we create and the activities to be undertaken in them.

—Jørn Utzon

Design Guidelines

All organisms tend toward life-enhancing forces and away from life-constricting conditions. Therefore, map the building's daily activities in time, and, if relevant, how these change by season. Organize the building so that these event timings correspond to the sun's orientation and people's fundamental shade-seeking or sun-seeking desires.

Program for experience. Building uses can be mobile (migration) or located in particular spaces. For each type, graphically schedule by day and season. For each room, especially if the use is fixed in place, determine whether direct sun would be an asset or a liability for either experience or heat gain. This may vary by season.

Start with predictable timings, for example, sleeping rooms oriented to the east help occupants wake more easily with the rising sun, while an office lunch-room is predictably used for one to two hours during mid-day when patterns of sun and shade could animate a room and not interfere with critical tasks.

Consider orienting the building diagonally to the cardinal directions, which allows each room to get some sun at some time during the day during March to September and for the SE and SW walls to get sun all year.

Orient rooms in cool climates so that activities that can tolerate direct sun follow the timing of the sun's path. Rooms with equator-facing exposure can usually easily heat themselves with passive solar gains, whereas rooms such as storage, garage, mechanical and rest rooms needing less heat can be zoned to the polar edge to serve as a buffer.

Orient rooms in hot climates to arrange morning events on the west and afternoon to the east. This is inverse to sun path. See diagram of Activity locations + sun path

Refine with R4 Circadian Space, C4 Inhabited Periphery and R4 Dawn and Dusk Places. Help build G6 Engagement and Retreat.

R6

Cooling Conversions

connects occupants to climatic rhythms by integrating finely calibrated passive and active cooling approaches.

274 **David + Lucile Packard Foundation Headquarters**

Los Altos, California, 2010
EHDD Architects

Two narrow, 40 ft (12 m) wide wings surround a court that connects workers to outdoors via large moveable glass walls on the ground floor and through operable windows on upper floors. Occupants are linked with the seasonal and daily rhythms by options for natural ventilation and mechanical cooling.

photo Jeremy Bittermann/JBSA

video + images see Packard 2022

loci warm and cool
circumstance and atmosphere
I participate

Architects often refer to building envelope as the *third skin*. Like the physical skin and second-skin, clothing, building skins mediate human relationships with the environment. In mechanically-cooled buildings, the envelope isolates, while permeable naturally-ventilated walls connect. Night-cooled mass structures alternate between thermally closed during the day and open to cool outdoor air at night. The nexus of climate, use and form, however, can be more complex than any of these individually. Hybrid, *mixed-mode* buildings exploit a spatial and temporal passive cooling strategy suite before using machine cooling. In the process, this schema relates occupants intimately and ontologically to climatic rhythms. Affluent societies have become accustomed to air-conditioning (AC) at the first seasonal warmth; in contrast to such conditioning monarchy, cooling strategies tuned in time to local conditions also attune inhabitants. Consider a sequence from natural ventilation to night-cooled mass to AC and back, adjusting strategies by week or hour, or spatially by use pattern. For long periods machines fall silent. Just imagine.

Makers Quarter Block D

San Diego, California, 2018
BNIM architects

Cooling coverts on a daily and seasonal basis from cross-ventilation to night-cooled mass to air-conditioning. Manual and automated shades and ventilation achieves net-zero energy and occupant climate connections.

photo Nick Merrick
Hall + Merrick + McCaugherty

AIA Top 10 report: BNIM 2019

Packard Foundation Headquarters is a net zero energy, mixed-mode building that provides employees with strong connections to the outdoor environment. The narrow 40 ft (12 m) wide floor plate of the two wings allows for ample daylighting and cross-ventilation. When the weather is too hot for ventilative cooling, an active chilled beam system fed by stored night-chilled water from a compressor-free rooftop cooling tower is engaged. While a sophisticated, automated control system manages the mechanical side, window operation remains relatively simple; a dashboard on laptops and in break rooms informs users to operate windows and sliding doors for natural ventilation — a degree of personal control essential to reap adaptive comfort benefits (CBE 2014; ILFI 2013; AIA 2014).

Makers Quarter Block D houses flexible office suites cooled by mixed-mode natural ventilation and efficient mechanical cooling. Motorized windows and garage doors on each level combine with exposed concrete slabs and frame to enable night-cooled thermal mass. Building circulation and cores are unconditioned, often exterior. The high-performance facade utilizes manual and automated shades to reduce cooling loads. Ceiling fans can raise comfort temperature by 6°F (3.3°C), reducing AC hours. The rhythms of thermally open/closed, combined with conditioned/unconditioned zones bring occupants to a calibrated relationship with climate (ArchDaily 2020).

Active cooperation, direct contributions to the effort, however small, is far more satisfying and effective than passive cooperation, mere acceptance of conditions imposed by others.

—Robert Knapp 2013

Adaptive Comfort Model

Field study results showing occupants' preferred comfort temperature in relation to seasonal shifts in outdoor temperature. 80 and 90% acceptability zones rise with climatic trends. This holds for NV, MM and AC buildings (Parkinson et al. 2020).

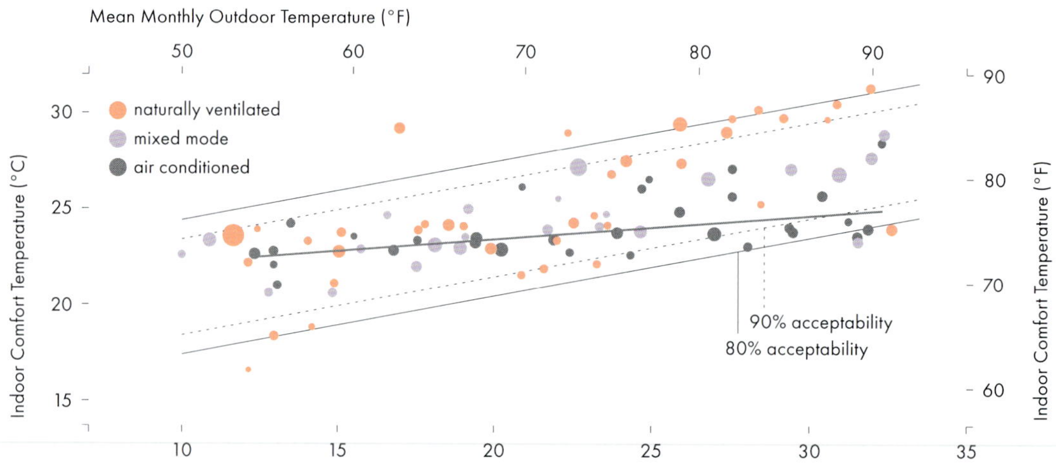

Supporting Evidence

When people can control cooling modes, fans and operable windows, they are more connected to Nature's rhythms of the day and season. In this context, they prefer a wider seasonal variation of indoor temperatures. The comfort zone in naturally ventilated and mixed mode buildings shifts as occupants adapt to seasonal conditions.

Cooling abbreviations

NV	Natural ventilation
AC	Air-conditioned
NCM	Night-cooled mass
MM	Mixed-mode
MV	Mechanical ventilation
ASHRAE	American Society of Heating, Refrigeration + Air-conditioning Engineers
Std 55	ANSI/ASHRAE Standard 55: Thermal Environmental Conditions for Human Occupancy

Warm climate traditions can be seen in homes where inhabitants delight at Spring's first opportunity to open windows, hear birds and feel the approaching rain's atmosphere. As Summer waxes, residents yearn to prolong openness and its pleasures, practicing a ritual of opening windows at night and closing in the morning, allowing the building's mass to coast through the day's rising heat. As summer wanes, again windows open during the day to enjoy, as the circuit inverts. Natural ventilation (NV) offers savory connections to outdoor nature and a familiar daily cycle in what was a fundamental aspect of pre-AC US Southern culture, expressed architecturally in vernacular porches, high ceilings, breezeways and large operable windows (Arsenault 1984).

The adaptive comfort model, described in Chapter 3, originally applied to just NV buildings. Along with Parkinson, Brager and colleagues (2020) conducted new analysis of the Global Thermal Comfort Database II, showing that comfort responses in mixed-mode (MM) buildings are similar to those in NV; the adaptive comfort standard in ASHRAE Std 55 (2020) now applies to MM. The same study found that people adapt most strongly to prevailing indoor temperatures, regardless of the building conditioning strategy. People adapt to higher AC setpoints, therefore over-cooling can be avoided.

Occupant satisfaction in MM buildings was found by Brager and Baker (2009) to be higher than that in the CBE Occupant Survey database overall. The best performers were moderate climate buildings with radiant (rather than air) systems, that allowed high degrees of direct user control without automated window locks.

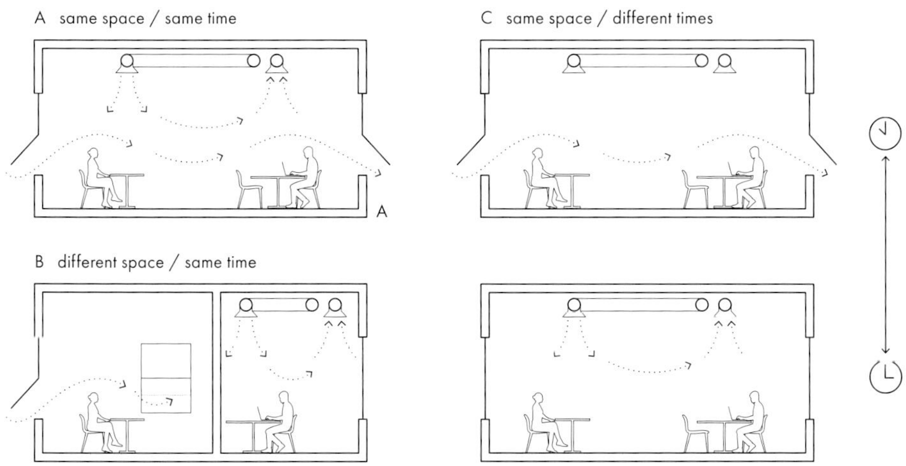

Mixed-mode cooling typology

Three common MM operational schemes combining NV and AC. A building may use one, two or all three schemes (Brager 2006).

A **Concurrent** schemes use AC and NV in the same space at the same time.

B **Zoned** schemes simultaneously use NV in one area and AC in another.

C **Change-over** schemes switch from NV to AC as conditions warm on a daily or seasonal basis—or as occupancy changes.

Design Guidelines

Use experiential programming to establish cooling zones. Minimize loads and develop a climate-calibrated cooling strategy suite that prioritizes passive when feasible, then integrates AC only when and where necessary. Preference user-activated manual controls.

Mixed-mode cooling typology schemes are shown in the diagrams. *Concurrent* schemes (A) operate NV and AC simultaneously in the same space. Mechanical ventilation may serve supplementally, with or without AC, while occupants are free to open windows based on individual preference. In an open-plan office with variable air volume systems, perimeter zones may go to minimum air when a sensor indicates window opening. *Zoned* schemes (B) employ different conditioning modes in areas with divergent loads or criteria, such as NV in perimeter offices and AC in conferences rooms. *Change-over* schemes (C) convert between NV and AC on a seasonal or even daily basis, in response to climatic or occupancy loading conditions. These designs are ideal for discreet offices with local AC that shuts down when windows open or in the case where inlet vents open when HVAC is in economizer (100% outside air) mode.

Combine automated and manual controls. Building automation can determine cooling modes based on outdoor temperature, occupancy sensors, window sensors or operator feedback. Use automated windows in high places difficult to reach, such as stack-vent outlets, atria, clerestories or roof vents. Employ in public spaces, where none feel ownership to operate manually. Automation is commonly used to provide minimum fresh air, night ventilation when unoccupied and controlled ventilation during high wind or rain, or to control overall ambient conditions. Place manual windows lower in occupied rooms for easy access. Give occupants direct control.

Refine with C5 Thermal Enclave and S5 Territorial Tuning. Also see G4 Zephyr Spectrum and F3 Fans First.

We are most alive when we experience subtle cycles of difference in our surroundings. The building itself becomes the *pattern which connects* us to the change and flow of climate, season, sun and shadow, constantly tuning our awareness of the natural cycles which support all life.

—Sim Van der Ryn 2020

Rhythm Sources

R2 Aperture Engagement

85 Design. 2020. 58 House. *85 Design*. 85architecture.com

ArchDaily. 2014. 242 State Street/ Olson Kundig. *ArchDaily*, 24 Mar, archdaily.com/489035/

ArchDaily. 2020. 58 House/ 85 Design. *ArchDaily*, 17 Jul, archdaily.com/943766/

ASHRAE 2020. *Standard 55: Thermal Environmental Conditions for Human Occupancy*. Atlanta, GA: American Society of Heating, Refrigerating and Air-Conditioning Engineers

de Dear, Richard + Gail S Brager. 1998. Towards an Adaptive Model of Thermal Comfort and Preference. *ASHRAE Transactions* 104 (part1)

Domus. 2014. 242 State Street. *Domus*, 1 Apr. domusweb.it/en/architecture/

HPC. 2021. *58 House/85 Design*. video. The House Plan Company. youtube.com/watch?v=ocbTENQF9fE

ILFI. 2019. Living Building Challenge 4.0. *International Living Future Institute*. living-future.org

IWBI. 2020. *WELL Building Standard v2*. New York: International Well Building Institute. wellcertified.com

Murcutt, Glenn. 1996. in Frampton, Kenneth, 2002. Glenn Murcutt 2002 Laureate Essay: The Architecture of Glenn Marcus Murcutt. The Pritzker Architecture Prize. pritzkerprize.com

OlsunKundig. 2014. 242 State Street. olsonkundig.com/projects/242-state-street/

Parkinson, Tom, Richard de Dear + Gail Brager. 2020. Nudging the Adaptive Thermal Comfort Model. *Energy and Buildings* 206(Jan):109559.

Tartarini, Federico, Stefano Schiavon, Toby Cheung, & Tyler Hoyt. 2020. *CBE Thermal Comfort Tool: Online Tool for Thermal Comfort Calculations and Visualizations*. SoftwareX 12:100563

R3 Biorhythmic Radiance

arc. 2015. Novo Nordisk headquarters wins Danish Lighting Award. arc: *Lighting in Architecture*, 4 Feb. arc-magazine.com

ArcDog. 2017. Novo Nordisk Headquarters. *ArcDog*. arcdog.com

Augustesen, Christina. 2017. Architecture for the Senses. *The VELUX Group*. thedaylightsite.com/architecture-for-the-senses-2/

Begemann, Simon H A, Gerrit J van den Beld + Ariadne D Tenner. 1997. Daylight, Artificial Light and People in an Office Environment: Overview of Visual and Biological Responses. *International Journal of Industrial Ergonomics* 20(3): 231–239

Brown, Timothy M, George C Brainard, Christian Cajochen, Charlies A Czeisler, John P Hanifin, Steven W Lockley, Robert J Lucas et al. 2022. Recommendations for daytime, evening, and nighttime indoor light exposure to best support physiology, sleep, and wakefulness in healthy adults. *PLoS Biol* 20(3): e3001571

Burling, Stacy. 2018. The Era of Circadian Lighting in Health Care is Dawning. *The Philadelphia Enquirer*, 27 Jun. inquirer.com/philly/

Cajochen, Christian, Mirjam Münch, Szymon Kobialka, Kurt Kräuchi, Roland Steiner, Peter Oelhafen, Selim Orgül + Anna Wirz-Justice. 2005. High Sensitivity of Human Melatonin, Alertness, Thermoregulation, and Heart Rate to Short Wavelength Light. *Journal of Clinical Endocrinology + Metabolism* 90(3) Mar: 1311–1316

Chellappa, Sarah Laxhmi, Roland Steiner, Peter Blattner, Peter Oelhafen, Thomas Götz + Christian Cajochen. 2011. Non-Visual Effects of Light on Melatonin, Alertness and Cognitive Performance: Can Blue-Enriched Light Keep Us Alert? *PLoS ONE*, 6(1): e16429

CIE. 2019. *Position Statement on Non-Visual Effects of Light: Recommending Proper Light at the Proper Time*. Vienna, Austria: International Commission on Illumination

De Kort, Yvonne + Karin Smolders. 2010. Effects of Dynamic Lighting on Office Workers: First Results of a Field Study with Monthly Alternating Settings. *Lighting Research and Technology* 42(3): 345–360

DeKay, Mark + G Z Brown. 2014. *Sun, Wind + Light: Architectural Design Strategies*, 3rd ed. Hoboken, New Jersey: Wiley. #A2 Sun Path Diagrams, E.374–404

Escofet, Jaume + Salvador Bará. 2017. Reducing the Circadian Input from Self-Luminous Devices Using Hardware Filters and Software Applications. *Lighting Research and Technology* 49(4): 481–96

Figueiro, Mariana G, Barbara A Plitnick, Anna Lok, Geoffrey E Jones, Patricia Higgins, Thomas R Hornick + Mark S Rea. 2014. Tailored Lighting Intervention Improves Measures of Sleep, Depression, and Agitation in Persons with Alzheimer's Disease and Related Dementia Living in Long-Term Care Facilities. *Clinical Interventions in Aging* 9:1527–1537

Figueiro, Mariana G, Claudia M Hunter, Patricia Higgins, Thomas Hornick, Geoffrey E Jones, Barbara Plitnick, Jennifer Brons + Mark S Rea. 2015. Tailored Lighting Intervention for Persons with Dementia and Caregivers Living at Home. *Sleep Health* 1(4): 322–330

Figueiro, Mariana G, Kassandra Gonzales + David Pedler. 2016. Designing with Circadian Stimulus. *L D + A (Lighting Design + Applications)* 46(10) Oct: 30–34

Figueiro, Marianna G + D Overington. 2016. Self-Luminous Devices and Melatonin Suppression in Adolescents. *Lighting Research and Technology* 48(8): 966–75

Mondo Arc. 2015. Circulating Color: Novo Nordisk, Krogshøjvej, Bagsværd, Denmark. *MONDO ARC*, 83(Feb/Mar): 54–58, mondoarc.designandgo.net

Riemersma-van der Lek, Rixt F, Dick F Swaab, Jos Twisk, Elly M Hol, Witte J G Hoogendijk + Eus J W Van Someren. 2008. Effect of Bright Light and Melatonin on Cognitive and Noncognitive Function in Elderly Residents of Group Care Facilities: A Randomized Controlled Trial. *Journal of the American Medical Association* 299(22): 2642–2655

Schwartz, Richard S + Jacqueline Olds. 2015. The Psychiatry of Light. *Harvard Review of Psychiatry* 23(3):188–94

Stefani, Oliver, Marlène Freyburger, Simon Veitz, Tamara Basishvili, Martin Meyer, Janine Weibel, Kumpei Kobayashi, et al. 2021. Changing Color and Intensity of LED Lighting across the Day: Impacts on Circadian Melatonin Rhythms and Sleep in Healthy Men. *Journal of Pineal Research* 70(3): e12714

UL. 2019. *Design Guideline for Promoting Circadian Entrainment with Light for Day-Active People*, 1st ed, 19 Dec, Underwriters Laboratories, Inc. DG 24480

Velux. 2013. *Circadian House: Principles and Guidelines for Healthy Homes*. Velux, Nov. thedaylightsight.com

Vetter, Céline, P Morgan Pattison, Kevin Houser, Michael Herf, Andrew J K Phillips, Kenneth P Wright, et al. 2022. A Review of Human Physiological Responses to Light: Implications for the Development of Integrative Lighting Solutions, *LEUKOS* 18(3): 387–414

Zeitzer, Jamie M, Derk-Jan Dijk, Richard E Kronauer, Emery N Brown + Charles A Czeisler. 2000. Sensitivity of the Human Circadian Pacemaker to Nocturnal Light: Melatonin Phase Resetting and Suppression. *Journal of Physiology* 526(3)1 Aug: 695–702

ZGF Architects LLP. 2017. First of Its Kind Pediatric Approach: Children's Hospital of Philadelphia, Medical Behavioral Unit. *ZGF*. zgf.com

R4 Dawn + Dusk Places

BlueHourSite. 2018. bluehoursite.com

Corfidi, Stephen. n.d. The Colors of Sunset and Twilight, NOAA/NWS Storm Prediction Center. spc.noaa.gov

Daily Moon Position. 2021. Monthly Moon Position by Latitude and Longitude. *Daily moon position.* dailymoonposition.com

DeKay, Mark + G Z Brown. 2014. *Sun, Wind + Light: Architectural Design Strategies,* 3rd ed. Hoboken, New Jersey: Wiley. #A2 Sun Path Diagrams, E.374–404

Giesen, Jürgen. 2020. Moonpos spreadsheet, Position and illuminated fraction of the Moon. jgiesen.de/moonpos/

Hoffman, Torseten. 2021. MoonCalc. MoonCalc.org

Hoffman, Torseten. 2021. SunCalc. SunCalc.org

Human Point. 2019. Shapes Luxury Suites. humanpoint.eu

Joy, Rick. 2018. *Studio Joy Works/Rick Joy.* New York: Princeton Architectural Press, 20–31

Karatzas, Pygmalion. 2019. Shapes Luxury Suites, Syros Island, Greece. pygmalionkaratzas.com/fotopoulosshapessuites

Kossmagk, Jens. 2019. Twilight Calculator. JekoPhoto. jekophoto.eu

Lynch, David K + William Livingston. 1995. *Color and Light in Nature.* Cambridge, UK: Cambridge University Press, 39

Marquès, Germán. 2017. Understanding Golden Hour, Blue Hour and Twilights. *PhotoPills.* photopills.com

Reijs, Victor. 2020. Calculating the Declination and Set/Rise Azimuth (of celestial objects). *Archaeocosmology.* archaeocosmology.org

USNO. n.d. Rise, Set, and Twilight Definitions. Astronomical Applications Department. US Naval Observatory. aa.usno.navy.mil/faq/RST_defs. Accessed 10.25.2022

Vincent, Foina. 2015. Lunar Standstills. St. Andrews University Astronomy Group. star-www.st-and.ac.uk/~fv/sky/standstill.html

R4 Circadian Space

DeKay, Mark + G Z Brown. 2014. *Sun, Wind + Light: Architectural Design Strategies,* 3rd ed. Hoboken, New Jersey: Wiley. #48 Direct Gain Rooms, E.132–133; #49 Sunspaces, E.134–136; #41 Daylight Zones, E.115

Figueiro, Mariana + Mark Rea. 2017. Quantifying Circadian Light and Its Impact. *Architect Magazine,* 13 Feb. architectmagazine.com

Joy, Rick. 2018. *Studio Joy Works/Rick Joy.* New York: Princeton Architectural Press, 120–127

Knoop, Martine, Oliver Stefani, Bruno Bueno, Barbara Matusiak, Richard Hobday, Anna Wirz-Justice, Klaus Martiny, et al. 2020. Daylight: What Makes the Difference? *Lighting Research and Technology* 52(3): 423–442

Leoncio, Ella. 2013. Luxury Studio Apartment by Studio Rick Joy/ Chelsea, USA, *Yellowtrace,* 17 Sep. yellowtrace.com.au

LRC. 2016a. *Results Report: Measuring Personal Light Exposures, Health and Wellbeing Outcomes, Federal Center South, Seattle, Washington.* Lighting Research Center, Renssalaer Polytechnic Institute, 18 May. LRC.RPI.edu

LRC. 2016b. *Results Report: Facility Lighting—Winter, Federal Center South, Seattle, Washington.* Lighting Research Center, Renssalaer Polytechnic Institute, 18 May. LRC.RPI.edu

Wirz-Justice, Anna, Francesco Benedetti + Michael Terman. 2013. *Chronotherapeutics for Affective Disorders: A Clinician's Manual for Light and Wake Therapy,* 2nd ed. Basel, Switzerland: Karger Medical and Scientific Publishers

ZGF Architects LLP, Studio SC + GR Plume Company. 2012. Federal Center South Building 1202. archello.com

ZGF Architects LLP. 2012. Meet You in the Commons: US General Services Administration, Federal Center South Building 1202. *ZGF*. zgf.com

R4 Radiant Sailing

Andersen, Flemming Bo. n.d. Can Lis. *Guide to Utzon*. utzonphotos.com

Arkitektur DK. 1996. Can Lis. *Arkitektur DK*, 40(2): 80–95

Bainbridge, David A + Kenneth L Haggard. 2011. *Passive Solar Architecture: Heating, Cooling, Ventilation, Daylighting and More Using Natural Flows*. White River Junction, Vermont: Chelsea Green, 31

Balcomb, J Douglas. 1984. *Passive Solar Heating Analysis: A Design Manual*. Atlanta: ASHRAE

DAH (Dept. of Arkansas Heritage). 1999. *Outside the Pale: The Architecture of Fay Jones*. Fayetteville, Arkansas: University of Arkansas Press

DeKay, Mark + G Z Brown. 2014. *Sun, Wind + Light: Architectural Design Strategies*, 3rd ed. Hoboken, New Jersey: Wiley. #54 Night-Cooled Mass, E.147–149; #60 Mass Arrangement, E.163–166; #75 (solar) Thermal Mass, E.203–207; #102 Mass Surface Absorptance, E.266

Grondzik, Walter T + Alison G Kwok. 2019. *Mechanical and Electrical Equipment for Buildings*. 13th ed. Hoboken, New Jersey: Wiley

Gunay, H Burak, Weiming Shen, Guy Newsham + Araz Ashouri. 2018. Modeling and Analysis of Unsolicited Temperature Setpoint Change Requests in Office Buildings. *Building and Environment* 33: 203–212

Heschong, Lisa. 1979. *Thermal Delight in Architecture*. Cambridge, Massachusetts: MIT Press

Ivy, Robert A, Jr. 1992. *Fay Jones: The Architecture of E Fay Jones*, FAIA. New York: McGraw-Hill, 18–127

Loftness, Vivian. 2013. Environmental Surfing: Delight and Nature's Renewable Energies. in Braham, William W + Daniel Willis, Eds. *Architecture and Energy: Performance and Style*. London: Taylor + Francis

Mazria, Edward. 1979. *The Passive Solar Energy Book, Expanded Professional Edition*. Emmaus, Pennsylvania: Rodale Press, 65

Mendell, Mark J + Anna G Mirer. 2009. Indoor Thermal Factors and Symptoms in Office Workers: Findings from the US EPA BASE Study. *Indoor Air* 19: 291–302

Rempel, Alexandra. 2020. Personal communication, 20 July

Samuel, D G Leo, S M Shiva Nagendra + M P Maiya. 2013. Passive Alternatives to Mechanical Air Conditioning of Buildings: A review. *Building and Environment* 66: 54–64

Wilcox, Danica. 2016. An Architect's Indoor/Outdoor Dreamscape in Mallorca, Spain. *Remodelista* 15, 11 Apr

R5 Habitat Fringe

Barba, Federico García. 2013. Palmyra House. Bijoy Jain. Studio Mumbai Architects. *Arquiscopio*, 14 Jul. arquiscopio.com/archivo

Brillon, James. 2018. Creek House by Faulkner Architects Preserves Boulders on Steep Site in California. *deZeen*, 18 Mar. dezeen.com/2018/03/18

Chalmin-Pula, Lauriane Suyin, Jenny Roob, Alistair Griffiths, Nina Smyth, Timothy Heatone, Andy Claydena + Ross Camerona. 2021. It Made Me Feel Brighter in Myself—The Health and Well-being Impacts of a Residential Front Garden Horticultural Intervention. *Landscape and Urban Planning*. 205:103958

Rhythm Sources

Cox, Daniel T C + Kevin J Gaston. 2015. Likeability of Garden Birds: Importance of Species Knowledge + Richness in Connecting People to Nature. *PLoS ONE* 10(11): e0141505

Cox, Daniel T C + Kevin J Gaston. 2016. Urban Bird Feeding: Connecting People with Nature. *PLoS ONE* 11(7): e0158717

DAH (Dept of Arkansas Heritage). 1999. *Outside the Pale: The Architecture of Fay Jones*. Fayetteville, Arkansas: University of Arkansas Press

Darke, Rick + Douglas W Tallamy. 2014. *The Living Landscape: Designing for Beauty and Biodiversity in the Home Garden*. Portland, Oregon: Timber Press

Frampton, Kenneth + Kengo Kuma. 2012. Kengo Kuma: Complete Works. New York: Thames + Hudson, 290–301

Frearson, Amy. 2013. Optical Glass House by Hiroshi Nakamura + NAP. *deZeen*. 27 Jan. dezeen.com/2013/01/27

Gorlin, Anton. 2018. *Photography Composition: The Definitive Guide*. Australian Landscape Photography, Anton Gorlin Photography. antongorlin.com

Hall, Charles R + Madeline W Dickson. 2011. Economic, Environmental and Health/Well-Being Benefits Associated with Green Industry Products and Services: A Review. *Journal of Environmental Horticulture* 29(2) Jun: 96–103

Hall, Charlie. 2011. Health and Well-being Benefits of Plants. ellisonchair.tamu.edu

Ivy, Robert A, Jr. 1992. *Fay Jones: The Architecture of E Fay Jones, FAIA*. New York: McGraw-Hill, 128–137

Low, Kevin. 2010. Palymyra House, Alibag, India: 2010 On Site Review Report. Aga Khan Trust for Culture. archnet.org/sites/6454

Lymeus, Freddie. 2019. Mindfulness Training Supported by a Restorative Natural Setting: Integrating Individual and Environmental Approaches to the Management of Adaptive Resources. Doctoral thesis. Uppsala Univ, Dept of Psychology

Matusiak, Barbara Szybinska + Christian A Klöckner. 2015. How We Evaluate The View Out Through the Window. *Architectural Science Review* 59(3):1–9

Ryan, Richard. 2009. Nature Makes Us More Caring, Study Says, Univ. of Rochester, 30 Sep. rochester.edu/news/show.php?id=3450

The Plan. 2019. Sand House, Around the Dissolution of Architecture Into Its Surroundings. Studio Mk27. *The Plan*. theplan.it

Trapasso, Emilia. 2021. Mindfulness-based Connection to Nature as a Tool to Improve Perceived Stress and Connection to Nature. PhD dissertation, University of Liverpool

Weinstein, Netta, Andrew K Przybylski + Richard M Ryan. 2009. Can Nature Make Us More Caring? Effects of Immersion in Nature on Intrinsic Aspirations and Generosity. *Personality and Social Psychology Bulletin* 35(10) Oct: 1315–1329

R5 Heliotropic Rooms

Constant, Caroline. 2000. Working Independently: Tempe a Pailia, *Eileen Gray*. London: Phaidon, 144–163, quote 149

Denzer, Anthony. 2014. *Modern Architecture and Theories of Solar Orientation*. 2014 ASES National Solar Conference. Boulder, Colorado: American Solar Energy Society

Escribano, Miguel Ángel Rupérez. 2014. Utzon and the Sun Path as an Organizing Element of Life in a House. *What Would Utzon do Now?*. 4th International Utzon Symposium, Sydney, Australia, 7–9 Mar, University of New South Wales

Fernandez-Galioano, Luis, ed. 2018. Fredensborg Houses, Selandia, in *Jørn Utzon, 1918-2008. AV Monographs* 205: 46–51 Madrid: Arquitectura Viva SL. arquitecturaviva.com

Jacobson, Max, Murray Silverstein + Barbara Winslow. 2012. A House that Follows the Sun, in *Patterns of Home: The Ten Essentials of Enduring Design*. Newtown, Connecticut: Taunton Press, 112–119

Leatherbarrow, David. 2021. Well-Timed Openings: Eileen Gray's Tempe à Pailla. in *Building Time: Architecture, Event and Experience*. New York: Bloomsbury, 31–48, quote 49

Mazria, Edward. 1979. *The Passive Solar Energy Book, Expanded Professional Edition*. Emmaus, Pennsylvania: Rodale Press, 90–92

Utzon, Jørn. 1948. The Innermost Being of Architecture, in Weston, Richard, *Jørn Utzon: Inspiration, Vision, Architecture*. Hellerup, Denmark: Bløndal, 10–11

Wurster, Catherine Bauer. 1934. *Modern Housing*. Boston: Houghton Mifflin Company

R6 Cooling Conversions

AIA. 2014. The David and Lucile Packard Foundation Headquarters. Top Ten Project. American Institute of Architects Committee on the Environment (COTE). aiatopten.org/node/403

ArchDaily. 2020. Makers Quarter Block D Office Building/ BNIM. *ArchDaily*, 4 Aug, archdaily.com/944795

Arsenault, Raymond O. 1984. The End of the Long Hot Summer: The Air-conditioner and Southern Culture. *Journal of Southern History* 50(4): 597–628

ASHRAE 2020. *Standard 55: Thermal Environmental Conditions for Human Occupancy*. Atlanta, GA: American Society of Heating, Refrigerating and Air-Conditioning Engineers

BNIM. 2019. Block D Makers Quarter, San Diego, California [Cote Top 10 Measures]. BNIM/issuu. issuu.com

Brager, Gail + Lindsay Baker. 2009. Occupant Satisfaction in Mixed-Mode Buildings. *Building Research + Information* 37(4) Jul/Aug: 369–380

Brager, Gail. 2006. Mixed Mode Cooling. *ASHRAE Journal* 48: 30-37

CBE. 2014. Livable Buildings Award Winner: The David + Lucile Packard Foundation Headquarters, Los Altos, CA. *CBE Centerline. Center for the Built Environment*. University of California, Berkeley. cbe.berkeley.edu/livable-building/david-lucile-packard-foundation-hq/

ILFI. 2013. David + Lucile Packard Foundation Headquarters. *International Living Future Institute*. living-future.org

Knapp, Robert H. 2013. Sustainability in Practice: Building and Running 343 Second Street, The Packard Foundation Headquarters, Los Altos, California. David + Lucile Packard Foundation. www.packard.org/about-the-foundation/our-green-headquarters/energy-reports/

Packard. 2022. About Our Green Headquarters. David + Lucile Packard Foundation. packard.org/about-the-foundation/our-green-headquarters/tour-our-building/

Parkinson, Tom, Richard de Dear + Gail Brager. 2020. Nudging the Adaptive Thermal Comfort Model. *Energy and Buildings* 206(Jan): 109559.

van der Ryn, Sim. 2020. Gregory Bateson Building. simvanderryn.com/bateson

284 **Hospital of San Sebastián**

Badajoz, Spain, 1694
Nicolás de Morales Morgado
architect

renovation 2017
José María Sánchez García,
renovation architect

The changing condition of sky color, clouds, daylight intensity and character from diffuse to direct can be seen directly in portions of the roof and indirectly projected on surfaces.

photo Roland Halbe

Flux Schemas

A breeze, with its inherent randomness, can be more pleasant than a constant mechanical fan, and an oscillating fan can be more pleasant than a fixed one. This unpredictable variability acts on the nervous system and awareness to keep one alert, awake and interested. Sometimes occupants want to exclude from buildings certain forces, such as wind on a cool day. Closing the window is an isolating response, disconnecting inhabitants in a single operation from scent, sound, moisture, air-movement and temperature outdoors. However, if vegetation or fabric elements moving in the wind can be seen, they give relief to one's attention while keeping a visual connection with the dynamic life outside. When sun or shadow's variability are unwanted—for instance on a work surface, on a book being read or directly on the body—shades or curtains may be employed. Ideally this is done in a way that provides at least a partial connection to view, sun or light. For example, if the light is reflected onto walls or ceilings, particularly off of water disturbed by wind, then the dynamics of the vibrant outdoors can be enjoyed indoors without discomfort.

The design schemas in this section articulate recurring ways that designers have brought non-recurring patterns of environmental conditions into architectural experience. F1 Melodic Materials employs sound to tell of other elements. F2 Current Prehension and F3 Fans First harness air movements to shift perception in the delight direction, at the elemental and building system scales, respectively. F2 Water as Mirror and F3 Water-Animated Surfaces utilize the nature of the fluid—in both its still and undulating modes—to converge consciousness on a charismatic Nature. F3 Revealed Conveyance and F4 Compluvium Shower visibly manifest the process of rainwater collection and its attendant sound and motion.

The designer's challenge with flux schemas is to manage randomness so that it does not become disturbing chaos. A gentle lilac-scented spring breeze, waxing and waning, delights. Yet, if the weather turns and the breeze becomes a strong wind, it becomes annoying. If a cold-front moves in and the temperature drops, even the gentle breeze becomes unwanted. Then again, if the trees outside the window can be viewed swaying in the same cold breeze, seen but not felt, pleasure and connection return. In this way, fluxes are often multi-sensory and, like many other of the design schemas, benefit from occupant choice and control.

F1

Melodic Materials

bring weather awareness by responding to rain and wind forces, translating their patterns into sound.

286 **Wind Museum**

Jeju Island, South Korea, 2006
Itami Jun (Yoo Dong Ryong)
architect

Dedicated to experiencing the wind through sound, the wind itself is the art.

photo Sato Shinichi

the world breathes outside
it hearkens and drinks the rain
sharing we rejoice

Comfortably sitting in a living room and hearing rain pattering on the metal roof, or resting near an open window seeing the trees blowing, hearing whispering leaves rustling against each other—these sounds alert us to weather activity without being physically touched by natural elements. Modern buildings shelter us, but can also isolate occupants from what is happening outdoors. Buildings are increasingly air tight and insulative, with the effect of silencing rain and wind. Everyone feels the shift of atmosphere and mood during rainfall—if we are not cut off by our shelter. To reconnect with weather, occupants need some places in buildings where the effects can be heard or seen, or both. Architecture can indirectly transmit the sounds of nature. We know the force of wind by its effect on us and on other objects. Sound-responsive materials keep inhabitants connected to wind and rain from a safe place. Melodic materials convert Nature's forces into tones and percussion, such as when revealing a slight breeze not normally noticed. Hard materials intensify the rain experience into an emotionally moving event.

Rain-hearing Pavilion

Hefei, Anhui, China, 2019
TJAD, architects
Qiang Chen + Wen Ye

The structure is designed simply for people sitting and listening to rain sounds on the tile roof, stone floor and in the basin as it fills.

photo Yuan Ma

Wind Museum is one of three PINX Museums (2017) in which the natural forces and materials of Jeju Island *are themselves* the exhibit: the Wind, Rock and Water Museums of the Biotopia complex. The Wind Museum, designed as a place for meditation on Nature, is organized as a long thin gabled shed (Space 2006). Jun explains, "The structure is much like an instrument. Wooden slats 10 mm (0.4 in) apart from each other create a small gap with which the wind can howl or whisper, depending on the climate. It is a space for the wind to sing....What I am communicating with this architecture is the world which exists inbetween nature and mankind. Thus, I present a way to see a new world, to see a world which cannot be seen" (Jun 2010).

Rain-hearing Pavilion, located at a university campus in a rainy climate, centers on an old well. Pitched hard-tiled roofs slope to a 30 cm (12 in) linear *tianjing* (heavenly well) opening, creating a rain curtain falling to stone and a rock-lined trench (Arch2o 2020). The axis leads to a compluvium-roofed well room known as *si shui gui tang* (four waters return to the hall), symbolizing plentiful resources (Knapp 2013). The architects explain, "People's acoustical and visual perception will be inspired to experience the relationship between ...humans and nature (daylight, wind, rain, hill and vegetation)" countering "indifference to nature in contemporary society" (Chen + Ye 2020).

Melodic Materials

Material acoustic characteristics

left
Sound absorption vs frequency
Fiberglass absorbs the most sound over a wide frequency band. Harder materials are more reflective, less absorptive. Glass absorbs low frequencies and reflects high frequency.

adapted from
Engineering Toolbox 2003

right
Rain noise vs frequency
Stiffer denser materials transmit less rain noise, while more drum-like construction transmits more.

adapted from BRE 2004, Toyoda + Takahashi 2013 and Pyrotek 2018

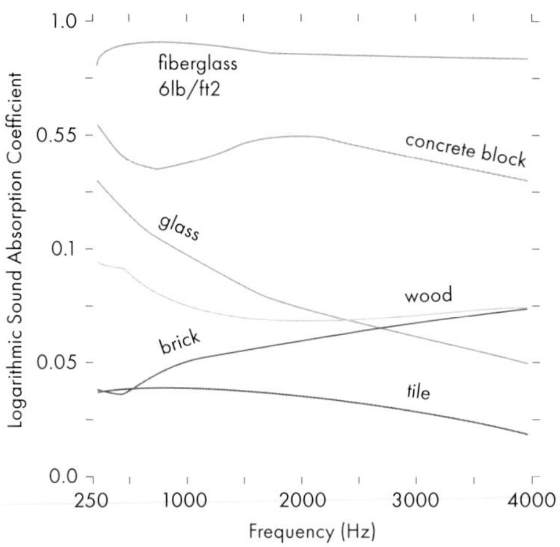

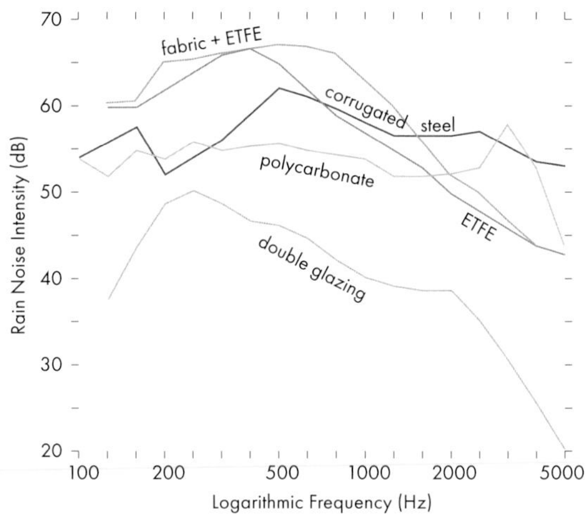

Supporting Evidence

Most studies of outdoor sound transmission into buildings focus on minimizing them; the same principles, inverted, can be used to engage wind and rain as enlivening nature connections with positive psychological affect.

Rain at Bellagio

The omnipresence of the sound
of water: rain
on the graveled walks, the
lakeside terraces,
the red pantiles of Bellagio.

—Amy Clampitt 1982

Rain can be considered as a form of impact loading, its vibrations of materials generated by the force of falling drops (Donohue + Pearse 2019). The sound can be pleasurable and relaxing or occur as unwanted noise, depending on the hearer or context. Intense rainfall sound has been shown to increase arithmetic skills for extroverts working hard problems (Proverbio et al. 2018).

Rain sound volume varies with rainfall intensity (Donohue + Pearse 2019), material, construction and surface geometry. Flatter is louder. Loudness is increased by harder rain, lighter weight (nonmassive) construction, lower material stiffness (a function of composition and mounting rigidity), uninsulated construction (contrasted to a sound absorptive layer) and acoustic holes (openings) between inside and outside (Ballagh 1991). Clearly, a low slope metal roof will transmit much more rainfall sound than a steep-sloped insulated asphalt shingle roof with a ceiling.

Tensile fabrics used for roofs are characterized by high sound reflectivity, particularly in the frequency range of 500–2000 Hz (high and mid-frequency sounds), while low frequencies pass through the fabric (Huntington 2013).

Pink noise, in which every octave carries the same power, helps with relaxation and deep sleep if steady rather than intermittent, as in "rainfall, wind and flowing brooks" (Suzuki et al. 1991). It "has significant effect on reducing brain wave complexity and inducing more stable sleep time to improve sleep quality" (Zhou et al. 2012).

Tranquility induced by falling water sounds seems to be maximized by "natural sounds rather than...more artificial" and with low levels of low frequency noise that are variable in nature, with the sense of "water splashing onto rocks or a relatively fine water spray falling on pebbles or gravel" (Watts et al 2009).

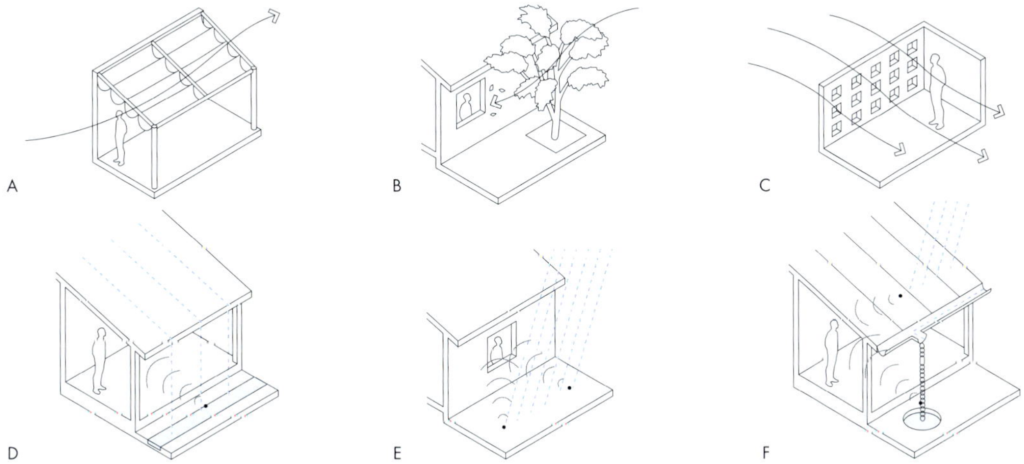

Bring wind and rain sounds to occupants

A fabric

B foliage

C perforated wall

D water

E hard surfaces

F metal roof, visible rain-chain

Design Guidelines

Choose melodic material locations and space uses where admitted or amplified nature sounds are desirable. Choose roofing materials that audibly amplify or visibly showcase rain and bring awareness to wind and weather.

Bring wind and rain sounds to occupants indoors or out: A. *Wind-disturbed elements*: blinds and looser awnings; B. *Wind-disturbed vegetation*: leaves, vegetation; C. *Wind focused sounds:* whistling, whispering or other sounds channeled via porous walls and grilles or by breezeways, dogtrots, cracked windows, spaces between buildings; D. *Rain falling in water*, yielding complex distinctions. E. *Reflected impact sounds* from rain hitting hard materials like paving; F. *Drum-like sounds* from rain on transmissive roofs (like metal), tents and taut fabric awnings.
Distinguish uses such as sleeping, contemplation, focused work and relaxation spaces where masking of urban background noises is beneficial and nature sounds will not distract. Spaces where speech intelligibility is critical, such as classrooms and conference rooms, are not good candidates. Consult with the client and occupants.
Select material density. Use dense materials as envelope isolators for airborne sound or as reflectors of outdoor impact sounds. Use soft materials as sound absorbers for dampening. Fabrics in high tension move little in the wind, while suspended canvas awnings may audibly and visibly flap; flags are the extreme example.
Choose roof construction and materials to enhance rainstorm effects. Solid roof decking and insulation dampens sound, while spaced strapping on an uninsulated open porch roof transmits significant rain impact. Low slope roofs are noisier than steep roofs. Skylights in insulated roofs or glazed roofs, such as in conservatories, also make the sound of rain available indoors and add the benefit of seeing moving water patterns from below.
Choose outdoor locations for wind effects based on wind orientation. Use isolating switches to reject if needed.
Refine with N1 Perceptible Provenance. Help build N2 Authentic Matters and F2 Current Prehension.

When the breeze is accompanied by some rain, then you're going to get the smell of the forest. You can listen to the sound of the rain on a metal roof, from a beautiful pitter-patter to a heavy sound to the gurgling of the water as it gets into the gutter and the throbbing of it as it goes into the water tank.

—Glenn Murcutt 2021

F2

Current Prehension

engenders occupant breeze awareness with visual and auditory animations of built and natural elements.

290 **Vertical Canal [facade]**

Westraven, offices for Rijkswaterstaat [Dutch Ministry of Infrastructure and Water Management]
Utrecht, Netherlands, 2008
Ned Kahn Studios (facade)
Cepezed, architects

Invisible breezes are rendered visible by the wave-like movement of flaps on suspended panels.

photo Ned Kahn Studios
video see Kahn 2008

seeking Aeolus
his presence invisible
purely to marvel

The Greek wind-god, *Aeolus*, ruled the winds. Sometimes his wind feels like a friend, sometimes an enemy, but usually a delight to see its invisible force expressed. Experiencing the wind on a brisk fall day has one feel alive and invigorated. The breeze's sound and animation from swaying branches amplifies its felt influence. Loosening crisp rusted leaves to fall, they swirl and map the air, tussling with the Earth. As part of this elemental dance, human beings immerse themselves in the generative fluxes and transformations of the *weather-world* (Ingold 2007). On this same cool delightful day, windows close to keep out wind and air. How then can occupants experience the wind minus its sometimes deleterious effects? How can a summer zephyr subtly enter one's awareness and trigger deep associations of coolness? Waving flags, jingling wind chimes, inflating wind socks, spinning weather vanes, anemometers and turbine ventilators alert us to moving air—yet, more integral and natural than these devices are the ways vegetation and building elements alert inhabitants to the wind's presence, intensity and pattern.

Villa White [Villa Alexy]

Porto Heli, Argolis, Greece, 2014
Harald Nürnberg, architect

Fabric movement and whispering sounds tell of the breeze and its pleasures brought to a quiet, shaded stone retreat.

photo Pygmalion Karatzas

Vertical Canal, a kinetic facade animated by wind hovers over the main entrance of the Westraven office building. The name refers both to the Amsterdam-Rijn Canal on site and to the work of the water ministry. MacArthur fellow Kahn's facade installations display the forces of nature, in this case, wind. 13,000 extruded plastic flaps are hung on 15 cm (6 in) grids of stainless-steel wires. The translucent panels are barely visible until a breeze arises, creating wind waves as "movement of the flaps become visible in the reflection of the light and colours of the sky" (Cepezed 2014). The suspended panels gently sway by wind turbulence, animating the building and bringing by-passers' attention to the presence of an otherwise invisible breeze. "When you stand there, the work is very much itself, it does not refer, it does not symbolize. It is" (van Ool 2014).

Villa White master bath and dressing room opens to a west-facing prospect on the Argolic Gulf and the multi-sensory experience of its air with full-height sliding glass walls. Ceiling-to-floor translucent curtains provide privacy while undulating in gentle breezes. The large opening links to a shaded outdoor lounge, framing a landscape and sea vista with raised seating and deep overhang. The fabric, animated by air currents, becomes susurrous, whispering of the thermal relief to the day's heat come riding on the sea breeze (Ktirio 2018; Nürnberg 2018).

Current Prehension

292 **Presence effects of wind-generated movement**

Both shadows projected from wind moving foliage and wind-animated reflections from water onto building surfaces can help people feel connected to the present more than static conditions.

adapted from Nute + Chen 2020

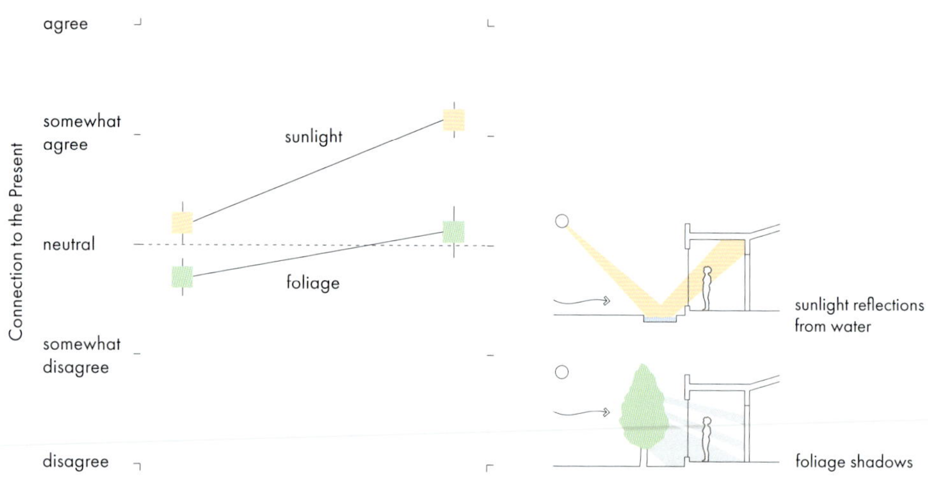

Supporting Evidence

Early human survival required assessments of ambient and future weather. Literature abounds with admiration of wind-animated foliage. Animation effects from wind can increase occupants' feelings of being present.

Environment of evolutionary adaptation (EEA) denotes characteristics of the environmental context in which humans are adapted to live (Crawford 1997). Discord and stress can occur if the mismatch between the inhabited environment and EEA is too great (Grinde + Patil 2009). One key mismatch is the lack of natural variability. As environmental psychologist Judith Heerwagen (1990) puts it, "Our indoor environments are largely devoid of sensory change, and deliberately so..... there have been relatively few attempts to provide indoor environments that deliberately mimic sensory change as it exists in the natural world. While most humans do not wish to return to living most of life outdoors, one solution is to bring such natural change into inhabitants' indoor experiences."
Communicating weather information to people is one of the roles plants play when interacting with moving or still air or when transforming with the seasons. Wind-animated vegetation, falling leaves, swirling maple pips, changing fall color and spring greens all locate people in their ecological place and time. One traditional weather proverb foretells rain: *When leaves show their undersides, be very sure that rain betides.* The US National Park Service (2021) explains that, "Some trees, such as oak and maple, have leaves that will curl when the humidity is very high and the wind is blowing strongly. Both these conditions indicate an approaching storm." Similarly, many plants have leaves that are darker green on the top side and lighter underneath. The silver maple is an extreme version. In breezes, the leaves move, revealing the underside and adding color information to their movement. The faster the wind, the more leaf movement and the more the lighter under-surfaces are revealed.
Psithurism means a whispering sound (OED 2021), more particularly, the "sound of wind in the trees or rustling

leaves" (Macmillan 2021). Numerous writers refer to the experience (Winson 2017). John Muir (1878) wrote, "Winds are advertisements of all they touch, however much or little we may be able to read them", and further, "There is always something deeply exciting, not only in the sounds of winds in the woods, which exert more or less influence over every mind, but in their varied waterlike flow as manifested by the movements of the trees". Presence effects of wind-generated movement were studied by Nute and Chen (2020) who found that shadows from wind-animated foliage projected on interior surfaces (this schema) and light reflected from wind-animated water (F3 Water-Animated Surfaces) had multiple effects on participants' feelings: 1. Increased connection to the present moment; 2. Decreased awareness of time passing; and 3. Sense that time passed faster. Movements observed outside the room had somewhat more effect than similar movements inside. Effects were greater in larger than in smaller rooms. The conclusion was that such visual movement has effects similar to mindfulness practice—lower stress by being more present and greater pleasure by being distracted from time's passage.

Design Guidelines

In addition to the direct experiences of natural ventilation indoors and air-flow in outdoor rooms, design to give inhabitants visual and auditory cues to the dynamic wind environment. Use plants in the foreground view of windows or in courts to which indoor rooms connect. Further connect occupied rooms with opening windows and doors to the outdoor wind regime. Reinforce with fabric layers of curtains, awnings and canvas roofs. If views in and out are not called for, use back-projected shadows from exterior vegetation.

Bring movement indoors. In addition to a view from indoors or from in-between spaces to outdoor vegetation, Nute et al. (2012) identified "three simple strategies for effectively bringing weather-generated movement indoors while maintaining physical protection from the elements": 1. *Vegetation in spatial enclosure,* as in a court with good visual linkage, which lessens the felt separation of in and out; 2. *Casting moving shadows* from wind-animated foliage onto interior surfaces; and 3. *Rear-projected animated shadows* on translucent glazing or exterior building skin.
Locate vegetation for view of breeze-induced movement from indoor places where occupants spend time. Nute suggests that foliage located in a courtyard can be designed to seem continuous with the indoor space, even when windows are closed, heightening the sense that the movement of the foliage is actually part of the interior.
Select plants for their effects. Evergreens can track wind year-round, leafless branches can still be moved by wind, yet with a dampened effect. Plants with lighter structures, such as vines, and smaller leaves, such as flowering dogwood, respond to the gentlest of whiffs. Climbing vines like Carolina jessamine and bougainvillea, can grow at windows' edges in close view by utilizing wire grids on walls, shading trellises and pergolas.
Signal aeolian action with fabric layers moved by air pressure. These include shading elements, such as curtains, awnings or mesh sun shades and fabric roofs of porches and outdoor rooms. Fabric has the additional feedback of sound and can also alert occupants to rainfall. When foliage or fabric is used for operable shading, it further connects occupants to the rhythms of nature expressed in these daily or seasonally responsive elements.
Refine with C1 Thermic Hues, F1 Melodic Materials and R2 Aperture Engagement. Help build F3 Fans First.

F2

Water as a Mirror

dynamically reflects images of adjacent buildings, vegetation and moving Nature in the sky.

294 **Villa Melana**

Tyros, Greece, 2014
Valia Foufa + Panagiotis Papassotiriou, architects

Both sea and infinity pool reflect the sky, creating an extended vista to the horizon and adding to the site's immersive dynamism. Reflections of the static building contrast with moving sky.

photo Pygmalion Karatzas

sun clouds geese maples
upon a sheet of glass skate
'til a ripple forms

Still water reflects the dynamic natural world around it. The nature of the sky and its changes are fundamental to place experience. Yet, people don't look up to the sky very often. The human head, neck and eyes naturally look ahead and slightly downward. Indoors, ceilings, roofs and overhangs further focus our attention to the horizon and obscure the sky. A simple reflecting pool, located effectively, brings the dynamic sky and surrounding vegetation back to awareness. Water reflects the movements of Nature, the circulation of people and the stillness of buildings. When a breeze moves across still water, the ripples distort the reflected images, adding motion to the sky's motion. Water as mirror provides literal moments of reflection, calling occupants to pause and contemplate Nature's changes. Frank Lloyd Wright (1928) wrote of glass and mirrors, "The mirror is seen in Nature in the surfaces of lakes, in the hollows of mountains and in the pools deep in shadow of the trees; in winding ribbons of the rivers that catch and give back the flying birds, clouds and blue sky... It may be as refreshing and beautifying in architecture."

Windhover Contemplative Center

Stanford University, Stanford, California, 2014
Aidlin Darling Design, architects
Andrea Cochran Landscape Architecture

The reflecting pool enhances a serene ambiance, capturing forested surrounds, sky and rammed earth images.

photo Matthew Millman

Villa Melana, perched on a narrow rocky plateau, has a shallow swimming pool located to visually merge the pool with the Mediterranean Sea some distance below. Its shaded terrace directs the view toward the horizon, framed between two horizontal planes. In complement and contrast, reflections from the expansive, dynamic sky and clouds are emphasized in the pool's surface against the static house. Depending on the viewer's position, either the massive Arcadian stone wall or the underside of the minimalist wooden pergola is replicated. The pool's infinity edge and light-colored border stone eliminate dark coping reflections (Contemporist 2015, Karatzas 2015).

Windhover Contemplative Center employs its reflecting pool to support a spiritual refuge on the Stanford University campus. It is meant to "inspire and promote personal renewal", a place to establish balance and find tranquility. Intended as an aid for meditation, its pool, which can be viewed from both indoors and outside, is bounded by garden walls and vegetation. It reflects static built form, dynamic sky and trees, swaying or still. "Corten steel, rammed earth walls, stone, glass and water are brought together to deepen the natural feeling, immersing visitors in a calm state" (Windhover 2021). The center combines aspects of sanctuary, art gallery and contemplative garden to create a "unique typology for contemplation and reflection" (Aidlin Darling Design 2015).

Water as a Mirror

Reflecting pool geometry

left
Reflected images appear equal in height to objects. Best reflections are beyond 45° view angle, enhanced by shallow edges and a deeper pool middle.

top right
A larger pool in the direction of view captures more image.

bottom right
Viewing position affects which reflections can be seen. Angles of incidence and reflection are equal.

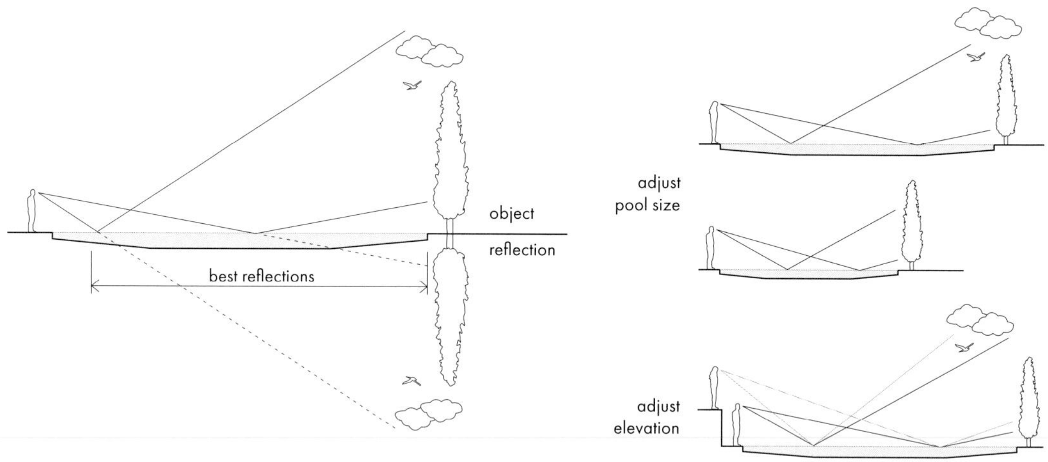

Supporting Evidence

Mirrored reflections from water are controlled by keeping the water surface still and minimizing reflections from the bottom. The result is generally a feeling of calm and fascination.

Inner calm. Still water is a metaphor for a still mind. As Indra Devi (1963) said, "Like water, which can clearly mirror the sky and the trees only so long as its surface is undisturbed, the mind can only reflect the true image of the self when it is tranquil and wholly relaxed." This water-mind correspondence goes further. Marine biologist Wallace Nichols (2014) argues in *Blue Mind* that nearness to water induces "a mildly meditative state characterized by calm, peacefulness, unity and a sense of general happiness and satisfaction with life in the moment."
Creativity. Water seems to give the brain a rest from over-stimulation. Nichols also finds that being near water stimulates creativity as the brain switches into a *default network mode* and new connections among ideas emerge.
Attraction. Eliel Saarinen wrote of Kleinhans Music Hall pool, "Well, doesn't water have a rather commonly felt attraction? Really, there is something enigmatic in this attraction .....to linger near water and to look into its waving and reflecting mirror. ......And there is reflection on this mirror, reflection of life that surrounds us, there is glimmer and glitter of our own life, there is sparkling of color and sunlight" (Schloop 2020).
Well-being. A review of 35 studies found that outdoor *blue spaces* (lakes, rivers, sea, etc) are good for well-being, especially mental health (Gascon et al 2017). A study of people's preferences for five different kinds of urban water features found that still water was rated as the most calming type (Nasar + Lin 2003).
Reflecting pool geometry. Vertical objects reflected in a flat mirrored surface appear the same height as the object. The tree's reflection height will appear the same as the actual tree. As objects are further away from the viewer, both the object and the reflection diminish. When standing at the edge of a pond, one can often see the bottom, but

looking toward the horizon, as the view angle drops below 45°, the water's reflectivity increases (Martin nd).
Depth and color. To prevent wave formation,"the edges of the pond are slightly shallower than the center of the pond." At the very large Lincoln Memorial reflecting pool in Washington, DC, the water is 18 in (46 cm) deep at the edge and 30 in (76 cm) in the center (Exterior Worlds 2015). Dark materials for surfaces below water reflect less light back to the surface, intensify the reflected image and minimize view of the pond bottom.

Design Guidelines

Place the pool strategically for views of reflected objects to the east or west of structures, if possible. Make its center deeper than the edges to reduce waves, with a dark-colored bottom and a thin coping or infinity edges.

Intend what is to be reflected. The mirror doubles the impact of objects reflected, gathering the visual environment around it. The reflections produced will be a result of the relationship between viewing place, water location, reflected objects and sun position. Reflections reveal the underside of trees or built structures, whether bridges or ceilings; make sure these undersides are something worth seeing.
Set a shallow depth of 6–12 in (15–30 cm); less than 18 in (46 cm) avoids code safety issues. Very shallow depths invite public access; some are 1 in (2.5 cm) or less. Pools deeper in the center reduce wind-induced waves.
Color the bottom dark for best reflections, because less light is reflected back to the surface to lighten and defocus the image. An added nontoxic black dye may create better reflections. Waterscape designer Kirk Bianchi (2017) argues, "going with a darker color will dramatically support reflection."
Forego fountains. Smooth water surfaces reflect well; fountains destroy the effect. To supplement for evaporation, supply a constant slow water input below the surface. If filtering, water can overflow at edges and recirculate.
Minimize edge depth that can reflect as doubled height. Vanishing (infinity) edges eliminate such dark reflection, making the water appear even more mirror-like. The Still Water pattern (Alexander et al. 1977) recommends a gradual feathered edge that provides water access and safety for wading children.
Tailor sight lines to intent, from occupied places or paths toward desired reflected objects. Downward view facilitates sky reflections. Sunset reflections require an open view to the west and a lower view angle. A low view angle also reflects objects or plantings on the far side of the pool.
Orient appropriately. In the northern hemisphere, a north-facing pool reflects light on the scene beyond the pool, lightening an area ordinarily in shadow; a south-facing location reflects onto ceilings, but the landscape beyond may appear silhouetted and bring reflected glare. Reverse for the southern hemisphere. Landscape artist Anthony Wills (2021) recommends water placement to the east or west of viewpoints and buildings: "If it's to the west, there will be wonderful, cool reflections in the morning, and in the evening trees and landforms on the other side of the water will be revealed in exciting black silhouette with beautiful colors behind them......Conversely, if the water's to the east of the house, the rich golden evening light will provide spectacular warm reflections of foliage beyond."
Refine with N1 Perceptible Provenance and C1 Thermic Hues. Help build C3 Water You Can Touch. The pool might also serve as visible rainwater storage fed via F3 Revealed Conveyance.

F3

Fans First

prioritizes air movement and raises AC setpoints as an operational strategy for pleasure and fast-acting comfort.

298 **L N R Associates Staff Canteen**

Bangkok, Thailand
3 m (10 ft) diameter low-energy brushless fan supplements natural ventilation in a large room shared by many employees.

Larger diameter fans can move the same volume of air at lower rpm, thus quieter than smaller fans. They produce more airflow over larger area with greater uniformity.

photo Mr. Ken

ardent or nipping
current choices abound near
instant contentment

Gentle breezes on a warm day, sitting on a swaying porch swing or under a fan, offer familiar outdoor sensory delights. A similar indoor pleasure strategy employs fans to move air and provide occupants local, personalized, fast-acting comfort control. Fans and natural ventilation are used as the first coooling strategy until insufficient. As conditions warm further, integrating intelligent fans with air-conditioning (AC) initiated at a higher-than-conventional setpoint offers benefits of both in an energy-efficient, sequenced operation. During periods when the AC is operating, fans enhance comfort, better distribute air and improve perceived air quality. Contemporary fans can provide steady, variable or intermittently stronger flow. Increasing air movement provides almost instantaneous cooling relief by efficiently evaporating even unnoticed perspiration; this compares to fifteen minutes or more response time after thermostat adjustments to AC alone. Reducing fan speed similarly results in immediate warmer sensations. In either case, inhabitants feel renewed during thermal transitions or when moving between spaces.

Bullitt Center

Seattle, Washington, USA, 2013
Miller Hull, architects

Ceiling fans supplement natural ventilation and integrate with AC to enhance occupant comfort more pleasurably and much quicker than centralized AC alone.

photo left Big Ass Fans
photo right Nic Lehoux

see also Bullitt 2013

L N R Associates Staff Canteen uses large-diameter, *high volume, low speed* (HVLS) fans, referring to diameters greater than 7 ft (2 m). HVLS fans enhance comfort in nonresidential occupancies. They sometimes use *winglets* or blade tip fences to minimize noise and maximize airflow, thus creating higher and more uniform felt airspeeds in large spaces. HVLS fans are useful in places with larger numbers of people where local control is impractical (Raftery + Douglass-Jaimes 2020). A single large fan versus several smaller fans is a major visual design choice.

Bullitt Center was designed to have exceptionally low energy use to meet net zero-energy targets and Living Building Challenge standards (ILFI 2015; Gonchar 2013; AIA 2015). It combines ceiling fans with automated windows for passive cooling and to provide natural ventilation. The fans use only 2% of end use energy but allow higher cooling setpoints to reduce AC reliance, offsetting about 750 hours of annual mechanical cooling in a marine climate. Sensors and controls coordinate windows to optimize indoor thermal comfort and air quality, reducing reliance on mechanical cooling. The ceiling fans enhance comfort by cooling occupants much quicker than a centralized system can. It has been shown to be an extremely comfortable building, placing in the top 15% of 500 commercial office buildings in the CBE Occupant Survey database (Raftery + Douglass-Jaimes 2020).

Fans First

Integrated fan operating strategy

As conditions warm, a smart fan turns on; speed increases as temperature rises. AC setpoint can then be higher, saving energy and providing greater comfort control.

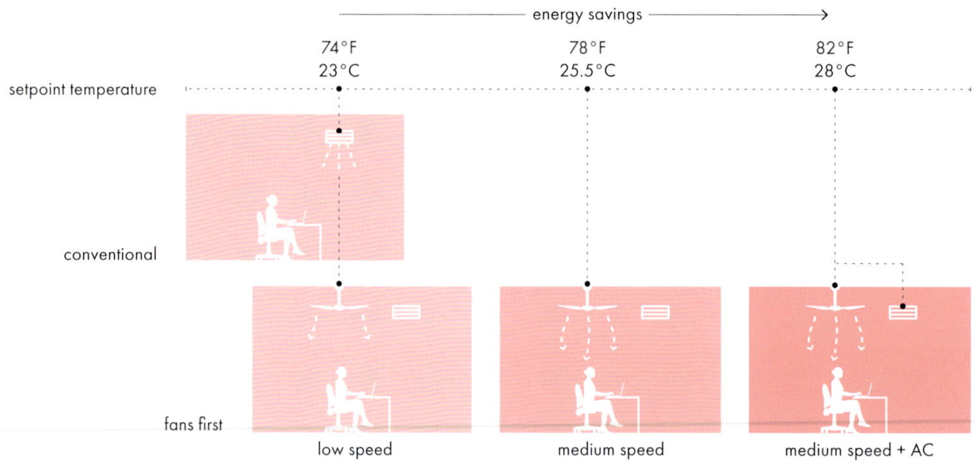

Felt air speed estimate

1 Divide rated airflow by fan diameter to get fan air speed (note associated units of each). This represents the average airspeed that passes through the circle swept by the fan blade

2 Multiply fan air speed by 1.3–1.5 to get the maximum velocity felt by occupants below. This generally occurs below the fan blade tip, slightly inside the fan blade diameter.

Recommended minimum fan speed <80 ft/min (0.4 m/s)

Raftery + Douglass-Jaimes 2020

Supporting Evidence

Standards minimize air movement perception, but occupants prefer air movement they can feel. Multiple benefits are documented, including providing comfort at warmer temperatures, raising the comfort zone upper limit.

Integrated fan operating strategy diagrams show an example sequence beginning with setting AC at 82°F (28°C), so that AC *begins as off.* A smart fan with temperature sensors (or connected to the building management system) starts on *low speed* at 74°F (23°C) and gradually increases speed as the space warms (78°F/25.5°C). Finally, at 82°F/28°C), the AC comes on and runs with the fan. This reduces AC run time, energy use and potentially, plant size and ductwork. Other combinations of velocity and temperature are possible. Controls may be automated with manual overrides in smaller zones for occupants to adjust fan speed and AC switchover (Chen et al. 2020).
Multiple benefits in field studies show that people: 1. Generally desire to have more air movement than they currently experience (Arens et al. 2009); 2. Find air flow particularly refreshing when just entering a space after walking (Zhai et al. 2019); 3. Perceive air quality is significantly enhanced at increased flow rates (Arens et al. 2011); and 4. Improve their productivity with higher air speed (Liu et al. 2018).
Reasonable speeds achieve positive effects. A ceiling fan air speed of 100 ft/min (0.5 m/s) creates about 5°F (2.8°C) cooling effect, at less than half the relative air speed felt when walking (Tartarini et al. 2020).
Verification was shown by a study with 100 smart ceiling fans in multi-family residences with average daily summer highs >90°F (32°C). Researchers raised AC thermostats to 80°F (26.7°C) and set fans to turn on in occupied rooms at 74°F (23.3°C), automatically increasing speed as temperature rose. 93% of occupants were comfortable with the elevated air temperatures and air movement, compared to 82% at 72°F (22.2°C) without fans. Compressor energy reduced by 39% (Miller et al. 2021).

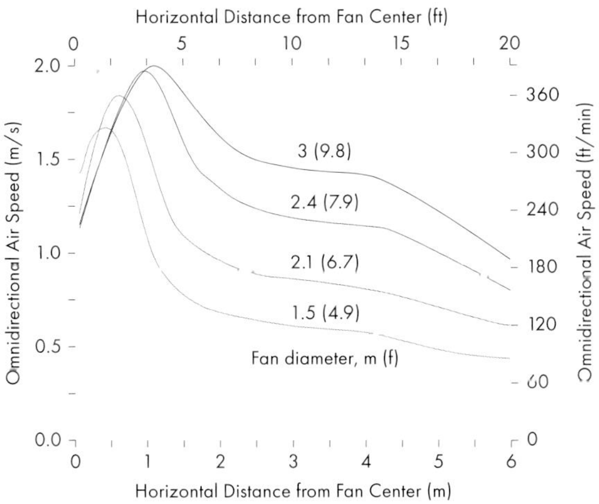

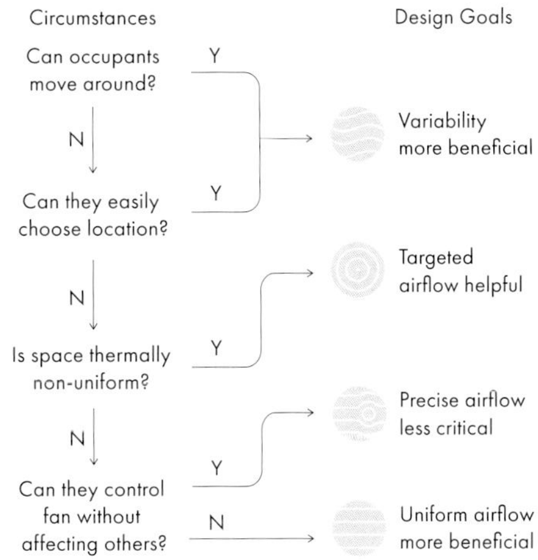

left
Felt room airspeed

Velocity varies with fan diameter and distance from fan center. Even lowest shown speed has 3°F (1.7°C) cooling effect.

Raftery et al. 2019

right
Fans first decision chart

Use the flow chart to help determine the best air flow distribution regime.

adapted from Raftery + Douglass-Jaimes 2020

Design Guidelines

Select smart fans and layout for response to dynamic conditions, spatial airspeed variety and user control. Integrate operation with AC controls, natural ventilation and mixed mode ventilation and cooling.

Fit experiential goal to context. For summer entry spaces, locate fans for maximum airspeed and rapid cooling of overheated people coming from outside. In longer occupancy rooms, design for subtle velocity variation.
Create spatial variation with different combinations of velocity and temperature to enable personal locational choice. Existing thermal non-uniformity, such as higher solar loads near windows, or higher internal gains in a conference area, can be met with increased air flow relative to other zones. User controls enhance local variety.
Select fan specifications using the *CBE Ceiling Fan Design Guide* and online *Fan Design Tool* (Raftery 2019) to configure fan type, diameter, blade style and configuration, motor and drive. Experience depends most on felt air speed at a person's location. A larger diameter fan produces greater airflow, greater average air speeds and uniformity than a smaller one. Airflow and room airspeed generally increase linearly with fan rotational speed
Design for felt air speed. While fans are typically rated for volumetric airflow in ft³/min (l/s), what inhabitants feel is air speed. To estimate felt air speed, occurring below and slightly inside the fan blade diameter, see sidebar. Using fan air speed, not airflow rate, allows comparing fans with different specs.
Use large fans for uniformity. The larger the ratio of diameter to room size, the more uniform the air distribution. For small rooms of plan aspect ratio 1.5:1 or less, set fan diameter at 0.2-0.4 times the smaller side; center it in the room. For larger spaces, subdivide the area into zones of up to 1.5:1,and use the same rule for each cell.
Provide multiple speed control levels, insuring low enough setting for long occupancy, such as in an office.
Refine with R2 Aperture Engagement and F2 Current Prehension. Help build G4 Zephyr Spectrum.

Sources

All design guideline recommendations in this schema come from the *CBE Ceiling Fan Design Guide* (Raftery + Douglass-Jaimes 2020)

F3

Revealed Conveyance

expresses the movement of rainwater from catchment to storage, manifesting the hydrologic process in daily life.

302 **Gando Teacher's Housing**

Burkina Faso, 2004
Kéré Architecture

At the Gando Primary School, houses collect harvested rainwater in channels atop stabilized earth block common walls. The exposed conduits testify to water's significance and connect to several shared cisterns.

photo Erik-Jan Ouwerkerk

below
Conveyance + storage
plan diagram

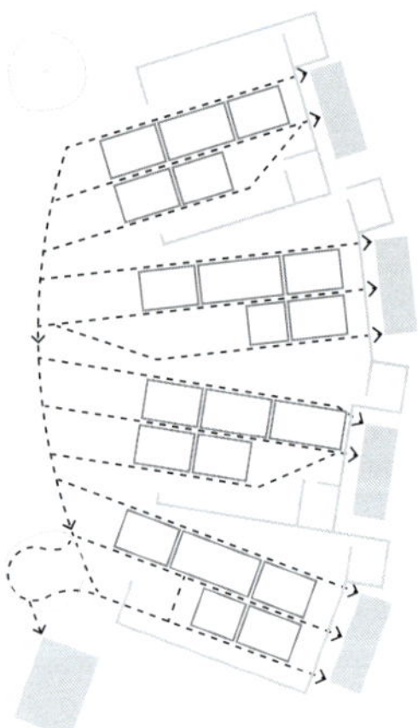

uplifting movement
gentle flows a showers' yield
enraptured we are

Moving water is emotionally moving. In its flows one sees infinite self-similar patterns. Even a loose fascination while watching and hearing its dancing motifs opens psychic access to a calming state. Beyond such direct experience, when rainfall conveyance is exposed to view, occupants engage in and relate to natural processes. In this awareness, the secure pleasure of belonging in a larger world arises. This schema supports both of these experiences. Ordinarily, people seek shelter, rarely thinking about the relationship between rainfall and its containing ecosystem. Most contemporary buildings keep water out of sight and out of mind. Instead, buildings can express how they interact with the water cycle, making pleasurable, educational and meaningful the architectural elements that manage runoff and harvest rainwater. Water, with its ability to take the shape of its vessel, has been celebrated by architects with scuppers, rain chains, gargoyles or other sculptural features, gutters, downspouts, cascades, swales and trenches, each directing water in an intentionally visible and auditory way.

House on a Pond

Dallas, Texas, USA, 2000
Max Levy, architect

Visible pathways, water falling to a pool, overflowing to embankment cascades, the path from sky to pond complete.

photos Charles Davis Smith

next page
Conveyance diagram

Gando Teacher's Houses, in a Burkina Faso village without running water, fan out in a wide arc. Vaulted roofs drain to channels at the top of bearing walls. The runnels flow along the walls, turning to dramatic sloped, open down-channels that connect to an exposed in-ground network. Combined, they visibly relay how water is being gathered and directed to storage cisterns. When dry, the channels still serve as a sculptural element while bearing witness to the promise of rains yet to come. During the rainy season, the rainwater is collected on both ends of the houses, fed to multiple water tanks and used primarily for agriculture (Lepik + Beygo 2019; Divcaro 2013).

House on a Pond has a simple gable roof. Each plane drains to a detached curved-profile 4 in (10 cm) deep outrigger gutter, which in turn leads to a central cross-gutter connected to a gang of four metal down-pipes. These empty to a circular collecting pool on the open breezeway *rain terrace* that serves as entrance. The gap between gutter and roof edge lets residents watch the process begin. The pool overflows down cascading concrete runnels, along the embankment stair to the quarry pond (Baum 2003). Architect Levy (2012) explains: "In this way, the house is connected to that site in a much more profound way than if the house simply enjoyed a view. The house... becomes an intermediary between the sky and the pond. The house gives its share of rain back to the pond."

Revealed Conveyance

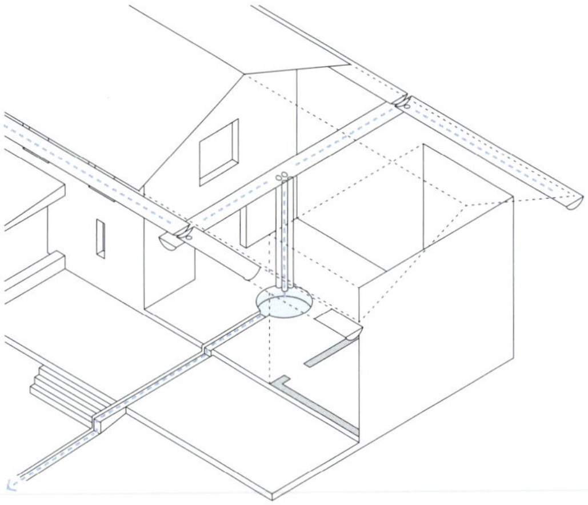

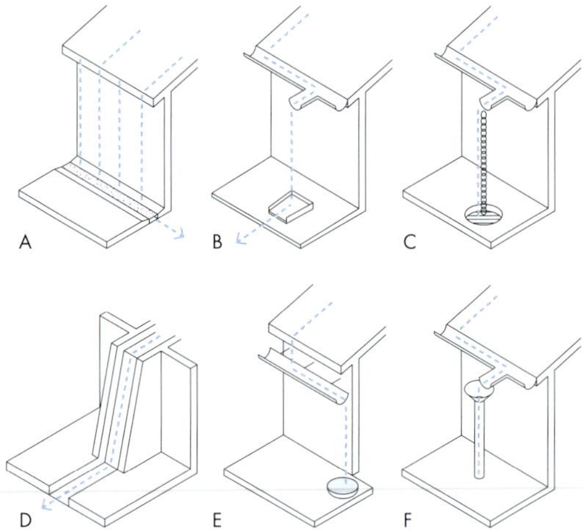

left
House on a Pond conveyance

right
Exposed rainwater pathways

A Gutterless rain curtain + exposed gravel trench

B Expressed gutter + scupper free-fall

C Expressed gutter + rain chain + grated catch basin

D Gando Teacher's Houses: Open channel on wall + sloped down-channel + ground drain

E Outrigger gutter + free-fall to splash vessel

F Expressed gutter, scupper, leader-head + rain-leader

Supporting Evidence

Stormwater design can transform awareness. Visible natural processes manifested in the built environment's form connect people to Nature and raise sensitivity to the living world. People prefer naturalistic water sounds.

Making nature visible. In the classic, *Architecture of the Well-Tempered Environment,* Reyner Banham (1969) distinguished *concealed power* and *exposed power* as two approaches the architect might use for mechanical conditioning systems and other services. These polarities are also present in how buildings make rainwater and drainage systems visible or invisible. Van der Ryn and Cowan (1996) articulate five principles for ecological design, the fifth being, *Make Nature Visible,* arguing that concealment of Nature's processes creates *nowhere places* in which people lose sensitivity to the natural world. In contrast, ecologically-expressive and transparent design weaves "nature back into everyday life" and "breaks down destructive dichotomies between the built world and wild nature."

Visible ecology as regenerative. Robert L Thayer, Jr, coined the term *visual ecology* (1976) to refer to an aesthetic vocabulary of the landscape that "reflects humanity's total dependence upon the land system." Water is one of the most expressive and accessible ecological elements for the designer. Thayer made a career developing the idea that ecological process, clearly-expressed, was a healing and regenerative practice that "allows us to see into, understand, and sustain ourselves and other life forms dependent upon that ecosystem" (Thayer 1998).

Types of water sounds. Patón and researchers (2020) tested 16 different water sounds at the same volume and showed that people find the sounds of natural streams and rain more pleasant than structured fountains or waterfalls. They recommend "water channels with small jumps, whose acoustic characteristics are ideal, causing deep and sustained relaxation." The pleasurable, relaxing sounds were characterized as "ever natural and consequently produced by many small [sound] structures as resultant lack of harmonics," meaning that there is a narrow range of frequency bands and many frequencies blend together, thus perceived as "unstructured and unpredictable. Not being able to differentiate patterns in our mind, an intense relaxation is produced." Within the context of this schema, revealed conveyance could be designed withe these characteristics, offering sonic pleasure added to ecological awareness. See additional water sound evidence in G4 Euphonic Water.

Design Guidelines

Use conveyance to link catchment surfaces to storage cisterns or pools. Reveal the path of runoff and the order of its network. Where possible, give occupants the opportunity to see, hear and touch the water.

Expose rainwater pathways. Whether or not the gutters, downspouts and other elements are enclosed, make them visible. Similarly, avoid having conveyance elements terminate by going underground; rather, reveal the flow along the ground surface. This can be accommodated in shallow channels at the perimeter of courtyards, across terraces or along the edges of buildings—or with less structured swales or streams. Small bridges or grates can be added where pedestrians cross and if handicapped accessibility is required. Note some of the many possible design options for revealed conveyance shown in the diagrams.

Design interaction so that people can touch or play with the water safely. Circulate runoff parallel to pathways or collect it in pools, ponds and fountains where steps or benches provide access. Locate some of the conveyance where the runoff can be observed from indoors or from a protected rain porch. Even better, as in the *rain terrace* of the House on a Pond, runoff brought under cover can maximize occupants' access during rain events.

Retain runoff rhythmically. Like House on a Pond, rainfall can be collected in an open pool, its level indicating whether rainfall was recent or not. As pools fill, let them overflow and initiate episodic drama, or let the water be held for a time and drain slowly, as in the Dai-ichi Yochien Preschool (shown in the Chapter 4 Introduction). Longer-term storage can be directed to cisterns or a reservoir. Linking stored rainfall to landscape irrigation or the building's water use continues the water cycle.

Celebrate with sound. Conveyance elements can be F1 Melodic Materials, such as metal roofs, gutters and downspouts that reproduce the pings or swirls of runoff. Rain chains, cascading steps, small dams or other obstructions can serve a similar purpose of added visual and auditory communicative delight. Research about sound preferences suggests small terraces or cascades with some randomness in flow create a blended pink noise masking sound with a naturalistic frequency profile.

Refine the schema with N3 Roof Terrain and F2 Water as a Mirror, whose pool might receive the conveyance. When the flows of conveyance can be focused in fewer places, the experience can be amplified and could be more engaging with C3 Water You Can Touch. Help build G4 Euphonic Water, F4 Compluvium Shower and C4 Engage the Rain.

There is in much of nature this mysterious, soothing quality. Architecture, of all things, has this natural capacity to re-frame our awareness of it, quietly reminding you of what's there. Over the years we have gotten more fluent at finding ways of building one's awareness of rainfall, or of breezes, or passages of the sun and shadows....so they can quietly take away the aggravations of your routine and give you a little lift.

—Max Levy, architect

F3

Water-Animated Surfaces

receive dancing sunlight reflections from water when it is disturbed by wind.

306 **Porsche Pavilion at the Autostadt**

Wolfsburg, Germany, 2012
HENN, architects

Compound curvatur es meet fluctuating light dancing off an undulating pool skimmed by breezes.

photo HG Esch

gliding over the sea
a mild whiff introduces
itself to my eye

Inhabitants are connected to Nature not only when they experience its forces directly, but also when buildings inform of their movements indirectly, when one force tells of another's presence. Such is the case when flat water, as in a pool, reflects sunlight onto walls or ceilings of nearby structures. When breezes disturb the water, its surface undulates, and the room becomes animated by light reflecting from the water at varying angles. This playful luminous quality informs occupants of wind movement and the changing qualities of sky and clouds. Such animation rarely fails to bring delight, fascination and a more subtle satisfaction of being aware of conditions outdoors. In warm weather, a well-shaded building blocks direct sunlight from striking glazing, isolating the interior from the sun's harshness. This shading can reduce daylight penetration; the contrast between darker indoors and bright outside sometimes feels too much like a cave. Giving up its heat, the water-reflected sunshine transforms to softer, cooler light. Brought inside, the room rebrightens, reconnecting inhabitants to sun, wind and water.

Damushan Tea House

Lishui, China, 2015
DnA, architects

A view of tea gardens and mountains—sunlight casts through a circular opening and bounces from a shallow pool to animate the concrete ceiling—minimalist design with much to contemplate.

left
View from west. Meditation room is on the right side.

right
Meditation room interior looking west.

photo left Chen Hao
photo right Wang Ziling

Porsche Pavilion exhibits reflections from a constructed lagoon onto compound curvatures of wall and ceiling overhanging the water in a 25 m (82 ft) cantilever. Both wind and periodic fountains disturb the water's surface to cast moving light reflections onto the continuous matte-finished stainless steel skin (ArchDaily 2012). The architects articulate the intention: "It creates the impression of a homogeneous unity, whilst creating a continuously changing appearance depending on light and weather conditions." Based on a *monocoque* (single shell) construction, "the architecture and landscape, interior and exterior, roof and facade are designed as a uniform, flowing continuum" alluding to Porsche styling (HENN 2012; Arca 2013).

Damushan Tea House sits on the edge of Xujing irrigation pool located between tea plantations in the Songyang tea valley. The teahouse faces west, enfronting the reservoir; an open-air meditation room at the southern end overlooks the pool through an unglazed circle that frames the sunset. Light reflecting from the lake and a shallow pool just outside the wall animates the rough concrete ceiling (Hudson 2015; Arkinka 2015). "The circular opening is... a converter for borrowing nature: the afternoon sun and its effects in the water....The two [projections] follow the sun's trajectory and slowly converge until the light becomes warmer and finally darkens" (DnA 2018).

Water Animated Surfaces

308 **Caustic reflections + projections**

Caustic patterns are reflected from the water surface and projected to the pool bottom.

adapted from Taylor 2017

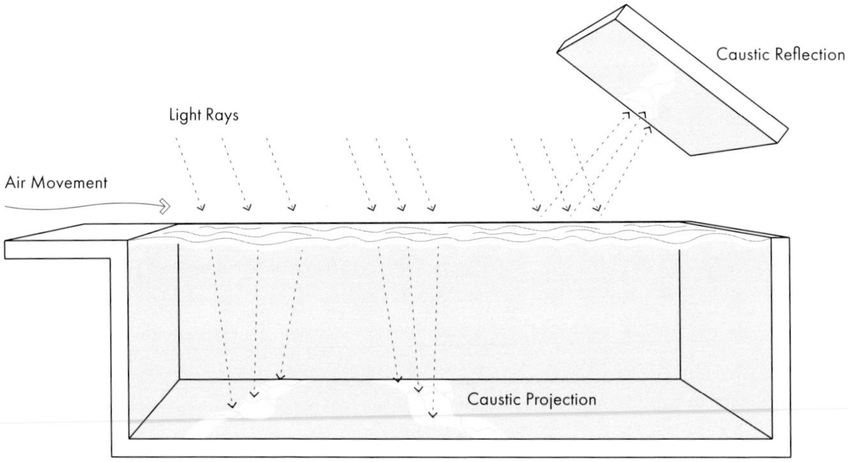

Supporting Evidence

The surface of a moving body of water has concave and convex conditions. Light is reflected from the wavy surface, refracted through the water and/or reflected back from the pool bottom (Upstill 1979). In optics, the phenomenon is known as *caustic reflections* (see diagram).

Caustic reflections + projections. When wind disturbs the water's surface, it creates waves that reflect at varied and changing angles. "The undulating water surface projects patterns of sunlight called *caustic networks* onto nearby surfaces," while light passing through the water is focused and dispersed by the water surface acting as "a series of positive and negative lenses" (Taylor 2017). Taylor's tests provide several useful observations:

1. Areas of the projection that are in focus are lighter, while out-of-focus reflections are darker.
2. Glossy receiver surfaces focus the projections more than matte surfaces.
3. Darker surfaces create more contrast with the caustic patterns than light surfaces.

Geometry. Lighter and more reflective pool bottom surfaces produce brighter, more contrasting projections. Kevin Nute (2014), one of the few researchers on the topic notes that, "At angles of incidence of less than 70° from the vertical...80% of the direct sunlight hitting a water surface enters the water rather than being reflected." This makes the schema especially effective at higher latitudes.

Calming effects. Nute and team (2012) studied the effects of wind-animated light, simulated artificially with fans disturbing a water pool in a controlled environment, and found average heart rates in waiting room occupants noticeably lower in animated versus static rooms with no reflections. Similarly, heart rates of people induced to stress by math problems recovered quicker with lower heart rates in such animated spaces. The researchers hypothesize even greater calming effects under natural conditions. In a small study testing wind-animated sunlight reflections from a *water light shelf* onto a ceiling in a hospital waiting room, most survey respondents described their feeling response as calm or fascinated (most common) or neutral, while a few described it as distracted or nauseous.

Cognitive effects. In other tests using the same laboratory setup described above (Nute et al. 2012), water-animated spaces increased mental response time in visual-mental tests after a 30 minute exposure gap. In contrast, response time decreased when videos of natural or artificial moments were seen on the participant's computer screen as a background while doing mental testing.

Time effects. Nute and Chen (2020) found that participants in rooms with wind-animated movement of sunlight reflected from water had greater feelings of *connection to the present*, less *time awareness* and increased sense of *time passing fast*. See the evidence graph in F2 Current Prehension.

Design Guidelines

Make shallow pools adjacent to windows or covered outdoor rooms, with light-colored bottoms, located where low angle-sun will not cause reflected glare in occupants' eyes. Arrange the geometries to cast reflections on surfaces where inhabitants' viewing is not fixed, such as ceilings or in spaces of short-term occupancy.

Avoid glare. Higher sun tends to reflect at angles without the glare of low-angle rays. When location of the pool is between southwest and southeast (in the northern hemisphere), make sure the pool is shallow and light-colored, so that light will be reflected back out, rather than transmitted and absorbed. This is the opposite of the dark bottom recommended for F2 Water as a Mirror. Glare can also be avoided when the low angle sun is obscured from view, such as by the use of high window sills.

Animate the effect using naturally moving water or make certain not to block incident breezes from reaching the water. Again, this guidance is the inverse of the surface stillness required for images in a reflecting pool. Moving water creates dynamic caustics but forms images poorly.

Detail the pool depth at less than 18 in (20 cm); for more varied and complex projections, form irregular bottoms, such as with stones, especially for shallower pools.

Locate and color receiving surfaces carefully. They can be light or dark, matte or glossy, depending on the results desired. Arrange surface areas to catch the refracted and reflected light from the pool and avoid the reflections reaching the occupants eyes directly. Avoid animated light patterns within the direct field of view for work or critical tasks, such as on a wall in front of a desk. Instead, create animation in non-critical spaces (lobbies, circulation, bedroom ceilings) or in portions of rooms where visual attention is optional.

Refine with F2 Water as a Mirror and understand how they can complement or conflict. Make the pool an opportunity for C3 Water You Can Touch. Help build F4 Compluvium Shower, whose pool might, once the rain ceases, also reflect light for this schema.

F4

Compluvium Shower

captures rainwater's sound and motion as it cascades from flow-focusing roofs into a court or pool.

310 **Copper House II**

Chondi, Maharashtra, India, 2012
Studio Mumbai, architects

If you go back through civilization, you will find that the absence or presence of water was at the core of what established inhabitation of space. All of my projects include a vessel of water, something that can, in anticipation, contain or collect water.
— *Bijoy Jain* in Burritcher 2020

photo Enrico Cano
video see Marucci 2012

next spread
Building section diagram

the ancients knew well
let Nature draw us a bath
singing timeless hymns

When people feel safe, experiencing the rain brings pleasure, centering and a dreamy atmosphere. Architecture can intensify or dampen these delights. Roofs that fall toward the outer building edges disperse runoff away from the structure; in contrast, roofs sloped to interior courts—what the ancient Romans called a *compluvium*—focus the same flows toward the building interior. When rainfall is light, this greater concentration brings heightened experience. During a rainstorm, the aural and visual effect is intensified by the roof's funneling, especially when water falls in sheets directly, without gutters, into the pool or court. Inhabitants become connected to the life-giving, primordial rain. Deep eaves, covered porches and rooms freely open to the court link life to vitalizing force. Hard court surfaces and/or a collecting pool can add to the chorus. They fill and drain, further marking the rain event cycles as a visible gauge. Revealed conveyances, as ground runoff channels, map the watershed's finest dendritic structure. Storage in a court pool or linked cistern completes the hydrologic language.

Cloister House

Johor Bahru, Malaysia, 2018
Formwerkz Architects

Organized as twelve open-to-rain courts, one a roof terrace, this may be the ultimate compluvium house.

photo Fabian Ong

Copper House II has four copper-clad roofs, rimming the court, that begin the symphony and funnel rainfall to gutterless eaves, sheeting runoff in water curtains that amplify in the valley corners. The court's hard surfaces add percussive sound and create dramatic splashing in the South Indian rains. Events can be viewed from adjacent rooms through wooden screens, an open breezeway dining room and perimeter circulation. Intense rainfall can be temporarily collected in the slightly sunken court and conveyed to surrounding stone swales below the raised plinth (avoiding monsoon flooding) and onward to a seasonal stream (Márquez + Levene 2019, ArchDaily 2012).

Cloister House is organized around twelve compluvium courts that bring light, ventilation and tropical rain to the thick plan's interior. The undulating roof is exposed below, foregrounding the shelter experience as a fundamental spatial feature. Each courtyard is unique—water ponds, graveled gardens of varied plantings, enclosures of sliding glass panels or brick, or openings to the larger garden (Ren 2019). The architects frame the intent: "We were interested in spaces that inspire and sensitise one to the beauty of Nature, adapting their living spaces with the changing sun-path and taking notice that the sound of rain is distinct in the different courtyards" (Design City 2021).

Compluvium Shower

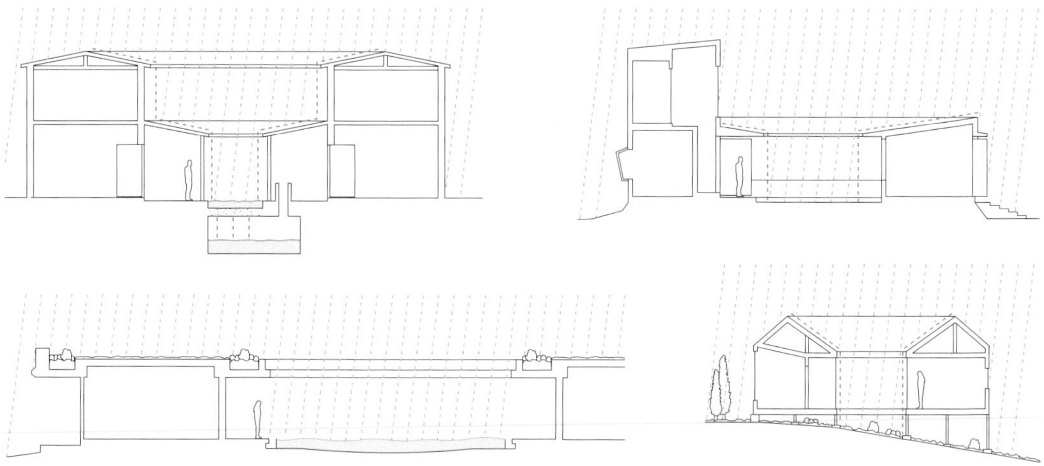

Compluvium variations

top left
Roman Atrium House
Diagram is typological composite.
Pompeii, 1st century CE

top right
Copper House II
Chondi, Maharashtra, India, 2012
Studio Mumbai

bottom left
Benesse House
Naoshima, Japan, 1995
Tadao Ando

bottom right
Impluvium Cabin
Neltume, Chile, 2019
SAA Arquitectura + Territorio

Supporting Evidence

Numerous historic and contemporary examples support the focusing of runoff and its internalized exposure for both utility and delight. Many variations are possible, with and without impluvium roofs or cisterns. The surrounding court walls determine the visual and auditory connections or isolations from the rainfall events.

Roman Atrium Houses, about 40% of Pompeii houses, had a court bounded by sloped roofs, the *compluvium*, which drained into a shallow pool, the *impulvium,* both referring to *pluvia* (rain). The open *atrium* brought light and ventilation, while the impulvium drained, often through a porous stone floor and sand, to a below-court cistern for domestic and evaporative cooling use. Excess water overflowed via a channel to the street. Many houses may have been retrofitted after a aqueduct-destroying earthquake (Tomlinson 1992; Draycott 2019).
Copper House II and its experiential response to rainfall is described previously. An excellent video by Daniele Marucci (2012) documents the house during the rain.
Benesse House is the guest house of the Benesse Museum. Its oval shaped courtyard is open to the sky and filled to the roof's edge with a shallow pool that overflows along the entire edge to exposed conveyance (Jodidio 2006). Covered circulation on the perimeter gives protected access to guest rooms while fully open to the court and rain. A green roof retains runoff, so only direct rain reaches the pool. From the path, the experience is both visual and aural. From the guest rooms, only the dampened sound is present. Nute (2018) recorded video of rain at Benesse.
Impluvium Cabin, in Chile's rainy zone, conducts rain to fall in sheets from precise gutterless edges and pass just outside the fully glazed skin, which as the architects put it, "creates in its transparency an open window to contemplate the treetops, the sky, and the rain." Perched on a light frame above the undisturbed terrain, there is no pool, resulting in a primarily visual effect (Silva 2021).

Psychological effects. In Hong Kong, Lau + Yang (2009) concluded that user experiences, such as "visual connection, privacy and security, [and] transparency from indoor to outdoor", are enriched by courtyards. Studies in Yazd, Iran of courtyards with pools indicate that water plays a significant role in promoting psychological restoration. If the court is secured from outsiders, then inhabitants feel safer opening windows and doors and even sleeping *plein air*.
Passive cooling. In arid climates, plants and water elements can increase evaporative cooling, especially in semi-contained spaces, such as courtyards. Sun and wind increase this evaporation. When the impluvium is dry, a thin layer of water can be returned from the cistern to promote rapid evaporative cooling (Beazley 1990). Natural elements such as water pools, fountains, trees, shrubs and lawns contribute to a cooling microclimate in a courtyard building (Givoni 1998).

Design Guidelines

Organize rooms on three or four sides around one or more open-to-sky courts. Slope roofs to focus runoff into the courts without gutters. If possible, add further animation with an impluvium pool that fills to overflow with rainwater and slowly drains to a covered cistern. Balance hard and soft surfaces in the court to complete the sensual variety. Locate enclosed and in-between rooms opening to the court under protected eaves or through an arcade.

Combine an impluvium (pool) with the compluvium, either with water storage or without. The filling water is made visible by the standing water in its splashes and ripples. Using the pool as temporary retention with slow drainage can indicate the rainfall rhythms and dampen stormwater runoff peaks. Similarly, a rainwater pool used for local landscape irrigation provides a visible cyclic cistern.
Amplify or dampen with material choices. Resonant roofing, like metal, can be an F1 Melodic Material. Hardscape surfaces of stone, brick, tile or concrete can amplify the sound of rainfall and intensify splashing in a controlled space. Conversely, softer ground and vegetation can lightly disperse sound and dampen the aggressiveness of heavy rains. Hard and soft can also be combined. Plants have the added effect of responding to raindrops on their leaves with visible motion.
Design courts for delight. Multiple aspects of courtyard comfort and aesthetics are covered in depth in Reynolds (2002). DeKay + Brown (2014) address organizations of Interwoven Buildings and Water to reduce ambient air temperature. Courts with one or more edges along circulation routes and with adjacent rooms having doors opening to the court will be more activated, appreciated and alive, as described in the Courtyards Which Live pattern (Alexander et al. 1977). Compared to exterior walls, the relative protection and privacy of the court allows walls facing the court to be more transparent visually and to be designed for greater openness to air movement and sounds, including those from water.
Refine with C3 Water You Can Touch, N3 Roof Terrain, F3 Revealed Conveyance and C4 Engage the Rain. Help build C5 Thermal Enclave.

Flux Sources

F1 Melodic Materials

Arch2o. 2020. Rain-hearing Pavilion of AUA: TJAD. *Arch2o.* arch2o.com/rain-hearing-pavilion-of-aua-tjad/

Ballagh, Kevin O. 1991. Noise of Simulated Rain on Roofs. *Applied Acoustics* 31: 245–264

BRE. 2004. *Test report: Measurement of Rain Noise on Roof Glazing, Polycarbonate Roofing and EFTE Roofing.* Test report number 220312, 24 Nov, Gaston, UK: Building Research Establishment

Chen, Qiaung + Wen Ye. 2020. Rain-hearing Pavilion of AUA/ TJAD. *ArchDaily*, 31 Aug, archdaily.com/946521

Clampitt, Amy. 1982. Rain at Bellagio. *The Kenyon Review*, New Series 4(3) Summer: 6–14

Donohue, Brian + John Pearse. 2019. Rain Noise. *Proceedings of the 23rd International Congress on Acoustics*, 9–13 Sep, Achen, Germany, 5050–5056

Engineering ToolBox. 2003. Sound—Room Absorption Coefficients. www.engineeringtoolbox.com/accoustic-sound-absorption-d_68.html

Huntington, Craig G, ed. 2013. *Tensile Fabric Structures: Design, Analysis and Construction.* Reston, Virginia: American Society of Civil Engineers, 131–132

Jun, Itami. 2010. The Architecture Of Yoo Dong Ryong (Itami Jun). Itami Jun Jeju Museum, 8 Nov. itamijun.com/en/museum/#jeju

Junhong, Zhou, Dongdong Liu, Xin Li, Jing Ma, Jue Zhang + Jing Fang. 2012. Pink noise: Effect on complexity synchronization of brain activity and sleep consolidation. *Journal of Theoretical Biology* 306: 68–72

Knapp, Ronald G. 2013. *The Peranakan Chinese Home Art and Culture in Daily Life.* Tokyo: Tuttle Publishing

Murcutt, Glenn. 2021. In Linda Cheng, Glenn Murcutt, the 'Pavilion Architect,' on His M Pavilion. *Architecture AU.* Jan 25. architectureau.com/articles/glenn-murcutt-mpavilion/. Original pub Architecture Australia, Mar, 2020

PINX Museum. 2017. Water, Wind, Rock Museum: Elegant Art Found in Everyday Life. thepinx.co.kr/en/biotopia/web/museum.px

Proverbio, Alice M, Francisco De Benedetto, Maria V Ferrari + Giorgina Ferrarini. 2018. When Listening to Rain Sounds Boosts Arithmetic Ability. *PLoS ONE* 13(2): e0192296.

Space. 2006. Pinx Museum, Water, Wind, Stone, Duson: Itami Jun. *Space* 458(Jan): 60-93

Suzuki, Shosuke, Tomoyuki Kawada, M Ogawa + S Aoki. 1991. Sleep Deepening Effect of Steady Pink Noise. *Journal of Sound and Vibration* 151(3): 407–413

Watts, Greg R, Rob J Pheasant, Krill V Horoshenkov + Laura Ragonesi. 2009. Measurement and Subjective Assessment of Water Generated Sounds. *Acta Acustica United with Acustica* 95:1032–39

F2 Current Prehension

Cepezed. 2014. *Westraven: Office Building for Rijkswaterstaat.* 1 Jan. Architectenbureau Cepezed, 010 Publishers. issuu.com/cepezed/docs/l_westraven_eng_issuu, 63–67

Crawford, C + D Krebs. 1997. *Handbook of Evolutionary Psychology: Ideas, Issues and Application.* New York: LEA

Grinde, Bjørn + Grete Grindal Patil. 2009. Biophilia: Does Visual Contact with Nature Impact on Health and Well-Being? *International Journal of Environmental Research and Public Health* 6: 2332–2343

Heerwagen, Judith. 1990. The Psychological Aspects of Windows and Window Design, *Proceedings of the Twenty-First Annual Conference of the Environmental Design Research Association* (EDRA 21). Champaign-Urbana, Illinois, 270

Ingold, Tim. 2007. Earth, Sky, Wind, and Weather. *Journal of the Royal Anthropological Institute* 13: S19–38

Kahn, Ned. 2008. Vertical Canal: Rijkswaterstaat, Utrecht, Netherlands. Ned Kahn Studios. nedkahn.com/portfolio/vertical-canal

Ktirio. 2018. Residence in Porto Heli: Villa White, Harald Nürnberg [in Greek]. Ktirio: Greek Technical Editions. ktirio.gr/el/κτιρια/κατοικιες/κατοικία-στο πόρτο-χέλι-villa-white

Macmillan. 2021. Macmillan Dictionary. Macmillan Education Ltd, macmillandictionary.com

Muir, John. 1878. A Wind Storm in the Forests of the Yuba. *John Muir: A Reading Bibliography by Kimes*. scholarlycommons.pacific.edu/jmb/70

Nürnberg, Harold. 2018. Villa White. *archello*. archello.com/project/villa-white

Nute, Kevin + Zhuo Job Chen. 2020. Wind-generated Movement as a Potential Means to Psychological Presence in Indoor Work Environment. *The International Journal of Design in Society* 14(2) June: 31–38

Nute, Kevin, Aaron Weiss, Jagdeep Kaur-Bala + Richard Marrocco. 2012. The Animation of the Weather as a Means of Sustaining Building Occupants and the Natural Environment. *The International Journal of Environmental Sustainability* 8:1

OED. 2021. *Oxford English Dictionary*. Oxford, UK. Oxford University Press

US National Park Service. 2021. Weather Lore Sayings, Mountain Weather (lesson plan). Grand Teton National Park. nps.gov/common/uploads/teachers/lessonplans/Weather-Lore-Sayings1.pdf

van Oel, Marcel. 2014. An Endless Performance. *BuitenPlaatsen* [OutdoorPlaces]. 1 Jul. buitenplaatsen.wordpress.com/2014/07/01/een-eindeloze-voorstelling/

Winson, Adam. 2017. Psithurism: the sound of wind whispering through the trees. AWA Tree Consultants. awatrees.com

F2 Water as a Mirror

Aidlin Darling Design. 2015. Windhover Contemplative Center/Aidlin Darling Design. *ArchDaily*, 18 Mar. archdaily.com

Alexander, Christopher, Sara Ishikawa + Murray Silverstein. 1977. *A Pattern Language: Towns, Buildings, Construction*. New York. Oxford University Press, #71 Still Water, 358–362

Bianchi, Kirk. 2017. The Pool as Mirror, *Aqua magazine* 27 Jul, 78–90

Contemportist. 2015. A Contemporary Greek Home Clad In Local Arcadian Stone. *Contemporist* 7 Jun. contemporist.com

Devi, Intra. 1963. *Renew Your life Through Yoga*. Crows Nest, Australia: Allen + Unwin

Exterior Worlds. 2015. Reflecting Pool, Swimming Pools: Exterior Worlds. *Landscaping + Design*, 20 Oct. Exteriorworlds.com

Gascon, Mireia, Wilma Zijlema, Cristina Vert, Mathew P White, + Mark J Nieuwenhuijsen. 2017. Outdoor Blue Spaces, Human Health and Well-being: A systematic Review of Quantitative Studies. *International Journal of Hygiene and Environmental Health* 220(8) Nov: 1207–1221

Karatzas, Pygmalion. 2015. Villa Milana. pygmalionkaratzas.com/villamelana

Martin, Bill. n.d. Reflections, in *Guide to Drawing*. Guidetodrawing.com

Nasar, Jack + Yi-Hsuan Lin. 2003. Evaluative Responses to Five Kinds of Water Features. *Landscape Research* 28(4): 441–450

Flux Sources

Nichols, Wallace J. 2014. *Blue Mind: the Surprising Science that Shows how Being Near, In, On, or Under Water can Make you Happier, Healthier, more Connected and Better at What You Do*. New York: Little Brown + Co

Schloop, Connor. 2020. Commemorative Booklet, Kleinhans Music Hall, 1945. *The Kleinhans Reflecting Pool: an Architectural Treasure*. Buffalo Philharmonic Orchestra, 5 Jun. bpo.org

Wills, Anthony Archer. 2021. Graceful Reflections. *WaterShapes*. watershapes.com

Windover. 2021. Windover Contemplative Center. orsl.stanford.edu

Wright, Frank Lloyd. 1928. In the Cause of Architecture, VI. The Meaning of Materials—Glass. *Architectural Record* 64 (Jul): 10–16. architecturalrecord.com

F3 Fans First

AIA. 2015. The Bullitt Center. Top Ten Project. American Institute of Architects Committee on the Environment (COTE). aiatopten.org/node/427

Arens, Edward, Stephen Turner, Hui Zhang + Gwelen Paliaga. 2009. Moving Air for Comfort. *ASHRAE Journal* 51(5):18–28

Arens, Edward., Hui Zhang, Wilmur Pasut, Ashley Warneke, Fred Bauman + Hirosh Higuchi. 2011. Thermal Comfort and Perceived Air Quality of a PEC System. *Proceedings of Indoor Air 2011*, Austin, TX, 5–10 Jun

Bullitt. 2013. Bullitt Center. *Bullitt Foundation*. bullittcenter.org

Chen, Wenhua, Hui Zhang, Edward Arens, Maohui Luo, Zi Wang, Ling Jin, Junjie Liu, Fred Bauman + Paul Raftery. 2020. Ceiling-Fan-Integrated Air Conditioning: Airflow and Temperature Characteristics of a Sidewall-Supply Jet Interacting with a Ceiling Fan. *Building and Environment* 171, 15 March:106660

Gonchar, Joann. 2013. A Deeper Shade of Green: A Seattle Office Building Aims to Be Self-Sustaining, Offering a New Model for Commercial Development in Dense Urban Settings. *Architectural Record* 201(6): 217–222, 224

ILFI. 2014. Bullitt Center. *International Living Future Institute*. living-future.org

Liu, Shuo, Aleksandra Lipczynska, Stefano Schiavon + Edward Arens. 2018. Detailed experimental investigation of air speed field induced by ceiling fans. *Building and Environment* 142 (Sep): 342–360

Miller, Dana, Paul Raftery, Mia Nakajima, Sonja Salo, Lindsay T Graham, Therese Peffer, Marta Delgado, Hui Zhang, Gail Brager, David Douglass-Jaimes, Gwlene Paliaga, Sebastian Cohn, Mitch Greene + Andy Brooks. 2021. Cooling Energy Savings and Occupant Feedback in a Two Year Retrofit Evaluation of 99 Automated Ceiling Fans Staged with Air Conditioning. *Energy and Buildings* 251(15 Nov):111319

Raftery, Paul + David Douglass-Jaimes. 2020. *Ceiling Fan Design Guide*. Mar. Center for the Built Environment. University of California, Berkeley. cbe.berkeley.edu/wp-content/uploads/2020/04/CBE-Ceiling-Fan-Design-Guide-V0.pdf

Raftery, Paul, Jay Fizer, Wenhua Chen, Yingdong He, Hui Zhang, Edwards Arens, Stefano Schiavon + Gwelen Paliaga. 2019. Ceiling Fans: Predicting Indoor Air Speeds Based on Full Scale Laboratory Measurements. *Building and Environment* 155(May): 210–223

Raftery, Paul. 2019. *CBE Fan Tool*. Center for the Built Environment, University of California, Berkeley. cbe.berkeley.edu/fan-tool

Tartarini, Federico, Stefano Schiavon, Toby Cheung + Tyler Hoyt. 2020. *CBE Thermal Comfort Tool: Online Tool for Thermal Comfort Calculations and Visualizations*. SoftwareX 12:100563

Zhai, Yongchao, Fengyu Miao, Liu Yang, Shengkai Zhao, Hui Zhang + Edward Arens. 2019. Using Personally Controlled Air Movement to Improve Comfort After Simulated Summer Commute. *Building and Environment* 165(Nov):106329

F3 Revealed Conveyance

Banham, Reyner. 1969. *The Architecture of the Well-tempered Environment.* Chicago: University of Chicago Press

Baum, Edward M. 2003. Watercourse: Cascading Water Links Sky to Earth and City to Nature in a Classical Villa Set Beside a Pond. *Texas Architect* 53(5) Sep–Oct: 28–31

Divsare. 2013. Kéré Architecture: Teacher's Housing. *Divasare*, 30 Oct. divisare.com/242941

Lepik, Andres + Ayça Beygo. 2017. *Francis Kéré: Radically Simple.* Berlin: Hatje Cantz Verlag, 40–41

Levy, Max. 2012. Materials and Meaning. *Dallas Museum of Art.* video. vimeo.com

Patón, Daniel, Pedro Delgado, Carmen Galet, Javier Muriel, María Méndez-Suárez + Matías Hidalgo-Sánchez. 2020. Using Acoustic Perception to Water Sounds in the Planning of Urban Gardens. *Building and Environment* 168 (15 Jan): 106510

Thayer, Robert L Jr. 1976. Visual Ecology: Revitalizing the Aesthetics of Landscape Architecture. *Landscape* 20(2): 37–43

Thayer, Robert L Jr. 1998. Landscape as an Ecologically Revealing Language. *Landscape Journal* 17:118–129

van der Ryn, Sim + Stewart Cowan. 1996. *Ecological Design*, 10th anniversary ed. Washington, DC: Island Press, 84–197

F3 Water-Animated Surfaces

Arca. 2013. Porsche Pavilion in Wolfsburg Germany: Henn Architekten. *L'arca International: La Revue Internationale D'architecture, Design et Communication Visuelle = the International Magazine of Architecture, Design and Visual Communication* 111: 36–43

ArchDaily. 2012. Porsche Pavilion at the Autostadt in Wolfsburg/HENN. *ArchDaily*, 22 Aug. archdaily.com/265034

Arkinka. 2015. Casa de Té, Plantacion de Te de Damushan, Songyang, China, 2015 = Tea House, Damushan Tea Plantation, Songyang, China, 2015: DNA_Design and Architecture Studio. *Arkinka*, Nov: 38–49

DnA. 2018. Damushan Tea Room. *DnA_Design and Architecture.* designandarchitecture.net/project/1526018054

HENN. 2012. Wolfsburg Prosche Pavillion. HENN Arhitekten. henn.com/en/project/porsche-pavillon

Nute, Kevin + Zhuo Job Chen. 2020. Wind-generated Movement as a Potential Means to Psychological Presence in Indoor Work Environments. *The International Journal of Design in Society* 14(2) Jun: 31–38

Nute, Kevin, Aaron Weiss, Jagdeep Kaur-Bala + Richard Marrocco. 2012. The Animation of the Weather as a Means of Sustaining Building Occupants and the Natural Environment. *The International Journal of Environmental Sustainability* 8(1): 27–40

Nute, Kevin. 2014. *Vital: Using the Weather to Bring Buildings and Sustainability to Life.* Apple Books, 74. books.apple.com

Taylor, Sally Dawn. 2017. Caustics in Architecture: an *Investigation into the Reflection of Light: Off Water, Creating Caustic Patterns.* MArch Thesis, Bartlett School of Architecture, University College London, 42, 60–65

Flux Sources

Upstill, Colin. 1979. Light Caustics from Rippling Water. *Proceedings of the Royal Society A: Mathematical, Physical and Engineering Sciences* 365(1720): 95–104

F4 Compluvium Shower

Alexander, Christopher, Sara Ishikawa + Murray Silverstein. 1977. *A Pattern Language: Towns, Buildings, Construction.* New York: Oxford University Press, #115 Courtyards Which Live, 561-564

Amirbeiki, Fatemeh + Azadeh Khaki Ghasr. 2020. Investigating the Effects of Exposure to Natural Blue Elements on the Psychological Restoration of University Students. *International Journal of Architectural Engineering + Urban Planning* 30(1) Jun:1–10

ArchDaily. 2012. Copper House II/ Studio Mumbai. *ArchDaily*, 16 Apr. archdaily.com/225365

Beazley, Elizabeth. 1990. Sun, Shade and Shelter: the Forgotten Art of Planning with the Microclimate in Mind: Part Three. *Landscape Design*, Dec 1990/Jan 1991, 196: 41–43

Burritcher, Felix. 2020. Interview: Bijoy Jain, Founder of Studio Mumbai is Inspired By Air, Water, And Light. *Pin-Up*, Spring-Summer. Pinupmagazine.org

Cecilia, Fernando Márquez + Richard C Levene. 2019. *Studio Mumbai, 2012-2019: espacios intermedios* (in-between spaces). Madrid: El Croquis Editorial

DeKay, Mark + G Z Brown. 2014. *Sun, Wind + Light: Architectural Design Strategies*, 3rd ed. Hoboken, New Jersey: Wiley, #10 Interwoven Buildings + Water, E.27

Design City. 2011. Cloister House/ Formwerkz Architects. *ArchDaily*, 15 Nov. archdaily.com/951257

Draycott, Jane. 2019. Roman Domestic Medical Practice in Central Italy. *The Roman House and Garden.* London: Routledge, 64–66

Givoni, Baruch. 1998. *Climate Considerations in Buildings and Urban Design.* New York: Van Nostrand Reinhold

Jodidio, Philip. 2006. *Tadao Andō at Naoshima: Art Architecture Nature.* New York: Rizzoli

Lau, Stephen S Y + Feng Yang. 2009. Introducing Healing Gardens into a Compact University Campus: Design Natural Space to Create Healthy and Sustainable Campuses. *Landscape Research* 34(1): 55–81

Marucci, Daniele. 2012. *Studio Mumbai/Copper House II.* video. vimeo.com/53087257

Nute, Kevin. 2018. *Naturally Animated Architecture: Using the Movements of the Sun, Wind and Rain to Bring Indoor Spaces and Sustainable Practices to Life.* London: World Scientific Publishing Europe

Ren, Chu Lik. 2019. Formwerkz' Modern Take On Traditional Architecture. *Habitus Living*, 23 April. habitusliving.com

Reynolds, John S. 2002. *Courtyard: Aesthetic, Social and Thermal Delight.* New York: John Wiley

Silva, Valeria. 2021. Impluvium Cabin/SAA Arquitectura + Territorio. *ArchDaily*, 6 Jan. archdaily.com/954160

Tomlinson, Richard. 1992. Ch 12, Pompeii. in *From Mycenae to Constantinople: the Evolution of the Ancient City.* London: Routledge, 184–186

320 **Hospital of San Sebastián**

Badajoz, Spain, 1694
Nicolás de Morales Morgado
architect

renovation 2017
José María Sánchez García,
renovation architect

Varied daylighting character and spatial enclosure reinforce the experience of moving from interior room to arcade to sunlit court. Moving from room to room using the arcade or the gallery above brings the occupant rhythmically into a sequence of brighter and dimmer.

photo Roland Halbe

Sequence Schemas

Sequences as we use them in this book come in many forms. They can be related to each of the other five conditional distribution types. Sequential transitions can be relatively gradual, like a lighting *gradient* down a passageway, or more abrupt, like a temperature *contrast* between a conditioned and an unconditioned space. They can also be constructed in alternating, repeating or complex patterns, analogous to those found in the *rhythms* schemas, or even potentially in a rather random set of experiential *fluxes*. In this regard, experiential sequences are more complex constructs of simpler or more discreet distribution patterns of conditions. As literary narratives are structured in time, design narratives may also include a time element. For example, S5 Ingress Transitions could be designed as a sensorial sequence, with or without an overt narrative.

The design schemas in this section identify how space can be ordered to orchestrate human experiences arranged as progressions of varied conditions yielding the potential for satisfaction, attraction, biophilia, bodily awareness and sensory pleasure. Inhabitants on these sequential journeys meet the possibility for a moment-to-moment awareness of Nature's forces arising in the field of their awareness.

Sequences can occur when a person moves through conditions or by the conditions themselves changing over time. Both are dynamic experiences that can operate over varied periods. Examples of these are illustrated by S5 Phototropic Catenation, in which inhabitants move toward brighter light, compared to S1 Veridical Patina, in which the building surfaces change over longer periods. Sequences can be movements from one of any number of conditions to another. S2 Aromatic Transit engages the transitory nature of the smell sense. In S5 Territorial Tuning, temperature, air movement and other forces vary from space to space, while lighting levels vary in S5 Light + Dark Procession. Sequences orchestrate movement through manifold settings of one sound, thermal, light, olfactory or haptic condition to another. Spatial sequences in buildings require walking, engaging the pressure sensors in the feet and the dynamic imbalance that is upright locomotion. S6 Topophilic Perambulation directs design attention to these existential phenomena.

The designer's challenge with sequence schemas is to keep conditions appropriate for each space while linking these varied experiences into a delightful progression. In some situations, this may imply that occupant control of conditions in sequenced spaces might need to be limited, so as not to destroy the effect. For example, the smooth experiential transition from bright outdoors to dimmer indoors, designed to allow eyes to adjust naturally, could be destroyed if the lighting level in the transition space is adjusted too high or low.

S1

Veridical Patina

records long-term weathering effects on buildings, embracing entropic process and refinishing.

322 **Centre de Suport Territorial Pirineus**

Institut Cartogràfic i Geològic de Catalunya (ICGC), Tremp, Pallars Jussà, Spain, 2012
Oikosvia Arqutiectura

Perforated weathering steel facade rusts initially, then forms a protective surface and changes color slowly for years.

photo Manuel Ortiz Alba

weather ravages
so aging lovely becomes
time and life, compressed

Gracefully aging materials remind inhabitants that architecture is a conversation across time. *Veridical* means truthful and coinciding with reality. It is easy to think of buildings as something permanent or immovable; however, they are actually in constant interaction and dialogue with Nature. Natural materials have variable surface—wood grain, stone veining, etc. Controlled weathering-by-design extends this inherent resonant beauty and furthers human biophilic affinity as direct experience and as wider awareness. When architecture forwards through the record written in its materials how it relates to its climatic context, inhabitants are reminded that what they see in any moment is a single point in a matrix of dynamic processes. Architecture, like people, inevitably ages. Designers can respond accordingly, utilizing materials that elegantly illustrate weathering interactions and, in their patina, express a compressed history of Nature's presence and by association the human lives lived there. In turn, especially when the materials are local, this contributes to a place-empathetic architecture at once regional and site-specific.

Loblolly House

Taylors Island, Maryland, 2006
KieranTimberlake, architects

left
new construction western red cedar, west facade
photo Peter Aaron/OTTO

right
west facade, weathered
photo Matthew Krissel

video see Howard 2014

Instituto Geológico de Cataluña is wrapped in an exterior skin constructed of weathering steel plates perforated with various diameter holes, configured in a pattern representative of the region's geological map, providing both shading and symbolism (ArchDaily 2014). The low-carbon steel alloy (known in the US by its trade name Cor-Ten) is naturally oxidizing, and after several years of useful corrosion, it achieves a protective coating with a matte orange-brown rust-like appearance that needs no paint or other finish (Structure 2005).

Loblolly House employs untreated western red cedar for its slatted rain screens on three sides, overlapping both windows and opaque skin. The layered facade becomes a metaphor of the surrounding pine forest's structure while simulating the forest's patterned daylight (Timberlake + Kieran 2008). The architects explain, "A study of the natural characteristics of the material, available water-repellents and preservatives, and detailing strategies led us to leave the cedar untreated..." (KieranTimberlake 2009). The example shows both the aged silver-gray that cedar can achieve and the darker staining that is possible. Such darkening and variability may be more or less desirable, depending on one's preferences. Here, the difference is mostly due to variations in the detailing of drainage and drying.

Veridical Patina

Exterior materials weathering

Many factors influence weathering, including climate, site context, facade or roof orientation, UV and rain exposure, atmospheric pollution and architectural detailing.

Each material shows its own life span and weathering process. Samples are representative only.

cedar wood, western red, rough sawn

new — 3 months UV + rain — 2 years, UV + rain

cor-ten steel

unexposed — 6 months — 40 years

limestone

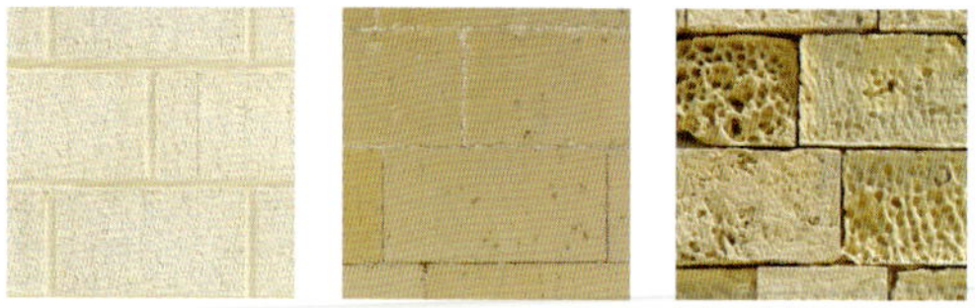

new — 15th century — ancient

copper

unexposed — 2 years — 10 years

Supporting Evidence

All construction weathers. Mechanical and chemical changes to surfaces and materials can be degrading or preservative, depending on application. In embracing Nature's circularity and negotiating the tensions between human purpose and natural forces, buildings help occupants aesthetically experience site and climatic time spans.

Responsiveness. Mostafavi + Leatherbarrow (1993), in *On Weathering*, provide a postmodern theoretical basis for reinterpreting Modernism's preoccupation with image, appearance and resisting time. With numerous examples, they suggest that solutions "could respond to the effects of the weather by creating situations that both recognize and utilize the ever-changing characteristics of materials as a way of renewing beginnings by allowing refinishing."
Cooperation with nature. The eloquent architect Alfred Browning Parker (1965) employed the precept: "Great architecture avoids the disillusionment of time" by "cooperating with nature, instead of trying to thwart her efforts"; thus "man learns to realize the highest values in his buildings." Rather than a maintenance expense, Parker saw weathering handled well as an enhancing factor. Constant maintenance is the "antithesis of enduring architecture."
Weathering variables. KieranTimberlake (2017) has conducted lab and field studies to develop an original predictive wood weathering tool to understand how cedar and other woods age over time as a result of sunlight and ultraviolet (UV) exposure, wind-driven rain, temperature, humidity and airflow. The research suggests that wind-driven rain and UV exposure are the most significant abiotic variables impacting cedar weathering. However, these forces can be modified significantly by the natural and built context, such as microclimatic shading or wind flow patterns from adjacent buildings, trees, or even the overhangs and facade depth of the building itself.
Preservation. A weathered finish is not necessarily an inferior material condition or structural issue. It can be a representation of age, metaphorically associated with wisdom. In historic building preservation, the preservation of

weathered, aged but functional materials is often preferred over replacement (HLC 2012).

Metals. Wright (1928) considered copper to be the only permanent sheet metal: "Its verdigris is always a great beauty in connection with stone or brick or wood..."

Design Guidelines

For experiential impact, design to manifest—in the time-record of its surface—the building skin's long-term relationship with climatic forces. Select exterior materials that age beautifully, such as natural stone, brick, copper, bronze, teak, cedar and weathering steel (Cor-Ten). Place materials in appropriate applications and detail to minimize moisture issues, allowing facades to dry.

Select for elegant aging. Redwood, cedar, and teak all develop a complex, subdued color as they age. Metals, especially copper, can form patinas over time. Weathering steel, zinc, and bronze all can produce pleasing visual qualities over the years. Travertine, sandstone, brick and marble, among others, age beautifully, lasting centuries.

Choose by location. Select the most durable materials for locations most exposed to the elements. Stewart Brand (1994) details that all building elements have a life span. Exterior skins have traditionally protected more long-lived structural elements. Masonry skins can last centuries if maintained, while wooden cladding is often more sacrificial unless protected from weather by deep overhangs and carefully detailed. Choose materials for horizontal applications that resist and deflect water. Unprotected wooden decks, even if constructed from treated lumber, for example, will not last a generation in dry climates and not a decade in warm-humid climates like the US Southeast.

Control wood cladding exposure. For cedar, exposure drives the resulting weathered color. General design guidelines (Escott + Faircloth 2021) include the following: To achieve a light silver-gray weathered color, expose cedar to both UV and penetrating (wind-driven) rain. Architectural researcher Efrie Escott (2021) elaborated that "Wet wood allows deeper UV ray penetration, leading to increased speed and intensity in coloration". For a darker orange/brown, expose the wood to rain, but keep it shaded, and for a dark gray result, place the cedar in sunlight (for UV), but protect it from rain. Detail to allow drainage from the bottom of exposed vertical wood grain and thus avoid stagnant moisture that can cause lignin and tannin accumulation and its blackening effects.

Detail for water. Protect all horizontal and low-sloped wood with roofs or flashing. Ideally, wood siding can hang with the end grain down in its natural position to facilitate even drying. Vented rain screen layering can allow more absorbent materials to dry out. Flashings, sealing the tops of masonry walls, drip edges, complementary fasteners and providing for drainage routes at the scale of details can all support materials aging relatively evenly.

Select coating for desired effect. The degree of aging can often be controlled or modified by surface treatments. For exposed wood, coating opacity is correlated with UV protection and durability, but also with maintenance (repainting or restaining). Transparent stains or penetrating treatments can visually age well, but need frequent re-coating; in general, the more opaque, the more long-lasting.

Refine with schemas N1 Perceptible Provenance. Help build N2 Authentic Matters.

S2

Aromatic Transit

builds a scent space as passageway or threshold, inciting immersive, transcendent moments.

326 **Biltmore House, Pergola**

Asheville, North Carolina, 1895
Frederick Law Olmsted
landscape architect
Richard Sharp Smith, architect

A shady retreat and resting place beneath ancient wisteria vines, the pergola provides a cool passageway from the house to the Shrub and Walled Gardens.

photo Biltmore Company

just breathe and wonder
through perfumed thresholds enter
adventures retold

Fragrance is one of the great pleasures in life. Gardens and living walls offer a variety of psychologically restorative effects. Smells evoke emotions and memories, yet the human olfactory sense quickly adapts to new scents. A single lily can fill a room with intense scent on entry and in the next minute, its influence fades. This episodic nature of smell suggests designing aromatic impacts for moments when occupants circulate or transition, such as a forecourt, porch, entrance, lobby or other spaces inhabited for short duration, like a resting bench or observation vantage. Redolent thresholds announce departure from one realm and arrival into another, along with signals for the regular ritualistic psychological transition between contexts. Commonly these thresholds include vegetation, such as flowering pergolas and arbors that provide visual and aromatic stimulus. Carefully placed olfactory moments provide focal points; the ephemeral nature of scent sensation requires an intervallic scentscape, rather than continuous fragrant planting. The height of noses intimates the value of elevating the aroma sources.

Living Wall, Foundry Square III

San Francisco, California, 2013
STUDIO architects
SWA, landscape architects
Habitat Horticulture, living wall
David Brenner, wall designer

A fragrant living wall creates an entry experience accessible by the public and employees.

photo Tim Griffith

Biltmore House Pergola abuts the south terrace and opens to the shrub garden with spring pastels (Biltmore 1980). Limestone columns and a massive wooden trellis support climbing wisteria vines planted in 1895. "The look of being festooned" was Olmsted's original intent (Ross 2018; Messer 1990). Luxurious sugary-scented purple pendulous wisteria blossoms cover overhead in Spring. The walk leads on one end to an overlook and on the other to a stairway to the Italian Garden and residence above. In the US, American wisteria, which often repeat blooms in late summer or early fall, is preferred over the invasive Asian varieties (Flanders).

Foundry Square III lobby is a breath of calm fresh air, contrasting San Francisco's bustling streets. Employees encounter two full height living walls with 12,500 plants on their way to the office; exterior glass facades invite the public for a gentle respite (Habitat Horticulture 2013; Wand 2014). The 2500 square feet (230 m^2) of plantings exude notes of geranium, mint and citrus that suspend in greeting. David Brenner, the wall's designer intends the project to have an aromatic element that varies at different times of the year, both as a public experience and as a ritual for building occupants passing through at least twice a day. "Just take a deep breath," he says. "We need actual vegetation...for reconnecting with nature, for our mental well-being" (Brenner 2017).

Aromatic Transit

Aromatic transit types

Activate scents by walking on, touching, or brushing past planting. Raise fragrance closer to the nose and for those in wheelchairs. Contain a redolent domain with partial enclosure so the air slows and smells linger and intensify.

A stepping scents

B raised beds

C vertical trellis

D arbor gate

E pergola path

F living wall

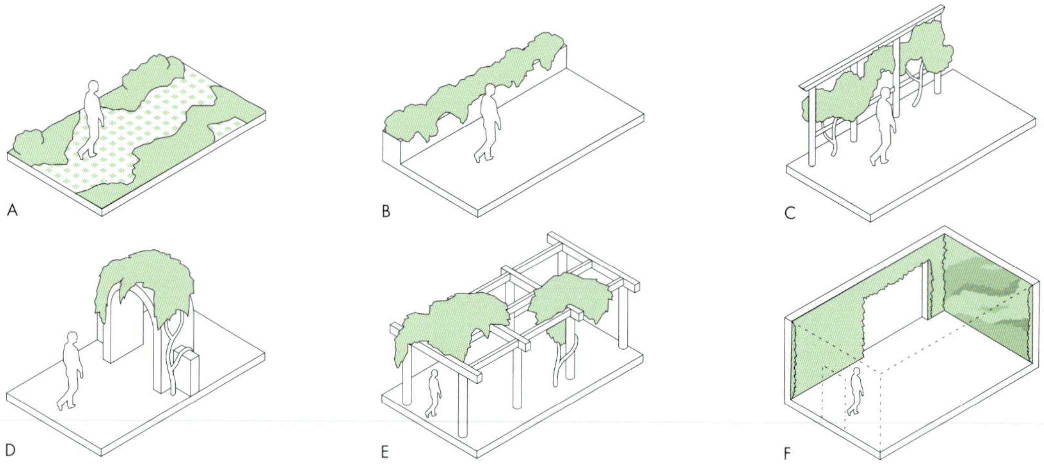

Top choice scented plants
Druse 2019, 2020

heliotrope
cottage pinks
licorice sweet flag
heirloom roses
lemon balm
tuberose
lilac

Supporting Evidence

Scent conveys spatial information and defines its own space. People perceive a scent's source and spatial diffusion. Aroma carries mood, associates with memories, stimulates emotions, brings pleasure and can improve health.

Information olfactation, a concept proposed by Patnaik and team (2018) as a compliment to information visualization, uses a prototype system of olfactory channels for analysis, including *molecular bouquet, direction, saturation* (intensity), *burst frequency, air flow rate* and *air quality* (climate) factors, such as temperature and humidity. While their model focuses on multi-modal virtual reality, it seems informative for designing multisensory lived reality. They write, "All of our senses create a spatial mapping of the world around us; a chemical topography view sees olfaction as no different" (El Mountassir et al. 2016).

Spatial perception. Humans can localize objects and track by scent, improving with practice. Dual nostrils supports spatial perception and scent directionality (Porter et al. 2007). Maggioni and team (2019) identified four key features from scientific literature for *smell space* design in human-computer interactions: *chemical, emotional, spatial* and *temporal*. Scents convey spatial information "including place, orientation, and movement" in spaces.

Emotions and health have been linked to scent, both positive and negative, including influences on mood, anxiety, happiness and relaxation (Diego et al. 1998; Vernet-Maury 1999). Lavender is often aligned with relaxation, decreased anxiety (anxiolytic effects) and promoting calm. Inhalation of essential oil seems effective in the reduction of anxiety levels (Donelli et al. 2019). "Numerous studies now confirm the potent relaxing effects of *linalool*, a fragrant alcohol found in lavender extracts" (Prior 2018; Harada et al. 2018). Rosemary improves alertness. Plant smells, especially citrus-scented pelargonium (commonly called geranium) facilitates stress reduction and supports mental recovery in real-life contexts (Pálsdóttir et al. 2021).

Olfactory mood. Elizabeth Diller argues against, "the kind of controls that neutralizes everything into nothing, a flat line condition", and considers smell essential to "the mood set by the architecture". Clino Trini Castelli advocates the olfactory: "We should work to bring the rationale of design into the world of odors. It would be an experience like the one that led to the Slow Food movement" (Barbara + Perliss 2006).

Design Guidelines

Built scentscape transits along travel paths and at thresholds. Employ aromatic herbal or highly-scented flowering plants raised above ground, in tall varieties or climbing as vines. Alternately, brushing by or walking on certain plants activates scent. Select species for successive seasonal blooming, climatic and solar context, and for layering.

Aromatic transit types diagrams present a few of the many options. *Stepping scents* (A) plant fragrant ground cover, such as Corsican mint or creeping thyme, inbetween pathway stones to release the herb's perfume underfoot. *Raised beds* (B) with soil at 24–30 in (60–75 cm) bring flowers closer to the nose than ground planting, where body-brushing and hand touch can bring forth scents from sage and juniper. A *vertical trellis* (C) or *pergola path* (E) provide a continuous head height sniffing potential. An *arbor gate* (D), climbing roses around a front door or at an entry porch concentrate the aroma as an episodic event at the threshold moment. *Living walls* (F) require greater maintenance and attention to irrigation technology, but can be interior or exterior multisensory planar garden artworks. See Alexander and team's (1977) Raised Flowers, Climbing Plants and Trellised Walk patterns.
"Focus on the most traveled paths," (Druse 2020), planting a succession of smells on high-traffic routes in staggered succession that mixes shrubs, perennials and annuals. If the aromatic path is along the street or public edge, or at a public entry or residential front door, then the plants become a gift to everyone on the street.
Intensify scent pockets at thresholds, near outdoor seating, at overlooks, vista points or as punctuations on a path.
Add variety with touchable fragrance, brushable bushes, stepped-on scented ground covers, native and night-perfumed plants. Select for scent and context, both climate and solar exposure. See the sidebar sample list.
Structure for climbers or other species needing support for orientation and training using wires or cables, trellis or lattice. Integrate the armatures with building elements at entrance transitions, on garden and building walls, especially in sunny locations, as living fences, around windows, as pergola shade for outdoor rooms or at courtyard arcades. Nothing like climbing plants has quite the same effect to help buildings become part of sites.
Layer flowers in time and with aromatic perennials. Set a foundation with aromatic trees, herbs, shrubs and perennials, allowing annuals and seasonal bloomers to accent and mark time. Create a temporal progression: "I have dwarf late-winter viburnums with their clove-scented flowers in March and April. Then, fragrant peonies and bearded iris. Next come the roses. In summer, the rich aroma of regal lilies intensifies in the evening (Druse 2020).
Make special with scent memory by distinguishing significant places with aroma, as bouquet memory is significantly stronger than visual memory.
Refine with S1 Veridical Patina and F2 Current Prehension. Help build C3 Scintillating Sun, G3 Existential Datum and N3 Distinguishable Durability. An aromatic transit may also be an element in S5 Ingress Transitions.

Aromatic options sampler

Natives
mountain mint
prairie dropseed grass
wintergreen
perennial black cohosh
milkweed

Native shrubs
Carolina sweetshrub
Virginia sweetspire
fringetree
azaleas (Rhododendron)
summersweet

Touchable
mints
rosemary
patchouli
anise hyssop
bee balm
pelargonium
big root geranium
catmint
lavender
creeping thyme

Climbing vines
climatis
wisteria
jasmine
Carolina Jessamine

Night bloomers
moonflower
Nicotiana
evening primrose
night-blooming jasmine
climbing petunia
angel's trumpet
Cestrum nocturnum
potato vine

Taste associations
lemon verbena
chocolate cosmos
pineapple sage
alpine strawberry

For many more options, plus varietal recommendations, consult *The Scentual Garden* by Ken Druse 2019

S5

Territorial Tuning

diversifies thermal zones for inhabitants' elective agency and transitional enjoyment.

 School of Design + Environment

National University of Singapore
Singapore, 2019
Serie Architects + Multiply Architects + Surbana Jurong with Transsolar KlimaEngineering

A large overhanging roof provides shade for "a porous architecture structured in a juxtaposition of *platforms and boxes,*" envisioned as "a very transparent volume in which the outside and the inside spaces are ambiguous; where nature and landscape play an important part" (Lee 2019).

photos Rory Gardiner

pause brings vital rest
yet journeys too may bestow
peace by divergence

Few souls enjoy eating the same foods at every meal. So it is for identical thermal experiences in every room, as a steady-sate interior may feel somniferous. In contrast, variability enlivens. People can easily sense 1 °C (1.8 °F) of temperature difference and feel very small changes in air speed, which means that moving from one set of conditions to another brings body and environment to awareness, accompanied by delight, alertness or invigoration if done well. Such pleasure transits are built with multiple thermal zones, which combine different passive and active cooling strategies and varied blends of conditions. Short-term occupancy spaces, such as circulation, can be warmer or cooler, breezier or more humid than the ambient context. This engenders ephemeral moments of thermal delight—as short-lived imbalance provides greater appreciation when returning to previously unremarkable conditions. Whether created by passive or active means, inhabitants savor the choice to modify or migrate, to opt for situational preference or simply to enjoy epicurean thermal variety that transcends comfort.

School of Design + Environment

left
Horizontal and vertical circulation is all 100% naturally ventilated.

right
Mixed-mode zone with hybrid cooling supplying warmer and more humid air than usual AC, 100% fresh air supply, no return ducting, variable speed ceiling fans, operable windows and access to outdoor terraces.

explanatory lecture *see* Kessling 2019
video *see* NUS 2020

NUS School of Design + Environment provides a high level of comfort in a warm-humid tropical climate using paradigm-shifting strategies that produce both a net-zero energy performance and an architecture of thermal delight. SDE4, as it is known, incorporates a mixed-mode hybrid cooling system in 26% of its area, including library, studios, theatre and office. The system supplies 100% fresh air tempered at 29°C (84°F) operative temperature with variable air movement from ceiling fans to achieve 27°C (81°F) effective temperature (NZEB 2019). With air movement and adaptation to the local climate, this is actually a comfortable condition. Engineers at Transsolar make the point that temperature alone is a poor measure of comfort, while their holistic approach inlcudes 6 parameters: air temperature, air speed, relative humidity, mean radiant temperatures, clothing and activity levels (Kessling 2019). There are no return air ducts or suspended ceilings; the air exits into corridors, creating a tempered zone. Large portions of facades are operable. Two additional thermal zone types are used: labs are fully air-conditioned, while the social plaza, modeling areas, workshops and all the circulation are naturally ventilated. The result is a range of zones where temperature, humidity, and air speed vary and enclosure transforms. The building coaxes inhabitants to choose their adaptive comfort locus, to engage more with the ambient biophilic environment and to luxuriate in transitional phenomenal moments (ArchDaily 2019; Lee 2017).

Territorial Tuning

Expanded comfort strategies

Bars show potential for broader comfort temperatures. Based on CBE Thermal Comfort Tool (Tartarini et al. 2020)

Radiation indicates heat added to the body.

Adjusting clothing shows a modest range from winter indoor clothing level (1.0) to summer (0.5).

Air speed max. with no user controls is 0.8 m/s, or with user controls, no upper velocity limit.

Adaptive comfort range can also be extended with air movement.

Personal comfort systems are typically active and local.

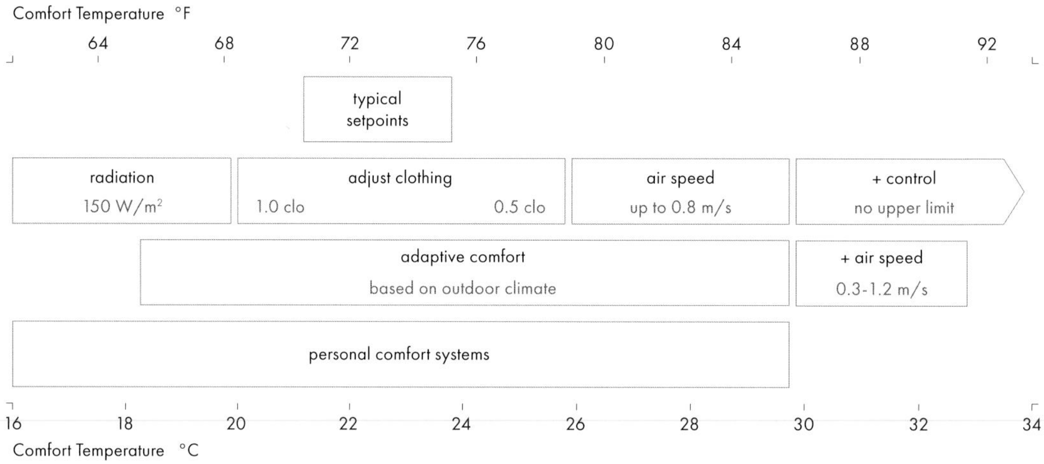

Supporting Evidence

Several studies indicate that thermally monotonous indoor environments hinder "cultural and microclimate thermal adaptations to a place" (Dahlan et al 2020). Deliberate step changes or ramps/drifts can create noticeable pleasure (alliesthesia). The range of adaptive comfort can be significantly extended on both warm and cool ends.

Spatial transients is the term building scientists use to describe a sequence of thermal conditions between spaces. People's responses to new conditions depend on their previous environment (Chun + Tamura 2005). Moving from a hot to a warm room or from a cold to a cool room may induce a neutral sensation (Luo et al. 2016). Moving from an AC environment to a warm outdoors can feel warmer than it actually is (Jitkhajornwanicha + Pitts 2002).
Step changes describe abrupt rather than smooth transitions. Their magnitude makes a difference in how pleasurable a transient is perceived (Xiong et al. 2015). Down-steps toward coolness are felt more than up-steps toward warmness (de Dear et al. 1993), but this also depends on the starting temperature.
Occupancy time. Occupants who work in a place for a long time tend to prefer narrower thermal comfort zones, than others passing through, such as in airports (Kotopouleas + Nikolopoulou 2016). It takes 20-30 minutes to fully adjust to a new set of conditions. Short duration spaces can be more variable over broader conditions. "To avoid overwhelming burdening of thermoregulatory system, the magnitude of step changes from main area to transition spaces may be limited to ±3 °C (5.4 °F)" (Mishra et al. 2016).
Variation examples. A sunspace varies on a winter day from colder at night to warmer in the afternoon than adjacent rooms. In summer, an earth-cooled basement, a ground floor and upper stories warmed by sun on the roof or buoyant warm air provide significant thermal contrast. Natural ventilation can be designed G4 Zephyr Spectrum. Evaporative strategies (shower towers or misting systems) provide bursts of moisture and cooler air.

Design Guidelines

Program for thermal pleasure. Zone spaces with similar needs, occupancy periods and tolerances together. Select conditioning strategies for each zone. Organize the zones to provide delightful sequences and adaptive choices.

Be intentional about the varied thermal conditions and inhabitant experiences for each space. Sequences can be more abrupt with contrasting conditions or more gradual using a gradient of conditions.
Allow comfort conditions to float over a wide range that tracks with outdoor rhythms, saving energy and providing more variety. Modulating temperatures in smooth changes over as little as 4 °F (2.2 °C) can lead to greater thermal pleasure in cooling situations than a constant temperature (Traylor et al. 2019). Test comfort variables using the CBE Comfort Tool (Tartarini et al. 2020) using the ACM or with PMV on a psychrometric chart.
Distinguish occupancy periods as long or short-term. Temporarily occupied spaces include circulation, atria, lounges and toilet rooms; allow conditions at the edge of comfort or beyond. 30-seconds in an unconditioned stairwell invigorates if cool or, if the stair is warm, can provide alliesthesia on return to more comfortable conditions.
Determine conditioning zones based on both standard heating and cooling load factors, such as the rate of internal gains, solar orientation and envelope heat transfer rate, and on two additional criteria: 1. *Length of occupancy*, short or long, and 2. *Allowable comfort range*, large versus small. Set comfort parameters for each zone. See Heating Zones, Cooling Zones and Energy Programming in DeKay and Brown (2014).
Associate zones with strategies for heating, ventilation and cooling. As a starting point, consider the Spectrum of Space Conditioning (sidebar), among many options. Strategies closer to free-running in the list use less energy.
Organize zones into thermal sequences, which can be more linear, such as in S5 Ingress Transitions, or more random, such as moving from an office to an adjacent veranda. Some example sequence types include:
1 *Journey and return:* a sequence from bodily thermal balance to imbalance (beyond comfort conditions) and return to balance. Example: the stairwell sequence described above.
2 *Odyssey and arrival*: a common transit from bodily thermal imbalance, usually outdoors (cold or hot) to a large thermal step (indoors) for maximum delight, then return to neutral. Example: an entry sequence with a significant difference between inside and outside conditions.
3 *Hedonic migration:* elective relocation from a zone with less preferred to more pleasurable conditions. Example: when sun over-warms one side of a building, and the occupant moves to the cooler side's zone.
4 *Promenade sensorielle:* choreographed movement from one zone to another, or in series. Perhaps for the pleasure of it, whith all conditions comfortable, but pleasantly contrasting. Example: a museum with cooler dimmer exhibits alternating with warmer brighter public spaces with sunshine.
5 *Extempore adjacency:* impromptu transiting across the building enclosure through multiple conditions from indoors to in-between space to outdoors. Example: precedents in C4 Inhabited Periphery.
6 *Nadir and summit*: descending to earth-influenced coolness and climbing multiple levels toward light and sky, accompanied by the thermal gradient of stratifying warm air. Example: a multi-story atrium building.
Refine with G4 Incalescent Center, G4 Zephyr Spectrum and C4 Inhabited Periphery. Link laterally with S5 Ingress Transitions and C5 Thermal Enclave. Help build G6 Engagement and Retreat and R6 Cooling Conversions.

Spectrum of space conditioning

1 Mechanical heating
2 Mechanical + passive heat
3 Passive heating
4 Free-running (unconditioned)
5 Passive cooling
6 Passive cooling + fans
7 Natural + mech ventilation
8 Mechanical ventilation
9 Mixed-mode cooling
10 Mechanical cooling + fans
11 Mechanical cooling

Thermal sequences

1 Journey and return
2 Odyssey and arrival
3 Hedonic migration
4 Promenade sensorielle
5 Extempore adjacent
6 Nadir and summit

S5

Ingress Transitions

organizes time-based zones of luminous adaptation and thermal delight on the path from outdoors to in.

334 **Kimbell Art Museum**

Fort Worth, Texas, 1972
Louis I Kahn, architect

top
Court of trees + portico

center
Entrance lobby

bottom
South gallery

photos Peter J Sieger

below
Entry sequence plan

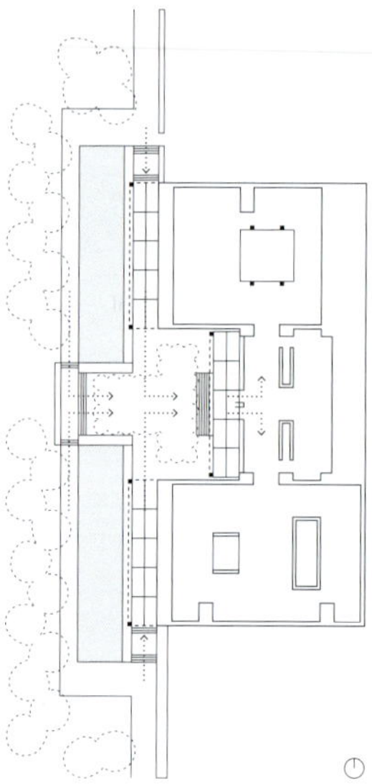

a simple passage
ordered flows light air thou
temple gloried path

Transitions from outdoors to inside, and vice-versa, are both sensory and psychological. Thoughtfully orchestrating progressions of light, sound, air and temperature between the outdoors and indoors facilitates inhabitants' adaptation and engenders alliesthesial moments—the pleasure of thermal contrast. Eyes react relatively slowly when moving from bright exterior to dimmer illuminance, the interior feeling at first darker than intended. Entry disorientation from quick high contrast change is common. Visual adaptation requires extended time and incremental darkening, expressed architecturally as travel distance and increasing enclosure. In contrast, the thermal steps during entry transit can be intentionally abrupt and bring delight. In warm weather, a person's over-heating can be offset by temporary, more intense cooling. In cool weather, their chill can be countered with a punctuated ardent arrival. Both scenarios precipitate transitory relief approaching thermal bliss and are followed by arranging return in subsequent spaces towards a normative comfort zone.

Kimbell Art Museum choreographs a primary entry sequence that creates "a transition between the vast, intense, bright, hot world outside and the contained, restrained, dim, cool world inside" (Millet 1996). Its west-facing entrance can be approached by arrival routes via the lawn and gardens along an old tree-line or on walks from the north or south bounding streets. The C-shaped plan surrounds a forecourt that Kahn called *Entrance of the Trees*. From either street, a split path leads to a vaulted attached porch or the visitor can circumambulate a pool to arrive on the central axis. In either route, one ascends three feet (90 cm) to a raised platform and passes along the water with its reflections, cascading sounds and cooling effects. Most of the day, the porches, which Kahn described as "an offering", provide cooling shade and offer respite or contemplative prospect from a long travertine bench with a view across the pool and garden. The routes intersect again for welcome shade and filtered light in the gravel court of gridded yaupon holly trees. Spatially, it is both an interruption of inertia and a low green ceiling. The way is clear, but the destination and entrance facade, uncertain. The shady path leads up a few more steps to the entrance portico, enclosed now on the ends, for deeper shade, reduced light and cooler air. This approach, where the visitors' ambling paths weave architecture and site, Benedikt (1991) argues, deeply "appeals directly to... our most physical/biological selves." Passing through the glass doors in the glazed wall to the entrance lobby, the vaulted lobby bay repeats the portico, but now also lighted from above with diffuse daylight spread over the vault—a space linked by its glass wall to the outdoor condition, but dimmer, and transitioning to the now famous interior toplighting. Simultaneously, the patron enters the controlled world of mechanical cooling, where on a summer afternoon, the temperature might drop 20 °F (11 °C) or more. Still, with no airlock and a 100 ft (30 m) long wall of full-height glass, the lobby is a zone of thermal transition. From this calm and mostly void space, one can proceed forward to the gift shop or, more commonly, turn either direction to the toplighted, vaulted galleries where illuminance is lower and isolation from outdoor thermal conditions, greater. Here, Millet describes the gallery condition where "sacred light emerges from the meeting of daylight and structure."

Ingress Transitions

Paths to thermal pleasure
adapted from
Parkinson et al. 2016

Pleasure in transitions between environments increases with greater thermal contrast.

Vertical lines show five different before + after experiments. Thermal pleasure axis indicates participants' perceptions. Arrows indicate directional change in pleasure from a warm or cool environment under *initial conditions* and then after experiencing a *post-transition* contrast. SET conditions combine effects of air and radiant temperature, moisture and air movement.

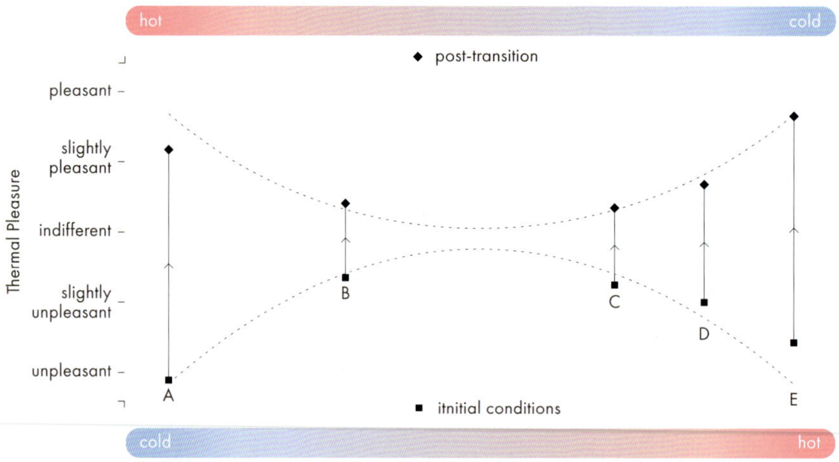

Standard Equivalent Temperature (SET)

		■ initial	◆ post
A	°C	14.7	25.3
	°F	58.5	77.5
B	°C	19.3	22.3
	°F	66.7	72.1
C	°C	20.9	22.6
	°F	69.6	72.7
D	°C	25.9	20.8
	°F	78.6	69.4
E	°C	27.7	20.2
	°F	81.9	68.4

Supporting Evidence

Entry sequences support one of the most fundamental social and psychological demarcations of human life: outside to inside and public persona to private. Thermal pleasure is best achieved when transitioning to conditions that quickly move a person in the opposite direction of discomfort. Visually, occupants prefer an opportunity to adapt slowly when transiting to darker settings.

Thresholds can be expanded from simple momentary transitional spaces moved quickly through to become *places* for lingering and occupancy, as recommended by Pierre von Meiss (1990). Sociologist Pierre Bourdieu (1970) described them as places "in which the world reverses itself," that is, where exterior domain becomes marked interior, public becomes private and permeability is controlled.

Psychological transitions. Susanka (2004), referring to residences, expresses it well, "The whole sequence needs to be designed to allow you to change from the public person that you are when outside in the world to the much more private person that you are once inside."

Temperature or air movement? In a warm environment, cooler temperature alone will eventually accommodate the person entering but may create discomfort for others. A classic example is an over-cooled lobby that will feel too cool for longer-term occupants and even for the new arrival after some time, especially if they were perspiring outdoors. Air movement is more effective to provide fast-acting relief; at 28°C (82°F) it improves comfort 2–10x faster than does cold air cooling at 24°C (75°F) without fans (Zhai et al. 2019). Skin temperature recovers in 5–10 min with fans, compared to 30 min without.

Visual transitions. When moving from a bright to dim space, full *dark adaptation* takes 20–30 minutes (Caruso 2007). More discussion and evidence about visual adaptation is presented in S5 Light and Dark Procession.

Design Guidelines

Design a series of occupiable places for visitors and inhabitants to pass through en route from arrival to interior destination. Choreograph each place in the promenade as moving, pausing, or resting with changes in direction, elevation and view. Build in perceptual transitions of light, temperature and air movement experiences. Use the transitions from one place to another to support the intimacy gradient and social patterns of the building.

Express welcome with an identifiable entrance that can be seen from the street or approach with taller massing or extensions from the main volume. Make it an offering of the building to the street and the public. Mark the site as a territory with a gateway or thickened threshold to mark passage into the landscape of the building. Surround a portion of ground to create an entrance court or forecourt as a welcoming in-between zone. Locate the entrance facing toward or away from the breeze, depending on climate.

Sequence places from arrival to destination in the interior. In buildings where the destination is private (individual office, residential quarters), arrange a gradient of public to private spaces in which degrees of associated social activities transpire. Link entrance gate to building entry with an integrated path. In both residential and non-residential buildings, create a covered outdoor entrance room with places to wait, shaded and dry. Make the door like another gate, a framed moment larger and thicker than the actual door. In cooler climates, especially in public buildings, an airlock or weather vestibule and a second set of doors is called for. Inside, place a receiving place, a foyer or lobby as greeting and opportunity for orientation. Offer a preview of coming attractions.

Order clear paths + goals. Along the exterior path, change directions once or twice and elevate the visitor a few steps up. Use these to shift views of the building and landscape. The entire path does not need to be seen from any point, but the next destination in the sequence should not require visitors to guess. Use the approach and sequence of outdoor places to build shade, reduce daylight and increase wind shelter, if appropriate.

Bias toward air movement with tempered air for warm climates, as this provides fast-acting cooling and accommodates people already in the building. Provide people-based conditioning in localized areas, rather than over-cooling large areas with air-conditioning alone. Condition an entrance transition zone within a range of indoor operative temperatures of 26–30°C (78–86°F), assuming that's on par with or not significantly warmer than the outdoor air people are coming from, with air speed of about 0.5–0.8 m/s (1.6–2.6 ft/s).

Gradually reduce illuminance from brighter outdoors to dimmer indoors to support comfort, orientation and wayfinding, ideally in steps no greater than 3:1 (Baker + Steemers 2002). Lengthen the entry path, especially in bright sky climates, giving occupants' vision time to adjust. This is especially important in buildings where the end goal is a dimly lighted space such as a theatre or archival museum galleries. Use small areas of more brightly-lighted objects or surfaces within a darker space to assist in conveying visual information and to balance the scene for a brightness-adapted person in transition (Tregenza + Wilson 2011).

Refine with G4 Shades of Brilliance, G4 Zephyr Spectrum and C4 Inhabited Periphery. This schema is a special case of S5 Territorial Tuning and of S5 Light + Dark Procession. Help build S6 Topophilic Perambulation.

S5

Light and Dark Procession

varies light intensity among spaces, both defining significant features and enlivening the luminous experience.

338 **Hill House (Blackie Villa) entry and hall**

Helensburgh, Scotland, 1904
Charles R Mackintosh, architect

A subdued north side, dark-paneled entry hall, stair lighting filtered through wood screen, dark trim and furniture, cool soft diffuse north light, contrasting window casing.

photo National Trust of Scotland

As we move around the house, we find it full of alternations and gradations of light which reinforce the masculine/feminine scheme of meanings: gloom in the vestibule, half-light in the hall, bright light beckoning us on the stairs and welcoming us in the drawing room and bedroom.

—María González Mínguez 2008

weaving with its rods
miracles from the eye's loom
lustrous warp and weft

Humans perceive their world predominantly through vision. Light reveals architecture, or as Kahn put it, light is the "giver of all presences." Modern lighting standards specify illuminance quantity, an impoverished notion with no reference to pattern, yet every beginning designer can see that light and shadow belong to each other. Luminous variety stimulates human contrast-biased sight, brings greater alertness and enhances interest. More significantly, light's qualities constitutes the essence of an architectural atmosphere. Brighter areas signal places of orientation, destination and social congregation. Functionally, people can see over an astonishingly wide range of light levels; therefore, maintaining the same illumination throughout a whole building is both pragmatically unnecessary and experientially monotonous. Lighting characters—light and dark, sun and shadow, direct and reflected, specular and diffuse, monochrome and colored, crisp and indistinct—these are the meter, structure and syntax of light's poetics employed in designing luminous sequences with significance and feeling.

Hill House drawing room

An energized and uplifting south-side, high-reflectance living space with larger windows and direct sun potential provides a dramatic contrast to the entry sequence. The sunny window seat, daylit from three sides, amplifies the effect.

photo Historic Environment Scotland

next spread
Lighting section diagram

additional precedent see
Ny Carlsberg Glypotek
in Chapter 4 introduction

Hill House's recessed front door and generous north entryway are daylit but relatively dim, leading to the main stair. The daylight from the stair landing window filters from the side through a wooden screen. A few steps lead past the stair to a wide hall that acts as reception area and access to the main ground-floor rooms. The entry zone is paneled in dark-stained pine that is also used for deep window sills and jambs. The dark wood is contrasted with lighter plaster and relieved by beige carpeting. A moderately-sized north window brings diffuse light and begins to raise the overall illumination. From this realm of dark oak furniture and diffuse north light, the visitor traverses south to the light-filled drawing room with its light-colored rose stencil motifs on white walls. The room amplifies its southern light with cream carpet, white ceiling, translucent white curtains and light chair upholstery. At the southern sunny edge, a long window seat is set in an alcove below a broad bank of tall windows and flanked by full-height glazed doors opening to the roofless terrace, open to the full sky. The North American or Southern European designer might wonder as to Mackintosh's seeming obsession with the white room. However, the psychological effect of moving between these rooms could not be more powerfully dramatic and uplifting, especially when set in the usual dim greyness of the western Scotland sky, where rain dominates every forecast and winter days shrink to only a few hours. Hill House lighting engages a psychological procession (Macaulay 1994; Ellis 1999).

Light and Dark Procession

Visual adaptation to contrast

Adaptation from dark to light conditions happens very rapidly, while moving form light to dark requires much longer for the eyes to adjust.

adapted from Lucas et al. 2014

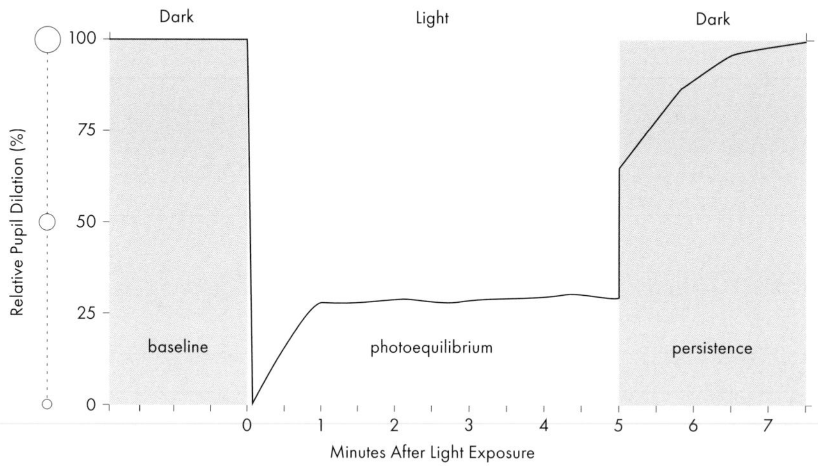

Supporting Evidence

Humans associate brighter light with safety, social settings, wayfinding and orientation in the world. The human eye takes longer to adapt moving from light to dark than it does from dark to light. Transitions that are too extreme can cause discomfort and disorientation.

...to plan the building as a pure mass of shadow, then, afterwards, to put in light as if you were hollowing out the darkness, as if the light were seeping in.

—Peter Zumthor 2006

Visual adaptation to contrast. When moving from lighter to darker spaces, the time it takes for people's eyes to adapt is particularly important for design. The eyes' adaptation mechanism is complex. The familiar pupil diameter change (from 1–2 mm to 8 mm) comprises a small part of adaptation. Other mechanisms include rod to cone switchover, photopigment bleaching and feedback from horizontal cells to control photoreceptor responsiveness. Combined effects make the retina more sensitive at lower than higher light levels (Lucas et al. 2014).

Brightness ratios used judiciously can create sparkle and drama or—if too high—visual glare and fatigue. Common lighting design practice suggests brightness ratios between room surfaces exceeding10:1 can induce glare. Ratios beyond 3:1 within the immediate field of view (between book and desktop) can be uncomfortable.

Shadows' significance to the psyche is a theme argued by Bachelard (1964), Tanazaki (1977) and others. Pallasmaa (2012) articulated, "The imagination and daydreaming are stimulated by dim light and shadow" and that clear thought requires both vision's sharpness to be suppressed and heterogeneous patterns, both light and dark.

Social patterns result from orchestrated lightscapes, find Bille and Sørensen (2007): "Light may be used as a tool for exercising social intimacy and inclusion, of shaping moral spaces and hospitality, and orchestrating movement, while working as a metaphor as well as a material agent in these social negotiations." Space, light, activity and the order of intimacy and sociality seem inseparable. Meditation calls for a cave; intense reading, a focused light; the kitchen, a sunny counter; social discourse, a glare-free brightness for understanding and togetherness.

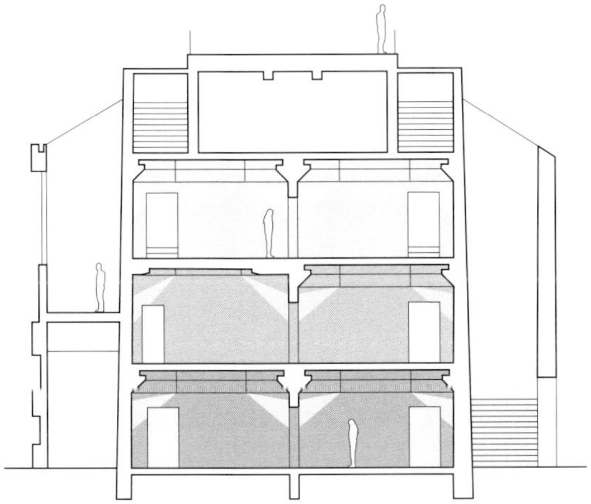

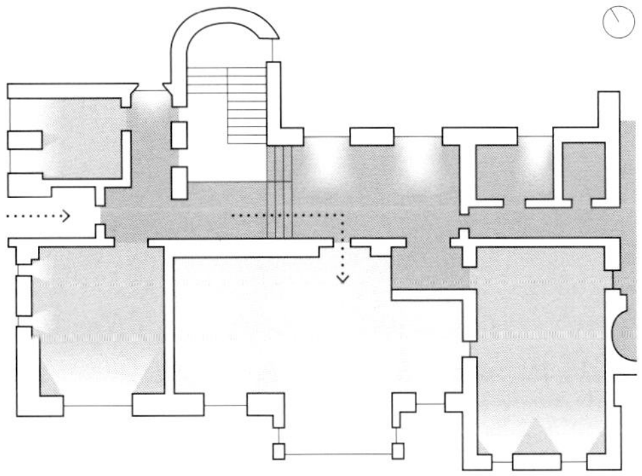

left
Ny Carlsberg Glyptotek Extension
Copenhagen, Denmark, 1996
Henning Larsens, architect

Visitors circulate through darker galleries alternating with skylighted circulation, transitioning upward towards brighter light. See images and text in Sequences section of Chapter 4 Introduction.

right
Hill House
Helensburgh, Scotland, 1904
Charles R Mackintosh, architect

Occupants progress from darker entry and north-side hall to bright south-facing living room and an even brighter window seat.

Design Guidelines

Envision a choreographed sequence of daylit atmospheres, subtle or dramatic, that delights and orients inhabitants. Manifest this vision by organizing the rooms and ordering orientation, aperture size, materials and color to control light levels and character. Provide illuminance contrast between adjacent spaces and link them with transitions.

Link lighter and darker spaces with spatial transitions that increase travel time and path distance. As the contrast between illuminance levels increases (especially from light to dark), plan even longer transitions. This allows the eyes time to adjust and creates gradients that reduce glare. The time required to adapt to large magnitudes of change influences whether one experiences progression as unpleasant (being blinded by too much light or having difficulty seeing in too little), or as a pleasant sequence of variation.

Alternate dark and light spaces along circulation routes, as Alexander and colleagues (1977) recommend in their Tapestry of Light and Dark pattern. They suggest that places in buildings, as settings for human events, are defined by light and that brighter places are defined in contrast to darker places.

Construct order following light, considering that, as Larsens did in Ny Carlsberg Glyptotek, access to daylight often increases on upper floors. Therefore, locate brighter portions of the sequence on higher levels. Similarly, like Mackintosh, some orientations have different lighting qualities, intensity, directionality, timing and color. Match the orientation and location of spaces to their planned qualities in the sequence.

Organize rooms for daylight, locating spaces requiring more lighting in places on the site and within the plan and section that have the greatest access to daylight resources (DeKay + Brown 2014, Daylight Zones strategy).

Refine with C4 Inhabited Periphery, R4 Circadian Space and C4 Lightrooms. S5 Ingress Transitions and S5 Phototropic Catenation become more specific types of procession. Help build S6 Topophilic Perambulation.

S5

Phototropic Catenation

links desirable places with circulation paths that engender occupants' curiosity and draw them toward light.

342 **Stockholm Public Library Annex**

Stockholm, Sweden, 1928
Gunnar Asplund, architect

A dark entry leads to dim stairs, narrowing as they ascend to "a temple of light and knowledge when they enter the rotunda" (Olsson 2020).

photo left Jon Hoem
photo right Arquitectura Viva

Aurora's bright gleam
such fecund site assured
no wolves in the light

Phototropic means attracted to light. To *catenate* is to link together, to form into a connected series. Thus, this schema uses the hardwired human attraction toward light to give structure and orientation to building inhabitation. Given this phenomenon, architects often orchestrate illuminance and circulation in what Sarah Susanka (2004) terms, "light to walk toward." This might take the form of higher Illuminance at the end of a corridor or punctuated brighter places along a darker passage. Contrast distinguishes forms, and the eye is attracted to brighter areas within the field of view. Light can lead to significant rooms, give meaning to a building's organization and reinforce the order of space. Conversely, uniform lighting conveys undifferentiated meaning, thus no meaning. Patterns of co-defining light and dark work together geometrically with forms to promote wayfinding and cognitive mapping. In common practice, daylighting and electric lighting are designed at the room scale; luminous effects considered in multi-room sequences can become generative of architectural order at the scale of plans and sections.

Bahrain Pavilion, Expo 2015

Milan, Italy, 2015
Studio Anne Holtrop, architect

A curving path with white-walled sunlighted court suggests a mystery beyond draws visitors.

photo Pygmalion Karatzas

more images see Divasare, 2017

Stockholm Public Library orchestrates citizens' passage, either through the main stair or by two darkened side radial staircases. From the dim, polished black art-deco carved stucco-walled entry vestibule, visitors ascend through a staircase compressed between converging dark side walls that visually amplify the depth, rising towards the alluring light of the lending hall rotunda and the "enlightening power of its books" (Plummer 2012). Within the cylindrical reading room, the dark-to-light progression continues from the warm wood and books at its base, to the solid, white, textured masonry drum and upward to high surrounding windows. Although initially only for librarians, the path continues today for patrons up curving stairs to the upper tiers of the amphitheater-terraced stacks. The progression becomes a "delivery to a higher order of thought" (Bennett 2013).

Bahrain Pavilion, also known as *Archeologies of Green*, is "a poetic interpretation of the cultural agrarian heritage of the country", organized as a sequence of linked courts and rooms accessing ten different fruit gardens (Holtrop 2015). The dry-jointed white precast concrete arcs, fitted with brass details, lead either to beckoning sun-drenched courts or large-windowed rooms looking onto the courts and gardens. The white garden walls reflect bright light through the openings, enticing the journeying visitor with mystery and glimpses of what lies just beyond.

Phototropic Catenation

 Phototropic movement

A **Toplight, repeated on path**
Jyväskylä University
Jyväskylä, Finland, 1959
Alvar Aalto

B **Sidelight at path end**
St Henry's Ecumenical Art Chapel
Turku, Finland, 2005
Sanaksenaho Architects

C **Top + sidelight, punctuated**
Gug Church
Aalborg, Denmark, 1972
Inger and Johannes Exner

D **Sidelight, repeated**
Santa Fe Visual Arts Center (plan)
New Mexico, USA, 1999
Legorreta + Legorreta

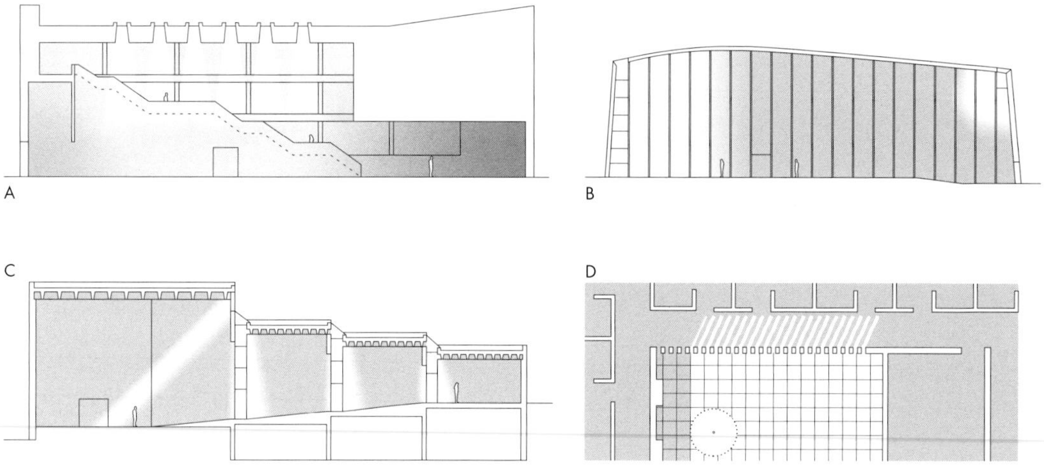

Supporting Evidence

For many reasons, measured and unmeasurable, people are both physiologically and psychically phototropic. They long for life-giving light with its character of clarity, but also for the way it generates meaning and mystique. Non-uniformly lighting the way assists navigation, orientation and helps occupants feel safe .

Archetype. Susanka (2004) writes, "our attraction to light subliminally draws us toward the brightness at the end of a walkway or passage and makes the space accessed along the route more engaging as a result." Plummer (2012) argues that the *primal image* of "beckoning light" resonates deep in the psyche as it carries a "metaphoric rebirth" of the new day, of spring, where "a radiant world appears within a dark void."
Phototropism. Humans are daytime, not nocturnal, beings and see poorly in the dark. Light is associated with safety—there are no unseen wolves howling in its brightness. Light reveals information necessary for both survival and pleasure. Light is associated with summer, with the warmth of the sun—and of fire.
Wayfinding is promoted by clear sight lines between decision points. Visual links through windows to the outside, or directionality understood by incoming light, can reduce stress and help orientation (MBIE 2019). People prefer higher light levels (250–500 Lux) when making orientation decisions in unfamiliar buildings (Hidayetoglu et al. 2012). They choose brighter paths in normal (Taylor + Sucov 1974) and emergency situations (Vilar at al. 2013).
Mystery + enticement, recommends Joye (2007), are nature-based phenomena that bring positive human affective responses. Mystery, he suggests, is most straightforwardly accomplished in building by the *deflected path*, (identified in Ulrich's 1983 psychoevolutionary framework) where the bending path encourages curiosity and exploration. Enticement occurs when occupants in darker areas see "a partially visible and enlightened area or setting", drawing attention and triggering "exploitative behavior".

Design Guidelines

The essential intention of this schema is to orchestrate light and shadow in rhythms that invoke emotional reactions. Bring light to attract attention, to guide the way, to invoke curiosity and anticipation. Shadow becomes the context and origin for movement toward light. In reverse, moving gradually toward darkness allows apprehension its time.

> Light directs movement and attention, creating hierarchies and points of importance and focus.
>
> *—Juhani Pallasmaa*

Intend emotional patterns generated by dark and light in sequence, however formally ordered and depending on the project circumstance, that move the participant from mystery to order, reverie to clarity, the unknown to the known, past to future, contrasting "feelings of tension and release, gloom and exhilaration, suspense and relaxation, even fear and hope" (Plummer 2012), from the subconscious toward the light of consciousness.

Promote movement with luminously non-uniform spatial sequences by varying brightness levels and changing ambient lighting and accent lighting. "Lighting has the task of directing the viewer's gaze, helping to indicate the direction of motion and building up atmospheric tension." In contrast, a more uniform homogeneous lighting is often associated with a calmer and quieter atmosphere without implied movement. The two schemes can be combined in to larger patterns (Krautter + Schielke 2009).

Light the nodes. Alexander and colleagues (1979) suggests in their pattern, Tapestry of Light and Dark, that nodes of circulation—entries, stairs and orientation places—be given more light, while the places around them remain contrastingly darker. Define circulation routes from one important decision or orientation point to another. Increase the lighting at the nodes. Light the end of routes with windows and views, but avoid direct brightness sources.

Punctuate the paths with sidelight or toplight, which helps define a rhythmic path and orients the moving occupant to the outdoor environment. Conversely, internal corridors without external reference points are disorienting.

Organize interior views from room to room that terminate in light and views to the exterior. Along the circulation route and at path turns, provide alternate views and *end-lighting* perpendicular to the primary path.

Follow circulation design principles, as conceived by lighting design expert Thomas Schielke (2013), which offer numerous precepts and concepts relevant to this schema:

1. Wall washing accentuates and expands the space, while focused light creates zones as "islands of light".
2. Differential illuminances create perceptual hierarchies that emphasize zones.
3. Windows and skylights in corridors create a more user-friendly environment.
4. A brightly illuminated end wall helps with directing view and spatial orientation.
5. "A window at the end of a corridor makes a connection to the exterior...and emphasizes the direction..."
6. Room to room transitions become more significant if illuminated with a bright light cone, creating a "welcoming impression", even if the door itself is not visible from a distance.

Detail carefully. Avoid designs that have occupants walk directly toward a bright window from a darker corridor. This *light at the end of the tunnel* effect is most often glare-inducing, unless gradients around the window and on the approach are handled carefully. Alternately, bring light from the side so that the surfaces seen are brighter, while the more intense source of the daylight is obscured until arrival.

Refine with C4 Lightrooms and G4 Shades of Brilliance. S5 Ingress Transitions is one specific type of this schema. S5 Light + Dark Procession is also related. Help build S6 Topophilic Perambulation and S6 Engagement + Retreat.

S6

Topophilic Perambulation

relates occupants to body and site by their traverse of floor plane changes fit to the variations in ground elevation.

346 **Casa Palicourea**

São Jorge, Brazil, 2020
BLOCO Arquitetos

Terraced in small intervals, its floors follow the land's form. Exterior covered circulation wraps the two long sides, one with steps, the other with ramps.

photo Joana França

next spread
Section diagrams

rising and falling
focused steps to balance
dwelling truly now

Earth underfoot, the surface roughness and slightest slope sensed, relates the walker in intimate moments to their body and place. To walk or stand is a fundamental able-bodied mode of human existence, one that registers elevation, profile and solidity in terms of effort and embodied skills. Traversing nature's floor, one comes to inhabit a landscape as a participant, yet to walk on earth is an uncommon occurrence for contemporary urban humans. If at all, the ground is found between buildings. Once a building is entered, the feeling of terrain typically disappears in the abstractions of floors flattened by cut and fill in full storey-height increments. Alternatively, on flat ground, a building's ground floor extends the site's plane. On even gently sloped sites, if a building's floor levels can translate the landscape to a congruent inhabitable topography, adjusted incrementally with existing terrain—then an intrinsic human place-empathetic satisfaction presences. Navigating ramps and stairs in a few steps or partial storeys brings moments of organic awareness and the enjoyment of breath, blood, muscle and mind in league, alive.

Ray + Dagmar Dolby Regeneration Medicine Building

University of California San Francisco (UCSF)
San Francisco, CA, 2010
Rafael Viñoly Architects

A single storey building stepped and contoured with the topography creates an indoor and rooftop analog to the ground on an extreme site.

photo Bruce Damonte

next page
Section diagram

Casa Palicourea consists of a house and a separate small design studio. "The internal spaces were placed at different levels and adapted to the existing topography, slightly suspended from the ground to prevent the entry of small wild animals... A system of stairs and ramps connect the house's internal and external levels." In the studio building, the end stairs transform into an amphitheater (BLOCO 2021). A core of concrete frame and brick walls is spanned by a single slope roof that "follows the general topography of each side of the hill." The parasol PV-clad, rainwater-harvesting shed accommodates spaces below that are carefully fitted to the terrain by four levels of the main house and two for the studio, each with small increments of 4–7 steps in-between (C3DIZ 2022).

UCSF Regeneration Medicine Building takes an alternate approach from Casa Palicourea, as it occupies a more treacherous, nearly 45-degree slope, "a site that essentially doesn't exist," and perches on steel space trusses (Viñoly 2011). Sited at the eucalyptus forest edge, it curves in a ribbon and steps down with the topography. Occupants descend four research areas in half-flight stairs. Scientists can meander through linked rooftop terraces accessible from each research level, with city and forest view, traversing and emulating the land-form profile. Suspended walkways and open cable rails add to the optional vertiginous experience (CBE 2013).

Topophilic Perambulation

Incrementally terraced floors

A Casa Palicourea, main house

B Casa Palicourea, studio

C UCSF Dolby Regeneration Medicine Building

See images and descriptions of both projects on the previous spread.

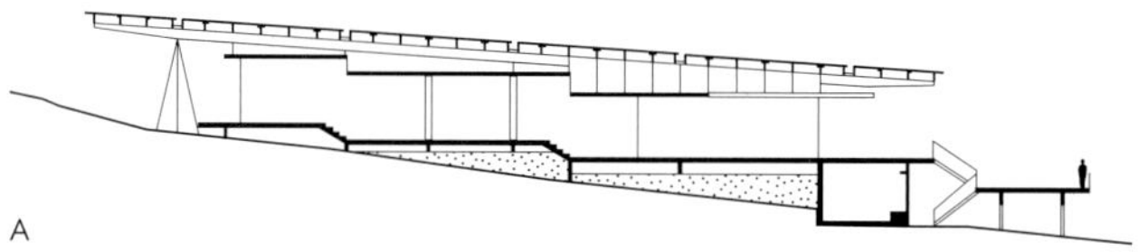

A

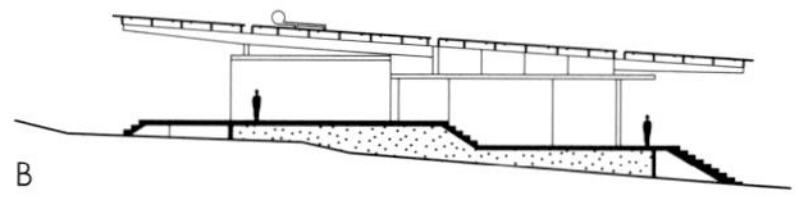

B

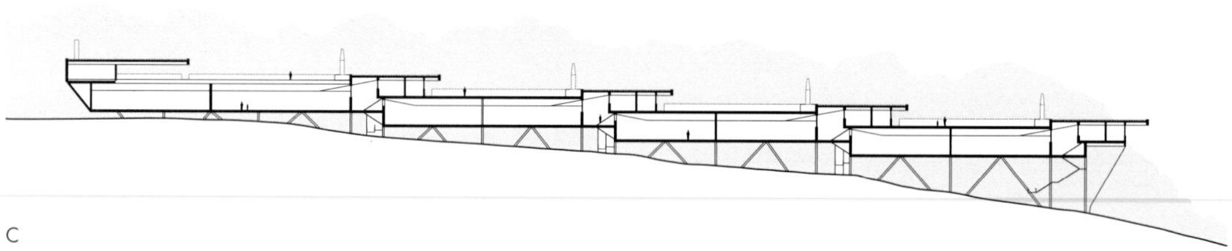

C

Supporting Evidence

While the feeling of groundedness is fundamental, the experience is surprisingly poorly researched. Ubiquitous sterile flat floors create a deadening steady-state uniformity, putting inhabitants' kinesthetic abilities to sleep. Evolutionarily, humans are self-satisfyingly agile and crave feeling rooted.

Monotony of predictable ground. As sensory variability is beneficial to mind, nervous system and emotions, walking and changing levels must also contribute to vitality, aliveness, alertness and body awareness. Long machine-like marches on hard concrete of big-box shopping is the extreme opposite of this. In many buildings, the uniform ground of flat floors and repetitive, equally-spaced and sized steps "subjects us to monotonous, mechanical movement, dissociating power from the body....The habitual ground that conserves life by eliminating risk is in reality a mechanism that, when universal, depletes and perverts the human spirit" (Plummer 2016).
Environmental awareness. Humans have agile bodies by evolution. Walking "generates [much] multisensory information about walked-upon objects" (Giordano et al. 2012), including haptic, kinesthetic, visual and auditory feedback. Gravity's pull is felt three-dimensionally in the body, even with slight changes in slope or elevation.
Rootedness, speculate Alexander and team (1977) in the pattern Connection to the Earth, may be helped or hindered by "the extent to which our physical world is itself rooted and connected to the earth." They recommend an ambiguous boundary between building and site with paths, steps and terraces around building edges.
Proprioception and kinesthesia. *Proprioception is* an individual's awareness of where one's body is positioned in space, while *kinesthesia* is a related faculty that provides useful information about how the physical body moves in space (Reed + Ziot 2018). "Kinesthetic perception of architecture refers to the capacity of architectural space to

stimulate our kinesthetic sense" (Yiannoudes 2006). Shusterman (2012) insightfully explains this mode of sensory environmental perception as "the tactile and muscular sensations of walking through space, feel of the surface material beneath our feet; the rhythm of our footsteps, the kinaesthetic feel, proprioceptive balance, and muscular effort of traversing a courtyard or ascending or descending a staircase or adjusting one's gait and posture to negotiate a narrow corridor or low door."

Surface. Floor material influences walking speed and sound pleasure. People walk more slowly on carpeted surfaces than on hard floors (Bitgood 2011), while they find the sound of walking on ceramic tile more pleasant than carpet (Tonetto et al 2014).

Grounded color. Living on Earth, humans' evolutionary preferences expect darker colors on lower surfaces, mid-range colors higher, and lightest colors overhead, thus reducing stress and increasing comfort (Stewart 2015). Monochromatic schemes signal environmental danger associated with approaching storms.

Design Guidelines

Engender groundedness and earth-connection primarily by peripatetic (meaning moving from place to place) design, floor relationship to topography and transitions between inside and outside. Shape the floors to bring awareness to the terrain. Promote both accessibility and bodily interaction options, engaged curiosity and improvisation with some surprise and allure.

Fit levels to slope to bring awareness of moving up and down indoors in relation to elevation changes outdoors. Smaller increments from a few steps to half storeys encourage stair and ramp use rather than elevators.

Connect indoors and out with floor levels that encourage moving directly across the enclosure at the same level or with only a couple of steps. On slopes, terrace the gardens with the site contours and around buildings to make them occupiable. Use terraces at the inhabited periphery to transition to the land-form.

Create playful terrain with variable stairs, different intervals for landings, widening treads near the bottom and variety that forwards the delight of negotiating uneven terrain—as children often remind us.

Balance certain and uncertain terrain such that accessibility is maintained but employing "ingenuity in combining flat floors with small concentrations of daring movement so that people may move about with ease yet occasionally return to their bodies in manoeuvres that can reach high-wire intensity" (Plummer 2016).

Supplement with haptic surfaces, such as the unevenly spaced stepping stones used in a Japanese garden, rough and cobbled paving, or other surfaces that attune the gait and body to variations. Soften surfaces with brick, gravel, tiles and earth on surrounding paths and terraces to transition to the landscape.

Ground the floor with relatively earth-hued and dark materials, medium-tone walls and "light is up" ceilings, as Stewart (2015) recommends. Contrasting floors with walls is especially important for elderly people because contrast perception decreases dramatically with aging.

Refine with N5 Three Realms, S5 Phototropic Catenation and S5 Ingress Transitions.

Sequence Sources

S1 Veridical Patina

ArchDaily. 2014. IGC Tremp/Oikosvia Arqutiectura. *ArchDaily*, 29 May. archdaily.com/509876

Brand, Stewart. 1994. *How Buildings Learn: What Happens After They are Built.* New York: Penguin

Escott, Efrie + Billie Faircloth. 2021. Personal communication, 19 Oct

Escott, Efrie. 2021. Personal communication, 28 Oct

HLC. 2012. *A Preservation Handbook for Historic Residential Properties + Districts in Salt Lake City.* Salt Lake City, Utah: Salt Lake City Historic Landmark Commissioners, part II, 2:1

Howard, Edgar B + Tom Piper. 2014. *KieranTimberlake: Loblolly House.* video. San Francisco, California: Kanopy Streaming

KieranTimberlake. 2009. The Long-Term Beauty of Untreated Western Red Cedar, 28 May. kierantimberlake.com

KieranTimberlake. 2017. Predictive Wood Weathering at the University of Washington, 1 Dec. kierantimberlake.com

McEleney, Bill. 2005. A Primer on Weathering Steel. *Structure*, Oct, 41–44

Mostafavi, Moshen + David Leatherbarrow. 1993. On *Weathering: The Life of Buildings in Time.* Cambridge, Massachusetts: MIT Press

Parker, Alfred Browning. 1965. *You and Architecture: a Practical Guide to the Best in Building.* New York: Delacourte Press, 93–98

Timberlake, James + Stephan Kieran. 2008. *Loblolly House: Elements of a New Architecture.* New York: Princeton Architectural Press

Wright, Frank Lloyd. 1928. In the Cause of Architecture, VIII. Sheet Metal and a Modern Stance. *Architectural Record* 64(Oct): 334–342

S2 Aromatic Transit

Alexander, Christopher, Sara Ishikawa + Murray Silverstein. 1977. *A Pattern Language: Towns, Buildings, Construction.* New York: Oxford University Press. #245 Raised Flowers, 1132–1134; #246 Climbing Plants, 1135–1137; #174 Trellised Walk, 809–811

Barbara, Anna + Anthony Perliss. 2006. *Invisible Architecture: Experiencing Places through the Sense of Smell.* Milano: Skira

Biltmore. 1980. *Biltmore House + Gardens.* Asheville, North Carolina: Biltmore Estate

Brenner, David. 2017. in Angela Hill, Getting Vertical with the Bay Area Expert on Green "Living Walls". *East Bay Times*, 19 May

Diego, Miguel A, Nancy Aaron Jones, Tiffany Field, Maria Hernandez-Reif, Saul Schanberg, Cynthia Kuhn, Mary Galamaga, Virginia McAdam + Robert Galamaga. 1998. Aromatherapy Positively Affects Mood, EEG Patterns of Alertness and Math Computations. *International Journal of Neuroscience* 96(3–4): 217–224

Donelli, Davide, Michele Antonelli, Caterina Bellinazzi, Gian Franco Gensini + Fabio Firenzuoli. 2019. Effects of Lavender on Anxiety: A Systematic Review and Meta-Analysis. *Phytomedicine* 65(Dec):153099

Druse, Kenneth. 2019. *The Scentual Garden: Exploring the World of Botanical Fragrance.* New York: Abrams

Druse, Kenneth. 2020. in Margaret Roach, The 'Invisible' Garden of Scent. 14 Jun, Section RE, 10 [print], Jun 10 [online]. *The New York Times.* nytimes.com

El Mountassir, Fouzia, Christine Belloir, Loïc Briand, Thierry Thomas-Danguin + Anne-Marie Le Bon. 2016. Encoding odorant mixtures by human olfactory receptors. *Flavour and Fragrance Journal* 31(5): 400–407

Flanders, Danny. nd. Growing American Wisteria. HGTV. hgtv.com

Habitat Horticulture. 2013. Foundry Square III. Habitat Horticulture, LLC. habitathorticulture.com/projects/foundry-square-iii

Harada, Hiroki, Hideki Kashiwadani, Yuichi Kanmura + Tomoyuki Kuwaki. 2018. Linalool Odor-Induced Anxiolytic Effects in Mice. *Frontiers in Behavioral Neuroscience* 12, Article 242, 23 Oct

Maggioni, Emanuela, Robert Cobden, Dmitrijs Dmitrenko, Kasper Hornbæk + Marianna Obrist. 2019. Smell Space: Mapping out the Olfactory Design Space for Novel Interactions. *ACM Transactions on Computer-Human Interaction* 37(4) Article 111, August

Messer, Pamela Lynn. 1990. *The Biltmore Estate (1888–1895): a Historical Documentation of the Landscape Development Designed by Frederick Law Olmsted*. MS Thesis, University of Tennessee, Knoxville

Pálsdóttir, Anna María, Sara Spendrup, Lennart Mårtensson + Karin Wendin. 2021. Garden Smellscape–Experiences of Plant Scents in a Nature-Based Intervention. *Frontiers in Psychology* 12 (Jun 29): 667957

Patnaik, Biswaksen, Andrea Batch + Niklas Elmqvist. 2018. Information Olfactation: Harnessing Scent to Convey Data. *IEEE Transactions on Visualization and Computer Graphics* 25(2): 726–736

Porter, Jess, Brent Craven, Rehan M Khan, Shao-Ju Chang, Irene Kang, Benjamin Judkewitz, Jason Volpe, Gary Settles + Noam Sobel. 2007. Mechanisms of Scent-Tracking in Humans. *Nature Neuroscience* 10(1): 27

Prior, Matthew. 2019. The Smell of Lavender is Relaxing. Science Confirms. *Frontiers Science News*, 6 Nov. blog. frontiersin.org

Ross, Judy. 2018. Enjoying the Shady Pergola. *All Things Biltmore* [online], 6 July. biltmore.com/blog/enjoying-the-shady-pergola

Vernet-Maury, Evelyne, Ouafae Alaoui-Ismal Íli, Andre Dittmar, Georges Delhomme + Jacques Chanel. 1999. Basic Emotions Induced by Odorants: a New Approach Based on Autonomic Pattern Results. *Journal of the Autonomic Nervous System* 75(2):176–183

Wand, Lucy. 2014. Habitat Horticulture Completes Largest Indoor Living Wall in California. *Inhabitat*, 14 Dec. inhabitat.com

S5 Territorial Tuning

ArchDaily. 2019. NUS School of Design + Environment/ Serie Architects + Multiply Architects + Surbana Jurong. *ArchDaily*, 5 Feb. archdaily.com/912021

Chun, Chungyoon + Akihiro Tamura. 2005. Thermal Comfort in Urban Transitional Spaces. *Building and Environment* 40(5): 633–639

Dahlan, Nur Dalilah, Amirhosein Ghaffarianhoseini, Amirhosein + Norhaslina Hassa. 2020. Sensory and Physiological Assessment of Spatial Transient Thermal Environment Changes at a Tropical University Campus. *Smart and Sustainable Built Environment* 11(3) 5 Nov: 516–531

de Dear, Richard J, James W Ring + Povl Ole Fanger. 1993. Thermal Sensations Resulting from Sudden Ambient Temperature Changes. *Indoor Air* 3(3) Sep: 181–192

DeKay, Mark + G Z Brown. 2014. *Sun, Wind + Light: Architectural Design Strategies*, 3rd ed. Hoboken, New Jersey: Wiley; #26 Cooling Zones, E.76–78; #28 Heating Zones E.81–82

Hoyt, Tyler, Edward Arens + Hui Zhang. 2015. Extending Air Temperature Setpoints: Simulated Energy Savings and Design Considerations for New and Retrofit Buildings. *Building and Environment* 88 (Jun): 89–96

Jitkhajornwanich, Kitchai + Adrian C Pitts. 2002. Interpretation of Thermal Responses of Four Subject Groups in Transitional Spaces of Buildings in Bangkok. *Building and Environment* 37(11):1193–1204

Sequence Sources

Kessling, Wolfgang , Martin Engelhardt + Nirmal Kishnani. 2016. Developing the Net Zero Energy Design for the School of Design and Environment of the National University of Singapore. *PLEA 2016 Los Angeles—36th International Conference on Passive and Low Energy Architecture: Cities, Buildings, People: Towards Regenerative Environments*

Kessling, Wolfgang. 2019. SDE4 in Singapore: Net-Zero By Design [Webinar lecture], 30 Sep. youtube.com/watch?v=g2qLogpa2Xg

Kotopouleas, Alkis + Marialena Nikolopoulou. 2016. Thermal Comfort Conditions in Airport Terminals: Indoor or Transition spaces? *Building and Environment* 99 (Apr):184–199

Lee, Christopher. 2017. Net-Zero Energy Complex, School of Design and Environment, London, UK: Serie Architects, London and Multiply Architects, Singapore. *Architecture + Design* 34 (6): 46–50 [India]

Lee, Christopher. 2019. in NUS School of Design + Environment/ Serie Architects + Multiply Architects + Surbana Jurong. *ArchDaily*, 5 Feb. archdaily.com/912021

Luo, Maohui, Wenjie Ji, Bin Cao, Qin Ouyang + Yingxin Zhu. 2016. Indoor Climate and Thermal Physiological Adaptation: Evidences from Migrants with Different Cold Indoor Exposures. *Building and Environment* 98(Mar): 30–38

Mishra, Asit K, Marchel G L C Loomans + Jan L Hensen. 2016. Thermal Comfort of Heterogeneous and Dynamic Indoor Conditions—An Overview. *Building and Environment* 109 (Nov): 82–100

NUS. 2020. NUS College of Design and Engineering. National University of Singapore. youtube.com/watch?v=lpk-wn8ybXk

NZEB. 2019. SDE4 in Singapore: Net-Zero By Design, Redefining Thermal Comfort for Design in a Tropical climate. Net Zero Energy Buildings. nzeb.in/webinars/design/sde4/

Tartarini, Federico, Stefano Schiavon, Toby Cheung + Tyler Hoyt. 2020. *CBE Thermal Comfort Tool: Online Tool for Thermal Comfort Calculations and Visualizations*. SoftwareX 12:100563

Traylor, Caleb, Weihuan Zhao + Yong X Tao. 2019. Utilizing Modulating-Temperature Setpoints to Save Energy and Maintain Alliesthesia-Based Comfort. *Building Research and Information* 47(2):190–201

Xiong, Jing, Zhiwei Lian, Xin Zhou, Jianxiong You + Yanbing Lin. 2015. Effects of Temperature Steps on Human Health and Thermal Comfort. *Building and Environment* 94, part 1(Dec): 144–154

S5 Ingress Transitions

Baker, Nick + Koen Steemers. 2002. *Daylight Design of Buildings*. London: James + James, 170

Benedikt, Michael. 1991. *Deconstructing the Kimbell: an Essay on Meaning and Architecture*. New York: Sites Books

Bourdieu, Pierre. 1970. The Berber House or the World Reversed. *Social Science Information* 9(2):151–170

Caruso, R. 2007. Why Does It Take so Long for Our Vision to Adjust to a Darkened Theater After We Come in From Bright Sunlight? *Scientific American*, 13 Aug. scientificamerican.com

Emden, Cemal. 2021. *The Essential Louis Kahn*. Munich: Prestel

Futagawa, Yukio + Marshall D. Meyers. 1976. *Yale University Art Gallery, New Haven, Connecticut, 1951-53: Kimbell Art Museum, Fort Worth, Texas, 1966-72*. Tokyo: ADA Editors

Kimbell Art Museum. 1987. *In Pursuit of Quality: the Kimbell Art Museum: an Illustrated History of the Art and Architecture*. Fort Worth: Kimbell Art Museum

Millet, Marietta S. 1996. *Light Revealing Architecture*. New York: Van Nostrand Reinhold

Parkinson, Thomas, Richard de Dear + Christhina Candido. 2016. Thermal Pleasure in Built Environments: Alliesthesia in Different Thermoregulatory Zones. *Building Research + Information* 44(1): 20–33

Sieger, Peter J. 2021. Kimbell Art Museum. *Peter J Sieger Architectural Photography*. siegerarchphoto.com/kimball-art-museum

Susanka, Sarah. 2004. *Home By Design: Transforming Your House Into a Home*. Newtown, Connecticut: Taunton Press, 126

Tregenza, Peter + Michael Wilson. 2011. *Daylighting: Architecture + Lighting Design*. London: Routledge, 24

von Meiss, Pierre. 2008. *Elements of Architecture: From Form to Place*. Abingdon, UK: Spon Press

Zhai, Yongchao, Fengyu Miao, Liu Yang, Shengkai Zhao, Hui Zhang + Edward Arens. 2019. Using Personally Controlled Air Movement to Improve Comfort After Simulated Summer Commute. *Building and Environment* 165(Nov):106329

S5 Light + Dark Procession

Alexander, Christopher, Sarah Ishikawa + Murray Silverstein. 197). *A Pattern Language: Towns, Buildings, Construction*. New York: Oxford University Press, #135 Tapestry of Light and Dark, 644–646

Bachelard, Gaston. 1964. *The Poetics of Space*. New York: Orion Press

Bille, Mikkel + Tim Flohr Sørensen. 2007. An Anthropology of Luminosity: The Agency of Light. *Journal of Material Culture* 12(3): 263–284

DeKay, Mark + G Z Brown. 2014. *Sun, Wind + Light: Architectural Design Strategies*, 3rd ed. Hoboken, New Jersey: Wiley, #41 Daylight Zones, E.115–116

Ellis, Anne. 1999. *The Hill House*. Edinburgh: National Trust for Scotland

Lucas, Robert J, Stuart N Peirson, David M Berson, Timothy M Brown, Howard M Cooper, Charles A Czeisler, Mariana G Figueiro, Paul D Gamlin, Steven W Lockley, John B O'Hagan, Luke L A Price, Ignacio Provencio, Debra J Skene + George C Brainard. 2014. Measuring and Using Light in the Melanopsin Age. *Trends in Neurosciences* 37(1):1–9

Macaulay, James. 1994. *Hill House: Charles Rennie Mackintosh*. London: Phaidon

Mínguez, María Teresa González. 2008. Dark/Masculine—Light/Feminine: How Charles Rennie Mackintosh and Margaret MacDonald Changed Glasgow School of Art, *Proceedings 31st AEDEAN Conference*. M J Lorenzo Modia, Ed, 85-91. A Coruña, Spain: Universidade

Pallasmaa, Juhani. 2012. *The Eyes of the Skin: Architecture and the Senses*. 3rd ed. London: John Wiley + Sons

Tanizaki, Jun'ichirō. 1977. *In Praise of Shadows*. New Haven, Connecticut: Leete's Island Books

Zumthor, Peter. 2006. *Atmospheres: Architectural Environments, Surrounding Objects*. Basel: Birkhäuser

S5 Phototropic Catenation

Alexander, Christopher, Sara Ishikawa + Murray Silverstein. 1977. *A Pattern Language: Towns, Buildings, Construction*. New York: Oxford University Press, #135 Tapestry of Light and Dark, 644–646

Bennett, Hannah. 2013. The Psyche of the Library: Physical Space and the Research Paradigm. *Art Documentation: Journal of the Art Libraries Society of North America* 32(2) Sep:174–185

Divisare. 2017. Studio Anne Holtrop: Bahrain Pavilion, *Divsare*, 20 Sep. divisare.com/projects/366682

Hidayetoglu, Mehmet Lutfi, Kemal Yildirim + Aysu Akalin. 2012. The Effects of Color and Light on Indoor Wayfinding and the Evaluation of the Perceived Environment. *Journal of Environmental Psychology* 32(1)Mar: 50–58

Holtrop, Anne. 2015. Bahrain Pavilion—Milan Expo 2015/ Studio Anne Holtrop. *ArchDaily*, 17 May. archdaily.com/631908

Joye, Yannick. 2007. Architectural Lessons From Environmental Psychology: The Case of Biophilic Architecture. *Review of General Psychology* 11(4): 305–328

Krautter, Martin + Thomas Schielke. 2009. *Light Perspectives, Between Culture and Technology: Light, Space, Perspectives.* Lüdenscheid, Germany: ERCO GmbH/Tim Henrik Maak + Kay Pawlik

MBIE. 2019. Planning for Internal Circulation, *Buildings for Everyone: Designing for Access and Usability.* New Zealand Ministry of Business, Innovation and Employment, 28 Jan

Olsson, Lasse. 2020. Stockholm Public Library—Gunnar Asplund's Masterpiece, Newsletter 34. app2.editnews.com

Plummer, Henry. 2012. *Nordic Light: Modern Scandinavian Architecture.* London: Thames + Hudson, 76

Schielke, Thomas. 2013. Lighting Design for Orientation and Direction, in Schittich, Christian, Ed, *DETAIL—Designing Circulation Area: Stairs, Ramps, Lifts—Routing, Planning Principles.* Munich: Edition DETAIL, 34–37. issuu.com

Susanka, Sarah. 2004. *Home By Design: Transforming Your House Into a Home.* Newtown, Connecticut: Taunton Press, 126-133

Taylor, Lyle H + Eugene W Sacov. 1974. The Movement of People Towards Light. *Journal of IES* (Illumination Engineering Society) 3(3)Apr: 237–241

Ulrich, Roger S. 1983. Aesthetic and Affective Response to Natural Environment. in *Behavior and the Natural Environment,* Human Behavior and Environment, Eds. I Altman + J F Wohlwill. Boston, Massachusetts: Springer US, 85-125

Vilar, Elisangela, Francisco Rebelo, Paulo Noriega, Julia Teles + Christopher Mayhorn. 2013. The Influence of Environmental Features on Route Selection in an Emergency Situation. *Applied Ergonomics* 44(4): 618-627

S6 Topophilic Perambulation

Alexander, Christopher, Sara Ishikawa + Murray Silverstein. 1977. *A Pattern Language: Towns, Buildings, Construction.* New York: Oxford University Press, #135 Tapestry of Light and Dark, 644–646

Bitgood, Stephen. 2011. *Social Design in Museums: The Psychology of Visitor Studies.* Edinburgh: Museums Etc

BLOCO. 2021. Palicourea House. *Bloco Arquitetos.* bloco.arq.br

C3DIZ. 2022. A Home and Studio Suited for Life in a Tropical Savannah, *C3DIZ,* 4 Jan. c3diz.net

CBE. 2013. Liveable Buildings Award Winner: UCSF Ray and Dagmar Dolby Regeneration Medicine Building, San Francisco, CA. *Center for the Built Environment,* University of California, Berkeley. cbe.berkeley.edu/livable-building/ucsf-ray-dagmar-dolby-rmb/

Giordano, Bruno L, Yon Visell, Hsin-Yun Yao, Vincent Hayward, Jeremy R Cooperstock + Stephen McAdams. 2012. Identification of Walked-Upon Materials in Auditory, Kinesthetic, Haptic, and Audio-Haptic Conditions. *Journal of the Acoustic Society of America* 131(5) May: 4002–4012

Plummer, Henry. 2016. *The Experience of Architecture.* New York: Thames + Hudson, 21, 24, 35

Reed, Catherine L + Mounia Ziat. 2018. Haptic Perception: From the Skin to the Brain. *Reference Module in Neuroscience and Biobehavioral Psychology.* Elsevier

Shusterman, Richard. 2012. *Thinking Through the Body: Essays in Somaesthetics.* Cambridge, UK: Cambridge University Press, 235

Stewart, Barbara Lyons. 2015. *Flooring Psych: How to Avoid (Literally) Slipping and Tripping Through Life.* San Anselmo, California: Architectural Design Psychology Press, 45–59

Tonetto, Leandro, Cristiano Klanovicz + Charles Spence. 2014. Modifying Action Sounds Influences People's Emotional Responses and Bodily Sensations. *I-Perception* 5:153–163

Viñoly, Raphel. 2011. In Mimi Zeiger, Ray and Dagmar Dolby Regeneration Medicine Building, San Francisco/ Rafael Viñoly Architects. *Architect, Journal of the American Institute of Architects*, 2 May. architectmagazine.com

Yiannoudes, Socrates. 2006. Exploring Kinesthetic Spatial Experiences in the "Active Room". *2nd IET International Conference on Intelligent Environments, IE 06*, Athens, 253–258

356 **Hospital of San Sebastián**

Badajoz, Spain, 1694
Nicolás de Morales Morgado
architect

renovation 2017
José María Sánchez García
architect

17th and 21st centuries coexist. A contemporary minimal whiteness with a lightweight contemporary roof layer onto stereotomic forms anchored by the archaic well. The scheme narrates the sensitive transformation yet respectful inclusion of history.

photo Roland Halbe

Narrative Schemas

N1
Perceptible Provenance

N2
Authentic Matters

N3
Roof Terrain

N3
Distinguishable Durability

N4

N5
Three Realms

N6
Situated Scenes

The narrative schemas are categorically different than all the other schema types, which are based on mappable distributions of mostly dynamic and non-uniform conditions. Distinctions of qualities and materials in these narrative schemas do not necessarily vary in time or space. Often they are quite static to human perception, yet offer potentials for deeper significance, less ephemeral states and the time to contemplate their stories.

The opening chapter, Beyond Comfort, presented three levels of an expanded experiential aesthetic: visual, phenomenological and process; all three reside in the narrative schemas. The smaller scale narrative schemas like N1 Perceptible Provenance and N2 Authentic Matters bring to awareness the material and structural processes and forces at play in buildings. Building systems become the elements of the chronicle in N3 Distinguishable Durability, which identifies the many time frames of a structure's physical layers. N3 Roof Terrain suggests means to visually recount how roof and rain interact in a purposive dance. The schema N5 Three Realms brings to the surface for human consideration metaphoric cosmological ideas embodied in form that otherwise may exist for occupants only tacitly. Finally, N6 Situated Scenes challenges designers to consider what is communicated by a contextual approach to views from and views of a building. In each case, the sensorial phenomena reveal elements that can be understood as moments in a process as elucidated by the backgrounds of interpretation offered by living in a time, culture and place.

Narratives and their readings are always set in the context of cultural worldviews. For example, ideas of *what nature is* and how architectural design ethically and practically relates to that idea of nature have evolved as cultures developed. Traditional pre-Modern Western thought understands Nature as the *primeval garden* or as *wilderness*, while Modernism sees Nature as *natural resources* for human use and (healthy) Postmodernism knows Nature as web-of-life *community*. The nature of Nature and the nature of design-with-Nature both depend on cultural metaphoric narratives.

The designer's challenge when working with narrative schemas is, like all good literature, to have something important and meaningful to say. The story should be worth the telling. The challenge is also to have the building convey its messages in ways that lay people, not just expert interpreters, can read and understand, beginning with how it is experienced in the body. This suggests the possibility of designing for varied degrees of interpretive skill and background knowledge. The essential, deep, mythic architectural narratives are accessible to all, yet unfold across many meaning-making levels. Like Joseph Campbell's (1949) *The Hero with a Thousand Faces*, architects' narratives are never personal or original; rather, they are timeless and archetypal, available for creative retelling in a thousand new ways.

N1

Perceptible Provenance

reveals the natural origin of materials by minimal processing or a preserved record of workmanship.

358 **Estudio Iturbide**

Mexico City, Mexico, 2016
Taller de Arquitectura
Mauricio Rocha + Gabriela
Carrillo, architects

Four types of local bricks reflect regional soil and building traditions transformed into contemporary expression.

photo Rafael Gamo

mere clay building blocks
terra with Agni's burning
ancestry's presence

As inhabitants are literally surrounded by them, construction materials are the most direct and immediate experience of design. Building materials can connect people to Nature when they are fashioned from natural origins and remain visibly, intuitively so. This relatedness and pleasure depends on occupants being able to see and feel Nature in the materials. As such, inhabitants are connected to Nature as the source of human sustenance through their intellectual linking from tool and surface back to mine, tree, clay and quarry, and from there back to Nature's events that brought them into being (DeKay 2011). The relationships of economy and ecology are made available for the human mind directly by the fragment of such processes that the foundation or column or floor surface exhibit, while also metaphorically conveying (or at least implying) the larger network. In the same way, traces of the human hand and tools for shaping evince a history of nature connection. There is something mysteriously satisfying for people about the recognition that their material habitat is sourced from the living world.

Low Energy House

London, England, 2021
Architecture for London, architects

Oak, limestone, lime plaster, wood joists and decking appear minimally processed, just as they are.

photos Christian Brailey

Estudio Iturbide, a photographer's workspace, combines four types of reddish-brown bricks, clay blocks and pavement clinkers, handmade in nearby Puebla (Santibañez 2021). Double rows of flat sleepers alternate with thick standing bricks, creating both opaque and screen walls. The architect explains, "Brick is a common material and very connected to certain areas of the country and especially to the city of Mexico...... For us it is important that the composition of materials is organic and comes from local soil. And it is worth mentioning that nowadays we think about such topics, like sustainability, using the soil and transforming it into a wall" (Rocha 2020). The image also shows exposed, unpainted wood grain in the table, roof joints and ceiling.

Low Energy House, a renovation and extension of a three storey Edwardian terrace in London reveals the original wood joist roof and floor structure while improving energy performance dramatically to Passivehaus standards. "Natural materials including stone, timber and lime plaster were used throughout rather than cement-based products" (A4L 2022). Finishes are exposed and natural: clear finished oak cabinetry and pale gray limestone for counters, window seat, floors, and textured in bathroom and hearth wall panels. The hand-applied lime-based plaster inevitably provides a subtly varied finish that records the hand of the crafter (Levy 2022).

Perceptible Provenance

left
Degrees of processing
In general, less processed materials are visually understood as more natural.

right
Sidwell Friends School
Washington, DC, 2006
KieranTimberlake, architects
photo Halkin/Mason Photography

Untreated recycled western red cedar is allowed to weather naturally. "The red cedar fins extend all the way to the walkway, abstractly referencing the origin of the tree in the forest prior to its use in the wine barrel" (Kieran 2008)

see *also* KieranTimberlake 2009
Detail 2009.

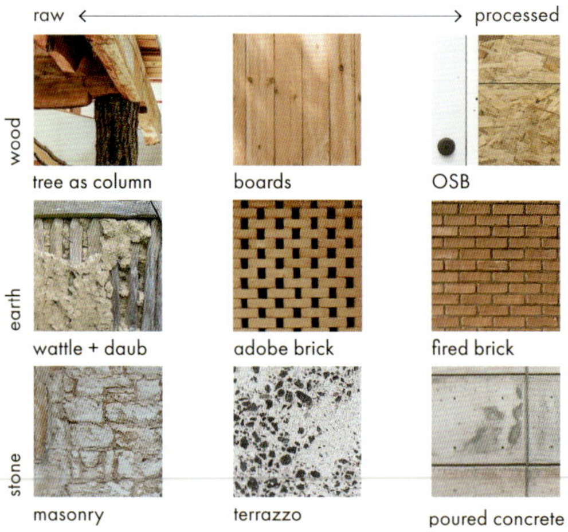

Supporting Evidence

Nature can be understood in materials and building craft. People prefer authentic natural materials, which can also connect them to place and region.

Tangible transactions. LaVine (2001) articulated how building technology constitutes a metaphor for nature as *tangible transactions*, by which nature becomes manifest and available in human understanding. "Abstractions of the structure of the world arise from these acts of the human hand" (LaVine 2001). He describes such metaphors as ideas of *felt force* reshaped—"felt harvesting of resources from nature, the ability to understand the modification of these resources...as the felt action of hand tools," and inhabited form as empathetic with the human body.
Degrees of processing. More raw, less processed materials are generally perceived and interpreted as more natural. Bysheim and partners (2017) found people in and outside of the building community ranked wood materials from most to least natural in the order of: knot-free pine decking, painted pine, oriented strand board (OSB) and medium density fiberboard (MDF). The degree of transformation the wood had undergone, significantly impacted participants' visual understanding of its naturalness. They conclude that people understand the material's origin and connect with something familiar and personal, experiencing space as also more personal.
Natural origins and hand traces. Often materials bear the signs of their origin or creator. The imprints left on a sun-dried brick reveal the hands that shaped it. The material's appearance can connect occupants with the craftsmen who fashioned the material and, thereby bring them a step closer to the origin of the material itself. In his *Seven Lamps of Architecture*, Ruskin (1877) explains that the hand of the skilled artisan apparent in the work is necessary to embed life in architecture, writing,"The effect of the whole, as compared with the same design cut by a machine

or a lifeless hand, will be like that of poetry well read and deeply felt..." Michael Benedikt, in his influential *For an Architecture of Reality* (1987), observes, "Part of our appreciating the materiality of an object has to do with our appreciation of the natural origin of its substance and the manufacturing or forming process it has undergone."

Sense of place. In describing *critical regionalism*, Doug Kelbaugh (2002) articulates *sense of place* as a fundamental principle: "It honors local climate, topography, vegetation, building materials, and building practices. It prefers local authenticity to sophisticated imitation."

Psychological impacts. Visible wood grain influences mental states. Fell (2010) found that "wood provides stress-reducing effects similar to the well-studied effect of exposure to nature..." Browning and Ryan (2020) created a *health-to-impact grid* for biophilic design strategies that suggest a range for natural materials from *high impact* (raw, unprocessed, textured, local, patina) to *medium* (furniture, finishes, millwork, exposed structure) to *low* (faux and skeuomorphic materials). People discern differences between real and imitation materials; they overwhelmingly prefer real oak flooring over printed laminates on a variety of measures (Jimenez et al. 2016).

Design Guidelines

To narrate a relationship to Nature, choose real, natural and organic materials, expressed to visibly retain their origin and workmanship.

Selection. Choose materials that require little processing such as wood that reveals its grain, stone with its veins, brick with its reddish porousness that tells of its origins as clay (DeKay 2011). Other options include adobe, terra-cotta, ceramic tile, rammed earth and other stabilized earth products, such as compressed blocks, bamboo, cork, rattan, leather, lime plaster, canvas and exposed aggregate concrete. In the Good Materials pattern from *A Pattern Language,* Alexander and colleagues (1977) argue for ultra-lightweight concretes with densities of 40–60 lb/ft^3 (640–960 kg/m^3) and aggregates from vermiculite, perlite, pumice, etc, which can be cut and nailed.

Reality. Browning and co-authors (2014) recommend "real materials....over synthetic variations because human receptors can tell the difference between real and synthetic, so minimally processed materials from real nature are preferred." Such a narrative is subversive in its choices that reverse contemporary trends. To paraphrase Douglas Kelbaugh's (2002) observations about construction today, choose slate over asphalt, copper over aluminum, marble over plastic laminate, solid wood siding over profiled plywood and plaster over gypsum wallboard—each choice opting for natural, substantial materials and greater human care opportunity.

Evidence and degree of processing. Reveal traces of the tools, hands, forming and processes of making that shaped or refined the material. Specify types of processing or working that expose the craft of making: the hand of the trowel in plaster, chisel marks revealed in stonework, mortar strikes of the mason and joinery expressed (DeKay 2011). In general, less processing makes the origin of the material more evident.

Refine with S1 Veridical Patina. Help build N2 Authentic Matters and C2 Haptic Connection.

N2

Authentic Matters

conveys the nature of architectural substances by employing their inherent expressive, felt and functional qualities.

362 **Phillips Exeter Academy Library**

Exeter, New Hampshire, 1972
Louis Kahn, architect

Elegant, calm visual order reveals empirical gravity loads as the intersection of columns and jack arches in a single material.

photos Cemal Emden

see also
Shih et al 2010
Kahn + Futagawa 1975

next spread
Eelments Shaped Authentically
Diagram F

wood stone steel three tongues
without compelled translations
hear these walls speak truth

Each material has its nature, its intrinsic characteristics, and from these each has construction logics that work with and express its particular material nature. Designers possess powerful tools for nature affiliation in their selection, shaping, assembly and composition of materials. Inhabitants are connected to Nature when design develops material authenticity by fitting the use of materials to the forms made with them. A brick, as Kahn said, "likes an arch." Said another way, an arch tells us an authentic visual story about bricks working together, while a soldier course over a concealed steel L-section lintel narrates a fiction, occluding the powerful tensile nature of steel and suppressing the logics of bricks' compressive character. A genuineness of tectonic allegory honors with the eye and mind, in felt and rationally transparent ways, the quintessence of architecture's constituents. When inhabitants engage with well-shaped components, they learn something of Nature by the way the architecture interacts with the fundamentals of gravity and grain, heaviness and hardness. Form and its shaping process reveal Nature's order.

Kiln Tower, Brickworks Museum

Cham, Switzerland, 2021
Boltshauser Architekten

The composition reveals compression and tension in relationship: rammed earth blocks set on concrete foundation, stacked with wood sills, stressed by tension cables.

photo Kuster Frey

Phillips Exeter Library's four brick facades are load-bearing. The brick piers thicken at each level while windows change proportions and increase in width on upper levels. The window openings are spanned by jack (flat-bottom) arches; their spring-line radial as it intersects the column determines the width increase in the piers. Of the facade Kahn (1972) said, "The brick was always talking to me, saying you're missing an opportunity ... The weight of the brick makes it dance like a fairy above and groan below. Arcades crouch." Principle, material and form align to resolve the composition of arches and columns while revealing gravity's requirements (LaVine 2008).

Brickworks Museum's Kiln Tower walls are constructed of prefabricated rammed earth-blocks, prestressed with steel cables to resist seismic loads. Unfired compressed clay blocks alternate with timber sills extending slightly beyond with water drip edges that "protect the earth from erosion and illustrate the joining principle", say the architects (ArchDaily 2021). The exhibition room ceiling is solid timber, its character "defined by the presence of earth and the monumentality of the concluding kiln wall. Thanks to the light slits of the open joints, in front of which the prestressing elements run, visitors can experience the whole solidity of the rammed earth walls, that contrasts with the delicacy of the tension bars" (Divasare 2021). Felt compression and tension partner elegantly.

Authentic Matters

364 **Elements shaped authentically**

A **Mgt. Development Ctr.**, 1989 Ahmedabad, Anant Raje. Bhatt + Scriver 1990; Raje + Raje 2012

B **Indian Inst. of Management** Ahmedabad, 1974, Louis Kahn ArchEyes 2019; Kahn et al 1975

C **Farmers' Training Institute**, Palanpur, 1983, Anant Raje. Bhatt + Scriver 1990; Raje + Raje 2012

D **Indian Inst. of Mgt. Dorms**, Ahmedabad, 1974, Louis Kahn ArchEyes 2019; Kahn et al 1975

E **Entrepreneurship Develop. Inst.** Ahmedabad, 1985, Bimal Patel Arch Rev 1992; Patil 2022

F **Phillips Exeter Academy Library**

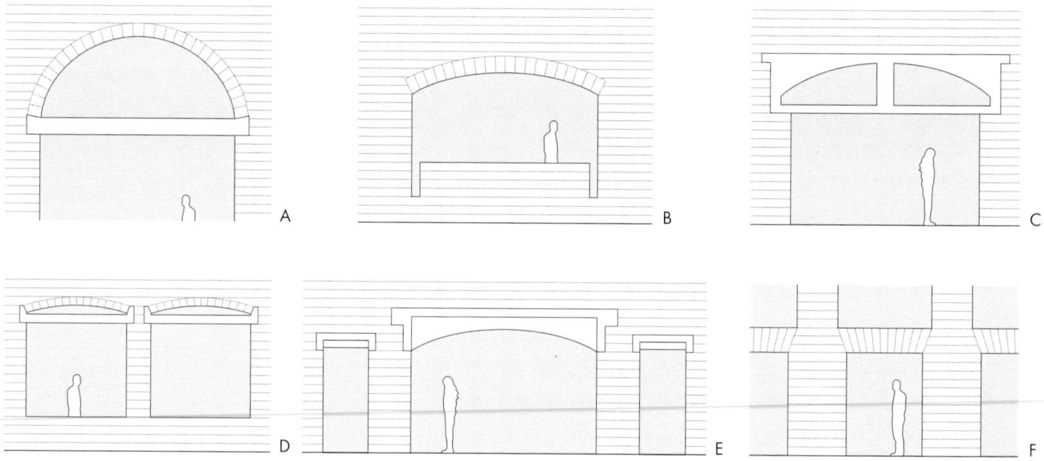

Supporting Evidence

Architectural materials and construction technologies both guide flows of empirical natural forces and provide felt, readable metaphors for how people are located within an understandably ordered Nature context.

Symbolic distinctions. The architectural technologies of wall, window and structural frame fundamentally constitute both symbolic and empirical distinctions as, respectively, separator from climate, connector of interior and exterior domains, and visible expression of humans' experience of the natural world as symbolized by architecture's response to gravity (LaVine 2008). Of these, gravity as expressed in the hierarchical order of structure, especially the roof, is the most visible expression of Nature's order. Buildings, as an inhabited nature-responsive technology, always serve to help their inhabitants understand the aspects of Nature to which the technology responds.

Organic architecture. Fay Jones practiced that, "the nature of materials is a very fundamental principle of organic architecture... Materials should be used in a way that conveys their strength and best qualities, letting each material—whether it is wood, stone, or steel—express its basic nature" (Dept. of Arkansas Heritage 1999).

Structural and material honesty is a Modern-era construct that can be linked to sustainability. Architect Ray Kappe (2009) expresses it as: "All of the material is expressed as it is, and it's not covered over." He advocates, therefore, a *non-layered* construction with fewer or even a single material performing all roles.

Empathetic Structure. Jacobson and co-authors (1990) argue that people can empathize with a building's structure if the form it takes expresses—or we might say *narrates*—the structural forces and roles at work. They suggest: "The bases of walls contract somehow with the top of walls. Make the bases wider and thicker, heavier and harder, composed of bulkier, larger-scaled elements that are darker, rougher and colder by contrast, the tops of walls will be lighter and more delicate, composed of small-scale details and elements."

Gravitational expectations. Steve Mouzon, author of *The Original Green* (2010) declares that humans "resonate with natural laws, such as the law of gravity. In other words, they don't just expect for things to stand up, but also to look like they are capable of standing up. Nobody except an architect wants to walk into a building built so thinly that it appears to be in imminent danger of collapse."

Design Guidelines

Employ an empathetic narrative that selects materials and configures them for the ways in which they contribute, by their nature, to an expression of visual structural logic reshaping gravity that is both readable and deeply psychologically satisfying.

Make space with structure, rather than with surfaces, as structure originates the fundamental order in a building. Begin the space-making process by thinking inside the logics of a particular construction system. This contrasts with the conventional practice of shaping with the surfaces of planes. Transcend reduction of space as arrangements of point, line and plane. Instead, build compositions from intentional systems, such as parallel bearing walls with wooden floor joists, heavy timber post and beam frames or concrete frames with composite steel and brick-vaulted floors. Each gives both unique expression and order, in plan and section, arising from its construction.
Shape structure expressively. Allen and Zalewski (2010) articulate a series of expressive principles, among them: 1. *Expose structure* as integral to the architecture: "A concealed structure is opportunity lost." 2. *Express structural action*: "People enjoy *reading* a structure that is self-explanatory." 3. *Express connections* to give "life and excitement" as they "are the adjectives and adverbs of a structure." 4. *Demonstrate how it was built:* "People enjoy seeing how a structure is put together." 5. *Establish structural rhythms* to enhance architectural experience.
6. *Show force defiance*: A structure is more satisfying when it gives the appearance of carrying the loads with ease.
7. *Intensify primary character:* Enhance reading primary elements with chamfers, recessed panels, color and joints.
Layer less to support occupants at more effectively reading the structure. Fewer materials is almost always more elegant. In skeletal structures, the exterior skin, interior finishes or fireproofing may easily occlude the structure and its connections. Select systems that building codes allow to be uncovered. Slender steel columns encased in seemingly thick gypsum wrappers isolate inhabitants from the meaning possible in unconcealed construction
Shape elements authentically. Arches and their derivatives, vaults, domes and buttresses, arise from the nature of compressive materials spanning wall openings or spaces. A monolithic structure can "express itself and the natural load paths are revealed to demonstrate support" (Lewis 2020). Form them veraciously from massive components, or from concrete, rather than wood or high-tensile materials tortured into shape. Use brick and stone primarily for their load bearing; veneers reveal themselves. Lintels are seen and not hidden
Relate span to space. Each material has spatial constraints and opportunities that give it characteristic order. Patterns of primary to tertiary spans suggest the hierarchical order of gravity as proportional to mass and distance.
Refine with N1 Perceptible Provenance and S1 Veridical Patina. Help build N3 Distinguishable Durability and G3 Existential Datum.

N3

Roof Terrain

can be shaped to collect rainwater and to direct it to storage, visibly narrating the building's role in the hydrologic cycle.

366 **Thread Artist Residency and Cultural Center**

Sinthian, Senegal, 2015
Toshiko Mori, architect

The thatched roof carefully and clearly focuses the path of rainfall towards open public spaces. From underneath, it provides a clear visual map of flows.

photo Iwan Baan

as land shapes rivers
so our canopies conduct
the tears of heaven

Buildings can express or occlude how they interface with rainwater. In some buildings the occupants' awareness of the hydrologic cycle is found only in the six inches (150 mm) between faucet and basin drain. Yet, in truth, buildings form an important link in the hydrology of developed areas—and, potentially, in inhabitants' understanding. They also provide shelter, meaning that most of the time people are indoors while rain falls on the roof. Even so, one can look at some buildings on a dry day and visualize how rain falls on the roof and what paths runoff would take. In others, the process is hidden behind parapets, the roof itself can not be easily seen or it is so flat as to conceal its primary reason for being. Hiding the building's relationship with rainwater suppresses the potential conveyed significance of water's cycle. Alternatively, we are connected to nature when we understand and celebrate the ways that human constructions integrate functionally—via formal pattern—with the ecological system's cycles. Both the fundamental shelter feeling from within and the hydrologic order of building as a watershed express in the roof.

Josey Pavilion
Dixon Water Foundation

Decatur, Texas, 2014
Lake | Flato, architects

Simple roofs, exposed detached gutters and visible storage combine for rational transparency of rainwater flows, expressed with simplicity and elegance.

photo Casey Dunn

Thread Artists' Residences and Cultural Center inverts the regionally typical pitched thatch roof to define two oval courts and direct rainwater to water canals ringing the courts that convey runoff to two covered water reservoirs. The dipping slopes of the bamboo-structured roof system can be seen from outside and experienced from underneath, as the interior volume follows the roof. Rainwater provides about 40% of the villagers' needs in a dry area with 200 mm/yr (8 in) rainfall. The scheme aligns shaded social space under roofs and in open courts, with a clear narrative emblematic of the importance of water (Divasarc 2015; Fixsen 2015).

Josey Pavilion is a demonstration and education project to promote sustainable livestock management that restores its dry landscape watershed. Two offset gabled-roofed volumes with exposed structure cover indoor and semi outdoor spaces. Metal roofs direct rainwater outward to half-pipe metal outrigger gutters, detached from the roof edge to reveal runoff; gable roofs share a detached gutter at their joint. Each connects to visible vertical rain-leaders that feed a cistern or, in one case, to a rain chain and concrete channel leading to a visible swale. Rainwater supplies non-potable building uses and irrigation. Rationally transparent, the project manifests the meaning of a ranch architecture integrated with the site hydrology (ILFI 2021; AIA 2015, ArchDaily 2020).

Supporting Evidence

Roofs are significant symbols, primordial conveyors of felt shelter and a typological place signifier. Their interaction with rainfall gives occupants an understanding of and participation in one of nature's essential processes.

Expression of shelter. Max Jacobsen and co-authors (2005) go so far as to say that, "One of the defining comforts of home is the feeling of being enveloped by a simple, sloping roof." In their pattern, *Sheltering Roof*, they argue that the roof is the primary meaning-carrying element, especially for homes, and that the experience of its volume, inside *and* outside, expresses how the building is inhabited.
Roof meanings. Gaston Bachelard (1994) described that the roof "tells its *raison d'etre* right away: it gives mankind shelter from the rain and sun he fears. Geographers... [remind] us that, in every country, the slope of the roofs is one of the surest indications of the climate. We *understand* the slant of a roof." Norberg-Schulz writes that a roof "emphasizes horizontal and vertical relations as they express a particular mode of connection between heaven and earth," and saw roof shape as playing "a significant role in distinguishing one place from another" (van Nes 2012). Roof form, therefore, combined with local construction can be place-empathetic.
Revealing nature's order. Heidegger (1993) extolled the *self-revealing* of nature's order, contrasting, for example, wind mills with hydro-elecrtic dams, arguing for a transparency rather than concealment of primordial forces. The bringing forth of otherwise invisible infrastructure can be made visible by architectural form. Roof shape is somehow a contentious issue for Modernist architects who, like Le Corbusier (1931) in his *five points* of modern architecture, argue for flat roofs. While expressive of 20th century architecture and technology, the flat roof can neither express a sense of shelter nor provide a biophilic metaphor of connection to nature's water events.
Poetic participation. Dwelling within architectural form that responds to natural force, residents come to know Nature's dynamics and participate in it. Philosopher Henry Dicks (2014) describes such human participation as "a distinctly poetic dimension". "The poetic metaphor of *rainwater harvesting*, for example, implies a renewed connectivity to the seasons, as well as a sense of autonomously reaping what one sows..."

Design Guidelines

Shape the roof, as ordered catchment, such that it directs runoff to discernible points or lines of conveyance. Make sure the roof shape is visible from both outside the building and from the occupied underside within the building.

Roof terrain schemes can creatively narrate the building's relationship to rain in diverse ways (see diagrams).
Shape to chronicle flow. While water will flow across a smooth roofing membrane at a slope of 1/4 in per ft (1.2°) or less, a flat roof does not connote that flow for occupants. Increase the roof slope to dramatize the effect. Historically, roof slope is correlated to both building materials (thatch needs a steep slope) and to rainfall (steeper in wet climates); therefore regional influences might nuance the symbolism. Thousands of variations among roof types and collection types are possible, as exemplified in the diagrams. In all cases, strive to construct the forms

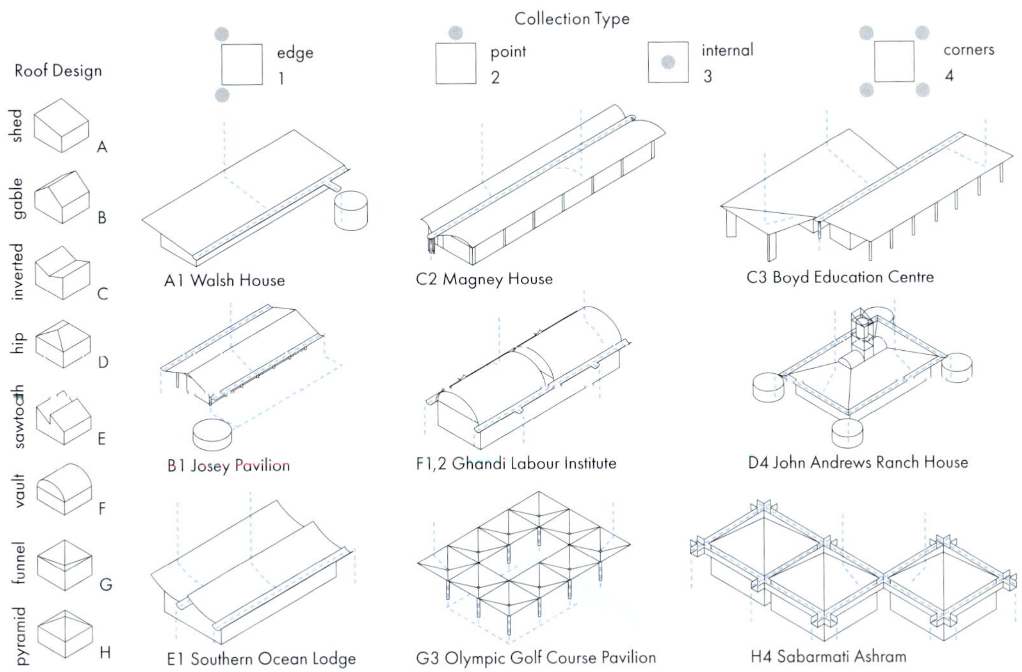

Roof terrain schemes

Each example is a combination of primary roof design type and rainwater collection type. Many other variations are possible.

A1 Glenn Murcutt
Kangaroo Valley, Australia, 2005

B1 Lake|Flato
Decatur, TX, 2014

E1 Max Pritchard
Kingscote, SA, Australia, 2008

C2 Glenn Murcutt
Bingie, NSW, Australia, 1984

F1,2 Balkrishna Doshi
Ahmedabad, India, 1986

G3 RUA Arquitetos
Rio de Janeiro, Brazil, 2015

C3 Glenn Murcutt
Illaroo, NSW, Australia, 1999

D4 John Andrews
Eugowra, NSW, Australia, 1980

H4 Charles Correa
Ahmedabad, India, 1915

visibly and logically, such that occupants can mentally map the flow of rain runoff to the conveyance elements, such as valleys and gutters, runnels, rain chains, etc.

Construct visibility from outside. The roof narrative can be emphasized by designing it for visibility from building entrances or other common vantage points, such as pedestrian routes, balconies or roof terraces from which occupants are more likely to view the building.

Construct visibility from within. Organize the building in section such that portions of the outdoor roof and outdoor terraces are visible from indoors, such as from dormer windows. Most importantly, in the most significant space—and anywhere on upper floors—shape the interior ceiling volume congruent with the exterior roof form. Then, from under the roof volume, an occupant imagines the roof terrain's watersheds and rivulets above.

Shape the roof to enclose inhabited space. Much has been written on the essential psychological effects of the sheltering roof. From within, a more enclosing shape creates greater feelings of shelter and protection. Bring the edges down and expose the structure, as it is the visible map of gravity.

Refine with N2 Authentic Matters and F3 Revealed Conveyance. Help build F4 Compluvium Shower and C4 Engage the Rain to create a fully expressed rainwater system.

N3

Distinguishable Durability

visibly and formally expresses differences among a building's more durable and its less permanent elements.

370 **Monterrey Incremental Housing**

Santa Catarina, Mexico 2010
Alejandro Aravena
ELEMENTAL, architects

Durable structural frames give rhythm to public space and orders incremental self-build infill construction.

photo Ramiro Ramirez

skeletons and skins
decay and near permanence
rollick in banter

Both durability and impermanence can express connections to Nature. Buildings are situated within a dynamic living system with forces of climate, biodegradation and human use, among others, acting on them constantly. The apparent static nature of buildings is a temporal illusion when, in fact, maintenance is perpetual; architecture is more fugacious, more fleeting, than typically imagined. All life manifests in cycles, including the life of building materials and systems. For plant-based materials, the longer a building element lasts, the longer it sequesters carbon. For abiotic materials, such as metals, a durable life span means less life-cycle embodied energy in manufacturing and recycling and a more responsible use of finite resources. The design challenge of this schema is to narrate and evince the range from durable, long-lasting elements and systems to those with shorter life. In doing so, buildings serve to metaphorically chronicle the processes in which architecture immerses inhabitants. This, in turn, situates people in a visible field where they may affiliate with Nature and sense cultural continuity.

Harvard Art Museums Expansion

Cambridge, Massachusetts, 2014
Renzo Piano Building Workshop + Payette Assoc (Boston), architects

Lightness contrasts against mass; durable fixity, with assembled flexure.

photo Pygmalion Karatzas

Monterrey Incremental Housing was built as a porous structure of solids and voids, with only 50% of the affordable units enclosed (ArchDaily 2010; Arkinka 2013). The difficult half—stairs, kitchens and baths—is part of the initial construction phase; owners self-build additional space over time within the covered voids. The initial structure is concrete floors and roofs with concrete masonry walls, while infill can be wood or any construction the inhabitants choose. Ground floor flats and two storey apartments above have space to grow. Durable structural components and dividing service walls provide urban unity, rhythm and continuity, while the infill portions allow for variety, adaptation and owner expression. Durability denotes community while impermanence and individuality align.

Harvard Art Museums Expansion combines the 1927 Fogg Museum with a new addition on one side, while a glazed roof bridges old and the new over a courtyard, creating an atrium, allowing controlled daylight for labs, study centers and galleries. The extension adds three stories, using concrete, structural steel and cedar siding in a distinct contemporary expression that contrasts the preserved historic brick exterior and replicated Renaissance marble courtyard facades. By articulating the landmarked stereotomic original against the addition's light, airy flexibility and more ephemeral feel, relatedness and time become visible (GA 2015; Bucci 2014; Domus 2016).

Distinguishable Durability

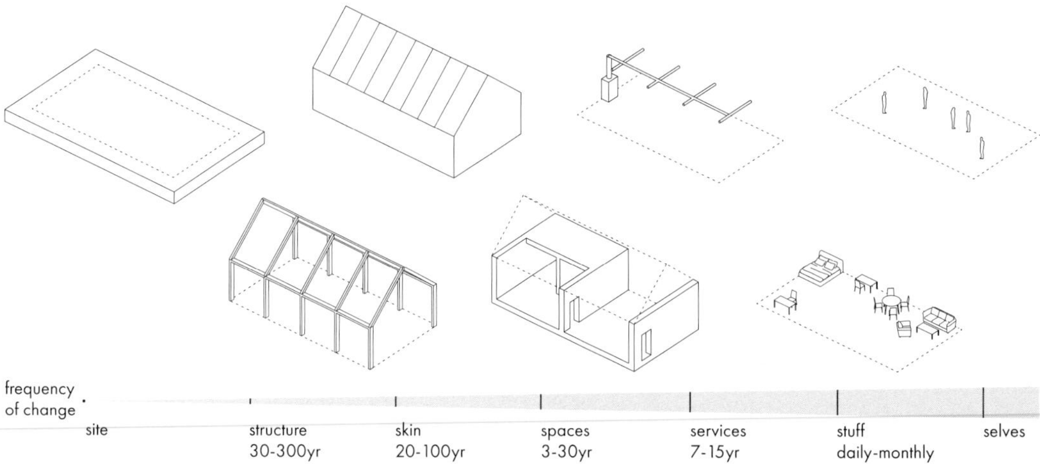

372 **Shearing layers of change**

Different building components have vastly different life spans and change rates.

developed from concepts in Brand 1994

Supporting Evidence

Increased durability and longer service life impact sustainability in terms of materials consumption, embodied energy and life-cycle cost. Building components have various service life spans, which is more complex than material characteristics. Perdurable buildings with life spans measured in centuries expresses a continuity of culture and a stewardship ethic toward built and natural environments.

Building life span averages in Britain, Australia and New Zealand 50–60 years; in the US, 35 years and in some parts of Japan, 20 years (Storey 2002), due to a combination of use changes, materials and maintenance. **Shearing layers of change** was outlined by Stewart Brand in *How Buildings Learn* (1994), writing that, "Because of the different rates of change of its components, a building is always tearing itself apart". Layers have to be replaced at different rates. *Site* and property definitions are long-lived, often seeing a series of buildings erected on them. "The site is eternal." *Structure* ideally lasts the life of the building, 30-300 years, or more. Foundations may actually be reused in subsequent buildings. Contemporary exterior *skin* lasts about 30 years, but brick or stone can last 100 or more. Windows have a life of 50-80 years, depending on maintenance. *Services*, such as wiring and plumbing, are often upgraded in less than 50 years, while HVAC components and elevators might have a life of 15 years. *Space* plans, including interior walls, doors, ceilings, etc, churn from a low of three years in some commercial spaces to perhaps 30 years or more in houses. Surfaces like paint and carpet change frequently. *Stuff*, such as furniture, changes daily or monthly, and the *Selves* inhabiting spaces are changing moment-to-moment. **Environmental impacts**. Durability can be considered a cornerstone of sustainability. Durability plans are required under LEED for Homes and the nonresidential LEED Canada. "A durable building—one that lasts a long time—

provides a long period of time to amortize the environmental and economic costs that were incurred in building it" writes Alex Wilson (2005). Construction cost, raw materials, embodied energy, and carbon footprint are all reduced when components last longer.

Maintenance drives durability in many cases (Wilson 2005), particularly for exterior skin materials and floors.

Lovable Buildings. "If a building cannot be loved, it will not last; it does not matter what the carbon footprint of a building is once its pieces have been carted off to the landfill" argues Steve Mouzon (2018). Such lovable nature transcends design as fashion and depends on incorporating "patterns that reflect timeless aspects of our humanity."

Design Guidelines

Design buildings to express at once long-lasting durability and an elegant adaptability to change. This argues for buildings that begin life more *conventionally*, that is, fit to their present, and through time become more *radical*, as unforeseen changes impact their adaptation (Brand 1994). The structural frame and structural walls, interior or exterior, have to be durable. Non-structural components offer adaptive affordance.

Intend timeless buildings with quality meant to last that Brand describes as *high-road* buildings, while *low-road* buildings can also be durable if designed as readily adaptable to changing circumstance. Reveal and express primary structure so that reconfiguration and change are easier to imagine.

Keep the least durable the most accessible. Separate services from skin and structure. Cables, wires and power have shorter life spans. Owners will need access, therefore design for maintenance and replacement with solutions such as cable troughs, surface-mount wire mould, dedicated chases and conduits in baseboards.

Honor the past. Borrow from vernacular local traditions that are fit to stable conditions of climate. Employ traditional materials and well-known construction techniques that wear well and are unlikely to fail. More timeless expressions of contextual responsiveness provides cultural continuity and a buffer against future calls for demolition based on the passing style of the once avant garde.

Allocate more budget to the durable (structure) than to finishes. Financially plan for long-term maintenance and ongoing adaptations, along with replacements to the more short-lived layers.

Choose durable, low-maintenance materials. Considering maintenance, environmental and replacement costs, investing in more durable materials is often justified on a life-cycle basis.

Plan adaptive opportunity by organizing structure and space in rectangular patterns that are easier to subdivide and add on to. In contrast, unique shapes and complex geometries might be used for uses and spaces that, with certainty, will not need to be reconfigured. Make the roof simple. Simple roofs have fewer leaks and are easier to add on to when the inevitable expansion occurs.

Avoid room use overspecialization. Timeless structure is more associated with a strategy of *long-life/loose-fit* in which the primary construction and spatial order is robust enough to accommodate some changes in use.

Refine with C2 Haptic Connection and N2 Authentic Matter. Help build R4 Radiant Sailing.

N5

Three Realms

connects occupants to the diverse natural and symbolic worlds of subterrane, surface and sky.

374 **Antinori Winery**

Bargino, Italy, 2012
Archea Associati, architects

The project integrates three levels of occupancy with the earth and sky of its productive landscape.

photo top Leonardo Finotti
photos mid + lower Pietro Savorelli e Associati

see also
Turtle Creek House
Chapter 4 Introduction

starry canopy
telluric plane, chthonic realms
vast vicinity

This schema describes three interrelated experiences that metaphorically enact a representation of the cosmos, potentially in a single building. The connection, both symbolic and physical, is among subsurface space, the earth's surface and the sky. Each zone offers a distinct visual opportunity, climatic affordance and relationship to nature. Archetypally, the underworld, the horizontal plane of the Earth and the dome of heaven form the ancient cosmos—a mythical conception extrapolated from human experience lived on ground, pervasive across many global cultures, told in story and illustrations.

Each arouses distinct feelings. Below ground, people may feel rooted, a distinct protection (such as from storms), a sense of calm from minimized sensory inputs and greater access to their subconscious. The horizon orients them with the plane of human inhabitation and the thin layer of green life. Looking down from high places (as if in the heavens), life appears with greater clarity as taking this prospect offers a god-like perspective of integrating wholeness. Looking up to contemplate the sky, clouds and stars changes the occupant's perspective once again and takes finite humans' thoughts outward to infinite worlds. Environmental conditions also vary with level. Underground, earth and stone elements dominate; light is at its minimum; temperatures, cooler and more stable. The wind is calm. Noises rarely penetrate, but reverberation abounds. In ground-floor rooms, one feels the sun. Daily cycles reign. The breeze can be admitted, and views to nature can be impelled. Above ground, and especially from high places, climate is the most extreme, but that price buys a new sense-making view on the world below. While the contemporary mind can comprehend the abstract facts of a heliocentric planetary system, the sense-making derived from life as a sensate, sentient being remains today a powerful influence on the body and mind.

Antinori Winery deeply roots its structure into its rural hillside in the Chianti hills of Tuscany and attempts to merge with its landscape (wikiarquitectura, nd). From the exterior, the building almost disappears with only two thin strips of facade following the contours, each with a planted roof terrace. Multiple realms each carry a unique atmosphere. A circular staircase connects the vaults below, where wine is stored, to the upper-level terrace that provides an elevated view of the landscape beyond its edge and is itself planted, becoming occupiable farmland, cultivated with vines. Circular openings in the roof planes admit daylight. The level between is the most highly trafficked. Here, sky views are framed. Downward, a deep well into the Earth emphasizes the connection among all three levels and "conveys, with its darkness and the rhythmic sequence of the terracotta vaults, the sacral dimension of a space which is hidden." With wine storage in the cool earth, the winery building type holds the perfect potential for this schema. The architects describe the project as having the most authentic expression of "a desired symbiosis and merger between anthropic culture, the work of man, his work environment and the natural environment" Their intent: "to pursue, through architecture, the enhancement of the landscape and the surroundings as expression of the cultural and social valence of the place where wine is produced." (ArchDaily 2013; AV 2014).

Supporting Evidence

Environmental psychologists tend to associate each realm's conditions with different evolutionary preferences for prospect, refuge, mystery, awe and aesthetic complexity.

Phobias and philias. Some people may feel *claustrophobic* in more enclosed underground space, *agoraphobic* if places feel too open, or *acrophobic* at heights. In contrast, well-designed buildings can make use of human attractions to various spatial conditions: the comforting sense of *hygge* (Billie 2019), coziness and *claustrophilia* possible in the subterrane (Boschi 2022); *topophilia* (Tuan 1974) and *biophilia* (Wilson 1984) at the landscape level and the *acrophilia* (LeBlanc 2011) seen as people flock to observation towers and penthouse lounges atop high-rise buildings.

Below ground spaces insulate occupants from much external stimuli, such as sound, light, and daily temperature rhythms, even social connections. Such places of low arousal promote some degree of sensory deprivation (Paulus, 1976), a potential problem for long-term occupancy, but not for intermittent use. They can also be an aid to focus, productivity and stress reduction (Carmody + Stirling 1984).

Sinking Floors, the term used by Thiis-Evenson (1987), suggests a depressed condition that intuitively is the same as penetrating the ground. To build into the ground, he finds, is to have an encounter and experience of "the earth's primeval forces, with the rough and natural, with death, water and fire," and with confinement rather than freedom.

High Places. In contrast, a raised floor, the occupiable roof being its extreme, is associated by Thiis-Evenson with the sky, nature's roof, creating an experience of absolute freedom. Alexander and co-authors (1977) in the High Places pattern understand "the instinct to climb up to some high place, from which you can look down and survey your world" as seeming to be "a fundamental human instinct." Such high places also function as an orienting device that can be seen from far away. Corbu's advocacy of roof terrace living was not simply to gain more functional space, but to take a vantage on the world.

Design Guidelines

Design the project in section to have occupants experience all three realms and to physically move among them with ramps or stairs. Activate the physical spaces with uses and sensory experiences fit to the nature of each realm.

Three realms in two houses suggest several design alternatives for essential prospect and enclosure typologies:

Casa Cala uses the *raumplan* prototype of spiraling overlapping double height spaces. The submerged level looks onto walled gardens east and west. "As we go up we feast our eyes on a panoramic view of the urban landscape of the east of Madrid" (Baeza 2016). The main level looks north to a terrace and garden and south to a pool terrace. Rooftops are planted with jasmine and vines. Upper levels offer both prospect on the city and sky view framed by the walled court (AV 2021a; Jauze 2015).

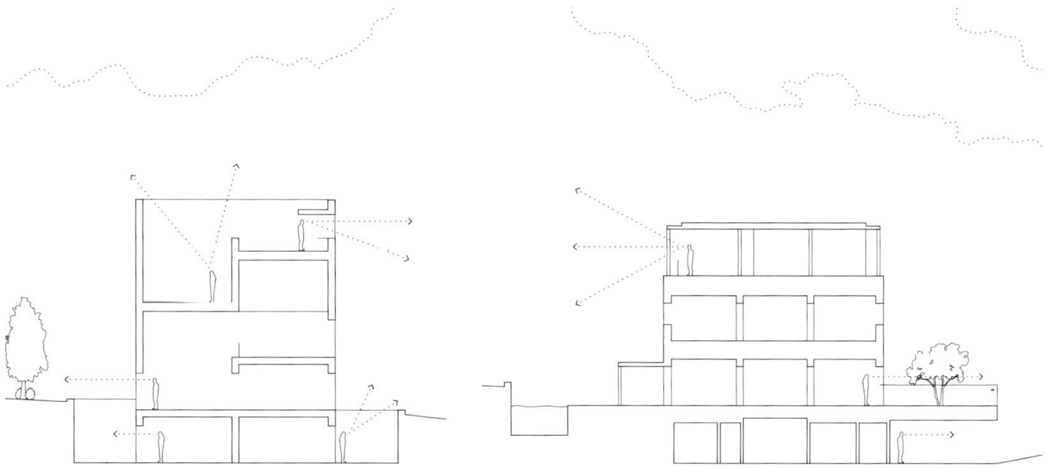

Three realms in two houses

left
Casa Cala
Madrid, Spain, 2015
Alberto Campo Baeza, architect

right
Casa Rotonda
Madrid, Spain, 2021
Alberto Campo Baeza, architect

Casa Rotonda sits on a sloping site, its three storeys on a podium, with rooms opening to walled courts carved into the earth. The main level establishes connection to the horizon with extended garden terraces and pool. The upper level provides 360° panoramic landscape views from a glass belvedere wrapped with roofed balconies and a deeply shaded terrace (AV 2021b; Arias 2022).

Embed meaning. Narrative schemas depend on the meaning embedded in the design becoming a real potential to be experienced. Therefore, articulate the contrasts in intended perceptions and feelings, the ways that the design helps the occupant to view and relate to the world differently from each perspective.

Distinguish each realm. Use materials (perhaps a range from massive to lightweight), degrees of enclosure (from close views and controlled daylight to expansive views and openness) and biotic nature (a range of vertical habitats) to emphasize connections to nature in three distinct ways.

Provision light, view and ventilation. As some people suffer from claustrophobia, consider that underground space can still have natural light, views to the outside or courtyards and good ventilation. For strategies, see Earth Edges in DeKay + Brown (2014). Alleviate these issues by offering options to easily connect the below ground spaces with above ground spaces and designing them for short-use occupancy.

Consider the alternatives.

1 *Subterrane*: basement, wine cellar, grotto, sunken court, terraced slope, crypt, cave.
2 *Surface*: earthen floor, veranda, picture window, extended roof, continuous floor surface.
3 *Sky*: tree house, balcony, widow's walk, roof terrace, open-to-sky court, observation deck.

Refine with G3 Existential Datum, C4 Inhabited Periphery and R4 Habitat Fringe. Help build S6 Topographic Perambulation and N6 Situated Scenes.

N6

Situated Scenes

steward visual resources, touching the earth lightly with a relating, non-consumptive gaze to nature.

378 **Pine Forest Cabin**

Methow Valley, Washington, 1999
Cutler Anderson, architects

The arrangement of framework elements blends partially with the surrounding forest, yet also delineating and emphasizing it —as in a good dialogue.

photos Art Grice

see also in chapter 2
Nordic Pavilion, Venice Biennale

subtle frames curate
fitting view to this domain
no thoughtless vistas

Buildings offer the inhabitant an intimate experience of participating in and belonging to Nature. This can include an individual dwelling in the lived moment and, by narrative extension, humanity at large—as the collective embrace belonging to a larger natural order. Architecture frames humans' Nature experience in the contemporary world; what it *means* depends on the design. How people understand Nature is largely determined by how architecture presents and interprets it *visually*—as an object in perspective or, instead, as a continuity of life where the built and natural environments constitute a co-defining network. In the former, the building communicates the relative identity, position and power of observer and observed; in the latter, a wholeness. Design can narrate an objective view of building-in-Nature *and* a more participatory view, with neither primary. Additionally, Nature occurs as what is seen out the window and as the view from afar of architecture in context. Both are important as visual resource and psychological support; each can be treated in consumptive or in conservative ways.

Pine Forest Cabin

A view though expressed, naturally finished, vertically-dominant wood framing recalls the elements' origins in the view.

photo Art Grice

see also
View + habitat layering
diagram in R4 Habitat Fringe

Pine Forest Cabin, situated in its eponymous biome, offers superb views to the surrounding woods via large windows with carefully articulated glazing divisions. While designed to connect inhabitant via view to the forest, the scale of the window framing is delicate, more expressed and related visually to the trees outside. The scale, siting and minimal tree-cutting give a connected visual relationship to Nature. The structural support members mimic the verticality of the exterior trees and, in form and material, suggest continuity and arboreal origins. From the outside, the house further blends into the site context, appearing neither in stark contrast nor incognito, rather, in subtle conversation with the forest. Trees are not clear-cut to maximize a view to beyond; rather the developed view is layered. The tempering of both internal and external views, along with scale and siting, help promote the over-arching idea of participating in the natural landscape (Wheeler et al. 2009; Olson et al. 2008; Olson 2004).

The visual nature of the pine trees on this site, with trunks of spare verticality and airy branches in the upper reaches....would provide little opportunity for discreetly placing a structure. Instead, the residence had to become an object that was of its surroundings, embodying the characteristics of the landscape.

—Beth Wheeler 2009

Post-modern thought emphasizes understanding all phenomena in context. Rather than the analytic subdivision, understanding a building requires placing it into its larger context. Contextual thinking profoundly impacts designing *views to* and *views from* buildings. To Moderns, views become visual resources to be consumed—thus extensive glass intended to connect occupants to Nature, yet in all non-visual ways isolating them.

WELL standard for view

> 75% of workstations and conference room, lecture hall and classroom seating [shall] have direct line of sight to indoor plants, water features and/or nature views (IWBI 2020).

Supporting Evidence

The construction of views to and from buildings narrate ideas of the relationship between people and Nature as context. Elements can be both literal and metaphoric.

Narrative elements. Stephen Kieran (2008) develops an environmental aesthetic "derived from an integral, not an additive relationship with the natural world" that expresses an innate biophilic resonance with Nature. In terms of views from buildings, he advocates for the skin as a filter of dynamic processes, both functionally, such as shading and daylight penetration, and as natural metaphor. For example, two such situated metaphors associated with view are filtering light, as though trees in a forest, and looking out among columns, suggestive of the site's trees. Similarly, some of KieranTimberlake's buildings viewed from the outside, give expression to site geology, hydrology and vegetation, such as this description of the Loblolly house as "among and above the trees, a tree house," and "as seen from the east or land side, is of the forest and in the forest." Such scenes narrate a relation among building, human occupancy and Nature.

Liminal linking. Kent Bloomer (2008) distinguishes the Modern large *picture* window as allowing occupants to see Nature, interpreted as subordinated, without actually engaging it. In contrast, he makes a case for constructing a thickened threshold with liminal elements of the natural world or symbolic ornamented abstractions of plants at the edges of windows or as mullions and subdivisions. To Bloomer, window designs, such as seen in Wright's houses, are "critical thresholds of viewing" that "establish a visible and touchable moment of mediation between inside and outside." The building skin is an extended psychological boundary, and a perceptually thick edge can link inside and outside and establish occupants in significant relationship.

Multiple benefits. Views of living landscapes are known to have multiple benefits. Studente and co-authors (2016) found that visual creativity was improved by subjects' exposure to natural views and plants. Mental fatigue, arising from information inherent in the surrounding world and within one's cognitive landscape, can be combatted with appropriately engaging views, as "fascinating situations... provide time to recover from mental fatigue" (Kaplan et al. 1998). Views provide occupants opportunities for wayfinding and orientation as well as aesthetic pleasure (Kaplan et al. 1998). Connections with Nature, such as green views, are associated with improved mood, stress and overall health (Browning et al. 2014; Ulrich 2001). Shemirani and colleagues (2011) found that children (age 9–11) prefer to work or sit near windows for access to daylight and interesting landscape views.

Connectedness to Nature. Some of the beneficial outcomes associated with Nature may be explained by a person's sense of their connectedness to Nature. People vary in the extent of their subjective connection to Nature, and studies suggest that those who report feeling more connected tend to have more pro-environmental attitudes and behavioral similarities, such as greater engagement in outdoor activities (Nisbet et al. 2008). A person's sense of Nature connectedness appears to be positively correlated with psychological and social well-being, as well as happiness (Capaldi et al. 2014; Howell et al. 2011).

Design Guidelines

Construct views to and from buildings to express dynamic integration and connection between building and site, viewer and Nature. Layer natural elements, materials and even abstracted site or natural forms to create linking transitions between inside and outdoors.

Design views to the building from the site or on approach that set it within and as a member of its built and natural context. Do not treat the building merely as a formal visual object, which often emphasizes contrast with its surroundings. Situated views emphasize the relatedness of forms and processes across scales.

Design views from the building that help inhabitants understand the building as situated in its context. Communicate a relationship between people and Nature as living community in which neither viewpoint position nor photographic-like moments are fixed. Postmodern Nature is not the *natural resources* of Modernism but a participatory web-of-life. It follows that views will be less like formal compositions that privilege sight and treated more as a visual component of a whole-body continuity from indoors to outdoors.

Frame views and vistas. To keep the view fresh and exciting, utilize smaller, choice framing of views to the exterior rather than vast, expansive ones; overconsumption of a view deadens the senses to it. Balance framed views with at least one vista that allows an overview of the surrounding area.

Calibrate layered interior views from one space to another such that internal spaces produce dialogue with each other. This engages occupants more than when the space is presented all at once or when rooms are discretely isolated from each other.

Shape windows to indicate important aspects of what is on the other side. For example, a vertical proportion is read as related to the human form and can emphasize the verticality of trees or the height of a mountain. A horizontal proportion can emphasize a relation to the horizon or a lake and is associated with the primarily horizontal gaze of the human pivoting head.

Thicken building edges by using natural materials in the view that either correspond abstractly or literally in form or material to natural site elements. In different locations these might refer to trees, native plants, earth or rock.

Layer views both horizontally and vertically. *Vertical layers* include sky, landscape and ground. *Horizontal layering* refers to depth: foreground, middle ground and background. Whether in a single view or in a series of several views, variability applies here also. Refer to the *View + habitat layering* diagram in R4 Habitat Fringe.

Make view a standard criteria. Ensure that the majority of occupied space has access to unobstructed external views. To optimize student performance, natural light and unobstructed window views of at least 50 ft (15 m) are recommended; it is preferable if those views "overlook some form of life" (Tanner 2008).

Refine with N5 Three Realms and G5 Pockets of Shadow.

Narrative Sources

Introduction

Campbell, Joseph. 1949. *The Hero with a Thousand Faces*. New York: Pantheon

N1 Perceptible Provenance

A4L. 2022. Low Energy House. Architecture for London, architectureforlondon.com

Alexander, Christopher, Sara Ishikawa + Murray Silverstein. 1977. *A Pattern Language: Towns, Buildings, Construction*. New York: Oxford University Press, #207 Good Materials, 955–961

Benedikt, Michael. 1987. *For an Architecture of Reality*. New York: Lumen Books

Browning, William D + Catherine O Ryan. 2020. *Nature Inside: A Biophilic Design Guide*. London: RIBA Publishing, 250

Browning, William D, Catherine O Ryan + Joseph O Clancy. 2014. *14 Patterns of Biophilic Design: Improving Health + Well-being in the Built Environment*. New York: Terrapin Bright Green

Bysheim, Kristian, Anders Nyrud + Kristen Strobel. 2016. *Building Materials and Well-Being in Indoor Environments. A Focus Group Study*. Oslo: Norsk Treteknisk Institutt, 88

DeKay, Mark. 2011. *Integral Sustainable Design: transformative perspectives*. Ed. Susanne Bennett. London: Earthscan, 367, 369

Detail. 2009. Sidwell Friends Middle School in Washington, DC, *Detail* 49(9): 920–921, 998

Fell, David. 2010. *Wood in the Human Environment: Restorative Properties of Wood in the Built Indoor Environment*, PhD Dissertation, University of British Columbia

Jiménez, Paul, Anita Dunkl, Kerstin Eibel, Elisabeth Denk, Vincent Grote, Christina Kelz + Maximilian Moser. 2016. Wood or Laminate?—Psychological Research of Customer Expectations. *Forests* 7(275): 11

Kelbaugh, Douglas S. 2002. *Repairing the American Metropolis: Common Place Revisited*. Seattle: University of Washington Press, 84–85

Kieran–Timberlake. 2009. The Long-Term Beauty of Untreated Western Red Cedar, 28 May. kierantimberlake.com

Kieran, Stephan. 2008. Evolving an Environmental Aesthetic, in Kellert, Stephen R, Judith H Heerwagen + Martin L Mador, Eds, *Biophilic Design: The Theory, Science, and Practice of Bringing Buildings to Life*. Hoboken, New Jersey: Wiley, 243–251

LaVine, Lance. 2001. *Mechanics and Meaning in Architecture*. Minneapolis, Minnesota: University of Minnesota Press, 111–113

Levy, Natasha. 2022. Architecture for London Uses Natural Materials to Renovate Studio Founder's Home. *deZeen*, 31 Jan. dezeen.com/2022/01/31

Patil, Manali. 2022. Entrepreneurship Development Institute by Bimal Patel: A Sequence of Spaces. *Rethinking the Future*, 19 Mar. re-thinkingthefuture.com/case-studies/a2649

Rocha, Mauricio. 2020. Brick Award 2020 Winner: Iturbide Studio, Mexico. video. brickaward.com

Ruskin, John. 1877. *The Seven Lamps of Architecture*. New York: John Wiley

Santibañez, Danae. 2021. Iturbide Studio/ Taller de Arquitectura Mauricio Rocha + Gabriela Carrillo [Estudio Iturbide/ Taller de Arquitectura Mauricio Rocha + Gabriela Carrillo]. *ArchDaily*, 22 Oct. archdaily.com/906832

N2 Authentic Matter

Allen, Edward + Waclaw Zalewski. 2010. *Forms and Forces: Designing Efficient, Expressive Structures*. Hoboken, New Jersey: Wiley, 601–602

ArchDaily. 2021. Kiln Tower for the Brickworks Museum/ Boltshauser Architekten. *ArchDaily*, 24 Nov. archdaily.com/972419

ArchEyes. 2019. Louis Kahn's Indian Institute of Management in Ahmedabad. *ArchEyes*, 17 Sep. archeyes.com

Architectural Review. 1992. Courageous Criteria [Aga Khan 1992 Award winners]. *Architectural Review* 191(1148) Oct: 50–65

Bhatt, Vikram + Peter Scriver. 1990. *Contemporary Indian Architecture: After the Masters*. Ahmedabad, India: Mapin Publishing

Department of Arkansas Heritage. 1999. *Outside the Pale, The Architecture of Fay Jones*. Fayetteville, Arkansas: University of Arkansas Press, 78

Divisare. 2021. Boltshauser Architekten: Kiln Tower for the Brickworks Museum. *Divasare*, 23 Dec. divisare.com/projects/452787

Jacobson, Max, Murray Silverstein + Barbara Winslow. 1990. *The Good House: Contrast as a Design Tool*. Newtown, Connecticut: Taunton Press, 70–71

Kahn, Louis I, Yukio Futagawa + Romaldo Giurgola. 1975. *Indian Institute of Management. Ahmedabad. India,1963–; Exeter Library, Phillips Exeter Academy, Exeter, New Hampshire, USA, 1972*. Tokyo: ADA Edita

Kahn, Louis. 1972. in Ada Louise Huxtable, New Exeter Library: Stunning Paean to Books, *The New York Times*, 2 Oct, 33

Kappe, Ray. 2009. in *The First Living Home and Its Sustainable Approach with Steve Glenn and Ray Kappe*. video. re:Source Network films

LaVine, Lance. 2008. *Constructing Ideas: Understanding Architecture*. Dubuque, Iowa: Kendall/Hunt, 139, 114–115

Lewis, Nigel C. 2020. *Design and Order: Perceptual Experience of Built Form, Principles in the Making of Place*. Hoboken, New Jersey: Wiley, 551

Mouzon, Steve. 2010. *The Original Green: Unlocking the Mystery of True Sustainability*. Miami: New Urban Guild Foundation

Raje, Shubhra + Amita Raje. 2012. *Anant Raje Architect: Selected Works 1971–2009*. New Delhi: Tulika Books

Shih, Chih-Ming, Fang-Jar Liou + Robert E Johnson. 2010. The Tectonic Integration of Louis I Kahn's Exeter Library. *Journal of Asian Architecture + Building Engineering* 9(1) May: 31–37

N3 Roof Terrain

AIA. 2015. The Dixon Water Foundation Josey Pavilion. Top Ten Project. American Institute of Architects Committee on the Environment (COTE). aiatopten.org/node/476

ArchDaily. 2020. Dixon Water Foundation Josey Pavilion/ Lake|Flato Architects. *ArchDaily*, 2 Nov. archdaily.com/772041

Bachelard, Gaston. 1994. *The Poetics of Space (La poétique de l'espace): The Classic Look at How We Experience Intimate Places* (Maria Jolas, trans). Boston, Massachusetts: Beacon Press

Dicks, Henry. 2014. A Phenomenological Approach to Water in the City: Towards a Policy of Letting Water Appear. *Society and Space* 32(3): 417–432

Divsare. 2015. Tokisho Mori: Thread Artist Residency and Cutural Center. *Divisare*, 18 Mar. divisare.com/284611

Fixsen, Anna. 2015. THREAD: Artists' Residence + Cultural Center. *Architectural Record* 203(6)16 Jun: 82–87. architecturalrecord.com

Narrative Sources

Heidegger, Martin. 1993. The Question Concerning Technology, in Krell, David Farrell, Ed, *Basic Writings: Martin Heidegger*. Oxford, UK: Routledge, 311–341

ILFI. 2021. Betty and Clint Josey Pavilion. includes video. *International Living Futures Institute*. living-future.org

Jacobson, Max, Murray Silverstein + Barbara Winslow. 2005. *Patterns of Home: The Ten Essentials of Enduring Design*. Newtown, Connecticut: Taunton Press

Le Corbusier. 1931. *Towards a New Architecture* (Frederick Etchells, trans). New York: Dover

van Nes, Akkelies. 2012. The Heaven, the Earth and the Optic Array: Norberg Schulz's Place. Phenomenology and its Degree of Operationability. *Environmental and Architectural Phenomenology* 23(1) Winter: 7–12

N3 Distinguishable Durability

ArchDaily. 2010. Monterrey Housing/ELEMENTAL. *ArchDaily*, 9 Mar. archdaily.com/52202

Arkinka. 2013. Elemental Monterrey, Monterrey, México: Elemental—Alejandro Aravena, Gonzalo Arteaga, Fernando García-Huidobro, Ramiro Ramírez (arquitectos)—2007–2009. *Arkinka* 17(215) Oct: 18–25

Brand, Stewart. 1994. *How Buildings Learn: What Happens After They are Built*. New York: Penguin Books, 13, 190

Bucci, Federico. 2014. Tutto è Riproducibile Anche Il 'Rinascimento'—Una Serra Per Una Esotica Concezione Americana: [Renzo Piano, Harvard Art Museums, Cambridge, Massachusetts]. *Casabella* 844(20 Dec): 30–51

Domus. 2014. RPBW: Harvard Art Museums. *Domus*, 19 Nov. domusweb.it/en/architecture

GA. 2015. Renzo Piano: Harvard Art Museums Renovation and Expansion, Cambridge, Massachusetts, USA, design 2006–09, construction 2010–14. *GA (Global Architecture) document* 131: 60

Mouzon, Steve. 2018. Buildings Should Comprise a Visible Base, a Middle No More Than Seven Stories Tall, and a Top, in Farr, Douglas, Ed, *Sustainable Nation: Urban Design Patterns for the Future*. Wiley, Hoboken, New Jersey, 216–217

Storey, John B. 2002. Designing for Durability, in Janis Birkeland, Ed, *Design for Sustainability: A Sourcebook for Integrated Ecological Solutions*. London: Routledge, 46–51

Wilson, Alex. 2005. Durability: A Key Component of Green Building. *Environmental Building News* 14(11) Nov: 1, 11–19

N5 Three Realms

Alexander, Christopher, Sara Ishikawa + Murray Silverstein. 1977. *A Pattern Language: Towns, Buildings, Construction*. New York: Oxford University Press, #62 High Places, 315–318

ArchDaily. 2013. Antinori Winery/ Archae Associati. *ArchDaily*, 13 May. archdaily.com/371521

Arias, Javier. 2022. Tribute to Palladio: Rotonda House by Alberto Campo Baeza. *Metalocus*, 3 Jan. metalocus.es

Arquitectura Viva. 2014. Hipogeo de Vides—Antinori Winery, San Casciano Val Di Pesa [Italy]: Archea Associati. *Arquitectura Viva* 160: 52–55

AV. 2021a. Casa Cala = Cala House, Madrid, Spain, 2013–2015: [Alberto Campo Baeza]. *AV Monografías* 236: 94–99

AV. 2021b. Casa Rotonda = Rotonda House, Madrid, Spain, 2017–2021: [Alberto Campo Baeza]. *AV Monografías* 236: 108–111

Baeza, Alberto Campo. 2016. Cala House: A Raumplan houseMadrid/ Spain/ 2015. *Archilovers*, 5 May. archilovers.com

Bille, Mikkel. 2019. *Homely Atmospheres and Lighting Technologies in Denmark: Living with Light*. London: Bloomsbury Academic

Boschi, Antonello. 2022. *Poetics of Underground Space.* Abingdon, UK: Routledge

Carmody, John + Ray Sterling. 1984. Design Considerations for Underground Buildings, *Underground Space* 8(5–6): 352–362

DeKay, Mark + G Z Brown. 2014. *Sun, Wind + Light: Architectural Design Strategies*, 3rd ed. Hoboken, New Jersey Wiley, #76 Earth Edges, E.208–210

Jauze, Colette. 2015. Casa Cala in Madrid. *Domus*, 1 Nov: 74–83

LeBlanc, Jim. 2011. The Acrophobe and the Funambulist: Existential and Cinematic Perspectives on the Phenomenology of Extreme Vertical Space. *Emotion, Space and Society* 4(1):1–7

Paulus, Paul B. 1976. On the Psychology of Earth Covered Buildings. *Underground Space* 1(2):127–130

Thiis-Evensen, Thomas. 1987. *Archetypes in Architecture.* Oslo: Scandinavian University Press, 75–83

Tuan, Yi-fu. 1974. *Topophilia: a Study of Environmental Perception, Attitudes, and Values.* Englewood Cliffs, New Jersey: Prentice-Hall

Wikiarquitectura. nd. Antinori Winery. en. wikiarquitectura.com

Wilson, Edward O. 1984. *Biophilia.* Cambridge, Massachusetts: Harvard University Press

N6 Situated Scenes

Bloomer, Kent. 2008. The Picture Window: The Problem of Viewing Nature Through Glass, in Kellert, Stephen R, Judith H Heerwagen + Martin L Mador, Eds, *Biophilic Design: The Theory , Science, and Practice of Bringing Buildings to Life.* Hoboken, New Jersey: Wiley, 253–261

Browning, William D, Catherine O Ryan + Joseph O Clancy. 2014. *14 Patterns of Biophilic Design: Improving Health + Well-being in the Built Environment.* New York: Terrapin Bright Green

Capaldi, Colin A, Raelyne L Dopko + John M Zelenski. 2014. The Relationship Between Nature Connectedness and Happiness: A Meta-analysis. *Frontiers of Psychology* 5: 976

Howell, Andrew J, Raelyne L Dopko, Holli-Anne Passmore + Karen Buro. 2011. Nature Connectedness: Associations with Well-Being and Mindfulness. *Personality and Individual Differences* 51(2):166–171

IWBI. 2020. WELL v2, Q2 2020, Concepts/Mind/Feature 09, Enhanced Access to Nature, Part 1, Provide Nature Indoors. *International Well Building Institute.* v2.wellcertified.com

Kaplan, Rachel, Stephan Kaplan + Robert L Ryan. 1998. *With People in Mind: Design and Management of Everyday Nature.* Washington: Island Press, 18, 99–100

Kieran, Stephan. 2008. Evolving an Environmental Aesthetic, in Kellert, Stephen R, Judith H Heerwagen + Martin L Mador, eds, *Biophilic Design: The Theory, Science, and Practice of Bringing Buildings to Life.* Hoboken, New Jersey: Wiley, 243–251

Nisbet, Elizabeth K, John M Zelenski + Steven A Murphy. 2008. The Nature Relatedness Scale: Linking Individuals' Connection with Nature to Environmental Concern and Behavior. *Environment and Behavior* 41(5): 715–740

Olson, Sheri, Alicia Kennedy + Theresa Morrow. 2008. *The best of Cutler Anderson Architects.* Gloucester, Massachusetts: Rockport

Olson, Sheri. 2004. *Cutlor Andorson Architocts.* Gloucoctor, Massachusetts: Rockport

Narrative Sources

Shemirani, Seied, Gholam Memarian, Shahnaz Naseri, Hashem Nejad + Vahid Vaziri. 2011. Investigating the Behaviors of the Elementary School Students in Reference to Factors Associated with Daylight. *Asian Social Science* 7(3): 237–248

Studente, Syvie, Nina Seppala + Noemi Sadowska. 2016. Facilitating Creative Thinking in the Classroom: Investigating the Effects of Plants and the Colour Green on Visual and Verbal Creativity. *Thinking Skills and Creativity* 19:1–8

Tanner, C Kenneth. 2008. Explaining Relationships Among Student Outcomes and the School's Physical Environment. *Journal of Advanced Academics* 19: 444–471

Ulrich, Roger. 2001. Effects of healthcare environmental design on medical outcomes. *Proceedings of the Second International Conference on Health and Design*, 1 Jan, Stockholm

Wheeler, Beth, James Cutler, Tom Schworer + Art Grice. 2009. *Searching for True: Cutler Anderson Architects*. New York: Rizzoli, 258–269

5

Reflections and Prospects

With all the problems of the world that could be addressed by buildings, why do we focus on human experience? It might seem an ephemeral luxury or something superfluous to the utility of buildings, perhaps merely a more complex way to talk about aesthetics. The answer is that our *Why*, our shared intention, is to contribute to solving the climate crisis while ennobling the human experience. We are activists in all our academic work.

We have spent our careers focused on making a measurable difference in the ways buildings use resources, how buildings can fit with Nature and on improving the satisfaction of occupants. As it turns out, these realms are mutually reinforcing. For example, when buildings can use natural ventilation for some or all of the warm season, inhabitants are inherently more related with and connected to their climate and place. Passive heating, cooling, lighting and ventilation reduce energy use and greenhouse gases while bringing greater variability of environmental conditions, which as we have outlined already, gives many opportunities for delight. The same is true for active systems tuned to climatic rhythms and employed only as needed. We see a direct connection between designing for delight and reducing greenhouse gases.

In addition to this linkage, there is evidence that when people have meaningful Nature experiences, they act in environmentally proactive ways. We are confident that there is truth in this, so much so that essentially all the schemas are oriented to bring building inhabitants into more significant relationships with Nature (broadly defined) and ultimately to foster greater care for Nature. This form of activism is a call to the whole building community to recognize, celebrate and act from humanity's profound connection to Nature. Architects, engineers, builders and other members of the community that build our places have an enormous contribution to make, one that simultaneously helps solve the climate crisis and deepens the beauty in the world.

The means to this end has for us, and we believe for most building professionals, seemed elusive up until now. What has been missing was a way to communicate about experience, something missing in our disciplinary languages. More than that, in a professional context of collaborative team-produced practice, we found little means in the professional literature—or in the daily conversations and critiques that fill design school review rooms—to clearly express and share the design intentions for subjective, qualitative slippery human experiences. Within our horizons, we found few tools or methods to help shape buildings to deliver delight. We offer in this book a beginning.

Villa Melana

Tyros, Greece, 2014
Valia Foufa + Panagiotis Papassotiriou, architects

photo Pygmalion Karatzas

Distinctions as empowering design conversations

To fill in the gap in the disciplinary vocabulary for architecture-Nature experience, we have begun the process of defining schemas in a particular way. In this way of thinking, naming stands for the complex articulation of a distinction. To generate a distinction is to name and define it such that something shifts from an undifferentiated background to occur in the foreground of awareness (Landmark 2004). The distinction of the schema generates a field of possibility for experience that is always situated in space and in Nature. In this approach, distinguishing a schema begins in a clear, open body-mind state that is as free as possible from an overabundance of previous concepts. Once a schema is named or distinguished, supported by its precedents and exposition, the creative design process can be accelerated. Architectural experience concepts come into being. Similar to the way that ecology became possible when biology had thoroughly classified and observed the varieties of life, as we name experiences in buildings and discover their spatial patterns, the potential emerges for more complex and sophisticated languages of architectural experiences—what can be imagined as spatial ecologies of felt form.

Schemas, when effectively distinguished, empower the designer by bringing forth new possibility from previously unidentified patterns, thereby transforming the sensed into the known. Schemas provide conceptual access in a form such that the qualitative may be cognized and incorporated into a design process. In presenting the schema concepts and their conceptual frameworks (described in Chapter 1), the response from professionals was often something like, "This is what we have been trying to do in our firm, but we had no language to communicate about it with each other."

Distinguishing as a developmental capacity

With practice, anyone can distinguish a new schema. To become conscious of the connections among space, forces and experiences, one constructs a first-person awareness for *feeling-in-form*. To distinguish is itself experiential in the same way that riding a bicycle cannot be learned by studying about it or conceptualizing it or intellectually understanding it—the bicycle must be ridden until the embodied phenomena of balance it felt. Once one *gets* bike riding, one permanently owns the distinction. Like the development of any type of intelligence, developing a fine-tuned ability for architectural experience requires attention, effort and practice over a long time. This discovery (or rediscovery) of inhabitation's felt qualities may seem challenging to some current beliefs, to particular disciplinary or cultural convention or to Modernist-mechanist comfort ideas. However, such an enhanced awareness can also feel personally intuitive, empowering and supportive. Designers, as the formers for inhabitants of the possibility of feeling, must build their own direct understanding of architectural experience. Otherwise, the concepts in the schemas will remain inanimate and empty. Instead, designers' experiential consciousness, born of careful sensory curation and reflection, animates the form and embeds it with life, giving rise to the possibility of transferring the same experiences to others. One practices experiencing in order to practice experiential designing.

Distinguishing schemas begins with sensation. Sensations and emotions are bodily and automatic—instantaneous—below and before thought. The emotions are the building blocks of cognition. The sea of unspecified pre-cognitive phenomena, when distinguished and identified, gives being to the thought objects on which cognition operates. If emotion is thought about, it becomes feeling. Thoughts about feelings can become ideas. Ideas ordered in the mind become systems of thought, ecologies of ideas. Sensation begins the chain.

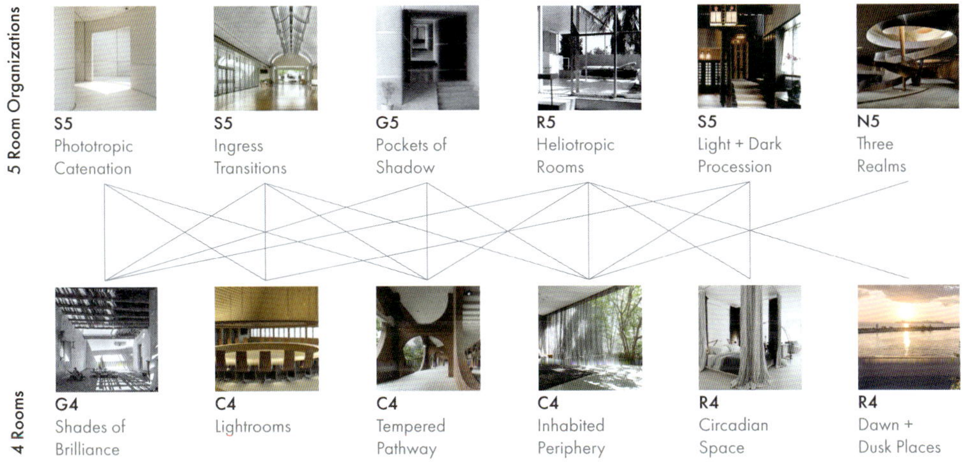

Schemata language map, excerpt

full map in Front Matter

Distributions of conditions

C Contrast
G Gradient
R Rhythm
S Sequence
F Flux
N Narrative

Designing sensory experiences also therefore begins with developing sensitivity to sensations. Forming designs to engender feeling compels the designer to develop on the emotional intelligence line, to attend to a rich inner life of affect, sentiment and empathy. We suggest that designers explore the schemas as potential experiences for themselves, as realities that many times can be found in the buildings one inhabits, visits or passes by every day. The more one directly apprehends the schemas as clearly articulated experiential distinctions, and explores how their effects are created in space, the more agile one can become as a designer of experience.

Design languages as co-arising contexts

Each schema distinguishes a realm of complexity and scale in a network of larger and smaller, more and less complex territories. In this sense, each schema exists in a language-like context that depends on mutual definition with other schemas. In physical terms the schema language forms a nested spatial network, as outlined in the Schemata language map (above). More complex schemas organize less complex ones. Less complex schemas help build more complex ones. Each sensory condition—sun, light, sound, heat, moisture, air, earth, life—crosses scales from small to large, linking schemas from materials to site complexity.

The schema distinctions name and call out while also making use of the more specific vocabularies of psychological, physical and biological phenomena, spatial order and interpretive backgrounds. Each of these vocabularies also constitutes a system of naming and defining, that is, of distinguishing, with its validity established by its respective discipline and by the awareness level employed within a particular disciplinary perspective. A language of experiential design schemas is, therefore, intertwined with other languages.

In distinguishing from the complicated noise of human life the nexus of space-conditions-experience that defines a schema, the designer is empowered to both become the *former of feeling* and to connect human experience to the other essential design progenitors. Design composes form, utility and idea; it engages social, technical and aesthetic agendas, and has been classically characterized by the essential criteria of firmness, commodity and delight. The schemata language, therefore, contributes to design's wholeness, but does not define its entirety. How an experiential schemata language interweaves and co-arises with other design languages emanating from alternate perspectives is a thorny question considered in the subsequent section on Four Languages. However, first, we need to address the question of how individual schemas might be related or combined to support larger ideas, more encompassing atmospheres. Consider the following constellation hypothesis.

Constellations as related families of schemas

To address how schemas come together in related families that construct more complex or sophisticated compositions we propose the idea of *constellations*. In one sense, design schemas are building blocks of larger entities. Individual schemas are not, in most cases, significant enough to drive a building's primary form and organization. Schemas work in concert with each other, clustered around larger integrating themes or motifs. These may be mostly focused on experience or integrated with other agendas.

Experiential design schemas can be organized to generate larger, more consistent or impactful human experiences, especially in typological situations and where human response is relatively consistent. This is a domain for much future research and development, as we are just beginning to understand how little is known about the complexities of how designers create the most powerfully moving architecture. At present, two types of schema interactions generating ideas of greater complexity occur as possibilities:

1 *Related combinations of design schemas at approximately the same scale*, such as schemas that activate multiple senses to create intensified experiential nodes, as in a great courtyard oasis.

2 *Related combinations of design schemas across multiple scales* that build experiential sequences or build a more pervasive and encompassing atmosphere.

Let us call these families of related schemas *constellations*. For example, multiple schemas might be combined and aligned in schema constellations to generate a matrix field of possible experiences such as, among many:

- The expression of the hydrologic cycle in a building designed as rainwater harvesting system
- A sacred atmosphere in a house of worship
- The sense of an integrated world that comes from connecting people to Nature in multiple ways
- A series of encounters that builds Nature awareness and higher levels of Nature consciousness

Knowledge Domain		Design Knowledge Module	Related Modules Family	Compositional System
Experiences	[I]	Schema	Constellation	Schemata language
Cultures	[WE]	Narrative	Suite	Metaphoric language
Behaviors	[IT]	Strategy	Bundle	Performative language
Systems	[ITS]	Pattern	Community	Pattern language

Four architectural languages

From each fundamental knowledge domain, the design knowledge that occurs can be organized and shared as discreet modules, families of related modules and ultimately in a language-like compositional system. Together these form an integral design meta-language.

Perspectival languages integrated as meta-language

A schema is a type of knowledge module for designing experiences. To speculate on integrating schemas with other kinds of design knowledge, consider the proposition that schemas combine in related families as constellations and constitute elements in a *schemata language* that is much larger than the set of schemas in this book. We offer a further proposition that experiential schemas can, when combined with other design knowledge systems, help construct a meta-language of architecture.

Four architectural languages (table), summarizes diverse perspectival knowledge systems. Using the four fundamental perspectives (Behaviors, Systems, Culture and Experiences) explained in Chapter 2 Integral Experience, each perspective can be considered in parallel, each with its own knowledge modules arising from its respective (quadratic) methods and values as outlined next.

Experiential design schemas constitute the distinctions that arise from the value proposition of the Experiences Perspective (I-realm, individual subjective). Thiis-Evensen's (1987) archetypes are phenomenological in intent and frame a system complementary to schemas, one linking feeling and space.

The strategies from *Sun, Wind + Light* (DeKay + Brown 2014) are one example of knowledge modules based in scientific and engineering knowledge and originating from the Behaviors Perspective (It-realm, objective) of how things work and behave in the empirical world. They combine as *strategy bundles* in a complex *performative language*. Bundles are families of strategies that work together to solve some recurring architectural problem of heating, cooling, ventilation, daylighting or microclimate. Example bundles include: Neighborhood of Light, Passively Cooled Building, Outdoor Microclimate and Responsive Envelope.

The Systems Perspective (Its-realm, interobjective) is well represented by the design *patterns* in the classic, *A Pattern Language*, the structure of which Alexander and colleagues (1977) describe as a cross-scalar semi-lattice. Its full expression is a *pattern language*, which refers both to the totality of design patterns and to the specific set of patterns that forms the language for a building. Similarly, Roös's (2021) *Regenerative-Adaptive Design for*

Sustainable Development employs a pattern language approach that sets big design ideas in a reconstructive and integrally-informed view that connects systemic ecological patterns with beauty, cultural meaning and performance. Pattern thinking is also employed in his recent (2022a) *A Biophilic Pattern Language for Cities*. Roös employs the term pattern *community* for an association of patterns (Roös 2022b).

Finally, in architecture, the Cultures Perspective (We-realm, intersubjective) employs signs and symbols to create built *narratives*. These are linked to the interpretive contexts of worldviews. Five worldview narratives about design with Nature are unpacked with their design implications in *Integral Sustainable Design* (DeKay 2011) and further elaborated more specifically for climate change in a later paper (DeKay 2018). More complex interweaving of narratives can be thought of as a *suite*, analogous to a suite in music, which is an ordered set of instrumental movements. Collectively this perspective primarily employs a *metaphoric language*. Comprehensive narrative systems as shared building language are most easily seen in place-empathetic building cultures (described in Chapter 2), such as advocated by LaVine (2010).

Of these four architectural design languages, the metaphoric language and schemata language, arising from the subjective perspectives, are the least developed for contemporary application. The language of architectural experiences has been initiated in this book, a logic of multisensory and process aesthetics and atmospheres. In doing the work, we found a gaping hole in the literature. We could not find any comprehensive works that were simultaneously focused on human experience and offered a strategic approach framed in applicable design terms. We found little if anything that explicitly offers design guidance for multi-sensory aesthetics or how to induce joy—thus, our efforts here.

Architectural experience as construct-challenging

Writing a book about designing for experience, we sought explanations for what people feel in buildings and how they get related to Nature through architecture. In digging through the scientific and disciplinary literatures in search of evidence that could connect design to positive experiences, we found that some things are well-understood, while other ideas are more speculative or poorly researched. In short, the knowledge in this territory is very unevenly developed.

From five years of investigation, what follows are some assessments that bear directly on the scientific knowledge-based approach to designing experience. These caution the designer that the field is adolescent and imply fertile domains for future research. They identify key areas where scientific research tends to under-examine precisely the questions for which a knowledge-based designer wants answers. Although it came as somewhat of a surprise to us, it remains one of the primary lessons taken from our attempts to connect research evidence to design guidance.

Finding the *philia*

Messolonghi Lagoon,
Greece, 2017

The Messolonghi-Aitoliko lagoon complex in the Gulf of Patras, with its shallow area between Acheloos and Evinos Rivers, is an important Mediterranean wetland. The Tourlida settlment is named for a marine bird species, the *tourlides* (eurasian curlew). Local stilt houses, *pelades*, are built by fishermen.

photo Pygmalion Karatzas

Chapters one and three have already outlined in some detail that the building disciplines—in research, practice and in industry standards—have been much more attuned to avoiding occupant discomfort in buildings than in the study and creation of inhabitants' positive experiences. We have addressed in-depth the building community's propensity to promote neutral and comfort conditions, rather than delight and even more positively valent states beyond comfort. In addition, we offer the following assessments and correlated questions, not in the mode of a literature review for an academic journal, rather, as generalizations gleaned from study and experience.

State of experiential scientific evidence (table on next spread) summarizes what is more and less currently known about the knowledge domain of this book.

Nature outside/nature inside. For many people, the most meaningful Nature experiences occur when immersed outdoors, also the setting of most Nature-response research. Nature inside needs equal study, even more if we weight toward where people spend their time. This book argues for a nondual idea of Nature that does not begin at the building envelope. Rather buildings are human habitat where Nature interpenetrates as abiotic forces, as biota that can live in and on architecture and ultimately as participatory human ecosystems. Nature is in buildings as much as buildings are in Nature. Much more study of the physiological, cognitive and emotional responses to biophilic design as indoor Nature is needed (Browning + Ryan, 2020). What elements of biophilic design in what building typologies need more investigation? Can building science dissolve the culture inside/nature outside duality while also adopting a more sophisticated form language for building enclosure, such as shown in C4 Inhabited Periphery?

Finding the missing *philia*. Scientific evidence confirms the general value to people of Nature connections but few of its details or mechanisms. It is particularly silent on the *philia* of biophilia, the love-of-Life. Beyond stress reduction and attention restoration, how can philia be engendered by design? How does the love in *love-of-Life* get catalyzed by design-with-Nature? How can biophilic design lead to greater environmental stewardship and care of built and natural environments?

Accessing the absent affinity. From the literature, it occurs that the more complex the human response, the less it can be predicted by scientific methods. It seems that—in order of how much researchers know about and are able to describe and predict—we find a wide range. Drawing on a previously outlined model from Chapter 1, the Nested Experiential State Complexity, that sequence of topics, from greater to lesser evidence is: sensation, emotion, awareness, affinity. Sensation is more predictable than affinity. Can building research create a new construct for complexity? Could such a construct deeply interrogate human interiors, penetrate the nature of peak experiences in buildings, and steer knowledge explorers to investigate states well beyond comfort?

Reclaiming the rhythms of place. Traditionally, people responded to climate first by behavioral change, such as clothing patterns, daily schedules and flexible uses of architectural space. As technological advances in mechanical heating and cooling systems and international building practices permeate a culture, indoor inhabitants become more isolated from daily and seasonal Nature rhythms and lose their socio-cultural sense of place. We ask researchers to ask, "To what extent do culture and social norms affect building practices, standards and individuals' comfort attitudes or expectations?" and "How might comfort attitudes, experience and conditioning practices affect culture?" (Brager and deDear 2003). What would a collaborative, transdisciplinary building research agenda look like that explored connecting culture experientially to place?

Experiential delight as social justice. The book's approach embraces equity, diversity and inclusion. Everyone deserves delight regardless of relative prosperity of people or place. Both research and design focus too heavily on discovering and providing acceptable conditions (minimizing dissatisfaction) for average or standard populations. However, humans run the gamut from hyper-sensitive to hypo-sensitive. Can our disciplines not enable sensory diversity? Designing for neurodiversity—the range of brain function and behavior from neurodivergent to neurotypical—needs accurate knowledge to inform it. In buildings, what drives dissimilarities in perception and feeling? How different are people and, in being more inclusive, how much range can architecture accommodate? Can neurodevelopmental research be translated for the design community and applied to the larger population? What schemas can design for the desire spectrum from serenity to stimulation? (HOK 2019, LMSa 2022)

Toward manifold time scales. Studies of human response to environmental conditions frequently and more easily focus on momentary experience. Much less is known about longer-term experience, particularly relevant to residential and workplace settings where people spend most of their time. How does exposure to the dynamic

More Known	Less Known
Avoiding discomfort	Creating positive experiences
Neutral + comfort conditions	Delight + beyond-comfort states
Single senses	Multiple senses interacting
Single room	Sequences of rooms
Simple spaces	Complex spatial order
Momentary experience	Manifold time scale expereinces
Conditions steady-state	Conditions dynamic in time
Conditions indoors	Conditions in-between indoors + out
Conditions uniform in space	Conditions non-uniform in space
Conditions passively received	Conditions actively engaged or controlled
Conditioning by air delivery	Conditioning by radiant delivery
Comfort produced mechanically	Comfort produced passively or hybridly
Nature outside	Nature inside

State of experiential scientific evidence

Less-studied topics offer frontiers for investigation and challenges to develop better investigative methods.

fluctuations of a place—hourly, daily, seasonal—impact physiological, psychological, emotional and cognitive responses? Does multi-year inhabitation with quality schemas have cumulative impact on neural mechanisms, expectations and preferences? Do these contribute to sustained positive experience and overall life quality? How does regular daytime circadian light exposure, as well as other patterns of environmental conditions, impact sleep quality and the following day's health or over longer run?

From environmental patterns to their effects. Distributions of conditions, such as wind flows around buildings, acoustic behaviors, daylight distribution, envelope heat and air flows, or indoor temperature and air movement fluctuations, can be predicted (with some user expertise required) by contemporary simulations with relatively dependable probability. Knowledge about how these patterns are created by natural or mechanical forces, or about their objective impacts, such as on energy use, air quality, sound reverberation and carbon emissions, far exceeds that about how the same environmental patterns are perceived. How does occupant behavior, such as actively modifying forces by adjusting façade elements, affect their experience of conditions in space? How do designers find feelings in the figures of Nature's forces?

From physiological to psychological response. The present state of scientific evidence shows that the link between indoor or outdoor environmental conditions and correlated physiological response is more predictable than researchers' current understanding of how conditions in buildings and Nature are linked to perception and emotional responses. For example, interest in architectural neuroscience is relatively recent. Can building research questions and methods be expanded from a focus on the physical and relatively simple subjective responses to study the psychologically sophisticated phenomena of happiness, well-being and awe? How can findings about hedonic and eudaemonic experience be translated to building design and operation? (Altomonte et al. 2020)

Researching the (whole) human being. Individual senses are more well-studied than their combined effects. The more complex the sense interactions, the less in known about their effects on human feeling. This appears to be especially the case for architectural settings. As an inquiry system is required that engages more complex human affect, so is a disciplinary core of principles that values the whole human being in well-being. What new research questions (and therefore methods) would arise from a shift in the essential understanding of humans toward more complex, developmental, multi-sensory, body-mind-spirit-integrated beings inhabiting buildings as their native habitat? How can researchers from the building, social and health sciences better collaborate to address these vexing issues? Can knowledge about alliesthesia and interactions between sensory modalities provide insights into the complexity of whole-being response?

Manifesting multi-sensory experience. There is a wealth of human response research studying singular environmental stimuli in isolation (for example, thermal, lighting or air quality). Yet this does not adequately reflect people's complex multi-sensory reality, which is especially pronounced in Nature-connected environments. A window view on a warm summer day can be comprised of static or moving objects accompanied by shaded and reflected delightfully cool daylight or by overheating solar radiation. A cooling breeze via an open window also conveys outdoor smells and sounds, pleasant or otherwise. The building community needs more multi-domain or multi-perceptual research that investigates stimuli interactions and crossed effects. Such studies link perception with behavioral outcomes and include the impacts of contextual and personal variables (Schweiker et al. 2020). Many studies lack a theoretical foundation; how can multi-disciplinary approaches, with building scientists, psychologists and neuroscientists collaborating, develop such foundations to add more explanatory power to the findings and help them become more generalizable? While conducting field studies in realistic settings is ideal, it is fraught with challenges; how can researchers introduce more realism in laboratory studies?

Escaping spatial poverty. Building science research most often studies human response in controlled or simple spatial situations. Examples include an environmental chamber (close in spatial terms to a primitive hut), a single room or an open office. While whole building field studies are becoming increasingly common, their associated research questions are often relatively bounded. Habitation patterns (behavior, movement, physiological and feeling responses) in complex spatial arrangements are rarely studied. Scientifically we currently know little about them. This is particularly relevant in hybrid buildings where occupants move between zones of actively-controlled relatively consistent conditions and passive zones where conditions follow climatic rhythms. What knowledge becomes possible when building science evolves its fundamental spatial constructs from Rooms (level 4 in the schemas network) to the complexity of Room Organizations (L5) and Whole Buildings (L6)?

Driving in the dynamic direction. Building inhabitants experience dynamic environments when stationary in a room where conditions are changing and when they move between spaces. While both are less well-studied than responses to steady-state conditions, there is a particular paucity of research on transient conditions in spatial sequences. A conception of spatial complexity is prerequisite to a study of the dynamic experience of sequences. For a few examples, consider the distinctions among single and double-loaded corridors, room-to room circulation with no corridors, sectionally-connected multi-level space with internal vertical circulation, and loggia-tempered circulation connecting rooms around a courtyard. Given a construct of spatial complexity aligned with the architectural subjects of study, what can building science then learn about designing positive experiences for occupants moving in sequences, such as the thermal sequences described in S5 Territorial Tuning? As one example, these thermal sequences include Journey + Return, Odyssey + Arrival, Hedonic Migration, Promenade Sensorielle, Extempore Adjacent, and Nadir + Summit.

Knowledge framework as generating investigations

Every project, certainly a book, answers some questions and uncovers others. We have set out new frameworks for dynamic and non-uniform conditions, experiential states, the experiential design schema itself and a network of scalar relationships among schemas. We generated one means to connect experience to space and environmental conditions, to link evidence to subjective opportunity, and to place science in dialogue with architecture in its expressive, spatial and cultural expressions. A new experiential design knowledge base domain has been initiated. What we offer in this book is a beginning, an opening to a larger conversation that we will not complete. It is a start that we know is imperfect and incomplete. We hope you will build on it, critique it, improve it and expand it. The work of this book and the implications we see at the end of the process, such as the propositions about constellations and design languages, suggest several prospects for further investigation by scholars, researchers and by designers:

The four languages are unevenly developed in the disciplinary literature and their intersections poorly studied. The whole of the Four Architectural Languages table can be seen as a meta-hypothesis awaiting further study and testing. Experiential schemas and cultural narratives operationalized for design occur as domains in particular need of further development.

The constellations concept is speculative, awaiting development by future research and scholarship—or future exploration by designers. In theory, there are fewer complex constellations than simpler schemas. The typology for modes of relationships among schemas is yet to be defined. Open topics include the nature of more complex experiential themes and motifs, an area ripe for study. We think of such motifs as generative subjective themes employed by designers to achieve intended inhabitant experiences.

Schema design process is open for theoretical and methodological definition. Design processes and methods have been historically difficult and thorny to research and to generalize about. Adding experience as a primary issue does not simplify the problem, but we believe that schemas provide a potentially powerful basis as elements that might be integrated into many ways to design.

Grammar principles of a schemata language need development in system, syntax and structure. For example, how are schemas linked horizontally at a given scale and vertically to larger and smaller scales and complexities? Do the linkages among schemas, which are intended for design ideas that address subjective human interiors (the Experiences quadrant), follow the same or different principles of relatedness and connection as do the links within systems of design strategies for the objective-exterior physical (Behaviors quadrant), such as the *Sun, Wind + Light* strategy bundles?

Gaps in the schema vocabulary are evident in the mapping of this book (see the Schemata language map). Many more schemas are possible and needed. This is true for each of the senses.

Representation of architecture-Nature experience needs tremendous new attention, both during design process and in concept communication. Conditions are often dynamic in time and space and invisible—air, heat, moisture and sound. How can experience be represented, studied and kept in design awareness as projects develop?

Experiential programming is in its infancy. Articulating intentions depends on accessing a robust experiential vocabulary. Lighting and acoustic design language is more developed than that for thermal experience. The terminology and distinctions of feelings and emotions, despite being well-studied in psychology, are poorly developed as they relate to engendering positive experiences in buildings. This important pre-design theme is developed in the next sections.

Experiential programming as qualitative design assignment

As the project stage in which the design team's assignment is set and the stakeholders align behind shared intentions, programming begins the experiential design process.

Early design decisions based on programming choices have profound, often irreversible effects on many factors, from energy performance to lighting quality. In conventional terms, programming defines the building's purpose, the human activities that it supports and the spaces that respond to those needs. The building's spatial elements are outlined by engaging the questions:

- What are the parts?
- What are their sizes?

Programming Precept	Conceptual Support
Transform your fundamental practice commitments.	Ch 1 From conventional realities to experiential possibilities
Aspire to engage the appreciative faculties: visual, phenomenological and process.	Ch 1 Experiential aesthetics
Target physiological or emotional states—from sensation to affiliation.	Ch 1 Nested experiential state complexity
Aim to enhance positive feelings and states beyond comfort.	Ch 1 Spectrum of occupant experiences Ch1 Framework for affective states in buildings
Eschew monotony in favor of spatial and temporal variability.	Ch 1 Framework of environmental conditions in and around buildings Ch 3 Valuing variability
Connect people to the to the varieties of Nature in the living world.	Ch 1 Degrees of Nature complexity
Connect people to Nature as it occurs in their current and emerging worldview.	Ch 1 Connecting to varieties of Nature
Employ multiperspectival thinking to unpack the holistic nature of intended experiences.	Ch 2 The integral context of architectural experience
Offer means for inhabitant experiential choice and/or control.	Ch 3 Adaptive opportunity toolbox Ch 3 Adaptive comfort

– How are they related in spatial and temporal organization?

These are good questions that every building needs to address. They arise from valuing the building as human habitat shaped to support human life.

In organizing the complex body of information and criteria that defines the design agenda, it is easy to postpone qualitative objectives, such as the desired sensory qualities of space or an aspirational atmosphere. Yet, in addition to the function and use-oriented questions, an experiential expansion of programming asks:

– What are the feelings intended for inhabitants?
– What are the environmental conditions that support such affects?
– What architectural qualities and organizations influence these conditions?

The answers to both sets of questions, conventional and experiential, yield potential organizations defined by design narratives, adjacency, movement sequences, zones and rhythms of time.

Experiential programming precepts (table) outlines a few of the recommendations we offer for the critical setting of the qualitative agenda that we hope design schemas help to address.

Dynamic

- o Distinguish times for desirable steady-state or dynamic sensory conditions.
- o Engage Nature's daily or seasonal rhythms.
- o Map occupancy schedules to environmental rhythms.
- o Employ punctuated intensity, but avoid sensory saturation, especially in long occupancy spaces.
- o Consider movement between adjacent spaces as experiential opportunity.

Control

- o Avoid uniform criteria for "all spaces, all people and all periods".
- o Distinguish zones for conditioning with active, passive and hybrid strategies.
- o Identify zones for centralized vs localized control.
- o Identify zones for automatic, manual and hybrid controls.
- o Plan for manual override to automatic controls.

Spatial

- o Choose places for desirable uniform or non-uniform sensory conditions.
- o Consider a range of sensory scales, from body to room to spatial sequence.
- o Attend to indoor, outdoor and in-between spaces.
- o Zone larger spaces into sensory subspaces.
- o Give different experiences to primary occupation, transition and circulation spaces.
- o Distinguish fixed vs flexible locations for activities, people, furniture and equipment. Is use tied to location or mobile? Does a space have a single use or can it accommodate changing uses?
- o Generate intentions for individual spaces and multiple spaces together.

It might be tempting to throw out the objective/functional aspects of traditional programming or to want to make qualitative programming get equal time with its more practical counterpart. We see it differently. No performance metric, technical criterion or form that follows its function can be separated from the human purpose, value or feeling it serves. Much, if not all, of objective architectural programming exists to serve subjective aspects and aspirations, even if often tacit or unstated. Therefore, during pre-design, the project team can be explicit about shared intentions for human experience, revisiting during the whole design process. These can be refined into specific objectives, expressed as inhabitants' physiological or emotional states and as the spatial and temporal qualities of the physical environment that support them. Performance serves people *and* pleasure.

Experiential programming checklist (next page) offers suggestions for the design team to consider while developing the building program.

Sensory diversity as indoor civil rights

When a single approach to sensory intensity dominates public and work places, the health and well-being of the neurodiverse population is compromised by design. We see this emerging issue as both a new civil right, akin to accessibility, and as an area for future design and research.

This book emphasizes creating fields of experiential possibilities in buildings that provide greater variety and options by designing environmental conditions more dynamic and spatially non-uniform than found in common practice approaches. This conditional diversity aligns well with a social-political goal of what we call sensory diversity. When buildings are uniformly stimulating, many people lose focus, productivity and equipoise. Some even suffer psychologically.

Individuals perceive and react to sensory stimuli with a range of responses based on both personality and neurological difference. Physiologically, a college athlete and a frail great grandmother may feel the same conditions differently. Cognitively and psychologically, humans also vary in significant ways. People can have low sensory thresholds (sensation avoiding) or high thresholds (sensation seeking). Everyone exists on a spectrum of sensitivity to sensory stimuli. To complicate matters, sensitivity can vary by each sense. Individuals also have different experiences and preferences depending on momentary factors, such as mood or activity.

One design response to this spectrum of individual sensitivity and predilection is *sensory intensity zoning*—a range of conditions within a space or a set of spaces providing varying amounts of sensory stimuli. A diversity of low to high intensity conditions allows for migration and offers adaptive opportunity, particularly well-suited to the growing trend of agile workspace design. Many of the schemas lend themselves to being applied in a relatively gentle, a moderate or a potent manner. Sensory intensity zoning can also be utilized in a choreographed sequence of experiences, described in schemas such as S5 Ingress Transitions or S5 Territorial Tuning. As a motif, Intensity Zoning is a prime candidate for new schemas and schemas constellations.

Early conversations as generative and enrolling

The futures that human beings create emerge in generative language. New ideas and models emerge and unfold in purposeful conversation by investigating what gets created when a group collectively generates a new contextual field. For example, the ideas and frameworks of this book have emerged from the field generated by thousands of conversations between us, the authors, and with colleagues. The emergent ideas generated have been surprising

Emergent ideas in this context means that the most successful and adaptive responses to complex problems arise from a situation in which three conditions are present (Darling, 2015): Diverse individuals as members in a system working around a shared goal, acting with their own agency (meaning a degree of independence), and interacting with each other as much as possible (the thousands of conversations).

Architects can facilitate conversations about creating rich sensory experiences for building inhabitants, involving different stakeholders at select points along the way. The experiential design conversation is both a *generative*

Suggestions for experiential early design conversations

Build a language for experiential design. Understand the language used by and priorities of different stakeholders. Practice speaking to the *listenings* present. Frame conversations first in terms people already use; then introduce new ideas to build a shared understanding.

Integrate essential ideas early and holistically. Incorporate key experiential themes such that they are integral and essential to the design scheme, rather that attributed to smaller components or incremental gestures at risk of removal during value engineering.

Frame sensory variability as affirmative. Natural ventilation, fresh air and sunlight are positively perceived. Explaining their experiential impact is less tangible, but important. Alliesthesia, a basis for thermal delight, once explained, often resonates with people.

Connect experiential intentions to design responses. Intending to have inhabitants feel delightfully alive and empowered by choice might generate a built luminous gradient, as in Shades of Brilliance, allowing the primal pleasure of positioning oneself in sun, shade or in-between.

Connect environmental forces to feelings. Guide client and design team to think about multiple environmental elements linked to feelings, such as conditions-in-space where people feel relaxed, contemplative, safe, energetic, stimulated, joyful, creative, focused or collaborative.

Align experiential intent with project priorities. Connect felt states with objectives, such as energy saving, Nature connection, employee retention, a welcoming lobby or a calming hospital. Durability and resilience can be aligned with increased care for enjoyable places.

Motivate with memory. Guide team players to connect personal experiences to proposals for environmental and felt qualities. A Nature connection intent can be tied to memories of inspiring moments in Nature and linked to intentions for creating analogous events indoors.

Frame feeling as flexibility. Good sensory design adds flexibility to the project's programming, often a boon under constrained budgets. Occupant locational choice suggests multi-use space, while temporally and spatially-variable conditions yield operational savings.

dialogue to set the qualitative design agenda and an *enrollment conversation* to align the players behind shared ideas and goals. In contrast to a marketing conversation, a sales pitch or an argument to convince others, an enrollment conversation is one in which other people get inspired by the possibility of the ideas on the table and want to align with them and take action. Authenticity, enthusiasm and ideas bigger than the proponent are its hallmarks.

Individual clients, builders, inhabitants, engineers and architects most often represent a diversity of worldviews and a range of fundamental value perspectives (the quadrants of Chapter 2). Recognizing this, pre-design and early design stages will necessarily engage conversations for aligning on shared intentions in qualitative and quantitative, prophetic and pragmatic, cultural and contextual domains.

While building users are the ones most impacted by experiential quality, they are often the least likely to have a voice during the design process. If not possible to engage them directly, someone on the team can serve as the occupants' advocate, such as by standing for commitments to provide adaptive opportunity. What is most important in a culture of collaboration is team alignment on a purpose, one might say *diversity aligned*. Simply collecting the stakeholders, getting diversity at the table, is like inviting the guests to dinner. Yet, the host also has to serve the fare—what is on the table—and often, provide a good question to frame the conversation. Enrollment in a vision creates the new *context of alignment and meaning* in which diverse stakeholders can have generative dialogue.

To guide us in offering concluding suggestions for generative experiential design conversations, we engaged twenty sensory-based architectural practitioners in a series of focus groups. Our overall questions to the participants were:

– How do you approach sensory experience in your work throughout the design process?
– How do you explicitly state the experience(s) you are trying to create during the early stages of your design?
– How do you communicate those ideas verbally and visually, both within your design team and when presenting sensory design to a client?

Discussions were lively and illuminating! Participants agreed on the essentialness of declaring experiential goals and communicating with clients and the whole design team about them early in the design process.

Suggestions for experiential early design conversations (opposite) summarizes some of their recommendations that we found to be most relevant to this work.

Invitations to readers as open-ended theory building

We invite you, students and building professionals of all types, to experiment with the schemas and to generate your own experiential intentions. Try them on. When creating experiences for inhabitants of your projects, allow the experience to generate or alter the form. While designing, test the formal propositions you make against the criteria you generated for human feeling. If you design and build something using the schemas and concepts from this book, please share it with us. It may inspire others. We would like to know what worked, where you got stuck and what could be improved.

We invite you to generate new design schemas. Those in this book are only a beginning, just a fraction of the possible whole schemata language. Use the schema template outlined in the beginning of chapter four, Experiential Design Schemas, as a guide. See if you can articulate some particular occupant experiences, the distribution of forces or Nature conditions that people sense and the patterns of space that shape those conditions. Can you find precedents where other architects or vernacular builders have built with the schema elegantly? Sometimes this is a great place to start; great precedents embody an architectural wisdom. Is there scientific, historical, vernacular or professional evidence and wisdom you can draw on? What are the core characteristics that the schema needs in order to generate the field of possible experiences? Can these be framed as design guidelines that transcend particular projects?

Even if you don't develop new schemas in detail, we invite you to share with us your ideas for new schemas and to help us identify the gaps in the schemata language. Where do you see missing schemas? What would you add?

406 **Iuav Materials Testing Laboratory**
New schemas await distinguishing.

Venice, Italy, 1995
Francesco Venezia, architect

photo Mark DeKay

We also invite graduate students and researchers at all levels, from both design and non-design disciplines, to engage with the frameworks we have created here to help the discipline fill out the knowledge base of experiential design. If you are a Master's student looking for a research topic, write a schema or two. It is harder than you think, and yet your work will make a contribution. If you are an advanced researcher, we invite you to take on whole schema constellations or to expand the territory to larger scales or new experiential topics. Consider developing experiments, surveys or field studies to explore human response to multi-sensory stimuli. We hope that we have created an open-ended system that can grow and develop in the hands and minds of our expanded learning community.

Let us see more joy, delight and pleasure in buildings! We hope for greater Nature awareness and connection, affiliation, biophilia and love to be present for more people in our designed world—and for this deep beauty to bring each inhabitant to care for the planet and act to solve the climate crisis. We invite you, in your own way, wherever you find yourself, to contribute to that vision.

Sources

Alexander, Christopher, Sara Ishikawa + Murray Silverstein. 1977. *A Pattern Language: Towns, Buildings, Construction.* New York: Oxford University Press

Altomonte, Sergio, Joseph Allen, Philomena M Bluyssen, Gail Brager, Lisa Heschong, Angela Loder, Stefano Schiavon, Jennifer A Veitch, Lily Wang + Pawel Wargocki. 2020. Ten Questions Concerning Well-Being in the Built Environment. *Building and Environment* 180(Aug):106949

Brager, Gail S + Richard J De Dear. 2003. Historical and cultural influences on comfort expectations. in Cole, Raymond J + Richard Lorch, Eds. *Buildings, Culture and Environment: Informing Local and Global Practices.* Oxford, UK: Blackwell Pub, 177–201

Browning, William D + Catherine O Ryan. 2020. *Nature Inside: A Biophilic Design Guide.* London: RIBA Publishing, 250

Darling, Marilyn. 2015. What's the Value Proposition of Emergence? Center for Effective Philanthropy. cep.org/whats-the-value-proposition-of-emergence/

DeKay, Mark. 2018. Designing Relationships to Nature: Five Kinds of Stories and Five Kinds of Connection. Integral European Conference. Siofok, Hungary

DeKay, Mark. 2011. *Integral Sustainable Design: Transformative Perspectives.* Ed. Susanne Bennett. London: Earthscan

HOK. 2019. Designing a Nuerodiverse Workplace. hok.com/workplace

Landmark Education. 2004. Landmark Forum Course Syllabus (Day 2). Landmark Education. landmarkworldwide.com/the-landmark-forum/syllabus

LaVine, Lance. 2010. *Architecture, Place, Empathy: the work of Enrique Lastra + Danile Lopez.* Mexico City: Editorial Piso + Daniel Escotto Editores

LMSa (Leddy Maytum Stacy Architects). 2022. *Practice with Purpose: A Guide to Mission-Driven Design.* San Francisco: ORO Editions

Roös, Phillip B. 2022a. *A Biophilic Pattern Language for Cities: Creating Healthy Urban Environments.* Cham, Switzerland: Springer

Roös, Phillip B. 2022b. Personal communication, Nov 28

Roös, Phillip B. 2021. *Regenerative-Adaptive Design for Sustainable Development: a Pattern Language Approach.* Cham, Switzerland: Springer

Schweiker, Marcel, Eleni Ampatzi, Maedot S Andargie, Rune Korsholm Andersen, Elie Azar, Verena M Barthelmes, Christiane Berger, et al. 2020. Review of Multi-domain Approaches to Indoor Environmental Perception and Behaviour. *Building and Environment* 176:106804

Thiis-Evensen, Thomas. 1987. *Archetypes in Architecture.* Oslo: Scandinavian University Press

408 **Pyrgos Village**

Santorini Island, Greece

photo Mark DeKay

Appendices

Acknowledgments

In a work that has taken a career to be able to write and then several years to produce, there are many generations to acknowledge. First peoples first:

Mark acknowledges the Traditional Owners of the land and waters he lives and works on and pays respects to Elders past and present. The land upon which the University of Tennessee-Knoxville is built is part of the traditional territory of the Tsalagi peoples (now Eastern Band of Cherokee Indians, Cherokee Nation of Oklahoma and United Keetoowah Band of Cherokee Indians in Oklahoma), Tsoyahá peoples (Yuchi, Muscogee Nation) and Shawnee peoples (Absentee Shawnee Tribe of Oklahoma, Eastern Shawnee Tribe of Oklahoma, and the Shawnee Tribe).

Gail recognizes that Berkeley sits on the territory of Huichin (Hoo-Choon), the ancestral and unceded land of the Chochenyo (Cho-chen-yo) speaking Ohlone people, the successors of the historic and sovereign Verona Band of Alameda County. This land was and continues to be of great importance to the Muwekma (Muh-wek-muh) Ohlone Tribe and other familial descendants of the Verona Band.

Thanks to Hansjörg Göritz, architect and Professor of Architecture at the University of Tennessee, for a great, elegant book design with the precise degree of complexity fit to tell the story. He also set the standards and provided many hours of critique working with the UT illustrators. He has been simultaneously a great supporter and a challenging critic in the best way, always pushing for the highest possible vision and outcome.

Susanne Bennett read each page multiple times offering, as usual, her deep command of English and experience with communicating to architects, combined with a gift for transforming academic language into intelligible prose.

A great staff of graduate and undergraduate students have contributed directly to the project over several years Zachary Dulin was on the case for three years, beginning with illustrations and then managing all the page layouts and intricacies of InDesign and coordinating the graphics standards among the many players. He played a significant role with generative conversations and graphic design to evolve the Schemata Language Map. His absolute commitment, creativity and precision were key to the project. Emily Miller worked with us for two years, providing support for a variety of tasks, including but not limited to literature review research, writing/editing, professional outreach, focus group lead, Zotero expert, InDesign assistance and overall project management. Her attention to detail and exemplary organizational skills were essential to keeping Gail and Mark on task. Brittany Bluel joined us for the final push, playing an indispensible role to get us to the finish line, managing time-critical tasks with finesse, joy and grace.

The many original illustrations were contributed by Ethan Guthrie, Megan McConnell and mostly by Zach Dulin and Matea Montanaro. Translating technical principles and conceptual design thought into visual communication is both central to our approach and a rare skill. Thanks go to our creative and thoughtful graphics team.

Acknowledgments

Many other students provided research and varied support, including Tathya Abe, Ethan Guthrie, Noelle Hayward, Phoebe Johanassen, Won Hee Ko, Amy Loy, Isabela Mesquita, Stephanie Robertson, Kevin Saslawski, Cullen Sayegh, Aaron Waldrupe, Jing Yuan and Yuhan Zhang. Amy and Cullen worked as summer research fellows sponsored by the University of Tennessee.

The majority of the haikus in the schemas were written by Aaron Waldrupe, several by Ethan Guthrie and a few by Mark. These were all written early in the schema development process and were later edited by Mark as each schema idea became clearer.

Mark worked on content for the book during a faculty development leave in fall of 2017, supported by the University of Tennessee, while a visiting scholar with Integrated Environmental Solutions (IES) in Glasgow, an amazing mission-driven company. Thanks go to the IES hosts Don McLean, Craig Wheatley and Ruggiero Guida. Additional work was completed during a teaching release during Spring 2022, sponsored by the UT School of Architecture and a UT Chancellor's Grant for Faculty Research.

Pygmalion Karatzas co-taught with Mark and Susanne Bennett a 2018 travel course in Greece on architectural photography for UT students. He has supported the development of the schemas and their visual exploration over several years, first in the course, then as part of a collaborative photographic video exhibit for the Integral European Conference in Hungary. His professional images are scattered throughout the book. As we bring the book to completion, Pygmalion continues his collaboration with sponsorship of Mark's 2023 faculty development leave to work on more schemas with photographic and video techniques.

Emily Miller helped Gail organize a series of focus groups with architects who incorporated sensory design in their practice. The participants brought images, illustrations, and inspiration to a lively set of discussions. Their sage contributions went far beyond the snippets we summarized in Chapter 5, and we are grateful for their time and guidance. Thanks go to Katie Ackerly, Nathan Brown, Kit Elsworth, Billie Faircloth, Gwen Fuertes, Shruti Kasarekar, Linda Lam, Anica Landreneau, Michael Martinez , Marsha Maytum, AJ Paron, Mark Perepelitza, Matt Piccone, Carol Rickard-Brideau, Erik Ring, Jenna Ritz, Mark Santaana, Kay Sargent and Pauline Souza.

Gail is deeply indebted to her professional family—the Center for the Built Environment (CBE). A good deal of their research findings are incorporated in these pages, and several provided technical reviews or additional analysis. More importantly, the CBE research team is what makes Gail's clock tick, offering an intellectually rich, unconditionally supportive and fun place to work that feeds her mind and spirit. Heartfelt gratitude goes to Ed Arens, Fred Bauman, Carlos Duarte, Allison Herbert, Lindsay Graham, Charlie Huizenga, David Lehrer, Tom Parkinson, Therese Peffer, Paul Raftery, Stefano Schiavon, Jessica Uhl, Tom Webster and Hui Zhang. An additional shout-out to the CBE Industry Partners (too many to list, you know who you are), who sustain this unique university-industry collaboration with both their financial support and valued expertise.

We are not the first to engage the challenging topics in this book. We have to acknowledge many who have engaged in the holistic search for how pleasure and performance are related in buildings. Among those who have influenced us directly as teachers and colleagues are Ed Arens, Cris Benton, G Z Brown, Clark Brockman, Bill Browning, Ginger Cartwright, Paul Clark, Gary Coates, Richard de Dear, Barbara Erwine, Mary Guzowski, Judi Heerwagen, Lisa Heschong, Ralph Knowles, Allison Kwok, Marietta Millett, Rob Peña, John Reynolds, Astrid Roetzel, Phillip Roös, Catie Ryan, Stefano Schiavon, Lance LaVine, Vivian Loftness and Susan Ubbelohde. There are no doubt many others not listed here who have touched us along the way. We are so grateful for you all.

We cannot finish without deep and profound acknowledgments to our devoted and patient spouses and family.

Mark: Susanne, you are the partner no one could deserve but I was lucky enough to be blessed with. You endured a writing process much longer than imagined and provided sustenance and encouragement all along the way. Your belief and enthusiasm are ever-empowering.

Gail: Suzy, my soul-sister, your wisdom lights my path and grounds me. Adam and Carolyn, my adventurous children who constantly amaze, your infectious joy makes my heart sing and your compassionate leadership gives me hope for the future. Geno, my beloved, your decades of unwavering warmth, selfless support, persistent positivity and karmic kindness provide me tranquility in the tumult. You are my favorite person.

Abbreviations + Units

°C	degrees Celsius
°C/m	degrees Celsius per meter
°F	degrees Fahrenheit
°F/ft	degrees Fahrenheit per foot
AC	air conditioning
ADA	Americans with Disabilities Act
APL	*A Pattern Language: towns, buildings, construction*
AQAL	all-quadrant / all-level
ART	Attention Restoration Theory
ASHRAE	American Society of Heating, Refrigerating and Air-Conditioning Engineers
BMS	building management system
CBE	Center for the Built Environment
CCT	correlated color temperature
CIE	International Commission on Illumination
CLA	circadian lux
clo	clothing insulation
cm	centimeters
CO2	carbon dioxide
CS	circadian stimulus
DB/dBA	decibels
DOAS	dedicated outdoor air system
EDI	equivalent daylight illuminance
EEG	electroencephalogram (brain activity recording)
EML	equivalent melanopic lux
ERPs	event-related potentials
fc	foot-candle
FMRI	functional magnetic resonance imaging
Ft	feet
ft/min	feet per minute (fpm)
HVAC	heating, ventilation, and air conditioning
HVLS	high volume, low speed
HZ	hertz
IAQ	indoor air quality
IEA	International Energy Agency
IEQ	indoor environmental quality
In	inches
IpRGCs	intrinsically photosensitive retinal ganglion cells
ISD	*Integral Sustainable Design: transformative perspectives*
ISO	International Standards Organization
IWBI	International Well Building Institute
K	degrees Kelvin
LEED	Leadership in Energy and Environmental Design
LRC	Lighting Research Center
lux	luminous flux per unit area
m	meters
m/s	meters per second
m2	square meters
m-EDI	melanopic equivalent daylight illuminance
met	metabolic rate (of activity)
mm	millimeters
MM	mixed-mode
mph	miles per hour

Abbreviations and Units

MRI	magnetic resonance imaging
NCM	night-cooled mass
nm	nanometer
NV	natural ventilation
PLEA	Passive and Low Energy Architecture
PMV	Predicted Mean Vote
POE	post-occupancy evaluation
PV	photovoltaic
RH	relative humidity
RPM	rotations per minute
SAD	seasonal affective disorder
SBSE	Society of Building Science Educators
SET	Standard Equivalent Temperature
SRT	Stress Reduction Theory
Std 55	ANSI/ASHRAE Standard 55: Thermal Environmental Conditions for Human Occupancy
SWL	*Sun, Wind + Light: architectural design strategies*, 3rd ed
UTCI	Universal Thermal Climate Index
UV	ultraviolet
VAV	variable air volume

Glossary

Note. Cross-referenced definitions also found in the glossary are *shown in italics.*

Adaptive Comfort Model (ACM). Based on extensive field studies, predicts the range of temperatures that people will find comfortable in buildings with operable windows, showing that a connection to the outdoors and control over one's immediate environment leads to a preference for a wider range of thermal conditions.

Adaptive opportunity. The options provided by a building that allow people to change environmental conditions or move within or between spaces to find more comfortable situations.

Adaptive thermal comfort. The theory that subjective thermal comfort depends on the physical environment and also contextual adaptation—physiological (acclimatization), psychological (expectation) and behavioral (personal or environmental adjustments). For naturally ventilated buildings in particular, comfort is influenced by personal control and one's historical indoor thermal patterns.

Affective states. The transitory body-mind experience of feeling, emotion or mood. Can be mapped along axes of valence (pleasure-displeasure) and arousal (calm-energetic). Also, the second class of nested experiential state complexity, feelings and thoughts about sensation. Includes the class of sensation. Helps build understanding states.

Affiliation. A class of high-level experiential complexity manifesting significant relationships to Nature and place, such as empathy, connection and oneness. Includes complexity levels of *sensation, affect* and *understanding.*

Alliesthesia. A psychophysiological phenomenon, specifically in reference to thermal experience as enhanced feelings of pleasure or delight beyond neutrality or comfort. Thermal pleasure sensations, induced by variability, come from the skin rather than core body temperature.

Alliesthesia, spatial/asymmetric. Pleasure arising from differences in temperature across the skin's surface, tending to occur when localized on the body.

Alliesthesia, temporal. Pleasure arising from dynamic thermal conditions where a contrasting stimulus helps the body return to heat balance from an initial state of feeling too warm or too cool.

Archetype. In general, a primary architectural form or spatial pattern tending toward being universal. In particular here, how common forms, such as flat vs gabled roofs, are correlated with human psychology.

Architecture-Nature experience. The concepts that, in most of contemporary life, humans do not experience buildings and Nature independently but, rather, as a synthesis in an integrated whole where each acts to co-define the other's patterns.

Arousal. The degree of feeling energy in an affective state, from calmness to excitement.

ASHRAE Standard 55. "Thermal Environmental Conditions for Human Occupancy." Specifies the range of indoor environmental conditions that will provide acceptable thermal comfort for the majority of occupants. It is intended for use in design, operation, and commissioning of buildings.

Atmosphere. As used here, refers to the affective atmosphere, the sensorial qualities or the overall mood and emotion evoked by a space.

Attention Restoration Theory (ART). One scientific explanation for biophilia that proposes that mental fatigue and concentration can be improved by time spent in or looking at Nature.

Backgrounds of interpretation. The context of meaning and value for inhabitant experience, situated in cultures and worldviews, that also constrain the *fields of possible experiences.*

Behaviors perspective. In Integral Theory, the singular, objective perspective of how anything (forces, Nature, people, buildings) behave in the empirical world.

Biophilia. The innate human tendency to connect with nature and affiliate with other living beings. Love of life.

Glossary

Biophilic design. Designed buildings and landscapes that intentionally connect people directly or indirectly with Nature.

Brown noise. The frequency spectrum of sound adjusted for the human hearing in a similar but stronger way to *Pink Noise*. Higher frequencies have lower and more random power, leading to deeper sounds like thunder or a strong waterfall.

Circadian rhythms. A biological process where physical, mental and behavioral processes follow a 24-hr cycle.

Cognition. The mental process of knowing. In architectural experiences, when precognitive phenomena of *sensations* and bodily *emotions* are thought about, *feeling* arises. Thoughts about feelings can become ideas.

Conditions-in-buildings. The expression that, in architecture, the environmental stimuli for *sensation* always exist in patterns of *distribution* that are inseparably situated in and influenced by spatial organizations.

Constellation. Families of related *schemas* working together to achieve complex, sophisticated or powerful *atmospheres* or *affects*.

Contrast conditions. An organizing subcategory of schemas, when opposing environmental stimuli, such as warm and cool, humid and dry, or dark and light are experienced simultaneously or in rapid succession.

Comfort. In the framework of affective states (Ch 1), a class more positively valent (attractive) than *neutrality* but less so than *pleasure* states.

Comfort zone. Used here to refer specifically to the thermal comfort zone, defined as the combination of personal and environmental conditions in which a specified percentage of people will express satisfaction with the thermal environment.

Cultures perspective. In *Integral Theory*, the *intersubjective* perspective of shared understanding, worldviews, myths and meanings. The culture can be any scale of group. Here, it gives the view from which the *backgrounds of interpretation* for schemas can be seen and understood.

Deadband. Used in reference to a thermostat, referring to the temperature range around a setpoint temperature in which neither the heating nor cooling system turns on.

Delight. One of the three Vitruvian elements of architecture, associated with aesthetic quality. Specifically here, one of the *pleasure* states beyond *comfort.*

Development. The process in humans of transformation from one stage of consciousness to another more complex, inclusive, aware stage. Here, it applies to levels of *worldview* and their ideas of Nature and also to the three levels of experiential aesthetic complexity (visual, phenomenological and process).

Distinctions. As used here, to name and define something such that it shifts from an undifferentiated background to occur in the foreground of awareness. Specifically, design schemas distinguish a nexus of environmental conditions, spatial organization and human experiences.

Distributions of environmental conditions. The patterns of environmental stimuli, shaped by *organizations of architectural space,* that provide the basis for *fields of possible experiences.*

Dynamic conditions. Refers to physical environmental stimuli that change over time, such as daylighting, solar radiation or wind velocity. For building thermal patterns in particular, also referred to as transients, often in terms of step change, drift and ramp, cycle, and sawtooth patterns.

Emotion. Used both in general terms and more specifically to mean real-time, immediate, precognitive biological responses to conditions and situations encountered, such as the sensory-spatial environment in buildings. Distinguished from *feelings* as mental experiences. Although prelinguistic, basic positive emotions include safety, rest, happiness and surprise.

Environmental adaptation/flexibility. A subcategory of behavioral *adaptive opportunity* where individuals modify local conditions by technical or operational controls, including opening a window, operating blinds or other shading, using a fan, turning on sound masking or accessing individualized task lighting.

Evidence. Used here broadly to describe knowledge supportive of schemas that comes from the sciences, humanities, arts, and architectural disciplines.

Experience. The lived direct, personal apprehension of and encounter with the environment, in physiological, psychological or cognitive dimensions. Can be understood as transitory body-mind states and more permanent consciousness stages.

Experiences perspective. In *Integral Theory*, the subjective viewpoint of individuals, the domain of feeling, aesthetic perception and thought.

Experiential aesthetics. A system of regarding aesthetic perception and response that recognizes the full range aesthetic objects, encompassing visual aesthetics, phenomenological aesthetics (multi-sensory), and process aesthetics (events in time set in patterns of form and space).

Experiential programming. A pre-design activity to generate the design assignment and its analysis that includes an experiential perspective. States intentions for inhabitant feelings in space along with assertions about environmental conditions and architectural qualities, zoning and organizations to support experience.

Experiential state. Transitory body-mind conditions or modes of being. Can be described as nested levels of complexity, from bodily *sensation*, to *affect* or mental perception, to *understanding* and direct knowledge, to *affiliation* and connection.

Fecundity. The capacity for creativity and generating novel ideas.

Feeling. Conscious experiences as the product of thinking about *sensation* and (precognitive) *emotion*. In neuroscience terms, equivalent to affect. Here, used in general terms to include both affect (pleasure, joy, wonder, awe) and higher order affiliation (boding belonging, identity).

Fields of experiential possibilities. The situations that give rise to potential inhabitant experiences, as *conditions-in-buildings* that are also influenced by *backgrounds of interpretation*. The concept recognizes that human experience may be impelled but not compelled.

Flux conditions. An organizing subcategory of schemas, defined as continuously changing stochastic environmental stimuli perceived as random or chaotic, such as cloud movements, rain sounds or leaves blown in the wind.

Gradient conditions. An organizing subcategory of schemas, defined as relatively smooth transitions across a significant degree of environmental stimulus (brighter to dimmer, for example) within the field of one's perception.

Habitability. Used in the spectrum of occupant experiences to describe the fundamental level of shelter, providing enough protection from the elements to ensure health and safety, such as avoiding extreme heat and cold *stress*.

Hedonic. Related to feelings of pleasure.

Integral model. In Wilber's approach, includes the basic frameworks of *quadrants*, levels, lines, states and types. Used here mainly as quadrants and *levels of complexity*. Quadrants refer to fundamental perspectives (see *quadrants*). Levels refers to developmental levels (see *development*).

Integral Theory. Here, as developed by philosopher Ken Wilber to provide a general framework for a theory of everything integrating the truths and workability from as many perspectives as possible.

Interobjective. Complex objective phenomena interacting in a system or network, such as an urban or ecological system, as disclosed by a view from the *systems perspective*.

Intersubjective. Complex subjective phenomena interacting in a collective, such as a group awareness or shared *worldview*, as disclosed by a view from the *cultures perspective*.

ipRGCs. Intrinsically photosensitive retinal ganglion cells are a third class of photoreceptors in the eye, in addition to rods and cones, and play an essential role in the biological impacts of light's circadian rhythms.

Glossary

ISO 7730. Presents methods for predicting the general thermal sensation and degree of thermal dissatisfaction of people exposed to moderate thermal environments. It has parallels to *ASHRAE Std 55*.

Kinesthesia/Kinesthetic. Awareness of the feeling of movement of a joint or limb, often used interchangeably with proprioception. Kinesthesia is often characterized as more behavioral; *proprioception*, more cognitive.

Levels of complexity. A nested framework of organization such that each more complex level transcends and includes less complex levels. Seen in *worldviews*, human consciousness, *experiential aesthetics*, and in particular used as an organizing framework for schemas in six levels of the *schemata language* map: Material, Element, Building System, Room, Room Organization and Whole Building.

Lightscape. Visual elements of the environment distributed in space and sensed by the eyes.

Metaphoric thought. A means of expression employing symbols (here architectural forms and composition) to make implicit comparison, referral or linkage with ideas not literally present. For example, a minimalist modern aesthetic as metaphoric for the idea of ecological efficiency on a finite planet. See *narrative* schemas.

Mixed-mode building. Refers to a specific hybrid approach to space conditioning that uses a combination of natural ventilation from operable windows (either manually or automatically controlled) and mechanical systems that include air distribution equipment and refrigeration equipment for cooling.

Narrative. An organizing subcategory of schemas, in which the characteristics and organization of space and form tell visual stories that convey meaning beyond the immediate sensory experience, such as how a building and site are designed-with-nature or to bring to awareness the material and structural processes and forces at play.

Natural forces. The abiotic elements of Nature, such as air, light, sun, water and earth.

Nature. In general, the web-of-life, including the physiosphere, biosphere and noosphere. Here, a complex living system with degrees complexity including abiotic natural forces, biotic living organisms (humans, too) and more complex ecosystems, all occurring with both spatial and temporal variations.

Nature connection. To be affiliatively related to Nature, especially here, as mediated by buildings. Each worldview has a different idea of what Nature is and a distinct mode of connecting to it via architecture.

Nature deficit disorder. Coined by Richard Louv, not as a medical term, but to describe the human costs of disconnection from Nature. Can include diminished use of senses, attention difficulties and long-term physical and emotional illness.

Neutrality. Used here to describe a sensory state where one barely notices if the temperature is warm or cool, the light dim or bright, etc. Sensory monotony. Also used here as a class in the framework of affective states that is more positively valent than *stress*, but less than *comfort*. Can be more energetic (alertness) or less (drowsy).

Neutrality fallacy. The mistaken belief that maintaining neutral, uniform, steady-state conditions in buildings is preferred by occupants or constitutes an ideal goal.

Organizations of architectural space. Here, used to refer to the shape and organizations at multiple scales that influence the *distributions of conditions* in buildings and help provide the basis for *fields of experiential possibilities*.

Overcooling. To cool excessively, either to temperatures that are too cold for comfort or for unnecessary hours .

Peak experiences (states). Used in the framework of affective states as the class of extreme positive states beyond *pleasure*. Can also be described as a transcendent moment or an altered state of consciousness characterized by awe, peace, ecstasy, unity, etc.

Perception. The psychological awareness and mental interpretation of the physical environment as known and apprehended through the senses.

Person-based conditioning. To keep human bodies comfortable at a local scale, in contrast to heating or cooling the volume of space overall. Can be achieved with local personally-control of building elements, fans, foot warmers, heated/cooling chairs, etc.

Personal adaptation/flexibility. A subcategory of behavioral *adaptive opportunity* in which occupants adapt to their surroundings by altering personal variables such as clothing, activity, posture, warm/cool beverage or food intake, or by moving to a different location to maintain comfort.

Philia. One of the four ancient Greek words for love. Used here as part of *biophilia.*

Pink noise. The sound frequency spectrum adjusted for the human hearing deficit to low-frequency. In contrast to a flat spectrum, lower frequencies have more power and the higher frequencies less, therefore sounding relatively balanced in loudness to the human ear.

Pleasure (states). Used in the framework of affective states as a class of states more positively valent than *comfort* and less than *peak experiences.* Examples include happiness, joy, serenity and delight.

Predicted Mean Vote (PMV). An index developed in laboratory experiments that predicts the mean value of the votes of a large group of people on a seven-point thermal sensation scale

Proprioception. Awareness of the feeling of movement of a joint or limb, often used interchangeably with *kinesthesia.* Kinesthesia is often characterized as more behavioral, proprioception, more cognitive.

Prospect-refuge theory. People's preference for environments with unobstructed views (prospect) while seeking places offering concealment and retreat (refuge). Implies being able to see without being seen.

Quadrant. In *Integral Theory,* one mode of understanding defined in a diagram distinguishing four fundamental perspectives and knowledge domains (*behaviors perspective, systems perspective, experiences perspective* and *cultures perspective*) on any occurrence. See *integral model.*

Rhythm conditions. An organizing subcategory of schemas in which environmental stimuli vary periodically, such as the daily, seasonal and annual cycles of Nature and its forces.

Scentscape. Olfactory elements of the environment distributed in space and time and smelled by the nose.

Schema. A generalized design knowledge module that aids in experiential design. It helps a designer to organize form and space that disposes environmental conditions to create a field of potential positive human experiences.

Schemata language. The full set of design schemas available for experiential design. Theoretically, organizes schemas and their constellations with system, syntax and structure, including as a nested spatial network. Used here as one of the four architectural design languages.

Sensation states. Used here as the most fundamental class of nested experiential state complexity, the response of sensory organs to environmental stimuli. Helps build *affective states.*

Sensescape. Environmental conditions distributed in space and time that can be sensed, perceived, felt and interpreted by people.

Sensibility. The capacity for feeling, an individual's ability to perceive and respond to stimuli.

Sensory diversity. The range of perception and responses in a population to sensory stimuli based on personality and neurological difference. Used here to broadly include physiological, neurological, cognitive and psychological origins for variation in response.

Sequence conditions. An organizing subcategory of schemas, in which environmental stimuli vary when people move from one space to another or when the stimuli change over time in a space but occupants don't relocate.

Glossary

Sound colors. *White noise, pink noise* and *brown noise* are the most common terms used to describe different power spectra, the amount of vibration at each individual frequency, of various types of sounds that are perceived differently.

Soundscape. Acoustic stimuli in the environment distributed in space and time and heard by the ears.

Space-based conditioning. Conventional approach of heating or cooling space, such as centralized air- or radiant-conditioning, in contrast to *person-based conditioning.*

Spatial adaptation/flexibility. A subcategory of behavioral adaptive opportunity that encourages and facilitates occupants to migrate to areas that they find most comfortable at different times of the day and year.

Spatially non-uniform conditions. Environmental stimuli that change across or between spaces.

Spatially uniform conditions. Environmental stimuli that do not change across or between spaces.

Stages of consciousness. Relatively permanent and stable, sequential structures of growth and maturity, characterized by transcending and including the previous stage, decreasing ego-identification and increasing awareness.

Std 55. See ASHRAE Std 55.

Steady-state conditions. Environmental stimuli that do not change over time.

Stochastic. Here, synonymous with a randomly distributed pattern. Stochasticity refers to the modeling approach of a random probability distribution. See also *Flux conditions.*

Stress (state). Used in the framework of affective states as a class of states most negatively valent (below *neutrality*), including depression and pain.

Stress Reduction Theory (SRT). One scientific explanation for *biophilia* that focuses on how connection to Nature can reduce physiological stress and aversive emotion, lowering anxiety and promoting relaxation.

Sufficiency. The second level in the spectrum of occupant experiences, equivalent to the *comfort zone* of many codes and standards. The aim is to provide conditions that a majority of occupants will find acceptable, reducing dissatisfaction but not necessarily enhancing positive feelings.

Systems perspective. In *Integral Theory*, the *interobjective* view that studies interactions of components or members in relationship, such as social and natural ecologies and contexts. Here, it gives schemas relationships across scales and spatial organization.

Temporal adaptation/flexibility. A subcategory of behavioral *adaptive opportunity* in which occupants can shift their schedules, either as a group or individually.

Temporal variability (dynamic or transient). See *dynamic conditions.*

Thermal satisfaction. Often considered synonymous with *thermal comfort.* A subjective experience, broader than *neutrality,* where a person feels neither too cold nor too hot.

Thermscape. Thermal factors of the environment distributed in space and time and sensed by the skin.

Understanding states. Used here as the third class of nested experiential state complexity, the knowledge of abiotic, biotic and ecologic nature. Includes the classes of *sensation* and *affect.* Helps build *affiliation* states.

Variability. Environmental conditions that change over time or across space.

White noise. A flat frequency spectrum of sound that has equal energy intensity across all audible frequencies. The perception of white noise is not a flat pattern, however, as the higher frequencies are heard more strongly, perceived as a high-pitched, radio static sound.

Worldview. The values, meanings and explaining stories of a culture that set the *backgrounds of interpretation* for individual experiences. Also used here to articulate differing *metaphoric thinking* for and modes of connecting to Nature. In *Integral Theory*, the domain of the *cultures perspective.*

Recommended Reading + Watching

Ackerman, Diane. 1990. *A Natural History of the Senses.* New York: Vintage Books

Aidlin Darling Design. 2022. Architecture for the Senses. Film Director Braden King. https://vimeo.com/720808726/1b2d6b4b3c

Alexander, Christopher, Sara Ishikawa + Murray Silverstein. 1977. *A Pattern Language: Towns, Buildings, Construction.* New York: Oxford Univ. Press

Allen, Summer. 2018. *The Science of Awe.* Greater Good Science Center at UC Berkeley

Altomonte, Sergio, Joseph Allen, Philomena M Bluyssen, Gail Brager, Lisa Heschong, Angela Loder, Stefano Schiavon, Jennifer A Veitch, Lily Wang + Pawel Wargocki. 2020. Ten Questions Concerning Well-Being in the Built Environment. *Building and Environment* 180

Barbara, Anna + Anthony Perliss. 2006. *Invisible Architecture: Experiencing Places through the Sense of Smell.* Milano: Skira

Behling, Stefan. 2016. Architecture and the Science of the Senses. TEDxTalk. https://youtu.be/FbfPWalO_ss

Blesser, Barry, and Linda-Ruth Salter. 2009. *Spaces Speak, Are You Listening?: Experiencing Aural Architecture.* Cambridge, Massachusetts: MIT Press

Brager, Gail, Hui Zhang, and Edward Arens. 2015. Evolving opportunities for providing thermal comfort. *Building Research & Information*, 43(3), 274 - 287.

Browning, William D, Catherine O Ryan + Joseph O Clancy. 2014. *14 Patterns of Biophilic Design: Improving Health + Well-being in the Built Environment.* New York: Terrapin Bright Green

Browning, William D + Catherine O Ryan. 2020. *Nature Inside: A Biophilic Design Guide.* London: RIBA Publishing. 250

Cabanac, Michel. 2010. *Fifth Influence or the Dialectics of Pleasure.* Union City, NJ: BookWhirl

Capaldi, Colin A, Raelyne L Dopko + John M Zelenski. 2014. The Relationship Between Nature Connectedness and Happiness: A Meta-analysis. *Frontiers of Psychology* 5: 976–976

DeKay, Mark. 2018. Designing Relationships to Nature: Five Kinds of Stories and Five Kinds of Connection. *Integral European Conference.* Siofok, Hungary

DeKay, Mark + G Z Brown. 2014. *Sun, Wind + Light, Architectural Design Strategies*, 3rd ed. Hoboken, New Jersey: Wiley

DeKay, Mark. 2011. *Integral Sustainable Design: Transformative Perspectives.* Ed. Susanne Bennett. London: Earthscan

Erwine, Barbara. 2017. *Creating Sensory Spaces: The Architecture of the Invisible.* New York: Routledge

Heschong, Lisa. 1979. *Thermal Delight in Architecture.* Cambridge, Massachusetts, USA: MIT Press

Heschong, Lisa. 2021. *Visual Delight in Architecture: Daylight, Vision and View.* New York: Routledge

Jacobson, Max, Murray Silverstein + Barbara Winslow. 2012. *Patterns of Home: The Ten Essentials of Enduring Design.* Newtown, Connecticut: Taunton Press

Jacobson, Max, Murray Silverstein + Barbara Winslow. 1990. *The Good House: Contrast as a Design Tool.* Newtown, Connecticut: Taunton Press

Kaplan, Rachel, Stephan Kaplan + Robert L Ryan. 1998 *With People in Mind: Design and Management of Everyday Nature.* Washington: Island Press

Kellert, Stephen R. 2018. *Nature by Design: The Practice of Biophilic Design.* New Haven, Connecticut: Yale University Press

Kellert, Stephen R, Judith Heerwagen + Martin Mador. 2008 Biophilic Design: *The Theory, Science and Practice of Bringing Buildings to Life.* Hoboken, New Jersey: Wiley

Recommended Reading + Watching

Knowles, Ralph. 1981. *Sun Rhythm Form.* Cambridge, Massachusetts, USA: MIT Press

LaVine, Lance. 2010. *Architecture, Place, Empathy: the work of Enrique Lastra + Danile Lopez.* Mexico City: Editorial Piso + Daniel Escotto Editores

LaVine, Lance. 2001. *Mechanics and Meaning in Architecture.* Minneapolis, Minnesota: University of Minnesota Press

Loftness, Vivian. 2013. Environmental Surfing: Delight and Nature's Renewable Energies. in Braham, William W + Daniel Willis, Eds. *Architecture and Energy: Performance and Style.* London: Taylor + Francis

Lyle, John T. 1994. *Regenerative Design for Sustainable Development.* New York: John Wiley

Millet, Marietta S. 1996. *Light Revealing Architecture.* New York: Van Nostrand Reinhold

Mishra, Asit K, Marchel G L C Loomans + Jan L Hensen. 2016. Thermal Comfort of Heterogeneous and Dynamic Indoor Conditions—An Overview. *Building and Environment* 109: 82–100

Nute, Kevin. 2014. *Vital: Using the Weather to Bring Buildings and Sustainability to Life.* Apple Books.
Also published as:
Nute, Kevin. 2018. *Naturally Animated Architecture: Using the Movements of the Sun, Wind and Rain to Bring Indoor Spaces and Sustainable Practices to Life.* World Scientific (WSPC)

Pallasmaa, Juhani. 2012. *The Eyes of the Skin: Architecture and the Senses.* 3rd ed. London: John Wiley + Sons

Parkinson, Tom, Richard de Dear + Gail Brager. 2020. Nudging the Adaptive Thermal Comfort Model. *Energy and Buildings* 206(Jan): 109559.

Plummer, Henry. 2016. *The Experience of Architecture.* New York: Thames + Hudson, 21, 24, 35

Raje, Shubhra + Amita Raje. 2012. *Anant Raje Architect: Selected Works 1971-2009.* New Delhi: Tulika Books

Rasmussen, Steen Eiler. 1962. *Experiencing Architecture.* 2nd ed. Cambridge, Massachusetts, USA: MIT Press

Reynolds, John S. 2002. *Courtyards: Aesthetic, Social and Thermal Delight.* New York: John Wiley

Roös, Phillip B. 2021. *Regenerative-Adaptive Design for Sustainable Development: a Pattern Language Approach.* Cham, Switzerland: Springer

Schreuder, Eliane, Jan van Erp, Alexander Toet + Victor L Kallen. 2016. Emotional Responses to Multisensory Environmental Stimuli: A Conceptual Framework and Literature Review. *SAGE Open* 6(1): 2158244016630591

Steane, Mary Ann + Koen Steemers. 2004. *Environmental Diversity in Architecture.* New York, NY: Routledge

Susanka, Sarah. 2004. *Home By Design: Transforming Your House Into a Home.* Newtown, Connecticut: Taunton Press

Tanizaki, Jun'ichirō. 1977. *In Praise of Shadows.* New Haven, Connecticut: Leete's Island Books

Thiis-Evensen, Thomas. 1987. *Archetypes in Architecture.* Oslo: Scandinavian University Press

Watchman, Mélanie, Mark DeKay, Claude M H Demers + André Potvin. 2022. Design Vocabulary and Schemas for Biophilic Experiences in Cold Climate Schools. *Architectural Science Review* 65(2):101–19

Wilber, Ken. 2000. *A Theory of Everything: An Integral Vision for Business, Politics, Science, and Spirituality.* Boston, Massachusetts: Shambhala

Wilber, Ken. 2000. *Sex, Ecology, Spirituality: The Spirit of Evolution.* Boston, Massachusetts: Shambhala

Zumthor, Peter. 2006. *Atmospheres: Architectural Environments, Surrounding Objects.* Basel: Birkhäuser

Index

Index

Index

Index

F

Index

Index

Index

Index

Index

Additional Image Credits

Unless specified otherwise, all images are courtesy of and copyright by the image source or photographer listed in captions and used by permission or license. Additional details for particular images are below.

44 Villa Sarabhai left, courtesy Manuel Bougot FLC-ADAGP ©

55 Casa del Fuerte, copyright, R L Castro, 1978

33 Gando Primary School Library, GandoIT, Share Alike 3.0 Unported license, creativecommons.org/licenses/by-sa/3.0/

76 Stamp Museum, Courtesy Mark Aronica www.aronica.com

131 Smells of Auld Reekie, © 2011 Kate McLean courtesy artist/designer

186 Light Zones, analysis + illustrations Merete Madsen 2004

211 Casa de Ritero Esperitual, courtesy Emilio Ambasz

234–235 Sea Ranch Condominium One, ©2023 The Morley Baer Photography Trust, Santa Fe. All rights reserved. Used by permission.

270 Fredensborg Houses, Share Alike 3.0 Unported license, creativecommons.org/licenses/by-sa/3.0/

271 Tempe a Pailla, © CNAC/MNAM, Dist. RMN-Grand Palais/Art Resource, NY

298 LNR Associates Staff Canteen, Courtesy of Mr Ken L N R ASSOCIATES BKK

326 Biltmore House, used with permission from The Biltmore Company, Asheville, North Carolina

342 Stockholm Public Library Annex, left, Jon Hoem (Joho commons), Share Alike 3.0 Unported license, creativecommons.org/licenses/by-sa/3.0/